# The Innovation of Economic Theory in China

"The edifice of economic theory has long been marked by the proliferation of diverse schools of thought, which is both a strength and a limitation. The relationship between the market and the government has been a central issue of debate among economic schools for centuries. However, the Chinese narrative offers a unique key to unlocking innovation in economic theory. The author builds a mathematical framework by combining the effective market and the efficient government, proposing a rational synthesis of economic logic. This approach not only provides a unified analysis of economic theory but also offers a compelling explanation for the logic behind China's success."

—Professor Liu Yuanchun, President of
*Shanghai University of Finance and Economics*

"The author integrates the Western binary thinking of "yes or no" with the Eastern concept of "degree", constructing a self-contained economic theoretical model. By assigning parameters to the model, the author derives specific theories and skillfully addresses the relationship between general theory and various schools of thought. This book tells the story of how China's successful practice intersects with modern economic theory, offering new perspectives on China's market economy model and theory. It represents an important exploration of transforming the relationship between the market and the government from opposition to unity."

—Professor Liang Qi, Member and Deputy Secretary of the Party Committee of
*Nankai University*

"The rapid development of China's economy has not only contributed to global economic growth but also brought new ideas to the international economics community. Dr. Zong Liang has long been deeply engaged in observing and reflecting on China's economy from the front line. His new work sheds light on summarizing the experiences of China's economic development! He breaks away from the traditional paradigm of "either-or" between the market and the government, but builds a theoretical model where the two hands work together. By addressing the relationship between the general and the specific in economic theory through weighting, he presents a highly creative research approach. This is an important attempt to tackle theoretical challenges in economics by using China's practical experiences."

—Professor Li Daokui, Director of the
*Academic Center for Chinese Economic Practice and Thinking,*
*Tsinghua University*

"The author elevates China's practice of organically integrating the effective market and the efficient government into a universal logic and paradigm, constructing a rational synthesis of economic models and establishing a corresponding theoretical system. This represents a significant innovation in thinking. The book not only reveals the dilemmas of Western economic theory but also draws on related important theories, arriving at many new conclusions, such as the balance point between the market and the government and the golden period of development. It is a distinctive innovative contribution to economic theory."

—Professor Su Jian, Director of the
*National Economic Research Center, Peking University*

Zong Liang

# The Innovation of Economic Theory in China

## Theoretical Perspectives

palgrave
macmillan

Zong Liang
Bank of China
Beijing, China

ISBN 978-981-95-2712-0 ISBN 978-981-95-2713-7 (eBook)
https://doi.org/10.1007/978-981-95-2713-7



Jointly published with China Renmin University Press Co., Ltd.
ISBN of the Co-Publisher's edition: 978-7-300-30420-5

Translation from the Chinese language edition: "经济学理论创新的中国探索——基于理论模型视角" by Zong Liang, © China Renmin University Press Co,. Ltd. 2022. Published by China Renmin University Press Co,. Ltd.. All Rights Reserved.



This Palgrave Macmillan imprint is published by the registered company Springer Nature Singapore Pte Ltd.
The registered company address is: 152 Beach Road, #21-01/04 Gateway East, Singapore 189721, Singapore

# Foreword to the English Edition

Why this book? This book is an effort to explain how China's rise means for the evolution of economic theories. Theoretical breakthroughs and innovations in economics usually are closely associated with global dominance of specific economies, such as the United Kingdom in the nineteenth century and the United States in the twentieth century. It may be expected that China's tremendous success and emerging as global economic powerhouse would generate breakthroughs and innovations in economic theory through unique Chinese-style perspectives. Against this backdrop, Professor Liang Zong, the former chief economist of the Bank of China Institute, led a young team to complete the book, *Innovation of Economic Theory in China: A Perspective Based on Theoretical Models* (the Chinese version was published by the Renmin University of China Press in 2022). This book has five distinctive features of innovations in economic theories.

## Viewing the Relationship Between Government and Market as Organic, Not Oppositional

For centuries, economic theories have revolved around the relationship between the market and the government. Starting with Adam Smith, economic thoughts have often framed this relationship as a binary opposition. Whether in the century-long debate between Hayek and Keynes or the disputes between the so-called saltwater and freshwater schools of thought, the central question has been whether to prioritize the market or the government. Thus, the market-government dynamic lies at the heart of economic theory. Since its reform and opening-up began in 1978, China's economy has grown rapidly and become the globally second largest in terms of exchange rate in 2009 and the world largest in purchasing power parity in 2016. Such exceptional miracle in human economic history offers a new perspective on the market-government relationship: the "two hands" of the market and the government are no longer in opposition but can instead form a dynamic, dialectical unity.

## Combining Quantitative and Qualitative Methods to Assess the Market-Government Relationship

This book breaks away from the "either-or" dichotomy that has long dominated discussions of the market and the government. Instead, it constructs a theoretical model that integrates the invisible hand of the market with the visible hand of the government, achieving a synthesis of qualitative and quantitative analysis. This represents a novel approach to understanding China's successful practice of combining an effective market with an efficient government. Drawing on major Western economic theories and methods, the book employs a new framework that unifies the roles of the market and the government, establishing a self-contained economic theoretical system. Based on the quantifying approach, the book reveals that China's market economy theory is not only quantifiable but also represents a more universal analytical framework rather than a special case, which is very meaningful. More specifically, the book creates new criteria for evaluating market economy models. When the market's role exceeds a certain threshold or when a system combining an effective market and an efficient government is established—where the market plays a decisive role—it qualifies as a market economy model. This leads to the important conclusion that market economy models are diverse. Clearly, China's market economy model differs from other typical models not in a binary "yes or no" sense but in terms of "degree," offering the world a new choice.

## Emphasizing the Integration of Modern Economic Theory and the Theoretical Elevation of the Chinese Story

For over 200 years since Adam Smith, economic theory has revered the guiding role of the market's invisible hand while marginalizing the role of the government. Yet, it has undoubtedly built a magnificent edifice of economic theory, with various schools delving deeply into related theories and playing significant roles in practice. In China's reform and opening-up, many theories and policies on the market economy and government roles have been adopted, bringing about positive results. Similarly, in the process of China's reform and opening-up and its theoretical innovation, it is essential to draw on and adapt modern Western economic theories.

## Developing a Unified System and Logic with Preliminary Empirical Analysis

By employing quantitative methods, this book achieves a mathematical elevation of the logic underlying China's market economy theory, proposing a self-contained and formally unified economic theoretical system and methodology from the perspective of theoretical models. The book comprehensively analyzes the development and transformative prospects of macroeconomic theory, arguing that economic research methodology should shift from one-dimensional to multi-dimensional approaches. It elucidates the logical connections between contemporary economic theories and methods, advocating for a rational synthesis in economic thinking. From the perspective of the Chinese story and economic theory innovation, this book constructs a rational synthesis model for economic theory, explores the corresponding policy framework system, and examines the balance between government and market roles. Building on this foundation, it conducts innovative analyses of dimensions such as economic growth theory and economic cycle theory, supported by mathematical models and empirical evidence.

## Analyzing the Conditions for Say's Law Based on an Extended Multiplier-Accelerator Model

Say's Law is a pivotal proposition in economic theory, often regarded as the cornerstone of modern economic thought, particularly in market economy theory. The French economist Jean-Baptiste Say (1767–1832), in his work *A Treatise on Political Economy* (published in 1803), articulated Say's Law, succinctly summarized as "supply creates its own demand." For a long time, Say's Law has been one of the most debated topics in economic theory and its history, with many supporters, opponents, and scholars exploring its conditions of validity. Theoretically proving or validating Say's Law is a significant challenge. With empirical evidence, the book finds that under certain specific conditions, situations very close to those supporting Say's Law exist, demonstrating its explanatory power for real-world phenomena.

In sum, this book presents China's market economy model and theory to the world with vibrant vitality. While allowing the market to play a decisive role, effectively exercising government functions within reasonable boundaries is both a rational choice and an effective path for economic development. China's practical experience and theoretical innovation represent a universal exploration, not only applicable to China but also offering the world new options in economic theory models and fair evaluation criteria. It is expected that China's economic development model and theory as a new development-path gain greater attention in the world, contributing to the building of a global community with a shared future.

Economics Professor, Illinois State University, Normal, IL, USA

May 2025 Kevin H. Zhang

# Foreword (to the Chinese Edition)

Reform and opening-up have shaped China's economic development model and motivated the innovation and advancement of economic theory. Through reform and opening-up, China has systematically integrated into globalization while driving the globalization and the innovation in international trade theory. Therefore, the essence of the Chinese story lies in the successful practices of reform and opening-up over the past 40 years, which represents a "gold mine" for advancing economic theory innovation.

Are the market and the government in opposition or in unity? What should the macroeconomic policy aim for? In this book, the author systematically reviews and conducts logical analysis upon the related questions raised by some renowned economists.

## The Market Economy Model with Chinese Characteristics: A Great Innovation in China's Practice

Over more than 40 years of reform and opening-up, China's economy has maintained steady growth. In this course, China has overall played the roles of the market and the government, allowing the effective market and the efficient government to function together, thereby forming a market economy model with Chinese characteristics. This is a great innovation of China's practice. Meanwhile, drawing on various theories and practical methods, China has developed a set of reasonable reform principles and approaches tailored to its own realities. These include steadfastly advancing reform and opening-up; adhering to the principle that practice is the sole criterion for testing truth; maintaining a problem-oriented approach; embracing strategies such as "crossing the river by feeling the stones" and the "black cat and white cat theory"; coordinated planning; and upholding the general principle of seeking progress while maintaining stability. As a result, there are different combinations of solutions in practice, implementation of pilot programs, and promotion or adjustment of relevant policies based on practical outcomes.

## Addressing Confusions in the Development of Economics

As economics continues to evolve, it faces many confusions, and some renowned economists have raised related questions. The author has systematically reviewed and conducted logical analysis upon the following questions:

1. **Are the Market and the Government in Opposition or Unity?**
   For centuries, economic theory has been revolving around this question. Since Adam Smith, Western economics has grappled with the tension between the government and the market. Subsequently, the debate between economic liberalism and state intervention has revolved around choosing between the market and the government. In practice, the market mechanism can increase the effectiveness of utilizing social resources through the "invisible hand", but it also has its limitations, necessitating the government to timely play its regulatory role through the "visible hand". It must be acknowledged that different schools of thought have their rationality when expressing their views and their limitations when criticizing others. A better approach is to turn to a higher-level unified relationship, i.e., a dialectical relationship between opposition and unity. Therefore, the government and the market are not in absolute opposition.
2. **Is It Reasonable for Economic Theory to Focus on the State of Equilibrium?**
   Absolute equilibrium has never existed in human history, yet the primary theories of economics take this as their study topic. This

means that economic theory typically examines specific states. Theoretical research conducted under different specific states yields different conclusions, leading to diverse schools of thought in economics. If different people can arrive at different conclusions about a defined research object, the justifiability of such a theory must be questioned.

3. **Should Growth Theory Study Potential or Actual Economic Growth?**
   The Solow growth theory, which has been popular for decades, studies potential rather than actual economic growth. Studying potential growth has its rationality, but it is not equal to actual growth research, just as one cannot judge whether someone is a military strategist based on the standards of a potential strategist.
4. **What Should Macroeconomic Policy Aim For?**
   The well-known macroeconomic policy objectives include economic growth, full employment, price stability, and balance of payments. These four objectives stem from Keynesian theory, but Keynesian theory only considers the demand side. Macroeconomic regulation requires a comprehensive consideration of both the supply and demand sides, casting doubt on the rationality of these four objectives. There are no, nor can there be, indicators that reflect structural changes on the supply side.

## The Claim That China Is Not a Market Economy Is Unfounded

In the development of macroeconomic theory, the construction of economic models is crucial. Marx and Engels highly valued the role of mathematics. Economics can establish corresponding theories from the dimensions of the market economy and macroeconomic regulation. In this book, the author integrates the effective market and the efficient government to construct a corresponding theoretical model. This model differs from previous economic theories that focused solely on a pure market economy, as it considers the relatively independent yet important roles of the market and the government. This represents an innovative research approach.

In fact, a system (combining an effective market and an efficient government) where the market plays a decisive role is a market economy model. Each market economy models in the world today have their own unique characteristics: the "liberal" market economy model represented by the United States; the social market economy model represented by Europe; the government-guided market economy model represented by Japan; the welfare-oriented market economy model represented by Sweden; and the socialist market economy model represented by China (combining an effective market and an efficient government). The US and Europe often criticize China for not being a market economy, but this claim is unfounded. In fact, governments in the US and Europe also play significant roles, and the difference lies only in the proportion of market-related components in their economic models.

## China's Practice Has Driven Innovation in Macroeconomic Regulation Theory

China's innovation in macroeconomic regulation theory acknowledges the role of Keynesian macroeconomic policies while aligning with Samuelson's logic of comprehensively considering aggregate supply and demand. However, based on China's practical experience, it has refined a regulatory system that organically integrates supply-side and demand-side policies, ensuring that macroeconomic policies address both demand-side and supply-side structural reforms. Consequently, macroeconomic regulation theory has become a system that integrates supply-side and demand-side management, with both aspects consistently present but emphasized differently depending on the prominence of aggregate or structural issues in the economy at different stages. In recent years, China's combined use of supply-side and demand-side policies is telling evidence in this regard.

Renmin University of China
Beijing, China
January 2022

Liu Wei

# Contents

# About the Author

## Author

**Zong Liang** is a professor and former chief economist of the Bank of China Research Institute and a senior researcher at the world finance forum (WFF). He has degrees from Wuhan University, Renmin University of China, Fudan University (China and America Economics Training Program), Wudaokou Financial Institute, and Tsinghua University. In recent years, he took part in more than 20 important projects and released over 200 papers. He has published *Innovation of Economic Theory in China—A Perspective of Theoretical Model, Manufacturing Finance, The Future of Globalization for Economic Internationalization, Theories and Prospects for RMB Internationalization*. He has also been an adjunct professor or instructor at Peking University, Renmin University of China, University of International Business and Economics and other universities. He has been working at the Bank of China for a long time, mainly responsible for macroeconomic research, financial and banking research and other related work. His awards include 2020 Outstanding Contribution Expert in News Propaganda of China's Banking Industry and 2022–2024 Leading News Propaganda Expert of China's Banking Industry.

## Translators

**Fan Ruoying** is a researcher at the Bank of China, having graduated from Wuhan University and Nankai University. Her primary areas of research are China's macroeconomics and policy, commodities, and prices.

**Li Yingting** is a researcher at the headquarters of the Bank of China. She obtained her bachelor's and master's degrees from the London School of Economics and Political Science (LSE) and holds a PhD from the Chinese Academy of Social Sciences. Her primary research focuses on international finance and international trade.

**Ping Jing** is a researcher at the headquarters of the Bank of China. Her primary stream of research focuses on Environment, social and governance (ESG) and organizational performance. She also studies capital market.

# List of Figures

# List of Tables

CHAPTER 1

# Macroeconomic Theory: History and Outlook

"This is the way of the world: what has long been divided must be united, and what has long been united must be divided." This opening quote from the *Romance of the Three Kingdoms*, the classical Chinese novel written in the fourteenth century, illuminates the vicissitudes of life, and the seemingly simple sentence is truly thought-provoking and enlightening. Human civilization can be roughly divided into Eastern civilization and Western civilization, both of which have created miracles and have their own advantages and disadvantages. In general, what primarily sets the two civilizations apart is the emphasis on union or division. Western civilization, marked by division, is more focused on "yes or no," while Eastern civilization, centered on union, emphasizes "balance." The models fitting with the social development stages influence the characteristics and progress of civilization. In comparison, division is more characteristic of a slave society or capitalist society. Western civilization has reached a higher level of development, while Eastern civilization largely boomed in feudal society. The US in the nineteenth century had the dual features of slavery and capitalism, but capitalism later took hold.

Similar to the progress of civilization, the logic of economic theory has evolved along the path of division and union, and the crux lies in whether to emphasize "yes or no" or "balance." At the two extremes are the pure market economy and the traditional planned economy, with the real-world economies in between. From Adam Smith's free market economy theory to the Keynesian Revolution and the rise of neoliberalism, the evolution of



Z. Liang, *The Innovation of Economic Theory in China*,
https://doi.org/10.1007/978-981-95-2713-7_1

economic theory reveals the seesaw, rather than an either-or, in the role of market and that of government. Hence, there is no use in arguing about the role of market and that of government, and the key lies in how to balance the two. Generally, neither option is advisable over the long time; the rational choice and also the most effective path of economic development is to let the market play the decisive role and the government do its part.

Theory comes from practice, guides practice, and constantly innovates in practice. Debates among different schools of thought have been prevalent during the evolution of macroeconomic theory. At times, these schools of thought are isolated from or completely opposite to one another, while at other times, they exhibit different degrees of continuity and progression. In advanced capitalist societies which have evolved rapidly, Western economics examines the role of market or government from a single-dimensional perspective rather than adopting a multidimensional, integrated approach. As such, there has been persistently a fundamental tension between market and government. In the long-term debates among different schools of thought, economists have come to realize the limitations of single-dimensional thinking, or an either-or between market and government, which forces a choice between two extremes. It is because of this realization that the thinking of rational synthesis has emerged. Practice has shown that neither the pure market economy model nor the planned economy model is flawless. Since the launch of reform and opening up in 1978, China has embarked on a road featuring the combination of market mechanisms and government regulation, which is also a road of innovation.

## 1 Evolution and Major Schools of Macroeconomic Thought

Hailed as the "king of social sciences," economics is the science that studies the principles governing economic functioning. It has indeed constructed a spectacular "edifice" of theoretical frameworks, but the absence of unified logic across numerous schools of thought somewhat dims its glitter as a robust science. Economics demands a coherent and homogeneous framework; otherwise, its nature as a science would not be fully justified. For any country, the relationship between economic variables and the principles of economic functioning should be basically settled, and should not be interpreted with two or more kinds of economic theories.

The origin of economic thought can be traced back to ancient times. Ancient Greece, Rome, and China all engaged in early explorations, which were just the embryo of economic research due to the limited economic conditions at the time. Although some thinkers offered opinions on economic problems back then, their ideas were mostly piecemeal and unsystematic. For this reason, economics had yet to be an independent discipline before Adam Smith. It is widely accepted that economics came into being in the fifteenth century and developed rapidly after the eighteenth century; especially since the 1870s onward, theories about economic operations and government regulation have abounded. Based on the practices of liberal capitalism in the UK, Adam Smith published *An Inquiry into the Nature and Causes of the Wealth of Nations* (commonly referred to simply as *The Wealth of Nations*) in 1776. The Great Depression in the 1930s and its response gave birth to Keynes's macroeconomic theory. After the 1970s, stagflation caused by a spike in effective demand, a concept articulated in Keynesianism, underlined the limitations of this theory. Monetarism, supply-side school, and other schools of thought emerged consequently. Despite the stark differences between the Great Depression of the 1930s and the 2008 international financial crisis, the two crises both wreaked havoc on the economy and brought to light the flaws of economic theory and market failures, which also reflects the basic logic of the evolution of economic theories.

Ancient economists in Eastern countries represented by China view economics as the practical knowledge that guides people to create value and meet people's demands. Guan Zhong (c. 720–645 BC) was a rare economist in history who put his economic thought into practice. Guan Zhong's economic thought encompasses market mechanisms, macroeconomic regulation, and international trade theory, providing insights for the interpretation of modern economic theory and economic theoretical innovation. During a period when the interconnectivity among various economic issues was relatively limited, early-stage economic research was inclined to single-dimensional thinking and even overgeneralization. Actually, economic thinking should be multidimensional rather than single-dimensional.

## *1.1 Evolution and Schools of Macroeconomic Thought*

With the evolution of economic thought, typical schools composed of economists in different contexts and with different viewpoints emerged at a particular stage. In fact, the emergence of various schools of economic thought and economic theories is based on the varying development stages and economic issues (Woodford, 2009). An in-depth study on the schools of macroeconomic thought and their evolution is conducive to a full and thorough understanding of debates among different schools of thought, and can also provide insights for comprehensively and dynamically observing and comprehending the evolution logic of macroeconomic thought from multiple perspectives.

1. Emergence of classical economics and its advocacy for Say's Law

Adam Smith, widely regarded as the father of classical economics, put forth the concept of the "invisible hand" in his masterpiece, *The Wealth of Nations*. He argues that the result of everyone pursuing their own self-interests will be the maximization of interests within a society, and this process is spontaneous. Classical economists assert that the market regulates itself through the "invisible hand." That is, employment and output disequilibrium is temporary, and in the case of any deviation from the equilibrium levels of employment and output deviate, the market mechanism will respond and regulate itself promptly so as to restore equilibrium in economic operations. In brief, classical economists consider a complete market mechanism as the optimal way of resource allocation, and believe in Say's Law, which states that supply creates its own demand.

2. Keynesian revolution brought about by the Great Depression and the rise of Keynesianism

The Great Depression of 1929–1933 presented an enormous challenge to the classical view of free markets and eventually gave rise to the Keynesian Revolution. In his book, *The General Theory of Employment, Interest and Money*, Keynes argues that because prices and wages are rigid, relying solely on the spontaneous operation of market mechanisms is not sufficient in a capitalist economy; instead, government regulation and market forces should be combined. Keynes was against Say's Law, believing that demand creates its own supply – this is called Keynes' Law. It uses comparative statics analysis instead of classical static equilibrium analysis and puts forward the output and employment theory as opposed to the classical price theory. Moreover, the theory of effective demand was produced, which holds that demand determines output. After World War II,

Keynesian views about government intervention and full employment could be found in the macro control policies adopted by most Western countries. The emergence of Keynesian economics prompted the shift of Western countries from free markets to government intervention, marking the birth of modern macroeconomics.

3. Return of neoclassical economics in the era of stagflation

During the 1970s and 1980s, the US economy experienced severe stagflation, causing Keynesian economics to be called into question. Amid the criticism of Keynesian views from neoclassical economists, Lucas's monetary theory of business cycles and Barro's real business cycle (RBC) theory emerged (Huang Shuren, 2002). Based on the hypothesis of price-wage elasticity and the rational expectations hypothesis, this theory emphasizes general equilibrium analysis and the micro foundation of macroeconomics. The hypothesis of price-wage elasticity originated from classical economics. It is believed that when there is a temporary imbalance between supply and demand in the commodity and labor markets, prices and wages can adjust swiftly to ensure continuous market clearing. The rational expectations hypothesis represents a breakthrough in neoclassical macroeconomics, stating that economic agents exploit the best available information to form their expectations. Neoclassical economics also emphasizes the use of modern mathematical statistical techniques and behavioral analysis under uncertainty, playing an enormous role in promoting the microscopic development and econometric development of macroeconomic research. Neoclassicalism believes that the market can regulate itself and possesses inherent stability, and that the government is practically no smarter than rational actors, so government intervention in economic operations is ineffective.

4. Evolution of new Keynesian economics

Building on the existing theories along the two paths, neoclassical macroeconomics came into being under the market economy model. New classical economist Robert Lucas (1972, 1988) has put forth the Lucas aggregate supply curve on the basis of the rational expectations hypothesis and microeconomic hypothesis. Long and Plosser (1983) have put forward the RBC theory, believing that the most important sources of economic fluctuations are supply shocks and government expenditure shocks.

However, they presume that a free market economy is in perfect conditions, and the role of government is merely to intervene in short-run market fluctuations. Under the model of government action, new Keynesian economics emerged relative to old Keynesian economics. The main proponents include N. Gregory Mankiw and Joseph Stiglitz. New Keynesian economics also deals with the key issues of unemployment and economic fluctuations, but it expands upon old Keynesian economics in some ways (Wang Yaozhong and Tong Wenjun, 2003). Information asymmetry and rational expectations are used to explain "price stickiness" in Keynesian economics and on this basis, a theoretical system is constructed with the key features of wage and price stickiness, imperfect competition, asymmetric information, and rational expectations. New Keynesian economics believes that policy ineffectiveness is based on immediate market clearing, but due to wage and price stickiness, immediate market clearing cannot be guaranteed in the process of the spontaneous operation of the economy. Therefore, market mechanisms are not necessarily effective, thus requiring government regulation.

The mid-to-late 1990s saw new consensus and integration between neoclassical economics and new Keynesian economics, resulting in the emergence of the new neoclassical synthesis. Neoclassical economics began to recognize the existence of market failure, while new Keynesian economics started to acknowledge the significance of market mechanisms, marking a gradual convergence of the two. New neoclassical synthesis integrates the RBC theory with new Keynesian economics, culminating in a landmark consensus on the optimal approach to explaining short-term economic fluctuations – the dynamic stochastic general equilibrium (DSGE) model after prolonged debates between neoclassical and new Keynesian economists (Giese, Guido, and Wagner, 2006; Woodford, 2009; Romer, 2016). The core idea is that a market economy operates as a DSGE system, and short-term market operations can deviate from the optimal allocation of resources due to wage and price stickiness and asymmetric market information. Nevertheless, over the long haul, market mechanisms remain the optimal means to regulate economic activity, allocate resources, and drive economic growth. In terms of policy propositions, the new neoclassical synthesis believes that monetary policy plays a greater role than fiscal policy, and that the primary goal of monetary policy should be to stabilize inflation.

The evolution of major schools of macroeconomic thought is shown in Fig. 1.1.

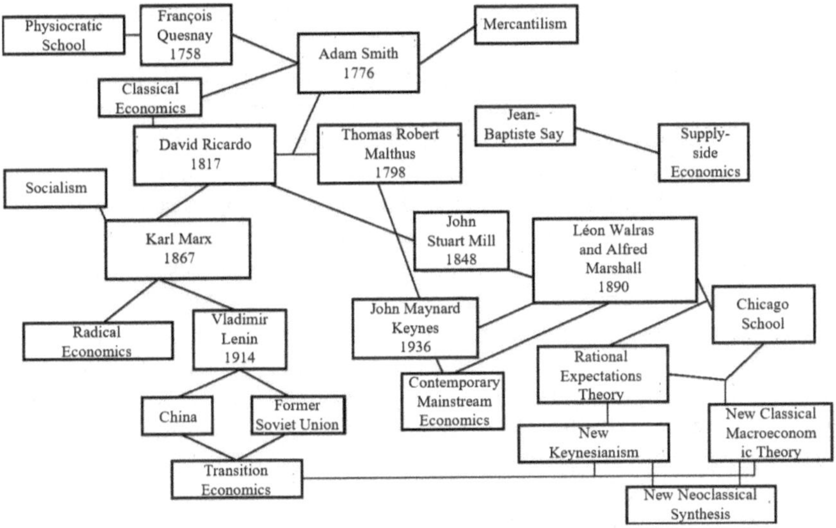


**Fig. 1.1** Evolution of major schools of macroeconomic thought. (Source: Paul A. Samuelson and William D. Nordhaus. *Economics*. 18th Edition. Beijing: Posts & Telecom Press, 2008)

## *1.2 Great Debate Between Hayek and Keynes*

Friedrich August Hayek and John Maynard Keynes were both prestigious economists in the twentieth century. Keynes is best known as the father of modern macroeconomics. His book, *The General Theory of Employment, Interest and Money*, published in 1936, gave rise to the Keynesian Revolution. Keynes is a pioneer in advocating the government's role in regulating the economy, bringing attention to the "visible hand," with many countries becoming the testing grounds. Hayek gained fame for his great book, *The Road to Serfdom*, arguing that the healthy functioning of human society must rely on the free market. Hayek is a leading figure of liberalism who gave an incisive criticism on big government while enthusiastically advocating liberalism. The great debate between Hayek and Keynes in the 1930s is deemed as the most important economic debate in the twentieth century, with a sizable and far-reaching impact on economic and social development.

1. Background of the great debate between Hayek and Keynes

World War I is a pivotal turning point regarding the UK's international status. Due to a sharp spike in government spending during the war, the UK had to go off the gold standard. After World War I, the UK fell into decline as the workshop of the world and a colonial empire. The Great Depression of 1929–1933 is regarded as the most severe crisis in the history of capitalism, distinguished by novel characteristics that set it apart from previous downturns. Over a prolonged five-year period, the Great Depression was marked by a sharp decline in productivity and a significant surge in unemployment, at an unprecedented scale compared to earlier crises, leading to a prolonged era of economic desolation. This crisis dragged the world's industrial production back to the level of 1900–1908 and even before 1900 for the UK. How to unravel the underlying causes of this prolonged depression thus emerged as a key challenge to economic theory.

In this context, Keynes began to question the two pillars of economic theory at the time: one is whether a currency must have a solid foundation, which is the gold standard; and the other is about Say's Law, which posits that supply creates its own demand to establish an equilibrium itself. The Keynesian theory then gathered wide attention in the academic community. After World War II, it was embraced by major developed countries, shaping their policies to regulate economic operations. In the wake of the Great Depression of the 1930s, the Keynesian Revolution emerged, giving rise to Keynesian economics, the Western mainstream economic theory for a long time after World War II. Amid the stagflation facing Western countries in the 1970s, Keynesian economics was called into question, while Hayek's theory received growing attention.

2. Great debate between Hayek and Keynes: a brief outline and key areas of contention

The great debate between Hayek and Keynes began with a paper published by John Maynard Keynes in 1926 – "The End of Laissez-Faire," and later, Keynes published a series of essays such as the "Treatise on Money." A great economic debate hence unfolded, with the bone of contention revolving around whether the government should intervene in the market. The two both studied the boom and bust cycles by looking at the economy after World War I, but they came to totally different conclusions.

Hayek argued that changing the "natural equilibrium" of the economy would lead to severe inflationary pressures, while Keynes contended that government economic policy could to some extent ease unemployment. From 1932 to 1936, Hayek published several treatises on monetary theory, industrial volatility, the relationship between savings and investment, and other topics, launching an exhaustive critique of Keynes's theory. Keynes published *The General Theory of Employment, Interest and Money* in 1936 as a counterargument. After this book came out, a majority of economists were inclined toward Keynes's views, thinking that compared with Hayek's advocacy for monetary restraint, Keynes' theory of economic expansion could work better to address the mass unemployment and high inflation at the time. In 1944, Hayek published his great book, *The Road to Serfdom*, and in 1974, became a Nobel Laureate in Economics together with Robert Mundell. As an opponent of Keynesianism, Hayek launched into an extended criticism of Keynesian views, pointing out the maladies caused by government intervention in the economy. The two economists, until the end of their lives, were not on the same page.

In 1947, Hayek founded the Mont Pelerin Society (MPS), an influential group of economists and intellectuals who meet to discuss and advocate for neoliberalism. Well-known members of the society include Karl Popper, Ludwig von Mises, Frank Knight, and Milton Friedman. Hayek is a believer in the private enterprise system and free market economy, regarding them as the best means of maintaining individual and market freedom and continuously improving economic efficiency. This may mark a starting point of Western neoliberalism. Generations of politicians, from Franklin Roosevelt to George W. Bush, have wavered back and forth between the views of the two scholars.

The debate between Hayek and Keynes primarily revolves around currency, the economic cycle, capital theory, and government intervention, with the last one being the bone of contention. According to Hayek, market economies have self-regulatory capacity, and excessive government intervention can cause distortions in resource allocation and eventually hinder economic development. In contrast, Keynes advocates regulating the operation of market economies through active government intervention. He believes that government intervention can reduce the instability of economic operations, thus serving the purpose of overcoming an economic crisis and improving economic expectations.

3. Divergent opinions on policy measures

Hayek thinks that the role of macro policy is limited, and expansionary monetary policy may lead to over-investment and even trigger major economic crises in serious circumstances, so a more restrained and prudent monetary policy may work better. Compared with Keynes, Hayek considers himself an optimist. While not discounting the possibility of economic crises hitting market economies, he claims that market is more capable of averting such crises than government.

Keynes ascribes economic crises to insufficient effective demand, particularly insufficient consumer demand. He argues that the primary reason for economic stagnation is inadequate employment, and in order to spur economic growth through public investment and creation of more jobs, government must intervene in market operations, for example, adopt appropriate policies to drive economic development. This stands in stark contrast to Hayek's optimism about market. Keynes holds that a moderate increase in money supply can effectively stimulate demand. Hayek, however, argues that preserving the "non-state" nature of currency will prove more effective in maintaining the stability of capitalist economies. Hayek's critique of Keynesianism barely pays attention to expansionary fiscal policy, which is precisely at the core of Keynesian policy. That is perhaps because in the real world, expansionary fiscal policy is often accompanied by expansionary monetary policy, so a country's fiscal deficits are usually addressed by the central bank through money printing.

Keynesian economics became the mainstream school of Western economics after World War II, playing a vital role in the post-war economic reconstruction of Europe. In the aftermath of World War II, capitalist economies experienced decades of economic boom, which was widely regarded as a testament to the great success of Keynesian economics and policy. For this reason, Keynes was lauded as the "architect of post-war prosperity." However, after the late 1960s and early 1970s, Keynesian economics came under criticism from liberal economists for failing to explain stagflation. Economic liberalism took Western economics by storm, while traditional Keynesianism lost popularity (before it was pulled out of the predicament by new Keynesian economics that emerged later). Economic liberalism advocated by Hayek enjoyed a resurgence, and his theory gained unprecedented attention amidst shifting times and needs.

While Keynes and Hayek held opposing views, their intellectual duel contributed to the maturation of their respective theories, both exerting a profound influence on global economic and governance structures. During the 2008 international financial crisis, views of Keynesian economics prevailed around the world, while Hayek's ideas helped the economy recover and grow steadily from 2009 to 2019. It goes without saying that both Keynes' and Hayek's economic theories hold high relevance for China in building a socialist market economy. On one hand, the logic of Keynesian economics is in alignment with China's demand for effective government intervention. The country's macro control policy also echoes the fundamental direction outlined in Keynesian economics. On the other hand, although China's market economy model is different from Hayek's vision of the free market economy, Hayek's firm grasp of the generalities of market economies offers inspiration for China to building it. It can be said that the synthesis of their economic theories shares common ground with China's market economy model.

### *1.3 Debate Between Liberalism and Conservatism*

The history of macroeconomics is inherently intertwined with the evolution of schools of economic thought, and the vibrancy of macroeconomics is mainly manifested in the debates and alternations among different schools of economic thought. The abundant results in macroeconomics owe much to the evolution and competition among different schools of economic thought. The debates among different schools of macroeconomic thought have long been centered around whether the government should intervene in economic activity. As can be seen from the evolution of different schools of macroeconomic thought,[1] macroeconomic discourses have always focused on whether the government should intervene in economic activity (Stiglitz, 2018). By this measure, macroeconomics can be divided into liberals and conservatives: Liberalism advocates a laissez-faire economy and opposes government intervention, and schools of liberal thought mainly include classicism and neoclassicism. Conservatism acknowledges market failure and approves of government intervention, and schools of conservative thought include Keynesianism and new

[1] In addition to the aforementioned schools of economic thought, there are also monetarism, supply-side economics, new institutional economics, and Austrian economics, which have all played their part in understanding economic phenomena and addressing economic issues.

Keynesianism. The main differences between liberalism and conservatism are as follows:

First, they have different understandings of market equilibrium. Liberalism holds that wages and prices are elastic, and when a supply-demand imbalance occurs in the product market or labor market, supply and demand can reestablish an equilibrium through quick adjustment of wages and prices. Conservatism argues that in the case of economic disturbances, self-adjustment of wages and prices is a slow process, making it difficult to reestablish a market equilibrium quickly.

Second, they provide different explanations for economic fluctuations. Liberalism thinks that rational actors will promptly adjust their behavior when detecting discrepancies between expectations and reality, and since wages and prices are perfectly elastic, such adjustments can quickly eliminate economic fluctuations. Conservatism contends that wage and price stickiness tends to amplify the impact of economic fluctuations, resulting in periodic fluctuations in real total output and total employment.

Third, they diverge over economic policies. Being against government intervention in the economy, liberalism asserts that economic fluctuations are an effective reaction of rational actors to shocks rather than the result of market failure. Thanks to market mechanisms, the economy can reestablish an equilibrium itself and has the ability to self-recovery and self-regulation, and government intervention may actually aggravate the fluctuations. On the contrary, conservatism advocates for government intervention in the economy, thinking that the government can introduce discretionary macroeconomic policies and further stabilize through institutional design.

Over time, both liberals and conservatives have come to recognize their own deficiencies and virtues in the opposing views, trying to draw upon each other's valuable ideas. Nonetheless, they are fundamentally flawed in their attempts to reconcile the other's rationale within the confines of their own perspective. Therefore, it's destined that they alternated with varying economic issues in early-stage research, so a unified analysis framework has yet to be established.

## 1.4 Debate Between the Saltwater School and the Freshwater School

The debates among different schools of macroeconomic thought have long been centered around whether the government should intervene in economic activity. One case in point is the ongoing debate between the saltwater school and the freshwater school[2] in the mainstream economic world of the US since the 1970s. The two schools of thought mainly differ from each other in their understanding of the market-government relationship, interpretations of economic fluctuations, and propositions for government policy intervention. Fundamentally, the drawn-out debate between the saltwater school and the freshwater school epitomizes the evolution of modern macroeconomics amidst the debates among different schools of thought, and a closer look at the debate can offer deep and comprehensive insights into the evolution and transformation of macroeconomic theory. International practices show that the role of government and that of market are not flawless, but they are both essential. For example, typical market economies have emphasized the role of government, while government-dominant economies have gradually allowed the market to play a bigger role, reflecting the trend of convergence among economic models. The debate between the saltwater school and the freshwater school also shows that macroeconomic theory is evolving toward unity and synthesis. Following the 2008 international financial crisis, significant changes have taken place in the global economic landscape, prompting further reflection on macroeconomic theory. The main differences between the saltwater school and the freshwater school (see Table 1.1) are as follows:

First, they have different understandings about the market-government relationship. In view of liberal principles, economists of the freshwater school contend that wages and prices are elastic. When a supply-demand imbalance occurs in the product market or labor market, supply and demand can reestablish an equilibrium through quick adjustment of wages and prices. Therefore, economists of the freshwater school advocate for self-regulation of market mechanisms, believing that a free market can

[2] Economists of the saltwater school are concentrated in prestigious universities on the East Coast and West Coast of the US, such as the University of California, Berkeley, Harvard University, Massachusetts Institute of Technology, Stanford University, University of Pennsylvania, Princeton University, Columbia University, and Yale University. These universities are located near the sea, so they are collectively called the "saltwater school." Economists of the freshwater school are mostly from prominent schools in the interior of the US and adjacent to the Great Lakes region, such as the University of Chicago, Carnegie-Mellon University, the University of Rochester, and the University of Minnesota. These universities are situated around the Great Lakes region and far from the sea, hence the name "freshwater school."

**Table 1.1** Differences between the freshwater school and the saltwater school

| *School of economic thought* | *Freshwater school* | *Saltwater school* |
|---|---|---|
| Understanding about the market-government relationship | Wages and prices can be adjusted quickly, allowing supply and demand to reestablish an equilibrium; market mechanisms are able to self-regulate | Self-adjustment of wages or prices is a slow process, making it difficult to achieve a swift restoration of market equilibrium<br>Relying solely on the self-regulating ability of market will not work, and there needs to be regulation from the government over economic activity. |
| Explanations for economic fluctuations | The monetary theory of business cycles thinks that economic fluctuations are caused by expectation deviations of actors<br>The RBC theory argues that economic fluctuations are caused by real shocks | Wage and price stickiness |
| Whether the government should intervene in the economy | No | Yes |
| Main strongholds | The University of Chicago, Carnegie-Mellon University, the University of Rochester, the University of Minnesota, etc. | The University of California, Berkeley, Harvard University, Massachusetts Institute of Technology, Stanford University, University of Pennsylvania, Princeton University, Columbia University, Yale University, etc. |
| Representatives | Milton Friedman, George Joseph Stigler, Friedrich August Hayek, Robert Lucas, Robert Barro, etc. | Paul Krugman, Bradford DeLong, Joseph Stiglitz, N. Gregory Mankiw, etc. |

Source: Compiled by the author

achieve the optimal allocation of resources. Economists of the saltwater school argue that in the case of demand or supply disturbances, self-adjustment of wages and prices is a slow process, making it difficult to reestablish a market equilibrium quickly. To bring real output back to the normal is a long process, in which the economy will be in a protracted state of disequilibrium, characterized by a mismatch between supply and demand. Therefore, economists of the saltwater school maintain that relying solely on the spontaneous operation of market mechanisms will not work, and it is necessary to regulate economic activity through government intervention.

Second, they have different views about government intervention in the economy. As staunch liberals, economists of the freshwater school are against government intervention in the economy. They think that economic fluctuations are an effective reaction of rational economic agents to shocks rather than the result of market failure. Market mechanisms are inherently able to recover and regulate themselves, enabling the economy to reestablish an equilibrium itself, and overcapacity and outdated productive forces are eliminated in this self-correction process. If the government introduces counter-cyclical policies to intervene in the economy, that will prove ineffective and may actually aggravate the fluctuations. In contrast, economists of the saltwater school are staunch supporters of government intervention in the economy. They posit that market mechanisms are ineffective in balancing supply and demand and that relying solely on markets to adjust from disequilibrium to equilibrium is not only a slow process but also a costly one. As such, they emphasize the need for the government to play an active regulatory role. Economists of the saltwater school believe in the effectiveness of the government's demand management policy, and argue that since the shocks that cause economic fluctuations are random, the government needs to develop appropriate policy responses. The government can introduce discretionary macroeconomic policies and further stabilize an economy through institutional design.

Finally, they provide different explanations for economic fluctuations and cycles. The freshwater school thinks that with complete information, actors have rational expectations and will adjust their behavior when detecting discrepancies between expectations and reality. Under the condition that wages and prices are perfectly elastic, economic fluctuations can be quickly eliminated. The theoretical underpinnings of the freshwater school mainly include the monetary theory of business cycles and the RBC theory. Specifically, the monetary theory of business cycles explains economic fluctuations from the demand side, asserting that unexpected changes in money supply cause price fluctuations and discrepancies in the expectations of rational actors. These discrepancies subsequently prompt adjustments in market supply and bring disturbances to the total economic production, eventually resulting in economic fluctuations. In contrast, the RBC theory interprets economic fluctuations from the supply side, contending that economic fluctuations are triggered by real shocks that can shift the production function, such as technological innovation and the launch of new products. Economists of the saltwater school combine the explanations for economic fluctuations with wage and price stickiness. They posit that the sources of economic fluctuations are both supply shocks and demand shocks, and that wage and price stickiness tends to amplify such shocks, resulting in periodic fluctuations in real total output and total employment. The process of reestablishing an equilibrium in the aftermath of economic shocks is an economic cycle.

## 1.5 *Market-Government Relationship Is the Key Area of Contention Among Different Schools of Thought*

Throughout the evolution of economic theory, economic development models and theory have always been focused on "whether the government should intervene in economic activity" and evolved with the different combinations of the role of market and that of government, of which the main line is that the market plays the decisive role, while the government plays a supporting role rather than function independently. The crux is that this debate has shown no signs of abatement, from the great debate between Hayek and Keynes to the debate between the saltwater school and the freshwater school. Still, economists' inquiry has gone deeper amidst the ongoing debates and spurred the development of macroeconomic theory. Economic theory is constantly evolving. In this process, old theories are not completely discarded, and some rational and useful insights are retained and endowed with fresh interpretations in the new era.

Macroeconomics encompasses theories built from the perspectives of market economy and also theories from the perspective of government intervention. These theories shed light on economic models within their own frameworks. However, free market economy and planned economy are highly abstracted models of the real-world economic systems and represent two extremes. In general, an economy is neither a purely free market economy nor an economy purely relying on government intervention; to be more exact, it is a mixed economy. In order to facilitate a more appropriate and accurate analysis of economic realities, it is necessary to develop an economic theory based on mixed economy, taking into account both the role of market and that of government. Just as in the case of medicine, traditional Chinese medicine (TCM) theories and techniques have been established based on China's practices, while the theories and techniques of Western medicine have been developed based on Western practices. Both TCM and Western medicine have their own functions and limitations, so combining the two is the way forward. For another example, the wave theory of light was constructed based on the view that light behaves as a wave, while the corpuscular theory was established based on the view that light behaves as a particle. In fact, further research found that light has the twofold nature of particle-wave duality, and the wave-particle duality theory offers a more comprehensive understanding of light.

Internationally, market economies are not infallible but have limitations and are prone to market failure. Meanwhile, comprehensive government intervention poses challenges to traditional theories of capitalist economies, leading to significant political and ideological transformations. As can be seen from the bail-out policies following the 2008 international financial crisis, policymakers were no longer confined to Keynesianism, monetarism, or the rational expectations theory, and as a last resort, tried almost all policy solutions advocated by different theories. Underlying this is essentially the thinking of rational synthesis. China's practices over the past decades have shown that relying solely on the traditional planned economy will not work, and China must take the road of developing a market economy, in which the government should play its part. This sets it apart from the market economy in the West. Combining the two offers a more effective economic model, and the role of government should be appropriate.

Throughout the evolution of macroeconomic theory, when old theories fall short in making good explanations for the new things and problems in society, theoretical revolutions would occur, giving rise to new ideas. Following the 2008 international financial crisis, significant changes have taken place in the global economic landscape, posing new challenges to macroeconomic theory. In response, we need to dive deep into the evolution of the macroeconomic theory, reflect, innovate and create opportunities in a time of crisis, and put forward policy recommendations on employment.

## 2 The Dilemma of Macroeconomic Theory and Reflection

The market-government relationship has long been a matter of disputation among different schools of macroeconomic thought. Adam Smith's *The Wealth of Nations* highlights the crucial role of the "invisible hand," while Keynesianism emphasizes the "visible hand" of government. Now that there are two hands, using both hands should work better than using just one hand, yet the reality is that the "invisible hand" has been admired in parts of the world for hundreds of years. In fact, the role of government and that of market are both indispensable. How to deal with the relationship between market and government is a significant topic that needs further research.

Enormous success has been achieved in macroeconomic theory, as evidenced by relatively complete theoretical systems and in-depth discussions in various areas. For example, the macroeconomic theory looks deeply into market economy, government regulation, and the market-government relationship, and discusses the aggregate demand and aggregate supply (long-term and short-term) policy framework. Among them, the aggregate demand-aggregate supply (AD-AS) model actually goes beyond the scope of effective demand in Keynesian economics and extends the policy space to supply, laying solid groundwork for exploring the long-term mechanism of macroeconomic policy. The growth model that stems from classical economics takes into account relevant macro factors while highlighting potential economic growth, paving the way for the development of growth models characterized by the synergy between market and government. These explorations still have some limitations. For example, they have yet to come up with a unified model or express it in precise mathematical terms; the economic growth model is largely within the scope of classical economics and not a dynamic model that considers both the role of market and that of government; there is no framework for considering macro policies from a holistic perspective of aggregate supply and aggregate demand, and the relationship between economic growth and economic development is to be unraveled, indicating the absence of a theoretical basis for long-term or short-term policy design.

This has prompted reflections and discussions on macroeconomic theory among numerous prominent macroeconomists. In recent years, especially since the 2008 international financial crisis, significant changes have taken place in the global economic landscape, and the advent of the era of big data has offered new insights into complex macroeconomic models. Typical examples in recent years include the debate between Paul Krugman and John Cochrane and "the trouble with macroeconomics" put forward by Paul Romer. All these pose new challenges to macroeconomics while also setting the direction for future development. The main predicaments of macroeconomic theory and reflections are in the following.

### 2.1 Reflections on the Boundary Between the Role of Market and That of Government

The market-government relationship has long been a focus of macroeconomic research. The seesaw of the role of market and that of government has inspired a wide reckoning from economists. Although the two schools of neoclassicism and new Keynesianism were approaching each other, inquiry into the cause and spread of the 2008 international financial crisis reignited the debate between them, sparking further discussions about what government should do or should not do. Paul Krugman contends that the financial crisis reflects the fact that financial markets are not perfect and need to be regulated by the government, stressing the need to "embrace Keynesianism again." Joseph Stiglitz distinguishes between economic shocks by level of severity, arguing that markets often fail in the face of some massive, structural economic shocks so appropriate government regulation is required. John Cochrane, a representative of the freshwater school, is a staunch supporter of the free market, claiming that government control over the market would generate even worse outcomes. Hacker ascribes the economic prosperity and social stability in the twentieth century to the integration of government intervention and market functions, stressing the need to find a balance between the two in the future.

### 2.2 Concept of Economics and the Rational Economic Man Hypothesis

Economics as a science shouldn't be equated to Western economics. Conceptually, the subject of study in Western economics revolves around the concept of scarcity, which is seldom mentioned in the current context of economic practices, as scarcity is a thing of the past and we now live in a world of abundance. As such, it would make more sense to define economics as the science that studies the principles of economic functioning. Economics as a science should adhere to certain laws and its objective nature, although the differences between economics and physics should be acknowledged. Economic theory is notably packed with concepts borrowed from physics or biology (for example, competition is related to Darwin's theory of evolution), largely due to the profound impact of Newtonian mechanics, which even extended its influence to Adam Smith's thinking.

The rational economic man hypothesis is the basis of Western mainstream economics. The concept of equilibrium is exactly based on the rational economic man hypothesis. With the economic development, especially the recurrence of financial crises, the rational economic man hypothesis is being called into question. The two core ideas of the hypothesis are: first, economic agents are completely rational, and second, they seek to maximize their personal utility. The rational economic man hypothesis is justifiable to some degree, and the research process follows rigorous standards. However, in reality, people are not absolutely rational or always maximize their personal utility. Therefore, the rational economic man hypothesis alone is not enough to explain various economic phenomena; that is, the rational economic man typifies individuals who are exceedingly self-interested and astute. If the rational economic man is used to represent real individuals, how can we ensure that theories founded upon the hypothesis align seamlessly with the real world?

Herbert A. Simon is the first to systematically argue that economic agents are not completely rational. In his book *Administrative Behavior: A Study of Decision-Making Processes in Administrative Organization*, he introduces the concept of bounded rationality and points out that in practice, economic agents follow the "satisfying principle" rather than the maximization principle. Behavioral economists represented by Daniel Kanemann and Richard Thaler further state that under conditions of uncertainty, most individuals are not rational and risk-averse; in situations of incomplete information, economic agents tend to use heuristics, intuition, and habits to aid decision-making, resulting in cognitive biases. After the 2008 international financial crisis, more and more scholars started to reflect on and question the basic assumptions about market economies such as rational economic man. Paul Krugman contends that "if the profession is to redeem itself, it will have to reconcile itself to a less alluring vision – that of a market economy that has many virtues but that is also shot through with flaws and frictions," and that "flaws-and-frictions economics will move from the periphery of economic analysis to its center." Joseph Stiglitz outlines the inadequacies of the DSGE model on a microscopic basis, arguing that it failed to incorporate insights from information economics and behavioral economics; consequently, "the model neither predicted the most important macroeconomic event in the past three quarters of a century nor provided good guidance as to the appropriate policy responses."

The rational economic man hypothesis posits that the "invisible hand" facilitates self-regulation and undergoes a transition to "bounded rationality," a shift from utility maximization as proposed in classical economics to satisfaction maximization as emphasized in behavioral economics. In fact, any economic individual is a combination of rationality and irrationality, the weights of which vary for different individuals, at different times, and on different occasions. In general, we think the rational economic man as a combination of rationality and irrationality, who is dominated by rationality, and this portrayal is consistent with reality.

### 2.3 *Proper Use of Hypotheses*

The concept of hypothesis in physics is a reasonable approximation of reality, and the results based on a hypothesis are approximations of reality. Theory should be constructed to elucidate reality, and a hypothesis should serve as a reasonable approximation of reality. However, in economics, the concept of hypothesis is generalized, so the conclusions drawn from it may be inconsistent with reality or even completely irrelevant to reality.

In scientific research, hypothetical conditions are always required. When the hypothetical conditions are relatively lax and better aligned with reality, the conclusions derived tend to be more general and applicable. Western economics is strict with hypothetical conditions, to such an extent that in reality, they do not exist and are not measurable. The typical examples include the rational economic man hypothesis, equilibrium, and a Pareto optimum state. A theory built on unrealistic hypotheses is tantamount to a myth.

Moreover, theoretical research in economics entails reading recent literature. There is a prevailing notion that economics keeps advancing and refining itself. In fact, human history unfolds cyclically, with many old theories holding great value. This necessitates a scientific scrutiny of relevant theoretical works. For example, the price theory in neoclassical economics is indeed helpful in understanding the impact of supply and demand on prices and resource allocation, but it offers few guidelines for weighing between planned and market economies.

### 2.4 *Lack of Consistency and Coherence*

As a rule, there shouldn't be two or more conflicting viewpoints within a theoretical framework. However, in Western economics, contradictory ideas abound, particularly the opposing views about the role of market and that of government. Indeed, varying doctrines are permitted to exist temporarily in scientific research, but longstanding, unresolved theoretical contradictions, as observed in Western economics, are by no means a norm in scientific research. Testing ideas in practice is a vital principle, which is exactly what Western economics lacks.

The findings obtained from scientific research accumulate over time. With the advancement of scientific research, new theories emerge while old theories are retained, so scientific knowledge of a discipline keeps expanding. Take physics as an example. With the progress of scientific research, the conditions under which a particular theory applies will be unraveled, ensuring coherence of theoretical content; at the same time, relevant scientific knowledge constantly accrues. Innovation and development are materialized by standing upon the shoulders of giants. However, this is not the case with Western economics, where many new theories repel rather than complement one another, and new theories tend to fall short in being compatible with old ones. This consequently gives rise to a special situation where conflicting viewpoints in economic theory persist no matter how historical contexts evolve, thus hindering the formation of a unified system, much less incremental accumulation of knowledge.

## *2.5 Equilibrium and Disequilibrium*

Equilibrium is a core concept in economics. As a unique idea, does it make sense or not? The term "equilibrium" originates from physics, which refers to the special state of a certain position, equivalent to balance at a specific point in time. The equilibrium method used in mainstream economics takes no account of time and process and overlooks the complexity and diversity of varying economic systems. Based on this, Alfred Marshall established the foundation of classical economics. In economics, the concept of equilibrium dictates that there is bound to be diverse schools of economic thought, since attempting to explain the general state of an economy with a specific state will definitely not work. So, what is the way out? A new system of hypotheses has to be brought forward. Thus, equilibrium not only determines the success of economic theory but also fosters diverse schools of economic thought. Just like in the real world, no one can precisely tell what the equilibrium exchange rate of the Renminbi is, but at most give a ballpark figure. The Austrian school of economics criticized equilibrium-focused economics long ago, viewing the market as a process rather than an ensemble of prices, qualities, and quantities adjusted to reach a market equilibrium.

### 2.6 Non-dynamic Theory Dominated by Static and Comparative Static Analysis

Overall, the macroeconomic policy framework is constructed based on non-dynamic theory dominated by static and comparative static analysis. This has something to do with the tendency in Western economics to overemphasize equilibrium analysis. Although equilibrium analysis is indeed intuitive and easy to understand, it can only be used to analyze some special states and is unable to address key issues such as economic growth and economic cycles given an obvious disconnect with the real-world economy. Different schools of macroeconomic thought diverge over aggregate supply and aggregate demand, and have different views about macro control or macroeconomic policy. Some even go to extraordinary lengths to substantiate the argument that monetary policy is useless, which is clearly at odds with practice. This is closely related to the context of Western economies (especially the US economy) and their logical basis of pure market economy, without giving due consideration to the role of government.

### 2.7 Reflection on the Application of Mathematical Tools

Underlying a good economic theory must be a rational logic, and the supreme form of logic is mathematical expressions. As the language of science, mathematics is extensively used and revered in economic research. Economic ideas expressed in concise and explicit mathematical terms are generally considered reliable and credible. For this reason, economic literature is increasingly riddled with mathematical and statistical techniques, to such an extent that people not good at math have trouble understanding them. Nonetheless, more often than not, what economists convey through intricate mathematical notation is just some simple content about economic realities. This in fact is a kind of formalism in economics. Paul Krugman incisively points out that mathematics has been overly used in the economics profession, remarking that "economists, as a group, mistook beauty, clad in impressive-looking mathematics, for truth." John Cochrane holds an opposing view. As he asserts, the problem is that we don't have enough math; math in economics serves to keep the logic straight, and frictions are just bloody hard with the mathematical tools we have now.

### *2.8 Differences Between Statistical Relationships and Economic Causality*

There are differences between statistical relationships and economic causality in econometrics. Given the non-experimental nature of economic data, any statistical relationships portrayed by econometric models are just correlations or predictive associations, and should not be misconstrued as economic causality. Statistical relationships make it easier for scholars to construct corresponding models, and there is relatively sufficient data, giving rise to a multitude of models based on statistical relationships. It should be noted that causality is the fundamental relationship, while statistical relationships are subordinate and mainly serve to validate.

## 3 Outlook of Macroeconomic Theory

Macroeconomic theory often sees great strides by solving new problems in the real-world economy. When old theories couldn't make good explanations for new things and phenomena in society, theoretical revolutions would occur, giving rise to new ideas. Since the 2008 international financial crisis, significant changes have taken place in the global economic landscape, and the advent of the era of big data has offered new insight into the construction of complex macroeconomic models. All these pose new challenges to macroeconomics while also setting the direction for future development. Looking to the future, macroeconomic theory is poised to seek out new avenues based on the latest theoretical and practical findings. Taking into account the roles of both market and government and making proper use of mathematical tools, it will evolve toward rational synthesis in order to construct dynamic models incorporating the roles of market and government and bring forward integrated policy frameworks capable of adapting to a variety of scenarios.

### *3.1 Concept of Mixed Economy as a New Breakthrough*

The market-government relationship has long been a matter of disputation among different schools of macroeconomic thought. The concept of mixed economy actually presents a unique line of thought, which remains understudied within conventional frameworks. However, the articulation of economic paradigms with this line of thought represents a new breakthrough in economic theory.

The macroeconomic system is in effect an extremely complex and nebulous system. Different schools of macroeconomic thought do their research from different perspectives, resulting in partial and one-sided viewpoints. In the longstanding debate and course of evolution, various schools of economic thought have come to realize their own shortcomings and deficiencies and started to draw on the valuable views and techniques of other schools of thought, spawning hybrid ideas.

In the late nineteenth or early twentieth century, the concept of "mixed economy" emerged. In response to crises in free markets, scholars like Arthur Cecil Pigou proposed that state authority should be combined with market forces, laying the groundwork for the concept of a "mixed economy." They posit that a mixed economy is a hybrid system of monopoly and competition, and a capitalist economy is neither a perfectly competitive economy nor a completely monopolistic economy, but a combination of the two. In his book *The General Theory of Employment, Interest and Money*, Keynes emphasizes the need to combine government intervention and market forces. Alvin Hansen and other scholars go further to point out that the economy of most capitalist countries is neither purely private nor public, but is a mixed economy that blends public and private economies. In a mixed economy, components in government control are intertwined with those left to the free market, so the price mechanism needs to play a fundamental role in the market economy while the government needs to appropriately intervene in the economy. The meaning of mixed economy is two-fold: first, a system of economic control is implemented by both government and private organizations. The price mechanism plays a fundamental role in the market economy. Second, the government intensifies its intervention in economic activity, and components of government control are intertwined with those left to the free market for the purpose of production and consumption. In the course of economic development, classicism that advocates free markets and Keynesianism that emphasizes macro control have become aware of their own limitations and made adjustments and improvements accordingly. In reality, all major countries share some key characteristics of a mixed economy despite their differences. That the "visible hand" and the "invisible hand" function simultaneously forms the basis for the functioning of a mixed economy.

When it comes to the concept of mixed economy, the contribution of Paul Samuelson must be mentioned for his attempts to synthesize classical economics and Keynesian economics, that is, the "mature synthesis" articulated by the neoclassical synthesis school. He has put forward the aggregate demand-aggregate supply model[3] to explain the stagflation in the US back then. Moreover, he produced a comprehensive account of what a mixed economy is. Samuelson's AD-AS model is a synthesis of various schools of economic thought at the time, covering Keynesianism, classicism, monetarism, supply-side economics, rational expectations theory, and modern macroeconomics. Regrettably, he clings to the view that the role of government is a supplement to market forces, believing that the goal of intervention by the "visible hand" is to bring into full play the role of the "invisible hand."

If a mixed economy is seen as the general case, then a pure market economy or planned economy is a special case. In view of this, the premise of economic research is no longer simply market economies but a framework where the general case precedes the special one. Consequently, a pure market economy is a rare case, which takes the entire economic theory a leap further. Future studies need to seek new ideas to reach a consensus instead of tinkering with existing viewpoints, shift the market-government relationship from opposition to high-level unity, and construct theoretical models based on the mixed economy and the combination of the role of market and that of government, so as to put forward a macro-policy system driving economic development.

### 3.2 *Imperative of Rational Synthesis for Transformation in Macroeconomic Theory*

Many theoretical constructs in Western economics are single-dimensional, for example, emphasizing the role of market over that of government, efficiency over equity, and rationality over irrationality. However, from a multidimensional or two-dimensional point of view, these seemingly opposing concepts should be complementary and exist as a dialectical unity. Therefore, some concepts in economic theory should shift from binary distinctions of all or nothing and yes or no to a nuanced

[3] In their co-authored book *Economics* (12th edition), Paul Samuelson and William D. Nordhaus propose the AD-AS model, trying to replace the original IS-LM model and use it as a core method or tool for analyzing macroeconomic issues.

consideration of "degree," that is, to strike the right balance, keep a neutral stance, and address conflicts and maintain social stability in mild, harmonious, and moderate approaches. This embodies a unity of principle and flexibility, and equilibrium and harmony are achieved through a unity of opposites, thus fostering stability and prosperity for all. This may seem easy but in fact, involves a transformation in mental models, which is manifested in the shift from dichotomous thinking to rational synthesis in the economic sphere, thus spurring innovation of economic theory on the basis of a better understanding of China's economic realities.

For example, China's emphasis on the importance of letting the market play the decisive role and the government play its role better echoes the fundamental contradiction in economics – the market-government relationship. China has embarked on the road of market economy, which requires the market to play a decisive role. So, is there a "golden ratio" regarding the extent to which the government should play its role and where is the boundary between the role of market and that of government? The ratio varies in different countries and at different stages but as long as the market mechanism plays the decisive role, it is a market economy model. As such, there is bound to be a variety of market economy models in the world, and China's market economy is one of them.

By horizontal comparison, the role of market and that of government vary significantly by country in the same period. Loose regulation from the US government and undue capital freedom before the 2008 international financial crisis led to government failure, which eventually resulted in the international financial crisis. Since the international financial crisis, the role of the US government has been enhanced notably. Conversely, to rein in the government's role, China is working to "streamline government administration and delegate power," while further highlighting the decisive role of the market.

By longitudinal comparison, the relationship between government and market in Western countries has been evolving in different periods, undergoing the process of "freedom – intervention – freedom – intervention" throughout history. It can be seen that the boundary and the degree of the role of market and that of government rest on the realities and should not be determined dogmatically or just based on values.

It follows that some contrasting concepts in Western economics can be better justified. For example, mathematical methods should be appropriately applied in economics, there may be a "golden ratio" of the role of market and that of government, and economic security and the expansion of opening up can be balanced. The main relationships in economic theory (such as the market-government relationship) may have a golden ratio or follow the 30/70 rule, which has become the norm for market economies to play the decisive role. Economics needs to change the dichotomous thinking and take all things into consideration, and should be flexible, resilient, and dynamic. Radical propositions at two extremes generally deviate from reality, and a compromise is a better option at many times. The same is true with economic life. What's important is to establish the appropriate "degree" – it's not an either-or but a transformation in mutual relationship.

### 3.3 *Shift of the Market-Government Relationship from Opposition to Unity*

One of the core issues in economic research is the relationship between market and government. Western economics thinks that market and government are in binary opposition and have a reciprocal relationship. However, China's economic practices since the launch of reform and opening up have proved that only by making good use of both the "invisible hand" and the "visible hand" can a new paradigm be fostered, in which the market and the government coordinate with, complement, and promote each other to ensure sustained and sound economic and social development. This goes beyond what Western economics perceives, pointing the way forward for the macroeconomic theory.

The roles of market and government are indispensable, and the key lies in the boundary. In their longstanding debate, different schools of macroeconomic thought have come to recognize their own shortcomings and others' advantages, showing the trend of confluence. However, confluence of two different economic theories is still not in sight, and there is a long way to go to achieve unity. Although the explorations in the integration of different schools of thought have yielded notable outcomes, there are still many limitations and challenges. First, different schools of thought still stick to their guns, refining their own propositions by selectively absorbing others' views. Second, earlier thought on integration lacks a unified research model, so the economic growth model still falls within the category of classical economics and is not a dynamic model that takes into account both the role of market and that of government.

In the future, macroeconomics is expected to evolve toward unity and integration based on a deeper understanding of the relationship between market and government. Such integration involves a relatively complete system. The first is to identify the subject of research better aligned with the real world, that is, the real-world economy (or mixed economy), which in essence is an integration of the role of market and that of government, not the market helping the government or vice versa, but a result of their working together in a reasonable and orderly manner. The second is to establish a unified dynamic model that considers both the role of market and that of government, which are reflected through different weights. The third is to develop a macro policy framework capable of adapting to different scenarios from the comprehensive perspective of aggregate supply and aggregate demand. This framework should be established on the basis of an in-depth analysis of the role of government, which is not a short-term role as articulated in Keynesianism. In fact, the role of government can influence long-term trends of economic growth; otherwise, there is no way to explain the phenomenon of sustained growth after a crisis. The fourth is to take a rational implementation path. A rational and synthetic innovation path works well both in theory and practice. For example, China has experimented with selected policy combinations on the basis of synthesis and comparison, tested their effectiveness in practice, and made adjustments accordingly to achieve better results. Additionally, the guiding role of plans and expectations should be taken into full account and highlighted in practice.

### *3.4 Constructing a Theoretical Model Considering the Roles of Market and Government Based on a Mixed Economy*

Market mechanisms often fail in resource allocation due to various factors such as incomplete information, externalities of economic activity, monopoly of producers or factor suppliers, and public goods. Furthermore, economic agents are not completely rational. Macroeconomic theories have seen growing reflections and doubts on the basic assumptions about market economies. People have become aware of the obvious discrepancies between the real-world economy and theoretical assumptions. Given that the real-world economy is a mixed economy, both market and government should play their respective roles. The construction of economic models is crucial to the development of macroeconomic theory, which should pay more attention to the construction or improvement of models and take into account imperfect factors in the real world. A theoretical model taking into account the roles of market and government should be constructed on the basis that the real-world economy is a mixed economy.

## 3.5 *Avoiding the Abuse of Mathematics in Economic Research*

At present, many economists are obsessed with constructing complex models using mathematical methods, while overlooking the essence of the models. Sociologist Albert points out directly that economics uses non-social methods to address social problems. Therefore, it is necessary to prevent the abuse of mathematics in economics, clearly identify the goals of economic research, avoid using complex mathematical methods to deal with simple economic problems, and pay more attention to the economic implications and logic underlying mathematics. Still, since mathematical analysis has the virtues of logic, conciseness, and accuracy, using mathematics is instrumental in promoting the advancement of modern economics. The advent of the era of big data has offered new insight into the construction of complex macroeconomic models and also put forward new requirements for the advancement of macroeconomics. To move macroeconomics forward requires greater importance attached to the application of mathematics, but the key lies in striking a balance between the proper use of mathematics and the nature of economic issues.

## 3.6 *Constructing a Complete Macro Policy Framework and Enriching the Connotation of Government Regulation*

With the advancement of macroeconomics, both new Keynesian economists and neoclassical economists have acknowledged the deficiencies and frictions in the real-world market. Based on their understanding of the flaws of market mechanisms, macroeconomists have come to realize the important role of government in regulating market activity. With a deepened understanding of government regulation, the connotation of government regulation is constantly evolving. Western economics encompasses theories built from the perspective of market economy and also theories from the perspective of government intervention. These theories shed light on economic models within their own frameworks. Given that the real-world economy is a mixed economy, the role of market and that of government should be both taken into account. In this book, we try to use the key findings of macroeconomic theory and "the simplest formula possible" to construct an economic development model.

### 3.7 China's Economic Success Contributes to the Innovation of Macroeconomic Theory

China's economic success is based on a strong theoretical foundation of economics and opportunity for innovation and plays a vital role in the transformation of the macroeconomic theory. It provides an alternative economic development model for other countries and regions and lays a profound basis for economic innovation.

(1) It embodies the basic logic and concept of balancing the role of market and that of government. The Third Plenary Session of the 18th CPC Central Committee pointed out that China should see that the market plays a decisive role in resource allocation and the government plays its role better. It summarized the socialist market economy model and in effect, put forward a rational mixed or hybrid economic model.

(2) It has opened up a path of rational development. In the early days, China's policy followed the basic logic of "crossing the river by feeling the stones." Today's top-level design aims to guide expectations by setting goals and implementing a macro control system that balances the supply side and the demand side to keep economic development stable.

(3) It has prompted major innovations in macro control. Macro control is a unique concept created by China, with no precise equivalent in Western economics. It is similar to macroeconomic policy in Western economics but has a richer connotation. It's fair to say that macro control is an innovation China has brought to Marxist economics and also represents new development of modern macroeconomic theory.

(4) It has propelled the shift of the market-government relationship from opposition to unity. Practice has proved that neither the planned economy nor the pure market economy is flawless. Since the launch of reform and opening up, China has embarked on a road featuring the combination of the roles of market and government. The Third Plenary Session of the 18th CPC Central Committee proposed seeing that the market plays the decisive role in resource allocation and the government plays its role better. General Secretary Xi Jinping stressed that "we must adhere to dialectical thinking and the doctrine that everything has two aspects,

> continue to better combine the basic socialist system and the market economy, and fully exploit the strengths of the two to achieve the goal of an 'efficient market' and a 'proactive government.' We should work hard to resolve this economic conundrum in practice." General Secretary Xi Jinping's instructions set the direction for the innovation of economic theory.

In the future, China's reform and opening up will be continuously deepened, and fresh practical outcomes will be produced. Therefore, it is imperative to further develop economic theory. On one hand, we should examine the relationship between market and government from a holistic perspective instead of looking at them separately, and should combine the roles of the two and carry out theoretical innovation. On the other hand, we should conduct an in-depth analysis of the connotation and value of the role of government to establish a more rational framework of policy combinations. Macroeconomic theory with the aforementioned characteristics can be referred to as "rational synthesis economics." We believe that "rational synthesis economics" born out of China's economic practices has a broader scope of application.

## 4 Overview and Change of Economic Paradigms

Given the differences in epistemology, methodology, and the worldview, the disputes and transitions among different schools of economic thought are often manifested as debates about different paradigms. Different research paradigms indicate different theoretical systems, and innovation of economic theory signals a transformation of research paradigms.

### *4.1 Main Economic Paradigms and Comparison*

Generally, the main schools of economic thought today can be classified into two economic paradigms.

(1) Market economy paradigm. This paradigm believes that a free, competitive market is the most effective way to allocate resources, where the balance between aggregate demand and aggregate supply is achieved itself through the "invisible hand." Essentially, the theory of this paradigm emphasizes "supply management," agreeing with Say's Law that supply creates its own demand. The main

schools of economic thought that believe in this paradigm include classicism, monetarism, neoclassical economics, and the Austrian school. See from neoclassical economics, the combination of a market economy and socialism is unthinkable.

(2) Government intervention (or macro control) paradigm. This paradigm contends that a free, competitive market has flaws, so the government should intervene in the economy. Keynesian and Marxist economics both identify with this paradigm. Specifically, with an emphasis on "demand management," Keynesian economics asserts that the root cause of economic crises is the lack of effective demand and explains this with the "three laws of human behavior." Keynesian economics also argues that free markets do not mean that equilibrium between aggregate demand and aggregate supply is obtained itself, requiring efforts to stimulate effective demand. Therefore, it has proposed expansionary fiscal policy and other measures for intervention. Marxist economics emphasizes the antagonism in capitalist economies and opposes free competition under capitalism, thinking that the "root cause" of economic crises is the capitalist system rather than the lack of demand.

It should be noted that the free market economy theory advocated by Adam Smith and the planned economy theory articulated by Karl Marx are two extremes of the real-world economy. The two look like the opposite, but they are integrated in the real world, and at the macro level, the roots of the two theories are woven together. Given that an economy is always a mixed economy, analysis from a single perspective is unable to give a full picture of social and economic activities. Neither the analysis model of market economy nor the analysis model of macro control can accommodate the rationality in others' theories, making it impossible to use the corresponding economic theory and model to accurately analyze the actual economic and market conditions and its operations. Therefore, these two models should be integrated appropriately to establish a unified theoretical system, so as to better explain the realities and address practical problems. Marxist economics is often regarded by Western mainstream economists as a political theory of class struggle or economic theory with political overtones, differing from Western economics in such aspects as research methods and structure. In fact, Marxist economics was established by drawing on and making revolutionary changes to the ideas of

British and French classical economics in the seventeenth and eighteenth centuries.

### 4.2 *Change in Economic Research Paradigms*

As mentioned above, previous economic studies all have limitations to varying degrees. In their longstanding debates, different schools of economic thought based on the two paradigms have come to recognize their own shortcomings and others' advantages, showing the trend of confluence. However, they still analyze the economy from a single perspective of market economy or macro control. Consequently, it is difficult for them to accommodate the rationality in others' theories, which will eventually lead to self-contradiction and obstruct an accurate analysis of economic theories and models. The real-world economy is, in essence, an integration of the role of market mechanisms and government regulation, not the market helping the government or vice versa, but a result of their working together in a reasonable and orderly manner. Therefore, it is necessary to develop a new-type, inclusive rational synthesis framework based on the evolving economic theories and ideas, in which economic growth is formulated as an organic unity of the roles of market and government.

To theoretically interpret the practices of the Chinese path requires breaking from the paradigm of Western mainstream economics. Different schools of Western economic thought have a long history of divergences and reconciliations. Now it's time for synthesis, integrating different macroeconomic theories, and such synthesis should be critical and revolutionary. Clearly, the new type of synthesis we anticipate goes beyond mere reconciliation; it should be a theoretical innovation in economics that derives from China's practices, reflects international theoretical advancements, and features a new paradigm with breakthroughs in methodology. It is hoped that the change in research paradigms brought about by China's economic success could open up new vistas for the development of economic theory.

## 5 Methodology of Economic Research: From Single-Dimensional to Multidimensional

The methodology of economic research is a fundamental pillar for the development of economic theory, involving the approaches and techniques through which people understand and interpret economic activity.

The rationality of research methods is key to constructing the "edifice" and improving the scientific rigor of economic theory. This requires a comprehensive consideration of the basic perspectives and logical structures upon which economic theory is built. The methodology of economic research has become a vital subject of urgency, which necessitates a systematic summarization and constant scrutiny of the approaches and techniques employed in economic research. An in-depth analysis from the perspective of philosophy is needed.

Assume that an experiment on sugar and water is to be carried out in an economic theory class at college. In the first step, divide the students into four groups and provide the first group with sugar, the second group with water, the third group with sugar water, and the fourth group with sugar, water, and sugar water. In the second step, ask each group to report on what they have observed and what the uses are, after the first group conducts an in-depth analysis of sugar, the second group examines water, the third group studies sugar water, and the fourth group makes a comprehensive study of sugar, water, and sugar water. In the second step, make an economic analog by thinking of sugar as a market economy, water as government regulation, sugar water as a mixed economy, and the last scenario of sugar, water, and sugar water as the situation in China, and then keep exploring to find out an optimal ratio of sugar and water. This is instrumental in understanding the evolution of economic theory. This chapter looks at the application of single-dimensional thinking and multidimensional thinking in economic research, compares their advantages and disadvantages, and tries to find better research methods, in the hope of providing insights into the development and transformation of macroeconomic theory in the future. A reconstruction of crisis economics entails improving the methodology of economics, which is expected to help develop more scientific and effective economic models.

### 5.1 *Scientific Hypotheses*

Making hypotheses in economics seems simple but is actually quite complicated. A prevalent problem at present is to make some assumptions, construct a model, and then carry out theoretical and empirical analysis. However, theory built in this way is of limited value, because hypotheses require strict conditions, just as in the real world, things can be done only when conditions permit. If the conditions are unrealistic, things may get complicated. When writing economic essays, scholars often make some assumptions to facilitate mathematical treatment of the corresponding economic issues, but whether those assumptions themselves are realistic or rational is questionable. If theoretical assumptions deviate far from real-world scenarios, even though the predictions of a theory pan out, it will not necessarily qualify as a good theory. It might just be a case of "a blind cat finding a dead mouse," which means blind luck.

### 5.2 Shifting Economic Research from Single-Dimensional Thinking to Multidimensional Thinking

In general, single-dimensional thinking is characterized by simplicity and straightforwardness and can work well in particular fields by fostering a refined approach to research. However, this mode of thinking tends to be one-sided, lacks a dialectical nature, and can even lead to extremism. It looks at things from a single perspective, angle, or level, resulting in conclusions akin to the parable of the blind men and the elephant, which implies that what each understands is only part of a broader picture. When used in comprehensive and intricate studies, single-dimensional thinking often distracts one from comprehending the whole, that is, they "can't see the forest for the trees." In the real world, single-dimensional thinking can lead to contradictory or oppositional actions and even the application of "double standards."

In contrast, multidimensional thinking is a more comprehensive and systematic mode of thinking that looks at things from multiple perspectives and in a multifaceted and multilayered manner. It is in essence the embodiment of a systematic approach in the cognitive domain, enabling one to perceive not only the overlaps and conflicts among various lines of thought but also their complementarities. This helps them seek dialectical unity amidst contradictions among these lines of thought and find a more effective way to solve problems.

Vladimir Lenin once said, in order really to know an object, we must embrace, study all its sides, all connections and "mediations." Multidimensional thinking exactly looks at an object from multiple perspectives, levels, and aspects to get the full picture, thus knowing the entirety of the object comprehensively.

As human societies advance at an unprecedented pace and economic operations become increasingly complex, economics has evolved into a vast, complicated, and dynamic system encompassing various dimensions and aspects. This objectively requires a more systematic and comprehensive approach to understanding economic dynamics. As single-dimensional thinking moves along a particular path or direction from one perspective or starting point, research findings based on single-dimensional thinking are too simplistic and one-sided in many cases. In contrast, multidimensional thinking looks at things from multiple perspectives and in a multifaceted manner and can give a comprehensive and holistic picture of the characteristics of the real-world economy and the principles of economic functioning, so research findings based on multidimensional thinking are closer to reality.

Economics is a science that studies the myriad economic activities and relationships in different development stages of human society, as well as the principles of economic operations and development. Different schools of macroeconomic thought have long been embroiled in heated debates over the market-government relationship. What this boils down to is clinging to single-dimensional thinking, as exemplified by an overwhelming emphasis on market mechanisms over the role of government. Consequently, the role of government (particularly that in other countries) is vulnerable to bias and is even demonized. Considering that the economic models of two countries feature the components of both market and government in roughly similar proportions, the question arises: why is one deemed a market economy, while the other is not? Even though Keynesianism addresses the role of government as the "visible hand" and this notion has prompted a shift in economic thought from the supply side to the demand side, government intervention is simply regarded as a condition for keeping market economies running. A multidimensional perspective brings awareness to the fact that a real-world economy is neither purely market-driven nor entirely planned, but is a hybrid economy in which market and government both play their roles. Subsequent developments in economic theory and practice show that the role of government and that of market are indispensable and that they are not antagonistic but rather complementary.

The debates among different schools of macroeconomic thought as mentioned above are largely due to single-dimensional thinking when it comes to research methodology. Over time, both liberals and conservatives have come to recognize their own deficiencies and virtues in the opposing views. However, single-dimensional thinking deters them from analyzing the real-world economy from systematic and comprehensive perspectives, despite their attempts to reconcile the other's rationale within the confines of their own perspective (market economy or macro control). The corollary is that all schools of macroeconomic thought can only spiral in their inquiry into economic issues, but are unable to put forward an analytical model best reflective of the real-world economy, together with a complete macro-policy framework. Therefore, macroeconomic theory based on the single-dimensional research approach is not exactly enough to explain the real-world economy, and the way out is a shift to the multidimensional approach.

### 5.3 *Rational Models and Appropriate Use of Mathematics*

Mathematics serves as an essential instrument in economic research to more precisely present the logic of economic connections and the principles of economic functioning, thus contributing to the advancement of economic theory. Nonetheless, contemporary economics has virtually become subservient to mathematics, which is primarily manifested in two tendencies. The first is to directly express some economic connections with mathematical formulas. An example is seen in the micro foundations of macroeconomics. While connections between macro and micro levels are a straight fact, describing them with overly precise mathematical formulas will inevitably go astray, resulting in conclusions that significantly diverge from reality. The second is to treat all economic issues mathematically. On the flip side, topics that are difficult to be dealt with through mathematical methods, such as division of labor and technological advances, are understudied. As Paul Krugman remarks incisively, "economics tends, understandably, to follow the line of least mathematical resistance." It should be noted that mathematics serves to facilitate more precise and effective economic research, so mathematics should be used appropriately in economics, and to subordinate economics to mathematics is a huge pitfall. To achieve true innovation in economics, it is necessary to avoid over-reliance on mathematics, but rather to use it properly to advance economic theory based on an in-depth analysis of the principles of economic functioning.

### 5.4 *Testing Theory in Practice*

Today, there exists a pervasive tendency in the world of economics to blindly follow authority and pundits while giving short shrift to reality. It is often the case that researchers expend considerable effort to substantiate conclusions that are already widely known or validate propositions that starkly deviate from reality. For example, they may construct refined theoretical models only to conclude that monetary policy is neutral or ineffective, or that industrial policy is of no use, despite the obvious effects of such policy in reality. In this regard, China has upheld the principle that "practice is the sole criterion for testing truth" and achieved great results. A case in point is the portrayal of monetary policy effects using the DSGE model. The earlier RBC model posited that monetary policy exerts no influence on real variables such as output, real interest rates, and employment, but only on the change in price levels. Building upon this, the DSGE models introduced the likes of price stickiness, but simulations from these models reveal that monetary policy has negligible impact on real variables. In practice, monetary policy can cause significant fluctuations and impacts on the macroeconomic landscape. However, the aforementioned models fall short in explaining the phenomenon but instead, attribute it to hypothetical exogenous shocks, which to some extent reflects the inherent flaws in DSGE models.

Therefore, how economic theory is effective should not be measured solely by model outcomes but instead, be verified with practical results. Discrepancies between theory and reality indicate theoretical inadequacies that need to be improved. Our proposal for a rational synthesis model is exactly based on the fact that market economies are not omnipotent and market failures can occur, so government intervention is necessary and beneficial, and it is also what all countries do. During the 2008 international financial crisis, policymakers in affected countries were no longer confined to Keynesianism, monetarism, or the rational expectations theory and as a last resort, tried to the fullest almost all policy solutions advocated by different theories. Underlying this is essentially the thinking of rational synthesis. After the crisis, Western countries escalated policy interventions in their economies, so the rhetoric about the so-called pure market economy model would undeniably be a sign of double standards.

CHAPTER 2

# Contemporary Economics and Rational Synthesis

This chapter summarizes some key theories and methods in economics, including the mixed economy theory, the aggregate demand/aggregate supply model, the Harrod-Domar model and the Solow-Swan model (neoclassical economic growth model), and the real business cycle theory. The mixed economy theory advocates implementing a mixed economy by combining market regulation and government regulation, private economy and public economy, as well as distribution according to labor and to production factors. The AD/AS model derived from the neoclassical synthesis school is used to analyze fluctuations in total output and price levels. The neoclassical economic growth model emphasizes the effects of savings, population growth, and technological advancement on economic growth and explains the conditions for economic growth to achieve steady-state equilibrium. The RBC theory explains economic fluctuations within the framework of general equilibrium, ascribing the root cause of economic fluctuations to technology shocks. The thinking of rational synthesis is closely related to these important theories, and on the basis of these theories and methods, performs relatively unified logical analysis. It can be said that the thinking of rational synthesis is built on and elevates these theories and methods. The basic logic of the thinking of rational synthesis is as follows: Based on the combined role of market and government, aggregate demand and aggregate supply are regarded as important forms of government involvement, the relations between short-term fluctuations and long-term economic growth are taken into account, and



Z. Liang, *The Innovation of Economic Theory in China*,
https://doi.org/10.1007/978-981-95-2713-7_2

dynamic analysis methods are used to construct a dynamic theoretical model with unified economic logic, with attention paid to disequilibrium analysis.

## 1 Mixed Economy Theory

A mixed economy is an economy featuring multiple methods of resource allocation, diverse forms of ownership of means of production, and multiple forms of distribution, involving the combination of market mechanisms and government regulation, private economy and public economy, as well as distribution according to labor and distribution according to production factors. In brief, a mixed economy is "a market economic system subject to government regulation that implements diverse forms of ownership and the system of distribution according to the contribution of various factors of production" (Cai, 2015).

The mixed economy theory is a product of the formation of monopoly capitalism in Western countries. During the period of free competition capitalism, the government primarily acted as a "night watchman," with very little intervention in the economy. State-owned enterprises were mainly concentrated in specialized sectors such as defense and postal services. The early twentieth century saw Western capitalist countries enter the stage of monopoly capitalism, and state monopoly capitalism emerged. After World War I, monopoly capitalism gained ground in Western capitalist countries. At that time, the characteristics of a mixed economy were already evident, and the government's management and regulation of the economy increased significantly. This included implementing countercyclical economic policies, developing economic plans, establishing state-owned enterprises, allocating raw materials and fuel, setting monopoly prices, intervening in income distribution and labor relations, and supporting the overseas expansion of monopolistic capital. In the wake of World War II, Western capitalist countries extensively intervened in market activities, leading to a significant increase in the share of the state-owned economy. Thus, they became genuine mixed economies.

The mixed economy theory came into being amid the changes of the Western capitalist economic structure and government functions. The mixed economy theory is a result of reflection on the flaws of market mechanisms and advocates combining market regulation and government regulation. For example, scholars like Arthur Cecil Pigou and John Maynard Keynes emphasize the necessity of government intervention from micro and macro perspectives. As the mixed economy theory evolves, its denotations and connotations are constantly enriched, involving other aspects of economic systems such as ownership of means of production and commodity distribution. The key figures include Alvin Hansen, Paul Samuelson, and Assar Lindbeck.

### *1.1 Mixed Economy Ideas of Pigou and Keynes*

In his book *The Wealth of Nations*, Adam Smith argues that social welfare can be maximized through the "invisible hand" of the market, with the government acting as a "night watchman" to ensure the smooth operation of market mechanisms. Adam Smith points out that "such regulation (government intervention in the economy) must, in almost all cases, be either a useless or a hurtful regulation." He believes that the government has three main duties: "providing for the national defense," "establishing an exact administration of justice," and "establishing and maintaining certain public works."

However, some economists gradually discovered that market mechanisms were not flawless. Pigou (1933) points out in his major work *The Economics of Welfare* that externalities frequently occur in economic activities, such as lighthouses, transportation, and pollution. When externalities exist, private marginal costs and private marginal benefits do not equal social marginal costs and social marginal benefits. Pareto optimality cannot be achieved by relying solely on market mechanisms; instead, taxes or subsidies are needed to address the externalities.

In his book *The General Theory of Employment, Interest and Money*, Keynes (1936) argues that the Great Depression in the 1930s is attributed to insufficient effective demand and full employment cannot be achieved solely by market regulation. The diminishing marginal propensity to consume, the declining marginal efficiency of capital, and the preference for liquidity led to insufficient consumption and investment demand. Among them, the declining marginal efficiency of capital was particularly important, and insufficient investment demand was the primary cause of the Great Depression. Keynes further states that the only effective way to save the capitalist system is to expand the role of government and combine government regulation and market mechanisms. Specifically, the government should adopt fiscal policy and monetary policy (especially fiscal policy) to stimulate investment and consumption, thereby achieving full employment. Hicks and Hansen developed Keynes's ideas into the IS-LM models, where fiscal policy influences the equilibrium in the product market, and monetary policy affects the equilibrium in the money market. Expansionary fiscal policy will raise both national income and interest rates, while expansionary monetary policy will raise national income and lower interest rates. When the economy is in a recession, a country should adopt expansionary fiscal policy and expansionary monetary policy, and vice versa.

### *1.2 Mixed Economy Ideas of Hansen and Samuelson*

In his book *Fiscal Policy and Business Cycles*, Keynesian economist Alvin Hansen (1988) argues that from the late nineteenth century, Western capitalist countries have ceased to be purely private economies and instead become a kind of "dual economy" where government is involved in business activities. Such a "dual economy" does not imply a gradual shift toward public ownership but rather emphasizes a "mixed economy" focused on social welfare. He further points out in *Economic Issues of the 1960s* that Western capitalist countries are "public-private partnerships" where the private sector produces material goods needed by society and government provides some public services and facilities. It is important to note that a "mixed economy" in the eyes of Hansen includes both private capitalism and a "socialized economy," of which the latter involves "socialized production tools" and "socialized income and consumption." It can be seen that a "mixed economy" in the view of Hansen includes not only the combination of regulatory means but also ownership of means of production, that is, the combination of private economy and public economy.

Samuelson, founder of the neoclassical synthesis school, also advocates a mixed economy. His mixed economy theory mainly covers three aspects: (1) The connotation of mixed economy. In the textbook *Economics*, Samuelson thinks that a mixed economy is a "combination of government and private enterprise," a "mix of monopoly and competition," and an economy in which both public and private institutions exercise economic control. (2) Government functions in the mixed economy. In their co-authored book *Economics* (19th Edition), Samuelson and Nordhaus note that government performs four economic functions: first, it remedies market failures such as monopoly, externalities, public goods, and imperfect information to improve the efficiency of economic operations; second, it redistributes income through taxation, transfer payment, and other means to promote economic equity; third, it establishes fiscal and monetary policies to stabilize the business cycle and promote long-term economic growth; and fourth, it manages international economic affairs. Samuelson also puts forward an AD/AS model to illustrate the impact of fiscal and monetary policies on macro-economy. (3) Strengths of a mixed economy. Samuelson thinks that a mixed economy combines market regulation and government intervention, effectively leveraging the strengths of market regulation while addressing its shortcomings through government intervention. This combination can overcome economic recessions and prevent overheating, while also avoiding resorting to war to expand domestic demand.

### *1.3 Lindbeck's Mixed Economy Theory*

Based on his observations of the economic systems around the world (especially the Swedish mixed economy), Assar Lindbeck, an economist of the Stockholm School, divides economic systems into three types: the Western mixed economy represented by Sweden, the market-oriented socialist economy represented by Yugoslavia, and the centralized economic model represented by the former Soviet Union. By comparing these three economic systems, Lindbeck argues that the ideal economic model is the Western mixed economy represented by Sweden, that is, the social democratic economic system.

1. Lindbeck's criteria for the classification of economic systems

Karl Marx divides economic systems into capitalism and socialism according to ownership of means of production. Lindbeck opposes such classification, thinking that the economic system is composed of multiple factors and is a "multidimensional" concept. He defines the economic system as "a set of mechanisms and institutions for decision-making concerning production, distribution, and consumption within a given geographical area." These mechanisms and institutions fall into the following eight categories.

(1) Decision-making bodies. Whether consumption, production, investment, and other decisions are made by individual units (such as households and businesses) or by central authorities involves the concentration in the decision-making process, that is, whether

decisions are made by decentralized institutions or by centralized institutions.

(2) Resource allocation mechanism. Lindbeck claims that there are two different mechanisms for providing resources, allocating resources, and coordinating economic decision-making: one is to take a market-oriented approach, that is, the market mechanism; the other is to take an administrative approach, that is, the administrative mechanism.
(3) Property ownership. Property ownership here refers specifically to capital ownership, which means the control, use, and management of capital. Lindbeck compares and analyzes two forms of ownership, namely, individual ownership and collective ownership.
(4) Commodity distribution mechanism. After being made by businesses, products reach consumers through the market equilibrium price mechanism or through directives and orders from superiors.
(5) The mechanism for motivating people. This refers to what method is used to arouse people's enthusiasm for production, either through economic stimulus or through administrative orders.
(6) Competition and cooperation. This refers to whether the relationship between people is competitive or cooperative.
(7) Competition and monopoly. This refers to whether the relationship between businesses is competitive or monopolistic.
(8) External Relations. This refers to the degree of openness of a country's economy to the outside world, meaning whether the country's economy is internationalized or self-sufficient.

In Lindbeck's view, an economic system comprises the above eight factors. As we see it, the differences in the above eight factors can basically be summarized as differences in resource allocation mechanisms. Under the market mechanism, decisions are made by decentralized individuals and businesses, the market price mechanism plays a role in distributing commodities, and economic stimulus can significantly motivate people. This mechanism mostly exists in the private economy. Under the administrative mechanism, decisions are made by the government centrally, and the distribution of products and people's enthusiasm for production depend on the government's plans and instructions. This mechanism primarily exists in the state-owned economy and collective economy.

2. Lindbeck's classification of three economic models

Lindbeck thinks that at present, there are three main economic models (see Fig. 2.1): the Western mixed economy represented by Sweden, the market-oriented socialist economy represented by Yugoslavia, and the centralized economic model represented by the former Soviet Union. According to Lindbeck's classification criteria, the main differences between these three economic models are as follows: (1) In terms of decision-making bodies, the Swedish model leans toward decentralized decision-making, the Soviet model is marked by centralized decision-making, and the Yugoslav model falls somewhere in between, slightly leaning toward decentralized decision-making. (2) In terms of resource allocation mechanisms, the Swedish model focuses on market institutions, the Soviet model focuses on administrative management, and the Yugoslav model falls in between, slightly leaning toward the market system. (3) In terms of ownership, the Swedish model is dominated by private ownership, the Soviet model is dominated by public ownership, and the Yugoslav model is somewhere in between, slightly leaning toward public-collective ownership. (4) As to the mechanism for mobilizing people, all three economic models are inclined toward economic stimulus; for businesses, the Swedish model focuses on economic stimulus, the Soviet model is dominated by administrative orders, and the Yugoslav model is somewhere in between, slightly leaning toward economic stimulus. (5) In terms of the relationship between competition and non-competition, for individuals, the Swedish model and the Soviet model focus on competition, and the Yugoslav model leans slightly toward competition; for businesses, the Swedish model is dominated by competition, the Soviet model by monopoly, and the Yugoslav model leans slightly toward competition. (6) In terms of external relations, the Swedish model is internationalized, the Soviet model is self-sufficient, and the Yugoslav model is somewhere in between.

3. The social democratic economic system

By comparing these three economic models, Lindbeck concludes that the ideal economic model is the Western mixed economy represented by Sweden, that is, the social democratic economic system. This economic system encompasses the following relationships and contents.

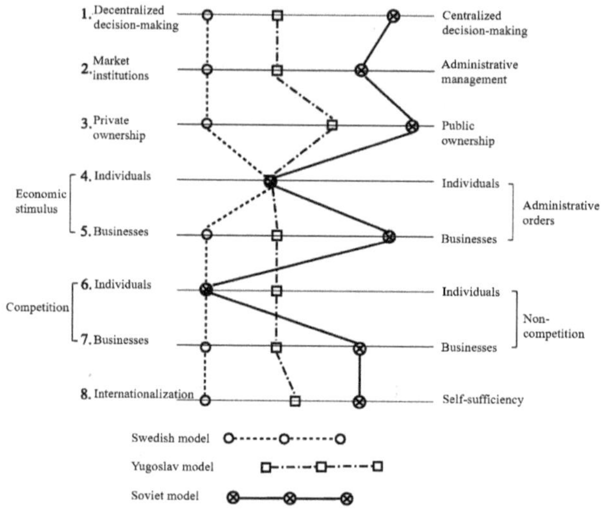


| | | | | |
|---|---|---|---|---|
| Decentralized decision-making | | | Centralized decision-making | |
| Market institutions | | | Administrative management | |
| Private ownership | | | Public ownership | |
| Economic stimulus | Individuals | | Individuals | Administrative orders |
| | Businesses | | Businesses | |
| Competition | Individuals | | Individuals | Non-competition |
| | Businesses | | Businesses | |
| Internationalization | | | Self-sufficiency | |
| Swedish model | | | | |
| Yugoslav model | | | | |
| Soviet model | | | | |

**Fig. 2.1** Three economic models divided by Lindbeck. (Source: Lindbeck, A. *The Political Economy of the New Left. An Outsider's View.* (Trans.). Beijing: The Commerce Press, 2013)

First, the relationship between decentralization and centralization. In analyzing the relationship between decentralized decision-making and centralized decision-making, Lindbeck thinks that the two should be combined, with neither being neglected. Decentralized decision-making involves two meanings: one is to delegate decision-making power to individuals and businesses, allowing them to make their own decisions concerning consumption, production, and investment; the other is to delegate decision-making power to individuals within a business, engaging them in business management and decision-making. Lindbeck thinks that the necessity of decentralized decision-making lies in the following: (1) In modern economies, only through decentralized decision-making can information on consumer preferences, production technologies, market supply and demand be collected in a timely manner. Such information is dispersed among numerous consumers and producers. The cost of collecting and processing information in a highly centralized system is higher than in a market system, and in a system based on central administrative management, unbiased information is practically unattainable at any cost. (2) In a decentralized system, the information collector is the same person as the decision-maker, who can make timely decisions based on market conditions; in a centralized system, however, the information collector and the decision-maker are different, making it hard to promptly respond to market conditions. Additionally, it is impossible to focus solely on decentralization without considering centralization, for the following reasons: (1) Certain economic activities require a centralized structure; for example, when it comes to national economic statistics, centralized institutions are more efficient than individuals and businesses. (2) Some public welfare undertakings are outside the scope of individual decision-making; for example, environmental pollution and public goods need to be dealt with by centralized institutions. (3) Certain macroeconomic objectives, such as fair distribution of income and economic stability, require centralized planning and handling. Lindbeck argues that any economic system is a combination of centralization and decentralization, and the principles that distinguish centralization and decentralization are as follows: consumption decision-making for consumer goods is up to consumers, and production decision-making for consumer goods to businesses; centralized institutions are responsible for providing public goods, maintaining economic stability, redistributing wealth and income, and conducting economic statistics.

Second, the relationship between market regulation and central planning. Lindbeck thinks that in a society with an extensive division of labor, for the economy to operate normally, it is necessary to exchange information, allocate resources, and coordinate the decisions of numerous consumers and producers so that the supply of each product equals its demand. Only by combining market regulation and central planning can these objectives be achieved. Relying solely on central planning, even with the aid of computers, would not only be insufficient to achieve these objectives but also lead to misallocation of resources, imbalance between inputs and outputs, inflexible planning adjustments, as well as product shortages, long queues for purchases, and abuse of ration coupons, ultimately resulting in a seller's market. The underlying reason is that there are multiple intermediary layers between individuals or businesses and central planners. Information becomes distorted as it passes through these layers. Decision-makers lack the time and energy to consider the many issues facing individuals and businesses, and they fall short in incorporating practical policy recommendations from individuals and businesses. In addition, relying solely on market regulation would fail to fully solve the problems in information exchange, resource allocation, and decision-making coordination. For example, since businesses generally lack insight into the macroeconomic situation, their production activities would be sightless to some extent if relying entirely on market regulation.

Third, the relationship between public ownership and private ownership. Lindbeck deems it necessary to take private ownership as the mainstay while implementing partial nationalization. Private ownership can give full play to the initiative and creativity of businesses, effectively addressing issues arising from bureaucracy. Nationalization includes two parts: the first is the nationalization of industries concerning public goods such as railways, post and telecommunications, and power stations; the second is the nationalization of income and consumption. This means incorporating a portion of national income into the government budget through a progressive tax system, which is then used for social insurance and collective consumption.

Fourth, the relationship between economic stimulus and administrative orders. Lindbeck thinks that economic stimulus and administrative orders should be combined to varying degrees to encourage people to work, produce, save, and invest. Economic stimulus comes in two forms: the first is the difference in profits, and the second is the difference in wages. The former is instrumental in promoting investment and improving enterprise management, while the latter is conducive to improving the work efficiency of individuals. Nonetheless, he points out that Sweden's experience shows that appropriately narrowing wage disparities helps maintain social stability and can increase efficiency rather than reduce it.

Fifth, the relationship between competition and monopoly. Lindbeck thinks that competition among countries, businesses, and individuals is common, and competition serves as a powerful driver for economic and social development. At the same time, within a country or business and among individuals, there is always an effort to establish a monopolistic position. The more stable the monopoly, the more intense the competition. If there is only monopoly without competition, it would lead to product shortages, poor quality, and a significant decrease in the efficiency of resource allocation. Competition and monopoly always coexist in modern economies.

## 2 AD/AS Model

The AD/AS model derived from the neoclassical synthesis school is used to analyze fluctuations in total output and price levels. Keynes' income-expenditure model and the Hicks-Hansen IS-LM model focus on analyzing aggregate demand, while completely neglecting aggregate supply. The AD/AS model combines the two to analyze how total output and price levels are determined.

### *2.1 Aggregate Demand*

1. Definition and components of aggregate demand

Aggregate demand refers to the quantity of total output that economic agents are willing to purchase at various price levels when all other conditions remain unchanged. In other words, aggregate demand represents the total expenditure by the household sector, the business sector, the government sector, and the international sector, including consumption, investment, government purchases, and net exports.

Consumption is the expenditure by the household sector on durable goods, non-durable goods, and services, which primarily depends on personal disposable income. Investment is the expenditure on capital assets, including fixed asset investment, inventory investment, and residential investment. Investment primarily depends on the cost of capital and the marginal efficiency of capital. Government purchases include the expenditure by the government sector on products and services, which is determined by the government's spending policies. Net exports equal exports minus imports and depend on factors such as domestic and foreign earned income, relative prices, and exchange rates.

2. Aggregate demand curve

The aggregate demand curve describes the total expenditure by economic agents at each price level. As shown in Fig. 2.2, the aggregate demand curve slopes down to the right, meaning that an increase in the price level leads to a decrease in the demand level when all other conditions remain unchanged.

On the aggregate demand curve, the price level is negatively correlated with aggregate demand. There are mainly four reasons.

(1) Interest rate effects. When prices rise, people need more money for trading, leading to an increase in the demand for money. If money supply remains unchanged, interest rates will rise, resulting in a decline in investment and output.
(2) Real balance effects. When prices rise, the real value of assets with fixed nominal value decreases, leading consumers to reduce their consumption expenditures, which in turn causes a decline in demand.
(3) Tax effects. When prices rise, consumers' nominal income also increases, moving them into a higher tax bracket, which reduces their disposable income and consequently decreases consumption expenditures.

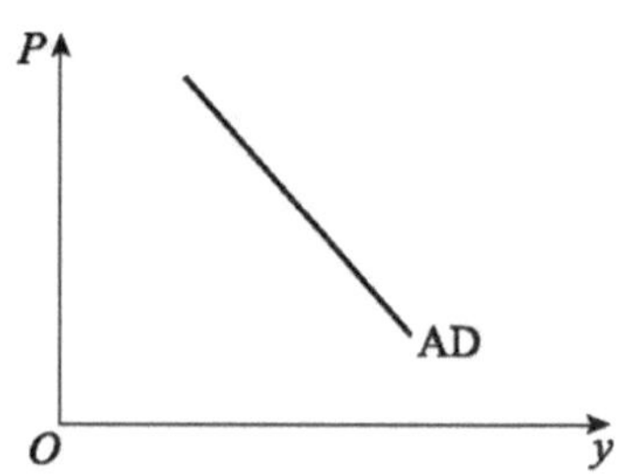

**Fig. 2.2** Aggregate demand curve

(4) Mundell-Fleming effects. If prices in a country rise, the nominal interest rate will also grow. According to the interest rate parity (IRP) theory, the country's currency would appreciate compared to foreign currencies, leading to a decrease in exports and an increase in imports. As a result, net exports and total output will decrease.

## 2.2 *Aggregate Supply*

1. Definition of aggregate supply

Aggregate supply refers to the quantity of total output that economic agents are willing to purchase at various price levels when all other conditions remain unchanged, that is, the total output produced by economic agents through the input of labor, capital, technology, and other means of production. The macro production function describes the relationship between the quantity of output and the quantity of input used in production, including labor, capital, and level of technology.

$$Y = AF(N,K) \tag{2.1}$$

Where $Y$ represents total output, $A$ represents the level of technology, $N$ represents employment in the whole society, and $K$ denotes capital stock of society as a whole.

The macro production function differs in the short and long run. In the long run, technology levels, capital stock, and employment can all change. In the short run, technology levels and capital stock do not change significantly and can be considered constants, so aggregate supply primarily depends on employment. Employment depends on labor demand and labor supply, with the latter being influenced by real wages. Under the condition that wages and prices are perfectly elastic, the equilibrium state where labor demand equals labor supply represents full employment. At this point, the output is known as full employment output. However, different schools of economic thought diverge over whether wages and price levels are perfectly elastic.

2. Three types of aggregate supply curves

The aggregate supply curve describes the total output that economic agents are willing to provide at various price levels. According to the time required for wages and price levels to adjust, the aggregate supply curve can be categorized into three types: the classical aggregate supply curve, the Keynesian aggregate supply curve, and the conventional aggregate supply curve.

(1) Classical aggregate supply curve. The classical aggregate supply curve is vertical at the full-employment level (see Fig. 2.3). Classical economics primarily studies the long-term state of the economy. Over the long term, wages and price levels have sufficient time to adjust, real wages are in an equilibrium state where labor supply and labor demand are equal, and the output is equal to full employment output. At this point, the classical aggregate supply curve represents the long-run aggregate supply curve. In addition, classical economics thinks that wages and price levels can be adjusted rapidly so that real wages and total output are at the levels of full employment. Under this assumption, the classical aggregate supply curve is also a short-run aggregate supply curve.
(2) Keynesian aggregate supply curve. The Keynesian aggregate supply curve is horizontal at a given price level (see Fig. 2.4). Keynesian economics mainly studies the short-term state of the economy. In the short term, there is not sufficient time for wages and price levels to adjust. When total output increases, neither wages nor price levels will change. At this point, the Keynesian aggregate supply curve denotes the short-run aggregate supply curve. In addition,

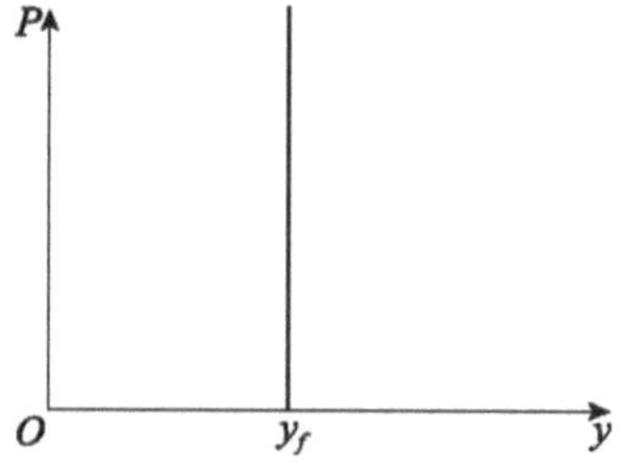


**Fig. 2.3** Classical aggregate supply curve

Keynesian economics believes that wages and price levels are "rigid," with no adjustments being made at all. In this case, the Keynesian aggregate supply curve is also a long-run aggregate supply curve.

(3) Conventional aggregate supply curve. The classical aggregate supply curve and the Keynesian aggregate supply curve are two extremes of the aggregate supply curve, while the conventional aggregate supply curve falls in between, as shown in the *CC* curve in Fig. 2.5. The conventional aggregate supply curve slopes up to the right, meaning that the higher the price level, the more the total output provided by economic agents.

**Fig. 2.4** Keynesian aggregate supply curve

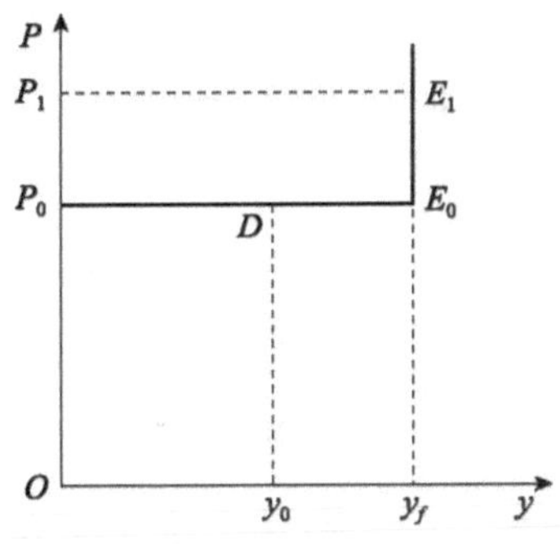


**Fig. 2.5** Conventional aggregate supply curve

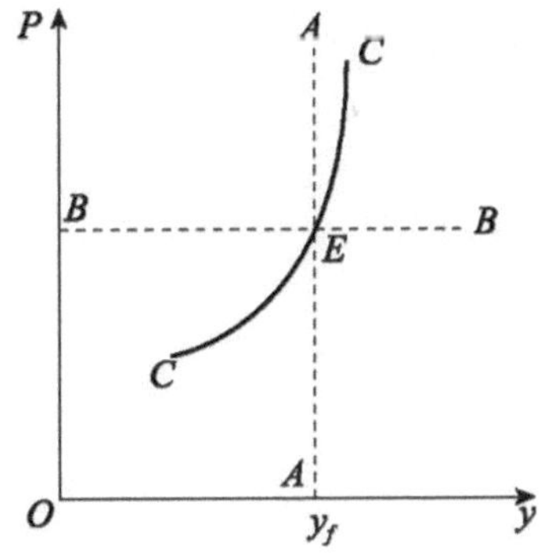

In the short term, the prices of production factors such as labor are relatively fixed; in other words, they are sticky. If prices rise, businesses will increase their output in order to increase profits. Under the assumption that the prices of production factors are sticky, the conventional aggregate supply curve slopes up to the right. An important reason for the stickiness of the prices of production factors is long-term contracts. In reality, labor contracts are typically signed for several years, with wages remaining fixed during the contract period. The prices of other production factors may also be fixed as a result of long-term contracts. How fast the prices of production factors adjust relative to product prices determines the slope of the aggregate supply curve. If the adjustment is slow, the aggregate supply curve will be relatively flat; otherwise, the aggregate supply curve will be relatively steep.

## 2.3 AD-AS Analysis

The intersection of the aggregate demand curve and the aggregate supply curve determines the equilibrium output and price levels (see Fig. 2.6). The short-term objectives of macroeconomic policy are full employment and price stability. However, the output equilibrium is not necessarily the output in full employment. The aggregate demand curve and the aggregate supply curve describe the relationship between price levels and total output. In addition to price levels, other factors can also affect aggregate demand or aggregate supply, which is reflected as the shift of the aggregate demand curve or the aggregate supply curve.

**Fig. 2.6** AD-AS analysis

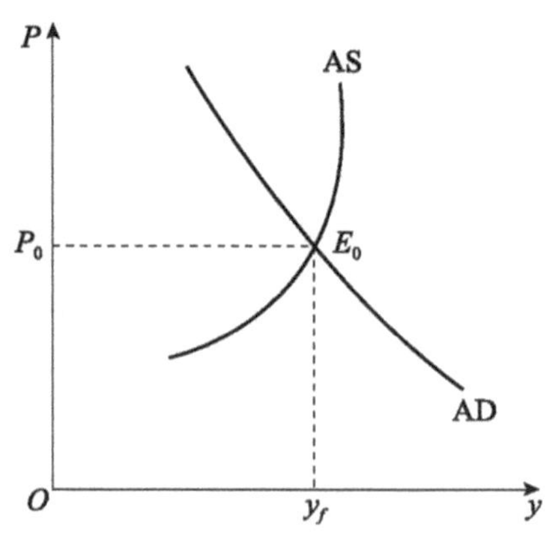

1. Shift of the aggregate demand curve

The shift of the aggregate demand curve can cause the price and output levels to change in the same direction. As shown in Fig. 2.7, when the aggregate demand curve shifts to the left, the price level and the output level both decrease; when the aggregate demand curve shifts to the right, the price level and the output level both increase.

Both government's macroeconomic policy and exogenous shocks can shift the aggregate demand curve. Expansionary fiscal or monetary policy shifts the aggregate demand curve to the right, while contractionary fiscal or monetary policy shifts the aggregate demand curve to the left. A core idea of Keynesian economics is demand management through macroeconomic policy. To be specific, contractionary policy is adopted to cool down an overheating economy, and expansionary policy is used during recessions to achieve full employment and price stability. Some exogenous shocks can increase aggregate demand, which in turn shifts the aggregate demand curve to the right; for example, war will increase government spending. Other exogenous shocks can reduce aggregate demand. For example, the COVID-19 pandemic harmed both consumer demand and investment demand.

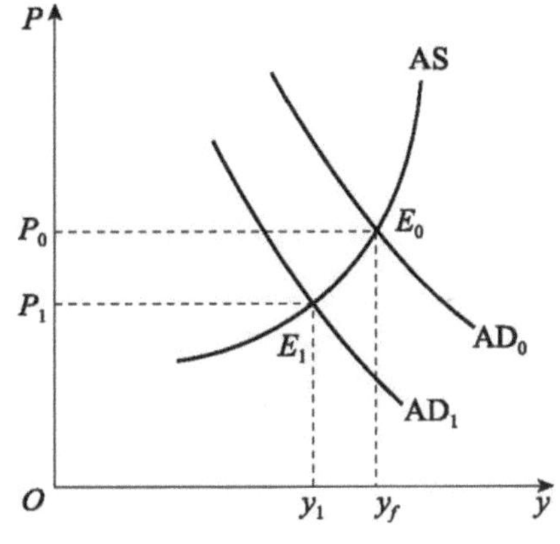


**Fig. 2.7** Shift of the aggregate demand curve

2. Shift of the aggregate supply curve

The shift of the aggregate supply curve can cause the price and output levels to change in the opposite direction. As shown in Fig. 2.8, when the aggregate supply curve shifts to the left, the output level declines while the price level rises, a phenomenon called "stagflation." When the aggregate supply curve shifts to the right, the output level rises while the price level falls. Macroeconomic policy relatively has less impact on the aggregate supply curve. Some adverse shocks can shift the aggregate supply curve to the left, such as the oil price hikes caused by the two oil crises. Some favorable shocks can shift the aggregate supply curve to the right, such as the "new economy" brought about by the advances in Internet technology in the United States.

## 3 Harrod-Domar Model and Solow-Swan Model

### *3.1 Harrod-Domar Model*

After Keynes published *The General Theory of Employment, Interest and Money* in 1936, some scholars tried to turn Keynes' short-term static analysis into dynamic analysis. Roy Harrod (1939 & 1948) and Evsey Domar (1946 & 1947) have established a dynamic economic growth theory, and the core of this theory is that the economic growth rate depends on capital stock. Keynes highlights the impact of investment on aggregate demand, and the Harrod-Domar model emphasizes the impact of investment on

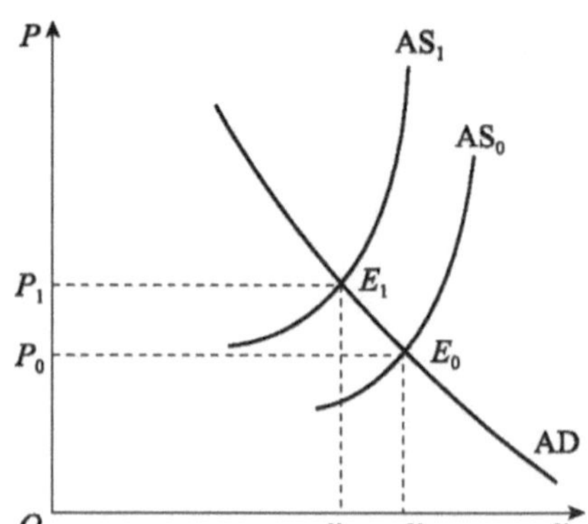


**Fig. 2.8** Shift of the aggregate supply curve

supply, that is, how investment affects capital stock and economic growth rates.

1. Main content of the Harrod-Domar model

The main assumptions of the Harrod-Domar model are as follows:

(1) This model deals with products produced by the household sector and the business sector that can be used for both consumption and investment.
(2) In an economy, labor ($L$) and capital ($K$) are used for production, the capital-labor ratio ($K/L$) and the capital-output ratio ($K/Y$) are constant over time, and the labor growth rate is exogenously given as $n$.
(3) Savings are a fixed proportion ($s$) of output.

In a two-sector economy, national income ($Y_t$) equals the sum of consumption ($C_t$) and investment ($I_t$).

$$Y_t = C_t + I_t \tag{2.2}$$

Savings ($S_t$) are a fixed proportion ($s$) of output.

$$S_t = sY_t \tag{2.3}$$

When the economy is in equilibrium, investment ($I_t$) and savings ($S_t$) are equal.

$$I_t = S_t = sY_t \tag{2.4}$$

Changes in capital stock are as follows:

$$K_{t+1} = (1-\delta)K_t + I_t \tag{2.5}$$

Where $K_t$ represents capital stock in the current period, $K_{t+1}$ represents capital stock in the next period, and $\delta$ is the depreciation rate. Capital stock in the next period equals capital stock net of depreciation plus investment in the current period.

Since the capital-output ratio, denoted by $v$, is constant, we get:

$$K_{t+1} = vY_{t+1} \tag{2.6}$$

$$K_t = vY_t \tag{2.7}$$

Substituting Eqns. (2.4), (2.6), and (2.7) into Eqn. (2.5), we get:

$$vY_{t+1} = (1-\delta)vY_t + sY_t \tag{2.8}$$

Dividing both sides of Eqn. (2.8) by $v$ and subtracting $Y_t$, we get:

$$Y_{t+1} - Y_t = (s/v - \delta)Y_t \tag{2.9}$$

Dividing both sides by $Y_t$, we get:

$$(Y_{t+1} - Y_t)/Y_t = s/v - \delta \tag{2.10}$$

In Eqn. (2.10), $(Y_{t+1}-Y_t)/Y_t$ implies that the output growth rate depends on the savings rate, the capital-output ratio, and the depreciation rate. Higher savings rates, lower capital-output ratios, and lower depreciation rates mean higher economic growth rates.

2. Policy Implications of the Harrod-Domar model

As can be seen from Eqn. (2.10), the Harrod-Domar model emphasizes the important role of capital accumulation in economic growth, and raising the savings rate can boost economic growth. The Harrod-Domar model was highly influential during the 1950–1975 period, becoming the basis for policy formulation in many countries. If a country's population growth rate is 2% and per capita GDP growth target is 2% per year, the GDP growth target should be set at 4% per year. Assume that the country's capital-output ratio is 4 and depreciation is ignored, the target savings rate is 16%. This means that when the actual savings rate is lower than the target savings rate, a "savings gap" occurs, which must be filled by policymakers.

According to the Harrod-Domar model, it is necessary to raise the personal savings rate to promote economic growth. Additionally, public savings can replace private savings, and fiscal policy can play a great role in promoting economic growth. If domestic savings are insufficient to achieve the set growth target, foreign investment can help fill the "savings gap."

3. Deficiencies of the Harrod-Domar model

The deficiencies of the Harrod-Domar model are mainly reflected in three aspects. First, this model assumes that the capital-output ratio is constant, which is at odds with reality. The reciprocal of the capital-output ratio is equal to the output ratio of capital. Many empirical studies find that the output ratio of capital is not fixed, so the relationship between economic growth and investment becomes "loose and unstable." Second, this model thinks that public savings and foreign capital inflows can make up for the domestic "savings gap" to increase investment. Some scholars find that in many cases, foreign capital inflows reduce domestic savings and investment productivity, without increasing the economic growth rate. In many developing countries, the public sector often faces "soft budget constraints," making it difficult to increase public savings by relying on profit accumulation of state-owned enterprises. Finally, this model assumes that the capital-labor ratio is constant, so it is difficult to achieve stable growth at full employment. In the Harrod-Domar model, the capital-labor ratio and the capital-output ratio are constant, and the labor growth rate is exogenously given. This means that when the economy is in equilibrium, the growth rate of capital and output is equal to the growth rate of labor. This is a balanced growth path "as narrow as a knife's edge" and is hard to reach. If the growth rate of output is lower than that of labor, massive unemployment will occur; if the growth rate of output is greater than that of labor, a lot of capital will stay idle, and the growth rate of output will decline.

### 3.2 *Solow-Swan Model*

Robert Solow (1956 & 1957) and Trevor Swan (1956) have put forward a neoclassical economic growth model on the basis of the Harrod-Domar model. The neoclassical economic growth model analyzes the effects of savings, population growth, and technological advancement on economic growth and explains the conditions under which output levels reach a steady-state equilibrium.

1. Assumptions of the Solow-Swan model

The main assumptions of the Solow-Swan model are:

(1) The economy consists of one sector that produces products that can be used both for consumption and for investment.
(2) The economy is closed, and the government sector is ignored.
(3) All savings will be invested, that is, ex-ante investment and ex-ante savings are equal.
(4) Prices are perfectly elastic, currency is neutral, and the economy is always at the level of potential output.
(5) This model abandons the assumption of the Harrod-Domar model that the capital-output ratio and the capital-labor ratio are constant.
(6) Technological progress, population growth, and depreciation are determined by exogenous factors.

2. Basic equations of the Solow-Swan model

The Solow-Swan model has three basic equations, namely, the production equation, the consumption equation, and the capital accumulation equation. In the Solow-Swan model, output depends on capital stock and labor, capital stock depends on investment and depreciation, and investment comes from savings, which depend on output (see Fig. 2.9).

(1) The production equation. For simplicity's sake, let us start with analyzing the production equation without technological advancement:

$$Y = F\left(K,L\right) \tag{2.11}$$

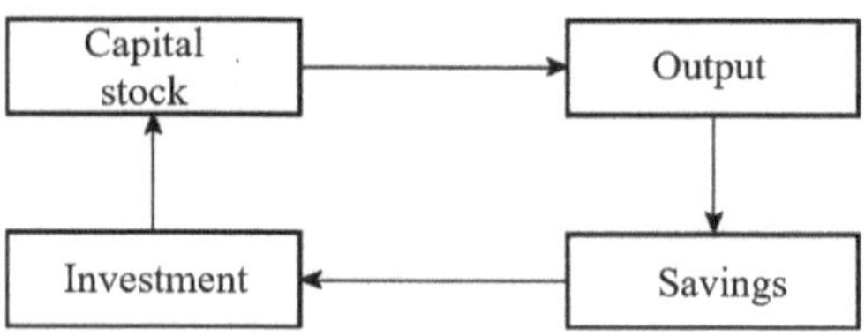


**Fig. 2.9** Relationships among output, savings, investment, and capital stock in the Solow-Swan model

Where $Y$ represents actual output, $K$ is capital, and $L$ denotes labor input.

Eqn. (2.11) implies that output depends on capital stock and labor input. The production function in Eqn. (2.11) has the following properties: first, the marginal product of capital and labor is positive, subject to diminishing marginal returns; that is, when $\partial F/\partial K > 0$, $\partial^2 F/\partial K^2 < 0$ and when $\partial F/\partial L > 0$, $\partial^2 F/\partial L^2 < 0$. Second, returns to scale are constant, that is, when $\lambda > 1$, $\lambda Y = F(\lambda K, \lambda L)$. Constant returns to scale imply that the economy is already sufficiently large, and benefits from the division of labor and specialization have been maximized. As a result, the scale of economy measured by labor has no effect on output per capita.

According to the property of constant returns to scale, let $\lambda = 1/L$, and we get $Y/L = F(K/L, 1)$. Let $Y/L = y$ and $K/L = k$, and Eqn. (2.11) can be written as below to describe the relationship between output per capita and output stock per capita:

$$y = f(k) \tag{2.12}$$

In Eqn. (2.12), $f'(k) > 0$ means that the marginal product of capital per capita is positive, and increasing the capital-labor ratio leads to higher output per capita; $f''(k) < 0$ implies that the marginal product of capital per capita is diminishing (see Fig. 2.10). Therefore, the marginal product of capital in developing countries where capital is relatively scarce is higher than that in developed countries with relatively abundant capital, and increasing capital per capita leads to higher output per capita.

(2) The consumption and savings equation. According to the national income identity, in a closed economy, total output is equal to consumption plus investment, and investment is equal to savings.

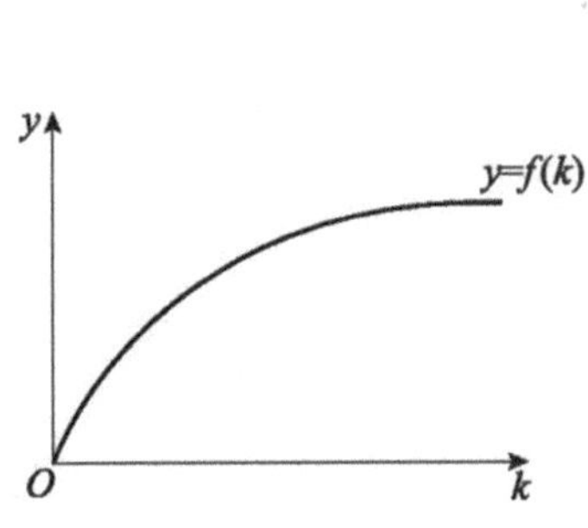


**Fig. 2.10** Per capita production equation of the Solow-Swan model

$$Y = C + I = C + S \tag{2.13}$$
$$Y = C + sY \tag{2.14}$$

Where $C$ represents consumption, $I$ investment, and $S$ savings; $S = sY$, where $s$ is the savings rate and $0 < s < 1$, representing the portion of income that is not consumed.

Equation (2.14) implies that under the assumption of a closed economy, domestic savings equal domestic investment:

$$\Delta Y_t = a\Delta Y^*_{Mt} \tag{2.15}$$

(3) The capital accumulation equation. Since output per capita depends on capital per capita, in order to analyze how capital per capita changes over time, the process of capital accumulation needs to be examined first. Similar to the Harrod-Domar model, changes in capital stock are shown in Eqn. (2.16). Capital stock in the next period ($K_{t+1}$) is equal to current investment ($I_t$) plus current capital stock net of depreciation ($K_t$-$\delta K_t$).

$$K_{t+1} = K_t - \delta K_t + I_t \tag{2.16}$$

Let $\Delta K = K_{t+1} - K_t$, substitute $I = sY$ into it, and we get:

$$\Delta K = sY - \delta K \tag{2.17}$$

Dividing both sides of the equal sign in the above equation by $L$, we get:

$$\Delta K / L = sY / L - \delta K / L = sy - \delta k \tag{2.18}$$

As $k = K/L$, the growth rate of $k$ can be written as:

$$\Delta k / k = \Delta K / K - \Delta L / L \tag{2.19}$$

Denote the growth rate of $L$ by $n$, i.e., $\Delta L/L = n$, substitute it into Eqn. (2.19), and we get:

$$\Delta k / k = \Delta K / K - n \tag{2.20}$$

$$\Delta K = \left(\Delta k / k\right)K + nK \tag{2.21}$$

Divide both sides of Eqn. (2.21) by *L*, we get:

$$\Delta K / L = \Delta k + nk \tag{2.22}$$

Combine Eqns. (2.18) and (2.22) and eliminate $\Delta K/L$, we get:

$$\Delta k = sy - \left(n + \delta\right)k \tag{2.23}$$

Equation (2.23) is a basic equation of the Solow-Swan model. This equation shows that changes in capital per capita ($\Delta k$) are equal to savings per capita ($sy$) minus $(n + \delta)k$. $(n + \delta)k$ can be understood as follows: a portion of savings per capita is to be allocated to the new workforce and is denoted by $nk$; the other portion is used to replace depreciated capital and is denoted by $\delta k$. The sum of the two is $(n + \delta)k$, which is called capital widening. When $sy > (n + \delta)k$ and $\Delta k > 0$, it is called capital deepening.

3. Steady-state analysis

When capital per capita and output per capita no longer change, the Solow-Swan model reaches a steady state. That is, when $\Delta k = 0$, capital per capita and output per capita reach a steady state. Therefore, the steady-state condition of the Solow-Swan model is:

$$sy = \left(n + \delta\right)k \tag{2.24}$$

This steady-state condition can be analyzed in Fig. 2.11.

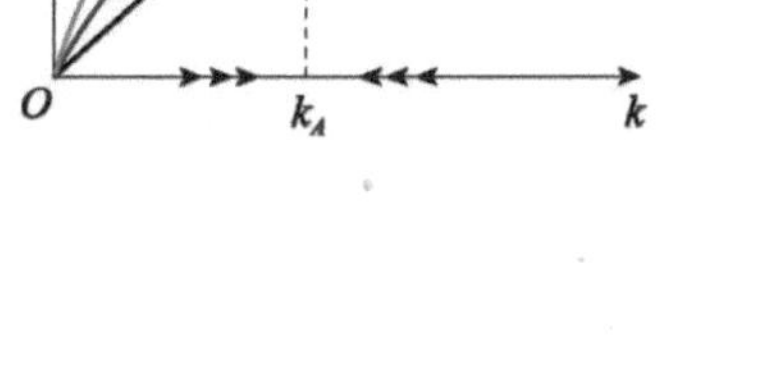


**Fig. 2.11** Steady state of the Solow-Swan model

$sf(k)$ represents the per capita savings curve, and $(n + \delta)$ represents capital broadening. As $s < 1$, $sf(k)$ has the same shape as $f(k)$, but lies under it. According to the steady-state condition, the intersection of $(n + \delta)k$ and $sf(k)$ can determine the steady-state capital per capita $k_A$ and output per capita $y_A$. When $k < k_A$, capital per capita shows an upward trend; when $k > k_A$, capital per capita shows a downward trend. This indicates that when the economy deviates from the steady state, capital per capita, whether it is too high or too low, will eventually return to equilibrium. Therefore, the Solow-Swan model demonstrates a steady dynamic growth process.

As $k = K/L$, $y = Y/L$, and growth rate is $n$, when $k$ and $y$ are in a steady state, *the growth rate of* $K$ and $Y$ is also $n$, so

$$\Delta K / K = \Delta Y / Y = \Delta L / L = n$$

4. The impact of savings rate, population growth, and technological advancement on economic growth

(1) The impact of savings rate on economic growth. As shown in Fig. 2.12, the economy is initially at the steady-state equilibrium point $C$, and the savings rate is $s$. If the savings rate increases to $s'$, $sf(k)$ shifts to $s'f(k)$, and the new steady-state equilibrium point becomes $C'$. By comparing points $C$ and $C'$, we can find that when the savings rate rises, steady-state capital per capita and output per capita both increase. Additionally, the growth rate of steady-state total capital and total output is still $n$, free from the impact of the savings rate. However, in the short run, an increase in the savings rate leads to growth in output and in the growth rate of output per capita. When the savings rate rises, capital per capita increases,

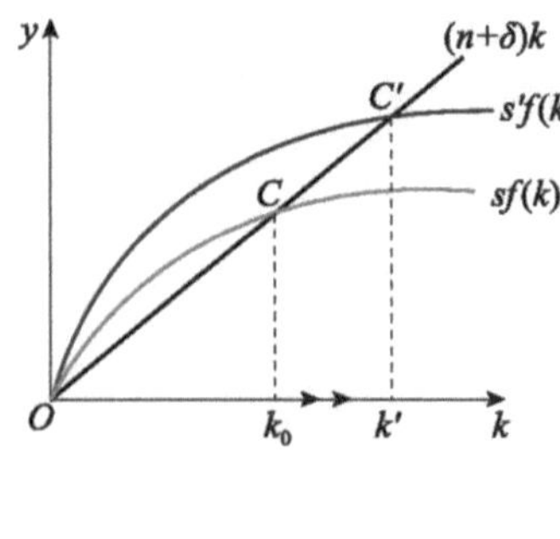


**Fig. 2.12** The impact of rising savings rate

meaning that capital stock grows faster than the labor force, which leads to a faster increase in output.

(2) The impact of population growth on economic growth. As shown in Fig. 2.13, the economy is initially at the steady-state equilibrium point $A$, and the population growth rate is $n$. If the population growth rate rises to $n'$, $(n + \delta)k$ shifts to $(n' + \delta)k$, and the new steady-state equilibrium point becomes $A'$. By comparing points $A$ and $A'$, we can find that when the population growth rate rises, steady-state capital per capita and output per capita both decline. Rising population growth rates and declining output per capita are among the challenges facing many developing countries. When the population growth rate rises, the growth rate of steady-state total capital and the growth rate of steady-state total output also increase.

(3) The impact of technological advancement on economic growth. Unlike the previous analyses, technological advancement is now taken into account. Take labor-enhancing technological advancement as an example. Technological advancement is tantamount to increasing the labor input of the economy:

$$Y = F(AL, K) \tag{2.25}$$

In Eqn. (2.25), $A$ represents technological advancement, the growth rate of $A$ is $g$, and $AL$ represents effective labor. Under this assumption, output depends on capital and effective labor. Let $k = K / AL$ represent average

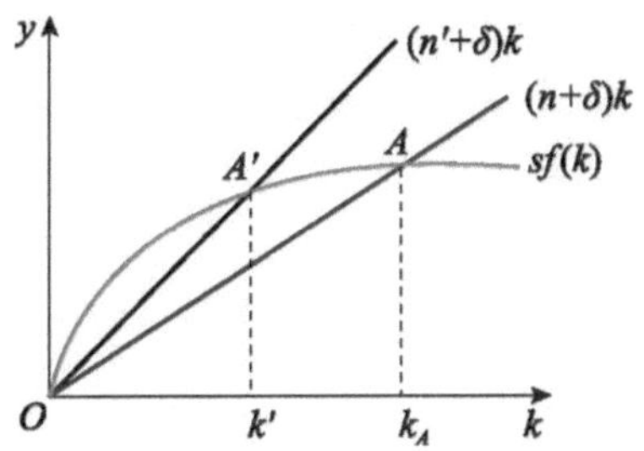


Fig. 2.13 The impact of rising population growth rate

capital in effective labor and $\tilde{y} = Y / AL$ represent average output in effective labor. Equation (2.25) can be written as:

$$\tilde{y} = f\left(\tilde{k}\right) \tag{2.26}$$

At this point, the basic equation of the Solow-Swan model turns into:

$$\Delta \tilde{k} = s\tilde{y} - \left(n + \delta + g\right)\tilde{k} \tag{2.27}$$

When $s\tilde{y} = \left(n + \delta + g\right)\tilde{k}$, the economy reaches a steady state (see Fig. 2.14). It can be seen that the steady-state analysis taking into account technological advancement is similar to the previous analysis. When the economy is in a steady state, the growth rate of average capital and output in effective labor is 0, the growth rate of capital per capita and output per capita is *g*, and the growth rate of total capital and total output is $n + g$. This indicates that technological advancement can lead to sustained growth in output per capita.

5. The Golden Rule level of capital

Many scholars believe that the fundamental purpose of economic development is to increase per capita consumption. In the Solow-Swan model, output per capita is equal to the sum of savings per capita and

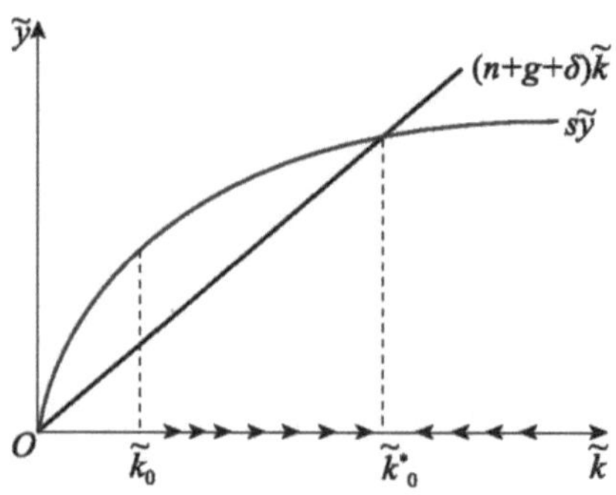


**Fig. 2.14** Steady state taking into account technological advancement

consumption per capita; savings per capita correspond to different levels of capital per capita, so different levels of capital per capita correspond to different levels of consumption per capita. American economist Edmund S. Phelps has proposed the Golden Rule of capital accumulation, in which the level of capital per capita should satisfy to maximize consumption per capita. The Golden Rule level of capital is shown in Fig. 2.15.

In Fig. 2.15, the horizontal axis represents the steady-state level of capital per capita, and the vertical axis represents the steady-state levels of output per capita, savings per capita, and consumption per capita. When the economy is in a steady state, $(n + \delta)k$ denotes savings per capita, and the distance between $f(k)$ and $(n + \delta)k$ represents consumption per capita. According to the first-order condition, the value of $k^*$ that maximizes $f(k)-(n + \delta)k$ should satisfy:

$$f'\left(k^*\right) = n + \delta \tag{2.28}$$

That is, in order to maximize steady-state consumption per capita, the marginal product of capital per capita should be equal to the population growth rate plus the depreciation rate. In Fig. 2.15, this question can be translated into how to determine $k$ to maximize the distance between $f(k)$ and $(n + \delta)k$. In the position of $k^*$, the tangent slope of $f(k)$ is equal to $n + \delta$, satisfying Eqn. (2.28). Therefore, $k^*$ is the Golden Rule level of capital.

According to the Golden Rule of capital accumulation, when the economy is in a steady state, if capital per capita is above the Golden Rule level, consumption can be increased by consuming a portion of the excess capital to bring capital per capita down to the Golden Rule level. Otherwise, consumption can be reduced and savings increased to raise capital per capita to the Golden Rule level.

**Fig. 2.15** The Golden Rule level of capital

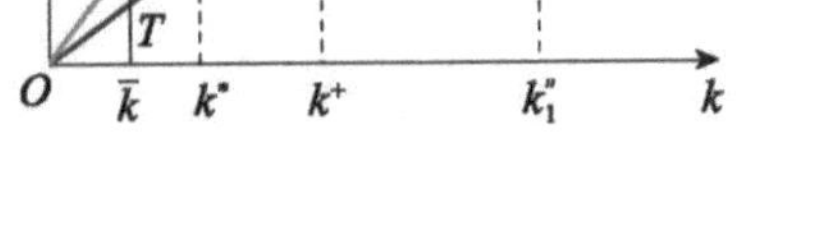

6. Reflection on the Solow-Swan model

To sum up, the key findings of the Solow-Swan model about economic growth are as follows:

(1) In the long run, the economy converges to a steady-state equilibrium, where the steady-state levels of capital per capita and output per capita are independent of the initial conditions.
(2) When the economy is in a steady state, the growth rate of output depends on the growth rate of population and the speed of technological advancement, while the growth rate of output per capita depends only on the speed of technological advancement.
(3) At a given depreciation rate, the level of steady-state output per capita depends on the savings rate and population growth rate. Higher savings rates will increase output per capita, and higher population growth rates will reduce output per capita.
(4) A one-time increase in the savings rate can raise the growth rate of output per capita in the short run, and has no impact on the growth rate of output per capita in the long run.
(5) The Solow-Swan model has a "convergence property." If rich and poor countries have similar structural parameters in terms of preferences and technology, poor countries tend to grow faster than rich countries.

According to empirical data, many findings of the Solow-Swan model have been verified. For example, cross-country data suggests that there is a significant negative correlation between population growth rate and income per capita, and a significant positive correlation between the savings to investment ratio and income per capita. The member countries of the Organization for Economic Cooperation and Development (OECD) generally grow at relatively low rates, but some developing countries have experienced rapid growth. There is strong evidence of convergence among OECD member countries and among the United States, Europe, and Japan. In empirical studies involving more diverse sample countries, the negative correlation between income per capita and population growth rate (i.e., absolute convergence) is not supported by data, while "conditional convergence" is supported by data.

However, the Solow-Swan model also has some deficiencies. First, the Solow-Swan model implies that only technological advancement can guarantee sustained growth in output per capita. Without technological advancement, the growth of output per capita would eventually stop because of the diminishing marginal product of capital per capita. In reality, output per capita in many countries has been growing for more than 100 years, with the growth rate showing no downward trend. Technological advancement in the Solow-Swan model is key to explaining long-run economic growth, but technological advancement is exogenously given in this model. Second, the Solow-Swan model thinks that the income disparities between countries can be explained by the difference in capital per capita. In reality, however, cross-country differences in capital per capita are not large enough to explain the income disparities between countries. For example, if the per capita output in the United States is 10 times that of India, then the per capita capital in the United States would need to be 1000 times greater than that in India. Moreover, the Solow-Swan model believes that under the premise that technological advancement is exogenous, the marginal product of capital in poor countries should be much higher than that in rich countries. If the gap in income per capita is entirely caused by the difference in capital per capita, a ten-fold per capita income gap between two countries means a 100-fold difference in the marginal product of capital. In reality, the difference in returns on capital between rich and poor countries is not that significant. Finally, the speed of convergence in practice is only half that projected by the model, while the impact of the initial conditions of the economy on the speed of convergence far exceeds what is predicted by this model. Generally, in the Solow-Swan model, capital per capita can neither explain the long-run growth of output per capita nor the income disparities between countries.

## 4 Real Business Cycle Theory

The real business cycle theory, proposed by Finn Kydland and Edward Prescott (1982), believes that real shocks, such as technology shocks, are the primary sources of economic fluctuations. The RBC theory interprets economic fluctuations within the framework of competitive general equilibrium, emphasizing the micro-foundation for the optimization of economic agents' behavior. The Dynamic Stochastic General Equilibrium models, which are based on the RBC theory, have become the mainstream approach in modern macroeconomics. Finn Kydland and Edward Prescott were awarded the Nobel Prize in Economics in 2004 for their contributions to the RBC theory.

### 4.1 *The Background of the RBC Theory*

1. The revival of the business cycle theory

At the beginning of the twentieth century, business cycle was a core topic in economics. Scholars put forward the pure theory of money, the overinvestment theory, the innovation theory, the underconsumption theory, and the sunspot theory, among others. Among them, Gustav Cassel's overinvestment theory and Joseph Schumpeter's innovation theory both argue that new inventions, technological changes, and organizational innovations are the primary causes of business cycles. After Keynes published *The General Theory of Employment, Interest and Money* in the 1930s, economists began to focus on the determination of short-run national income and how various policies can influence the equilibrium level of output. After World War II, Western countries experienced a prolonged period of economic prosperity, leading some to question whether business cycles had disappeared. However, stagflation occurred in major market economies in the 1970s, leaving Keynesian economics struggling to provide effective solutions. With the failure of Keynesian macro-econometric models and the influence of the "rational expectations revolution," business cycles were back in focus in economic research. Keynesian models are static models lacking a micro-foundation, while the RBC theory is a dynamic model that emphasizes the optimization of economic agents' behavior.

2. Lucas critique and his equilibrium model of the business cycle

In the late 1970s, Robert E. Lucas Jr. made a fierce critique of the IS/LM-AD/AS model, the main paradigm of macroeconomics. This is called the "Lucas critique." A typical IS/LM-AD/AS model includes a set of functions such as the consumption function, the investment function, the money demand function, and the money supply function. The impact of policy on output is analyzed by estimating fiscal policy multipliers and monetary policy multipliers. Lucas points out that the parameters in the consumption function and the investment function, for example, depend on the past consumption and saving decisions of economic agents, without considering the optimization of economic agents' behavior. In the wake of the new macroeconomic policy, constraints on economic agents will change, and the parameters in the consumption function and the investment function will change, as well. Fiscal policy multipliers and monetary policy multipliers estimated based on previous data can cause policymakers to misestimate the policy impact. As a result, the policy may fail to achieve the expected objectives. Lucas thinks that the utility function and the production function, which describe the behavior of economic agents, should be used to construct models so as to understand the actual response of economic agents to policy changes. To this end, Lucas applies the general equilibrium model to the study of business cycles, giving rise to the monetary surprise model of neoclassical macroeconomics. In this model, unexpected changes in money supply bring about changes in the real variables of the economic system. However, the assumption that economic agents lack information on general price levels and money stock is hard to believe, because, in practice, such information is easily accessible. As a result of dissatisfaction with the monetary surprise model, the business cycle theory of neoclassical macroeconomics starts shifting to a theory that highlights real factors.

3. Business cycles and random walks

Before the 1980s, Keynesianism, monetarism, and neoclassical macroeconomics all thought that the long-term trend of economic growth is smooth and determined by internal factors of the economy; short-run fluctuations around long-term trends are caused by demand shocks, and such deviation is temporary. In their research on macroeconomic time series, Charles R. Nelson and Charles I. Plosser find that despite the seeming tendency to revert to a trend, actual output is actually a random walk. Some random shocks are positive and others are negative, leading to upward or downward movements in the trendline. The business cycles that we observe are actually the result of the trendline itself moving upward or downward. In neoclassical economics, currency is neutral and unlikely to cause persistent changes in output, so the main driving force of economic fluctuations must be real shocks. Therefore, Nelson and Prosser believe that the business cycle model that attributes economic fluctuations to monetary disturbances is difficult to explain changes in output, while random variations caused by real factors are a core component of any macroeconomic volatility model.

4. The impact of business cycles—the framework of communication theory

In the 1930s, Eugen Slutsky and Ragnar Frisch pointed out that using completely independent random variables can generate time series that exhibit the characteristics of economic variables, specifically showing persistent fluctuations around a trend. Ragnar Frisch distinguishes between the stimulus mechanism and the communication mechanism of economic fluctuations. The stimulus mechanism refers to the initial shock to the economy that causes variables to deviate from their steady-state values. The communication mechanism transmits given shocks over time, resulting in variables persistently deviating from their steady-state values. It is an inevitable choice for research on business cycles within the framework of dynamic general equilibrium to incorporate the stimulation mechanism and the communication mechanism into the model. This approach is adopted in both the monetary surprise model and the RBC model. In the RBC theory, technology shocks serve as the stimulus mechanism, while the intertemporal substitution for leisure and investment lags act as the communication mechanism.

## 4.2 *Main Content of the RBC Theory*

1. Basic assumptions and premises

The RBC theory, which is based on the framework of general equilibrium, is also known as the equilibrium model of the business cycle. This theory has the following assumptions and premises:

(1) Using an analytical framework of representative agents circumvents the problem of macroeconomic aggregation. Economic agents are rational. Under resource and technical constraints, representative households will maximize utility, and representative businesses will maximize profits.
(2) All economic agents have rational expectations, and there is no information asymmetry.
(3) Prices and wages are perfectly elastic, and there is no friction or transaction cost, assuming that the market is complete and clears continuously.

(4) Since households engage in utility-maximizing behavior, employment fluctuations reflect voluntary changes in the number of working hours, and there is no involuntary unemployment.
(5) Currency is neutral, and monetary policy has no effect on real variables.
(6) Technology shocks serve as the source of fluctuations in output and employment. Given the current technology shocks, intertemporal substitution for leisure impacts future output by affecting future labor supply, and investment lags affect future investment, which in turn influences future output.
(7) Economic fluctuations and economic growth are incorporated in the same analytical framework, without distinguishing between the short run and the long run.

2. Basic model

The basic model of the RBC theory only involves the household sector and the business sector. The household sector chooses the optimal quantity of consumption and labor, with the aim to maximize utility. The household sector provides capital and labor to the business sector to get rent and wages. The business sector chooses the quantities of capital and labor to maximize profits, and the production function is subject to random technology shocks.

(1) Household sector. Assume that the economy consists of numerous homogeneous, infinitely lived households, representative households can therefore be selected for analysis. The utility of representative households depends on consumption ($C_t$) and leisure ($L_t$), and its utility function is $u(C_t, L_t)$. Representative households choose the consumption sequence $\{C_t\}_{t=1}^{\infty}$ and leisure sequence $\{L_t\}_{t=1}^{\infty}$, so as to maximize the expected utility:

$$E_0\sum_{t=0}^{\infty}\beta^t u(C_t,L_t) \tag{2.29}$$

Where $\beta$ is the subjective discount factor ($0 < \beta < 1$), reflecting household preferences for current consumption-leisure combinations over future consumption-leisure combinations. $E_0$ is the mathematical expectation operator, representing the mathematical expectation based on information available at time 0. The utility function $u(C_t, L_t)$ is concave, indicating that households prefer to smooth their consumption and leisure over time. Additionally, when interest rates and wages change, households will engage in intertemporal substitution for consumption and leisure.

(2) Business sector. In a perfectly competitive market, the objective of representative businesses is to maximize profits. The production function of businesses exhibits constant returns to scale, as shown below:

$$Y_t = z_t f(K_t, H_t) \tag{2.30}$$

Where $K_t$ represents capital investment; $H_t$ is labor input; $z_t$ denotes technology shocks and is a strictly positive random parameter. Since the production function exhibits constant returns to scale, an economy with a single business is similar to an economy with many businesses.

The capital accumulation process of the RBC theory is the same as that of the neoclassical economic growth model. Capital stock in the next period is equal to current investment plus current capital stock net of depreciation:

$$K_{t+1} = (1-\delta)K_t + I_t \tag{2.31}$$

Where $\delta$ is the depreciation rate of capital stock, and $0 \le \delta \le 1$; $I_t$ represents investment in the period $t$.

(3) Resource constraints. In each period, the household sector and the business sector face two resource constraints:

First, the sum of working hours and leisure time equals the total time endowment. By normalizing the household's time in each period to 1, the time constraint can be expressed as:

$$H_t + L_t = 1 \tag{2.32}$$

Second, in a closed economy without the government sector, according to the national income identity, output is equal to the sum of consumption and investment:

$$Y_t = C_t + I_t \tag{2.33}$$

(4) Technology shocks. In the RBC theory, a broad range of productivity shocks are collectively referred to as "technology shocks," including changes in the quality of capital and labor inputs, new management practices, the development of new products, and the introduction of new production technologies. Technology shocks $z_t$ involve a first-order autoregressive process, as shown in the following equation:

$$z_{t+1} = \gamma z_t + \varepsilon_{t+1} \tag{2.34}$$

Where $0 < \gamma < 1$; $\varepsilon_t$ follows a normal distribution with a mean of 0 and a variance of $\sigma_\varepsilon^2$, and it is serially uncorrelated. $z_t$ is practically random technological advancement and represents the portion of output changes that cannot be explained by changes in input.

3. Solution, calibration, and simulation of the basic model

Dynamic programming methods can be used to solve the aforementioned model.

First, the specific forms of the utility function and the production function are given. In most RBC models, the following utility function and production function are usually used:

$$u(C_t, L_t) = \log C_t + A \log L_t \tag{2.35}$$

$$f(K_t, H_t) = K_t^\theta H_t^{1-\theta} \tag{2.36}$$

Second, derive the equilibrium conditions and describe the decision variables using state variables:

$$C_t = C^*\left(K_t, z_t\right) \tag{2.37}$$

$$H_t = H^*\left(K_t, z_t\right) \tag{2.38}$$

$$I_t = I^*\left(K_t, z_t\right) \tag{2.39}$$

Where $C^*$, $H^*$, and $I^*$ are all continuous functions. Eqns. (2.37), (2.38), and (2.39) indicate that current capital stock and technology shocks determine consumption, labor, and investment. The capital rental and the real wage can be derived by solving the profit maximization problem. Assuming that $z_t = 1$ and consumption, labor, and investment are constant, as shown in Eqns. (2.40), (2.41), and (2.42), a steady-state equilibrium of the economy can be obtained.

$$\bar{C} = C^*\left(\bar{K}, 1\right) \tag{2.40}$$

$$\bar{H} = H^*\left(\bar{K}, 1\right) \tag{2.41}$$

$$\bar{I} = I^*\left(\bar{K}, 1\right) \tag{2.42}$$

In the above model, the solution to the optimization problem exists and is unique, but it cannot be expressed in a closed-form analytical solution. In order to obtain the solution for this model, the simplest method is to derive a linear approximation of the equilibrium conditions around the steady-state values ( $\bar{C}$ , $\bar{H}$ , $\bar{I}$ ) using first-order Taylor approximation. Therefore, the decision variables are expressed as linear functions of the state variables.

To derive quantitative implications of the research question from the general framework, the model needs to be calibrated. The calibration process involves selecting the values of the model parameters, so that the model's steady-state behavior aligns with the long-term characteristics of the data. This process can be divided into three steps: first, parameterize the model; second, establish a set of metrics consistent with the model parameters; and finally, assign values to the model parameters. The model parameters include the share of capital in income $\theta$, the discount factor $\beta$, the depreciation rate $\delta$, the weight of leisure in the utility function $A$, and the parameters related to technology shocks $\gamma$ and $\sigma_\varepsilon^2$ . These parameters are all obtained from other empirical studies rather than directly estimating the model.

After the relevant parameters are determined, the model can be simulated. First, generate realizations of the random process $\{\varepsilon_t\}\{\varepsilon_t, t = 1, 2, \ldots, T\}$ and consequently, the sequence of technology shocks. Second, combine the sequence of technology shocks, initial capital stock, and the decision function to generate the sequences for $K_t$, $C_t$, $I_t$, $H_t$, and $Y_t$. Finally, analyze the cyclical features of these sequences and compare them with the cyclical features of real economic data. Table 2.1 shows the cyclical features of the model of Kydland and Prescott (1982).

The RBC model uses stochastic productivity shocks to explain fluctuations in output, and the primary criterion for evaluating the effectiveness of the RBC model is whether it can simulate the cyclical features of real economic data. During the process of the simulation, the variance of the productivity shocks is selected to ensure that the fluctuations in the output sequence generated by the model align with those observed in real data. Therefore, the standard deviation of output in the model should equal the standard deviation of output in real data. As can be seen from Table 2.1, the basic model of the RBC theory can reflect the cyclical features of many key variables, and such cyclical features are quite close to the observed cyclical features. For example, the fluctuations in consumption are less than those in output, and the fluctuations in investment are greater than those in output. However, some cyclical features generated by the model vary notably from real data. For example, the correlation coefficient

**Table 2.1** Cyclical features of the model of Kydland and Prescott (1982)

| | *US Economy* | | *Model Results* | |
|---|---|---|---|---|
| | *Standard Deviation* | *Correlation Coefficient* | *Standard Deviation* | *Correlation Coefficient* |
| Output | 1.8 | 1.00 | 1.80 | 1.00 |
| Consumption | 1.3 | 0.74 | 0.63 | 0.87 |
| Investment | 5.1 | 0.71 | 6.54 | 0.99 |
| Inventories | 1.7 | 0.51 | 2.00 | 0.39 |
| Capital stock | 0.7 | −0.24 | 0.63 | −0.07 |
| Labor hours | 2.0 | 0.85 | 1.05 | 0.93 |
| Productivity | 1.0 | 0.10 | 0.90 | 0.90 |

Source: Kydland and Prescott (1982)

Note: The US economic data is quarterly data, covering the sample period between 1950 and 1979. The standard deviation is expressed as percentage, and the correlation coefficient is between the variables and output

between productivity and output in the model is much higher than that in real data.

4. Comparison with other macroeconomic theories

The AD/AS models of classical economics, monetarism, neoclassical economics, and new Keynesian economics have some similarities: The aggregate demand curve slopes down to the right, the long-run aggregate supply curve is vertical on the level of potential output, and the horizontal axis represents output, and the vertical axis represents price levels. The AD/AS model of the RBC theory is shown in Fig. 2.16. The horizontal axis represents the real output, and the vertical axis represents the real interest rate. The RAS curve and the RAD curve represent real aggregate supply and real aggregate demand, respectively. Real aggregate demand is a decreasing function of the real interest rate. An increase in government spending, autonomous consumption, or investment can shift the RAD curve to the right. Real aggregate supply is an increasing function of the real interest rates, and negative productivity shocks can shift the RAS curve to the left, leading to a decline in output and an increase in real interest rates.

In contrast, the RBC theory is different in the following aspects: (1) The RBC theory has only one RAS curve and does not distinguish between the short run and the long run. In the RAS curve, the labor market is always in equilibrium, and there is no involuntary unemployment. (2) The RBC theory posits that technology shocks can cause shifts in the RAS curve, and this is the root cause of fluctuations in output and employment. Classical economics, monetarism, neoclassical economics, and new

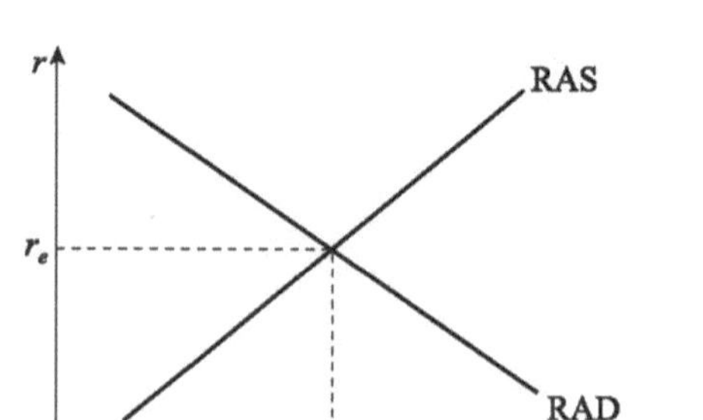


**Fig. 2.16** AD/AS model of the RBC theory

Keynesian economics consider aggregate demand shocks as the root cause of economic fluctuations. (3) The RBC theory incorporates the growth theory and the fluctuation theory within the same framework, believing that the observed fluctuations in output are fluctuations in potential output rather than the deviation of output from potential output.

5. Policy implications of the RBC theory

Before 1980, Keynesian economics, monetarism, and neoclassical economics reached the following consensus regarding business cycles: fluctuations in output reflect temporary deviations from the potential growth trend; fluctuations in output reduce social welfare, so economic policy should be implemented to reduce fluctuations in output; and monetary policy is an important factor influencing the business cycle. The emergence of the RBC theory poses challenges to the aforementioned consensus. First, the RBC theory contends that rational economic man's optimal responses to random technology shocks are the primary source of economic fluctuations. Output fluctuations reflect fluctuations in the potential economic growth trend, rather than temporary deviations from the trend. Facing technology shocks, workers will optimize their labor supply, so there is no involuntary unemployment. Second, since output and employment fluctuations reflect fluctuations in the potential output trend and are Pareto-optimal, they do not reflect any market failure. The RBC theory claims that government intervention intended to stabilize the economy is unnecessary and can reduce social welfare. Finally, the RBC theory emphasizes that technology shocks as a real factor are the primary source of output fluctuations. Currency is neutral, and monetary policy is unlikely to produce practical results.

To sum up, the RBC theory holds that output fluctuations reflect fluctuations in the potential output trend, and trying to stabilize the economy through countercyclical policy is meaningless. As the fluctuations in the growth rate of total factor productivity (TFP) are the primary source of business cycles, the most effective countercyclical policy is to reduce or eliminate the random fluctuations in the TFP growth rate. Regrettably, economists and policymakers are unclear about how random fluctuations in TFP growth can be reduced or eliminated. Policymakers can mitigate the impact of random fluctuations in TFP growth on individuals, but the RBC theory holds that such policies may worsen the situation.

### 4.3 Reflection on the RBC Theory

The contributions of the RBC theory are reflected in three areas. First, the RBC theory applies the general equilibrium theory to the study of business cycles, trying to establish a micro-foundation for macroeconomic theory. The DSGE models, which are based on the RBC theory, have become the mainstream approach in modern macroeconomics. Second, the RBC theory incorporates the economic growth theory and the business cycle theory in the same framework, and thinks that the factors influencing economic growth and economic fluctuation are the same, offering a fresh perspective for understanding business cycles. Finally, the RBC theory asserts that supply shocks (especially technology shocks) are the primary source of output fluctuations, leading economists to place greater emphasis on the impact of supply factors in macroeconomic research.

The RBC theory also has various deficiencies.

First, the importance of technology shocks lacks empirical support. Since technology shocks cannot be directly observed, the RBC theory generally uses the Solow residual as a substitute for technology shocks. In order to match the RBC model with the cyclical patterns observed in real data, technology shocks must be massive and persistent. This requirement has been subject to criticism from many scholars. The theory using technology shocks to explain economic fluctuations faces the challenge of how to explain economic recessions, as significant technological regress is unrealistic.

Second, the RBC theory cannot explain the cyclical features of output fluctuations. In the RBC theory, cyclical output fluctuations are driven by the exogenous technology shock cycle. Temporary productivity shocks will only cause output and employment to temporarily deviate from their long-term path, without bringing about cyclical fluctuations in output and employment. To generate cycles, productivity shocks must be specified as a first-order autoregressive process, which causes technology shocks themselves to exhibit cyclical features. However, the communication mechanism in the RBC theory is quite weak.

Third, some of the "characteristic facts" of business cycles on which the RBC theory relies are subject to debate and controversy. For example, the RBC theory believes that real wages are strongly procyclical, while prices are countercyclical. However, empirical research on the cyclical features of real wages has yet to reach generally accepted conclusions. The cyclical features of real wages vary from one country to another, and the countercyclicality of prices provides little information for identifying the nature of shocks.

Fourth, the Hodrick-Prescott (HP) filter used by the RBC theory may produce false business cycles. In the RBC theory, the predicted values of time series such as output, consumption, and investment are expressed as deviations from the steady state, and the HP filter is used to detrend the data on these variables. Some scholars find that the data generated by RBC models are nearly white noise, but the data exhibits cyclical patterns after being filtered using the HP filter. Moreover, the HP filter can amplify the correlations between time series, potentially leading to spurious correlations between two time series that are actually unrelated.

Fifthly, the calibration method used in the RBC theory has several drawbacks. The calibration method is unable to estimate the parameter uncertainty and determine whether a calibrated model is meaningful in some ways. The calibration method cannot provide an objective evaluation of a model's fit to the data, making it difficult to compare the fit of different models.

Sixth, the research method involving representative agents has considerable flaws. The RBC theory uses a representative agent method to circumvent the problem of macroeconomic aggregation. The condition for representative agents to accurately represent individuals is that all economic agents must have identical marginal responses, but it is impossible to meet this condition. The complexity of economic issues lies in coordinating the behaviors of various economic agents, but the research method used by representative economic agents completely rules out the possibility of coordination. However, it is from such coordination that many economists are able to identify the root cause of business cycles.

Seventh, the conclusions of the RBC theory about voluntary unemployment and the ineffectiveness of monetary policy are at odds with reality. As many economists see it, a large portion of unemployment is involuntary, and the labor market is not always in equilibrium. The anti-inflation practices in the United States and Britain in the 1980s demonstrate that the impact of monetary policy on output cannot be ignored.

## 5 Logical Connections Between Major Economic Theories and Rational Synthesis

Some typical theories and methods in contemporary economics are summarized in this section. Built on these theories and methods, the thinking of rational synthesis achieves an important innovation by translating the analysis of specific issues into a general statement. It treats specific issues as special cases of broader, more general issues, rather than starting with the analysis of specific issues and then extending them, for example, extending from static system analysis to dynamic analysis. In some sense, it represents a rational synthesis of these typical theories and methods and a step forward based on them. Here, we provide a brief analysis of these logical connections.

i. Rational synthesis entails a comprehensive analysis of the role of market and that of government and is a continuation and development of the mixed economy theory

The mixed economy theory is a result of reflection on the flaws of market mechanisms and advocates combining market regulation and government regulation. Arthur Pigou, from a microeconomic perspective, points out that market mechanisms are unable to address externalities. Keynes, from a macroeconomic perspective, posits that full employment can't be achieved solely by relying on market mechanism, and government intervention is necessary. As the mixed economy theory evolves, its denotations and connotations are constantly enriched. The mixed economy theories of Hansen, Samuelson, and Lindbeck involve the combination of market regulation and government regulation, private economy and public economy, distribution according to work and distribution according to production factors, as well as monopoly and competition. Samuelson and Lindbeck believe that the mixed economic system has several advantages, as it not only leverages the strengths of market regulation but also addresses its shortcomings through government intervention.

For quite a long time, a common misconception in the evolution of macroeconomic theory has been the tendency of scholars to accommodate the rationality of each other's theory from a single perspective of the market economy or the role of government, without realizing that a real-world economy is actually a mixed economy. Therefore, it's destined that early-stage economic theories alternated with varying economic issues, and a breakthrough analysis model and a complete policy framework have been absent so far. Given that economic operations are driven by both the "invisible hand" and the "visible hand," the shift of the market-government relationship from opposition to unity should be the fundamental direction of the development of macroeconomics. Drawing on the latest developments in Western economics and China's successful practices, we need to shift the market-government relationship from opposition to high-level unity, and construct theoretical models based on the mixed economy and the combination of the role of market and that of government, so as to put forward a macro-policy system driving economic development. The thinking of rational synthesis stresses the need to enable the market and the government to play their respective role. It emphasizes both the market regulation and government regulation to bring into full play the roles of an "efficient market" and a "proactive government" at the same time, taking the roles of market and government as a unity. The role of market and that of government can be reflected through different weights in the model.

ii. The thinking of rational synthesis requires the use of dynamic analysis methods and emphasizes disequilibrium analysis. It is a continuation and development of dynamic macroeconomic theory and DSGE models.

Overall, the macroeconomic policy framework adopted in Keynesian economics is constructed based on non-dynamic theory dominated by static and comparative static analysis, unable to provide precise analysis of economic issues. For example, Keynes' income-expenditure model, the Hicks-Hansen IS-LM model, and the AD/AS model are all static models. The Harrod-Domar model and the Solow-Swan model are based on the dynamization of Keynesian theory so as to analyze long-term economic issues. The dynamic macroeconomic theory of the Stockholm school emphasizes the role of time in economic analysis and advocates for dynamic economics. For example, Knut Wicksell's accumulation process theory posits that the difference between the natural rate of interest and the monetary rate of interest can lead to changes in the price level as well as expansions and contractions of economic activity. Wicksell extends microeconomic static equilibrium analysis to macroeconomic dynamic disequilibrium analysis, building a prototype of modern macroeconomic theory. The DSGE models, which are based on the RBC theory and emphasize intertemporal optimization, stochastic shocks, and general equilibrium, have become the mainstream approach in modern macroeconomics. The RBC theory interprets economic fluctuations within the framework of competitive general equilibrium, emphasizing the microfoundation for intertemporal optimization of economic entities' behavior. New Keynesian economics improves the RBC theory by adding Keynesian elements such as monopolistic competition and price/wage stickiness while retaining assumptions such as intertemporal optimal choice, general equilibrium, rational expectations, and market clearing. As such, a new Keynesian DSGE model is formed.

Just as dynamic macroeconomic theory and DSGE models, the thinking of rational synthesis emphasizes the use of dynamic analysis methods. Additionally, the thinking of rational synthesis emphasizes disequilibrium analysis, whereas the vast majority of economic models (including the AD/AS model, the RBC model, and the new Keynesian DSGE model) are all equilibrium models. Although equilibrium analysis is intuitive and easy to understand, the state of equilibrium is just a special state rather than a norm in economic operations. The dynamic transition between equilibrium and disequilibrium of aggregate supply and aggregate demand is a specific manifestation of market mechanisms at work and is also the crux of the issue. Particular attention must be paid to disequilibrium analysis of aggregate demand and aggregate supply.

iii. The thinking of rational synthesis requires a comprehensive analysis of short-term issues and long-term issues and incorporates economic fluctuations and economic growth in the same framework

The traditional approach in macroeconomics is to analyze short-term and long-term issues separately. Short-term analysis revolves around the determination of national income and economic fluctuations, while long-term analysis is centered on economic growth and business cycles. Keynes' income-expenditure model, the Hicks-Hansen IS-LM model, and the AD/AS model are all focused on studying the determination of short-run national income, assuming that aggregate demand determines output under the condition that the short-run aggregate supply curve is horizontal. The AD/AS model distinguishes between short-run and long-run aggregate supply curves, thinking that aggregate demand and aggregate supply together determine output. In the short run, the aggregate supply curve is horizontal, and aggregate demand determines output. In the long run, the aggregate supply curve is vertical, and aggregate supply determines output. The Harrod-Domar model and the Solow-Swan model deal with long-term economic issues. They emphasize the effects of savings, population growth, and technological advancement on economic growth and explain the conditions for achieving steady-state equilibrium. However, the Harrod-Domar model and the Solow-Swan model study potential economic growth rather than real economic growth. Building on the neoclassical growth model, the RBC theory incorporates the economic growth theory and the business cycle theory in the same framework, and thinks that the factors influencing economic growth and economic fluctuation are the same and economic fluctuations reflect the optimal responses of economic agents to random technology shocks.

The thinking of rational synthesis posits that economic growth, as manifested in economic operations, is driven by a combination of the long-term trend and short-term fluctuations. Therefore, it is essential to conduct a comprehensive analysis of short-term and long-term issues. Changes in the level of total economic output consist of two parts. One is potential output in a pure market economy, which forms the main part of the long-term trend. The long-term trend depends on both economic fundamentals and government policy. The neoclassical economic growth model analyzes the effects of savings, population growth, and technological advancement on potential economic growth. The RBC theory emphasizes the impact of technology shocks and policy shocks on real economic growth. Combining the neoclassical economic growth theory and the RBC theory gives a better picture of the long-term economic trend. The other is the part due to short-term fluctuations, which are generated by temporary shocks on the supply side and the demand side, including changes brought about by the role of government. This can be analyzed by referring to the AD/AS model. Combining and building on the AD/AS model, the neoclassical economic growth theory, and the RBC theory, the thinking of rational synthesis incorporates economic fluctuations and economic growth in the same analytical framework.

iv. The thinking of rational synthesis requires a comprehensive analysis of demand and supply and is the synthesis and development of the AD/AS model and the RBC theory

The AD/AS model derived from the neoclassical synthesis school is used to analyze how total output and price levels are determined. Aggregate demand and aggregate supply represent the demand and supply of economic agents for total output. The intersection of the aggregate demand curve and the aggregate supply curve determines the equilibrium output and price levels. As to the determination of short-term national income, Keynes' income-expenditure model and the Hicks-Hansen IS-LM model focus on analyzing aggregate demand, while completely neglecting aggregate supply. The AD/AS model combines the two to analyze how aggregate output and price levels are determined, but it still emphasizes aggregate demand analysis over aggregate supply analysis, highlighting demand management by government through macroeconomic policy.

Different from the other theories mentioned above, the RBC theory argues that technology shocks are the primary source of economic fluctuations. It emphasizes the impact of supply factors, but completely ignores demand factors. In the AD/AS model of the RBC theory, real aggregate demand and real aggregate supply determine the equilibrium output level and interest rate. Technology shocks can cause shifts in the RAS curve, and this is the root cause of fluctuations in output and employment. Using the analytical framework of dynamic general equilibrium, the RBC theory thinks that output fluctuations reflect Pareto optimality over time, and trying to stabilize the economy through counter-cyclical policy is meaningless. This view completely negates the role of macroeconomic policy in managing short-term demand.

The thinking of rational synthesis requires a comprehensive analysis of demand and supply, rather than emphasizing demand factors or supply factors alone. Under market mechanisms, prices play a role in resource allocation by influencing demand and supply. Likewise, government's macroeconomic policy serves the purpose of macro control by influencing demand and supply. In the short term, macroeconomic policy can impact aggregate demand, which is a key aspect of aggregate policy. Expansionary fiscal or monetary policy can increase aggregate demand, while contractionary fiscal or monetary policy can reduce aggregate demand. Macroeconomic policy can also influence aggregate supply. For example, industrial policies aimed at optimizing the economic structure are structural policies. In the long run, macroeconomic policy can impact the economic growth trend, that is, the potential economic growth or total factor productivity on the supply side. To sum up, government's macroeconomic policy can influence economic fluctuations through supply-side and demand-side shocks combined, and can also exert a notable impact on the long-term trend of the economy through supply-side adjustments. The thinking of rational synthesis posits that it is necessary to implement a macro control system that balances the supply side and the demand side, properly handles the contradictions between total economic output and structural issues, and develop a macro policy framework capable of adapting to different scenarios from the comprehensive perspectives of aggregate supply and aggregate demand.

CHAPTER 3

# China's Stories and Innovation in Economic Theory

Reform and opening-up is one of the most marvelous stories of China. Thanks to reform and opening up, China has boosted its economic development and improved people's wellbeing. China's reform and opening up has also reshaped the global economic and financial landscapes. China's stories depict its phenomenal economic development and the evolution of its market economy model since reform and opening up, as well as the continuous innovation in economic theory. More than 40 years into China's reform and opening up, our theoretical research on it remains in the stage of plain description and simple storytelling, commented an official of the International Monetary Fund. China's economic theory is not yet well studied and has a long way to go. This chapter will focus on the stories about China's reform and opening up and innovation in economic theory.

## 1 China's Economic Success and Root Cause Analysis

Over the past decades since reform and opening up, China's economy leaps forward, making China the world's second largest economy by GDP. It has escaped the Malthusian trap and become an upper-middle-income country, creating miracles which will go down in the annals of the world economy. These are China's stories, an account of its economic success and why it can make that happen. Taking reform and opening up as



Z. Liang, *The Innovation of Economic Theory in China*,
https://doi.org/10.1007/978-981-95-2713-7_3

the main line, China has established a sound economic development model, driving and inspiring innovation in economic theory. The main line and theoretical innovation based on China's practices involve two aspects. The first is reform. In the planned economy, market power was regarded as a supplement. Later, the combination of "government planning" and "market power" was emphasized. As reform further progressed, the "essential role" of market was stressed, and the wording has now been changed to the "decisive role" of market in resource allocation. Market-oriented reform as part of macro control has prompted social development, thus spurring innovation in the market economy theory. The second is opening up. From the establishment of special economic zones to China's accession to the World Trade Organization (WTO) and to the proposal of initiatives such as the Belt and Road Initiative and a community of shared future for mankind, thanks to the opening up policy under international trade rules, China has quickened its pace to integrate into the world economy, and fostered theoretical innovation.

Figure 3.1 illustrates a comparison of economic development between China and the US, and Fig. 3.2 is a comparison between the economy of China and that of the world.

First, China's economy has entered a golden period of development featuring sustained and rapid growth. In 1978, China was a typical low-income country with per capita GDP of merely RMB381. From 2019 to 2020, its per capita GDP exceeded USD10,000 for two consecutive years, rising into the ranks of upper-middle-income countries. The reform and opening up have led to tremendous economic success. China's economy has not only achieved leapfrog development but also been holding steady as the world's second largest economy, with a growing influence on the world economy. Meanwhile, China's industrial structure has transformed from extensive and labor-intensive to high-quality and innovation-driven. In the early days of reform and opening up, China had a relatively small economic size. Its GDP was still at low levels despite the high growth rate. In the past, the principal challenge facing Chinese society was that China's underdeveloped social production was unable to meet the ever-growing material needs of the people. Nowadays, what we face is the challenge of meeting the people's ever-growing needs for a better life. Such a shift will definitely drive the rapid development and profound change of China's economy and society. In 2018, China ranked first in the world by retail sales of consumer goods. During the 14th Five-Year Plan period (2021–2025), China will remain the world's leading consumer market,

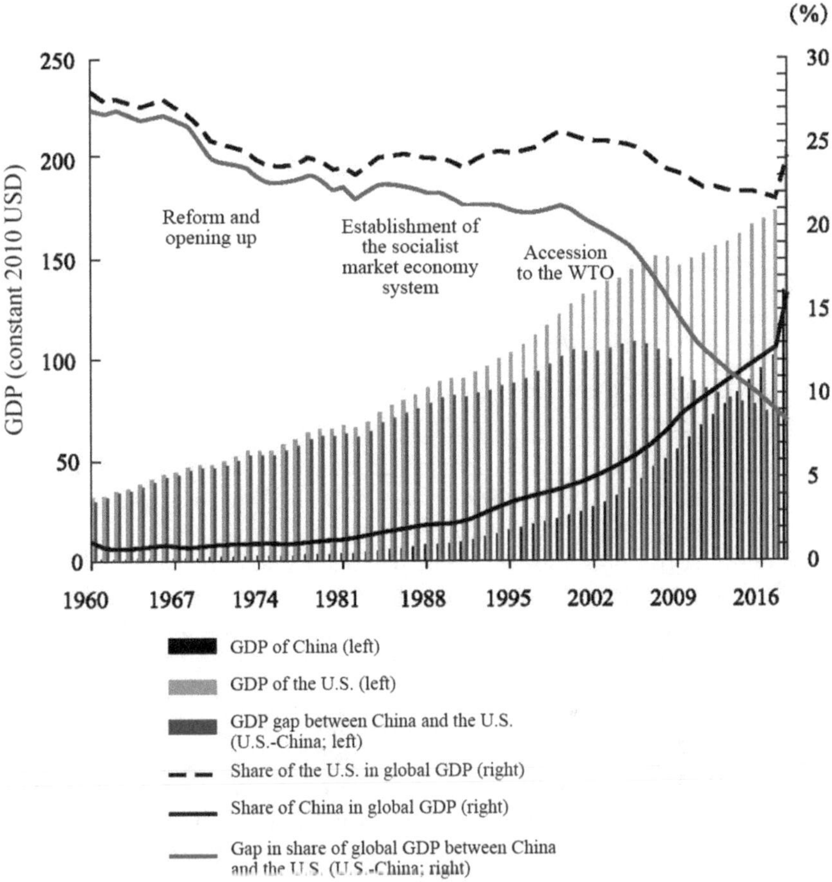


**Fig. 3.1** China vs. the US: a comparison by GDP and GDP growth

and its enormous consumer market will be a powerful engine for the economic development of China and the rest of the world. Over the past decades, no economic or financial crisis has occurred in China, which is a testament to the unity among the quality of economic development, the expansion of economic size, and the growth rate. From its accession to the WTO to the proposal of initiatives such as the Belt and Road Initiative and a community of shared future for mankind, China's status in the international arena has been rising. A thorough and objective understanding of

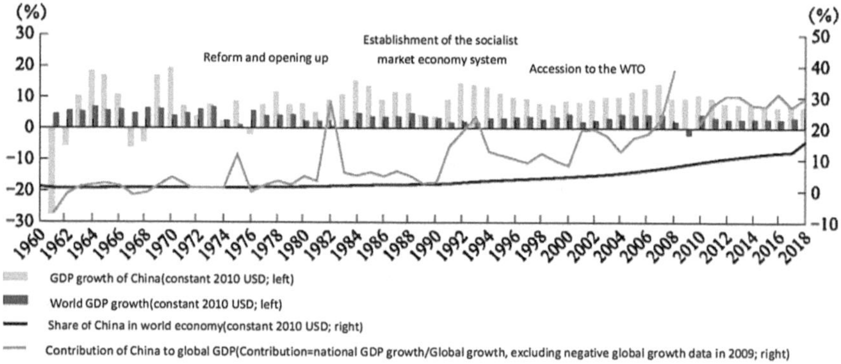


**Fig. 3.2** China vs. the world: a comparison (data from the World Bank)

China's development achievements since the start of reform and opening up is an important prerequisition for telling China's stories. In fact, China's development is well-recognized by the rest of the world.

Second, substantial improvement has been made in people's lives. In 1978, China had 250 million people living in absolute poverty. Since the start of reform and opening up, more than 700 million people have been lifted out of poverty. Further progress has been made in the critical battle against poverty since the 18th CPC National Congress in 2012. In 2020, China secured a complete victory in the fight against poverty, creating a miracle in human history. The Chinese people have secured adequate food and clothing, become better off, and achieved moderate prosperity in all respects step by step. Eradicating poverty is the goal the Chinese people have been pursuing for centuries. In just a few decades, China has gone through a process that took the developed countries centuries to complete, realizing historic leaps from access to adequate food and clothing to moderate prosperity. The principal challenge facing Chinese society is the gap between unbalanced and inadequate development and the people's ever-growing needs for a better life. Currently, social and cultural endeavors have been thriving, social harmony and stability has been ensured, and the people's sense of happiness has been significantly enhanced. China is on course to build a moderately prosperous society in all respects.

Third, reform and opening up has enhanced China's image and international status. Thanks to reform and opening up, China has got on the fast track of socialist modernization and quickened its integration into the world economy. Over the past four decades, the average annual growth rate of China's GDP has approached 10%. China has contributed over 30% to global growth for years, China's economic strength has grown significantly, and its role in the international arena has been enhanced. The share of China's GDP in the world increased from 1.8% in 1978 to about 17% in 2020. From 1979 to 2020, China contributed about 20% to global growth annually on average, second only to the US. Since 2006, China has remained the largest contributor to global growth. In terms of import and export, according to the *World Trade Report* published by the WTO, China became the third largest investor in the world in 2018. China has a tremendous consumer market. From 2013 to 2018, China contributed the most to global consumption growth. Regarding RMB internationalization, the RMB was officially included in the Special Drawing Rights (SDR) basket by the International Monetary Fund (IMF) on October 1, 2016. By pursuing high-standard opening up and promoting globalization, China is playing an active role in the world economic development and international governance, contributing China's wisdom and approaches to the world (especially to developing countries). Although a backlash against globalization is rising, China will further integrate into and promote economic globalization and do its part in building a community of shared future for mankind.

Fourth, China's reform and opening up offers a new market economy model for the world. China is a large developing country in the process of reform and opening up, and is also showing responsibility. Reform and opening up has promoted China's integration into the international community in an all-round way. The achievements of reform and opening up not only benefit China itself but are also shared by the whole world, making special contributions to the diversity of human civilization. The achievements of China's reform and opening up show that to improve people's wellbeing, there is more than one model; instead, multiple models can coexist at the same time. Only with inclusiveness, mutual learning, and harmony among different models can we have a diversified world. China has a new type of market economy and provides a new model and standard for the world. This standard is not based on particular values but the actual outcomes of growth. The key to China's economic success lies in combining the roles of "efficient market" and "competent government," integrating the roles of market and government, and exploring a set of systematic and appropriate approaches and methods in practice.

## 2 China's Fundamental Experience in Promoting Reform and Opening up

After the Third Plenary Session of the 11th CPC Central Committee in 1978, China embarked on a great journey of reform and opening up and began the historic transformation from a highly centralized planned economy into a socialist market economy. Over the past four decades, China has achieved tremendous success in reform and opening up and its economic strength has been significantly reinforced, propelling China into a leading position in terms of national strength. China's experience in advancing market-oriented reform and opening up can be summarized into the following nine aspects.

### 2.1 Focus on Productivity and Rely on the People

The *Decision of the CPC Central Committee on Reform of the Economic Structure* adopted in October 1984 for the first time put forward that the primary criterion for reform should be whether it can "benefit the growth of the productivity." Deng Xiaoping placed great emphasis on productive forces and summarized that the criteria for judging all work are that it must benefit the growth of productivity, be conducive to increasing China's overall strength, and help to improve the people's living standards.

The innovative spirit of the people is the most important source of strength for liberating and developing the country's productivity. There is no blueprint for reform and opening up in Marxist classics nor successful experience in practice. Therefore, we must respect the pioneering spirit of the people and encourage them to make pioneering attempts under the leadership of the Party, so as to secure a victory in reform and opening up. In the process of reform and opening up, the people's creative practices keep emerging. The practices and wisdom of hundreds of millions of Chinese people are valuable assets and fertile soil for reform and opening up, catalyzing breakthrough progress and news things. With full respect to the people's pioneering spirit, the report to the 18th CPC National Congress establishes the main framework of reform in key areas, keeps leading the people forward and vows to deepen reforms in key areas. As a result, the development and innovation vitality of the whole society has been significantly strengthened, and the country's governance system and capacity has been further modernized. The great journey of China's reform and opening up proves that the specific experience and practice of the people provide a solid ground for the launch of major reform measures.

### 2.2 *Push Forward Market-oriented Reform*

The great achievements of reform and opening up would not have been possible without the market-oriented reform. Over the past decades, the role of market in resource allocation has been rising. From the planned economy to an economy of guidance planning, and finally building a market-oriented economy, it is the market that plays the decisive role in resource allocation.

Sticking to market-oriented reform is the most central experience gained in the process of reform and opening up. The market economy can stimulate innovation, as evidenced by the fact that the number of patent applications filed by private enterprises is almost twice that of state-owned enterprises and collectively owned enterprises. In the era of the internet and big data, the market economy model goes beyond whether there is a plan or whether the plan is sound and enables China to stand out in the fierce market competition. The combination of technology and market power produces greater outcomes. Market-oriented reform has transformed the economic system and adjusted interest relationships. It is imperative to balance reform, development, and stability. Generally, China's reform and opening up and its economic miracle are in alignment with the growth logic and inner laws of market economy.

### 2.3 *Insist on the Approach of Pilot, Coordination and Progression*

A defining feature of China's reform is to carry out pilot reforms and then extend them on a larger scale. To be more specific, pilot programs are launched in selected regions of reform to accumulate experience, and then, the successful experience and best practice are introduced into other regions with adjustments made to adapt local conditions. This approach helps to control risks and to promote and replicate the successful experience effectively. It charts a path for comprehensively deepening reform and further opening up. Looking back, it can be seen that reform and opening up is a major issue of the overall reform, a complex process of breaking old systems and establishing new ones, and a cause to tackle long-term structural problems as well as short-term problems. As such,

China has taken the path of "gradual reform." Reform and opening up is a systematic project that requires a holistic approach and a balance between "breaking old systems" and "establishing new ones." While instituting new systems and mechanisms geared toward the growth of productivity, we need to remove deep-rooted institutional obstacles, coordinate different aspects of work according to the overall plans, and ensure overall progress while seeking breakthroughs in key areas. This way, we have pressed head with reform and opening up on all fronts as expected.

### 2.4 *Strike a Balance Between Reform, Opening Up, Development, and Stability*

Reform and opening up is a major driving force for economic and social development. Effective mechanisms provide a fundamental guarantee for steady and healthy economic development. Development and stability are the preconditions for deepening and advancing reform and opening up. To strike a balance between reform, opening up, development, and stability, it is necessary to take into account the intensity of reform and opening up, the pace of development, and the resilience of society in a coordinated way. These make up a coherent whole and none of them should be overlooked. Only in this way can reform and opening up be advanced in an orderly manner. China's reform and opening up provide important implications in terms of both methodology and values. CPC leadership is the hallmark of China's market-oriented reform, which is both historical choice and practical process. The CPC has played a pivotal role in reform and opening up, and emphasizes the balance between reform, opening up, development, and stability.

### 2.5 *Treat All Economic Entities as Equals*

The static status of market is the parity among people and equality among entities. Different property rights give rise to transactions and equal status prompts transactions. Active trading is bound to result in a prosperous market. As pointed out in the report to the 18th CPC National Congress, "The underlying issue we face in economic structural reform is how to strike a balance between the role of the government and that of the market." In a market economy, market entities under all forms of ownership are entitled to equal protection and treatment. The key lies in building a sound business environment. Therefore, the government should take solid steps to transform its functions, improve the business environment, and level the playing field for economic entities under all forms of ownership. The Fourth Plenary Session of the 18th CPC Central Committee made a decision to advance law-based governance across all fields of endeavor, laying a solid foundation for fair play among economic entities under all forms of ownership. The *Civil Code* enforced in 2021 provides a legal basis for developing the market economy and protecting market entities.

### 2.6 Free the Mind and Promote Theoretical Innovation

After reform and opening up was launched in 1978, China started learning from Western countries. China adopted the planned economic system at the time, and neither top-ranking officials nor economists had any practical knowledge about market economy. China came to realize the necessity of reform and opening up based on its own experience. Yet where reform and opening would be headed was unclear at the beginning – it was gradually established in practice. Especially as China was opening wider to the rest of the world, different sectors of society got a better understanding of the basic connotation and main characteristics of market economy, and the market economy models of major developed countries became a reference point for China's reform and opening up. Different from other countries in transition, China chose its own path based on its own exploration rather than copying solutions from other countries. China had no ready-to-use theory or experience to support its transformation from the planned economy to the market economy. Furthermore, China was a tremendous economy with high unpredictablility, so it was crucial to advance the endeavor in an orderly way. At that point, promoting theoretical innovation was of great significance, which would provide an important basis for the progress of reform and opening up.

Reform and opening up entails the freeing of minds and theoretical innovation. In the process of reform and opening up, China has abided by the principle that practice is the sole criterion for testing truth, insisted on freeing the mind and seeking truth from facts, promoted institutional innovation, theoretical innovation, and innovation in other areas of work in keeping with the times, and developed the theory and policy system of the socialist market economy. A series of Party conferences have laid the theoretical foundation for the socialist market economy, and some of the most important ones are as follows. The Third Plenary Session of the 11th

CPC Central Committee proposed the general idea of "reform and opening up." The 14th CPC National Congress and the Third Plenary Session of the 14th CPC Central Committee put forward the "socialist market economy system." The 18th CPC National Congress and the Third Plenary Session of the 18th CPC Central Committee determined the decisive role of market in resource allocation.

## 2.7 *The "Five-Year Plan" is a Vital Tool to Achieve Long-term Stability and Development*

Since 1953, China has developed plans for national economic and social development ("five-year plans") every five years, except for the period of economic adjustment from 1963 to 1965. The *14th Five-Year Plan (2021–2025) for National Economic and Social Development and the Long-Range Objectives Through the Year 2035* released in 2021 marked a new milestone of five-year plans. Over the past few decades, the five-year plans have played an essential role in promoting economic development and maintaining the continuity of economic planning, making them a good part of the story about China's economic success. Speaking of China's "five-year plan," Michael Spence, Nobel laureate in Economics, was quoted as saying that China has a comprehensive and flexible roadmap for reform, which is good for its economic and social development. The five-year plan combines "competent government" and "efficient market" and integrates top-down design and bottom-up vitality. It is an important recipe for China's rapid economic growth and a vivid reflection of its economic success.

## 2.8 *Develop a Dynamic and Replicable Chinese Model of Market Economy*

Historically, a highly successful model of exploration is generally named after the country. In the age of the industrial revolution, there were the British model, German model, and American model. In the second half of the twentieth century, the West German model, Japanese model, and the "Four Asian Tigers" model came into being thanks to the rapid economic growth of these countries. The successful practices of China's reform and opening up have led to the Chinese model. History has shown that the Chinese model is not merely a concept but involves Chinese culture, history, and political system. Certainly, the Chinese model is not fully fledged but is still evolving. Generally, the Chinese model has the following important characteristics: (1) The roles of market and government are combined, and the government plays a critical role to remedy market failures, as a way of exploring the tradeoff between the role of market and that of government. (2) To achieve sustained economic growth, the Chinese model pursues green and coordinated development, emphasizes a gradual approach to solving problems in development, and allows for the increase of some social costs in a period of time. (3) Policy is used as an instrument to guide reform and national governance. Policy effectiveness, stability, and sustainability are improved to promote high quality economic and social development. (4) Efforts are made to ensure social stability while cracking down on corruption at the proper time. (5) Particular attention is paid to promoting scientific and technological innovation and giving play to the "second-mover advantage," and the strategy for moving forward by leaps and bounds has been implemented. (6) China has established a sound social welfare system, expanded the social security system, pushed forward the poverty alleviation endeavor to achieve common prosperity and maintain social stability and harmony. (7) China stays committed to the policy of opening-up and is actively moving with the tide of globalization and pushing for a community of shared future for mankind. (8) The Chinese model stresses cultural confidence and advocates collectivism and patriotism.

### 2.9 *Advance Opening Up Steadily and Ensure Positive Interplay Between Opening Up and Reform*

The process of China's opening up has shown that continuing with globalization is of great significance. Opening up means actively integrating into globalization and aligning the country's institutions, legal system, and infrastructure with the Western world. In a move to step up opening up, the central government decided to establish special economic zones (SEZ) in Guangdong and Fujian. This move can make the best of the advantages of Hong Kong and Macao to develop an export-oriented economy and pilot reforms, and can also mitigate the political and ideological impacts brought by opening up. In June 1992, Deng Xiaoping, chief architect of China's reform and opening-up, said, "Shenzhen has a socialist market economy." In the early days of the Shenzhen Special Economic Zone, it was made clear that the SEZ should "follow international practice and connect to global markets." Opening up has changed the relationship between China and the rest of the world, enabling China to integrate into the world economic system, and it has to some extent deepened China's reform. In this sense, reform and opening up have worked together to shape China's market economic system. The relationship between China and the world is embodied in the ties between China and globalization. China should walk a fine line between independent opening up and forced opening up. China should maintain its autonomy when engaging with the rest of the world, and improve the system that suits its national conditions and is helpful to open to the outside world. Now, China has taken its place among the world's major countries by economic size. Opening up can bolster China's economic growth, according to some empirical researches. For example, Zhao Jinping finds that between 1983 and 1999, a 1% increase in foreign direct investment was associated with a 0.286% increase in China's GDP. Fei Wei's analysis shows that for every 1% increase in foreign direct investment from 1990 to 2003, China's GDP grew by 0.37%. From 2000 onwards, with the entry of a large number of multinational companies into the Chinese market, foreign direct investment in China was on the increase. From 2000 to 2007, the excess labor force of China's growing working population flew to multinational companies in the manufacturing sector, giving a strong impetus to China's sustained and rapid economic growth during the periods of the end of the twentieth century and the beginning of the twenty-first century. According to a report published by McKinsey in 2021, since China began to develop economic exchanges with other parts of the world, embrace market mechanisms, and draw on international best practice, China's economy has taken off.

Opening up has brought both impetus and pressure to China's domestic market and prompted the market-oriented reform. Over the past decades, China's financial market has made some qualitative leaps and emerged stronger. Summarizing the experience and practice in the journey of China's financial reform and opening up is of great significance and value in guiding future development. Financial openness has a bearing on the overall reform, development, and stability, and is an important part of the endeavor to expand opening up. China's best practice in opening its financial sector includes promoting opening up in various fields in a coordinated and orderly manner, taking a progressive approach, and boosting economic growth through financial opening up.

## 3 Key Strategies for China's Economic Success

China's success in reform offers a new option of economic reform and market economy model for the world, and provides a profound basis for innovation in economic theory. China's success is based on a strong theoretical foundation of economics and opportunity for innovation. That is, it provides an alternative economic development model for other countries and regions and provides a profound basis for economic innovation (Wu and Liu, 2013). China's economic success is an important example of theoretical innovation of macroeconomics. Economics is a science that examines the laws of economic operation, and at the core of it are theories of economic growth.

### 3.1 *Adopt a Problem-oriented Approach*

The development and innovation of economic theories is propelled by the aim of tackling prominent economic problems at the moment. Adam Smith' theory and Keynesian economics were both put forward in response to solve problems at the time, and they accounted for practical problems. In the course of reform and opening up, China has adopted a problem-oriented approach in order to solve problems effectively.

### 3.2 *Stick to the Market Economy Model Combining Market and Government Forces*

The Third Plenary Session of the 18th CPC Central Committee pointed out that China should let the market plays the decisive role in resource allocation and let the government plays a more effective role. It summarized China's economy model and put forward the framework of a mixed economic model, that is, while the market plays the decisive role in resource allocation, the government gives overall consideration to supply and demand and performs macro control in a timely and appropriate way to align economic and social development goals with macro-policies and to promote steady economic development. Aggregate supply and aggregate demand, the two sides are holding the key to market stability and balance.

### 3.3 Apply "Rational Synthesis"

Reform and opening up has led to the path of market-oriented reform and increased market openness. In the early days of reform and opening up, China adopted an approach of "crossing the river by feeling the stones." In the process of reform, it conducted systematic analysis and made rational explorations based on the actual situation. A pilot program or method that delivered good outcomes would be promoted on a larger scale; otherwise, it would keep trying alternative ways until the desired results are achieved. This approach can effectively solve problems while forestalling risks. In the later stage of reform, China placed greater emphasis on top-level design. By combining the roles of market and government, goals are set to guide expectations; reforms are deepened and a macro control system combining the supply and demand sides are in place to achieve a balance in economic development. Underlying this is a profound principle of "rational synthesis," that is, various rational concepts and measures can be synthesized for maximum effect.

From steadily improving China's economy to letting the market play the decisive role in resource allocation, China's reform has undergone a gradual process with obstacles in the way, but it has kept moving toward the right direction. This way, a market economy model with Chinese characteristics has taken shape. In this process, China has a good command of the following key parts. The first is the thinking of rational synthesis. For example, the "good cat theory" and the principle of "setting goals, prioritizing planning" are both manifestations of rational thinking. In addition, based on in-depth analysis of various theoretical and practical methods and in light of its own situations, China has devised different combinations of approaches. It has carried out pilot programs and then extended those with desired outcomes to other areas; otherwise, it would make adjustments accordingly. This is a vivid example of synthetic thinking. The second is to enable the market and the government to play their respective role. China emphasizes both the market and macro control to bring into full play, achieving "efficient market" and "competent government" at the same time. This is a major innovation of China's practices.

### *3.4 Innovate a Macro Control Model: The Macro Policy Framework*

The Chinese approach to macro control is neither entirely derived from Marxist political economics, nor completely reliant on Keynesianism or supply school economics. Instead, it is an innovation of Marxist economic theory and a step forward based on modern macroeconomic theories. Generally, Keynesian theory puts forward the demand side policy framework, and the supply school of thought come up with the supply side policy framework. However, there is still no comprehensive policy framework integrating aggregate supply and aggregate demand. China's logic of macro control is to appropriately integrate supply and demand management and adopt targeted strategies to tackle outstanding problems in different periods in which structural problems and cyclical problems coexist. Underlying this is rational synthesis, which synthesizes relevant measures in theory and practice. It is highly pertinent and practicle as a major innovation in thinking on macro policy making. China attaches great importance to macro control strategies in practice. Specifically, China stresses that the strategies are both principled and flexible to see that reform and opening up proceeds in an orderly way.

## 4 China's Stories and Innovation in Economic Theory

Since reform and opening up was launched more than four decades ago, China has made remarkable achievements in its economic development. However, innovation in economic theory is at the exploration stage. Reform and opening up has given rise to China's economic development model, providing a driving force for innovation in economic theory. In particular, the core of the reform is straightening out the market-government relationship, advancing market-oriented reform, streamlining administration to delegate power to lower levels, and innovating in the market economy theory. Meanwhile, China has constantly expanded opening up and integrated into globalization in an orderly way, prompting innovation in globalization and international trade theories. Therefore, the key to telling China's story well lies in outlining China's economic success well since the launch of reform and opening up. On this basis, a replicable model can be formed and innovation in economic theory can be achieved. Telling China's stories well and innovating in economic theory are interconnected to each other.

### 4.1 China's Stories as the Driver and Source of Economic Theory Innovation

The years of reform and opening up have brought about tremendous economic success. On the one hand, China's economy has not only achieved leapfrog development but also been holding steady as the world's second largest economy, with a growing influence on the world economy. Meanwhile, China's industrial structure has transformed from extensive and labor-intensive to high-quality and innovation-driven. In the early days of reform and opening up, China had a relatively small economic size. Its GDP was still at low levels despite the relatively high growth rate. In the past, the principal challenge facing Chinese society was that China's underdeveloped social production was unable to meet the ever-growing material and cultural needs of the people. Nowadays, what we face is the challenge of meeting the people's ever-growing needs for a better life. Such a shift means a profound change of China's development. Currently, China is the world's leading consumer market, and its enormous consumer market is a powerful engine for the economic development of China and the world. Over the past decades, no economic or financial crisis has occurred in China, which is a testament to the combination among the quality of economic development, the expansion of economic size, and the growth rate. On the other hand, from its accession to the WTO to the proposal of global initiatives such as the Belt and Road Initiative and a community of shared future for mankind, China's international status has been rising. We need to have a thorough understanding of China's development achievements since the introduction of the reform and opening up policy, put our strengths and achievements in perspective, and adhere to the general principle of telling China's stories well. At the same time, we should not overestimate China's national strength and capacity. The key to China's success lies in exploring a set of systematic and rational concepts and approaches in practice, for example, remaining committed to reform and opening up, abiding by the principle that practice is the sole criterion for testing truth, adopting the problem-oriented approach, the strategy of "crossing the river by feeling the stones," and the "good cat theory." These concepts and approaches prove effective in practice and involve profound economic logic.

### 4.2 *Predicaments of Economic Theory and the Way Out*

The first is about the scarcity of resources. It is generally known that "scarcity" is an important concept in Western economics, which was proposed based on the scarcity of resources and products in the past. Back then, economics was even defined as a science studying the allocation and utilization of scarce resources. Nowadays, excess supply happens in many cases as a result of improvement in productivity. Scarcity is no longer a concept in reality. Furthermore, the scarcity of resources is a relative concept, but the evaluation criteria for measuring scarcity are somewhat subjective. It is clear that determining the research object of economics from this perspective has some drawbacks. The second is about equilibrium and disequilibrium. Although absolute equilibrium has barely occurred throughout human history, it is studied in almost all mainstream economic theories. This means that an economic theory generally examines a particular state, and as the state varies, the conclusions will be different. In other words, there are bound to be different schools of thought. Even for a given economic object, different people can draw different conclusions. For example, eight economists can give nine answers to the same question, which poses barriers to decision-making. In that case, the scientific nature of an economic theory will inevitably be questioned. Last but not the least, a core issue of economics is whether the market and the government are opposite to or united with each other. This has been a key area of economic research in human history. Starting with Adam Smith, Western economists polarize the government and the market. From that onwards, the great debate between Hayek and Keynes and the debate between the saltwater school and the sweetwater school on the relationship between the market and the government either tilt toward the market or the government. Of course, the extent of opposition between the two varies in different periods of time. Different schools have different theories and can justify their own views, but exhibit limitations when criticizing others. As we see it, if two things have always been set against each other in human history with long debate over their relationship, then the two are definitely not in a substitution relationship (i.e. one cannot fully justify the other), but require unity (i.e. the opposite and united dialectic relationship). Therefore, the market and the government are not absolutely in opposition with each other as claimed in Western economics. In practice, the market mechanism can lead to the effective use of resources through the "invisible hand." However, it has limitations. Hence, the government needs to play a regulatory role through the "visible hand."

Many economists have shared their views in this regard. The famous economist Paul Krugman concludes that we have to "face up to the often idiosyncratic imperfections of markets and accept that an elegant economic 'theory of everything' is a long way off." To put it another way, we should acknowledge the imperfections of markets and seek some sort of unity among economic theories. Friedrich Hayek ascribes the economic prosperity and social stability in the twentieth century to the integration of government intervention and market functions, believing that the world economy ahead will still need to find a balance between market and government. Justin Yifu Lin's new structural economics is a theory built on the practice that one country can catch up with another. Cai Jiming thinks that there must be some unity between market and government, and the core is the labor theory of value. David Daokui Li argues that the economics of government and market aims to take a closer look at the government-market relationship. Samuelson's logic is typical and mainly has six characteristics. (1) The mixed economic theory culminates in Samuelson's logic. (2) It combines the roles of market and government, but he also underscores that the role of government is a complement to that of market. (3) Aggregate supply and aggregate demand are taken into overall consideration to construct the AD-AS model, which not only emphasizes the effective demand in Keynesian theory but also the supply side. (4) The rigorous mathematical logic is introduced to economics, and moderate mathematization holds high relevance to economic logic. (5) It is recommended that China take the path between planned economy and market economy (or the third path). There are multiple economic development models, and the most typical model should also be multifaceted. (6) Economic development is no longer regarded as static, but as a combination of various dynamic factors. It can be seen that combining the roles of market and government is the consensus among economists, though the weights of the two vary under different economic development models.

Robert Solow's growth theory has gained popularity in recent years, what it examines is potential economic growth rather than real economic growth. Potential economic growth has its merit, but it does not equate to real economic growth. This is a limitation of Solow's theory. Just as military strategists can't be judged by the criteria for prospective military strategists. The real business cycle theory (RBC theory) is also a theory of economic growth. It brings forward the factors that influence real economic growth, which is a good complement to Solow's growth theory. Given that potential economic growth is a poor indicator of the status of economic development, the theory proposes the second factor (technology shocks) and the third (policy shocks). In particular, fiscal policy has an obvious impact, while monetary policy makes no difference. It should be noted that to interpret the business cycle with external technology shocks is a bit contrived; fiscal policy can be used to adjust the economic structure, while monetary policy has no effective impact on potential economic growth largely because it relies on the logic of Solow's growth theory and virtually measures the potential economic growth. This is the logic behind the RBC model. Since the planned economy model and the pure market economy model both have drawbacks, the rational choice is to integrate the two. Since the launch of reform and opening up, China has embarked on the path of combining the role of market with that of government, rather than choosing one over the other. This represents an important exploration in shifting the relationship between market and government from opposition to unity.

### *4.3 Develop a Sound Market Economy Model with Chinese Characteristics*

The construction of economic models is crucial to the development of macroeconomic theory. Based on the key findings of macroeconomic theories on the role of market and government and China's experience in the development of the market economic system, we have established the rational synthesis economic model, giving overall consideration to "efficient market" and "competent government." Instead of examining the role of market and that of government separately or providing a qualitative description, this model is based on the setup of mathematical equations (see Chap. 5 for details). We have come to the conclusion that market economy goes beyond just a few models but manifests in the different weights of the role of market and that of government. Theoretically, there are an infinite number of models, which can be abstracted into several typical ones in reality. Unlike previous economic theories based merely on in pure market economy, the rational synthesis economic model is essentially a significant innovation in research paradigms. The equations for economic growth obtained from this model are consistent with the logic and factors of the mixed economic theory and the RBC theory.

The weight of the parameter denotes the difference in the market-government relationship between economies. A curve showing the change of economic models can be drawn, depending on the degree of difference between the role of market and that of government. Different economic models, which are at different points on the curve, can be displayed in a single graph. In fact, every modern economy is a mixed economy rather than a single-product economy. The five major market economy models in the world have their own characteristics: (1) the US model, which is a model of free market economy; (2) the European model, which is a model of social market economy; (3) the Japanese model, which is a government-guided market economy model; (4) the Swedish model, which is a welfare state model; and (5) the Chinese model, which is a socialist market economy model. From a perspective of combination of market and government, these models differ in the weight of the role of market – it is not about whether the market plays a role or not. Different as they are, these models still have things in common. An economic development model should be measured only by whether it can promote economic development.

## 4.4 The Inconsistency of Western Economics with the New Situation of Economic Development

First, the goals of macro policy or macro control should be adjusted. The macroeconomic goals include full employment, price stability, economic growth, and balance of international payments. These four goals stem from Keynesian theory, which, however, only looks at the demand side. Macro control takes into account both the demand side and the supply side, so setting macro control goals according to Keynesian theory cannot be justified. The goals need to be reconsidered: (1) economic growth and full employment can be merged into the goal of economic growth; (2) since the supply side is also examined, a goal for structural improvement or adjustment should be added; (3) the content of the goal of price stability should be further enriched, which needs to take into account both short-term and long-term economic and financial stability, and a case in point is the People's Bank of China's dual policy of macro control underpinned by monetary policy and macro-prudential policy; and (4) the goal of balance of international payments can be retained, but its content needs to be enriched. In this way, the four goals of macro control are adjusted to economic growth, structural improvement, financial stability, and balance of international payments.

Second, given the growing importance of macro control, a macro control system taking into account both the supply side and the demand side needs to be in place. This is a step forward from Keynesian macroeconomics and is congruous with Samuelson's logic that comprehensively considers aggregate supply and aggregate demand. Although Western economics touches on aggregate supply and aggregate demand, a complete theoretical system has yet to be constructed. China's practices are precisely an embodiment of the combination of supply-side and demand-side policies. The mixture of policies based on the model takes into account not only the economic cycle but also the changes in economic structure, while comprehensively considering the intertwining of structural problems and cyclical problems. When structural problems are more pronounced or cyclical problems are negligible, it is time to launch a new round of supply-side structural reform. When demand-side problems or cyclical problems stand out, the policy system proposed in Keynesian theory actually offers a solution. Therefore, the solutions to structural problems and cyclical problems are opposite during economic upswings and downswings. This is different from Keynesian theory that only looks at the demand side.

China's supply-side structural reform is designed to address structural problems, which can be said to be an expression of macro control in the context that demand-side contradictions are less prominent. However, this does not mean that demand-side management is not to be reckoned with. Synthetic thinking is required. To be more specific, we should focus on supply-side structural reform while giving attention to demand-side management and expanding aggregate demand appropriately. This is exactly the approach adopted in China's practices.

### 4.5 *Innovation in International Trade Theory and Globalization*

As can be seen from our theoretical model, what goods or services two countries trade are not simply determined by their factor endowments but by their dynamically synthesized competitive advantages. Dynamically synthesized competitive advantages are subject to change, and there is a breaking point. A country's comparable advantage in certain products or industries is not necessarily rock solid. It is common that one country is caught up with or even overtaken by another country benefiting from appropriate macro policies. In international trade, free trade under international rules plays the leading role, and there should be limited protection. Nonetheless, sometimes power interference are disguised as "international rules." International rules should not hinge on the interests of any particular country, but should truly represent a balance of global interests. Free trade is the cornerstone of mutually beneficial international economic and trade relations and is the trend of future development. There must be stringent conditions and procedures for trade protection, which should never be implemented under the pretext of "national security." Fair trade is not to maximize the interests of a particular country, no country's laws should be imposed upon others or above international rules, and bullying acts of using strength to intimidate the weak should be prevented.

Theoretical innovation is a significant tool to deal with the ongoing backlash against globalization and oppose trade protectionism. The US wages a trade war for political reasons rather than balanced foreign trade, with the aim of maintaining its competitive advantage while containing other countries. This runs counter to the direction of globalization, where fair competition should be the fundamental principle. China and the US should engage in fair competition, and their comparative advantages are not static. In fact, the transformation of the US itself from colony to a world great power is a good example.

## 5 Guan Zhong's Economic Thought and the Implications for Modern Economics

Guan Zhong was an important economist in history who put his economic thought into practice. Based on his years of practical experience as the chancellor of the state of Qi, Guan Zhong summarized and put forward a theoretical system that integrated Eastern and Western economic thoughts, covering market mechanisms, macroeconomic control by government, and international trade theory. It was one of the earliest economic elaborations in China. Below, we will analyze the relations between Guan Zhong's economic thought and modern economic theory, and the insights they provide for economic theoretical innovation, from the dimensions of market mechanisms, macroeconomic control, and international trade theory. It is worth noting that his economic thought corroborates, from the angles of theory and practice, the inherent logic behind the success of the Chinese market economy model in which market mechanisms and government policies are integrated with each other. Considering the world undergoing profound changes unseen in a century, a study of Guan Zhong's economic thought to search for the sources of Chinese economic thought and wisdom and strengthen Chinese-Western interactions concerning economic thought will not only help tell Chinese stories well but also give new insights into economic theoretical innovation and the process of globalization.

### 5.1 *Guan Zhong and the* Guanzi

Guan Zhong (c. 723-645 BC), named Yiwu and styled Zhong, was a famous economist, philosopher, politician, military strategist, and forerunner of the Legalist school of thought in ancient China during the Spring and Autumn period; born in Yingshang (present-day Yingshang County, Anhui) in the state of Qi, he was posthumously known as Guanzi. His work *Guanzi* is a collection of his essential economic thought on various fields, two-thirds of which are concerned with economic issues. Considered to be the world's first economic treatise,[1] it stands as one of the rare ancient Chinese classics that systematically discuss economic problems.

### 5.2 *Main Points of Guan Zhong's Economic Thought from a Modern Viewpoint*

1. Respecting market mechanisms

Guan Zhong points out that the pursuit of profit is inherent in human nature, and that the source of benefit can be grasped by providing guidance in the light of circumstances. He introduces the concept of division of labor, categorizing the people into four groups: scholars, farmers, artisans, and merchants. He also considers the market as a means of resource allocation and a mechanism for determining prices. It is stated in *Guanzi*, Chapter "Queries," that "The market is the treasure of heaven and earth, the common meeting place and source of profit for all people. It is the

[1] Harry Landreth and David C. Colander. *History of Economic Thought*. Beijing: Posts & Telecom Press, 2014.

right way." Guan Zhong believes that the market has its internal mechanisms for price adjustment and so the government should not forcefully intervene in prices of goods.

2. Stressing state involvement in the economy

Classical Western economics assumes that the market automatically achieves equilibrium, but in reality it can experience failures, for example insufficient effective demand, monopolies, excessive wealth gaps, negative externalities, and inadequate provision of public goods. While the market has the function of self-organization, according to the *Guanzi*, government regulation is indispensable, and government involvement in the economy could not only correct market failures but generate fiscal revenue, alleviating the tax burden on people. It is said in the *Guanzi*, Chapter "State Reserves," that "If nothing is done to regulate interest relations among people, no legal system works to achieve great governance."

3. Advocating the opening up of the economy

The middle of the Spring and Autumn period saw the court of the Zhou dynasty being in decline and the various states vying for supremacy, with productivity developing rapidly and inter-state trade flourishing. It is mentioned in the *Guanzi*, Chapter "Weight I," that "Therefore, if a state cannot attract wealth from under heaven and benefit all under heaven, it cannot prosper." Guan Zhong encouraged the circulation of commodities between Qi and other vassal states, implementing four major policies—establishing markets, reducing tariffs, providing services, and developing foreign trade. Simultaneously, he was adept at using the exchange rates between gold and knife money, a modern-day equivalent of exchange rates, to boost exports and accumulate wealth by depreciating the domestic currency.

## *5.3 A Comparison of Guan Zhong's Theory with Adam Smith's free Market Economic Theory*

Many of Guan Zhong's economic ideas coincide highly with those of modern economists, though they originated more than 2600 years ago in ancient society. Adam Smith's book, *The Wealth of Nations*, published in 1776, laid the theoretical foundation for capitalist free-market economics and has been celebrated as the Bible of Western economics. It is made clear in the book that "the political economy of every country is to increase the riches and power of that country."[2] In the *Guanzi*, Chapter "Ruling the State," there is a very similar formulation, which says that "The way to govern a state is, above all, to enrich the people. When the people are wealthy, governance becomes easy; when the people are poor, governance becomes difficult." Both thinkers consider self-interest as the fundamental purpose of productive activities, emphasize the inherent power of the market—i.e., the "invisible hand," and advocate free trade. From this perspective, Guan Zhong could be regarded as the Adam Smith of ancient China.

1. The "rational economic agent" hypothesis

The basic meaning of the "rational economic agent" hypothesis is that all agents are rational in both thinking and behavior, their purpose in different types of economic activity is to maximize individual self-interest. Based on self-interest, Adam Smith believes, the society forms a spontaneous economic order that directs the natural growth of national wealth.

It is written in the *Guanzi*, Chapter "On Maintaining Restraint," that "[i]n the feelings of ordinary people, when they see profit, they cannot resist pursuing it, and when they see harm, they cannot resist avoiding it. Merchants, in seeking profit, travel day and night at double speed, covering hundreds of miles without feeling the distance ... Therefore, wherever there is profit, no mountains are high enough to be an obstacle to merchants." It can be observed that Guan Zhong and Adam Smith's reflections on self-interest align remarkably well.

2. Division of labor

Based on ideas of self-interest, there emerged social division of labor and exchange theories. The division of labor, through improved skills on the part of workers, increased productivity and led to rapid growth of national wealth. It is observed in *The Wealth of Nations*, Chapter "On the Division of Labor," that "The greatest improvement in the productive powers of labor, and the greater part of the skill, dexterity, and judgment with which

[2] Adam Smith. *The Wealth of Nations*. Beijing: Central Compilation & Translation Press, 2010.

it is anywhere directed, or applied, seem to have been the effects of the division of labor."

Guan Zhong already had a deep understanding of the importance of the division of labor, though he lived in the Spring and Autumn period, a time when China was transiting form a slave society to a feudal society with an economy far less developed than the British economy of the time of Adam Smith in the early stages of the Industrial Revolution. It is stated in the *Guanzi*, Chapter "Correcting a Ruler from a Minor Error," that "The four occupations—scholars, farmers, artisans, and merchants—are the foundation of the state." By dividing the people into the four categories, people are required to live and work in separate areas and adhere to their own occupations across generations and that they be allowed no free migration, stressing the need to "keep the occupations separate from one another." On the one hand, the division of labor could increase labor productivity, and on the other, hereditary occupations could allow of cumulative experience.

3. Market mechanisms—"an invisible hand"

With the division of labor comes exchange in goods and services. In Adam Smith's view, only market exchange based on self-interest and on acts of exchange with equal footing could endure in the long run. It is believed in *The Wealth of Nations* that as rational beings individuals can achieve the maximization of personal and social interests by the direction of the "invisible hand" of market mechanisms. Adam Smith notes in *The Wealth of Nations*, Chapter "Of the Natural and Market Price of Commodities," that the "natural price" is the central price, around which the prices fluctuate, and while prices may sometimes deviate from the central price, they will eventually return to it.

In the *Guanzi*, Chapter "Weight II," Duke Huan of Qi asked Guan Zhong, "Are prices fixed?" Guan Zhong replied, "Prices are not fixed. Prices cause things to rise or fall, and they cannot be constantly fixed." Duke Huan said, "Then, can prices not be regulated?" Guan Zhong replied, "They cannot be regulated. Regulation leads to stagnation. Stagnation leads to constancy, and constancy leads to avoiding the alternation of rise and fall. If there is no alternation of rise and fall, then all things cannot be made stable." In Guan Zhong's view, prices are not fixed and unchanging. Prices keep fluctuating around a stable price, and absolute price stability is neither possible nor necessary. The statement "They

[Prices] cannot be regulated. Regulation leads to stagnation" emphasizes that the government should not forcefully intervene in prices, or it would result in an imbalance of supply and demand. This shows a similarity between Guan Zhong and Adam Smith's understanding of the "invisible hand," demonstrating a shared perspective on the recognition of market mechanisms.

It is pointed out in *Guanzi*, Chapter "Economic Consideration," that "[t]he market is the standard for goods. If all goods are cheap, therefore, no high profits can be gained. And so all things can be well managed. And so all uses can be well regulated." Guan Zhong deems that only with the normal circulation and stability of the market can the growth of national wealth be achieved. This view, which was very remarkable in ancient China where commerce was typically inhibited in favor of agriculture, bears a striking resemblance to Adam Smith's ideas of free guidance of the market and of the government playing the role of a "night watchman."

### 5.4 A Comparison of Guan Zhong's Economic Thought and Keynesian Macroeconomic Theories

Keynesian economics emerged during the Great Depression of the 1930s, and the historical background imbued Keynesianism with a strong sense of government intervention. While Keynes did not oppose the mechanisms of a free market, he lacked confidence in the self-sufficiency of market mechanisms, believing that market mechanisms could not automatically recover from economic crises—which necessitates vigorous government intervention. Keynes' book, *The General Theory of Employment, Interest and Money*, published in 1936, is widely regarded as a symbol of the establishment of modern macroeconomic theory. The book *Guanzi* contains a lot of discussions on government macroeconomic regulation, advocating for a combination of government and market forces to jointly promote the sound operation of the economy. Considering this, Guan Zhong could be considered as a Keynes of ancient China.

1. Theory of effective demand

In *The General Theory of Employment, Interest and Money*, Keynes points out that insufficient effective demand is the primary cause of economic recession and unemployment and that it is, therefore, crucial to increase effective demand and especially to boost the propensity to consume and stimulate consumption. It is advised in the *Guanzi*, Chapter "Extravagance," that "When grain is cheapened, and jewelry made useful, the people will be easy to rule" and "Those accumulating wealth should take out a substantial portion as surplus and engage in lavish consumption, adorning their vehicles and horses and indulging in the pleasure of speeding along, and abundantly acquiring wine and delicacies and fully relishing them. In this way, there will be no beggars for a thousand years, because that promotes agricultural production." To promote luxurious consumption is not to encourage excessive extravagance and indulgence but to encourage the wealthy to consume. It is stated in the *Guanzi*, Chapter "Discourse on Economic Matters," that "If no high buildings and magnificent palaces are built, materials will not be sold." This, in essence, is to increase effective demand, stimulate the economy, and boost employment through consumption.

2. Fiscal policy

Fiscal expenditure that Keynesianism advocates are intended, primarily through expansionary fiscal policies, to directly promote consumer demand and boost effective demand by increasing government purchases or transfer payments. Similar measures are found in the *Guanzi*, too.

First, emphasize government purchases. It is written in the *Guanzi*, Chapter "Economic Consideration," that "In years of severe droughts or floods, when the people lose their livelihoods, the government should build palaces and pavilions, hiring those who cannot afford to raise dogs or pigs. This is not for the sake of luxury but to stabilize the country's policies. Building palaces and pavilions is not for the sake of luxury but to implement the state's economic policy." This implies that the government seeking infrastructure development could increase government purchases, stimulating consumption, improving effective demand and boosting employment.

Second, stress transfer payments. In the *Guanzi*, Chapter "Weight I," it is stated that "Let each prefecture have a man in charge to see to it that each community has five cellars of grain stores, that poor families unable to pay taxes are given a long-term loan, and that those cannot afford a burial are given a burial fee. When hungry people have food to eat, those without clothing have clothing to wear, dead ones are properly buried, and those living in destitution are assisted, then all people will flock to us like flowing water. This is what it means to win over the people of the world" and that "Then the monarch can use forty times as much grain [as previously had] to aid orphans and widows and take in the poor and the sick." The various disaster relief measures undertaken by the government, as mentioned here, also reflect the idea of transfer payments.

Keynesianism advocates fiscal revenue policies that call for reforming the tax system and public debt policies to accommodate increased fiscal expenditure and the needs of interventionist economic policies. During his tenure, Guan Zhong consistently emphasized a light tax burden to alleviate the people's financial burdens. It is mentioned in the *Guanzi*, Chapter "Cultivating Authority," that "Goods should be kept with the people so that the government cannot accumulate goods," an idea that illustrates Guan Zhong's view that "Taxation should be reduced rather than be exacted excessively from the people" and "Whatever is taken from the people should be done moderately." His specific measures of light taxation include the following: imposing only the principal tax; opposing arbitrary and excessive exactions; refraining from forcibly levying miscellaneous taxes and labor services beyond the agricultural tax on the people; and implementing differential taxation based on poverty gaps. Guan Zhong's tax policy takes into consideration the varying abilities of individuals to bear tax burdens, and pays particular attention to tax fairness. In terms of the land or acreage tax, Guan Zhong applies different tax rates based on the degree of land fertility in a differential-taxation practice. At the same time, Guan Zhong considers the tax-paying abilities of people for prosperous and lean years, lowering tax rates or delaying tax collection in case of lean years (equivalent to modern economic crises).

It is important to note that the "mountain and sea monopolization" policy, which Guan Zhong thinks would "not cause public anger by taking it from the intangible," is intended in essence to address the issue of devel opment for state-owned enterprises in a market economy. The "mountain and sea monopolization" here refers to the state control of vital industries such as salt and iron, which could reduce the tax burden on the people while increasing fiscal revenue. The salt and iron monopolization system initiated by Guan Zhong produced far-reaching effects on later generations. It is mentioned in the *Guanzi*, Chapter "King of the Sea," that Duke Huan of Qi wanted to impose taxes, to which Guan Zhong was opposed, saying that "Only a mountain and sea monopolization is feasible." Guan Zhong's idea of nationalization does not mean complete monopolies but a combination of state ownership and private management, where ownership is separated from powers of management, allowing for part of profits to be shared with the people.

3. Monetary policy

Keynesian monetary policy involves influencing interest rates by controlling the money supply, a fundamental indicator, to regulate total demand. Guan Zhong considers money as a crucial tool for the state control of the economy. It is written in the *Guanzi*, Chapter "Calculations and Measures," that "The knife coins are like channels and ditches." Guan Zhong sees money as something like a channel or ditch that guides economic activities, implying that the ruler of a state controlling this channel controls all properties of the state. This insightful perspective is significant, as it took European philosophers around 2000 years to put forward similar views.[3]

First, Guan Zhong advocates that the state to issue money. It is stated in the *Guanzi*, Chapter "From Mountains to Amounts," that "The ruler possesses mountains, in which there is bronze that can be used to establish currency," and in Chapter "State Reserves," that "The money that the ruler casts to establish currency is the means of transaction among the people," both statements indicating that money issuance should be controlled by the state.

Second, Guan Zhong calls the measurement of money supply as "money planning." It is stated in the *Guanzi*, Chapter "From Mountains to Amounts," that "Money planning is to find an area with a radius of six *li* and figure out how much fertile land and infertile land it has, how much grain is yielded on it, what price limits of the grain are, how much money is demanded for the land, and how much is required based on the grain prices. Money planning, therefore, involves applying this demand across the state so that the amount of money corresponds to the state's amount of land. This is what is called money planning." In other words, a detailed survey is conducted in an area with a radius of six *li*, including land conditions and grain production and prices, and then national money demand is extrapolated from this area, forming the basis for determining the total amount of money to be issued. In the *Guanzi*, Chapter "State Roadways in Mountainous Areas," an account of state statistical work is given: "How

[3] William N. Goetzmann. *Money Changes Everything: How Finance Made Civilization Possible*. Beijing: CITIC Press Group, 2017.

much land does a township own, and what is its population? How many women in the township are engaged in spinning and weaving, and how much cloth is in surplus? Every prefecture and every community should be carefully inspected... Standard data must be worked out, and this is called overall statistics. And then it is planned to issue a thoroughly planned amount of money." Guan Zhong deems it necessary to work out standard data through a survey so that a thoroughly planned amount of money is issued. This shows the rigorousness and meticulousness of his calculation.

Third, Guan Zhong, rather than simply using money for market regulation, emphasizes a two-way method of goods and money regulation, with the government controlling most goods (grain and money) in agricultural society through reserves. Goods are purchased at low prices when there is an excess of goods on the market, and are sold at high prices when there is a shortage; in this way, the government could stabilize the market, prevent excessive speculation by merchants, and additionally generate fiscal revenue. It is noted in the *Guanzi*, Chapter "State Roadways in Mountainous Areas," that "When nine parts of the state money are kept in the treasury and one is circulated, the money's worth is high and goods are cheap. Put the money into circulation by purchasing goods of all kinds. When the money is in circulation and the goods are concentrated in the government, the prices of goods will increase tenfold." The purchasing power of money is closely linked to prices, and by regulating between money and goods—purchasing cheap goods at higher prices or selling them at lower prices, "the ruler can master the relations of balance between grain, money, and gold, and the state will enjoy a stable economic order."

4. Governance on market monopolization

The *Guanzi*, on multiple occasions, mentions that it is government responsibility to intervene in behaviors of market monopolization and address the issue of excessive wealth disparity. It is stated in the *Guanzi*, Chapter "State Reserves," that "Therefore, in a state with ten thousand chariots, there are merchants with ten thousand measures of gold; in a state with a thousand chariots, there are merchants with a thousand measures of gold. What does this mean? It means that the state has suffered a huge loss of property and profit, with ministers not giving their full loyalty, and warriors not risking their lives completely. Grain prices can fluctuate as a year can be one of calamity or abundance; the value of goods varies as decrees can be pressing or otherwise. However, if the ruler cannot govern properly, merchants will hoard and speculate in the market, taking advantage of the people suffering a plight, and reaping profits a hundredfold. The same land, the strong are good at defending it; the same property, the wise are skilled in using it to their advantage. The wise can achieve ten times what ordinary people can, while fools engage in unproductive activities. Yet, if the ruler cannot regulate, the people may have lives that differ by a hundredfold. When the people are wealthy, they cannot be spurred on by official positions and riches; when they are poor, they cannot be held back by punishments. It is because of disparity between rich and poor that laws cannot be enforced and the masses remain unruly."

## 5.5 A Comparison of Guan Zhong's Economic Thought and International Trade Theory

Adam Smith came up with the concept of absolute advantage, according to which a country should, based on its national circumstances, abandon production with high absolute costs and instead choose production with lower absolute costs, and through mutual exchange, would increase its labor productivity together with another country it trades with. Therefore, in his view, free trade is the optimal choice for increasing national wealth. David Ricardo's theory of comparative advantage further extends the understanding of international trade from the perspective of comparative advantages.

Similarly, Guan Zhong believes that free trade can improve people's situations, advocating for the circulation of goods between Qi and other vassal states and implementing four major policies—establishing markets, reducing tariffs, providing services, and developing foreign trade. "When things circulate, they move; when they move, they become inexpensive." The free market brings lower prices and the cross-regional sharing of interests, a viewpoint thought highly of by senior officials with the World Trade Organization.[4] Guan Zhong can also be seen as a proponent of international economic and trade theory.

First, Guan Zhong advocates a policy of low tariffs. He opposes a policy of isolationism, believing that there should be mutual exchanges between vassal states; to achieve this, he implements a trade policy with zero or low tariffs. It is mentioned in the *Guoyu*, Chapter "Discourses of Qi," that

[4] William N. Goetzmann. *Money Changes Everything: How Finance Made Civilization Possible*. Beijing: CITIC Press Group, 2017.

"Fish and salt of Qi were traded with Donglai, with tax officers ordered to only inspect the goods without collecting taxes, for the benefit of all vassal states." In other words, foreign merchants were encouraged to export Qi's aquatic products, salt, and handicrafts to other states, and only inspections were conducted at border ports without imposing taxes. The result was that "merchants and traders from all over the world flock to Qi like flowing water" (*Guanzi*, Chapter "Weight II"). The state of Qi consequently saw its commerce thriving and national strength increased, Linzi, its capital city, became a de facto free trade zone. An account is given in the *Zhan Guo Ce*, "Strategies of Qi," of the prosperous scenes in Linzi, Qi's capital at the time: "On the streets of Linzi, traffic is heavy, with carriages traveling closely one after another; people crowd around, their fronts—if joined up—forming curtains, their sleeves—if raised—becoming canopies, their sweat dropping like rain. All families are rich, and all people are high-spirited." It is mentioned in the *Guanzi*, Chapter "Correcting a Ruler from a Major Error," that "In the nineteen-year reign of Duke Huan, tariffs were relaxed, with a rate at one-fiftieth."

Second, Guan Zhong makes good use of exchange rate policy. During the Spring and Autumn period and the Warring States period, money used varied from state to state, with the primary bronze coins including knife money, spade money, ring money, and shell money; the main currency for international trade was gold, and Qi used gold and knife money (made of bronze) as its standard money. For the domestic circulation of money, Guan Zhong equated the purchasing power of Qi's knife money with that of gold. It is mentioned in the *Guanzi*, Chapter "Weight I," that "Gold is worth four thousand," and in Chapter "Weight II, that "Our state is located at crossroads, connecting the places where straw is transported, the routes of travelers, and the paths of merchants storing their goods. Therefore, if they use the grain and the money of our state, let them pay for it with gold. Consequently, increase the price of gold and use it to purchase everything at a discount, and possess everything and make good use of it, and the state's financial policy will be successful." Guan Zhong observes that by appreciating gold against the national currency, other imported goods would correspondingly depreciate, allowing the accumulation of wealth from across the world. The long-running bimetallic standard (gold and bronze, or silver and bronze) in ancient China was closely related to Gresham's law, that is "bad money drives out good," though no such phenomenon occurred during Guan Zhong's time in the Spring and Autumn period and Warring States period. The phenomenon did occur more than four centuries later, in the Western Han dynasty, as Jia Yi of the time observed that "[d]eceptive money is multiplying, while genuine money is dying"—where "deceptive money" was meant to be bad money, and "genuine money," good money. When the price parity between bad money and good money exceeds a certain range, good money will inevitably be out of circulation—either collected, melted, or exported abroad.

Also, in the *Guanzi*, Chapter "Weight IV," it is written that "As stone discs were everywhere circulated, all wealth under heaven flowed to Qi." Guan Zhong had stone discs sold to other states in exchange for gold, gems, grains, and cloth, among other things, making Qi's currency an international currency and allowing Qi to amass wealth from them.

## 5.6 *Insights Guan Zhong's Economic Thought Provided for Innovation on Modern Economic Theory*

Guan Zhong's economic thought, which was in advance of the age in which he lived, are undoubtedly a gem in ancient Chinese culture and represent a great milestone in history of economic thought. Guan Zhong's economic thought has great reference value, and we should make good use of their roles as we are improving China's economy system for now.

1. Market mechanisms and government roles are not opposed but can be integrated

For hundreds of years, a central theme in the history of Western economic thought has been the debate on the market versus the government. Adam Smith's *The Wealth of Nations* highlighted the crucial role of the "invisible hand," emphasizing market mechanisms and the supply side. Keynesianism brought attention to another "visible hand," emphasizing the role of government and the demand side. In its course of evolution, Western economic thought has shifted from the supply side to the demand side, moving from one extreme to another. Thus, the economic thoughts of Western economists like Adam Smith and Keynes are unidimensional, whereas those of Guan Zhong are multidimensional. In other words, the roles of the market and those of the government are not necessarily opposed to one another but can be integrated, with the market and the government being united with each other. Guan Zhong's successful economic governance practice demonstrates that both " competent government" and "efficient market" are indispensable. His economic thought and governance experience, which were in advance of his time, provide reference for the theoretical foundation of the socialist market economy with Chinese characteristics: the real-world economy is, in essence, an integration of the roles of market and that of government, not the market helping the government or vice versa, but a result of them working together in a reasonable and orderly manner. The core of Chinese market mechanisms is allowing the market to play its decisive role while letting the roles of government work more effectively.

2. Different economies can have their distinctive economic development models

We should view a country's economic development model dynamically and with open-mindedness. Typically, the success of an economic model is judged by its ability to adapt to its own circumstances and promote steady and healthy economic growth. From a historical perspective, a complete market economy model does not exist. All market economy models involve the government to varying degrees, and no country is an exception; each has its unique characteristics. The United States adopts a free market economy, Germany a social market economy, Japan a government-guided economy, and Sweden a welfare-oriented market economy, each with its distinctive features. Countries can learn from each other's market economy models, as there is no perfect market economy model that cannot be surpassed. China's economic miracle out of its over four decades of reform and opening-up practice, where market and government roles are integrated, demonstrates the tremendous economic success. This success is not only a great innovative practice in human history but also an innovative development of modern economic theory.

3. Economic opening up and free trade are absolute musts

Over 2600 years ago, Guan Zhong advocated free trade, opposing isolationist policies; he proposed the maximum use of zero or low tariffs and explored the role of currency in trade. In the process of globalization for now, it is essential to adhere to the fundamental principles of free trade, gradually reduce tariffs, and even create conditions for zero tariffs. Simultaneously, there should be enhanced coordination between international trade and monetary policies. Humanity shares the world as a global village, forming a community of shared future. While globalization may encounter challenges, it is ultimately bound to progress forward.

CHAPTER 4

# Rational Synthesis Economic Model and Policy Framework

A real-world economy is neither purely market economy nor planned economy but is a mixed economy, in which market and government both play their roles. Economic theory should accurately reflect and explain reality, and any theory from the perspective of a pure market economy model or a planned economy model would deviate from reality. China's successful practices over the past decades have shown that relying solely on the traditional planned economy would not work, and China must take the road of developing a market economy, in which the government should play its part. This sets it apart from the market economy model in the West. The combination of the role of market and government forms a relatively effective economic model, but the government should play an appropriate role. Throughout the years, economic development models and economic theory have evolved with different combinations of the roles of market and government. What is needed for constructing a rational synthesis economic model is the basic conditions in original theories, with no additional tough conditions required. The primary goal is to integrate the logic of existing theoretical models with China's successful practices and make proper adjustments in line with the thinking of rational synthesis to form a relatively unified economic logic. Through unified equations, important conclusions can be drawn from deductive reasoning and justified with relevant theories.



Z. Liang, *The Innovation of Economic Theory in China*,
https://doi.org/10.1007/978-981-95-2713-7_4

# 1 Background

Throughout the history of the global economy, macroeconomic theory always makes significant advancements by solving new problems in the real-world economy. When old theories were unable to provide good explanations for the new things and phenomena in society, theoretical revolutions would occur. Generally, new theoretical models derive from successful practices and are constructed on the basis of drawing on existing theories.

## *1.1 Innovation in Economic Theory is Needed to Adapt to the Trend of the Times*

Theoretical innovation is necessary for practice and guides practice. The history of Western economies has shown that although market mechanisms can spur innovation and improve the efficiency of resource allocation through the "invisible hand," their limitations are obvious if left unchecked. One example is that the Great Depression of 1929–1933 gave rise to the Keynesian theory of government intervention. After stagflation hit Western countries in the 1970s, Keynesianism which advocates demand management by the government gave way to neoliberalism, including monetarism and the rational expectations school. After that, Western developed countries (especially the US) saw weakening government intervention in the economy, with relaxed controls on financial innovation. After the US dot-com bubble of the 1990s imploded, financial deregulation and unchecked financial innovation led to the US subprime mortgage crisis and eventually triggered the 2008 international financial crisis. Because of the international financial crisis, neoliberalism experienced unprecedented challenges, while government interventionism made a comeback. The 2008 international financial crisis was a wake-up call for China—to blindly copy the development model of Western countries would lead nowhere. As the world's second-largest economy, China faces key issues including how to learn the lessons from the international financial crisis, actively participate in global governance, strengthen theoretical innovation, and ensure the steady development of the economy and the financial sector. In particular, existing macroeconomic theory has trouble in providing reasonable explanations for many new phenomena and situations in the process of China's economic development and transformation, heralding potential innovations and breakthroughs in macroeconomic theory.

China's economic success presents vast opportunity for innovation in macroeconomic theory. Since the launch of reform and opening up in 1978, China has achieved rapid economic development at an average annual growth rate of approximately 10%, creating a miracle in the human history. One hallmark of China's reform and opening up policy is the combination of the approach of "crossing the river by feeling the stones" and top-level design, with notable differences at different stages. The basic logic of earlier economic policy can be summarized as being guided by "crossing the river by feeling the stones." To be more specific, policy was first piloted on a small scale in a rational and pragmatic manner, and if the policy proved effective, it would be implemented on a larger scale; otherwise, timely adjustments would be made in order to achieve the desired effect. In the later stage, the logic of economic policy is dominated by top-level design, that is, goals are set to guide expectations, and a macro control system that balances the supply side and the demand side is implemented to keep economic development stable.

As Chinese President Xi Jinping pointed out, we live in an era where theory is needed and can be produced, and we must live up to the expectations of this era. When it comes to summarizing China's development experience and making theoretical innovations, Chinese economists definitely have a first-mover advantage. The Third Plenary Session of the 18th CPC Central Committee proposed that we must see that "the market play the decisive role in resource allocation and the government should play its role better," so market mechanisms and the role of government can be combined to form synergy. Looking ahead, we hope that innovation in economic theory can transcend the division between the East and the West while maintaining certain differences under different models.

### *1.2 Transformation in Macroeconomic Theory Requires New Ways of Thinking*

The market-government relationship has long been a matter of disputation among different schools of macroeconomic thought. Adam Smith's book, *The Wealth of Nations*, emphasizes the importance of the "invisible hand" of market rules, while Keynesianism highlights the active role of the "visible hand" of government. In fact, the role of market and government are both indispensable. As economic theory evolves, how to deal with the relationship between market and government is a key topic worthy of in-depth research.

Amidst the ongoing debates, the concept of a mixed economy emerged. Over time, liberals and conservatives have both come to recognize their own deficiencies and virtues in the opposing views, trying to draw upon each other's valuable ideas. Nonetheless, they are fundamentally flawed in their attempts to reconcile the other's rationale within the confines of their own perspective (market economy or macro control), and fail to realize that a real-world economy is always a mixed economy, which should be taken as the starting point of their research. Therefore, it's destined that they alternated with varying economic issues in early-stage research, and a unified analysis framework or a complete policy framework has yet to be established.

Since the 2008 international financial crisis, significant changes have taken place in the global economic landscape, and the advent of the era of big data has offered new insight into the construction of complex macroeconomic models. These pose new challenges to macroeconomics while also pointing out the direction for development. Macroeconomics needs to break new ground on the basis of incorporating the latest theoretical insights and practical outcomes in economics. Given that economic operations are the result of interplay between the "invisible hand" and the "visible hand," it is evident that the role of market and government are both indispensable. The shift of the market-government relationship from opposition to unity will be a basic path in the development of macroeconomics.

### *1.3 A Relatively Systematic Theory Combining Market Mechanisms and Government Intervention*

New theoretical models need to incorporate the latest developments in theory and practice. In Western economics, both Marxism and Keynesianism emphasize the role of government. Marxism addresses economic operations, but is short on theoretical models and quantification. The mixed economic theory (Pigou, 1933; Keynes, 1933) lays the basis for the construction of theoretical models. Samuelson, a student of Hansen, further expanded upon the mixed economic theory to form a relatively complete theoretical system. He established the AD-AS model and posited that government intervention only helps bring market economies to the due level, sending an unequivocal message that government just plays a supporting role. Economic operations should be the result of the "two hands" working together, with one coordinating with the other.

Innovation in economic theory will be rational and effective if it borrows from Western economics and is based on a dynamic model combining the role of market and government. The issue should be dealt with from a higher perspective, just like the respective strengths of Chinese traditional medicine and Western medicine and the gender division of labor. Therefore, the shift of the market-government relationship from opposition to unity represents the way forward in macroeconomics.

The views of different economists on the role of market and government can be roughly categorized into two economic analysis paradigms: the market-oriented model and the macro control model. A real-world economy is a combination of market mechanisms and government intervention. On one hand, the market mechanism promises steady economic growth in the long run, reflecting the long-term trend of economic growth, that is, potential economic growth. On the other hand, government regulation, which includes intervention on the supply side and the demand side, exerts an impact on not only short-term economic fluctuations but also the medium- and long-term trends of potential economic growth mainly through the supply side. As such, we can construct a model centered on economic growth and establish the basic relationship among various economic variables.

### *1.4 Reflection on Economic Theory Against the Backdrop of the COVID-19 Pandemic*

The global spread of COVID-19 exposed the limitations of mainstream economics. The pandemic was the trigger for many economists to reflect on economic theory: some modern mainstream economic theories seem to have a coherent theoretical framework, but in essence, they are simply "blackboard economics" that is based on the hypothesis of pure market economy and utility maximization of rational actors and can barely be applied in the real world. During the pandemic, the role of government was strengthened, and monetary policy was abused in some cases, which obviously runs counter to the principles of the market economy that people have long been required to comply with.

Although the theoretical models are increasingly more complex than before, there exist considerable discrepancies between theory and practice, and many of them cannot stand up to the test of practice in the event of major problems or external shocks such as the COVID-19 pandemic. In the early days of the pandemic, economists lacked relevant data to conduct research, despite having models on hand. Later, with the shutdown of the global economy and supply and industry chain disruptions caused by the pandemic, economists were struggling to bring forward powerful countermeasures, and government intervention became the primary means. Some economists who have long relied on "hypotheses" in research should reflect on what a "hypothesis" means. This is not meant to deny the necessary of hypotheses for economic research, but to draw attention to high-uncertainty practical problems so as to make hypotheses in alignment with reality.

The evolution of human civilization and the history of economic and social development have shown that philosophy forms a basis for analyzing problems and articulating logical relations. There should be more philosophical thinking in economics, and the basic logical relationships should be properly expressed in mathematical terms. These are the preconditions for economics being widely recognized as a science. Only in this way can economics go beyond the division of "Eastern and Western economics" and "different schools of economic thought" and be a science where economic laws apply equally to all. This is exactly the mission economists are endowed with by history.

### *1.5 Economists' Expectations*

There are myriad schools of economic thought, and many economists have voiced their views, or in other words, expectations. After the 2008 international financial crisis, some well-known macroeconomists began to reflect on the deficiencies of previous macroeconomic research. For example, Paul Krugman concludes that we should "face up to the often idiosyncratic imperfections of markets and accept that an elegant economic 'theory of everything' is a long way off," that is, we should acknowledge market imperfections and recognize that unity among economic theories will require time. Regarding modern economic growth theory, Joseph Stiglitz (2018) points out that the standard paradigm is often silent about market failure. He also changes the speculation on the government's willingness to intervene in the market, believing that when there is a market failure, the government is inclined to take action to correct the market failure. Hacker and Paul (2016) ascribes the economic prosperity and social stability in the twentieth century to the integration of government intervention and market functions, stressing the need to find a balance between the two.

Chinese scholars have explored this topic, as well. After scrutinizing Marxist economics and neoclassical economics and distinguishing the rationalities of the two, Jiang Yongji (2010) and Cai Jiming (2015) conclude that the two economic systems of socialism and capitalism are converging. On this basis, they construct a new value theory more capable of explaining reality—the generalized value theory—to eliminate the basis for opposition between the two economic systems. However, since their main focus is on the understanding of the value of factors and the differences and convergence of social systems, their theory revolves around the formation and determination of value and falls short in explaining the actual economic and market operations. Cai Jiming posits that there must be some degree of unity between market and government, but such unity should be grounded in the labor theory of value. Justin Yifu Lin (2017) thinks that to promote China's economic theory innovation, it is necessary to take structural differences as a starting point and integrate Marx's historical materialism with the research paradigm of Western mainstream economics. Nonetheless, he believes that the differences between the two different systems should not be overemphasized. In fact, Marxist economics was established by drawing on and making revolutionary changes to the ideas of British and French classical economics. Justin Yifu Lin's new structural economics is based on the practice that one country can catch up with another.

Samuelson's typical and distinctive logic to some extent reflects the vision of economic theory innovation: (1) The mixed economic theory culminates in Samuelson's logic. (2) It combines the roles of market and government, but also underscores that the role of government is a complement to that of market. (3) aggregate supply and demand are taken into overall consideration to construct the AD AS model, which not only emphasizes the effective demand in Keynesian theory but also the supply side. (4) The rigorous mathematical logic is introduced to economics, and moderate mathematization holds high relevance to economic logic. (5) It is recommended that China take the path between planned economy and market economy (or the third path). There are multiple economic development models, and the most typical model should be multifaceted. (6) Economic development is no longer regarded as static, but as a combination of various dynamic factors. It can be seen that combining the roles of market and government is the consensus among economists, although the weights of the two vary under different economic development models.

Although contemporary mainstream macroeconomics looks like a science on the surface, it is increasingly deviating from practice. As such, macroeconomics in the future should escape from the ivory tower and acknowledge its critical function in guiding policy decisions. This demands that economic hypotheses should better mirror real-world conditions. Only through the accurate correspondence between theoretical models and the intricate facets of reality can the bedrock of macroeconomics as a science be solidified in a real sense, so as to align with the purpose for which economics is designed: to solve practical problems and contribute to societal well-being.

## 2 Construction of a Rational Synthesis Economic Model and the Balance Between Market and Government

With an eye to addressing practical problems, The basic connotation of rational synthesis is that it gives overall consideration to various policy instruments in theory and practice, and categorizes, selects, and uses them, starting with addressing practical problems and following the principles of rationality and pragmatism. Then it makes the policy choice and determines the policy path according to the effectiveness of policy implementation, in order to achieve optimal outcomes.

### *2.1 Logic and New Perspective for Constructing a Rational Synthesis Economic Model*

The concept of economic growth is clear, but the factors affecting economic growth are complex. In order to better understand the factors of economic growth, Western economists divide them into direct factors and indirect factors. The direct factors are related to the accumulation of input factors (such as capital and labor) in the economy, as well as the variables that affect the productivity of these production factors (such as economies of scale and technological changes). Factors affecting economic growth include population, the macro environment, the trade system, government revenue and expenditure, and geographic, political, and social factors. As such, Western scholars have proposed the following equation:

$$Y_t = F\left(K_t, L_t, A_t, N_t, S_t\right)$$

where $Y_t$ is the total output of an economy; $K_t$, $L_t$, and $N_t$ represent the stock of capital, labor, etc. respectively; and $A_t$ is total factor productivity.

Essentially, $Y_t$ should be the real total output in general and can also be the potential total output. The above equation can be simplified in certain circumstances. If $Y_t$ is taken as the potential total output and complies with the law of market economies and the relationship of the Cobb-Douglas production function exists, it should be possible to derive the Solow growth model. Under the conditions of Keynesian economics, the initial focus was on short-term economic fluctuations, which can be construed as real economic growth, but in the HAROLD (hemispheric asymmetry reduction in older adults) model, potential economic growth is ultimately derived through the balance of several growth rates. From the perspective of government regulation, the impact on the economy is jointly determined by aggregate supply and demand, and the AD-AS model serves to illustrate the impacts of aggregate supply and demand on economic growth.

A dynamic analysis can be conducted from a general viewpoint. The dynamic macroeconomics of the Swedish School, represented by a Nobel laureate, has introduced several innovations: first, it takes monetary factors into account; second, it gives attention to dynamic situations; third, it looks at aggregate supply and demand; fourth, it acknowledges that government intervention works. However, this theory also has some limitations: first, there is ambiguity regarding equilibrium; second, it does not elaborate on total output determination.

We can break down how the factors impact economic growth. On the surface, the Real Business-Cycle (RBC) theory addresses business cycles, but essentially, it deals with the issue of economic growth. It takes account of potential economic growth rates from the perspective of classical economics, but external technology shocks can also affect economic growth rates. Considering the impact of policy, we can further identify the relevant roles and impacts to determine the exact sources. With that said, the view that external technology shocks have cyclical effects would not make sense.

### 2.2 *Building a Rational Synthesis Economic Model*

With reference to the key findings of macroeconomic theory, we try to use "the simplest equation possible" to illustrate the theoretical model in accordance with the logical relationship of rational synthesis. A real-world economy, as the subject of economic research, is always a mixed economy, where both market mechanisms and government intervention or macro control play their roles. In other words, market mechanisms and government intervention combine to drive the development of a real-world economy. A market economy is on track for stable economic growth in the long term, which is potential economic growth in the steady state of a market—it reflects the long-term trend of economic growth and can be expressed by potential economic growth in the steady state of a market. From the perspective of government regulation, the impact on the economy is jointly determined by aggregate supply and demand, and the AD-AS model serves to illustrate the impact of aggregate supply and demand on economic growth. Adjustments on the supply side and demand side, particularly on the supply side, exert both short-term and long-term impacts, while non-macroeconomic policy only affects the economy in the short run. To be specific, the impacts on short-term economic fluctuations primarily manifest on the demand side, echoing the ideas of Keynesian theory. Conversely, the impacts on medium- and long-term economic fluctuations are concentrated on the supply side, practically through the impact of government action on potential economic growth. This differs from what is generally known that Keynesian macroeconomic policy mainly has short-term effects. For a better understanding, assume that the natural conditions of two children are exactly the same, or the potential of the two persons is the same under natural conditions, but one of the two children is raised in a particular environment, while the other receives a different education and has different experiences. After a few years, their potential may be starkly different. Factoring in external opportunities, they may live completely different lives. People's course of life can be likened to real economic growth, their development potential to potential economic growth, education and experiences to supply-side reform, and external opportunities or challenges to demand-side changes.

In view of this, we can use the rate of change to establish a corresponding model following the principles in mathematics and physics.[1] The model consists of the following three equations:

$$\Delta Y_t = a\Delta Y_t^* + b\Delta \mathrm{Y}_t \tag{4.1}$$

$$Y_t^* = f\left(K_t, L_t\right) = \lambda K_t^{\theta} L_t^{1-\theta} \tag{4.2}$$

[1] See Chap. 5 for more general expressions.

$$\Delta Y_t = \Delta AS + \Delta AD \tag{4.3}$$

In Eqn. (4.1), $\Delta Y_t$ is the change in total output, and $\Delta Y_t = Y_t - Y_{t-1}$. $\Delta Y_t^*$ represents the change in potential output, considering only the steady state of a market, and it is the main part of the long-term trend. $\Delta \hat{Y}_t$ represents the change brought about by the role of government. Different from the Keynesian view that the government only affects short-term economic fluctuations, the role of government has effects on both short-term economic fluctuations and long-term economic trends, and shocks that come from the supply side and the demand side will be superimposed.

According to the rational synthesis economic model, to achieve an equilibrium requires both market regulation and government regulation, that is, the combination of the "invisible hand" and the "visible hand." in Eqn. (4.1), parameters $a$ and $b$ represent the weights, of which the sum is 1.

When $a = 1$ and $b = 0$,

$$\Delta Y_t = \Delta Y_t^* = Y_t^* - Y_{t-1}^*$$

This points to a pure market economy as articulated in classical economics, where an equilibrium is achieved through the self-regulation of the market itself.

When $a = 0$ and $b = 1$,

$$\Delta Y_t = \Delta \mathrm{Y}_t = \Delta AS + \Delta AD$$

This points to a fully planned economy, a model of distribution according to needs as stated by Marx, where the market is completely regulated through macroeconomic policy.

When $0 < a < 1$, $0 < b < 1$, and $a + b = 1$, it represents a mixed economy where market forces and government intervention both play a role, which is a model closer to the real-world economy. Depending on the varying weights assigned to parameters $(a, b)$, Eqn. (4.1) encapsulates the different perspectives of Keynesian economics, neoclassical economics, and new Keynesian economics regarding the role of market under different circumstances. For example, assume that a country adopts Keynesian economics to regulate its economy, and when $a = 0.8$ and $b = 0.2$, the equation will represent the relationship between market and government at a given stage.

In Eqn. (4.2), $\lambda$ is a constant, $K$ denotes capital, $L$ represents labor, and parameters $\theta$ and $1-\theta$ represent the elasticity of output with respect to capital and labor, respectively. This equation shows that the potential output of an economy is mainly determined by factors such as capital and labor. It should be noted that although $Y_t^*$ here is similar to the Solow growth model, the meaning is different.[2] There exists part of economic growth that cannot be explained by factors in the Solow growth model, but in the rational synthesis economic model, $Y_t^*$ denotes output growth owing to the role of market, excluding the unexplained portion of shocks.

In Eqn. (4.3), ΔAS represents the impact from the supply side, and ΔAD represents the impact from the demand side. The government's impact on economic fluctuations is the compounded effects of both supply-side and demand-side shocks. In light of the deviation between the expected output and real output of the previous period, the government carries out countercyclical macro control by introducing targeted policy on the demand side or supply side. Assume that the government's expectations are rational expectations, $E(Y_t) = Y_t$. Therefore, the policy of demand-side management can be expressed as:

$$\Delta AD = \mu_d \left(Y_t - Y_{t-1}\right) + \varepsilon_{dt} \tag{4.4}$$

where $\mu_d(Y_t - Y_{t-1})$ represents demand-side macroeconomic policy responses, $\mu_d$ is a constant, and $\varepsilon_{dt}$ is an unmeasured random factor.

Supply-side macro control will not only cause short-term fluctuations to economic growth, but also influence its long-term trend, that is, the path of economic growth in the long run. Here, the lag effects of the long-term impacts are simplified. The equation for supply-side reform policy can be expressed as follows:

$$\Delta AS = \mu_{sl} \left(Y_t - Y_{t-1}\right) + \mu_{ss} \left(Y_t - Y_{t-1}\right) + \varepsilon_{st} \tag{4.5}$$

[2] In the Solow growth model, the increase in total output is mostly attributed to the growth of labor and capital, but there remains an unexplained change known as the Solow residual, which economists predominantly ascribe to technological progress. In the rational synthesis economic model, the increase in total output attributable to the role of market is entirely explained by market-determined factors, excluding the unexplained portion of shocks. This is the key distinction in the assumptions of the rational synthesis economic model and conventional market assumptions.

On the right side of Eqn. (4.5), $\mu_{sl}(Y_t - Y_{t-1})$ and $\mu_{ss}(Y_t - Y_{t-1})$ represent supply-side macroeconomic policy responses. The former denotes long-term impacts from the supply side, and the latter is short-term impacts from the supply side. In particular, the response mechanism of short-term impacts from the supply side $\mu_{ss}(Y_t - Y_{t-1})$ is the same as that of macro control policy on the demand side. Not all supply-side macroeconomic policies have long-term impacts on economic growth. Here, let us assume that supply-side policies that act on technological progress can exert long-term impacts on economic growth. The long-term impacts of supply-side policy can be expressed as below:

$$\mu_{sl} = \frac{\Delta Y_t^*}{Y_t - Y_{t-1}} \times \Delta A_t \tag{4.6}$$

Therefore, the equation for supply-side reform policy can be rewritten as:

$$\Delta AS = \mu_{ss}\left(Y_t - Y_{t-1}\right) + \Delta A_t \times \Delta Y_t^* + \varepsilon_{st} \tag{4.7}$$

where $\Delta A_t$ represents technological progress, $\mu_{ss}$ is a constant, and $\varepsilon_{st}$ is an unmeasured random factor.

Combining Eqns. (4.4) and (4.7), we can get:

$$\Delta Y_t = \left(\mu_{ss} + \mu_d\right)\left(Y_t - Y_{t-1}\right) + \Delta A_t \times \Delta Y_t^* + \left(\varepsilon_{st} + \varepsilon_{dt}\right) \tag{4.8}$$

Combining Eqns. (4.1) and (4.8), we can get:

$$\Delta Y_t = \left(\mu_{ss} + \mu_d\right)\left(Y_t - Y_{t-1}\right) + \Delta A_t \times \Delta Y_t^* + \left(\varepsilon_{st} + \varepsilon_{dt}\right) \tag{4.9}$$

The above lays out the construction of the rational synthesis economic model, and the resultant Eqn. (4.9) carries profound economic implications: economic growth $\Delta Y_t$, manifested in economic operations is jointly driven by the long-term trend $(a + b\Delta A_t)\Delta Y_t^*$ and short-term fluctuations $b(\mu_{ss} + \mu_d)(Y_t - Y_{t-1}) + b(\varepsilon_{st} + \varepsilon_{dt})$. Specifically, the long-term trend depends on the fundamentals of the economy and is mainly determined by such market factors as capital and labor. Plus, technological progress owing to government actions (such as long-term industrial policy) can also influence the long-term economic trends. Short-term fluctuations are caused by a combination of temporary shocks on the supply side and demand side. Among them, supply-side reform and shocks mainly come from temporary industrial policy and exogenous random shocks, while temporary shocks on the demand side come from the changes in fiscal policy, monetary policy, and other unknown factors. The rational synthesis economic model is a unified, dynamic economic growth model and primarily differs from Keynesian theory in the understanding of the role of government. The rational synthesis economic model asserts that the role of government influences not only the short-term fluctuations of the economy but also the potential economic growth, thus exerting an impact on the foundation of the market economy. Macro control plays a role in promoting long-term economic growth or development, instead of being impotent. This also overcomes the limitations of existing economic growth models, as it reflects economic development rather than merely growth.

### *2.3 Policy Combination Analysis Under the Rational Synthesis Economic Model*

On the basis of the rational synthesis economic model, we can delve deeper into the impacts of various policy combinations. Below, we will look at different policy combinations and the corresponding real-world scenarios in a layered approach.

1. Compound effects of the role of market and government

Classical economics thinks that in extreme or ideal situations, the economy operates as a pure market economy, and the market is able to achieve an equilibrium itself. Marxist economics believes that the economy operates as a fully planned economy, and the government has a dominant position in the economy. However, real-world economic operations are the result of integration of market functions and government intervention. A real-world economy is always a mixed economy, where the market plays a fundamental role and the government a regulatory role, including the combined impacts of demand-side fiscal and monetary policies and supply-side changes (such as reform, industrial structure, and ownership). Normally, the market shows a positive trend, putting the economy on a path of benign development that is bolstered by moderate government regulation, as shown in the first quadrant in Fig. 4.1. However, if the market or government fails to function well, that may cause changes in the

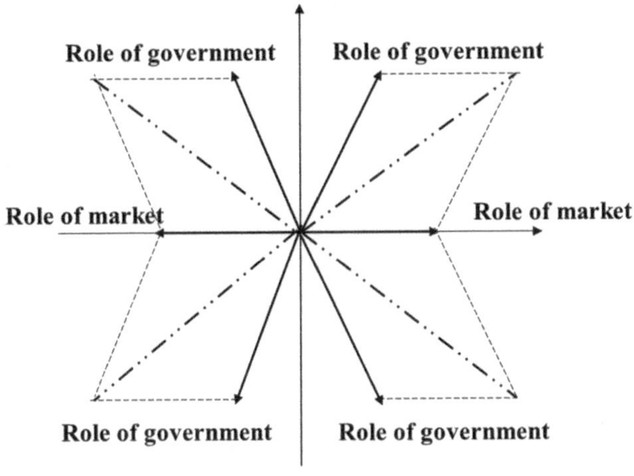


**Fig. 4.1** Different scenarios of the role of market and that government. (Source: Compiled by the author)

direction of economic operations, leading to an economic recession or depression. Therefore, we should allow the market to play the decisive role to ensure smooth economic operations and avoid systemic risks, and at the same time, let the government better play its role and use economic tools to set the stage for development.

2. Combination of demand-side management and supply-side reform

In the real world, demand-side management is emphasized in certain contexts, while supply-side reform is highlighted in others. According to $\hat{Y}_t = \Delta AS + \Delta AD$ in Eqn. (4.3), the government can carry out macro control on both the demand side and the supply side, so macroeconomic policy is a combination of supply-side policy and demand-side policy. Different from Keynesian theory, the rational synthesis economic model posits that demand-side management focuses on regulating short-term economic fluctuations, while supply-side reform exerts impacts on both short-term fluctuations and the long-term trend. As shown in Fig. 4.2, curve $\Upsilon$ can be approximated as the trajectory of economic operations, oscillating around the curve $\Upsilon^{*1}$ in the earlier stage. If government regulation works, it may influence the long-term potential economic growth rate, driving the potential economic growth curve to move upward from

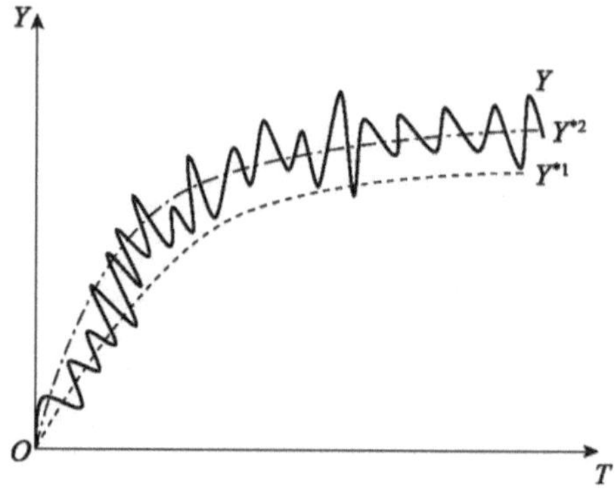


**Fig. 4.2** Short-term economic fluctuations and the long-term trend. (Source: Compiled by the author)

$\Upsilon^{*1}$ to $\Upsilon^{*2}$. That is, the curve $\Upsilon$ will fluctuate around the potential economic growth curve $\Upsilon^{*2}$ in the later stage. Therefore, a more effective role of government not only catalyzes economic growth by achieving a short-term equilibrium between supply and demand but also propels the transformation and upgrading of the economic architecture by shaping the potential economic growth trend.

Demand management prioritizes the regulation of aggregate demand, where the government plays a crucial role in revitalizing the economy, but this strategy is unable to tackle the imbalances in industrial structure or expand supply effectively. Conversely, supply-side reform emphasizes structural adjustment to increase effective supply and unleash business vitality, so as to develop a truly dynamic economy. Demand-side management policies generally consist of fiscal policy and monetary policy. Policies for supply-side reform include policies aimed at bolstering production (with respect to wages and raw materials and energy prices, for example), policies aimed at adjusting corporate profits (such as taxes, subsidies, rationing, and government purchase), institutional change policies (such as those with respect to business and personal motivation), and policies for state-owned enterprise reform. Of course, some policies may serve the purposes of demand management and supply adjustment at the same time. For example, although monetary policy is primarily a demand management policy, interest rates do affect production costs and consequently, aggregate supply. For another example, industrial policy, as a policy for supply-side reform, can impact the supply capacity of a particular industry in the short term, and affect the non-steady-state rate of potential economic growth (or total factor productivity) over the long haul. The overarching goal of macroeconomic policy is to inspire economic vitality and cultivate a good environment and a set of favorable and stable characteristics in favor of businesses and individuals.

3. Economic cycles and policy combinations

Macro control theory is a holistic regulatory system integrating supply-side reform and demand-side management. While the two run through the whole process, they have different focuses and functions depending on the levels of prominence of aggregate and structural issues in the economy, and different policy combinations of aggregate demand management and supply-side reform can be implemented at different stages of the business cycle. According to the characteristics of aggregate and structural issues, macro control can be categorized into two types: one prioritizes demand-side management over supply-side reform, and the other prioritizes supply-side reform over demand-side management. Moreover, policy combinations of demand-side management and supply-side reform can be orchestrated according to the characteristics of the business cycle. Certainly, some specific objectives can be incorporated into these policy combinations.

According to the rational synthesis economic model, in order to achieve the goal of "stabilizing economic growth and adjusting the economic structure," various policy tools should be used in a targeted manner to implement macro control in light of the characteristics of economic operations at the given stage, with a focus on the potential economic growth rate. In response to the stagflation of the 1980s in the US, the Reagan administration adopted a targeted macro control strategy which prioritized supply-side reform while emphasizing the supplementary role of demand-side management. This strategy reduced tax rates on a large scale to stimulate the vitality of businesses, eventually bringing the economy out of stagflation. To advance supply-side reform in the new normal, China should implement a proactive fiscal policy centered on tax cuts and a moderately easy monetary policy, and address soft budget constraints through economic system reform so as to reduce financing costs for small and medium enterprises (SMEs). SMEs serve as a major channel for employment, especially for people who lost their jobs as a result of the overcapacity reduction policy.

4. Overcapacity does not mean the ineffectiveness of industrial policy

As a matter of fact, industrial policy is effective in supporting supply-side reform and fostering new growth drivers, and can promote economic transformation and upgrading through its impact on potential economic growth. Overcapacity does not mean that industrial policy fails. In fact, industrial policy can drive an industry from its infancy all the way to overcapacity, which exactly testifies to the effectiveness of industrial policy. The crux of utilizing industrial policy lies in the right time for scrapping the policy. When an industry reaches maturity, the relevant industrial policy should be phased out in a timely manner, and preferential treatment be canceled to avoid overcapacity and adjust the industrial structure. From this perspective, combining demand-side management and supply-side reform policies is instrumental in adjusting the potential economic growth rate to a reasonable level while narrowing the output gap. This dual-pronged approach can help China get out of the current predicament and escape the middle-income trap.

### 2.4 *Realistic Simulation of Economic Development Models and Their Evolution*

According to Eqn. (4.1), the curve of economic model evolution is illustrated in Fig. 4.3.

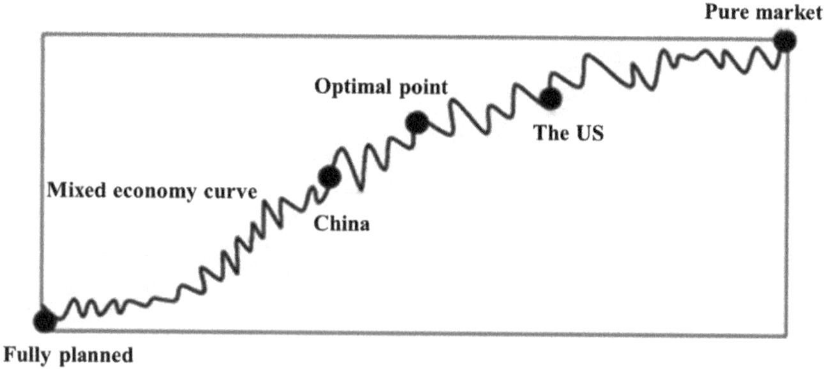


**Fig. 4.3** Dynamic curve of economic model evolution. (Source: Compiled by the author)

At the upper right of the rectangle in Fig. 4.3 represents a pure market economy, which falls under the scenario when $a = 1$ and $b = 0$ in Eqn. (4.1). At the bottom left represents a fully planned economy, which falls under the scenario when $a = 0$ and $b = 1$ in Eqn. (4.1). The points on the mixed market curve stand for mixed economies in the real world, falling under the scenario when $a < 1$, $b < 1$, and $a + b = 1$ in Eqn. (4.1). Different economies correspond to different points on the curve, depending on the degree of difference between the role of market and government. On one hand, the evolution of economic models is a dynamic process; on the other hand, it remains relatively stable in a given period, that is, the relationship between market and government is basically stable. Therefore, an economic model can be replicated and promoted within a relatively broad time span, and it is necessary to identify the critical point between the role of market and government at a particular stage.

### 2.5 *Analysis on the Balance Between the Role of Market and Government*

The boundaries between the role of market and government have long been a topic of much discussion and controversy in academia. We believe that in a certain period of time, there exists a critical point between the role of market and government in a mixed economy, which is reflected in the maximum or optimal role of market in Eqn. (4.1) under the rational synthesis economic model. Here the weight of the government's role in the market is referred to as the government activity index. Due to length constraints, we will focus on explaining the logic of rational synthesis and only make simple calculations of the government activity index.

With reference to the method developed by Fan Gang, Wang Xiaolu, and Zhu Hengpeng (2011), the proportion of government expenditure in GDP is used to measure the government's role in the total economy. By comparing data from China and the US, we find that the government activity index in China is 31.28%, and that in the US is 18.51%. To put it another way, the ratio of the market's fundamental role to the government's regulatory role is 68.72:31.28 in the Chinese economy, while the ratio is 81.49:18.51 in the US economy. It is believed that during a given period of time, the ratio of the role of market to the role of government has a reasonable level, which is roughly 75:25 at the current stage. To be specific, a government activity index of 25% indicates a relatively reasonable system allowing the market to play the decisive role and the government to better play its role. Given the realities of China and the US, the government activity index in the US is on the low side, indicating that its macro control has not achieved the desired effect. In comparison, China's government activity index is a little high, suggesting that its macro control has a strong impact on the economy, but market-oriented reform needs to be deepened to further raise the degree of marketization.

In view of the time span of data, the government activity index in the US (see Fig. 4.4) is examined, from which inferences can be drawn about the general evolution process of typical Western economic models. The US economy in the early stage was close to a pure market economy, and the role of market peaked during the Great Depression of 1929–1933, while the average government activity index was 10.54%, basically the lower limit of a general market economy. However, the Great Depression posed a huge challenge to the free market economy, raising awareness of the limitations of market forces and giving rise to the theory of insufficiency of effective demand and government intervention in Keynesian economics. As a result, government intervention was greatly strengthened in the wake of the Great Depression. The stagflation of the late 1970s in the US revealed the limitations of Keynesian economics.

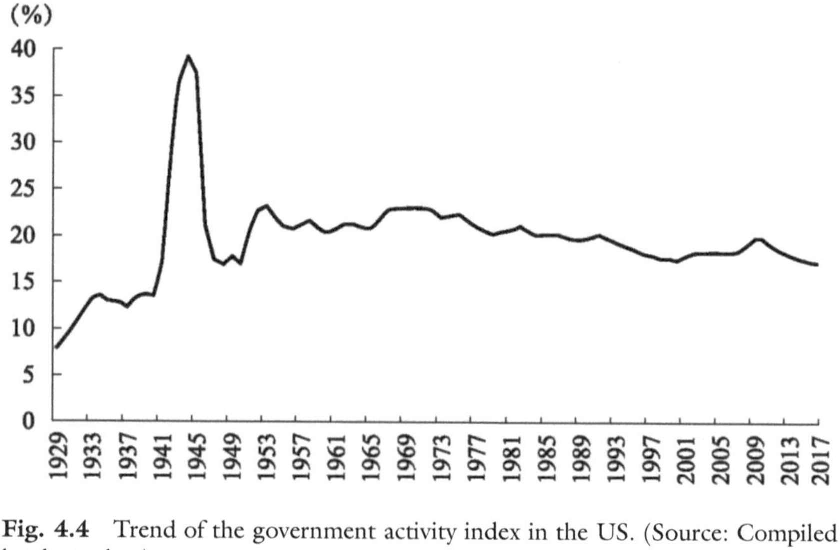


**Fig. 4.4** Trend of the government activity index in the US. (Source: Compiled by the author)

It can be seen that every time when an economic crisis occurs, Western economics tends to emphasize the importance of government intervention. However, after each crisis comes a renewed emphasis on the significance of market economy, requesting the government to leave room for the market. Therefore, in the later stage of the stagflation, the economy became market-oriented again, and the government activity index started to decline. However, the 2008 international financial crisis again raised questions about the free market, and the government strengthened its intervention in the economy, as reflected in an increase in the government activity index after 2008.

Evidently, the roles of market and government always co-exist, despite their different weights at different stages. At the stage of limited productivity, supply can barely match demand, so the economic structure based on the market economy model is more effective, and Say's Law, which posits that supply creates its own demand, holds true. When productivity grows mature, supply can fully match demand, and technological advances make it possible to quantify and calculate demand. In this case, the economic structure where the government plays its part is more effective.

The equilibrium point of an economic development model is not static but is inherently dynamic. As the supply capacity continues to grow, demand becomes the focus in the economy, and the cutting-edge big data technology ensures precise demand forecasting, so the "visible hand" plays a more important role. When productivity reaches an ideal level, people's demand will be fully met, and supply will no longer be a concern. However, before this ultimate goal is realized, the roles of market and government are both indispensable. The government exerts its role in both aggregate demand and aggregate supply, with varying policy combinations and emphases at different stages and in different contexts.

## 3 Macro Control Policy Framework from the Perspective of Rational Synthesis

Throughout the history of Western economics, the term "macro control" has never shown up. There are the concepts of macroeconomics and macroeconomic policy. However, the trajectory of modern socioeconomic development shows that government intervention always exists, and early mercantilist policies enacted by nations can be somewhat deemed as a kind of macro control. The notion of macro control finds its origins in China and has evolved into a comprehensive system deeply rooted in practice. Building upon extensive practices, China has pioneered theoretical innovation in macro control.

### 3.1 *The Origin and Evolution of Macro Control Theory*

1. Overview of macro control ideas in Western economics

The term "macroeconomics" was coined by Norwegian economist Rager Frisch in 1933. Keynes' book, *The General Theory of Employment, Interest and Money*, published in 1936, is widely regarded as a symbol of the establishment of the macroeconomic theoretical framework. Since then, macroeconomic policy has gained widespread attention and played an important role in the practice of government intervention in market economies. Centering on the roles of market and government, we sort out macroeconomic policies in different periods based on the viewpoint that macro control is a form of government action.

In the early days, classical economics founded by Adam Smith was held in high esteem. In *The Wealth of Nations*, he argues that a free market can achieve optimal allocation of resources and regulate itself through the "invisible hand." Therefore, advocates of the free market economy support Say's Law, positing that demand creates its own supply. They believe that actors hold rational expectations and that economic fluctuations can be quickly corrected. At the same time, they oppose government intervention in the economy and call for the minimum macro control by the government.

The Great Depression of 1929–1933 gave birth to Keynesian macroeconomics, resulting in the Keynesian Revolution. Starting from the insufficiency of effective demand, Keynes argued against the idea of relying solely on market self-regulation, but advocated for a combination of government intervention and market self-regulation, highlighting the importance of governmental intervention. On this basis, he proposed a systematic macroeconomic theoretical framework (see Fig. 4.5), exerting a significant impact on short-term macroeconomic policy. In the mid-twentieth century, the neoclassical synthesis school represented by Samuelson went further from Keynesian theory and constructed the AD-AS model. While they no longer confine themselves to aggregate demand analysis, there are

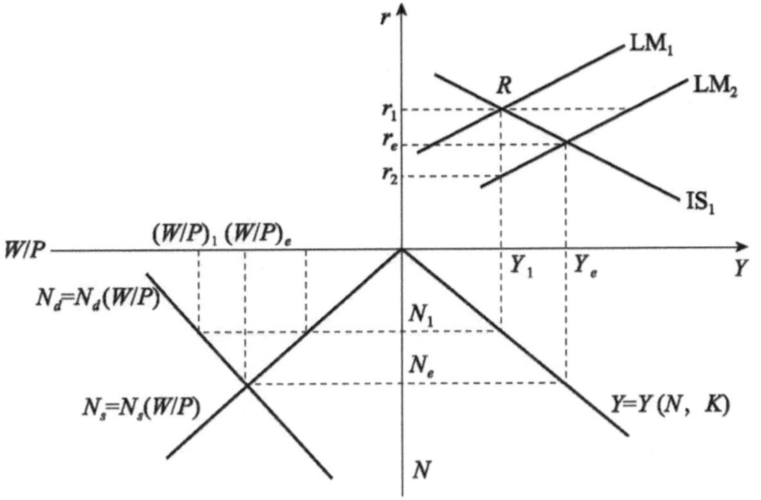


**Fig. 4.5** A complete Keynesian model. (Source: Compiled by the author)

limitations in their comprehension of the supply side. Samuelson thinks that in a market economy, the government's role is primarily reflected in its efforts to improve economic efficiency, promote social equality, facilitate steady economic growth, reduce unemployment, and stabilize prices, and the government mainly employs policy tools such as fiscal and monetary policies to achieve these objectives.

In the 1970s, the US economy was mired in stagflation, and the theory of neoclassical synthesis was called into question consequently. The neoclassical school launched a critique against Keynesianism. Based on a synthesis of Marshall's classical economics and Keynesian economics, neoclassicism emphasizes general equilibrium analysis and the micro foundation of macroeconomics and builds its arguments upon the price-wage elasticity and the rational expectations hypothesis, taking a quantitative approach to explaining the US stagflation. Neoclassicism advocates for a combination of aggregate demand management and aggregate supply management, arguing that when involuntary unemployment occurs, government intervention is necessary, and when the economy approaches or achieves full employment, the role of market self-regulation should be allowed to take precedence. The RBC theory conducts an in-depth analysis from the supply-side perspective and takes a deep dive into economic dynamics.

Overall, various policy frameworks have come into being during the evolution of Western economics, each playing a notable role at different development stages of the developed countries, but there are still some limitations:

(1) A complete framework of macro control has been absent. An integral whole as macroeconomic theory, Keynesian economics claims that the "visible hand" is a short-term policy system that only concerns demand management, and this view is in fact a far cry from the essence of macro control. Conversely, while recognizing the importance of the supply side, the supply school neglects the significance of demand and lacks rigorous logic, models, and policy frameworks.

(2) The macroeconomic policy framework still predominantly relies on static and comparative static analysis, so it remains a non-dynamic theory. This is closely connected to the prevalence of equilibrium analysis in Western economics. Despite the advantage of being intuitive and easy to understand, equilibrium analysis is confined to specific states and therefore, can only provide moderate descriptions rather than cogent explanations for economic growth, business cycles, and other key issues. The crux lies in the transition between equilibrium and disequilibrium between aggregate supply and demand, which is a specific manifestation of market mechanisms at work.

(3) There exists an obvious disconnect with the reality of economic operations. Different schools of macroeconomic have different thoughts about aggregate supply and demand and have different views about macro control or macroeconomic policy. Some even go to extraordinary lengths to substantiate the argument that monetary policy is useless, which is clearly at odds with practice. This is largely because Western economics grounds its logical basis on the pure market economy, without giving due consideration to the role of government.

2. Marxist economics provides a theoretical foundation for macro control

Marx elucidates on the necessity of macro control, stating that "All combined labor on a large scale requires, more or less, a directing authority, in order to secure the harmonious working of the individual activities, and to perform the general functions that have their origin in the action of the combined organism, as distinguished from the action of its separate organs. A single violin player is his own conductor; an orchestra requires a separate one." For a nation, the "conductor" is government, and government macro control is essential to ensure sound socioeconomic operations. Marx also points out the necessity of the distribution of social labor, saying that "the masses of products corresponding to the different needs required different and quantitatively determined masses of the total labor of society. The necessity of the distribution of social labor in definite proportions cannot possibly be done away with by a particular form of social production but can only change the mode of its appearance, is self-evident."[3] In addition, Marxism expounds on the theory of macroeconomic balance and operations, uncovering the essence and basic conditions of equilibrium and disequilibrium. According to the Marxist theory of social reproduction, the reproduction of the whole social capital is a unity of production and circulation, and only when the two branches of social production and various departments are in proportion can the reproduction of the whole social capital be conducted smoothly. Since a deep-rooted antagonistic contradiction between production and consumption is inherent in capitalism, disequilibrium in capitalist economies is a norm. Marx's equilibrium and disequilibrium theory serves as the theoretical roots of macro control in modern market economies.

Generally, the Marxist's thought about macro control involves equilibrium in aggregate and structure, which is a comprehensive analysis based on aggregate supply and demand, laying the theoretical groundwork for China to bring forth the concept of macro control. Nonetheless, due to the limitations of the era and other factors, Marxist economics did not establish a systematic theory of macro control.

3. The proposal and evolution of macro control in China

Macro control is a new concept China proposed during its economic system reform. In 1984, the term "macro control" appeared for the first time

[3] Karl Marx and Friedrich Engels. *Collected Works of Marx and Engels* (Vol. 32). Beijing: People's Publishing House, 1974: 541.

in the *Decision of the CPC Central Committee on Reform of the Economic Structure* in 1984. The Communique of the Fifth Plenary Session of the 13th Central Committee of the Communist Party of China adopted on November 11, 1989 stressed the need to "further deepen and improve various reform measures and gradually develop a macro control system that follows the principle of integrating planned economy and market regulation and comprehensively uses economic, administrative, and legal measures." In 1993, the term "macro control" was written into Article 15 of the *Amendment to the Constitution of the People's Republic of China*, which stipulates that "The state shall strengthen economic legislation and improve macro control." In the same year, the *Decision of the Central Committee of the Communist Party of China on Issues Concerning the Establishment of a Socialist Market Economy* proposed to establish a macro control system for the socialist market economy. In 2003, the Decision of the Central Committee of the Communist Party of China on Issues Concerning the Improvement of the Socialist Market Economic System called for efforts to further improve the macro control system that coordinates with national planning and fiscal and monetary policies." The *Outline of the 12th Five-Year Plan for National Economic and Social Development of the People's Republic of China* adopted at the National People's Congress in 2011 elaborated on "strengthening and improving macro control." The Third Plenary Session of the 18th CPC Central Committee in 2013 outlined a range of innovative approaches to macro control, stating that "The reform of the economic system is the focus of all the efforts to deepen the all-round reform. The core issue is to straighten out the relationship between the government and the market, allowing the market to play a decisive role in allocating resources and improving the government's role" and "Sound macro control, along with effective governance by the government, is essential to ensure that we can fully harness the institutional strengths of our socialist market economy."

It can be seen that macro control is a key economic concept that derives from China's economic practices, is based on Marxist economics, borrows valuable ideas from modern Western economics, and has evolved in the process of China's economic development and transformation.

### 3.2 The Connotation of Macro Control and its Theoretical Model Analysis

to enrich the connotation of government regulation and develop a more systematic macroeconomic policy framework is an important goal for transformation in macroeconomics theory and also provides a pivotal foundation for improving the system of economic theory. There is a consensus between New Keynesian economists and neoclassical economists that flaws and frictions exist in real-world markets. Acknowledging the flaws of market mechanisms, macroeconomists have come to realize that the government plays an essential role in regulating the market, and that the market and the government constitute the two indispensable pillars of market regulation. As former Under Secretary of the US Treasury David Malpass put it, there was no Keynesian back in 1929, and we are all Keynesians now. As the understanding of government regulation is being deepened, the connotation of government regulation is also constantly evolving. Keynes proclaims that government intervention can only regulate short-term economic fluctuations, but throughout history, there have been many times when government regulation pulls the economy out of crises, indicating that government policy has an impact on the long-term business cycle. By that token, it is crucial to accurately define the concept of macro control.

Analysis of aggregate supply and demand is at the heart of macro control. Although macroeconomic theory is not articulated in classical economics, due attention is paid to analysis of aggregate supply and demand as classical economics regards the equilibrium between aggregate supply and demand as an important condition. From a Marxist perspective, macro control should include the regulation of both aggregate supply and demand. Keynesian economics holds that macro policy revolves around effective demand, though the equilibrium between aggregate demand and aggregate supply is also an important condition. As seen from the evolution of modern macroeconomic theory, macro control should give consideration to both aggregate supply and demand, and the AD-AS model practically represents the logic and direction of macro control.

Based on the rational synthesis economic model's depiction of real-world mixed economies, we will illustrate macro control more specifically. Starting with Eqn. (4.3), we can get:

$$\Delta Y_t = \Delta AS + \Delta AD$$

The government's effect on economic fluctuations is the superposition of effects from both supply-side and demand-side shocks. Thus, supply-side and demand-side macro control are decomposed as shown below:

$$\Delta AD = \mu_d\left(Y_t - Y_{Gt}^*\right) + \varepsilon_{dt} \tag{4.10}$$

$$\Delta AS = \mu_{ss}\left(Y_t - Y_{Gt}^*\right) + \mu_{sl}\left(Y_{Gt}^* - Y_{Mt}^*\right) + \varepsilon_{st} \tag{4.11}$$

In Eqns. (4.10) and (4.11), $Y_t$ represents the real economic output curve, $Y_{Gt}^*$ the potential economic output curve with the government's role at work, and $Y_{Mt}^*$ the potential economic output curve in a pure market economy; $\mu_d$ is government regulation coefficient on the demand side, and $\mu_{ss}$ and $\mu_{sl}$ respectively represent the short-term and the long-term government regulation coefficient on both the supply and demand sides; $\varepsilon_{dt}$ and $\varepsilon_{st}$ are unmeasured random factors.

Specifically, on the one hand, government regulation is not powerless to influence the long-term economic trends. In the long run, government regulation will have an impact on the economy's potential output curve on the supply side, that is, the economic output curve will be adjusted from $Y_{Mt}^*$ to $Y_{Gt}^*$, which is reflected as $\mu_{sl}(Y_{Gt}^* - Y_{Mt}^*)$ in Eqn. (4.11). On the other hand, given the economic output curve with the government's role at work $Y_{Gt}^*$, the government's role can have short-term impacts on the demand side and the supply side, which presents as a deviation of the real economic output curve $Y_t$ from $Y_{Gt}^*$. Such deviation is reflected as $\mu_d(Y_t - Y_{Gt}^*)$ in Eqn. (4.10) and $\mu_{ss}(Y_t - Y_{Gt}^*)$ in Eqn. (4.11).[4]

Substitute Eqns. (4.10) and (4.11) into Eqn. (4.3), and we can get:

$$\Delta\hat{Y}_t = \mu_d\left(Y_{t^-} - Y_{Gt}^*\right) + \mu_{ss}\left(Y_{t^-} - Y_{Gt}^*\right) + \mu_{sl}\left(Y_{Gt}^* - Y_{Mt}^*\right) + \varepsilon_{dt} + \varepsilon_{st} \tag{4.12}$$

$$\Delta\hat{Y}_t = \left(\mu_d + \mu_{ss}\right)\left(Y_t - Y_{Gt}^*\right) + \mu_{sl}\left(Y_{Gt}^* - Y_{Mt}^*\right) + \left(\varepsilon_{dt} + \varepsilon_{st}\right) \tag{4.13}$$

The above illustrates a basic model of macro control. Further, the effect of government regulation on the potential output curve in a pure market economy can be considered:

[4] Certainly, macro control comes with a cost. This model is a reduced analysis and does not take into account the cost of macro control, but instead, assumes that such cost has no influence on policy selection and the achievement of regulatory objectives.

$$Y_{Gt}^{*} - Y_{Mt}^{*} = \Delta A_t f(K_t, L_t) = \Delta A_t Y_{Mt}^{*}. \tag{4.14}$$

In Eqn. (4.14), $\Delta A_t$ represents the change in total factor productivity. Not all supply-side macroeconomic policies have long-term impacts on economic growth. Here, let us assume that supply-side policies that act on technological progress can exert long-term impacts on economic growth. Thus, Eqn. (4.13) can be simplified as:

$$\Delta Y_t = (\mu_d + \mu_{ss})(Y_t - Y_{Gt}^{*}) + \mu_{sl} \Delta A_t Y_{Mt}^{*} + (\varepsilon_{dt} + \varepsilon_{st}) \tag{4.15}$$

The above illustrates a basic model of macro control. Equation (4.15) denotes the core connotation of macro control. On this basis, the economic growth equation can be transformed into:

$$\Delta Y_t = a \Delta Y_{Mt}^{*} + b(\mu_d + \mu_{ss})(Y_t - Y_{Gt}^{*}) + b \mu_{sl} \Delta A_t Y_{Mt}^{*} + b(\varepsilon_{dt} + \varepsilon_{st}) \tag{4.16}$$

Equation (4.16) is referred to as the dynamic macroeconomic growth equation.

Equation (4.16) carries profound economic implications: economic growth is jointly driven by the long-term trend and short-term fluctuations. Specifically, the long-term trend depends on the fundamentals of the economy and is mainly determined by such market factors as capital and labor. Plus, changes in total factor productivity brought about by government actions (such as technological innovation input, long-term industrial policy) can also influence the long-term economic trends. Short-term fluctuations are brought about by a combination of temporary shocks on the supply side and demand side. Among them, supply-side shocks mainly come from temporary industrial policy adjustments and exogenous random shocks, while temporary shocks on the demand side are caused by changes in fiscal policy, monetary policy, and other unknown factors. In fact, the dynamic macroeconomics of the Swedish School, the DSGE mode, and the RBC theory bear resemblance to the way how we research this topic. Our main originality lies in that we consider the roles of market and government as well as their combined effects from the perspective of rational synthesis, study disequilibrium as the norm rather than equilibrium, and give high attention to the fluctuations of economic aggregates. As such, we have constructed a complete dynamic equation.

### 3.3 Main Macro Control Models

Based on various definitions, macro control can be basically perceived from three levels, each with respective mechanisms of government intervention and theoretical roots. This gives rise to three main macro control models.

1. Macro control model 1

This is macro control in a narrow sense. Built on Keynesian economics, it usually refers to macroeconomic policy that regulates aggregate demand in the short term. It is applicable when aggregate supply is significantly greater than aggregate demand, and aggregate demand on the whole determines output. Based on the logic of effective demand theory, Keynes posits that the government intervenes in the economy by adopting policies to stimulate aggregate demand, and in this case, fiscal policy is regarded as a key instrument of macroeconomic policy (see Fig. 4.6). Accordingly, the objectives of macro control include economic growth, price stability, full employment, and balance of international payments.

2. Macro control model 2

This macro control model integrates the theoretical foundation of the AD-AS model and the supply-side and demand-side adjustments (see Fig. 4.7). This model shows the basic connotation of macro control, falling under the scenario when $a + b = 1$ in the aforementioned rational synthesis economic model, and is applicable to economies with a solid foundation and sound regulatory mechanism. For low degrees of disequilibrium between aggregate supply and demand, economic growth can be achieved by adjusting aggregate supply and demand to restore equilibrium. In this case, the government's role extends beyond short-term effects; in other words, it influences not only short-term economic fluctuations and also the long-term trends. From this perspective, it does not make sense if macroeconomic policy objectives are restricted to the four components articulated in Keynesian economics; instead, structural indicators and indicators of financial stability should be incorporated.

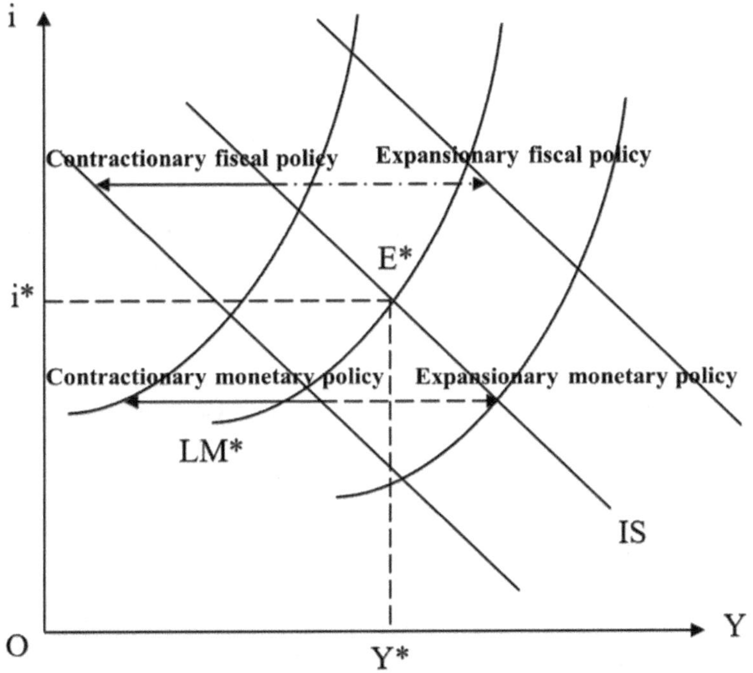


**Fig. 4.6** Macro control model 1. (Source: Compiled by the author

3. Macro control model 3

This is macro control in a broad sense, and falls under the scenario when $a + b \neq 1$ in the aforementioned rational synthesis economic model. It is an integral part of government intervention. In addition to the basic meaning, this model also encapsulates the role of reform, economic transformation, social distribution, and other factors. In fact, the nationalization or privatization policy, structural reform, or trade protectionism implemented by Western countries in different periods could be identified as this model. From this level, Macro control includes not only government intervention or regulation on the supply side and demand side, but also some policy actions aimed at inspiring social changes or advancing social equity, creating a complex tapestry of different economic development models. Economies that have yet to establish a sound market

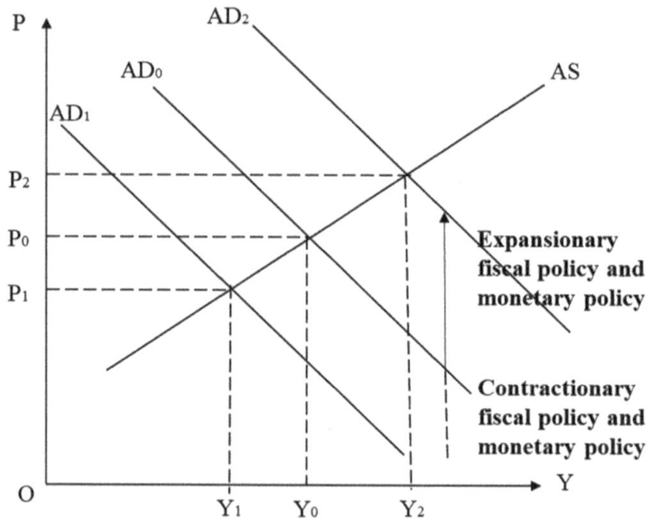


**Fig. 4.7** Macro control model 2. (Source: Compiled by the author)

mechanism or that are highly market-oriented but have undergone major structural adjustments need to employ such regulatory instruments. This essentially concerns a country's transformation or reform, and the key lies in properly handling the relationship between market and government. A country should take steps to develop an economic system that suits itself and combines the roles of market and government. On the one hand, market-oriented reform must be advanced unswervingly to allow the market to play a decisive role. On the other hand, the government should gradually reduce direct intervention in the economy and improve the macro control mechanism so as to better play its role. China's reform and opening up is a good example of this process. Based on the previous statement on the macro control model, transitory shocks and long-term impacts can be distinguished from supply-side impacts to better depict macro control at this level (see Fig. 4.8). As this type of macro control may have a fundamental impact on the long-term trends of a country's economy, the government needs to maintain an accurate perspective on the economic landscape and the domestic and international environments when drawing up policy, have an exact knowledge of the country's development stage, and exercise macro control in a targeted manner.

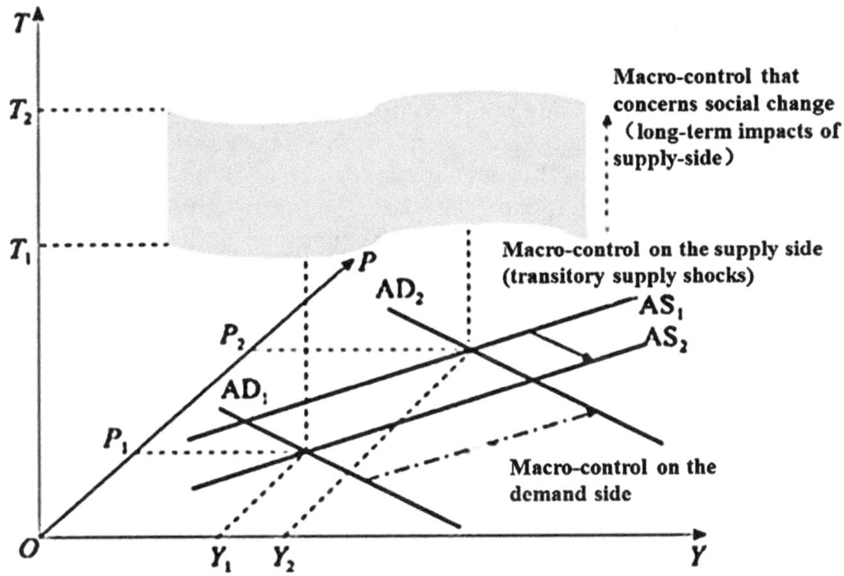


**Fig. 4.8** Macro control model 3. (Source: Compiled by the author)

In summary, the macro control model is essentially a dynamic model of the government's role and somewhat can be regarded as an economic growth model. The most striking distinction between macro control theory and Keynesian economics lies in their understanding of the government's role. Macro control can promote long-term economic growth, and the macro control model overcomes the limitations of existing economic growth models, as it is not only a manifestation of economic growth but also an expression of the connotation of economic development. Specifically, $b\mu_{sl}\Delta A_t Y^*_{Mt}$ in Eqn. (4.16) represents the impact of macro control on potential economic growth, which can improve total factor productivity through promoting technological progress and industrial upgrading, and therefore, promote the long-term economic restructuring and economic upgrading; $b(\mu_d + \mu_{ss})(Y_t - Y^*_{Gt})$ represents the impact of macro control on economic growth fluctuations and can also be regarded as the variation in the gap. Keynes' famous argument that "In the long run we are all dead" does have some grounds because, from the angle of effective demand, macroeconomic policy only exerts short-term impacts but no long-term impacts. However, from the perspective of macro control theory, such grounds are inadequate and diverge from reality. If macroeconomic policy only has short-term effects, that is, only influences short-term economic fluctuations but not long-term trends, then there would be no rationale for enacting policy to turn things around. Obviously, this does not align with reality. The macro control theory should not lead to the same conclusion as Keynes' argument. In addition to short-term effects, macroeconomic policy can exert long-term impacts, which are sometimes so significant that they bring about a shift in the potential economic growth curve.

### 3.4 Establishment of the Macro Control Policy Framework

1. Significant adjustments to macro control objectives

When it comes to macro control, we generally refer to its basic meaning, which is embodied in macro control model 2. In this case, the theoretical foundation of macro control diverges from Keynesian economics, so the objectives of macro control should also change accordingly. The four objectives laid out in Keynesian economics, namely, economic growth, price stability, full employment, and balance of international payments, should be revised. First, considering the demand side, the objectives of economic growth and full employment can to some extent be unified into economic growth. Second, considering the supply side, there should be an objective for economic restructuring. Third, in view of the equilibrium and disequilibrium between aggregate supply and demand, there should be a financial stability indicator to maintain price stability and forestall risks. Fourth, the objective "balance of international payments," as an external indicator, can be retained, but it should be enriched. As such, the four objectives of macro control are adjusted to economic growth, economic restructuring, financial stability, and balance of international payments. Therefore, the macro control or macroeconomic policy objectives changed significantly, and each objective has profound theoretical roots. In fact, China's three major tasks of stabilizing economic growth, making structural adjustments, and guarding against risks reflect the three objectives of economic growth, economic restructuring, and financial stability, respectively, while improving livelihoods and advancing reform should be the goals set for macro control in a broad sense. Furthermore, the combination of economic growth and economic restructuring is manifested in the shift of the Chinese economy from high-speed to high-quality development.

2. Macro control policy combinations

First, the combination of demand-side management and supply-side reform. The government can exercise macro control on both the demand side and the supply side. Therefore, macroeconomic policy is generally a combination of supply-side policy and demand-side policy. The short-term and long-term effects of macro control are illustrated as below(see Fig. 4.9). There are some differences between this curve and the curve drawn based on the Keynesian theory. The curve $Y_t$ can be approximated as the trajectory of actual economic operations. At the outset, it fluctuates around the potential growth curve $Y^*_{Mt}$. When government regulation works and influences the potential economic growth, the potential growth curve $Y^*_{Mt}$ undergoes an upward shift to $Y^*_{Gt}$, and consequently, the curve $Y_t$ fluctuates around the adjusted potential growth curve $Y^*_{Gt}$, which falls under the scenario in Eqn. (4.10). Therefore, an effective role of the government can not only drive economic growth by achieving a short-run equilibrium between supply and demand, but also promote economic restructuring by influencing the trend of potential economic growth.

Specifically, demand management prioritizes the regulation of aggregate demand, in which the government assumes a pivotal role in reviving the economy, but this strategy is unable to tackle the imbalances in industrial structure or expand effective supply. Conversely, supply-side reform emphasizes structural adjustment to increase effective supply and unleash

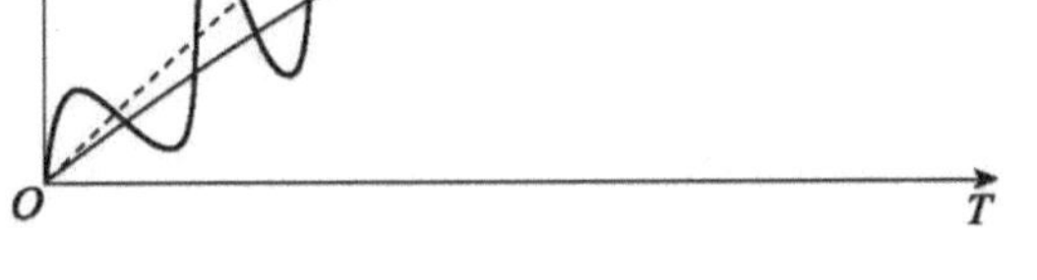


**Fig. 4.9** Curve of short-term fluctuations and long-term trends. (Source: Compiled by the author)

business vitality, so as to develop a truly dynamic economy. Demand-side management policies generally consist of fiscal policy and monetary policy. Policies for supply-side reform include policies affect production costs (with respect to wages and raw materials and energy prices, for example), policies aimed at adjusting corporate profits (such as taxes, subsidies, rationing, and government purchase), institutional change policies (such as those with respect to business and personal motivation), and policies for state-owned enterprise reform. Of course, some policies may serve the purposes of demand management and supply adjustment at the same time. For example, although monetary policy is primarily a demand management policy, interest rates do affect production costs and consequently, aggregate supply. For another example, industrial policy, as a policy for supply-side reform, can impact the supply capacity of a particular industry in the short term, and affect the non-steady-state rate of potential economic growth (or total factor productivity) over the long haul.

Second, the correspondence between the stage of the business cycles and policy combinations. Macro control theory is a holistic regulatory system integrating supply-side reform and demand-side management. While the two run through the whole process, they have different focuses and functions depending on the levels of prominence of aggregate and structural issues in the economy. According to the characteristics of aggregate and structural issues, macro control can be categorized into two types. One is policy combinations of demand-side management and supply-side reform based on the issues to be addressed. When cyclical issues are the primary concern and structural issues are secondary, policy emphasis should be placed on demand-side management, with supply-side reform playing a supplementary role. Conversely, when structural issues are the primary concern and cyclical issues are secondary, policy emphasis should be on supply-side reform, with demand-side management playing a supplementary role. The other is policy combinations of demand-side management and supply-side reform orchestrated according to the characteristics of the business cycles, and there are eight sub-types (see Table 4.1). For economies that have not completed institutional transformation or need to adjust their systems, the macro control is beyond the basic meaning, necessitating the consideration of institutional reform, social equity, economic transformation or model transformation, and other factors in carrying out comprehensive and flexible reform or regulation through policy combinations.

**Table 4.1** Overview of macro control policy combinations

| | *Aggregate issues > Structural issues* | *Structural issues > Aggregate issues* |
|---|---|---|
| Prosperity | Demand-side management plays a primary role, and supply-side reform plays a supplementary role<br>Tight fiscal policy and tight monetary policy<br>Supply-side reform | Supply-side reform plays a primary role, and demand-side management plays a supplementary role |
| Recession | Demand-side management plays a primary role, and supply-side reform plays a supplementary role<br>Loose fiscal policy and loose monetary policy<br>Structural adjustment | Supply-side reform plays a primary role, and demand-side management plays a supplementary role |
| Depression | Demand-side management plays a primary role, and supply-side reform plays a supplementary role<br>Tight and loose matching | Supply-side reform plays a primary role, and demand-side management plays a supplementary role<br>Expand demand |
| Recovery | Demand-side management plays a primary role, and supply-side reform plays a supplementary role<br>To prudently expand demand and conduct supply-side reform plays a supporting role<br>Prudently expand demand and steadily advance supply-side reform | Supply-side reform plays a primary role, and demand-side management plays a supplementary role<br>Prioritize supply-side reform and moderately expand demand |

Source: Compiled by the author

## 4 Application of the Rational Synthesis Economic Model: Case Studies

Underlying the rational synthesis economic model is a sound economic logic, making it possible to analyze various economic issues according to a relatively consistent logic, rather than in disparate approaches. It is important to develop a theoretical model that combines "efficient market" and "proactive government," articulate basic logical relationships using mathematical formulas, and conduct a systematic analysis of the models of economic development, macro-regulation, the theory of economic growth, the business cycle, the middle-income trap, supply-side structural reform, and new structural economics. Below are some case studies.

### 4.1 *Theoretical Model of Supply-side Reform and its Application*

As can be seen from the aforementioned derivation of theoretical models, the models of supply-side structural reform fall into two types: one is a single-dimensional thinking, as expressed in the following equation:

Similar to the emphasis on effective demand in Keynesian economics, the focus here is on the major changes brought about by supply-side reform. The second is the multi-dimensional thinking, as expressed in Eqn. (4.15):

When the economic fluctuations caused by $(\mu_d + \mu_{ss})(Y_t - Y_{Gt}^*)\mu_{sl}\Delta A_t Y_{Mt}^*$ are far smaller than those caused by $\mu_{sl}\Delta A_t Y_{Mt}^*$, the focus of macro control should be on supply-side reform. Logically, supply-side reform represents not only an application of the rational synthesis economic model, but also a special application of the macro control model. It falls under the scenario where structural issues are the primary concern and cyclical issues are secondary, and the corresponding strategy should focus on addressing structural issues while paying attention to balance on the demand side. The core task of supply-side reform is to adopt policies to improve total factor productivity and also ensure a dynamic equilibrium between supply and demand, that is, prioritizing supply-side reform while implementing demand-side management.

China's supply-side reform is mainly carried out using a multidimensional thinking approach, though there is also single-dimensional thinking in some cases. It emphasizes that the focus should be on addressing major structural issues, and attention should also be paid to ensuring an equilibrium between aggregate supply and demand. China has reiterated the need to "focus on supply-side structural reform while giving attention to demand-side management," and this is exactly a manifestation of multidimensional thinking. Multidimensional thinking goes beyond solving immediate problems, as it can illuminate the path forward for policies after supply-side reform succeeds, and this is beyond the capacity of single-dimensional thinking. During the stagflation in the 1980s, the US embraced supply-side economics to unleash business vitality through large-scale tax cuts, eventually bringing its economy out of dilemma. With its theoretical foundations rooted in single-dimensional thinking, the US practically adopted a strategy that focused on supply-side reform while giving attention to demand-side management. Single-dimensional thinking also exists in China in some cases, for example, when it focuses on supply-side issues.

It can be seen that China's supply-side reform is not exactly the same as the views of the Western supply-side school. While focusing on supply-side reform, China also moderately expands aggregate demand to achieve economic transformation and upgrading and bolster social productivity across the board. aggregate supply and demand policies are not isolated but evolve with the changing economic issues at different stages, which is in alignment with the intrinsic logic in the rational synthesis economic model that supply-side and demand-side controls should be balanced. In fact, the Western supply-side school does give consideration to demand-side issues when examining supply-side problems, but the logical frameworks of the two are not integrated or unified. For instance, when Keynesian economics analyzes effective demand, although the logical framework is not directly linked to aggregate supply, it in fact entails certain connection with aggregate supply to guarantee its rationality.

## *4.2 Coordinating Supply-side Reform and Demand-side Management*

*The Proposals for Formulating the 14th Five-Year Plan for Economic and Social Development and the Long-Range Objectives Through the Year 2035* adopted at the Fifth Plenary Session of the 19th CPC Central Committee and the Central Economic Work Conference both stressed the need to pursue supply-side structural reform as the main task while attaching importance to demand-side reform and management. It can be seen from the rational synthesis economic model that when both supply-side and demand-side issues are pronounced, it is necessary to advance supply-side reform and demand-side management in a coordinated manner. Demand-side reform is necessary if systems and mechanisms must be improved to solve demand-side issues. The main task of accelerating the creation of a new development pattern is to continuously improve the match between supply and demand.

On the one hand, the strategy of expanding domestic demand must be implemented unswervingly. As China has entered a new stage of development and is pursuing high-quality economic development, domestic demand is always the strategic priority for fostering a new development pattern. Therefore, efforts should be made to further accelerate consumption upgrading, strengthen the protection of consumer rights and interests, and improve the consumption environment. It is also necessary to enhance social security, increase employment, and further tap the consumption potential of low- and middle-income groups. Reform measures such as launching tax reform, increasing investment in education, and facilitating the flow of labor forces should be taken to improve the income distribution structure and expand the middle-income group. On the other hand, it is important to further deepen supply-side reform and better align the supply system with domestic demand, so as to ensure a dynamic equilibrium where demand drives supply and supply creates demand. Efforts should be made to ramp up the transformation and upgrading of the manufacturing sector, and promote the integration of manufacturing and services industries with the internet; accelerate the development of the digital economy, fully tap into its potential, and capitalize on China's advantages to get a head start in this regard.

### 4.3 Discussion on the Theoretical Model of New Structural Economics and the Effectiveness of Industrial Policy

Prof. Justin Yifu Lin's new structural economics studies the structure of an economy and the determinants of structural changes using the methods of modern economics. According to new structural economics, the industrial structures of countries at varying stages of development are inherently determined by their factor endowments, and if the factor endowments are specified at a given point in time, these endowment structures will dictate the industries with comparative advantage at that particular stage of development. Combined with appropriate infrastructure and institutional arrangements, these industries can translate into the country's dominant industries with competitive advantages. In this case, the development structure is deemed as a good structure. Indeed, this theory holds great value. First, it reflects on the limitations of structuralism and neoliberalism, and posits that a well-functioning country or economy must have both an efficient market and a proactive government; that is, the market plays a fundamental role, while the government plays an important role in industrial upgrading and restructuring. Second, it goes beyond the factor endowment theory and comparative advantage theory, but proposes that the factor endowments of an economy at a specific point in time can be used to identify potential industries with comparative advantage, which can translate into dominant industries with competitive advantage. As such, the following conclusions can naturally be drawn: the competitive advantage of a country or an economy is dynamic and variable, and the country or economy can gradually improve total factor productivity through industrial policy and other measures to catch up or overtake another country. This does work with reality. From a historical perspective, if that was not the case, there would not have been the rapid development of the UK at the early stage, let alone the subsequent height of the US. The original comparative advantage theory is inadequate in explaining the success of China's reform and opening up.

New structural economics illustrates pretty clear ideas and policies, but there is still room for improvement in terms of methodology and other aspects. New structural economics is based on the static comparative advantage analysis logic of neoclassical economics, which is unable to explain the dynamic processes of economic structure evolution and economic convergence. This gives the impression of applying a relatively outdated theoretical approach to interpret major economic issues in modern society. Furthermore, based on this logic, it is difficult to develop a robust and effective theoretical model, which consequently deters new structural economics from providing a comprehensive and systematic analysis.

From the perspective of the rational synthesis economic model, we can bring forward a basic approach to construct a theoretical model of new structural economics and provide relatively comprehensive explanations, which is actually a validation of Prof. Justin Yifu Lin's new structural economics. The basic approach to constructing a theoretical model of new structural economics is that the equation for economic growth based on rational synthesis combines the roles of market and government, taking into account the different roles of governments in different countries. This lays the mathematical groundwork for new structural economics. In the context of pure market economics, although the conditions of competition for a certain industry in two countries are basically set, the governments of the two countries can, as international rules permit, adjust the total factor productivity of the industry through macro control to alter the long-term growth trend. They can also build a relationship between supply and demand in favor of industrial development, thereby transforming the competitive advantage of that industry and achieving the goal of catching up. In this way, the comparative advantage theory based on static analysis can extend to the field of the upgrading of the entire industrial structure through factor accumulation and endowment structure changes, thereby turning growth potential into a real-world problem and shifting the focus of study from growth potential to real growth and catch-up.

The competitiveness of a certain industry in two countries is the dynamic result of change in comprehensive advantage, and it is not uncommon that the industry of one country catches up with that of the other. The key to industrial policy lies in properly determining the optimal timing for the withdrawal of policy support. When an industry reaches maturity, industrial policy should be phased out and preferential treatments canceled. This ensures sustained growth of the industry and also prevents overcapacity, ultimately achieving the goal of structural adjustment. Industrial policy can effectively support supply-side reform by fostering new growth drivers and also facilitate economic transformation by exerting an impact on potential economic growth. It can be seen that overcapacity does not prove the failure of industrial policy; on the contrary, industrial policy can drive an industry from its infancy all the way to overcapacity, which exactly testifies to the effectiveness of industrial policy. In this sense, comprehensive use of supply-side reform and demand-side management policies can adjust the potential economic growth rate to a reasonable level and narrow the output gap, thus enabling the country to overcome its current challenges and escape the middle income trap.

### 4.4 Theoretical Discussion on High-quality Development

Economic development theory studies the modernization process of a country's economic and social structures on the basis of economic growth. Ideas about economic development can trace back to the era of classical economics or even earlier, and those early ideas have had a profound impact on modern economic theory. The representative figures and their works include Adam Smith's *The Wealth of Nations*, David Ricardo's *On the Principles of Political Economy and Taxation*, Thomas Robert Malthus's *An Essay on the Principle of Population* and *Principles of Political Economy*, and Karl Marx's *Das Kapital*. After the 1980s, modern economic development theory entered a new stage of development, and new theories and models kept emerging, including new institutionalism, new growth theory, and sustainable development theory. These theories exhibit a new trend toward integration. Although such integration does not equate to complete convergence, it indeed can lead to the generation of new perspectives.

As indicated by the equation for economic growth $Y = A \times F(K, L)$, GDP growth is a complex process that involves both the pace of development and the improvement of total factor productivity. GDP growth is mainly reflected in the pace of development in the short run but manifests in the improvement of economic benefits from a long-term and evolutionary perspective. Economic development refers to the process in which the speed of development and economic benefits are coordinated for the better. If the two are well coordinated, that will signify high-quality development. In contrast, if the sole focus is on increasing quantity without giving due attention to the improvement of benefits, that can be referred to as growth without development. Governments around the world all hope to achieve high-quality economic development by taking effective measures.

The report to the 19th CPC National Congress pointed out that China's economy was transitioning from a stage of high-speed growth to a stage of high-quality development. The fundamental characteristic of the stage of high-speed growth is rapid expansion of quantity, while high-quality development emphasizes the quality and effectiveness of development. The report also highlighted that innovation was the foremost driving force to lead development. Through the equation $Y = A \times F(K, L)$, we can make a clear analysis: if the change in $A$ tends toward zero, it represents simple economic growth; if the change in $A$ exceeds a specified value, it signifies economic development. If the two are coordinated well, it will be in alignment with China's commitment to high-quality development and can guide the economy toward sound development. This is a crucial condition for China to avoid excessive economic turbulence and also gives a good answer to the ongoing debate about economic growth and economic development.

## 5 Empirical Analysis of the Rational Synthesis Economic Model and the Equilibrium Point Between the Roles of Market and Government

### 5.1 *The Equilibrium Point Between the Roles of market and Government Based on the US Data*

According to the rational synthesis economic model, considering the impact of government regulation on the potential output curve in a pure market, we can get:

$$Y_{Gt}^{*} - Y_{Mt}^{*} = \Delta A_t f\left(K_t, L_t\right) = \Delta A_t Y_{Mt}^{*} \tag{4.17}$$

Based on the key equation for macro control, the final economic growth equation can be transformed as below:

$$\Delta Y_t = a\Delta Y_{Mt}^* + b\left(\mu_d + \mu_{ss}\right)\left(Y_t - Y_{Gt}^*\right) + b\mu_{sl}\Delta A_t Y_{Mt}^* + b\left(\varepsilon_{dt} + \varepsilon_{st}\right) \quad (4.18)$$

We try to preliminarily verify the rationality of this model, that is, to prove Eqn. (4.17) on an empirical level. The verification process mainly involves the following three steps:

Step 1. For the stage of an almost pure market economy, verify Eqn. (4.2), that is

$$Y_t^* = f\left(K_t, L_t\right) = \lambda K_t^{\theta} L_t^{1-\theta}$$

Step 2. For the entire historical period, verify Eqn. (4.18), that is

$$\Delta Y_t = a\Delta Y_{Mt}^* + b\left(\mu_d + \mu_{ss}\right)\left(Y_t - Y_{Gt}^*\right) + b\mu_{sl}\Delta A_t Y_{Mt}^* + b\left(\varepsilon_{dt} + \varepsilon_{st}\right)$$

Step 3. Based on the degree of government involvement in the market at different stages, verify Eqn. (4.18) by stage.

Given that the US has a mature system of economic statistics and much higher data availability than that of other countries, we choose to analyze the US data using the indicators outlined in Table 4.2.

1. Stage of almost pure market economy

It should be noted that since the emergence of government, a genuinely pure market economy has never existed. As the government has always had some influence on the economy (for example, through taxation), a country can be said to have an almost pure market economy. Before the Great Depression, the classical school of economic thought dominated economic theory. Classical economists advocated for the free market, believing that the market has an inherent ability to self-regulate through the "invisible hand." Given the weak government intervention, the US had an almost pure market economy before 1930.

We use a nonlinear model to estimate the potential production function based on empirical solutions obtained from economic data including

**Table 4.2** Indicator descriptions

| *Indicator* | *Unit* | *Time Span* | *Description* |
|---|---|---|---|
| Year | Year | | |
| GDP | USD100 million | 1790–2017 | Dependent variable, nominal economic output[a] |
| jiuye | 10,000 persons | 1939–2017 | US non-farm payrolls (total, quarterly, annual)[b] |
| renkou | 10,000 persons | 1790–2017 | US population |
| drenkou | % | 1791–2017 | Annual growth rate of the US population |
| guzi | USD100 million | 1925–2017 | Net fixed assets (current costs; total) in the US |
| diffymt | USD100 million | 1926–2017 | Annual economic growth based on the potential production function |
| hpdata_n | USD100 million | 1925–2017 | GDP after government regulation, results using the HP filter |
| tfp | | 1925–2017 | Total factor productivity |
| preymt | USD100 million | 1925–2017 | Potential economic growth |
| quekou | USD100 million | 1925–2017 | GDP after government regulation |

Source: Compiled by the author

[a]Nominal GDP is adopted based on the following considerations: first, GDP deflator data far back in time is unavailable, so it is difficult to accurately calculate real GDP. Second, we think that despite the short-run validity of the GDP deflator, it may not fully capture the long-term impact of technological advances on prices, potentially distorting the real value and production structure of goods over a long time span (about 100 years)

[b]This indicator is adopted based on the following considerations: first, there is complete data. Second, it is a population-based indicator. Finally, in the industrial society, non-farm payrolls represent the effective labor force brought by technological advances in a pure market economy

nominal GDP, non-farm payrolls (representing effective labor force), and net fixed assets between 1925 and 1929 in the US. With regard to data processing, as countries varied significantly in the time when governments began to intervene in the economy and conduct statistics, there is a severe lack of relevant data during this period. To address this issue, we use the technique of data interpolation to fill in missing data points for non-farm payrolls between 1925 and 1938 based on the relationship among non-farm payrolls, population, and population growth rates from 1939 to 2017 (see Figs. 4.10, 4.11, 4.12, and 4.13). The adjusted *R-squared* value suggests a good fit and the variance inflation factor (VIF) is around 10, indicating no severe multicollinearity.

On this basis, we can get the empirical potential production function:

$$Y_t^* = 0.35K_t^{0.96}L_t^{0.04} \tag{4.19}$$

```
Coefficients:
                   Estimate Std. Error t value Pr(>|t|)    
(Intercept)      -3.320e+03  8.397e+02  -3.954 0.000172 ***
renkou            5.242e-01  3.915e-02  13.389  < 2e-16 ***
drenkou          -1.471e+05  7.277e+04  -2.021 0.046859 *  
renkou:drenkou    8.006e+00  3.832e+00   2.089 0.040056 *  
---
Signif. codes:  0 '***' 0.001 '**' 0.01 '*' 0.05 '.' 0.1 ' ' 1

Residual standard error: 509.4 on 75 degrees of freedom
Multiple R-squared:  0.9805,	Adjusted R-squared:  0.9797 
F-statistic:  1257 on 3 and 75 DF,  p-value: < 2.2e-16
```

**Fig. 4.10** Interpolation of non-farm payroll data between 1925 and 1938. (Source: Compiled by the author)

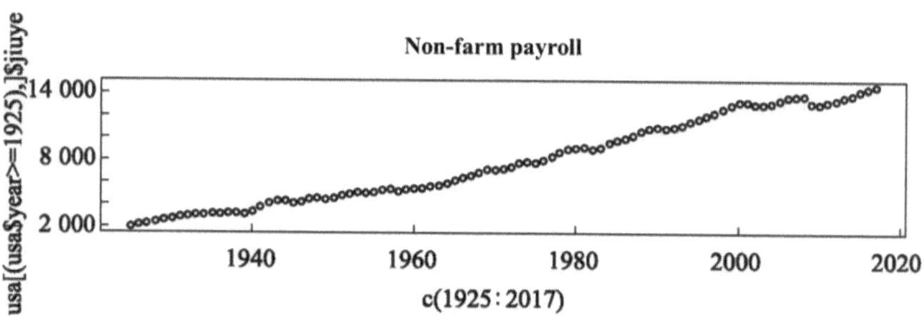


**Fig. 4.11** Trend of non-farm payrolls after data interpolation. (Source: Compiled by the author)

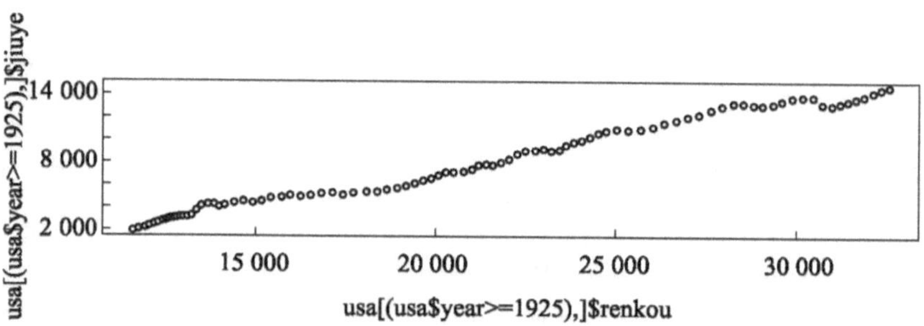


**Fig. 4.12** The relationship between population and non-farm payrolls (after data interpolation). (Source: Compiled by the author)

```
Formula: GDP ~ lambda * (guzi^theta) * ((jiuye)^(1 - theta))

Parameters:
       Estimate Std. Error t value Pr(>|t|)
lambda  0.35129    0.02232   15.74 0.000557 ***
theta   0.95984    0.27660    3.47 0.040343 *
---
Signif. codes:  0 '***' 0.001 '**' 0.01 '*' 0.05 '.' 0.1 ' ' 1

Residual standard error: 28.3 on 3 degrees of freedom

Number of iterations to convergence: 3
Achieved convergence tolerance: 2.673e-06
```

**Fig. 4.13** Model of the potential production function, 1925–1929. (Source: Compiled by the author)

It should be noted that given the unique circumstances of each country, it is not advisable to mechanically apply the empirical potential production function.

2. The entire historical period

Then, we create a data model for the US data from 1925 to 2017 based on the empirical potential production function (4.19) and apply the HP filter to GDP, treating it as GDP after government regulation GDP( $Y_{Gt}^{*}$ ), and the parameter is 6.25 (the empirical value 6.25 is generally used to treat GDP in China).

This model fits well, and the coefficients are statistically significant with high interpretability. During the entire historical period from 1925 to 2017, the contribution ($\alpha$) of potential economic growth to real economic growth reached 0.712 96 (see Fig. 4.14).

3. Analysis by historic stage

Based on economists' research on the policy of the US government, the 1925–2017 period can be divided into three stages.

(1) Stage 1 (1925–1929). As mentioned before, the US suffered the Great Depression around 1929, so the 1925–1929 period is designated as Stage 1. The coefficients in this model are not statistically

```
Call:
lm(formula = diffGDP ~ diffymt + I(GDP - hpdata_n) + I(tfp *
    preymt) - 1, data = data_n)

Residuals:
     Min       1Q   Median       3Q      Max
-2181.86   -29.13    79.79   297.27  2574.31

Coefficients:
                  Estimate Std. Error t value Pr(>|t|)
diffymt            0.71296    0.05108  13.957  < 2e-16 ***
I(GDP - hpdata_n)  0.32669    0.11406   2.864  0.00521 **
I(tfp * preymt)    0.14928    0.02415   6.182 1.87e-08 ***
---
Signif. codes:  0 '***' 0.001 '**' 0.01 '*' 0.05 '.' 0.1 ' ' 1

Residual standard error: 786.3 on 89 degrees of freedom
  (1 observation deleted due to missingness)
Multiple R-squared:  0.942,     Adjusted R-squared:   0.94
F-statistic: 481.4 on 3 and 89 DF,  p-value: < 2.2e-16
```

**Fig. 4.14** Rational synthesis economic model, 1925–2017. (Source: Compiled by the author)

significant, which, we believe, is partly due to a small sample size, and the data is also used in the modeling of the potential production function, resulting in higher variance and potentially affecting the effectiveness of hypothesis testing. It should be noted that the contribution ($a$) of potential economic growth to real economic growth hits 0.865 7 (see Fig. 4.15), a relatively high level. This is in line with the expectations of the "stage of an almost pure market economy."

(2) Stage 2 (1930–1974). In October 1973, the fourth Middle East war broke out, leading to the first international oil crisis. The three-year international oil crisis that lasted till 1975 triggered the most serious global recession after World War II, delivering a heavy blow to the economies of developed countries and dragging them into stagflation. From 1930 to 1974, Keynesian economics was at its peak, and governments generally regulated the economy through demand-side policy.

As for this stage, the rational synthesis economic model exhibits high interpretability. The contribution ($a$) of potential economic growth to real

```
Call:
lm(formula = diffGDP ~ diffymt + I(GDP - hpdata_n) + I(tfp *
    preymt) - 1, data = data_n)

Residuals:
       2        3        4        5
-14.7453  -0.1478   0.3824  23.9009

Coefficients:
                  Estimate Std. Error t value Pr(>|t|)
diffymt             0.8657     0.5185   1.670    0.344
I(GDP - hpdata_n)   1.9081     0.7918   2.410    0.250
I(tfp * preymt)    -2.3496     3.2377  -0.726    0.600

Residual standard error: 28.09 on 1 degrees of freedom
  (1 observation deleted due to missingness)
Multiple R-squared:  0.9192,	Adjusted R-squared:  0.677
F-statistic: 3.794 on 3 and 1 DF,  p-value: 0.3569
```

**Fig. 4.15** Rational synthesis economic model, 1925–1929. (Source: Compiled by the author)

economic growth is 0.616 18 (see Fig. 4.16), and the coefficient (*b*) for change brought about by the role of government is 0.383 82.

(3) Stage 3 (1975–2017). During this stage, neoliberal economics gained support again, with a growing influence on the government intervention in the economy. Representatives of neoliberal economics such as "Reagan's economics" and "Clinton's economics" emerged.

The rational synthesis economic model exhibits high interpretability for this stage. The contribution (*a*) of potential economic growth to real economic growth is 0.713 26 (see Fig. 4.17), and the coefficient (*b*) for change brought about by the role of government is 0.286 74.

Considering the impacts of government intervention on the economy in the entire historical period and by stage (see Table 4.3), the results of this model are in line with expectations. When the sample size reaches a certain level, the overall fitting statistical effect is better for the coefficients of the model. Let's look at the changes in coefficients. From the perspective of the entire historical period, the role of the US market and government on the economy is about 7:3; the government's macro control role

```
Call:
lm(formula = diffGDP ~ diffymt + I(GDP - hpdata_n) + I(tfp *
    preymt) - 1, data = data_n)

Residuals:
    Min      1Q  Median      3Q     Max
-202.62  -30.84   10.96  111.47  220.47

Coefficients:
                  Estimate Std. Error t value Pr(>|t|)
diffymt            0.61618    0.03738  16.486  < 2e-16 ***
I(GDP - hpdata_n)  0.61002    0.18519   3.294  0.00204 **
I(tfp * preymt)    0.35394    0.04303   8.226 3.25e-10 ***
---
Signif. codes:  0 ‘***’ 0.001 ‘**’ 0.01 ‘*’ 0.05 ‘.’ 0.1 ‘ ’ 1

Residual standard error: 116.5 on 41 degrees of freedom
  (1 observation deleted due to missingness)
Multiple R-squared:  0.9463,    Adjusted R-squared:  0.9424
F-statistic: 240.8 on 3 and 41 DF,  p-value: < 2.2e-16
```

**Fig. 4.16** Rational synthesis economic model, 1930–1974. (Source: Compiled by the author)

```
Call:
lm(formula = diffGDP ~ diffymt + I(GDP - hpdata_n) + I(tfp *
    preymt) - 1, data = data_n)

Residuals:
    Min      1Q  Median      3Q     Max
-2176.2  -154.8   392.7   813.8  2572.7

Coefficients:
                  Estimate Std. Error t value Pr(>|t|)
diffymt            0.71326    0.07817   9.125 3.21e-11 ***
I(GDP - hpdata_n)  0.32375    0.17165   1.886 0.066734 .
I(tfp * preymt)    0.14881    0.03670   4.055 0.000232 ***
---
Signif. codes:  0 ‘***’ 0.001 ‘**’ 0.01 ‘*’ 0.05 ‘.’ 0.1 ‘ ’ 1

Residual standard error: 1175 on 39 degrees of freedom
  (1 observation deleted due to missingness)
Multiple R-squared:  0.9424,    Adjusted R-squared:  0.938
F-statistic: 212.8 on 3 and 39 DF,  p-value: < 2.2e-16
```

**Fig. 4.17** Rational synthesis economic model, 1975–2017. (Source: Compiled by the author)

**Table 4.3** Coefficients of the roles of market and government in the US

| *Time span* | *Years* | *Stage* | *Contribution (a) of potential economic growth to actual economic growth* | *Coefficient (b) of change brought about by the role of government* | *F value of the rational synthesis economic model* |
|---|---|---|---|---|---|
| 1925–2017 | 93 | All stages | 0.712 96*** | 0.287 04*** | 481.4*** |
| 1925–1929 | 5 | Stage 1 | 0.865 7 | 0.134 3 | 3.794 |
| 1930–1974 | 45 | Stage 2 | 0.616 18*** | 0.383 82*** | 240.8*** |
| 1975–2017 | 43 | Stage 3 | 0.713 26*** | 0.286 74*** | 212.8*** |

Source: Compiled by the author

Note: *** represent significance levels at 10%, 5%, and 1%, respectively

on the economy has experienced a low, then a high, and then close to a long-term equilibrium state.

The above analysis gives a picture of the evolution of the role of government and that of market in the US economy. Before 1925, the role of the US government stood within the range of 0% to 13%, remaining at low levels for a long time. From 1925 to 1929, the figure went up to approximately 13.4%. From 1930 to 1974, the US government played a greater role in the economy, and Keynesian economies played an important role. During this stage, the government activity index reached about 38.4%, while the market's contribution to real economic growth was 61.6%. At the third stage from 1975 to 2017, neoliberal economics gained support, with a growing influence of government intervention in the economy. Representatives of neoliberal economics such as "Reagan's economics" and "Clinton's economics" emerged. At this stage, the market's contribution to real economic growth hit 71.3%, while the government activity index was 28.7%.

### 5.2 *China's Practices of Macro Control*

China's logic of macro control does not fully align with Keynesian economics, supply-side economics, or other Western economic theories, nor does it completely conform to Marx's theory of supply and demand management through planning. China's logic of macro control is problem-oriented. According to the risks and issues in the economy at different stages, China's government rationally would choose the combination and intensity of supply-side reform and demand-side management. After that, the government would implement appropriate measures, and making proper adjustments based on the implementation outcomes.

Since the reform and opening up in 1978, China's history of macro control can roughly be divided into eight periods, namely, 1979–1981, 1985–1987, 1989–1992, 1993–1997, 1998–2002, 2004–2007, 2008–2011, and from 2014 to the present. In the 1998–2002 period and the 2008–2011 period, macro control was expansionary, that is, expanding domestic demand through proactive fiscal policy. In other periods before 1998, macro control was contractionary policy. And since 2014 macro control has emphasized supply-side structural reform. Overall, these eight rounds of macro control have basically worked well and achieved the expected outcomes.

China's macro control from 1979 to 1992 prioritized supply-side reform, with demand-side management playing a supplementary role. With a focus on economic development, this round of macro control stuck to the basic direction of market-oriented reform, implemented the household responsibility system to release and develop rural productive forces, launched price reforms, and delegated relevant decision-making power to the market to increase the productivity of enterprises. During this period, the emphasis of supply-side reform was to release productive forces through market-oriented reform, and the emphasis of demand side management was to adjust the investment structure and curb excessive consumption according to the economic conditions, so as to restore an equilibrium between aggregate supply and demand.

China's macro control from 1993 to 2007 prioritized demand-side management, with supply-side reform playing a supplementary role. The surge in investment after 1992 contributed to an increase in economic output. During this period, the focus of demand-side management was on domestic demand, but inflation caused by price hikes of upstream products to some extent resulted in an overheating economy. In order to curb inflation without greatly undermining economic growth and to achieve a "soft landing" for the economy, the main growth driver after 1997 was to further release the dividends of institutional reform. At that time, China's economic development transitioned to a "dual-driver" model of upgrading the domestic consumption structure and encouraging external demand through demand-side management. Thus, China's economic development was alternately propelled by external demand and the upgrading of the domestic consumption structure, and government-led infrastructure investment played a vital role. As can be seen from the characteristics of macro control in this phase, demand-side management focused on intervening in and regulating short-term economic fluctuations, while also playing a key role in smoothing out excessive economic fluctuations.

China's macro control from 2008 to 2011 was dominated by demand-side management against the special background of the 2008 international financial crisis. As the global economy was stuck in a deep recession, China's 4 trillion yuan stimulus package and large-scale infrastructure construction played an important role in keeping the economy stable. In 2009, China set the macro control objectives to "expand domestic demand, maintain growth, adjust economic structure, and focus on people's livelihoods" and adopted a proactive fiscal policy and a moderately easy monetary policy, which showed the characteristic of Keynesian economics. Demand-side stimulus prevented China from falling into a deep recession because of the international financial crisis and achieved notable results. On the flip side, although this strategy spared China from an economic deceleration at the time, it resulted in the issues of redundant investment and overcapacity, bringing about long-term risks in the fiscal and financial systems.

The latest round of macro control since 2014 has been centered on supply-side reform while moderately expanding aggregate demand. On November 10, 2015, Chinese President Xi Jinping for the first time proposed the concept of "supply-side structural reform" at the 11th meeting of the then Central Financial and Economic Leading Group. Supply-side structural reform was defined as an initiative "to adjust structures through reform, reduce ineffective and lower-end supply while increasing effective and medium- and high-end supply, make supply structure more adaptive and flexible to changes in demand, and increase total factor productivity, so the supply system is more adaptable to changes in the demand structure." The main tasks are to cut overcapacity, reduce excess inventory, deleverage, lower costs, and shore up weaknesses. Unlike demand management in Keynesian economics, supply-side shocks from government action can influence both short-term economic fluctuations and long-term economic growth or development. Under the new normal, China is seeing a slowdown in economic growth, and the economic structure needs to be further adjusted. Given the new developments and changes, the government needs to act quickly to adjust the perspective and means of macro control, and the emphasis of macro control needs to transfer from demand regulation to supply-side structural reform. Therefore, based on China's actual situation, supply-side structural reform at this stage can increase potential economic growth and promote economic transformation and upgrading by improving total factor productivity, thus achieving the dual purposes of economic growth and economic restructuring.

In its practices of macro control, China attaches great importance to the art of regulation. First, in terms of guiding principles, China adopts a global vision and strategic perspective; exercises macro control from the perspective of development and adheres to the general principle of pursuing progress while ensuring stability; considers worst-case scenarios and works to maintain steady growth and forestalls systemic risks; gets better at thinking creatively and focuses macro control efforts on improving the quality of economic growth; takes a global perspective and sees it as an important goal of macro control to achieve the coordinated development of the domestic economy and global economy. Second, flexible regulation methods are adopted. For example, in terms of regulation methods, range-based regulation, targeted regulation, and a combination of the two are implemented. Counter- and cross-cyclical adjustments are also significant innovations. Third, the objectives of macro control have been enriched, and a new indicator system has been formed in practice.

The theory of macro control is the fruit of China's successful practices of macro control, an innovative development of macroeconomic theory, and also a significant contribution China has made to economic theory innovation, with the potential to propel more breakthroughs in macroeconomic theory. Such exploration is the important practice and theory innovation of the government by allowing the "visible hand" to better play its role. The construction of theoretical models for macro control and those for supply-side structural reform lays solid groundwork for innovation in macro control theory. China's successful practices are not only a crucial keystone for the innovative development of macro control theory, but also a testing ground for verifying the effectiveness of macro control theory. We believe that innovation in macro control theory born out of China's practices has extensive applicability that extends well beyond the Chinese context, and can provide an inspiration for the economic development practices of other countries.

CHAPTER 5

# Economic Growth Theory: Evolution, Change, and New Perspective

In the realm of economic theory research, economic growth theory occupies a significant position. First and foremost, economic growth is crucial for the improvement of human social welfare (Barro et al., 2004). Secondly, the temporal sustainability and spatial variability of economic growth captivate economists. It is no wonder that American economist Lucas (1988a) once remarked: "Once you start thinking about economic growth, it's hard to think about anything else." Over the long term, economic growth theory has undergone rapid development and yielded abundant results amidst its ups and downs, although there remain some areas that are less than satisfactory. This chapter will explore the developmental trajectory, key advancements, and future directions of economic growth theory.

In fact, the development of economic growth theory is intertwined with the evolution of economic theory. Adam Smith's *The Wealth of Nations* can be regarded as the foundational work of it. Marx, within the framework of his political economy theory, was among the earliest to propose corresponding economic growth theories. Economic growth theory-has experienced two major stages: classical theory and modern theory. Some commentators believe that Ramsey's (1928) paper divides economic growth theory into two stages: the former stage, generally viewed as classical growth theory, and the latter stage, generally viewed as modern growth theory. Other commentators argue that Keynes's *General Theory* markes the separation between classical and modern growth theory. Broadly speaking, modern growth theory can be divided into three



Z. Liang, *The Innovation of Economic Theory in China*,
https://doi.org/10.1007/978-981-95-2713-7_5

developmental stages: the first stage is represented by the Harrod-Domar model; the second stage is represented by the Solow economic growth model; and the third stage (the current stage) is represented by new growth theory models.

## 1 The Connotation and Basic Research Issues of Economic Growth Theory

Economic growth theory primarily focuses on the factors influencing economic growth and the underlying principles governing it. Economic growth is reflected in the increasing total output of goods and services produced by a country or region.

### *1.1 The Connotation of Economic Growth Theory*

Economic growth is typically manifested as an increase in gross domestic product (GDP) or per capita GDP. Thus, the economic growth level of an economy can be measured by the average growth rate of GDP or per capita GDP over a specific period. The corresponding equation is:

$$\mathrm{GDP}_t = \mathrm{GDP}_b\left(1+\mathrm{r}\right)^n$$

Wherein, $\mathrm{GDP}_t$ is the GDP at the end of period $t$, $\mathrm{GDP}_b$ is the GDP at the end of the base period, $n$ is the number of years from the base period to the end period, and $r$ is the average growth rate.

To avoid the effects of price changes, GDP or per capita GDP is usually adjusted for price changes and calculated using constant prices. In other words, the economic growth of an economy can be measured by the annual growth rate of GDP after adjusting for price changes.

Economic growth theory primarily investigates the intrinsic causes of economic growth and the fundamental laws governing it, focusing on understanding the patterns of actual economic growth and the driving forces behind sustained economic growth. The former emphasizes the outcomes of economic growth, while the latter analyzes the main factors influencing economic growth and quantitatively assesses the contribution of different factors to economic growth. Various economic growth models aim to analyze the laws of economic growth from different perspectives and explain the driving sources that promote economic growth. Generally speaking, the main factors influencing economic growth include:

1. Technological constraints: The level of technology directly affects production efficiency.
2. Resource constraints: These include capital stock, labor supply, natural resources, etc.
3. Institutional constraints: Institutions significantly impact income distribution, labor methods, labor organization, and the circulation of materials and commodities, setting the boundaries for economic operations.

### *1.2 Basic Issues in Economic Growth Theory*

The concept of "equilibrium" holds significant importance in economic growth theory. Equilibrium is a core concept in mainstream modern economics; hence, modern growth theory is also built on the framework of equilibrium analysis. In Arrow-Debreu's static general equilibrium, the equilibrium concept inherits Walras's equilibrium connotation. However, the Arrow-Debreu model construction method is suitable for illustrating static general equilibrium.

The evolution of the equilibrium concept from static to dynamic conditions began in the 1960s. This work not only contributed to dynamizing the equilibrium concept but also led to the emergence of the rational expectations school (actual economic cycle school) by dynamizing the equilibrium concept. Historically, Hayek and Myrdal initiated such pioneering research early on. Subsequently, economists such as Hicks, Harrod, Lucas, and Prescott introduced the concept of expectations into their research, extending the equilibrium concept to the dynamic study of economic growth. In static general equilibrium models, achieving equilibrium means all markets have achieved supply-demand balance, leaving no room for Pareto improvement. In modern economic growth models, achieving equilibrium signifies that the entire economy has achieved equality between aggregate supply and aggregate demand.

The notion of "equilibrium" in economic growth theory already embodies the characteristic of "optimality." When the macroeconomy reaches equilibrium, it has achieved the full utilization of all production factors, leaving no room for Pareto improvement, which is evidently "optimal."

Thus, the "growth" in economic growth theory refers to what is commonly called "balanced growth," and the theory itself isolates an important characteristic from a theoretical perspective—that the market mechanism can always reach an optimal clearing state. Consequently, modern growth theory based on this assumption indeed considers that economic growth under equilibrium conditions is optimal, not only achieving static optimality at a certain point in time but also achieving optimality over time. However, economic growth should be a dynamic process, so only by evolving the concept of static equilibrium to dynamic equilibrium can in-depth research on economic growth be conducted, which is inherently a paradox.

### *1.3 Potential Economic Growth and Actual Economic Growth*

These seemingly simple concepts actually pose significant issues that require deep contemplation: Are the actual economic growth rate and the potential economic growth rate equivalent? Mainstream economic growth theory often focuses on the potential economic growth rate, but is this always appropriate? Nobel laureate in economics, Kuznets, points out in his speech: "A country's economic growth may be defined as a long-term rise in the capacity to supply increasingly diverse economic goods to its population. This growing capacity is based on advancing technology and the institutional and ideological adjustments that it demands." The potential economic growth rate represents the process of a country's production possibility frontier continuously moving outward, indicating an increase in productive capacity, but this is merely quantitative growth. In contrast, actual economic growth is calculated based on actual output at constant prices. Thus, actual economic growth and potential economic growth are fundamentally different, and in some cases, the gap between them is significant. Potential is merely potential and does not equate to actual performance. Moreover, the potential economic growth rate cannot be directly measured.

## 2 Evolution of Economic Growth Theory

### 2.1 *The Foundational Stage of Economic Growth Theory: Classical Growth Theory*

Classical growth theory encompasses the paradigms of classical economics and neoclassical economics. Figures such as Adam Smith, Malthus, Ricardo, and Marx can be seen as representatives of classical growth theory. As early as the eighteenth century, Adam Smith proposes in *The Wealth of Nations* the important idea that economic growth stems from capital accumulation and the division of labor. He points out that capital accumulation facilitates the specialization of production, while the emergence of division of labor further promotes capital accumulation, with both processes mutually reinforcing each other to drive economic growth. In the late eighteenth century, Malthus demonstrated the relationship between population growth and economic development. Ricardo emphasizes that under constraints of capital and labor, national welfare can be enhanced through the development of international trade and the exploitation of comparative advantage, which inherently includes ideas promoting economic growth. Marx's theoretical framework, centered on the labor theory of value and the surplus value theory, became a significant component of classical economics. Schumpeter highlighted "creative destruction," emphasizing the role of innovation in economic growth, while Allyn Young underscored "Smith's theorem," which can be seen as part of the neoclassical economics paradigm of economic growth theory.

However, it should also be noted that while classical economics contributed profound ideas on economic growth, it lacked comprehensive economic growth models. Classical economics had a relatively vague approach to macroeconomic studies and did not propose a distinct economic growth theory; it only provided thoughts on economic growth and development. *The Wealth of Nations* explores the sources of economic growth, encapsulated in the idea that "land is the father of wealth, labor is the mother of wealth," implying that labor and land are the two critical production factors for creating wealth and promoting economic growth. Marx's labor theory of value suggests that labor is the sole cause of wealth creation, and increases in both the quantity and quality of labor lead to economic growth, driven by technological progress and deeper social division of labor. Consequently, specialized production and technological advancement are essential for promoting economic growth and development. Classical economics did not achieve a scientific or quantitative approach to macroeconomic theory, and its understanding of economic growth and macroeconomics was largely empirical. While classical economists such as Adam Smith, Malthus, and Ricardo were outstanding pioneers in the study of economic growth theory, their research generally focusing on the analysis of the influencing factors and processes of economic growth without conducting quantitative analysis through modeling. Mathematical modeling has become a hallmark of modern growth theory. However, it is important to note that the emergence of the neoclassical economics paradigm marked a significant shift in focus toward "static market equilibrium," guided by Marshall's direction of "equilibrium prices where supply equals demand." This shift led to the disappearance of economic growth theory from the neoclassical economic perspective, a controversial change in direction. In fact, it is economists outside the neoclassical school, like Young and Schumpeter, who have proposed significant economic growth theories. Thus, the neoclassical economics period was a low point for economic growth theory.

### 2.2 *The Mature Stage of Economic Growth Theory: Modern Economic Growth Theory*

When did modern growth theory begin? There are differing opinions within the academic community. Some scholars believe that the starting point of modern growth theory was Frank Ramsey's "A Mathematical Theory of Saving," published in the *Economic Journal* in 1928. In the 1960s and 1970s, Koopmans and Cass used Ramsey's model paradigm to give a neoclassical reinterpretation of the Solow economic growth model. However, other scholars argue that the Harrod-Domar model marked the beginning of modern growth theory. This model aimed to dynamize Keynesian theory by incorporating economic growth into short-term analysis and discussing the significant role of capital accumulation. Broadly speaking, the development of modern economic theory has gone through three major peaks.

The first peak occurred in the 1940s when Keynesian economists like Harrod and Domar sought to extend and dynamize Keynes's short-term analysis, leading economic growth theory into a new era. This undoubtedly marked an important milestone in the gradual maturation of economic growth theory, indicating that mainstream economists began to pay more attention to this field. The theory posits that the economic growth rate is influenced by the capital-output ratio and the savings rate. To achieve sustained economic growth, the growth rate needs to match the guaranteed growth rate determined by the collective will of capitalists and the natural growth rate that can achieve sustained full employment. The Harrod-Domar model points out that the coincidence of these growth rates is merely accidental, making long-term stable economic growth difficult to achieve in a capitalist market economy, often accompanied by significant fluctuations. In the long run, it is very challenging to maintain balanced growth with full employment, and once deviated from the path of balanced growth, the economy finds it difficult to self-correct, possibly leading to even greater fluctuations.

The second peak occurred in the mid-1940s when Robert Solow and Swan proposed the landmark neoclassical growth model, sparking a wave of research on economic growth theory. Many Western economists were dissatisfied with the conclusions and implications of the Harrod-Domar model and believed that substantial revisions were needed. Solow and Swan argued that the Harrod-Domar model's assumption that labor and capital are non-substitutable, making the capital-output ratio a fixed value, was a major flaw. Solow and others hypothesized that capital and labor were substitutable and developed the Solow model based on this premise. This model suggested that the capitalist market mechanism could facilitate long-term stable growth, a conclusion of significant importance.

The Solow model highlighted the indispensable role of technological progress, asserting that without technological advancements, economic growth would reach a steady state and eventually stagnate. However, with continuous technological progress, especially if it is Harrod-neutral, the macroeconomy could sustain growth. This model, rooted in the neoclassical economics paradigm, aligned with the rising trend of neoliberalism, quickly replaced the Harrod-Domar model and became the mainstream theory in Western economics.

The third peak began in the 1980s, represented by economists like Romer and Lucas. This wave led to the rise of endogenous growth theory. In the Solow model, technological progress is exogenous and unexplained by the model, which is a significant shortcoming of economic growth theory. Endogenous growth theory posits that technological progress is endogenous to the economic growth process, thus offering an important correction to the Solow model and forming the theoretical foundation of the "knowledge economy." This theory casts doubt on the market economy's ability to ensure that economic growth always follows the optimal path and suggests that appropriate government intervention would be beneficial for maintaining economic growth, as relying solely on the market might result in inefficient growth.

Overall, compared to classical growth theory, modern growth theoryexhibits two new characteristics: first, in terms of research methods, unlike the diverse approaches of the classical growth theory period, modern growth theory emphasizes standardized, mainstream, and mathematical methods in its evolution, fostering a tradition of focusing on optimal decision-making by microeconomic agents and dynamic analysis. Second, in terms of research conclusions, unlike the diverse conclusions of classical growth theory, modern growth theory's conclusions demonstrate good comparability and extensibility, allowing different explanations of the sources of economic growth to be judged by comparing different production functions. Thus, different economic growth theories can be more easily compared, facilitating further in-depth development of economic growth theory on the existing foundation.

## 3 The Development and Literature Review of Modern Growth Theory

The research of Harrod and Domar marked the beginning of the modelization of modern growth theory, reviving the study of economic growth within mainstream economics. Subsequently, the Solow neoclassical growth model and related endogenous growth models responded to the rise of neoliberalism since the 1970s.

### *3.1 Marx's Economic Growth Theory*

Reviewing the history of economic thought, Marx was the first to dynamize static analysis and the first to extend short-term analysis into the long term. On this basis, he constructed an economic growth theory that provided significant inspiration for later Western mainstream economists. Marx focused on the crucial issue of the reproduction of total social capital, pioneering the construction of a scientific theoretical framework that emphasizes the circulation and reproduction of total social capital. He also studied critical issues such as how the total social product should be compensated in both physical and value forms. Marx conducted a scientific and rigorous systematic study of total social production, proposing objective laws of reproduction that are significant for both socialist and capitalist societies. His method of long-term dynamic analysis and the resultant economic growth theory have profoundly influenced the development of modern growth theory.

### *3.2 The Harrod-Domar Model*

It is well known that Harrod and Domar have proposed the first mathematical model in the history of Western economic growth theory, a milestone achievement. Shortly after the Great Depression of 1929–1933, the Harrod-Domar model emerged, abstracting the problem of economic growth into a functional relationship among three macroeconomic variables: the economic growth rate, the savings rate, and the capital-output ratio. According to the Harrod-Domar model, a country's economic growth rate is positively influenced by the savings rate, which determines the level of total societal investment, and negatively influenced by the capital-output ratio. In a sense, the Harrod-Domar model extended Keynesian equilibrium theory into the long term. This is significant as it constructed an economic growth model from the perspective of government intervention. According to Keynes's short-term national economic equilibrium theory, $Y = C + I = C + S$, where $Y$ represents national income, the two $C$ terms represent consumption expenditure and actual consumption, $I$ represents investment expenditure, and $S$ represents savings. Since the two $C$ terms are identical, the simple condition for achieving national economic equilibrium is $I = S$, meaning savings equal investment. Based on Keynesian theory, this result holds. So, what is the long-term economic growth rate? The logic of the Harrod-Domar model is to extend Keynes's short-term model into the long term, where the long-term economic growth rate is $S/V$, with $S$ representing new investment and $V$ representing the output rate of assets, thus deriving the economic growth rate.

The Harrod-Domar model provided a simple equation: economic growth rate = new investment / capital-output ratio. This can be considered the core idea of the Harrod-Domar model. In practice, achieving stable economic growth requires satisfying a series of conditions, namely that the warranted growth rate, the actual growth rate, and the natural growth rate should be equal. At this point, the macroeconomy can achieve stable, sustained growth. The actual economic growth rate is achieved when savings equal investment, determined by the societal savings rate given a fixed capital-output ratio. The warranted growth rate refers to the growth rate desired by capital. The basic economic implication of this equation is that the economic growth rate grows to the point where the return on capital equals the cost of capital. Another growth rate is the natural growth rate, which is allowed by population growth. Harrod and Domar explained this model by stating that when the actual growth rate exceeded the warranted growth rate, economic growth would decelerate because the marginal efficiency of capital became negative; and when the warranted growth rate exceeded the natural growth rate, labor supply fell short and wages rised sharply, leading to inflation, and consequently, the economic growth rate declined.

The Harrod-Domar model holds milestone significance in the history of economic thought: first, it rigorously analyzed the factors influencing economic growth using a mathematical model; second, it emphasized the decisive role of the savings rate, or capital accumulation rate, in economic growth. This aspect has been cited by many theorists and seen in policy practice cases in China for a long period. However, the Harrod-Domar model also has many shortcomings, the most significant being overly strict assumptions that are far from reality. According to their model, any economy would experience continuous fluctuations, which does not align with actual conditions. The Harrod-Domar model is based on a series of assumptions: first, a fixed capital-output coefficient, implying non-substitutability between capital and labor; second, the production of only one product in society; third, no technological progress; fourth, savings always equal investment. These assumptions have some inadequacies: first, assuming a fixed capital-output ratio implies a constant technological state, without considering technological progress or capital depreciation, which is clearly unreasonable; second, considering only labor and capital as production factors in the production process, with no substitutability between them. Evidently, this production process lacks a reasonable micro economic foundation and is far from the actual production process. Although achieving simultaneous full employment of capital and labor in the Harrod-Domar model is challenging, leading to what is known as the "knife-edge" problem in the economic growth process, it is important to note that this model marks the beginning of using mathematical models to explain and study economic growth issues in the field of economics, holding milestone significance in the development of economic growth theory.

### 3.3 *Solow's Economic Growth Theory and Related Neoclassical Growth Theory*

As a benchmark reference model for many current theories, the classic Solow model considers a series of assumptions: first, it acknowledges Say's Law, which suggests that supply can automatically create demand; second, it assumes an economic model with homogeneous characteristics; third, it presupposes that capital and labor are completely substitutable. This model uses the Cobb-Douglas function as its production function:

$$Y = A \times F(K,L) = K^{\alpha} \times (AL)^{1-\alpha}$$

In this production function, the dependent variable is total output, while the independent variables are capital and labor, with the sum of the exponents of capital and labor equaling 1. In the Harrod-Domar model, economic growth is volatile and difficult to sustain in the long term. However, in the Solow model, the assumption of substitutability between capital and labor ensures stable economic growth. The Solow model delves into the impact of the growth of capital or labor stock on economic growth: if the total amount of labor remains unchanged but the capital stock increases, then the per capita capital stock will also increase, thus promoting economic growth; conversely, if the capital stock decreases, more labor can be invested in economic operations to stimulate growth.

According to this model, under market mechanism adjustments, it is always possible to achieve an equilibrium state where the economic growth rate, the marginal output of labor per unit, and the marginal output of capital per unit are equal. At this equilibrium, both capital and labor are fully utilized, and there is no exploitation in distribution. In the history of modern growth theory development, Solow's economic growth model holds a significant position, for which Solow was awarded the Nobel Prize in Economics. This model introduced modern mathematical tools into economic modeling and cleverly used the Cobb-Douglas production function as the starting point for analysis. The main contributions of the Solow model are as follows:

1. Influenced by this model, the neoclassical production function became a benchmark production function in modern growth theory, having a profound impact.

2. The model posits that the entire economy is in a state of dynamic general equilibrium, profoundly influencing subsequent theoretical development.
3. The model endogenizes labor productivity under given exogenous technological levels and introduces the famous total factor productivity representing the level of technology.

The Solow model's assumption of substitutability between labor and capital effectively resolves the "knife-edge" problem present in the Harrod-Domar model. However, the Solow model also has notable shortcomings: first, it suggests that high per capita capital stock in wealthy countries will lead to lower returns on capital, prompting capital to flow from rich to poor countries, which does not fully align with reality. Second, the Solow model predicts that a country's economic growth will converge to a balanced growth path but does not explain whether different countries will converge to the same equilibrium or what causes differences in equilibrium paths between countries. In this economic growth model, technology's influence on growth is still considered an exogenous variable; it views technological progress as given exogenously, attempting to explain economic growth through the assumption of "assumed economic growth," which makes it challenging to account for the true source of long-term economic growth. Furthermore, according to this model, economic downturns do not occur; however, in reality, Western developed countries have experienced multiple recessions since the publication of the Solow model.

### 3.4 New Growth Theory

In the mid-1980s, new growth theory emerged, represented by economists such as Paul Romer and Robert Lucas. This resurgence marked a new peak in the development of economic growth theory after nearly two decades of stagnation. A significant highlight of this theory is its expansion of the "labor" concept in the neoclassical growth model from merely the quantity of labor and the average level of technology in a country to include education levels, collaboration abilities, and production skills, collectively termed "human capital."

Paul Romer (1990) has first proposed the endogenous growth model of technological progress, characterized by the following points: first, it emphasizes that the core of economic growth is technological progress.

Second, it asserts that most technological progress is actively obtained by market micro-entities under the incentives of the market mechanism. Third, it considers the cost of knowledge products to be the expenses incurred during development, and once developed, knowledge products can be reused with a marginal cost of zero. In the new growth model, the dependent variable of the production function is total output $Y$, and the independent variables include capital $K$, labor $L$, human capital $H$, and technological progress $t$, expressed as $Y = F(K, L, H, t)$. The first generation of endogenous growth theory emphasizes that the technological progress and diffusion obtained from capital investment effectively resolve the dilemma of diminishing marginal returns on capital, making capital the core factor and driving force of economic growth. Arrow and Romer hypothesize that knowledge is a by-product of the production process, and Romer argues that knowledge can be separated in different uses, ensuring its exclusivity as a commodity, while externalities ensure sustained economic growth.

In addition to the Romer model, the Lucas model, and the Grossman-Helpman model, other scholars have proposed new growth theories from different perspectives. For example, Aghion and Howitt (1992) have developed an endogenous growth model of imitation and creative destruction, King and Robson (1993) have proposed a knowledge diffusion endogenous growth model, and Young (1991) has presented an international trade endogenous growth model. While these theories differ, they share similar ideas, namely that the ultimate driving force of economic growth originates from enterprises. These models analyze how enterprises accumulate knowledge achievements, including human capital and innovative technologies, mainly reflected in the increase in human capital, improvement in product quality, and production of new products. Meanwhile, these theories generally hold that the process of knowledge creation and accumulation requires appropriate government intervention. Although economic growth theory, built on neoclassical economics, has developed into new growth theory, it still implicitly assumes exogenous technological levels and denies increasing returns to scale. Like the Solow model, if the sole driver of economic growth is understood as an exogenous variable, such a theory is undoubtedly unsatisfactory. The economic thoughts and core features of this theory are threefold: first, almost all new growth theories use Solow's growth model as their analytical starting point. Second, they establish modern economic models to demonstrate their theories. Third, they believe that factors such as institutions, education, and technology should be included in the models, commonly recognizing technology as a crucial factor influencing economic growth.

Entering the 1990s, academic research on endogenous growth theory continued to advance, leading to new progress. Economic growth models attempted to construct models that endogenize total factor productivity and further improve existing endogenous growth models. This development is evident in two directions. The first direction involves exploring the relationship between technological progress and market structure (e.g., Aghion and Howitt, 1998). For instance, this includes relying on direct research on knowledge to accumulate technology, exploring externalities from capital investment, and internalizing total factor productivity in the Solow model through the production and accumulation of human capital. The second direction analyzes the interrelationship between economic growth and economic structural changes. For example, John Laitner (2000) proposes that during industrialization, a country's savings rate would endogenously rise, leading to changes in the economic growth rate. Essentially, this explores the role and impact of industrial policy on economic growth.

### *3.5 Economic Growth Conclusions Under the New Keynesian DSGE Model*

Due to obstacles in price adjustments in reality, changes in money supply have real effects. Dynamic Stochastic General Equilibrium (DSGE) models attempt to extend the micro foundation of imperfect price flexibility to dynamic macroeconomic growth. Common pricing models in New Keynesian DSGE models include the Calvo pricing model, predetermined price models (such as the Fischer model), fixed price models (such as the Taylor model), and state-dependent pricing models like the Caplin-Spulber model. These pricing models seek to explain the real impact of imperfect price flexibility on the economy from a microeconomic perspective. For example, both the Fischer model and the Taylor model assume that wages or prices are determined by multi-period contracts or commitments, and in each period, a proportion of these contracts terminate or renew. Thus, the core conclusion of these models is that multi-period contracts lead to gradual adjustments in the price level to nominal disturbances, resulting in persistent real effects from aggregate demand shocks.

Consider a standard three-equation New Keynesian DSGE model, which includes the following three basic equations: the New Keynesian IS curve illustrates the negative relationship between interest rates and output, the New Keynesian Phillips curve demonstrates the positive relationship between inflation and output, and the forward-looking central bank interest rate rule is based on the Taylor rule. Here, $u^{IS}$, $u^{\pi}$ and $u^{MP}$ represent demand shocks, inflation shocks, and monetary policy shocks, respectively.

$$y_t = E_t\left(y_{t+1}\right) - \frac{1}{\theta} \times r_t + u_t^{IS} \qquad \theta > 0$$

$$\pi_t = \beta E_t\left(\pi_{t+1}\right) + ky_t + u_t^{\pi} \qquad 0 < \beta 1, \kappa 0$$

$$r_t = \phi_{\pi} E_t\left(\pi_{t+1}\right) + \phi_t E_t\left(y_{t+1}\right) + u_t^{MP} \qquad \phi_{\pi} > 0, \phi_t \geq 0$$

Assuming that exogenous shocks follow an AR (1) process and degenerate into white noise disturbances, the simplest solutions are drawn from this model as follows:

$$y_t = u_t^{IS} - \frac{1}{\theta} \times u_t^{MP}$$

$$\pi_t = \kappa u_T^{IS} + u_t^{\pi} - \frac{\kappa}{\theta} \times u_t^{MP}$$

$$r_t = u_t^{MP}$$

From this, three clear conclusions can be drawn:

1. Monetary policy shocks can have real effects. Specifically, a contractionary monetary policy shock will reduce both total output and inflation.
2. Demand shocks also have real effects. Specifically, a positive aggregate demand shock will increase output and the inflation rate but will not affect interest rates because monetary policy is forward-looking.
3. Positive aggregate supply shocks or inflation shocks will only increase the inflation rate without affecting real output or real interest rates.

## 4 Developments, Limitations, and Outlook of Modern Growth Theory

Modern growth theory has made breakthrough progress in both theory and modeling over nearly a century of development. However, whether it is the Harrod-Domar model, the Solow model, the neoclassical growth models developed from Keynesianism, or the new growth theory, there are certain limitations accompanying these significant breakthroughs. Since the progress of these theories has already been introduced earlier, this section will focus on analyzing the major breakthroughs of the new growth theory.

### 4.1 *Major Breakthroughs of New Growth Theory*

1. Endogeneity of Economic Growth: New growth theory posits that economic growth is endogenous, primarily a product of endogenous technological change. It offers a detailed analysis of the mechanisms for achieving technological progress, demonstrating that knowledge accumulation and technological progress are decisive factors for economic growth, thereby filling a gap in economic theory. This theory regards technology as a core component of the economic system, being "endogenous," thus enabling government policies to influence human behavior. New growth theory argues that the focus of government policy should be on promoting long-term economic growth rather than on addressing economic cycles. Technological progress can enhance investment returns, and new investments can further augment the value of technological progress, creating a virtuous cycle that continuously drives economic growth.
2. Acknowledgment of Government Policy's Role: Unlike neoclassical growth theory, new growth theory revisits the role of government in economic development. It proposes a series of policy recommendations for achieving long-term sustained economic growth. New growth theory holds that market forces alone are insufficient to maximize societal innovation efficiency, and thus government intervention is justified and necessary to enhance economic growth rates. Governments should focus on supporting policies conducive to technological advancement, such as protecting intellectual property

rights, supporting research and development, and fostering education.

New growth theory acknowledges the existence of market failures and the potential role of government in addressing these issues, representing a progressive step. However, it cannot completely escape the fundamental principles of Western economics, still adopting the dynamic general equilibrium method, which limits the extent of its advancements. The theory acknowledges the imperfections of market mechanisms, due to externalities or monopolies, making it difficult for the macroeconomy to grow along the optimal path. Therefore, it seeks to leverage government intervention to address these market deficiencies. The theory aims to achieve optimal growth in a capitalist market economy through government intervention, but views the role of the government as supplementary, non-independent, and limited.

3. Focus on the Role of Knowledge: Incorporating human capital, knowledge, and other endogenous factors into economic growth models is a significant breakthrough and highlight of new growth theory. Additionally, this theory assumes that the marginal returns on factors may be increasing, implying that the rate of return on capital can remain constant or even increase, allowing for sustained growth in per capita output. The model holds that technological progress is not an exogenous variable independent of economic theory. Human societies can promote economic development by investing in technological progress.

### 4.2 *Limitations of Modern Economic Growth Theory*

1. Dynamic vs. Static Models: In a world that is entirely unbalanced, why must we seek an economic growth theory under "equilibrium" and then laboriously make it dynamic? The issue of dynamizing economic growth models itself is a problem. Is it necessary to follow the path of first establishing static models and then expanding them? Or can corresponding dynamic models be directly constructed?
2. Preference for Potential over Actual Economic Growth: Given that actual economic growth is the best research object, why do scholars favor potential economic growth? Existing models aim to derive bal-

anced growth paths, where each point on the path corresponds to an equilibrium state at a specific time, implying that the balanced growth path is not purely dynamic. In reality, factor markets and consumer goods markets do not always clear, and total production often does not occur in equilibrium. Hence, the paths derived from models greatly diverge from actual situations, making current economic growth models unrealistic. Potential economic growth rates differ from actual economic growth rates and are more theoretical concepts. Mainstream economic growth theory today primarily explores theoretical potential economic growth rates, often deduced from actual figures. Additionally, mainstream economic growth theory focuses mainly on potential economic growth rates or long-term economic growth, while paying relatively less attention to short-term economic fluctuations, a limitation that has existed since the existence of the Solow model.

3. Government's Role in Economic Growth: The existing economic growth models generally construct production functions from the perspective of production factors to study the aggregate supply from the supply side, seldom considering the combined effects of market and government on aggregate supply. This means the government's influence on aggregate supply and aggregate demand is often neglected. Given the clear and real impact of government policies on actual economic growth, they should have a defined role in the models. A reasonable approach would be to reflect Keynesian theories about the government's role in economic growth within these models.

### *4.3 Scientific Considerations on Endogenous and Exogenous Factors*

Neoclassical growth theory employs the Cobb-Douglas function as its production function, uses labor input and capital input as independent variables to establish an economic growth model, and considers technological progress an exogenous variable. This theory concludes that due to diminishing marginal returns, long-term economic growth will encounter bottlenecks. In contrast, endogenous growth theory, which emerged in the 1990s, posits that endogenous factors are critical to explaining long-term economic growth. It suggests that the accumulation of capital encompasses activities such as research and development and innovative inventions, leading to technological progress, while labor input includes human capital accumulated through education, on-the-job learning, and training, thereby internalizing technological progress. This theory posits that continuous technological progress may result in increasing returns on factors, leading to a positive long-term economic growth rate. Many economists recognize the crucial role of technological progress and human capital in promoting economic growth but still consider technological progress as an exogenous factor. New growth theory internalizes technological progress, providing a robust explanation for the driving forces behind sustained economic growth. However, issues such as the externalities of technological spillovers and the market incentives for technological progress are challenging to be explained solely through market mechanisms, and endogenous growth theory has not deeply explored these issues. Some commentators suggest that while endogenous growth theory offers an endogenous explanation for technological progress, it also reveals another "institutional" black box. To unlock this "black box," it is necessary to further integrate institutional analysis into economic growth theory. New institutional economics views technological progress and institutional evolution as endogenous variables of economic development, proposing that appropriate institutional arrangements play a crucial role in promoting economic growth. This perspective expands the research horizon of endogenous growth theory. The different logic of endogenous and exogenous factors can lead to varying policy implications in theoretical models: although it is clear from economic practices that fiscal policy can influence economic growth, neoclassical growth theory posits that exogenous variables determine long-term economic growth. In other words, it suggests that fiscal policy can only impact the economy in the short term, without long-term effects. In contrast, endogenous growth theory argues that a series of endogenous variables influencing long-term economic growth are significantly affected by government policies, particularly fiscal policies. Since long-term economic growth is determined by endogenous variables, further research is needed on how government influences economic growth rates and the impact of fiscal policy on economic growth. In reality, the effectiveness of fiscal policy is evident, and any discrepancies between theory and reality indicate shortcomings in the theory itself.

### 4.4 *Future Transformations in Economic Growth Theory*

Given that the actual conditions of economic growth are very clear, there is no need to make remote assumptions to justify potential economic growth. Instead, we should focus directly on studying dynamic actual economic growth, its influencing factors, and policy effects to achieve a unity of theory and economic practice.

1. Simplified Dynamic Models: We need to accurately represent dynamic economic growth using a concise mathematical model. Our assumptions should closely reflect reality, shifting away from expanding static models to dynamic models and directly using dynamic models to express dynamic economic growth. Economic growth theory should reflect its true nature by studying actual economic growth issues rather than primarily focusing on potential economic growth that reflects general trends.
2. Incorporating Government and Technology: Theoretical models must reflect the role of the government and the significant impact of science and technology on economic growth. According to traditional Keynesian views, government spending can only influence short-term effective demand and cannot produce long-term effects. This perspective fails to explain many important issues, such as the critical role of supply-side structural reforms. Beyond affecting short-term economic fluctuations, the government can also influence long-term economic growth trends. Only by thoroughly demonstrating the role of government in profoundly affecting trends in potential economic growth rates and enhancing total factor productivity can we theoretically justify the significant role of supply-side structural reforms. This understanding helps better explain the substantial improvement in labor productivity in China since the reform and opening up and logically align the concepts of an "effective market" and a "proactive government." Shifting the relationship between the market and the government from opposition to unity can facilitate a significant breakthrough in economic growth theory, serving as a starting point for influencing economic theory with China's narrative. This approach, elevated to the theoretical level, can promote the modeling and standardization of economic theory, providing robust theoretical support for the Chinese market economy model.

3. Accurate Consideration of Endogenous and Exogenous Variables: In discussions of economic growth, if some scholars consider a variable endogenous while others exogenous, both cannot be correct simultaneously. We need a clear logic to determine the nature of such variables. We believe the most important variables should be endogenous within the system to provide a comprehensive and effective explanation of economic growth. If an economic growth theory relies on special external shocks to explain actual economic growth, it is incomplete.
4. Dynamicization of Economic Growth Theory: According to Marxist growth theory, the capitalist system cannot provide an intrinsic mechanism to maintain stable economic growth, inevitably causing macroeconomic fluctuations, thus making stable and balanced economic growth difficult to achieve. In Western economic growth theories, aside from the Harrod-Domar model, mainstream growth theories represented by neoclassical growth theory and new growth theory generally believe that under market regulation, the macroeconomy can grow stably along the optimal path, although dynamic fluctuations may occur due to supply-side or demand-side influences.
5. Integration of Theoretical and Applied Research: Economic growth theory must effectively explain reality and should not be theoretical for its own sake. There should be a basic consistency between theory and practice, and the results given by theoretical models should closely resemble the actual economic growth landscape. In practice, we need to avoid using potential economic growth rates for theoretical analysis while using actual economic growth rate data for verification, as the significant differences between them usually lack strong persuasive power.

## 5 Economic Growth Model from the Perspective of Rational Synthesis

Economic growth results from the combined effects of various factors, and Western scholars have proposed the following equation:

$$Y_t = F\left(K_t, L_t, A_t, N_t, S_t\right)$$

Wherein, $Y_t$ is the total output of an economy; $K_t$, $L_t$, and $N_t$ represent the stocks of capital, labor, and population, respectively; $A_t$ denotes total factor productivity; and $S_t$ includes factors such as institutions, policies, and environment.

To some extent, this is a dynamic general economic growth equation. This equation can be further generalized, with the independent variables interpreted more broadly, giving them fewer specific meanings. Any economic growth model can be seen as a special case of the above equation under certain conditions. Following this line of thought, we will explore the establishment of a rational synthesis economic growth model and conduct corresponding empirical analyses.

### 5.1 Important Origins and Extensions of Economic Growth Models

In exploring the construction of a rational synthesis economic growth model, we find it closely related to existing economic growth theories and related economic theories, which we briefly explain here.

1. Expansion of Adam Smith's Economic Growth Theory: In fact, the title "An Inquiry into the Nature and Causes of the Wealth of Nations" can be considered, in some sense, an economic growth theory. The general economic growth equation mentioned earlier offers the most general summary of economic growth and its causes, which can be further considered based on this equation. Interestingly, this logic allows us to derive new equations. Suppose we assume only market and government factors, separating market and government effects, the equation can be divided into two parts. The economic growth equation can then be transformed into a combined economic growth equation. If the government's role is entirely removed, the entire economy would belong to a standard complete market economy model, becoming the logical foundation of the entire economic growth theory.
2. Expansion of Mixed Economic Logic: Modern market economies are essentially mixed economies, combining market economies with government intervention. If it were a complete market economy, the economic growth equation could be expressed using the Solow model; if it involved government intervention, the logic of Keynesian theory could be applied. By mixing the two economies, a mathe-

matical weighted combination can be used to express the model. Notably, the Solow model already considers the government's role in potential economic growth through factors such as technological changes.

3. Expansion of Paul Samuelson's Middle Road Theory: Besides mixed economic theory, Paul Samuelson emphasizes the logic of a middle road, considering it an important choice for China. In early 2009, he wrote in the *China Europe Business Review* that by 2050, China would become the world's largest economy. Based on his understanding of economic history and economic theory, he recommends that China follow a "limited centrist" path. Relying solely on market mechanisms would make effective supervision difficult, inevitably leading to income inequality and significant macroeconomic fluctuations. The "limited centrist" path requires effective regulation of enterprises and markets. Although regulation may not be perfect, it is a second-best choice. The middle path is neither left nor right; each region and society must design the compromises needed for a middle path. This means Paul Samuelson's basic logic includes both ideal market economies and traditional planned economies, suggesting that China can choose a middle path. From this perspective, we can think differently, describing economic models as general models and giving them corresponding mathematical expressions. The three specific models are just special cases; in theory and practice, there can be many economic development models, presenting a new landscape.
4. Refinement of Economic Growth Trend and Fluctuation Theory: This is a familiar equation and graph. From Fig. 5.1, we can see that economic growth at a certain point consists of three parts, which can be viewed as an overlay of three components: the first part represents potential output under laissez-faire, the second part is government intervention, and the third part is short-term economic fluctuations. If we directly use this overlay method to express economic growth at a certain point, a specific economic growth equation is presented.
5. Expansion of the RBC Model: This theory tells us that the starting point of the economic growth formula can be broadly expressed using the Solow formula, representing the initial potential economic growth rate. If there are technological shocks, we can add a term to

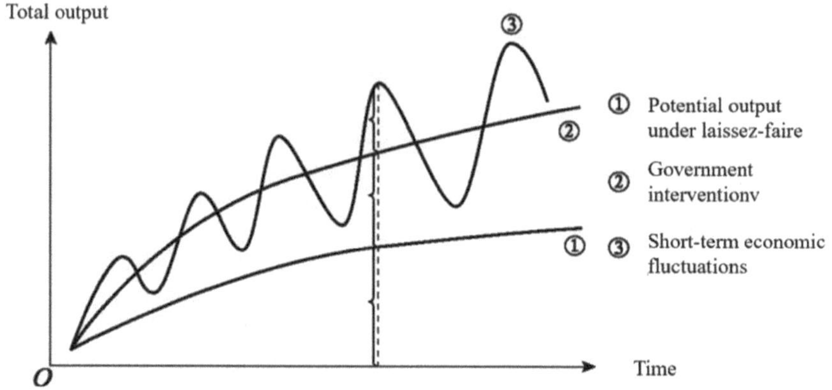


**Fig. 5.1** Decomposition of factors influencing economic growth

the formula; if there are policy shocks, regardless of empirical results, theoretically, we can also add this term. Consequently, the economic growth formula involves three main factors: the initial potential economic growth rate, corresponding technological shocks, and policy factors. Generally, we can express economic growth as an appropriate equation. This equation does not require many special assumptions, and the role of policy is reflected in the corresponding variables, eliminating conclusions like the ineffectiveness of monetary policy that do not align with reality.

## 5.2 Construction of the Rational Synthesis Economic Growth Model

Essentially, an economic growth model is an equation describing the factors influencing actual economic growth and its dynamic operating laws. Based on the results of the articles by Zong Liang and Fan Ruoying,[1] we obtain a dynamic economic growth equation by comprehensively considering the roles of the market and government. Here, we refer to the models they proposed, as shown in Eqns. (5.1) and (5.2).

[1] Zong Liang, Fan Ruoying. Innovative Thinking, Model Building and China's Practice of Macro-Control Theory. *Studies of International Finance*, 2018, 379 (11)

$$\Delta Y_t = \left(a + b\Delta A_t\right)\Delta Y_t^* + b\left(\mu_{ss} + \mu_d\right)\left(Y_t - Y_{t-1}\right) + b\left(\varepsilon_{st} + \varepsilon_{dt}\right) \tag{5.1}$$

$$\Delta Y_t = \Delta A_t \times \Delta Y_t^* + \left(\mu_{ss} + \mu_d\right)\left(Y_t - Y_{t-1}\right) + \left(\varepsilon_{st} + \varepsilon_{dt}\right) \tag{5.2}$$

In Eqn. (5.1), $\Delta \Upsilon_t = \Upsilon_t - \Upsilon_{t-1}$ represents the change in total output; $\Delta Y_t^*$ denotes the change in the potential output level of the economy under market conditions, representing the main part of the long-term trend; parameters $a$ and $b$ represent the weights of market effects and government effects, respectively, with their sum equal to 1. Equation (5.2) represents the effects of government actions, differing from the Keynesian theory, which posits that the government can only regulate short-term economic fluctuations, i.e., $(\mu_{ss} + \mu_d)(\Upsilon_t - \Upsilon_{t-1}) + (\varepsilon_{st} + \varepsilon_{dt})$. It can also affect the long-term economic growth trend, i.e., $\Delta A_t \times \Delta Y_t^*$, with impacts from supply-side and demand-side shocks.

Equation (5.1) has profound economic significance: the observed economic growth phenomenon $\Delta \Upsilon_t$ is driven by both long-term trends $\left(a + b\Delta A_t\right)\Delta Y_t^*$ and short-term fluctuations $b(\mu_{ss} + \mu_d)(\Upsilon_t - \Upsilon_{t-1}) + b(\varepsilon_{st} + \varepsilon_{dt})$. The long-term trend is primarily influenced by economic fundamentals such as labor and capital, with the government able to impact long-term economic growth. This overcomes the limitations of existing economic growth models by reflecting economic development rather than simple economic growth. The corresponding extendable equations align with the logic of rational synthesis thinking, serving as a good confirmation to some extent.

### 5.3 *Rational Synthesis Economic Growth Curve*

As shown in Fig. 5.2, $\Upsilon_t$ is the actual total output curve. We can see that the real-life total output curve often fluctuates around the trend line, indicating the existence of an output gap, while the model-derived curve is smooth. Some economists believe that institutional innovation and technological progress interact in their roles in economic growth. Institutional innovation can make economic operations infinitely approach the production possibility frontier from within, while technological progress can shift the production possibility frontier outward. Therefore, incorporating institutional innovation into economic growth models is also a field worth exploring for economists.

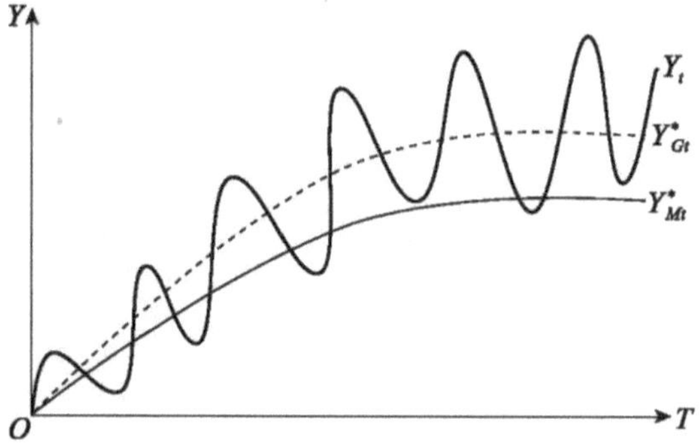


**Fig. 5.2** Variation curves of short-term fluctuations and long-term trends

The trend of a country's total output over time can be discussed from both long-term and short-term perspectives. In the short term, it exhibits economic fluctuations, as shown by $Y_t$ in Fig. 5.2, displaying certain economic cycles with output cycling between peaks, recessions, troughs, and recoveries. The long-term trend of total output over time shows a certain trajectory, which, in an idealized model of a pure market economy, can be understood as the potential output curve of that economy.

### 5.4 *Theoretical Analysis of the Rational Synthesis Economic Growth Model*

Actual economic growth can be explained through three critical stages and various factors.

1. Important Stages:

First Stage: The potential economic growth rate under zero government intervention, which is the potential economic growth rate under pure market conditions.

Second Stage: The potential economic growth rate under government intervention. Currently, the widely measured potential economic growth rate falls into this category, reflecting the basic trend of economic growth. Government policies or reforms in education, industry, technology, and other areas can significantly alter the potential economic growth rate. It is important to note that in this stage, the government can act as a brake, changing the growth path from a long-term perspective. The reforms, five-year plans, and medium to long-term plans promoted in China often fulfill this function.

Third Stage: The regulation of short-term economic fluctuations through macroeconomic policies. This stage addresses the impact of macroeconomic policies on economic fluctuations in the short term. In this sense, economic growth is essentially the result of the overlay of long-term trends and short-term fluctuations, forming a unified and complete system. However, our focus may differ depending on the context. The basic logic is: in the short term, focus on fluctuations; in the medium to long term, focus on trends.

2. Influencing Factors Such as Macroeconomic Policy: Each stage involves numerous influencing factors. Firstly, the potential economic growth rate without government intervention is under minimal government interference in the economy and market. Given the neutrality of technological progress under conditions of full market competition, explaining technological progress solely through market conditions is insufficient. Here, a relatively stable technological progress under market conditions is assumed, reflecting the basic trend and path of potential economic growth or long-term economic growth under natural conditions. Secondly, the potential economic growth rate under government intervention is influenced by factors such as capital, labor, and technology, similar to the existing potential economic growth rate. Therefore, such analyses are reasonable and realistic, with the main difference being the emphasis on the unique mechanisms of government influence. The most crucial role is the braking effect, where the government can enhance the potential economic growth rate by increasing investments in education and technology and implementing industrial policies, as shown in Fig. 5.3. From this perspective, we can also explain the random walk theory, whose role aligns with new growth theory. In practice, an economy requires such mechanisms to achieve transformation and significant recovery. The tremendous success of China's reform and opening up and the Keynesian policies adopted by the United States after the Great Depression align with the respective circumstances and achieved great success. Thirdly, macroeconomic regulation involves measures to maintain stable short-term economic growth, consistent with discussions in the macroeconomic regulation section, primarily reflected in the relevant content of macroeconomic policies.

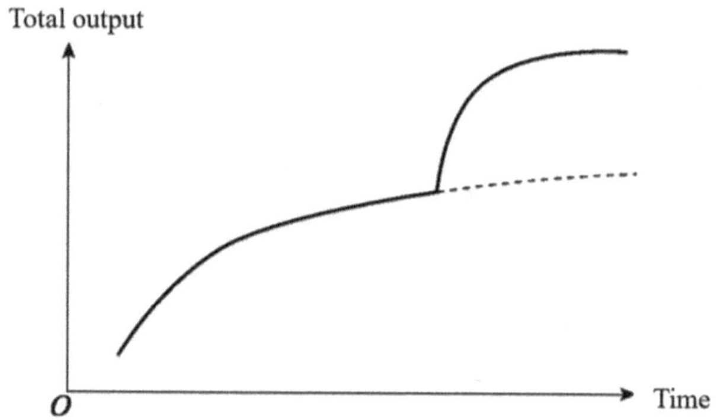


**Fig. 5.3** Curve of government braking effect

## 5.5 *Comparison Between the Rational Synthesis Economic Growth Model and Personal Career Development Model*

In reality, there is no economy without government, nor a purely planned economy without a market. Existing economic growth models, based on neoclassical economic logic, typically consider the potential economic growth rate under purely market conditions nominally, but what is actually calculated is the potential economic growth rate considering government intervention, which has certain limitations. From a market economy perspective, there will be a steady-state economic growth rate in the long term, reflecting the long-term trend of economic growth. This can be represented by the potential economic growth rate under a stable market condition. When considering the role of the government, it transforms into a new potential economic growth rate. Previously, we cited a new model that comprehensively considers the roles of the market and the government in economic growth, precisely quantifying and distinguishing their effects.

Here, we illustrate this with a vivid example. A person's career development is analogous to a country's economic growth. The quality of an individual's career development is influenced by the following factors, whose combined effects determine their career development level:

1. Innate Qualities: This includes their intelligence or talent, equivalent to potential qualities. It also encompasses their personal efforts,

analogous to the potential economic output under market conditions.

2. Education and Support: The education provided by teachers and parents is analogous to the role of the government. Generally, their potential quality is determined by their innate talents. With personal effort, the potential development trend can improve. If the education from teachers and parents is scientific and effective, their potential development ability will significantly increase. Conversely, if the education method is improper, their potential quality may decrease. Their career development quality may also be influenced by various external conditions (such as opportunities and timing), leading to fluctuations in their career development, analogous to the short-term effects of macroeconomic regulation.

In fact, economic growth follows a similar pattern. An economy's own conditions and endowments initially determine its potential output. The economy's inherent ability to innovate can drive economic growth. If the government can implement scientific and effective educational policies, technological policies, industrial policies and other policies, particularly utilizing its braking effect (e.g., through reforms and opening up), the potential economic output can significantly increase. Conversely, ineffective government policies may lead to economic decline. Furthermore, an economy's total output can fluctuate due to various policy shocks.

## 6 Empirical Analysis of China's Government-Market Relationship Based on Rational Synthesis Economic Model

The following section utilizes relevant data from China's reform and opening up period to demonstrate the rationality and significance of the economic growth equations from a rational synthesis perspective, specifically focusing on Eqns. (5.1) and (5.2) or their transformed forms [i.e., Eqn. (5.3)]:

$$\Delta Y_t = a\Delta Y_{Mt}^* + b\left(\mu_d + \mu_{ss}\right)\left(Y_t - Y_{Gt}^*\right) + b\mu_{sl}\Delta A_t Y_{Mt}^* + b\left(\varepsilon_{dt} + \varepsilon_{st}\right) \quad (5.3)$$

In practice, the impact of government macro control on potential output under pure market conditions is shown in Fig. 5.2. Below, we will verify the rationality of Eqn. (5.3) using China's economic data from 1978 to 2019, selecting the indicators listed in Table 5.1.

### *6.1 Acquisition of Various Indicators' Data*

The data of nominal GDP are sourced from the "China Statistical Yearbook," from which we also obtained the GDP deflator to calculate the real GDP. All data in this section are based on constant prices from 1978.

The population of young adults and those gradually entering the working age (15–64 years) is sourced from the "China Labor Statistical Yearbook." The reason for choosing this indicator instead of the employed population is mainly due to two factors:

1. The number of employed people shows a significant increase in census years, which, even after smoothing, remains quite abnormal and negatively impacts regression results.
2. This section mainly uses the employed population to estimate potential economic output rather than actual output. Therefore, using the potential working-age population better reflects the labor factor in the production function.

**Table 5.1** Description of indicators

| *Indicator* | *Unit* | *Description* |
|---|---|---|
| Year | Year | |
| GDP | 100 million yuan | Nominal gross domestic product |
| rGDP | 100 million yuan | Real gross domestic product |
| renkou | 10,000 people | Population of young adults and those gradually entering the working age (15–64 years) |
| guzi | 100 million yuan | Capital stock |
| ymt | 100 million yuan | Potential total output |
| hpdata_n | 100 million yuan | GDP after government regulation, the result after HP filtering |
| tfp | | Total factor productivity |
| preymt | 100 million yuan | Potential growth of market economy |

The method for calculating capital stock refers to Shan Haojie's "Re-estimation of China's Capital Stock K: 1952–2006," with a depreciation rate of 10%.

To calculate the potential economic growth rate, we first estimate the potential economic output. When estimating the potential economic growth of the United States, data from 1925 to 1929 was chosen because the US government had minimal intervention in economic development before the 1929 economic crisis, closely approximating a pure market economy. Unfortunately, it is difficult to find a similar period of near-pure market economy in China's economic development. Therefore, all relevant coefficients can only be estimated based on other scholars' research results. The mainstream view in China currently is that the comprehensive technical level technical coefficient is about 0.4, and the capital elasticity coefficient is between 0.6 and 0.7. Considering these two coefficients change with economic development, we use 0.37–0.42 and 0.55–0.7 for phase-based estimation. Finally, using the Solow model and previously calculated labor population and capital stock data, we estimate potential economic output and growth rate.

$$Y_{Mt}^{*} = f\left(M_t, L_t\right) = \lambda K_t^{\theta} L_t^{1-\theta}$$

For estimating GDP under government control, we use a similar method to the HP filter for processing GDP, with a parameter of 100 [Hodrick and Prescott (1980, 1997) used annual data, quarterly data filled 1600, monthly data filled 1440. Since we use annual data, we chose 100].

Currently, there are four main methods for estimating Total Factor Productivity (TFP): the algebraic index method, the Solow residual method, the latent variable method, and the potential output method. Here, we refer to the calculation process of Guo Qingwang and Jia Junxue (2005) and use the Solow residual method for estimation.

After calculating all indicator data, we will perform regressions for the entire historical stage and three sub-stages respectively to conduct empirical analysis.

### 6.2 *Full Historical Stage*

The overall fitting effect of this model is quite good, with significant and interpretable coefficients. During the full historical stage from 1978 to

2019, the contribution of potential market economic growth to actual economic growth (a) reached 0.51855, as shown in Fig. 5.4.

### *6.3 Different Historical Stages*

Based on economists' research on Chinese government policies, we divide China's history from 1978 to 2019 into three stages.

1. The first stage: 1978–1992

In 1978, the Third Plenary Session of the 11th Central Committee of the Communist Party of China was held in Beijing, confirming the new policy of focusing on economic construction and implementing reform and opening up. During this stage, the contribution of potential economic growth to actual economic growth was only 0.29778, at a relatively low level. This is because China's economic construction still followed the

```
lm(formula = diffGDP ~ diffymt + I(GDP - hpdata_n) + I(tfp *
    preymt) - 1)

Residuals:
      Min        1Q    Median        3Q       Max
-0.039775 -0.012694  0.005808  0.026628  0.083102

Coefficients:
                   Estimate Std. Error t value Pr(>|t|)
diffymt            0.518553   0.158335   3.275   0.0023 **
I(GDP - hpdata_n) -0.003318   0.005173  -0.641   0.5252
I(tfp * preymt)    1.464477   0.308593   4.746 3.09e-05 ***
---
Signif. codes:  0 '***' 0.001 '**' 0.01 '*' 0.05 '.' 0.1 ' ' 1

Residual standard error: 0.03148 on 37 degrees of freedom
  (1 observation deleted due to missingness)
Multiple R-squared:  0.895,     Adjusted R-squared:  0.8865
F-statistic: 105.2 on 3 and 37 DF,  p-value: < 2.2e-16
```

**Fig. 5.4** Empirical analysis of the full historical stage

principle of "planned economy as the mainstay, market regulation as a supplement" proposed by the 12th National Congress of the Communist Party of China.

2. The second stage: 1993–2001

In 1992, Deng Xiaoping proposed in his Southern Tour Talks that "planned economy is not equivalent to socialism since capitalism also has planning; market economy is not equivalent to capitalism since socialism also has markets." As a result, China vigorously promoted the reform of the market economy system.

During this stage, the Chinese government's influence on market economic development decreased, resembling the situation in Western countries in the 1960s and 1970s. However, China remained a socialist country with public ownership as the mainstay, and even though the government's influence on the market diminished, it was still significantly greater than that in Western economies. The test results showed that the contribution of potential economic growth to actual economic growth in this stage was 0.53706 (see Fig. 5.5); correspondingly, the coefficient of changes brought by the government's role was 0.46294.

3. The third stage: 2002–2019

In November 2001, the Fourth Ministerial Conference of the World Trade Organization (WTO) decided to accept China as a member, marking a new stage in China's economic development. The benefits of joining the WTO included facilitating further expansion of imports and exports, attracting investment, accelerating the adjustment and optimization of domestic industrial structures, and enabling China to participate comprehensively in international cooperation and competition. However, the impact of foreign macroeconomic conditions on China increased, significantly raising the risk level of China's macroeconomy. Additionally, the extensive development mode of the 1990s was no longer applicable, and the Chinese government needed to enhance its influence on the economy, fully leveraging macro control to promote healthy economic development.

After the 2008 international financial crisis, developed economies led by the United States gradually began to expand the government's influence on

```
lm(formula = diffGDP ~ diffymt + I(GDP - hpdata_n) + I(tfp *
    preymt) - 1)

Residuals:
      Min        1Q    Median        3Q       Max
-0.022041 -0.010839 -0.001538  0.016255  0.024945

Coefficients:
                  Estimate Std. Error t value Pr(>|t|)
diffymt            0.53706    0.21767   2.467   0.0486 *
I(GDP - hpdata_n)  0.01713    0.01029   1.664   0.1472
I(tfp * preymt)    0.89436    0.43209   2.070   0.0839 .
---
Signif. codes:  0 '***' 0.001 '**' 0.01 '*' 0.05 '.' 0.1 ' ' 1

Residual standard error: 0.02021 on 6 degrees of freedom
Multiple R-squared:  0.9707,	Adjusted R-squared:  0.9561
F-statistic: 66.28 on 3 and 6 DF,  p-value: 5.437e-05
```

**Fig. 5.5** Empirical analysis of the second stage (1993–2001)

economic development, such as the US Obama administration launching three rounds of large-scale quantitative easing and the Japanese Abe administration devaluing the yen to stimulate economic growth, bringing Keynesianism back into vogue. At the same time, this economic crisis made China realize that effective government control and management of the market is a necessary precondition for the healthy development of the economy. Hence, the role of macroeconomic policy in actual economic growth became increasingly important. China also promptly adjusted its economic development direction, no longer blindly pursuing the speed of economic growth but rather the quality of economic development. The government encouraged industrial transformation through supportive policies and prevented economic overheating through monetary and fiscal policies.

During this stage, the contribution of potential economic growth to actual economic growth showed an overall increasing trend, as shown in Fig. 5.6.

As shown in Table 5.2, considering the intervention effects of the government on the economy in the three stages, the fitting results of this

```
lm(formula = diffGDP ~ diffymt + I(GDP - hpdata_n) + I(tfp *
    preymt) - 1)

Residuals:
      Min         1Q     Median         3Q        Max
-0.017510 -0.004063  0.002207  0.005777  0.018182

Coefficients:
                  Estimate Std. Error t value Pr(>|t|)
diffymt           0.515343   0.122395   4.210 0.000873 ***
I(GDP - hpdata_n) 0.001904   0.002455   0.775 0.451038
I(tfp * preymt)   0.794470   0.204137   3.892 0.001628 **
---
Signif. codes:  0 '***' 0.001 '**' 0.01 '*' 0.05 '.' 0.1 ' ' 1

Residual standard error: 0.009445 on 14 degrees of freedom
  (1 observation deleted due to missingness)
Multiple R-squared:  0.991,     Adjusted R-squared:  0.9891
F-statistic: 515.1 on 3 and 14 DF,  p-value: 1.473e-14
```

**Fig. 5.6** Empirical analysis of the third stage (2002–2019)

**Table 5.2** Coefficients of government and market roles in China

| *Historical span* | *Number of years* | *Stage* | *Contribution of potential economic growth to actual economic growth* | *Coefficient of changes brought by government role* | *Rational synthesis model F-value* |
|---|---|---|---|---|---|
| 1978—2019 | 42 | Full Historical Stage | 0.518 55** | 0.481 45** | 105.2*** |
| 1978—1992 | 15 | First Stage | 0.297 78* | 0.702 22* | 28.57*** |
| 1993—2001 | 9 | Second Stage | 0.537 06* | 0.462 94* | 66.28*** |
| 2002—2019 | 18 | Third Stage | 0.515 34*** | 0.484 66*** | 515.1*** |

Note: *, *, and *** represent significance levels at 10%, 5%, and 1%, respectively

model meet expectations. With a sufficient sample size, the statistical effect of the overall fitting for this model's coefficients is good. Looking at the changes in the coefficients, on average, the roles of the Chinese government and the market in the economy are approximately in a 1:1 ratio, with the market role slightly exceeding 50%. The macro control role of the government experienced a decline after initially being high, gradually stabilizing in the later stages, with the market role coefficient exceeding 50%, reflecting the market's decisive role. After the international financial crisis, this ratio did not continue to increase, mainly due to the increased role of governments around the world, influenced by the international financial crisis and other factors.

## 6.4 *Main Conclusions*

Through theoretical models and related empirical analysis, we can draw the following conclusions:

(1) Reasonable Description of Economic Growth: The use of this formula to describe economic growth is fundamentally reasonable. It can broadly capture the basic laws of economic growth and is generally consistent with actual economic growth in simulations. It can be used to predict short-term adjacent periods, reflecting basic trends. Mathematical analysis results show that this formula can be regarded as an empirical formula for economic growth, consistent with graphical analysis.

(2) Reflection of Market Index Changes: This formula essentially reflects the basic situation of market index changes, showing differences across different stages of China's reform and opening up, thereby illustrating the extent of market and government roles. The market economy index has undergone a gradual increase, reflecting the deepening process of China's market economy. In recent years, China's market economy index has slightly exceeded 50%, indicating the decisive role of the market, with the government playing a better role. It also highlights the need for deepening reforms to further enhance marketization. This empirical perspective verifies the rationality and effectiveness of rational synthesis analysis.

(3) Comparison with the US Economic Empirical Analysis: By comparing this chapter with the empirical analysis of the US economy

in the fourth chapter, we observe that China's market economy index is lower than that of the United States, reflecting a higher degree of government intervention in China compared to the US. The fourth chapter combined the entire historical stage and the three stages of government intervention effects, showing that the roles of the US government and market in the economy are approximately 3:7, while China's overall market economy index just exceeds 50%. Therefore, the marketization degree of China's market economy model is still somewhat behind that of the United States, indirectly reflecting the insufficiency of marketization in China. Hence, deepening market-oriented reforms remains an important task for the future.

## 7 Correlation Analysis Based on Potential and Real Economic Growth Rates

In reality, when analyzing potential economic growth rates, short-term factors are not considered within this basic trend. However, the government can influence economic growth trends by affecting technological changes or labor productivity. According to our model, the core difference is that potential economic growth rates consist of two parts: one part represents a smooth curve that follows the convergence law, and the other part is influenced by technological changes, primarily reflecting government actions that can drive changes in the economic growth path. Thus, the actual potential economic growth rate is not simply a smooth curve but one that can be significantly redirected through government actions. This characteristic also serves as an important theoretical support for China's economic miracle achieved through reform and opening up. Therefore, calculating the potential economic growth rate is still profoundly significant for analyzing actual economic growth.

In recent years, we have calculated potential economic growth rates using two methods: the production function method and the trend method. Both methods require assessing the influencing factors of potential economic growth rates and the relative importance of each factor. In summary, the conclusions derived from different methods do not vary significantly, all indicating a downward trend in China's potential economic growth rate since 2006. In recent years, China's aggregate demand has been slightly insufficient. Since 2008, the slowdown in Total Factor Productivity growth and the deceleration of capital accumulation have led to a decline in China's economic growth rate. To estimate the future potential economic growth rate using the production function method (see Table 5.3), it is necessary to first predict the trends in TFP, capital stock, and labor force. Regarding the labor force, considering issues such as accelerated aging and declining birth rates, the proportion of the working-age population may continue to decline in the future (see Fig. 5.7), making it difficult for the labor force to become a significant engine for future economic growth.

By analyzing the regression relationship between the growth rate of capital stock and the share of the secondary industry in GDP, it can be predicted that the future capital growth rate will gradually decrease to about 8%, as shown in Fig. 5.8. Due to the potential continued increase in the share of the service industry in China's industrial structure, the capital growth rate in core cities like Beijing and Shanghai may also decline.

Based on regression analysis using panel data from provinces from 2005 to 2014, the impact coefficients of various factors on TFP can be calculated. Further analysis reveals the extent of the influence of each factor on TFP, with the main indicators shown in Tables 5.4 and 5.5.

Research findings suggest that the future growth rate of TFP could reach 1.8%. In an optimistic scenario, if urbanization accelerates, infrastructure investment speeds up, human capital rapidly accumulates, and technological progress continues to develop, China's TFP growth rate

**Table 5.3** Estimation of China's potential economic growth rate from 2015 to 2025 (unit: %)

| *Year* | *Optimistic scenario* | *Average growth rate* | *Baseline scenario* | *Average growth rate* |
|---|---|---|---|---|
| 2015 | 7.6 | 7.5 | 6.8 | 6.3 |
| 2016 | 7.7 | | 6.6 | |
| 2017 | 7.7 | | 6.4 | |
| 2018 | 7.5 | | 6.2 | |
| 2019 | 7.4 | | 6.0 | |
| 2020 | 7.2 | | 5.8 | |
| 2021 | 7.0 | 6.6 | 5.6 | 5.3 |
| 2022 | 6.8 | | 5.5 | |
| 2023 | 6.6 | | 5.3 | |
| 2024 | 6.4 | | 5.1 | |
| 2025 | 6.1 | | 4.9 | |

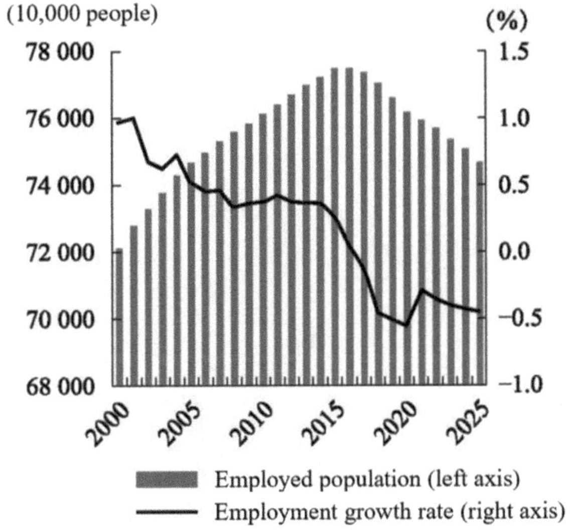


**Fig. 5.7** China's employed population and employment growth rate

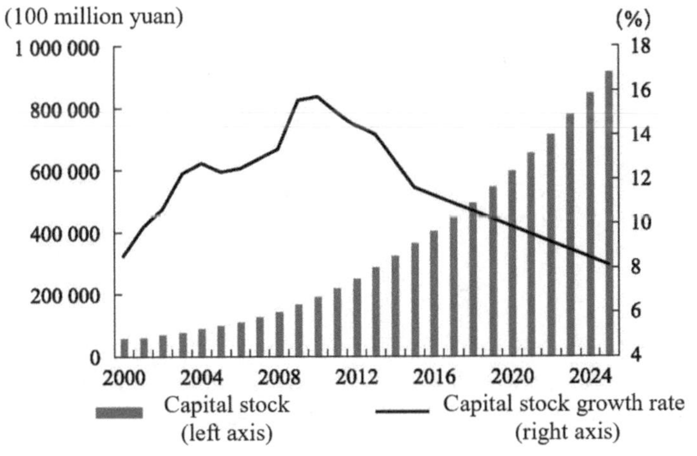


**Fig. 5.8** China's capital stock and capital stock growth rate

**Table 5.4** Impact of various factors on TFP

| *Indicator* | *Impact on TFP* |
|---|---|
| Urbanization Rate | TFP increases by 1.2% for each 1-percentage-point increase |
| Investment Rate | TFP decreases by 0.23% for each 1-percentage-point increase |
| Average Years of Education | TFP increases by 0.405% for each 1-percentage-point increase |
| Number of Authorized Invention Patents | TFP increases by 0.04% for each 1-percentage-point increase |
| Government Revenue/GDP | TFP increases by 1.08% for each 1-percentage-point increase |
| Comprehensive Transportation Facility Mileage/Square Kilometer | TFP increases by 0.128% for each 2-percentage-point increase |
| Credit/GDP | TFP increases by 0.268% for each 10-percentage-point increase |

**Table 5.5** Decomposition of potential economic growth contribution from 1979 to 2014 (unit: %)

| *Year* | *Potential Economic Growth Rate* | *Labor Income Share* | *Capital Growth Rate* | *Labor Force Growth Rate* | *Human Capital* | *TFP* |
|---|---|---|---|---|---|---|
| 1979–2007 | 9.9 | 50 | 4.86 | 0.87 | 0.41 | 3.80 |
| 2008 | 10.6 | 51 | 6.49 | 0.2 | 0.13 | 3.76 |
| 2009 | 10.5 | 52 | 7.41 | 0.2 | 0.13 | 2.72 |
| 2010 | 9.7 | 53 | 7.42 | 0.2 | 0.14 | 1.99 |
| 2011 | 9.2 | 53 | 7.03 | 0.2 | 0.47 | 1.50 |
| 2012 | 8.5 | 53 | 6.72 | 0.2 | 0.47 | 1.09 |
| 2013 | 8.0 | 54 | 6.52 | 0.2 | 0.47 | 0.84 |
| 2014 | 7.4 | 54 | 5.98 | 0.2 | 0.47 | 0.75 |
| 2008–2014 | 9.1 | 53 | 6.80 | 0.2 | 0.33 | 1.81 |

could rise to about 3%. Therefore, the growth rate of TFP will be significantly influenced by government reform measures.

The above research holds certain policy value. It is suggested that future efforts should focus on stabilizing the labor force, increasing capital, and particularly enhancing Total Factor Productivity to further promote market-oriented reforms. This will help maintain a steady rise in potential economic growth rates, thereby shifting the economic growth trend curve upward.[2] At the same time, corresponding macroeconomic policies should be implemented to maintain a basic balance between actual economic growth and potential economic growth, promoting high-quality development of China's economy. This requires effective coordination of fiscal and monetary policies as well as a relatively stable external environment to facilitate the basic coordination between actual and potential economic growth, achieving high-quality actual economic development.

[2] The new growth theory refutes the neoclassical growth theory's view that market mechanisms alone can ensure the economy follows an optimal growth trajectory and that government economic policies do not have a long-term impact on economic growth. Instead, it posits that appropriate government intervention can help promote economic growth. This refers to the trend of economic growth, which is consistent with our logic.

CHAPTER 6

# Economic Cycle Theory, Economic Crisis, and Golden Period of Development

The economic cycle refers to the phenomenon of alternating periods of economic expansion and contraction in an economy, recurring in a cyclical manner. Research on economic cycles is of significant importance for analyzing economic trends, predicting financial crises, and formulating government macroeconomic policies. Over time, economic cycle theory, as a crucial component of economic theory, has developed rapidly, but it also has certain limitations. Particularly after the 2008 global financial crisis, the Dynamic Stochastic General Equilibrium (DSGE) model, which has been the mainstream economic cycle theory and core analytical framework in macroeconomics since the 1980s, has faced strong criticism from various sectors of society. The primary criticism of the DSGE model lies in its deficiencies in predicting exogenous shocks and forewarning financial crises. This is because the theoretical core of the DSGE model is the theory of exogenous random shocks, which presupposes that such shocks are random and unpredictable. On one hand, within the analytical paradigm of the DSGE model, the economic cycle comprises exogenous shocks coupled with internal transmission, neglecting the significant role of the government in the economic cycle. Economic operations cannot solely rely on the "invisible hand" of the market, nor can they disregard the "visible hand" of the government. In the economic cycle, both the market and the government play indispensable roles. On the other hand, economists and policymakers have not attempted to overcome the theoretical shortcomings of the DSGE model. Instead, they have focused on clearly delineating


Z. Liang, *The Innovation of Economic Theory in China*,
https://doi.org/10.1007/978-981-95-2713-7_6

the transmission mechanism of exogenous shocks and the policy trade-offs in responding to such shocks, neglecting the study and prediction of the sources of economic fluctuations.

First, we will review the evolution and progress of economic cycle theory, and analyze the significant advancements and limitations of existing mainstream economic cycle theories. Based on this, we will construct a theoretical model of economic cycle from the perspective of rational synthesis, using new thinking to explain economic cycles and crises, exploring the conditions and prospects for the golden development period. We will theoretically discuss the logic of the existence of economic cycles, measure the length of economic cycles, and finally discuss methods of macroeconomic forecasting and counter-cyclical management.

## 1 Evolution of Economic Cycle Theory

The economic cycle is a regular alternation of expansion and contraction in overall activity levels (Chen Leyi, 1998). Its classic definition is: "An economic cycle is a type of fluctuation found in the aggregate economic activity of nations that organize their work mainly as business enterprises: a cycle consists of expansions occurring at about the same time in many economic activities, followed by similarly general recessions, contractions, and revivals which merge into the expansion phase of the next cycle; this sequence of changes is recurrent but not timed. The duration of economic cycles varys from more than one year to ten or twelve years" (Burns and Mitchell, 1946). There are four common types of economic cycles (see Table 6.1): the Kitchin cycle (Kitchin, 1923), lasting 3–5 years and also

**Table 6.1** Different types of economic cycles

| *Cycle name* | *Cycle duration* | *Average length* | *Source of cycle* |
|---|---|---|---|
| Kitchin Cycle | Short Cycle | Approximately 40 months (3–5 years) | Fluctuations in business inventory investment |
| Juglar Cycle | Medium Cycle | Approximately 10 years (9–10 years) | Fluctuations in fixed investment |
| Kuznets Cycle | Medium-Long Cycle | Approximately 20 years (15–25 years) | Fluctuations in construction investment |
| Kondratieff Cycle | Long Cycle | Approximately 50 years (50–60 years) | Cyclical development of technological innovation |

Source: Compiled by the author

known as the inventory cycle; the Juglar cycle (Juglar, 1862), lasting 9–10 years and also known as the fixed investment cycle; the Kuznets cycle (Kuznets, 1930), lasting 15–25 years and also known as the construction investment cycle; and the Kondratieff cycle (Kondratieff and Stolper, 1935), lasting 50–60 years and also known as the technological cycle. We will sequentially review these four types of cycles and their explanatory power for the China's economy.

### *1.1 Lengths and Types of Economic Cycles*

Classifying economic cycles based on their duration is a common practice among Western scholars. As shown in Table 6.1, Western scholars believe that 3–6 Juglar cycles constitute a Kondratieff cycle, and 2–3 Kitchin cycles constitute a Juglar cycle. Although the driving factors for each type of economic cycle are different, they are interconnected.

1. Kitchin Cycle

Kitchin (1923) is the first to propose the concept of inventory fluctuation cycles. By analyzing bill payments, price indices, employment conditions, and interest rate fluctuations, he discovered a short wave cycle with an average length of approximately 40 months in the economic fluctuations of the UK and the US from 1890 to 1922.

The core idea of the Kitchin cycle is that when the economy shows a positive trend and the overall demand increases, enterprises are compelled to increase production. When each enterprise increases production, overcapacity and inventory surplus will inevitably occur. This, in turn, will prompt enterprises to reduce production, thus leading to an economic downturn. After 1–2 years of consuming inventories, adjusting economic structures, and resolving overcapacity issues, enterprises start to increase production again, and the economy improves and sustains for about a year. Subsequently, enterprises will continue to experience inventory surplus and economic downturn stages. The Kitchin cycle, also known as the short wave cycle or inventory cycle, is characterized by its short duration, with inventory investment being the main driving factor.

2. Juglar Cycle

Juglar (1862) has discovered that there are regular fluctuations in economic life, and the cycle of each fluctuation is 9–10 years. He believes that the cyclical fluctuations occurring in the economy are normal phenomena in capitalist economies. These cyclical fluctuations can be foreseen and mitigated to some extent through certain actions but cannot be completely suppressed. The Juglar cycle, approximately ten years in length, is driven by fixed asset investment fluctuations and is also known as the medium cycle.

The core idea of the Juglar cycle is that economic cycle fluctuations are constituted by the repeated occurrence of three socio-economic movement phases—prosperity, crisis, and depression. External factors (such as natural disasters and wars) are not the main causes of economic fluctuations but only exacerbate them.

3. Kuznets Cycle

Kuznets (1930) finds, by organizing historical data on the output of 60 major industrial and agricultural products and the price changes of 35 major industrial and agricultural products in the US, UK, France, and Germany, that the cycle length of major capitalist countries is 15–25 years. Due to the high coincidence between the length of the Kuznets cycle and the length of housing price fluctuation cycles (many studies show that the average cycle length of housing price fluctuations is 18 years), the Kuznets cycle is also known as the construction investment cycle.

Kuznets believed that changes in the real estate market were an important driving factor for economic cycles. The cyclical fluctuations in real estate are divided into four stages: recovery, prosperity, crisis, and depression. After the market has passed a downturn (depression), increased demand leads to a rise in transaction volumes, which quickly reflects in real estate prices, causing rapid price increases (prosperity). When housing prices deviate significantly from their steady state, purchasing power decreases, transaction volumes drop, and housing prices fall, leading the real estate market into a period of simultaneous decline in both volume and prices.

4. Kondratieff Cycle

The Kondratieff cycle was identified through the study of statistical data, including wholesale price indices, interest rates, coal production, and consumption over more than a hundred years in the US, UK, France, and other countries. This research revealed that the economy oscillated at very low frequencies, manifesting as an economic fluctuation cycle lasting 40–60 years.

This long-term cyclical fluctuation is mainly caused by technological inventions and the resulting industrial structure changes, thus it is also known as the technological cycle. Kondratieff explained economic fluctuations from the perspective of over-investment: excessive investment leads to market oversupply, followed by recession, until new inventions bring about a significant increase in new investments. He believed that the factors leading to economic recovery and take-off include a high propensity to save, relatively large-scale supply of circulating capital at lower interest rates, accumulated capital in the hands of capable entrepreneurs and financial groups, and lower price levels.

5. Schumpeter's Three-Cycle Nested Theory

Schumpeter's three-cycle nested theory is based on the summary and induction of cycle theories such as the Kitchin cycle, the Juglar cycle, and the Kondratieff cycle, as shown in Fig. 6.1. The three-cycle nested theory posits that within the Kondratieff cycle, which spans 50–60 years, there

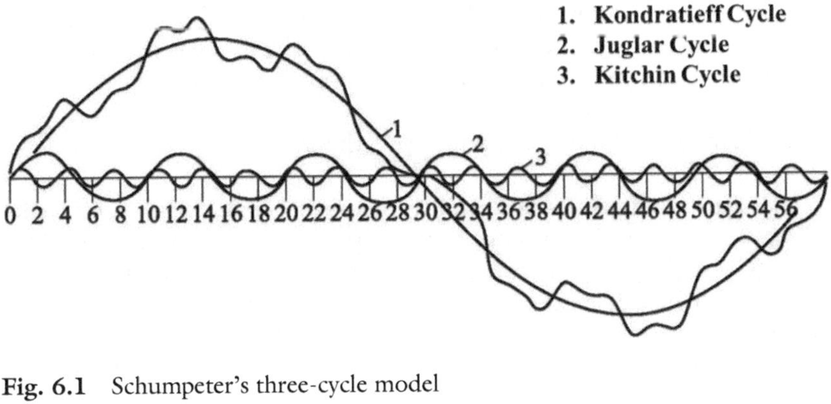


**Fig. 6.1** Schumpeter's three-cycle model

are six Juglar cycles, each averaging 9–10 years, and 18 Kitchin cycles, each averaging approximately 40 months. The three cycles are interwoven and mutually constrained. The Kondratieff cycle restricts the prosperity and depression levels of the Juglar cycle, while the Juglar cycle restricts the prosperity and depression levels of the Kitchin cycle.

Schumpeter's research found that the three most severe and prolonged depressions, occurring in 1825–1830, 1873–1878, and 1929–1933, were caused by the temporal overlap of the downward phases of the Kondratieff, Juglar, and Kitchin cycles. In the real economy, multiple vibrations occur simultaneously. The temporal overlap of the corresponding stages of the three cycles produces resonance phenomena. Particularly when the prosperous (or depressed) stages of different cycles overlap, the economy exhibits more intense phase characteristics.

### 1.2 Mainstream Economics' Explanation of Economic Cycles

1. Marx's perspective on economic cycles

Marx believed that economic cycles are the products of the "money-commodity" economy based on modern machine production, beginning with the categories closely linked to modern machine-based large-scale industry. He described the economic cycle as a "life process peculiar to modern industry." Marx's discussion of economic cycles is based on the sudden and substantial expansion and contraction capabilities of production scale induced by modern machine-based large-scale industry. This expansion and contraction capability is the material basis for the cyclical movement of the entire society's economic activities. The connotation of Marx's economic cycle concept is the crisis of relative overproduction, closely related to the imbalance between supply and demand.

2. Keynesian school's economic cycle theory

Keynes attributed economic cycles to the diminishing marginal efficiency of capital and the diminishing marginal propensity to consume (MPC). The "Great Depression" of 1929–1933 led to the development of Keynesian macroeconomics, which centers on stimulating aggregate demand. However, Keynesianism separates the study of long-term economic trends from short-term economic fluctuations, analyzing the influencing factors of each separately. Scholars studying economic growth theory focus on long-term growth issues and overlook short-term fluctuations, attributing the driving forces of long-term economic growth mainly to three factors: population growth, capital accumulation, and technological progress. Scholars studying economic cycles analyze only the short-term fluctuations after removing the long-term trend, attributing technological progress to smooth (linear), deterministic (non-random), exogenous trend terms, and assuming that technological progress does not influence economic fluctuations.

3. Schumpeter's innovation theory

Schumpeter's theory of economic cycle movement is based on technological innovation. In 1936, after conducting a comprehensive analysis of various cycle theories, Schumpeter proposed his "innovation theory." Schumpeter believed that each long cycle includes six medium cycles, and each medium cycle includes three short cycles. The short cycle lasts about 40 months, the medium cycle lasts 9–10 years, and the long cycle lasts 48–60 years. During the long-wave recovery period of the economic cycle, technological innovation brings new demand and new requirements for production equipment, leading the production sector to engage in new production, the capital sector to purchase equipment, and the labor sector to raise wages and hire more personnel. At this time, the economy enters the long-wave recovery period, characterized by continuous economic improvement, more capital equipment investment by enterprises, large-scale hiring, and a sharp increase in production capacity, leading to a period of prosperity. Subsequently, large-scale expansion results in over-investment and overcapacity, causing enterprises to reduce hiring, and a large amount of output becomes unsellable, leading the economy into a recession. After entering the recession period, the demand for consumer goods will decrease and severe overcapacity will cause the economy to enter a depression until new demand arises, ushering the economy into a new recovery phase. Innovation causes changes in the long-wave cycle, with revolutionary innovations leading to gradual technological changes that cause changes in the medium-wave cycle, and capacity fluctuations caused by technological changes leading to changes in the short-wave cycle.

Schumpeter marked three long cycles with significant innovations: the first long cycle from the 1780s to 1842, known as the "Industrial Revolution Period"; the second long cycle from 1842 to 1897, known as the "Steam and Steel Period"; and the third long cycle after 1897, known as the "Electricity, Chemistry, and Automobile Period." In each long cycle, medium cycles are caused by medium-sized innovations, and in each medium cycle, short cycles are caused by small innovations.

4. The Austrian school's economic cycle theory

Representatives of the Austrian School, such as Ludwig von Mises and Friedrich Hayek, argued that economic cycles are caused by monetary factors. They believed that central banks deliberately lower interest rates during credit expansion, leading to the misallocation of capital and causing economic cycles. This occurs because, after interest rates drop, investors' cost of obtaining funds decreases, leading to increased investment. Once the funding needs of investment projects with high returns and short production cycles are met, people will invest in new projects with longer production processes, creating a boom. However, over time, people find that certain production factors are in short supply, and the rising prices of these factors increase costs, further boosting credit demand. If investors withdraw their investments due to funding issues, the consequence is that the many costs already incurred cannot be recovered and become sunk costs, resulting in wasted resources. Meanwhile, workers associated with these resources will become unemployed, plunging the economy into a depression. The Austrian School holds that to respond to economic crises, monetary expansion should be halted, but there is no need for drastic contraction. They advocate allowing the economy to return to normal without artificially controlling wages, prices, consumption, or investment.

5. Real business cycle theory

Real business cycle (RBC) theory centers on technological shocks, attributing economic fluctuations to exogenous, random technological shocks. RBC theory posits that in a competitive economic environment, the dynamic effects of technological shocks are the primary cause of most macroeconomic fluctuations. RBC theory attempts to integrate long-term economic growth trends with short-term cyclical fluctuations, seeking to explain both simultaneously. Within the "shock-transmission" mechanism framework, RBC theory extracts technological shocks from long-term trends, viewing them as the source of economic fluctuations. Thus, RBC theory attributes economic fluctuations to supply-side technological shocks, differing from Keynesianism, which emphasizes demand shocks, and monetarism and rational expectations theory, which emphasize the short-term effects of monetary shocks.

### *1.3 The Interpretations of China's Economy by Various Economic Cycle Theories*

Currently, the academic community has not reached a consensus on whether the Juglar cycle is clearly present in the China's economy. Sun Xiaoying et al. (2009) and Ma Jiaxi (2011) have argued that, from the period of reform and opening up until 2005, China's economy experienced three economic cycles, lasting nine, nine, and ten years, respectively. By analyzing the length of these economic cycles, we can see that fixed capital investment drove China's economic cycles. Therefore, the Juglar cycle emerged as a typical economic cycle in China after the reform and opening up period. An Hongyu (2013) has contended that fluctuations in enterprise fixed equipment renewal investment and investment returns are the main drivers of the Juglar cycle, and China has experienced three rounds of Juglar cycles since 1981. However, other scholars believe that the approximately ten-year economic cycles observed in China are not typical Juglar cycles but rather "political" economic cycles based on the timing of official promotions. China's economic structure, dominated by public ownership and the significant market share of state-owned enterprises, means that political influences play a crucial role in the economy. Consequently, the "promotion cycle" combined with "macro control" forms the primary source of economic cycle fluctuations in China (Liu Ruiming and Bai Yongxiu, 2007).

Compared to fixed asset investment, the academic community primarily studies the relationship between inventory investment and economic cycles. Yu Jing et al. (2005) have found that external manifestations of economic fluctuations are seen in inventory investment fluctuations. Ji Min and Wang Yue (2009) have pointed out that industrial inventory fluctuations in China have exhibited pro-cyclical characteristics. Xu Zhiwei et al. (2012) have argued that previous research does not distinguish between finished goods and raw materials inventories. Raw material inventory investment is counter-cyclical, but finished goods inventory investment is pro-cyclical. The overall pro-cyclicality of total inventory investment is largely due to the strong pro-cyclicality of finished goods.

In recent years, with the increasing connection to the international academic community, Chinese scholars have started using the RBC models and DSGE models to study China's macroeconomic fluctuations. Huang Zelin (2005) has constructed a three-sector RBC model for China, incorporating government expenditure as an exogenous random shock variable. His empirical tests on China's economy post-reform and opening up have found that technological shocks and government expenditure shocks could explain over 70% of China's economic fluctuation characteristics. Li Hao et al. (2007) have extended the closed RBC model to an open economy and found that introducing government purchases into the open economy model can significantly improve its explanatory power for China's economic conditions. Lü Chaofeng and Huang Meibo (2012) have introduced belief shocks and uncertainty equilibrium into the RBC model and found that government expenditure shocks can explain 60% of China's economic fluctuations, making it a major source of macroeconomic shocks. Guo Jie and Guo Qi (2015) have differentiated between the state-owned sector and the private sector in the RBC model and discovered that after introducing financial intermediaries, the role of the government can cause increase in investment demand in the state-owned sector. This, through the loan pricing behavior of financial intermediaries, caused interest rate fluctuations, which were then transmitted to the private sector, ultimately altering the allocation structure of macroeconomic credit funds and consumption levels. As an improvement on the RBC model, the DSGE model has become an important tool for domestic scholars in conducting research related to economic cycles. Liu Bin (2008) turns out to be the first to establish a DSGE model based on China's actual economic conditions and estimate the model parameters using Chinese data for central bank policy analysis. Wang Guojing and Tian Guoqiang (2014) have studied the dynamic impact differences of financial shocks on real economic variables and financial variables, finding that financial shocks play a very important role in explaining output growth, investment growth, debt growth, wage growth, and employment fluctuations. He Qing et al. (2015) have constructed a DSGE model with nominal price rigidity and collateral constraints to study the relationship between the Chinese real estate market and macroeconomic fluctuations. Their results showed that shocks from the real estate market profoundly impact China's macroeconomy, becoming an important factor driving China's economic cycle fluctuations. Yang Xiaohai et al. (2017) have improved the latest research methods within the framework of a two-country DSGE model; at the same time, they conduct policy simulations based on economic fundamentals concerning the gradual opening of China's outward equity investment process and assess its potential risks. As China enters a "new normal" in its economy, more scholars are using the DSGE model to discuss uniquely Chinese economic issues such as shadow banking (Qiu Xiang and Zhou Qianglong, 2014; Hou Chengqi and Huang Tongtong, 2020), local government debt risk (Liang Qi and Hao Yi, 2019; Li et al., 2020), and the transformation of the monetary policy framework (Wang Xi et al., 2016; Bian Zhicun et al., 2019).

## 2 Key Developments and Issues in Economic Cycle Theory

Since the twentieth century, Western scholars' focus on economic cycle theory has gradually shifted from endogenous economic cycle theory to exogenous economic cycle theory. Initially, Western economists preferred to study the intrinsic causes of economic cycles. The "multiplier-accelerator" model, based on endogenous economic cycle theory, achieved significant success. Endogenous economic cycle theory posits that the demand for final products or changes in it will lead to changes in the demand for intermediate products, ultimately resulting in economic cycles. Although the endogenous economic cycle theory, analyzed through the "multiplier-accelerator" model, has made important contributions to explaining the occurrence of economic cycles, Frisch (1931) has found that the number of differential equations in the "accelerator" theory is less than the number of variables, leading to an indeterminate solution in the accelerator model. This shortcoming was magnified in the context of mainstream economics becoming increasingly mathematical and emphasizing empirical research. At the same time, the cyclical pattern of "boom-recession-boom" (i.e., economic cycle model) in macroeconomics should gradually converge to a steady state using alternating peaks and troughs. The DSGE model (and its predecessor, the RBC model) consists of first-order stochastic difference equations, allowing the DSGE model to better simulate the cyclical fluctuations and persistence of alternating peaks and troughs in economic cycles. This mathematical formulation led to the exogenous economic cycle theory replacing the endogenous economic cycle theory as the mainstream macroeconomic analytical framework. The direct result was a shift in academic research from focusing on the causes of economic cycles to analyzing the transmission processes of exogenous shocks within the economy.

Combining the exogenous random shock analysis framework with economic cycle theories of different eras led to the development of Real Business Cycle Theory (RBC theory), New Classical Economic Cycle Theory, and New Keynesian Economic Cycle Theory (DSGE model). Since the birth of the RBC model, the predecessor of the DSGE model, mainstream economic cycle theories of various eras have continued to explore and innovate upon the basic assumptions and core conclusions of this model, while the underlying analytical framework has consistently adhered to exogenous economic cycle theory. Exogenous economic cycle theory holds that economic cycles and financial crises result from the combined effects of exogenous shocks and internal transmission. It assumes that exogenous shocks are random and unpredictable. Under this assumption, short-term fluctuations in economic cycles can only be attributed to exogenous random shocks, making it impossible to explain the underlying causes of economic cycles. In the DSGE model framework, the fundamental source of economic fluctuations remains exogenous random shocks, which are modeled as stochastic difference equations to ensure that the DSGE model, when subjected to shocks and deviating from the steady state, can alternate between peaks and troughs before re-converging to a steady state. The DSGE model achieves the endogenization of the shock transmission mechanism through the optimal behavior of micro economic agents and the general equilibrium framework, but not the endogenization of the shock sources.

Exogenous shock theory posits that without shocks, there are no crises. Only when the intensity of exogenous shocks is large enough, or if there is some mechanism within the economy to amplify these exogenous shocks, can exogenous shocks evolve into crises. The DSGE model studies the general equilibrium issues of the economy under uncertainty, exploring how real shocks (such as technological shocks and interest rate shocks) are transmitted and cause economic fluctuations, while describing the dynamic changes of variables such as GDP, consumption, investment, prices, wages, employment, and interest rates. Given the uncertainty, the DSGE model employs dynamic optimization to characterize the decision-making behaviors of economic agents, coupled with constraints such as resource constraints, technological constraints, information constraints, and market clearing conditions, to construct a system of equations describing economic operations. By solving this system of equations, the DSGE model derives the expected economic growth under the general equilibrium framework (i.e., the steady state solution).

This is the fundamental reason why existing mainstream economic cycle theories and research paradigms failed to predict the 2008 global financial crisis: On the one hand, before the 2008 global financial crisis, the academic community had insufficient understanding of the impact of financial intermediary sectors on economic cycles. The mainstream DSGE models introduced financial frictions only through information asymmetry (Kiyotaki and Moore, 1997; Bernanke and Mihov, 1998), generally neglecting the modeling of the behavior of financial intermediary sectors and underestimating the vulnerability of economies with financial frictions when facing external shocks. The DSGE model originated from the RBC model and inherited the RBC model's research paradigm of using dynamic optimization methods to handle the optimal behavior equations of micro economic agents under uncertain environments. Subsequently, the New Keynesian School expanded the DSGE model's modeling approach by introducing market friction assumptions such as price rigidity and the financial accelerator. Whether it is the financial accelerator model or the credit constraint model, they both conduct macroeconomic analysis of financial markets at the level of nominal frictions, lacking discussion of the heterogeneous frictions existing among different types of financial institutions and various financial markets. This deficiency makes it difficult to predict the financial crisis and economic recession triggered by the subprime mortgage crisis. On the other hand, taking the 2008 global financial crisis as a turning point, policymakers before the crisis generally adhered to the dominant ideology of "post-crisis rescue." Theoretically, although the exogenous economic cycle theory represented by the DSGE model assumes that exogenous shocks are unpredictable, research on the shock transmission mechanism can reveal that certain links within the economy may have an amplifying effect on the impact of shocks. Monitoring these links within the economy can provide early warnings of crisis occurrences. Since exogenous shocks are unpredictable, the best policymakers can do is to wait for the occurrence of exogenous shocks and then mitigate the negative impacts of the crisis. However, the outbreak of the 2008 global financial crisis demonstrated that the presence of financial frictions not only increased the probability of crisis occurrence but also weakened the effectiveness of macroeconomic policies and increased the difficulty and cost of crisis rescue efforts, leading to comprehensive skepticism from the academic community regarding the exogenous economic cycle theory and the DSGE model analytical framework.

We believe that various economic cycle theories have played important roles in explaining cyclical phenomena in economic operations from different perspectives, but they also have clear limitations.

(1) Regarding the connotation of economic cycles: Is the connotation of economic cycles that the short-term trend fluctuates around the long-term trend, or the cyclical fluctuations of actual economic activities? From the perspective of Keynesian theory, the economic cycle prominently features two stages: rising (expansion) and falling (contraction), as well as two turning points: peaks and troughs (see Fig. 6.2). From the Keynesian perspective, the economic cycle refers to fluctuations around the potential economic growth trend. However, earlier economic cycle theories were derived from actual data, commonly using real economic growth data, naturally implying that the connotation is the fluctuations of actual economic activities. From the perspective of RBC theory, it refers to the cyclical fluctuations of actual economic growth and no longer distinguishes between long-term economic growth and short-term economic fluctuations, making RBC theory a typical real economic growth theory. In practice, many situations exhibit a mixture of the

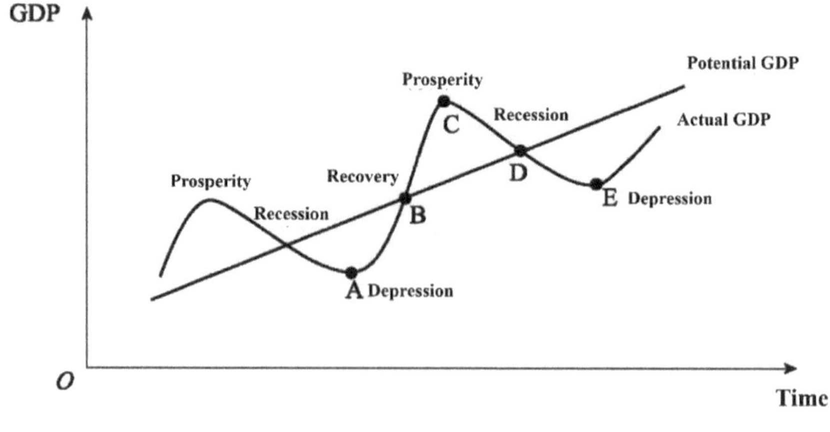


**Fig. 6.2** Economic cycle curve from the Keynesian perspective

two; for instance, some theories use the former in discussions but switch to the latter when it comes to verification or actual data. Therefore, the core issue is which of the two is more reasonable.

(2) The issue of whether the causes of fluctuations in economic cycle theory are exogenous or endogenous: We believe that explaining cyclical phenomena using exogenous shock factors is rather strained. By attributing the causes of economic cycle fluctuations to exogenous shocks, exogenous economic cycle theory addresses the issue of the causes of economic cycles. However, it fails to provide a reasonable explanation for the essence of exogenous shocks and why specific forms of exogenous shocks occur at specific times, which is its most serious flaw. At the same time, since exogenous economic cycle theory attributes the causes of economic fluctuations to exogenous shocks, it cannot capture the development brought about by internal changes in the economy, such as the interactions and mutual promotion among economic agents that lead to an overall improvement in economic quality. This is akin to attributing inexplicable phenomena and factors to mysterious forces. While we acknowledge that mysterious forces can cause shocks and that fluctuations are normal, it is unrealistic for such mysterious forces to exhibit such strong periodicity. If such good periodic phenomena truly exist, we can re-examine them by elevating the dimensional perspective, thus revealing that the so-called periodic mysterious forces are not exogenous shocks but endogenous natural phenomena. This is similar to the tidal phenomenon, which has strong periodicity. From the Earth's perspective alone, it appears as an exogenous shock, but when taking the moon into consideration, it becomes an endogenous shock, providing a reasonable explanation.

(3) The issue of whether the achievements of China's reform and opening up can be reasonably explained: Using exogenous economic cycle theory and DSGE models alone cannot explain the long-term and sustained economic growth that China has achieved since the reform and opening up. If we view the initial policy dividends and utilization of foreign capital during the reform and opening up as exogenous shocks, according to the economic principle of diminishing marginal returns on factor inputs, it is difficult to explain China's sustained and high-speed economic growth

driven solely by exogenous shocks (i.e., upward economic fluctuations), which has not shown significant signs of recession or depression. Exogenous economic cycle theory posits that shocks cause the economy to deviate from a steady state but eventually return to it, implying that after a period of prosperity, the economy would enter a state of depression and ultimately revert to pre-shock levels. Exogenous economic cycle theory overlooks the logical relationship between technological progress and the economic industrial structure, excessively focusing on the unpredictability and randomness of exogenous shocks, thereby weakening the model's explanatory power. Meanwhile, endogenous economic cycle theory lacks an internal connection between consumption structure upgrades, technological progress, and economic cycle fluctuations, and it does not consider many real-world constraints (such as demand constraints and resource constraints). Both economic cycle theories based on these two logic fail to provide a comprehensive and reasonable explanation for the significant economic achievements China has made since the reform and opening up, necessitating the use of new economic cycle theories for explanation.

(4) The logical basis for the internal relationship between various economic cycle theories and cycle lengths: Schumpeter speculated on the relationship between the lengths of various economic cycles. This involves several important questions: What is the logical mechanism for the internal connection and length relationship between these cycles? Why do they have a general proportional relationship? What is the logical mechanism behind this?

(5) The inherent difficulties in explaining economic cycles based on equilibrium theory: Equilibrium theory addresses specific states, while cycles emphasize the recurring process of change, presenting a natural contradiction between the two: If equilibrium is well-maintained, cycles are unlikely to exist; if cycles exist, equilibrium loses its significance to some extent.

In summary, while economic cycle theory has made considerable progress, its shortcomings are also evident. We anticipate the development of a relatively unified economic cycle theory model that can systematically explain these issues, elucidate their internal logical relationships and mechanisms through comprehensive analysis, and explain the scenarios and conditions for economic prosperity and crises within the model. This would enable us to predict macroeconomic trends, formulate appropriate economic policies, and more effectively regulate macroeconomic development.

## 3 Economic Cycle Model from the Perspective of Rational Synthesis

The construction of economic cycle models is crucial for the innovation of economic cycle theories. Below, we are going to establish a theoretical model from the perspective of rational synthesis to systematically analyze the issues of economic cycles.

### *3.1 Economic Cycle Model from the Perspective of Rational Synthesis*

As previously mentioned, we utilize the core results of macroeconomic theory to organically combine an "efficient market" and a "proactive government," establishing a rational synthesis model. The main part of this model consists of the following three equations:

$$\Delta Y_t = a\Delta Y_t^* + b\Delta Y_t \tag{6.1}$$

$$Y_t^* = f\left(K_t L_t\right) = \lambda K_t^{\theta} L_t^{1-\theta} \tag{6.2}$$

$$\Delta Y_t^* = \Delta AS + \Delta AD \tag{6.3}$$

Through derivation, we obtain the economic growth Eqn. (6.4), detailed in the fourth chapter of this book. From the perspective of economic cycles, this formula reflects the cyclical changes in actual economic growth. Based on this, we can analyze economic cycle theory.

$$\Delta Y_t = a\Delta Y_{Mt}^* + b\mu_{sl}\Delta A_t Y_{Mt}^* + b\left(\mu_d + \mu_{ss}\right)\left(Y_t - Y_{Gt}^*\right) + b\left(\varepsilon_{dt} + \varepsilon_{st}\right) \tag{6.4}$$

Seen from the above equation, the expansion and contraction phases experienced by various economic agents during the economic cycle are influenced by the third term in Eqn. (6.4), determined by the relationship between aggregate supply and aggregate demand, where effective demand plays an important role, reflecting Keynesian theory. In a simple economic model, the core factor influencing the economic cycle is fixed asset investment, which demonstrates the characteristics of the Juglar cycle, thus serving as the logical basis for considering the Juglar cycle as the primary cycle. The first and second terms together form the long-term economic growth trend, with the first term reflecting the role of market factors and the second term reflecting the role of government factors. Their "resonance" can be seen as a manifestation of the Kondratieff cycle. In extreme cases, a sharp imbalance between AS and AD often indicates economic prosperity or crisis.

### 3.2 *Analysis of the Connotation of Economic Cycles*

According to economic cycle theory, there is no clear explanation as to whether an economic cycle fluctuates around the potential economic growth trend or the cyclical fluctuations of actual economic growth. In most cases, the two are mixed. From the theoretical synthesis perspective, the fluctuations in actual economic growth are more important and more reasonable. Rational synthesis economic theory defines economic cycles as the cyclical fluctuations observed in actual economic activities. This is because the potential economic growth trend itself is uncertain and difficult to measure, as we typically do not know it in real time. Using it as a reference would undoubtedly bring many problems. In practice, major economic cycle theories are generally derived from continuous measurement of real economic data. Moreover, studying the cyclical fluctuations of actual economic growth is more meaningful as it provides better references for practical macroeconomic regulation and counter-cyclical management. Of course, according to our model, these two concepts of economic cycles also have their origins. The long-term economic growth trend is relatively stable, while short-term economic fluctuations generally represent common forms of economic cycles, which can meet general needs.

### 3.3 *Connotation and Internal Relationships of Economic Cycles*

From the perspective of rational synthesis, economic cycles are divided into three categories: The first category mainly consists of cycles influenced by demand-side changes, including the Kitchin cycle, Juglar cycle, and Kuznets cycle. The second category consists of cycles influenced by supply-side changes, including the Kondratieff cycle and Schumpeter's three-cycle nested theory. The third category considers comprehensive changes. The RBC theory actually encompasses a dual understanding of the logic of economic cycles, taking into account both the supply side and the demand side, but without deep model analysis. Schumpeter's three-cycle nested theory qualitatively explains the existence of different types of cycles and suggests that these cycles may have a specific quantitative relationship in terms of their lengths. For instance, there is a general proportional relationship between the Kondratieff cycle and the Juglar cycle.

The fundamental reason for the existence of economic cycles is the cyclical fluctuations in the relative relationship between supply-side and demand-side changes. Generally speaking, the first category of cycles originates from the demand side, where the supply side can be considered constant, and the fluctuations mainly reflect changes in the demand side. Factors such as inventory and real estate investment are important in the demand-side changes, but fixed assets are a more comprehensive factor. Therefore, we can conclude that the Juglar cycle is called the primary cycle based on theoretical grounds. The second category of cycles originates from the supply side, reflecting long-term trends in supply-side changes. In this case, the short-term effective demand fluctuations are not considered, and the root cause of the cycles can be innovation factors or technological changes, which are the bases for Schumpeter's three-cycle nested theory and the Kondratieff cycle theory. The third category can be seen as a comprehensive understanding of both demand and supply sides. Both the RBC theory and Schumpeter's three-cycle nested theory follow a logic that describes the entire system of economic cycles, but they do not clarify this analysis. Particularly, why do the cycle lengths of the two ccategories have a proportional relationship? This is because, under normal circumstances, the potential economic growth reflected by the supply side is related to both the market conditions and the changes in potential economic growth under the influence of the government, mainly related to changes in total factor productivity. It reflects the "resonance" state of potential economic growth caused by two different factors; that is, the effects of the government and the market on the supply side or potential economic growth are in the same "frequency" or cycle state. Mathematically, we assume that the government's role in supply-side changes is contemporaneous. In reality, these changes are not contemporaneous but lagged. We can assume they are realized through contemporaneous and one-period lag, and the potential economic growth rate with the government's role can be constructed as a second-order difference equation based on the principles of multiplier and accelerator, enabling systematic scenario and condition analysis. It is worth noting that the real business cycle theory makes a special assumption: the core transmission mechanism of economic fluctuations caused by technological shocks is the inter-temporal substitution of labor supply, meaning that people reallocate their working hours across different periods, forming the cyclical fluctuations of the economy in response to external shocks. The subsequent discussion in this chapter will reveal this assumption indeed leads to corresponding cyclical characteristics, which is significant. Given that detailed argumentation requires complex mathematical knowledge, we only provide a qualitative logical analysis here.

### 3.4 *Comprehensive Explanation of Economic Cycles*

Thus, we can summarize the economic cycle theory: Overall, economic cycles are the result of the superimposition of cycles triggered by various factors, and different cycles are the explicit manifestations of this superimposition. In a certain period, due to different dominant factors, different characteristics may be presented, which can be said to reflect different cyclical characteristics. The specific conclusions are as follows: First, from a long-term perspective, short-term economic fluctuations will not affect the long-term economic trend. The Kondratieff cycle, reflecting productivity changes, is closely related to the spontaneous action of the market and the continuous and reform-oriented inputs from the government, which can be seen as the cycle of the industrial revolution. Second, various factors can cause cyclical changes in economic growth, but under general economic conditions, the impact of fixed asset investment is most significant. However, fixed asset investment has different sources such as inventory and real estate, so the explicit characteristics of economic cycles are different in different periods. In subsequent empirical analysis, we can see the related results. When a cycle triggered by a specific factor plays a significant role in economic growth during a certain stage, we can call this cycle by that factor's name, such as the "pig cycle" or the "financial cycle," reflecting the significant role of pork prices or financial factors in economic growth during that stage. Third, economic crises and economic overheating are the results of the superimposition of cycle low points or peak points. The "Great Depression" of 1929–1933 is believed to have been caused by the coinciding downward phases of the Kondratieff cycle, Juglar cycle, and Kitchin cycle. By comparing and analyzing the stages of the "Great Depression" and the depressions of 1825–1830 and 1873–1878 within different economic cycles, we find that the Juglar cycle, as a medium cycle, plays a "linking" role; that is, during the depression period, the recovery of the Juglar cycle helps pull the economy back to normal, and during the prosperity period, the sustained prosperity of the Juglar cycle keeps the economy prosperous for a longer time.

## 4 Theoretical and Empirical Analysis of Economic Crisis and Golden Period of Development

To conduct a more comprehensive analysis, we will further examine economic crises and golden periods of development from both theoretical and empirical perspectives.

### *4.1 Theoretical Explanation of Economic Crisis and Golden Period of Development*

Based on the economic cycle logic of the rational synthesis model, we can conclude that major crises or major booms are specific manifestations of dynamic low points or peak points from both the supply side and the demand side. A major crisis results from the extreme imbalance between supply and demand, caused by the overlap of the low points of the long-term economic trend and the short-term economic fluctuations, while a major boom results from the dynamic balance between supply and demand, caused by the overlap of the peak points of the long-term economic trend and the short-term economic fluctuations. Generally, major crises and major booms typically occur at the troughs or peaks of the Kondratieff cycle. It should be noted that major crises or major booms are fundamental laws of economic operation and objectively exist, but their adverse effects can be mitigated through adjustments in macroeconomic policy to maintain more extended periods of economic prosperity.

According to the rational synthesis model, we can further conclude that if, during a particular period, the economic development of a country or major global economies has a solid foundation and environment, and with the transformation and upgrading of the supply and demand sides, total factor productivity can be continuously improved without significant imbalances or crises between supply and demand, then rapid development can be sustained for an extended period. Therefore, theoretically, whether it is the global economy or a single economy, if there is coordinated upgrading and development of the supply and demand sides, along with the advancement of globalization, a golden period of economic development can be anticipated.

### 4.2 *Panoramic Analysis and Empirical Evidence of Economic Crisis and Golden Period of Development*

As shown in Fig. 6.3, the first industrial revolution (Industry 1.0) marked by mechanization featured leading industries such as steam engines, textiles, coal, steel, and railways. The second industrial revolution (Industry 2.0) represented by electrification featured leading industries such as electricity, automobiles, oil extraction, and chemicals. The third industrial revolution (Industry 3.0) marked by automation featured leading industries such as computers, biotechnology, aerospace, and new materials. The predicted major crisis periods roughly align with the "Great Depression" of 1929–1933 and the global financial crisis of 2008. Figure 6.3 also shows that we are currently arriving at a new starting point or the early phase of a golden period of development, namely the fourth industrial revolution (Industry 4.0), marked by intelligence. The leading industries in this phase include the internet, new energy, intelligent technology, 5G, and quantum technology.

In the real economic practice, we can clearly observe periods of golden development. From the 1950s to the early 1970s, the United States,

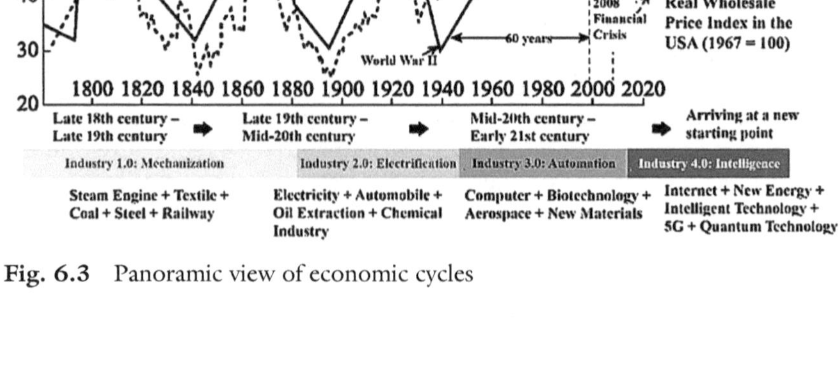


**Fig. 6.3** Panoramic view of economic cycles

Japan, and Western Europe experienced periods of rapid economic development, with an average growth rate of 5% in GDP, known as the golden age of capitalism. Since the reform and opening up in 1978, China has experienced a golden period of development. By adhering to reform and opening up, China has achieved continuous growth and upgrading of both the supply side and the demand side, leading to a prolonged period of rapid development. From 1978 to 2020, China's national economy averaged nearly 10% growth per year, creating a miracle in human history. The reform and opening up significantly stimulated consumption and effective supply, and opening up to the outside world has increasingly tightened China's economic relations with the global economy. China's sustained rapid growth over decades is not accidental but inevitable, embodying profound economic operational laws.

The golden period of development in the United States is also very typical. The US golden period began in the mid-twentieth century and lasted until the early tweny-first century, reaching a "peak" during the "Great Moderation" period of the 1980s. Specifically, during these several decades, the US economy exhibited moderate growth, low volatility, and low inflation. The US golden period also spurred the development of other countries, marking this era as the "third wave of global economic prosperity." Scholars attribute the US golden period to three main reasons: First, technological progress had a highly positive impact on the real economy. The information technology revolution had a massive influence on economic growth. Particularly since the 1980s, the US "Great Moderation" period coincided with the boom of the fifth world technology long cycle, creating a positive resonance effect on US economic development. Second, steadily increasing capital returns promoted investment. Rising capital returns significantly increased the actual investment rate during the "Great Moderation" period, stimulating more investment enthusiasm, and the continuously rising investment led to sustained stable economic growth. Third, improvements in inventory management model altered short cycles. The "Great Moderation" period saw significant improvements in inventory management systems, greatly enhancing inventory management efficiency and altering the inventory-driven short cycles. From the perspective of the rational synthesis model's economic cycle logic, the third industrial revolution drove the US's leading global position in technological innovation and product supply capability. The reconstruction of Europe, the easing of East-West relations, has provided a vast market for the US. Moreover, the US's unique geographic location allows it to avoid the ravages of war, providing a favorable development environment, ultimately leading to the US golden period of economic development.

### *4.3 A New Golden Period of Development Driven from Coordination of Supply and Demand Upgrades and Globalization Process*

The world today is undergoing profound changes unseen within a century, presenting significant strategic opportunities for China, which is in the stage of resurgence. The first centenary goal has been achieved, and the "14th Five-Year Plan" has been formulated. Not only in practice but also theoretically, China is likely to usher in a new and prolonged golden period of economic development in the future. In the new era of deepening reforms and expanding opening up, the driving force for supply-side transformation and upgrading stems from supply-side structural reforms. The new round of technological revolution, represented by artificial intelligence, 5G, and quantum technology, will drive industrial and supply-side transformation and upgrading. The driving force for demand-side upgrades comes from the grand goal of continually meeting people's needs for a better life, and the Belt and Road Initiative leading global market openness will bring rapid demand growth.

In the future, China will not only be a major manufacturing country but also a global super market. The "dual circulation" strategy proposed by China promotes both its own development and the continuous advancement of the global economy. China has signed the world's largest free trade agreement with ASEAN, strengthened cooperation with Africa, Latin America, and the Arab League, and the Belt and Road Initiative will bring enormous demand worldwide. The rapid growth of global demand dynamically matching the supply provided by the fourth industrial revolution will bring about a new golden period of global development.

A peaceful and stable development environment is essential for China to enter a golden period of development. This requires opposing trade protectionism and building a multilateral global governance system while upholding free trade. Since 2018, international trade protectionism has intensified, showing a clear trend of de-globalization. Particularly, the trade protectionism policies of the United States will have an impact on the global economy, including China's economy. As a developed Western country that has benefited the most from free trade, the United States constantly claims to be at a loss. A country that has long touted itself as a model of a market economy is now turning toward trade protectionism, treating multilateral mechanisms and international rules as trifles. If every country adopts "301" clauses against others, where will the world head? Therefore, to usher in a golden period of development, countries must unite, adhere to the direction of peaceful development, maintain the free trade mechanism, and steadily advance economic globalization. In the face of trade friction, China will continue to focus on the international landscape, uphold free trade and the global multilateral framework, maintain resolve, do its work well, and confidently embrace a new golden period of development.

## 5 Principles and Measurement of Economic Cycles Based on the Multiplier-Accelerator Model

Economic cycles are the alternating periods of economic expansion and contraction in economic operations, manifesting as fluctuations in national total output, total income, and total employment. A core issue in economic cycle theory is the length of economic cycles. Various economic cycle theories measure the length of economic cycles primarily based on empirical data or calculations from actual data. Establishing theoretical models and calculating the length of economic cycles based on real-world data is a significant issue worthy of study.

After a period of rapid growth, China's economy is currently transitioning to a new normal of medium-high growth. China's economic growth model has also shifted from being driven by exports and investments to being driven by consumption. The successful practice of China's economy is the foundation of macroeconomic innovation. China's success is a result of the organic combination of an "efficient market" and a "proactive government" (Zong Liang and Fan Ruoying, 2018a, 2018b). The government's counter-cyclical measures have become an important means of smoothing economic fluctuations (Liang Qi and Teng Jianzou, 2006). China's counter-cyclical fiscal policy has undergone stages of preparation, germination, development, and maturity, playing a significant role in promoting long-term economic growth (Liu Anchang, 2019). The fiscal expenditure multiplier during economic downturns is 2.3 times that during economic booms, showing significant counter-cyclical characteristics (Chen Shiyi and Chen Dengke, 2019). Therefore, calculating China's economic cycle must not overlook the roles of both the market and the government's guidance and direction in economic operations.

To determine the characteristics of China's economic cycles, Liu Wei and Cai Zhizhou (2019) focus on fluctuations in economic growth rates and inflation rates, concluding that China's economic growth can be divided into four major cycles. From a cyclical perspective, China is currently at the bottom of the fourth economic cycle and may enter a new growth phase shortly. Wang Qiaoru et al. (2019) have analyzed provincial-level economic cycles from a more micro perspective, concluding that China's overall economy exhibits a new pattern of low volatility and medium-high growth. Regarding the identification of driving factors of China's economic cycles, unlike developed economies where demand (Stock and Watson, 2002), labor (Chari et al., 2007), and credit constraints (Gambetti and Musso, 2017; López-Salido et al. 2017) are the main driving factors, investment, especially government investment, is the primary driver of China's economic cycles. Liu Ruiming and Bai Yongxiu (2007) have found that the promotion incentive system and the central government's macro control are the main causes of China's economic cycle fluctuations. Chen Xiaoguang and Zhang Yulin (2010) have constructed an RBC model to simulate China's economic cycle and found that government consumption is one of the major sources of economic fluctuations in China. Lü Chaofeng and Huang Meibo (2012) have studied the characteristics of China's economic cycles and found that investment fluctuations are higher than consumption and output fluctuations.

Measuring the length of China's economic cycles is also a topic of interest to scholars. Chinese scholars primarily measure economic cycles using actual economic data. Some scholars have attempted to use the multiplier-accelerator model to predict economic growth and explain economic cycle fluctuations. In using the multiplier-accelerator model to predict China's economy, Li Xingwei (2011) has applied the model to China's economy and made growth predictions. Li Lasheng and Guan Minfang (2010) have used the model to forecast the policy effects of the "four trillion" fiscal stimulus plan, concluding that the plan could achieve "maintaining growth," with macroeconomic contradictions shifting to "maintaining employment." In explaining China's economic fluctuations using the multiplier-accelerator model, Zhuang Liting (2010) has proposed using OLS regression to determine the model's parameters, successfully predicting China's economic fluctuations under the premise of significance testing. Hua Dongfang and Hong Min (2013) have examined the impact of marginal propensity to consume, accelerator, and spontaneous investment on economic cycle fluctuations using Chinese data, concluding that the greater the MPC, the longer the time required for economic cycle fluctuations to converge. Ji Yao (2017) has introduced a Markov switching model into the traditional multiplier-accelerator model, solving the issue of estimating time-varying coefficients and calculating that China's economic cycle length after 2003 is ten years.

Scholars continuously expand the theoretical framework of the classic multiplier-accelerator model to better align it with the operation of China's macroeconomy, with a focus on endogenizing government investment behavior. Zou Zhizhuang and Wang Xiaoliang (2016) have confirmed through econometric methods the significant impact of fiscal policy on China's macroeconomic operation since 2006, demonstrating that the traditional multiplier-accelerator model cannot accurately describe China's macroeconomic conditions post-2006. Qin Yu (2016) has endogenized government expenditure in the multiplier-accelerator model as inherent government investment and expected government investment, and analyzed the modified model using annual data from 1978 to 2012. The study found that sustained expenditure could have a lasting impact on China's economic growth, and when China's economy deviated from a reasonable range, government intervention had a strong corrective ability on economic operations.

In light of this, we used the basic principles of the multiplier-accelerator model to explain and calculate economic cycles. The contributions of this study are primarily reflected in three aspects:

First, we expanded the traditional multiplier-accelerator model by incorporating variable government expenditure and spontaneous consumption, enriching the behavior equations of both the household and government sectors, and endogenizing the macro control economic behavior of the government. This emphasizes the significant role of the government sector in the economy, making the model better reflect the operational characteristics of China's economy since the reform and opening up, specifically, the dual regulation of economic growth by an "efficient market" and a "proactive government."

Second, we expanded the multiplier-accelerator model to construct a corresponding economic cycle theoretical model, demonstrating the existence of economic cycles and calculating their lengths.

Third, we combined the model and calculation results to explain the economic implications of economic cycle formation and changes in economic growth rates, identified the driving factors of economic cycles and summarized China's successful economic growth experiences. This provides the necessary theoretical exploration and preparation for future macroeconomic regulation, smoothing China's economic cycles, and promoting China's successful experiences.

### 5.1 *Expanded Multiplier-Accelerator Model*

Samuelson (1939) starts with the simplest national income equation and proposes the multiplier-accelerator model, attempting to combine internal and external factors to explain economic cycles. In this model, the multiplier refers to the multiple between the increase in national income and the increase in spontaneous investment, illustrating the impact of investment on changes in national income. The accelerator indicates the multiple between the increase in capital stock and the increase in national income, reflecting the feedback effect of national income on investment. Samuelson's multiplier-accelerator model is a macroeconomic dynamic system built considering these interactions. It uses real data to reflect cyclical fluctuations, thereby depicting the actual economic cycles. This approach emphasizes the role of investment in economic operations, aligns with Marx's logic of economic cycle analysis, and serves as a simplified dynamic equation of economic operations with significant implications for analyzing economic cycles.

1. Multiplier-Accelerator Benchmark Model and Its Limitations

Based on the national income equation and the multiplier-accelerator principle, Samuelson (1939) has established the following dynamic equation of economic operations:

$$\begin{cases} Y_t = C_t + I_t + G_t \\ C_t = cY_{t-1} \quad t = 0,1,2,\dots \\ I_t = \dfrac{a}{c} \times \left(C_t - C_{t-1}\right) \end{cases} \tag{6.5}$$

Wherein, $Y_t$, $C_t$, $I_t$ and $G_t$ are total income, total consumption, total investment, and government expenditure, respectively. Samuelson set government expenditure as a constant, assuming that the government should not intervene in the market. Over the long term, government expenditure remains at an equilibrium level, i.e., $G_t = G$. $c$ is the marginal propensity to consume, and $a$ is the accelerator, defined as:

$$a = \Delta K / \Delta Y \tag{6.6}$$

Wherein, $K$ is the capital stock, and the accelerator $a$ is the net investment required to increase output by one unit.

However, from the perspective of modern economic theory and the practical experience of various countries, Samuelson's (1939) model has two main aspects needing improvement:

The first is setting government expenditure as a constant. In economic practice, government expenditure in most countries varies significantly from year to year and is closely related to the economic performance and fiscal situation. Additionally, many countries use government expenditure as a crucial tool to regulate the economy when facing various types of economic uncertainties, adjusting public spending to stimulate or stabilize the economy. Government spending behavior increasingly affects economic operations and even changes in economic cycles. Therefore, setting government expenditure as a constant in Samuelson's (1939) model has certain limitations and cannot accurately describe the recent reality of increasing economic downward pressure and expanding fiscal expenditure in China.

The second is that Samuelson's model assumes all investment and consumption are induced. From the viewpoint of modern economic theory, this assumption needs further exploration. Even without income, people will still consume to survive. We divide investment and consumption into spontaneous and induced parts: Induced investment and consumption are those generated due to income, directly related to income. Spontaneous investment and consumption refer to necessary investment and consumption that people undertake even when income is zero, unrelated to changes in income.

2. Adding Variable Government Expenditure and Spontaneous Consumption

To reflect the impact of government expenditure on economic operations, we define $G_0$ as the initial government expenditure and $g_g$ as the annual growth rate of government expenditure. Government expenditure increases at an annual rate of $g$, that is:

$$G_t = G_0 \left(1 + g_g\right)^t \tag{6.7}$$

At the same time, we describe consumption and investment from both spontaneous and induced perspectives:

$$C_t = C_{0t} + cY_{t-1} \quad t = 0,1,2,\ldots \tag{6.8}$$

$$I_t = I_{0t} + \frac{a}{c} \times \left(C_t - C_{t-1}\right) \tag{6.9}$$

Wherein, $C_{0t}$ and $I_{0t}$ are spontaneous consumption and spontaneous investment, respectively. We further assume that $C_{0t}$ is constant over a certain period, i.e.,

$C_{0t} = \overline{C}$; $I_{0t}$ is not constant but is determined by initial spontaneous investment and the annual growth rate of spontaneous investment $g_i$, expressed as:

$$I_{0t} = I_0 \left(1 + g_i\right)^t$$

Based on Samuelson's model, we establish an improved dynamic equation of economic operations:

$$\begin{cases} Y_t = C_t + I_t + G_t \\ C_t = \overline{C} + cY_{t-1} \\ I_t = I_0 \left(1 + g_i\right)^t + \dfrac{a}{c} \times \left(C_t - C_{t-1}\right) \end{cases} \tag{6.10}$$

3. Economic Cycle Calculation Based on the Extended Model

From the above system of equations, a recursive equation for total income can be derived, resulting in a second-order difference equation for period λ:

$$Y_{\lambda+1} = (c+a)Y_{\lambda-a}Y_{\lambda-1} + \bar{C} + I_0(1+g_i)^t + G_0(1+g_g)^t \tag{6.11}$$

To solve the difference equation, we analyze the discriminant of the corresponding characteristic equation to determine the existence of its roots. The discriminant is given by:

$$\Delta = (a+c)^2 - 4a \tag{6.12}$$

When the discriminant $\Delta < 0$, there is a pair of complex conjugate roots:

$$\lambda_1 = \frac{1}{2} \times \left[(a+c) + \sqrt{\Delta}\right] \tag{6.13}$$

$$\lambda_2 = \frac{1}{2} \times \left[(a+c) - \sqrt{\Delta}\right] \tag{6.14}$$

At this point, the general solution to the equation is:

$$Y_t = r^t\left(c_1 \cos \omega t + c_2 \sin \omega t\right) \tag{6.15}$$

Here, national income is a time-dependent equation involving trigonometric functions. The corresponding frequency and economic cycle can be determined as follows.

$$\omega = \text{arctg}\frac{\sqrt{-\Delta}}{a+c} \tag{6.16}$$

$$T = \frac{2\pi}{\omega} = \frac{2\pi}{\text{arctg}\frac{\sqrt{-\Delta}}{a+c}} \tag{6.17}$$

Based on Eqs. (6.16) and (6.17), the necessary condition for the existence of an economic cycle is $\Delta < 0$, meaning the accelerator $a$ must satisfy the following boundary conditions:

$$A_d = 2 - c - 2\sqrt{1-c} < a < 2 - c + 2\sqrt{1-c} = A_u \tag{6.18}$$

Wherein, $A_d$ is the minimum value of $a$ satisfying the condition for the existence of an economic cycle; $A_u$ is the maximum value of $a$ satisfying this condition. Based on the research by Ji Yao (2017) and actual economic data from China, we calibrate the marginal propensity to consume as 0.4, i.e., $c = 0.4$. Using the calibrated value, we calculate the boundary conditions for the accelerator:

$$A_d = 2 - 0.4 - 2\sqrt{1-0.4} = 0.05 \tag{6.19}$$

$$A_u = 2 - 0.4 + 2\sqrt{1-0.4} = 3.15 \tag{6.20}$$

We use cyclical fluctuations in economic growth rates to measure economic cycles. Figure 6.4 illustrates the economic growth scenarios and their characteristics as determined by different values of $a$. The possible values of $a$ are discussed in detail in the following three scenarios.

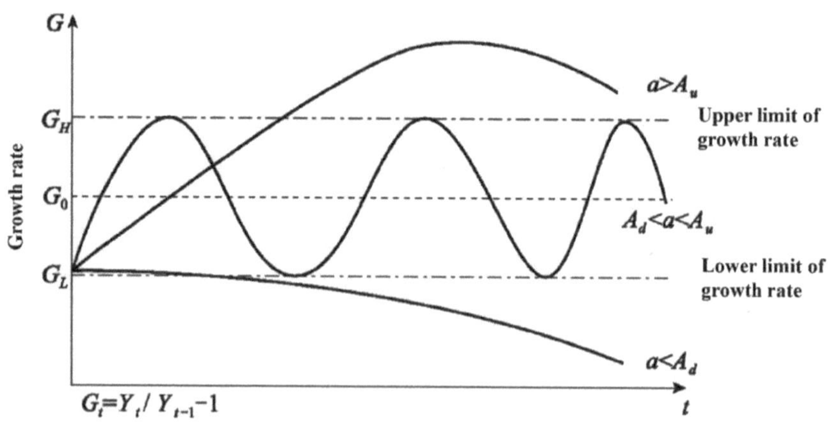


**Fig. 6.4** Relationship between accelerator $a$ and economic cycle. (Source: Compiled by the author)

Scenario 1: When investment willingness and investment amounts are within a reasonable range, with $a$ between the lower limit of 0.05 and the upper limit of 3.15, i.e., $A_d < a < A_u$, this can be seen as the critical condition for the economic cycle operation. At this time, the aggregate supply brought by aggregate demand and investment is roughly balanced, and the economy is in a stable operating state. In the short term, economic operations will exhibit fluctuations due to supply and demand imbalances, but these fluctuations are within a controllable range, allowing the market to spontaneously adjust supply-demand imbalances. In the long term, stable economic growth can be achieved, with the economic growth rate showing cyclical fluctuations.

In an ideal state, through market self-regulation and government macro control, the accelerator $a$ is maintained within the reasonable range of $A_d < a < A_u$, ensuring stable, healthy, and sustainable economic growth.

In his economic growth model, Hicks believes that the upper and lower limits of economic growth are due to limited labor resources, and the growth of spontaneous investment determines the average economic growth rate $G$. We believe that the growth of government expenditure also plays a significant role in economic growth. The average economic growth rate $G$ is determined by the annual growth rate $g_g$ of government expenditure $G_t$ and the growth rate $g_i$ of spontaneous investment $I_{0t}$, i.e., $G = f(g_g, g_i)$.

Scenario 2: Economic overheating occurs when invest willingness is so fervent that the total amount of investment far exceeds what is needed for normal economic functioning. At this point, $a$ exceeds the upper limit of 3.15, i.e., $a > A_u$. Under these circumstances, the economy will deviate from the economic cycle, with aggregate supply far exceeding aggregate demand due to increased investment, leading to supply-demand imbalances. In the short term, excessive investment will bring rapid economic growth, but in the long term, insufficient demand will reduce the economic growth rate, causing future economic recessions. At this time, the government needs to timely implement macro control measures to curb investment growth, reduce aggregate supply, and bring the accelerator $a$ below the critical value $A_u$, helping the economy return to the economic cycle.

Scenario 3: Economic overcooling occurs when the willingness to invest is so low that the amount of investment is far below that required for the normal operation of the economy. At this point, $a$ is below the lower limit of 0.05, i.e., $a < A_d$. Under these circumstances, the economy will similarly deviate from the economic cycle, but for the opposite reason to Scenario 2: aggregate supply is far below aggregate demand due to reduced investment, leading to supply-demand imbalances, and the economic growth rate significantly decreases, resulting in prolonged economic stagnation. At this time, the government needs to implement macro control measures to stimulate investment growth, increase aggregate supply, and bring the accelerator $a$ above the critical value $A_d$, helping the economy return to the economic cycle.

In summary, we conclude that investment is an important variable affecting economic cycles and a crucial tool for implementing macro control. When the economy is in Scenario 1, it can maintain a relatively balanced state. When the economy is in Scenario 2 or Scenario 3, economic growth will deviate from the economic cycle, indicating that for an economy to operate normally, investment should be maintained within a reasonable limit without excessively emphasizing consumption expansion. Some countries (especially developed ones) commonly face this situation. In the case of economic recession, economic stagnation, or new region development, initiating extraordinary investment is a relatively effective means to achieve economic advancement and cultivate new economic growth points.

During the early stages of reform and opening up, China placed significant emphasis on investment growth, achieving rapid economic growth. In the development of certain regions (such as Shenzhen and Shanghai Pudong), investment has played a crucial role. The expanded multiplier-accelerator model analyzes the successful experiences of reform and opening up, illustrating the rationale for measures such as the Belt and Road Initiative to launch infrastructure investments from both theoretical analysis and practical experience perspectives. Additionally, investment growth may cause changes in the accelerator, which can be seen as counter-cyclical regulation, leading to some changes in the economic cycle and achieving the goal of smoothing the economic cycle.

## 5.2 *Calculation the Length of China's Economic Cycle: Methods, Data, and Empirical Results*

1. Method for calculating China's economic cycle

For the model $I_t = I_0\,(1 + g_i)^t + \frac{a}{c} \times (C_t - C_{t-1})$, it is difficult to find a suitable method for regression. Therefore, we first estimate the $I_{0t}$ series, then calculate the $I_{1t}$ series using $I_t$-$I_{0t}$, and finally regress the equation $I_{1t} = \frac{a}{c} \times (C_t - C_{t-1})$. Thus, we establish the following regression model:

$$\begin{cases} C_t = \alpha_0 + \alpha_1 Y_{t-1} \\ I_{1t} = \beta_1 (C_t - C_{t-1}) \\ Y_t = \hat{C}_t + \hat{I}_{1t} + I_{0t} + G_t \end{cases} \tag{6.21}$$

For this model, we can directly use the three-stage least squares method for parameter estimation. The advantage of this method is that it effectively avoids the autocorrelation problem caused by the strong correlation of economic data. The specific method is as follows: first, regress the first two equations using the least squares method and calculate the estimated values $\hat{C}_t$ and $\hat{I}_{1t}$ of $C_t$ and $I_{1t}$, respectively. Then, regress $Y_t$ using $\hat{C}_t$ and $\hat{I}_{1t}$ (the regression coefficients here need to be set to 1). Finally, replace $\hat{C}_t$ and $\hat{I}_{1t}$ with $Y_{t-1}$ and $Y_{t-2}$ in the regression results to obtain:

$$Y_t = f\left(\alpha_0, \alpha_1, \beta_1; Y_{t-1}, Y_{t-2}, I_{0t}, G_t\right) \tag{6.22}$$

2. Data description

(1) Data source and outlier handling: We collected China's annual GDP, total household consumption, gross capital formation, government purchases, and GDP deflator from 1978 to 2017, all sourced from the "China Statistical Yearbook 2018" published by the National Bureau of Statistics. The Asian financial crisis in 1998 and the global financial crisis in 2008 caused data from adjacent years to deviate significantly from normal levels. Therefore, when estimating China's economic cycle using the three-stage least squares method, we excluded data from 1997 to 1999 and 2008 to 2009.

(2) Constant price processing: Using 1978 as the base year, we converted the nominal values of total output, consumption, gross capital formation, spontaneous investment, induced investment, and government expenditure to real values based on 1978 price levels using the GDP deflator. Ideally, the fixed asset investment price index should be used for constant price processing of gross capital

formation, but this data was not officially disclosed before 1990. To ensure consistency, we chose to use the GDP deflator instead.

(3) Estimating the spontaneous and induced investment: Referring to the research by Han Liyan and Wang Zhebing (2005), we define spontaneous investment as the investment made to offset the capital depreciation of the previous year. Therefore, we need to calculate the capital stock for each year and set the capital depreciation rate. The method used here to estimate the capital stock is the perpetual inventory method, commonly used in economics. First, estimate the initial capital stock:

$$K_0 = I_0 \times \frac{g+1}{g+\delta} \tag{6.23}$$

Wherein, $I_0$ is the gross capital formation of the first year, and $\delta$ is the capital depreciation rate.

In calculating China's capital stock, Shan Haojie (2008) has obtained a depreciation rate of 10.96%, while Zhang Jun (2003) has set the depreciation rate at 9.6%. Following their research results, we choose 10% as the depreciation rate. The initial growth rate of the capital stock $g$ can be estimated using the following formula:

$$g = \sqrt[n]{Y_t / Y_0} - 1 \tag{6.24}$$

Wherein, $Y_t$ is the total output at the end of the given period, and $Y_0$ is the total output at the beginning of the period. Using 1978 as the initial year and 1982 as the final year, the calculated $g$ is 7.41%. We then use the perpetual inventory method to estimate the capital stock for each year:

$$K_t = I_t - \delta K_{t-1} \tag{6.25}$$

According to the definition of spontaneous investment, i.e., investment to offset the capital depreciation of the previous year, spontaneous investment is calculated as:

$$I_{0t} = \delta K_{t-1} \tag{6.26}$$

Since spontaneous investment and induced investment together constitute total investment, induced investment can be easily calculated as:

$$I_{1t} = I_t - I_{0t} \tag{6.27}$$

(4) Sample regression interval selection: In the study of economic cycles, some scholars decompose economic data using filtering methods and then extract the decomposed cyclical sequences, observing economic cycles through charting. BK filtering is a Band-Pass filter that separates high-frequency irregular disturbances in calculations, while HP filtering is an approximate High-Pass filter that may miss high-frequency irregular movements. Therefore, we use BK filtering for processing. The specific steps are as follows. First, we take the natural logarithm of total output $Y_t$ to obtain $\ln Y_t$. Second, we calculate the first-order difference of $\ln Y_t$, the result of which approximates GDP growth. Finally, we decompose the GDP growth into trend (Trend) and cycle (Cycle) sequences, and extract the cyclical sequence for charting, as shown in Fig. 6.5.

As shown in Fig. 6.5, China's economic growth exhibits cyclical fluctuations, with two distinct cycles around 1995 and 1998 of different lengths. The first cycle, roughly 11 years long, closely resembles the Juglar cycle, while the second cycle, about 18 years long, aligns with the Kuznets cycle. Given the significant role of real estate in economic cycles, we divided the overall sample into two sub-intervals: 1978–1996 and 2000–2017, excluding the data from 2008–2009.

3. Empirical results

Here, we use the three-stage least squares method to estimate China's economic cycles since the reform and opening up in 1978. The results are shown in Table 6.2. Compared to 1978–1996, the marginal propensity to consume $c$ decreased slightly after 2000 (from 0.479 to 0.380). This is due to increased incomes, reflecting a significant improvement in people's living standards. However, the change in consumption habits of Chinese consumers took time, and the concept of frugality and saving still influenced consumers in China. As a result, the marginal propensity to

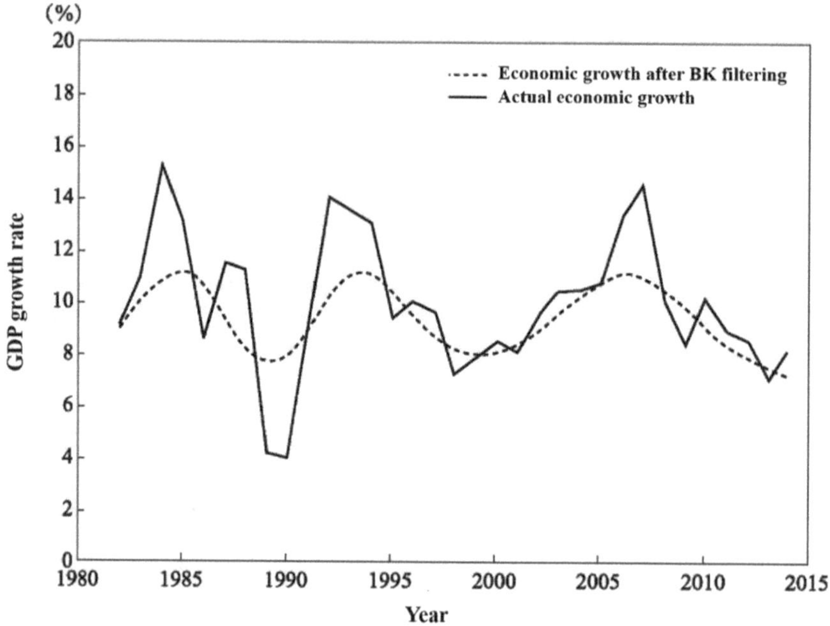


**Fig. 6.5** Comparison of economic growth after BK filtering and actual economic growth. (Note: The solid line represents China's actual economic growth, while the dashed line represents economic growth after BK filtering. BK filtering requires the removal of the first and last three observations. Additionally, calculating the growth rate requires using the first observation as the base period. Therefore, the sample period for the BK-filtered results is from 1982 to 2014)

consume during this period decreased compared to 1978–1996, directly causing the boundary conditions $[A_d, A_u]$ of the accelerator to increase slightly (from [0.077, 2.965] to [0.045, 3.195]), thereby raising the upper limit of economic growth. However, the accelerator $a$ itself grew rapidly (from 2.04 to 2.78), nearing the critical value, which significantly increased the economic cycle $T$ (from 12.8 to 19.3). The calculation of China's economic cycle length reveals that China's economic cycle has gradually transitioned from the Juglar cycle (a medium cycle of about ten years dominated by fixed investment) to the Kuznets cycle (a medium-long cycle of about 20 years dominated by construction investment). The earlier period approximating the Juglar cycle indicates that this stage was

**Table 6.2** Estimation result of China's economic cycle

| | *1978–1996* | *2000–2017* |
|---|---|---|
| $c$ | 0.479*** | 0.380*** |
| | (0.009) | (0.008) |
| Beta1 | 4.271*** | 7.300*** |
| | (0.307) | (0.438) |
| $a$ | 2.04 | 2.78 |
| | 1978–1996 | 2000–2017 |
| $A_d$ | 0.077 | 0.045 |
| $A_u$ | 2.965 | 3.195 |
| $T$ | 12.8 | 19.3 |

Note: Values in parentheses are t-statistics; ***, **, and * represent significance levels of 1%, 5%, and 10%, respectively

driven by cyclical fluctuations in fixed investment, while the later period approximating the Kuznets cycle was primarily due to the significant role of real estate-related investments in China's national economy during this phase. It is worth noting that China first allowed mortgage loans in 1998 and liberalized the real estate market. Since then, China's real estate industry has grown annually, increasing its influence on economic cycles. As China's investment becomes more balanced in the future, the prominence of real estate investment will diminish, and the nature and length of China's economic cycles will also change.

Meanwhile, we note that although economic growth depends on both investment and government expenditure, the size of the accelerator is positively correlated only with the size of investment. This is because $K_t = (1-\delta)K_{t-1} + I_t$, and when the capital depreciation rate $\delta$ is 0, $\Delta K = I_t$. In this case, the accelerator $a$ satisfies the equation of $a = \Delta K/\Delta Y = I_t/\Delta Y$, indicating that if investment $I_t$ overheats, $a$ will increase. Given a constant marginal propensity to consume $c$, $a$ will gradually approach and exceed the threshold, leading to a deviation from the economic cycle.

After 2000, as the marginal propensity to consume decreased, China's economic development increasingly relied on investment. Particularly after the 2008 global financial crisis, the global economic recession dragged down exports, and weak consumption led to insufficient domestic demand. In response, the Chinese government launched a "four trillion yuan" economic stimulus plan. This fiscal stimulus policy effectively supported the economic growth but also indirectly increased the accelerator. However, as shown in Table 6.2, the current accelerator in China is still below the threshold, indicating that the economy remains stable. As China's economy transforms, consumption will gradually replace investment as the key driver of economic growth, leading to an increase in the marginal propensity to consume and a reduction in the boundary conditions for the accelerator. If the accelerator remains high, economic growth may deviate from the economic cycle, necessitating active macro control by the government to curb investment overheating. Additionally, we should consider the crowding-out effect of government expenditure on private investment. When the government increases expenditure, private investment decreases, which can help suppress an excessively high accelerator to some extent. Since total output is a function of investment and government expenditure, i.e., $Y = f(I_t^+, G_t^+)$, the government can still maintain economic growth by increasing expenditure and restraining investment. In this case, the accelerator will decrease because the numerator decreases and the denominator increases.

Currently, China's economic growth rate is declining (i.e., $\Delta Y$ is decreasing), while total investment is increasing annually (i.e., $I_t$ is increasing), causing $a$ to increase annually and approach the threshold. This results in a significantly prolonged economic cycle and weaker cyclical fluctuations. In the coming years, as China's economic growth rate may further decline, $a$ will continue to increase. Given a constant marginal propensity to consume and a fixed upper threshold in the short term, there is a high risk that $a$ will exceed the threshold, causing the economy to deviate from the economic cycle. If $a$ breaks through the threshold, in the short term, aggregate supply will far exceed aggregate demand, leading to a supply-demand imbalance. In the long term, economic growth will further decline due to weak demand, entering a recession phase. Therefore, the Chinese government needs to actively use macro control measures: on the one hand, stimulate the economy by increasing government expenditure to curb investment overheating in the private sector and keep $a$ within a reasonable range; on the other hand, continue to expand domestic demand to ensure that aggregate demand and aggregate supply can match and remain relatively balanced.

## 4. Conclusions and policy recommendations

Based on our understanding and estimation of China's economic cycle, we have incorporated variable government expenditure and spontaneous consumption into the Samuelson (1939) multiplier-accelerator model to establish an improved economic operation equation. The main conclusions are as follows:

First, economic cycles objectively exist and have their boundary conditions. The length of economic cycles is constantly changing, and different dominant factors may result in different characteristics at various stages. Economic cycles are the explicit result of the superposition of various dominant factors and exist under critical conditions. Once investment grows too fast or too slow, exceeding certain boundaries, it will lose basic balance, which can be seen as a condition of market failure to some extent.

Second, economic cycles are jointly determined by the accelerator $a$ and the marginal propensity to consume $c$. Investment is an important variable affecting economic cycles and a crucial tool for macro control. The accelerator $a$ determines the stability of the overall economic cycle: overheated investment will lead to an excessively high accelerator, causing economic growth to lose its cyclical nature, with short-term aggregate supply far exceeding aggregate demand and long-term economic depression. Conversely, low investment will result in an excessively low accelerator, with short-term aggregate supply far below aggregate demand, leading to prolonged economic stagnation. Our analysis using the expanded multiplier-accelerator model suggests that China's Belt and Road Initiative, which starts with infrastructure investment, is reasonable. Investment growth may cause changes in the accelerator, leading to some changes in the economic cycle and helping to smooth the economic cycle to some extent.

Third, China's economic cycle can be divided into two stages, each with distinct driving factors and characteristics. The first stage, from 1978 to 1998, features an economic cycle close to the Juglar cycle, mainly influenced by fluctuations in fixed investment. The second stage, after 1998, saw rapid development in construction and real estate due to the implementation of mortgage policies, with the economic cycle gradually extending to exhibit characteristics of the Kuznets cycle. Regression results for the accelerators and economic cycle lengths for 1978–1996 and 2000–2017 show that compared to 1978–1996, the marginal propensity to consume decreased, and the accelerator increased after 2000, with the economic cycle tending to lengthen.

Our research has important policy implications: First, maintaining investment within a reasonable range is crucial for ensuring the stable operation of China's economy. Excessive or insufficient investment may cause the accelerator to increase or decrease, undermining economic stability. Given the slow recovery of the global economy and complex and volatile internal and external economic conditions, it is necessary to avoid the risks associated with the accelerator exceeding the threshold and keep investment within a relatively reasonable range to lay a foundation for stable economic growth. Second, the government should actively play a regulatory role, balancing short-term and long-term growth goals. In the short term, to prevent economic growth from deviating from the economic cycle, the government should actively implement macro control measures, maintaining the basic balance of the three major demands and promoting stable growth in investment and government expenditure. In the long term, it is essential to expand domestic demand, use measures such as fee reductions and tax cuts to transform China from an investment-driven economy to a consumption-driven one, and support high-quality economic development in China.

## 6 Business Cycle Forecasting and Counter-Cyclical Management from the Perspective of Rational Synthesis

Economic operation is the result of the dual roles of the market and the government, both of which are indispensable. In recent years, Western economies that advocate market economies have frequently experienced economic crises characterized by prolonged duration, high severity, and difficulty in policy rescue, with government intervention becoming the primary policy option. This highlights the importance of macro control.

Macro control needs to be based on accurate forecasts. It is important to acknowledge the long-term, cyclical, and complex nature of economic development. While planning for long-term economic growth, it is also essential to pay attention to the leap changes in the economy, represented by drastic changes in productivity and social relations. Here, we carefully consider the characteristics of economic dynamic non-linearity from the perspective of rational synthesis and explore the implementation of counter-cyclical economic policies.

## 6.1 Forecasting

The purpose of forecasting macroeconomics from the perspective of rational synthesis is to grasp future economic trends and provide potential directions for future economic activities, to develop optimal economic development plans from a long-term perspective. Currently, data-driven time series forecasting methods are the mainstream in macroeconomic forecasting. These methods are based on historical data and the assumption that events that occurred in the past are likely to happen in the future, indicating a link between the past and future. These methods statistically analyze historical data to predict economic trends. However, time series forecasting methods have inevitable errors or defects because they cannot consider external factors. If there is a significant exogenous shock in the economy, the forecast may deviate significantly, making time series methods more effective for predicting short- to medium-term economic fluctuations rather than long-term economic growth. The longer the forecast span is, the greater the possibility of changes in the external environment will be. If only time factors are considered while ignoring the impact of external factors on economic entities, the forecast results may significantly deviate from the actual situation.

The economic cycle theory from the perspective of rational synthesis is still based on the benchmark equation in the rational synthesis model framework, considering both the role of the "invisible hand" of the market economy and the importance of government regulation, the "visible hand." When used for forecasting, the rational synthesis economic cycle theory has better predictive ability because its endogenous logic-based modeling technique helps overcome the shortcomings of exogenous models, such as time series models, in economic forecasting. It considers the nonlinear dynamics of the economy. Forecasting within this analytical framework helps provide more reliable planning and policy tools. Equation (6.28) is the forecasting equation of the rational synthesis model. For the sake of analysis, the formula is quoted again below:

$$\Delta Y_t = a\Delta Y_{Mt}^* + b\mu_{sl}\Delta A_t Y_{Mt}^* + b\left(\mu_d + \mu_{ss}\right)\left(Y_t - Y_{Gt}^*\right) + b\left(\varepsilon_{dt} + \varepsilon_{st}\right) \quad (6.28)$$

Based on the analysis of the above equation, we can conclude the following: economic growth is driven by both long-term trends and short-term fluctuations, with economic cycles representing the cyclical fluctuations of actual economic growth. The first and second terms comprehensively consider the roles of both the market and the government, reflecting the Kondratieff cycle. $\Delta \hat{Y}_t$ represents the relative changes between aggregate supply and aggregate demand due to government actions and can also be seen as the result of the interactions of other cycles besides the Kondratieff cycle. In economic operations, changes in market factors such as capital and labor, government's roles, total factor productivity changes represented by technological innovation inputs, and long-term industrial policies all influence the long-term trend of economic growth. Temporary composite shocks from the supply side and demand side are the main sources of short-term fluctuations in economic growth. Supply-side shocks include temporary industrial policies and exogenous random shocks, while changes in fiscal policy, monetary policy, and other unknown factors constitute demand-side shocks.

When using the rational synthesis model for forecasting, the interrelationships between various cycles are taken into account. According to Schumpeter's three-cycle nested theory, the three types of cycles show interlocking and mutually restrictive relationships. There are interactions and interdependencies between long cycles, medium cycles, and short cycles. The interaction between medium and short cycles affects the mechanisms of long cycles, while long cycles influence the prosperity and depression levels of medium and short cycles. The interdependence between long, medium, and short cycles also affects forecasting, as previously analyzed. In a purely market economy and a fully planned economy, the structure of medium and short cycles is the same, with medium cycles playing a localized role and not affecting all areas of economic activities simultaneously. For accurate forecasting of an economy's future long-term trends, in addition to capturing short-term exogenous random shocks (short-term exogenous shocks from both supply and demand sides) and fully considering the fundamental characteristics of economic fluctuations, it is necessary to consider the qualitative changes in long cycles induced by quantitative changes in medium and short cycles. Medium cycles playing a localized role can trigger nationwide long cycle changes, driven by a country's substantial technological advancement and major economic structural changes. The rational synthesis model's forecast takes into account the medium and short cycle trends determined by economic policies (such as financial and tax policies) and the changes in the overall economic cycle shape brought about by long-term technological progress driven by supply-side changes. This will become an important reference for China's future economic operations and policy formulation.

## 6.2 Counter-cyclical Management

The outbreak of the 2008 global financial crisis made academia, industry, and supervisory departments realize that if the government adheres to a principle of post-crisis intervention, it not only increases the likelihood of financial crises by ignoring weak links in the financial market but also weakens the effectiveness of macroeconomic policies post-crisis, increasing the difficulty and cost of crisis management. Therefore, counter-cyclical management is of paramount importance for mitigating the destructiveness of abnormal economic fluctuations, ensuring the effectiveness of macroeconomic rescue policies during crises, and facilitating a swift economic recovery.

The theoretical research on counter-cyclical management generally includes the following two aspects. On the one hand, some scholars are dedicated to constructing dynamic macro control theoretical models to explore counter-cyclical management policies. By constructing theoretical models and derivation, the normativity and practicality of macro control are significantly enhanced. For example, insufficient effective demand is the theoretical foundation of Keynesian macroeconomic models, whose research methods include static analysis and comparative static analysis. However, given the exponential growth in economic data and the increasing richness of data dimensions today, classic Keynesian macroeconomic models struggle to accurately compare and analyze economic development processes. Therefore, the increasingly complex economic realities prompt theorists to shift the focus from demand-side macro control to exploring how macroeconomic policies can balance supply-side and demand-side adjustments to achieve dynamic equilibrium between aggregate supply and aggregate demand. On the other hand, some scholars attempt to establish policy framework systems reflecting the latest developments in macroeconomic theory to study counter-cyclical management policies. Currently, macroeconomic theory has developed to the aggregate supply-demand (AS-AD) model, but it is still based on the IS-LM model from the 1930s and 1940s. To reflect the latest advances in economic theory and more accurately depict the current economic operations, there is an urgent need to construct new policy frameworks. From the perspective of rational synthesis, macro control is an organic combination of supply-side and demand-side management, and addressing the contradiction between aggregate and structural issues is crucial to solving problems. The government should flexibly adjust policy tendencies, coordinate the heterogeneous demands of various economic entities in different economic cycles, effectively resolve structural contradictions, and ultimately achieve macro control objectives.

Here, we should base counter-cyclical management on the rational synthesis model's theoretical framework, carefully analyze and rationally coordinate the roles of the government and the market, replace equilibrium research with disequilibrium research, use dynamic research methods to examine changes in economic aggregates, and enrich the content of counter-cyclical management based on the aforementioned comprehensive dynamic equation. Counter-cyclical management is essentially a specific form of macro control aimed at smoothing economic cycle fluctuations and maintaining stable macroeconomic operations. It primarily has two modes:

Mode One: Regulating aggregate demand to smooth economic cycle fluctuations. This mode takes Keynesian theory as the guiding principle, regulating short-term aggregate demand to achieve economic growth and relatively stable economic operations, which is a narrow use of macro control policy. In an economic environment where aggregate supply significantly exceeds aggregate demand, and insufficient demand is a prominent issue, this mode is suitable for macroeconomic control, with fiscal policy being the core.

Mode Two: Based on the AD-AS model, this mode balances supply-side and demand-side adjustments. It comprehensively employs supply-side and demand-side measures to achieve stable economic growth, which is a broad use of macro control policy. When the imbalance between aggregate supply and aggregate demand is low and there are issues with both, dynamic equilibrium adjustment can achieve stable and sustainable economic growth. In this scenario, government regulation affects not only short-term economic fluctuations but also long-term economic trends and growth. Therefore, this mode requires attention to both monetary and fiscal policies and supply-side policies, particularly cross-cycle policies related to supply-side reform.

In summary, economic cycles should reflect the cyclical fluctuations of actual economic growth and activities. Although the lengths of economic cycles vary due to different factors, each cycle alternates between prosperity and depression, which is the commonality between cycles. The multiplier-accelerator interaction and its extensions explain economic cycles well and provide a good simplification of real economic operations. The endogenous analysis method is meaningful and provides a theoretical basis for economic cycles. The root of cyclical economic fluctuations lies within the economic system itself, rather than being caused by external factors. The delayed effect of relevant factors is an essential basis for the existence of economic cycles. That is, only endogenous variables can drive economic cycles, while exogenous variables can only influence economic fluctuations indirectly through endogenous variables. Government-driven supply-side reforms can affect a country's long-term potential economic growth cycles, while short-term economic intervention policies can mitigate cyclical fluctuations. Maintaining a dynamic balance between supply and demand sides is crucial to keep the economic operations stable.

CHAPTER 7

# Theoretical Modeling and Empirical Analysis of the Middle-Income Trap

The Middle-Income Trap (MIT) refers to the situation where a country's development prospects may diverge after reaching the middle-income stage (with a per capita GDP of approximately USD4000). The outcomes could be either continued development toward becoming a developed country or economic stagnation leading to the MIT. Therefore, studying the MIT is crucial. Practically, it affects the future of many developing economies and consequently the global economic outlook. Theoretically, existing literature lacks in-depth research on the MIT and fails to provide a theoretical model or scenario analysis. After over 40 years of rapid growth, China's per capita GDP continuously exceeded USD10,000 in 2019–2020, nearing the standard of high-income countries. China has set a significant goal of reaching a moderately developed country status by 2035, providing a solid subject for theoretical research. This chapter will construct a theoretical model of the MIT based on its connotation and international experiences, reveal possible scenarios and conditions theoretically, and conduct empirical analysis to offer references for China and other economies to smoothly pass through the MIT and advance into the high-income country club.



Z. Liang, *The Innovation of Economic Theory in China*,
https://doi.org/10.1007/978-981-95-2713-7_7

## 1 Literature Review

### 1.1 The Concept of the MIT

The MIT was first mentioned by the World Bank in the report *East Asia's Renaissance* in 2006. The report stated that "after a country's per capita income reaches the middle-income level, it fails to smoothly transition its economic development model, leading to a loss of sustained economic growth momentum, and resulting in prolonged economic stagnation." The report also highlighted that "the East Asian region faces widespread income distribution inequality, which further enlarges the wealth gap and hinders the transformation and upgrading of regional economic development models." Hence, caution against the MIT is warranted.

In 2008, the World Bank first announced quantitative sub-criteria for the MIT, which have been updated almost annually since then. According to the *World Development Report 2008*, the standards were as follows: low-income countries have a per capita national income of less than USD905; lower-middle-income countries range from USD905 to USD3595; upper-middle-income countries range from USD3595 to USD11,115; and high-income countries have a per capita national income exceeding USD11,115.

In 2020, the latest standards revised by the World Bank were: low-income countries have a per capita national income of less than USD1036; lower-middle-income countries range from USD1036 to USD4045; upper-middle-income countries range from USD4045 to USD12,535; and high-income countries exceeding USD12,535.

### 1.2 The Essence of the MIT

The essence of the MIT lies in the dual challenges of economic and social transformation that a country faces after moving from the low-income stage to the middle-income stage. Countries entering the middle-income stage often face problems such as the disappearance of the demographic dividend, resource and environmental constraints, and a lack of new economic growth drivers. These countries usually encounter structural imbalances characterized by upward rigidity in supply structures. In terms of industrial structure, there is often a persistent surplus of low-end capacity, while high-end capacity has not caught up. Spatially, there are imbalances in regional and urban-rural development. Socially, class solidification occurs alongside increasing income distribution gaps. Overall, mismatches or disconnections between the real economy and the financial economy are evident.

To address these issues, economic transformation is necessary to cultivate new economic growth drivers. Economic growth mainly stems from increased factor accumulation and improved total factor productivity (TFP). When a country enters the middle-income stage, relying on large-scale input of production factors and expansive economic development is no longer sustainable. Instead, promoting economic structural transformation and upgrading and improving TFP are essential for achieving economic growth. Social transformation is also required to perfect social institutions. Rapid economic growth and social wealth accumulation have widened income disparities and deepened social stratification. Without timely and effective reforms, social contradictions may intensify, leading to frequent conflicts. Transitioning from an era of essential goods to durable goods poses new requirements for social structure and institutions. Encouraging the growth of the middle class, improving social security and welfare systems, and fostering an innovation-friendly market system are necessary. Comprehensive and in-depth reforms targeting interest relations, distribution patterns, and governance levels are essential for smoothly passing the middle-income stage.

Typically, countries caught in the MIT do not experience absolute stagnation but rather exhibit slow growth and an unsustainable high input–low output economic growth model, incurring enormous social costs and irreversible environmental consequences, leading to long-term abnormal growth. Socially, the traditional development model loses credibility, with growing conflicts and contradictions between economic, social, political, and cultural fields due to imbalanced and asynchronous development.

To avoid the MIT, countries need to undergo comprehensive transformations in political, economic, and social aspects. Successfully overcoming the MIT requires multifaceted changes encompassing domestic and international political and economic factors and historical and cultural contexts. Thus, economic policies, whether domestic monetary and fiscal policies or external trade and exchange rate policies, must consider national conditions comprehensively. The implementation and effects of economic policies vary by country, reflecting the intricate interplay of various factors.

## 2 Key Developments and Issues

### 2.1 Debate on the Existence of the MIT

In 2006, the World Bank first introduced the concept of the MIT in its report "East Asia's Renaissance." Since then, research on the MIT has garnered widespread attention, and some studies have even questioned the theoretical existence of the MIT. Many studies suggest that the issue of the MIT is closely related to changes in economic development strategies. For example, in the 2010 World Bank report "Robust Recovery and Risks Accumulated," it emphasized that the strategies for economies to grow from low-income to middle-income were no longer applicable for advancing to high-income economies. The original growth mechanisms can no longer support further economic growth, making it easy for countries to fall into prolonged periods of economic stagnation, with per capita national income struggling to break the USD10,000 threshold. Countries falling into the MIT commonly exhibit characteristics such as economic growth stagnation, high unemployment rates, social unrest, fragile financial systems, serious corruption, widening income disparities, distorted urbanization, and shortages in public services.

Regarding the concept of the MIT, researchers have divided views into two categories. One view attributes the primary cause of falling into the MIT to the widening income gap. In China, scholars like Cai Fang have used statistical methods to analyze relevant cases, proving a certain correlation between the two. A country entering the middle-income stage finds it difficult to maintain high-speed economic growth, resulting in slow growth or even stagnation. Reports from the Organisation for Economic Co-operation and Development (OECD) on the middle class in Latin American countries, lessons learned internationally about Latin American countries falling into the MIT, and reports from the Andean Development Corporation on infrastructure all mention that when per capita income in Latin American countries reaches a certain level, excessive income disparity leads to social unrest, hindering economic development and even causing stagnation. Kenichi Ohno argued that crossing the MIT required going through four stages: market-driven, factor-driven, efficiency-driven, and innovation-driven. The essence of the MIT is the failure to transition from a "national wealth model" to a "people's wealth model" and from a "traditional developmental state" to a "welfare state." Another view posits that falling into the MIT is not necessarily due to income distribution disparities. Peng Gang and Miao Yongwang believed that in cases of countries trapped in the MIT, issues such as economic structure, industrial structure, technological innovation, human capital, and macroeconomic policies would be the obstacles to overcoming the MIT.

Rao Longxian contended that the essence of the MIT was a development trap, where the focus was solely on economic growth while neglecting changes in production methods. Only by achieving a certain level of accumulation can a country bring about meaningful technological revolutions and industrial upgrades. Liu Fuguang asserted that every country's income level must pass through the middle-income stage, and structural issues like income inequality did not necessarily imply problems with the total income level.

### 2.2 *Analysis of the Causes of Falling into the MIT*

Existing research commonly focuses on Latin American countries from various perspectives. Philip and others have studied the relationship between income distribution and economic growth. They believe that when institutional investment is constrained or capital markets are underdeveloped, it is difficult to balance efficiency and equity; when revolutionary technological advances occur, international trade relations change, further widening income disparities. Analyzing the reasons why Latin American countries fall into the MIT, in addition to the early "center-periphery" theory, Fatas and others have proposed the relationship between economic growth and institutional quality, including path dependence, crony capitalism, and development strategy failures. Additionally, large income distribution gaps, industrial structure constraints, trade imbalances, and financial risks are also major research directions.

Lin Yifu, in his analysis of "Latin Americanization," mentioned the development strategy failure. He believes that Latin American countries, in order to protect domestic industries, implemented an import substitution industrialization strategy, causing market price distortions and hindering the normal development of industrialization. Latin American political elites, manipulating state power and using the history of Latin American colonies, guided the masses to resist foreign capital and actively promoted capital nationalization. Liu Hong believed that the "Brazil cost" was the main reason why Brazil fell into the MIT, including overprotection leading to a lack of competitiveness in domestic industries, high interest rates leading to high debt costs, rigid wages, and weak currency leading to hyperinflation.

Fang Hao argued that the core reason why Latin American countries fell into the MIT was the obstruction by vested interest groups. To maintain the current distribution of benefits and price monopoly, these groups hindered technological progress and industrial revolution, thereby obstructing healthy market competition. While Latin American countries hope to emulate the welfare systems of developed countries, domestic income distribution becomes increasingly imbalanced, leading to declining government governance levels, prominent social conflicts, and weak social and economic development. Su Jingchun believed that the lack of labor mobility caused structural unemployment, and the massive accumulation of unemployed workers significantly expanded the informal sector, making the simple pursuit of welfare catch-up behavior unachievable.

The research team from the International Finance Institute of the Bank of China believed that to overcome the MIT, China faced four major challenges: the weakening of traditional growth drivers, the disappearance of the demographic dividend, unreasonable income distribution, and significant constraints on resources and the environment. Chen Liang believed that China's comparative advantages in basic factors such as labor and land were rapidly disappearing, and the role of its original comparative advantages was diminishing. Liu Wei believed that the key reason why China faced the MIT was a lack of innovation and technological development. Hu Angang argued that the main reason why China faced the MIT was the widening income gap, and the inability to deepen reforms was due to unresolved corruption issues.

The research team from the Institute of Economics at the Chinese Academy of Social Sciences pointed out that during the poverty alleviation stage, the goals of the government and enterprises were aligned. After reaching the middle-income level, the government shifted toward welfare expenditure goals, which conflicted with the profit-driven goals of enterprises. This conflict can seriously hinder economic transformation and upgrading, causing the country to fall into the MIT. It's generally believed that economic transformation faced two major problems: whether the market was mature and whether government transformation was successful and aligned with market development.

### 2.3 How to Successfully Pass Through the MIT

From the perspective of the research on other countries, Sun Zhangwei and Qiao Junfeng analyzed the experiences of Japan and South Korea. They concluded that fair income distribution policies were necessary to ensure social stability, while a free trade environment and technological innovation can provide new impetus for economic transformation and upgrading, helping nations to pass through the middle-income stage and enter the high-income stage. Some argue that the development of Japan and South Korea is related to their alliances with the United States and their unique geopolitical environments, but premature welfare policies have had adverse effects on their labor markets. Dou Baoguo believed that Chile's reform experience showed that implementing a free market under authoritarian rule, followed by economic reforms, can achieve sustained economic growth. However, the reform process requires a balance between market and government forces, as economic development is a complex system engineering that necessitates sound political systems and stable social environments.

Regarding China's strategies, Lin Yifu argued that to pass through the MIT, China needed to upgrade its industries, reduce income disparities, and maintain sustainable resource and environmental development. Gu Shengzu asserted that reforms should not be limited to short-term actions or confined to internal departmental adjustments but should actively break departmental interests that constrain reforms. He believed China needed to shift from low-end to high-end industries, from industrialization to urbanization, and from a manufacturing giant to a consumption-driven economy. China needs to transition from exporting goods to exporting capital, with the government significantly developing public services, rigorously addressing corruption, breaking class solidification, and narrowing the income gap.

The research team from the International Finance Institute of the Bank of China emphasized that successfully passing through the MIT required addressing four key issues: fair and reasonable income distribution with inclusive growth; ensuring the supply of energy and resources, developing a low-carbon economy, and emphasizing environmental protection; optimizing and upgrading economic structures, focusing on resolving structural imbalances; and changing the mode of economic growth by discovering new drivers and successfully transitioning from old to new growth drivers. The team believed that China's future economic and social development strategy should focus on balanced distribution, optimizing industrial structures, encouraging technological innovation, and protecting the ecological environment. Chen Liang, analyzing from the perspective of international division of labor, suggested that industrial transformation can help enhance a country's position in the international division of labor. Therefore, it is necessary to increase investment in scientific research and innovation, develop emerging industries, break down institutional barriers, and ensure economic development through strategic trade policies.

The research team from the Institute of Economics at the Chinese Academy of Social Sciences emphasized that the government should not rely on debt financing to promote welfare development. Welfare expenditure should match the level of social and economic development, and market competition should stimulate innovation and optimize resource allocation to achieve sustainable economic growth. Zhang Monan believed that the dollar trap caused emerging markets' economic and financial security to be dragged down by US debt risks. Emerging economies should establish sovereign currency settlement through currency swaps as a future development direction. Sun Liping and others argued that the game between power and market was crucial for transformation, and breaking the deadlock required reducing the gap between social forces and inclusively developing the economy. The World Bank's interpretation of inclusive growth emphasized fairness in opportunity, distribution, and rules.

## 3 The Middle-Income Trap Model from the Perspective of Rational Synthesis

Researching the MIT problem essentially means studying long-term national income issues, which have two primary determinants: the long-term growth trend of national income and the cyclical fluctuations around this trend. Generally, the trend component reflects the results of long-term economic growth, while the cyclical component reflects economic fluctuations. Economic cycles caused by aggregate demand fluctuations are short term, usually lasting several quarters or years, and are trend-stable. In contrast, supply-side shocks can have long-term effects, such as technological progress leading to economic cycles lasting several decades, akin to the Kondratiev wave described by Schumpeter. Nelson and

Plosser's research indicates that total output fluctuations may result from both permanent and short-term shocks, but are mainly influenced by permanent shocks. Long-term economic growth or development is not a trend-stable process but a difference-stable process characterized by a random walk model. These discussions align with our analysis for building theoretical models.

### 3.1 *Building Theoretical Models of the MIT from the Perspective of Rational Synthesis*

Based on our constructed theoretical model in Chap. 4, we can obtain the economic growth equation from a rational synthesis perspective:

$$\Delta Y_t = a\Delta Y_{Mt}^* + b\left(\mu_d + \mu_{ss}\right)\left(Y_t - Y_{Gt}^*\right) + b\mu_{sl}\Delta A_t Y_{Mt}^* + b\left(\varepsilon_{dt} + \varepsilon_{st}\right)$$

The economic growth phenomenon $\Delta Y_t$ is driven by the long-term trend $\left(a + b\Delta A_t\right)\Delta Y_t^*$ and short-term fluctuations $b(\mu_{ss} + \mu_d)(Y_t - Y_{t-1}) + b(\varepsilon_{st} + \varepsilon_{dt})$. The economic fundamentals influencing the long-term trend include capital, labor, government, and technological progress. Short-term fluctuations are affected by temporary supply-side and demand-side shocks. The core difference lies in the fact that the trend part is derived from the superposition of two parts, allowing the government to push for transformation through related policies, altering the nature of the problem. When discussing the long-term issue of the MIT, short-term fluctuations can be disregarded, allowing for simplified processing.

Assuming the change trend of total output $Y_t$ can be described by the following equation:

$$Y_t = \alpha + \beta t \tag{7.1}$$

Wherein, $\alpha$ and $\beta$ are constants, and Eqn. (7.1) indicates that the total output increases by $\beta$ units per time unit.

$$Y_t = Y_{t-1} + \beta \rightarrow \quad or \quad \Delta Y_t = \beta \tag{7.2}$$

If we express external shocks with a random variable $u_t$ and incorporate it into the equation, we get the total output equation reflecting the shock effect.

$$Y_t = \alpha + \beta t + u_t \text{ or } \Delta Y_t = \beta + u_t - u_{t-1} \tag{7.3}$$

$$Y_t = Y_{t-1} + \beta + u_t \text{ or } Y_t = \alpha + \beta t + u_{t-1} + u_{t-2} + \ldots + u_0 \tag{7.4}$$

Equation (7.3) indicates that the shock effect lasts only a short period before returning to the trend line, whereas Eqn. (7.4) indicates that any shock to total output has a cumulative effect or lasting impact. Variables conforming to Eqn. (7.4) are called "difference-stable" variables, dominated by permanent shocks, while trend-stable processes are primarily influenced by short-term shocks. Sustained steady growth in an economy provides more welfare to the residents of that economic region, and GDP can measure national or regional economic development and reflect the abundance of material products.

Therefore, we need to set up a model to examine the concept of the growth rate.

Let $Y_t$ represent the total output at time $t$, and $Y_{t-1}$ represent the total output at time $t - 1$. The growth rate in terms of total output is:

$$g_Y = \frac{Y_t - Y_{t-1}}{Y_{t-1}} \tag{7.5}$$

If $y_t$ represents the per capita output at time $t$, and $y_{t-1}$ represents the per capita output at time $t - 1$, the growth rate in terms of per capita output is:

$$g_y = \frac{y_t - y_{t-1}}{y_{t-1}} \tag{7.6}$$

Observing the per capita GDP growth rates of various countries, it is evident that countries with higher GDP growth rates over time can achieve higher income levels. Let $y_t$ and $y_{t+n}$ represent the per capita GDP of a country at time $t$ and $t + n$ respectively, then the average growth rate of per capita GDP over $n$ periods is:

$$g = \left( \frac{y_{t+n}}{y_t} \right)^{\frac{1}{n}} - 1 \tag{7.7}$$

Economic growth is the foundation of human welfare progress; even minor differences in growth rates can lead to significant differences in living standards among nationals over time. Table 7.1 and Fig. 7.1 show the income level differences for seven countries with various growth rates, starting from a per capita income of USD1000. After 50 years, the income levels of different countries vary greatly.

In a certain period, if a country implements significant macro control policies and causes substantial changes in influencing factors, this will alter the country's economic growth path. If an economy can change its growth path through reforms and technological innovations, raise the potential economic growth rate to a higher level, and simultaneously implement related macroeconomic policies and supporting measures, it can achieve long-term, high-speed steady growth, thereby successfully passing through the MIT, as shown in Fig. 7.2. Below, according to the World Bank's relevant standards, we conduct related scenario calculations using specific data.

**Table 7.1** Scenario calculations for passing through the MIT (growth rate = $g$) (Unit: USD)

| *Number of years* | *Country 1* $g = 1\%$ | *Country 2* $g = 2\%$ | *Country 3* $g = 3\%$ | *Country 4* $g = 4\%$ | *Country 5* $g = 5\%$ | *Country 6* $g = 6\%$ | *Country 7* $g = 7\%$ |
|---|---|---|---|---|---|---|---|
| 0 | 1000 | 1000 | 1000 | 1000 | 1000 | 1000 | 1000 |
| 10 | 1100 | 1220 | 1340 | 1480 | 1630 | 1791 | 1967 |
| 20 | 1220 | 1490 | 1800 | 2190 | 2650 | 3207 | 3870 |
| 30 | 1350 | 1810 | 2430 | 3240 | 4320 | 5741 | 7612 |
| 40 | 1490 | 2210 | 3260 | 4800 | 7040 | 10,277 | 14,974 |
| 50 | 1645 | 2692 | 4384 | 7107 | 11,467 | 18,420 | 29,457 |
| 60 | 1817 | 3281 | 5892 | 10,520 | 18,679 | 32,988 | 57,946 |
| 70 | 2007 | 4000 | 7918 | 15,572 | 30,426 | 59,076 | 113,989 |

Source: Calculated by the author

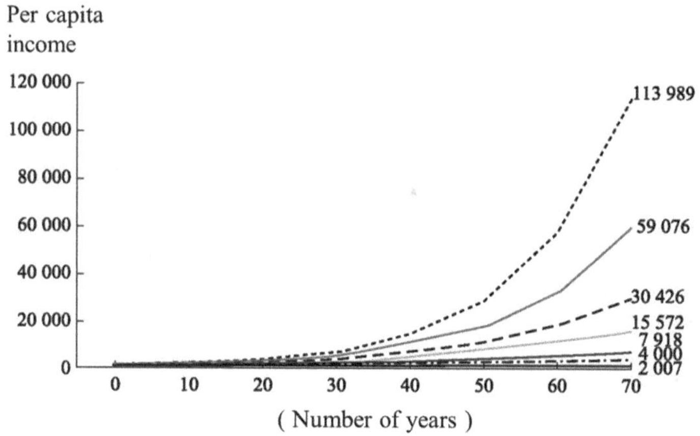


**Fig. 7.1** Economic growth rate calculations for passing through the MIT. (Source: Compiled by the author)

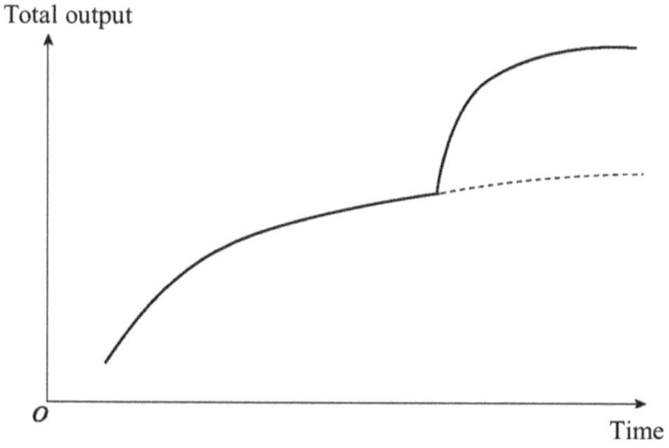


**Fig. 7.2** Possible paths for passing through the MIT

### *3.2 Scenario Assumptions for Passing Through the MIT*

Overall, whether an economy can pass through the MIT depends on its economic development level, growth rate, and duration. As shown in Table 7.1, a theoretical critical point can be determined: to increase per capita GDP from USD1000 to over USD10,000, an economy must maintain an economic growth rate of at least 4% for 60 years; to increase from

USD2000 to over USD10,000, at least 40 years are needed; and to increase from USD4000 to over USD10,000, at least 20 years are needed. Theoretically, maintaining a 4% growth rate should allow an economy to pass through the MIT. The time required for a country to pass through the MIT is related to its initial economic development level, growth rate, and duration. Relatively speaking, if initial conditions are better and growth rates higher, the time required is shorter; if initial conditions are worse and growth rates lower, the time required is longer. It should be noted that as the economy develops and per capita GDP increases, maintaining a high economic growth rate becomes increasingly difficult. For instance, once an economy reaches developed country status, growth rates typically range from 2% to 3%.

Through analysis, we can outline the following scenarios and conditions. When assessing whether economic growth rates can pass through the MIT, it is necessary to consider that the classification standards given by the World Bank are dynamically changing. Late-developing countries need to achieve relatively higher economic growth rates compared to early-developing countries to pass through the MIT. (In the model, for ease of classification, we simplified this consideration, but it will be taken into account in actual country-specific analyses.)

Scenario 1: Being able to pass through the MIT. Main conditions: For a developing economy with initial conditions, such as a per capita GDP of USD4000, an average potential economic growth rate of 6% or higher, combined with supportive policies and a stable external environment, achieving long-term sustained economic growth can allow it to pass through the MIT in 15–20 years. If a developing economy has an initial condition of around USD1000 per capita GDP, at least 40 years are needed. It is crucial that the government promotes the upward shift of the potential economic growth rate curve through reforms, educational investments, technological investments, and industrial policies, which can appropriately reduce the time needed.

Scenario 2: Being in the critical interval of the MIT. Main conditions: A developing economy with certain initial conditions but can only maintain an average economic growth rate of 4–6% for 40 years faces two possibilities: either it can pass through the MIT or fail to do so. In this case, the requirements for governments are high, and the key is whether the policies can effectively promote actual economic growth. If policies and the external environment remain stable, achieving long-term sustained economic growth results in a favorable outcome; otherwise, the economy will fall into the MIT. Simultaneously, if the initial conditions are around a USD1000 per capita GDP level, the chances of passing through the MIT are very slim. If the per capita GDP is already around USD2000, the chances of passing through the MIT are relatively higher, although slower economic growth will make the time needed slightly longer.

Scenario 3: Being unable to pass through the MIT. Main conditions: A developing economy with a long-term economic growth rate below 4% and average initial conditions, such as a per capita GDP of USD1000–2000, is almost certain to fail to pass through the MIT. Without significant reforms or technological innovation initiatives to drastically increase the potential economic growth rate, short-term measures to stimulate economic growth will not sustain long-term economic growth. Meanwhile, policies and the external environment need to remain stable to achieve actual economic growth.

### 3.3 *Analysis and Prediction of Whether Economies can Pass Through the MIT*

Table 7.2 shows the relationship between the economic development of some countries and their ability to pass through the MIT.

As shown by the actual data, the United States became a middle-income country in the 1920s and reached high-income status by the mid-1950s, taking nearly 40 years to pass through the middle-income stage with an average economic growth rate of only 4.96%. The US case has certain particularities: firstly, the United States experienced a 10-year period of super-high economic growth around the time of the Pacific War, with an average growth rate of 10.48% during this decade; secondly, the establishment of the Bretton Woods system in 1946 made the dollar the international currency, a factor that is incomparable to other countries and ensured the United States as the leading developed country. Germany passed through the middle-income stage in the 1940s–1960s, taking about 20 years with an average economic growth rate of 6.77%. Japan passed through the middle-income stage in the 1960s–1970s in less than 20 years, with an average economic growth rate of 6.9% (since the World Bank's classification standards for low-, middle-, and high-income countries were first given in 2008, adjustments were made considering inflation for older developed countries which mostly became developed before the 1970s). South Korea had a per capita GDP of USD834 in 1976 and USD10,385 in 1994, taking less than 20 years to pass through the

**Table 7.2** Relationship between economic development and passing through the MIT in selected countries

| *Country* | *Rapid development period (40 years)* | *Average economic growth rate (g)* | *Passed through the MIT or not* |
|---|---|---|---|
| USA | 1916–1955 | 4.96% | Yes |
| Germany | 1924–1963 | 6.77% | Yes |
| Japan | 1948–1987 | 7.10% | Yes |
| South Korea | 1961–2000 | 9.04% | Yes |
| Brazil | 1941–1980 | 7.07% | Yes |
| Mexico | 1941–1980 | 6.20% | No |
| Argentina | 1903–1942 | 4.18% | No |
| Indonesia | 1950–1989 | 4.15% | No |
| Malaysia | 1901–1940 | 5.39% | No |
| Thailand | 1953–1992 | 6.48% | No |
| India | 1980–2019 | 6.10% | Unknown |
| China | 1963–2002 | 9.57% | Unknown |

Note: During the calculations, extreme data from Germany (1945 and 1946) and the United States (1946) at the end of World War II were excluded

middle-income stage with an average economic growth rate of 9.04%. Brazil had a per capita GDP of USD775 in 1973, which rose to USD11,286 by 2010, but then fell back, with a per capita GDP of USD8717 in 2019, taking a long 50 years with an average economic growth rate of 7.07%. In 2019, Brazil chose to give up its developing country status and barely entered the ranks of developed countries.

However, even in the fastest 40 years of economic growth, the average economic growth rate of Argentina and Indonesia did not exceed 4.5%, thus remaining trapped in the MIT for a long time. Mexico, Malaysia, and Thailand had average economic growth rates of 4.5% to 6.5%, but due to the lack of a long-term stable domestic political and economic environment, these countries failed to smoothly pass through the MIT.

According to relevant forecasts, India's difficulty in passing through the MIT is greater than China's. India's per capita GDP first exceeded USD1000 in 2007, and its average economic growth rate over the following 13 years was 6.46%, with a per capita GDP of USD2100 in 2019. In the next 20 years or more, India's average economic growth rate must maintain at least 8% for it to have a chance of pass through the MIT. China reached a per capita GDP of over USD1000 in 2001, and over the following 19 years, its average economic growth rate was 9.04%, with a per capita GDP of USD10,973 in 2020. Although this is still below the World Bank's 2020 high-income country threshold of USD12,536, China is expected to soon join the ranks of high-income countries. If China can maintain an average economic growth rate of 5.5% or higher over the next 15 years, it will smoothly reach the status of a moderately developed country.

### 3.4 *Analysis of Differences in Economies' Ability to Pass Through the MIT*

Why do economic growth rates vary significantly across countries? We need to empirically test the impact of various factors on a country's economic growth. To do this, we intend to use the actual economic growth rate of a country to regress against the potential economic growth rate and various major factors. To conduct this regression, we need to obtain data on the potential economic growth rate; thus, we first estimate the potential output series.

$$Y_t = AK_t^{\alpha} L_t^{\beta} \tag{7.8}$$

$$\ln Y_t = \ln A + \alpha \ln K_t + \beta \ln L_t \tag{7.9}$$

Assuming economic output follows the Cobb-Douglas function as shown in Eqn. (7.8), taking the natural logarithm of both sides of it yields Eqn. (7.9). We select time series data for actual economic output $Y_t$, capital stock $K_t$, and actual employment $L_t$ for the countries to be tested. Regressing Eqn. (7.9) provides the parameter values $\alpha$ and $\beta$ for each country. We believe that the estimation of potential economic output should be based on capital stock and potential employment.

$$P_t = \text{hptrend}\_P_t + \text{hpcycle}\_P_t \tag{7.10}$$

$$\frac{L_t}{P_t} = R_t = \text{hptrend}\_R_t + \text{hpcycle}\_R_t \tag{7.11}$$

$$\text{LP}_t = \text{hptrend}\_P_t \times \text{hptrend}\_R_t \tag{7.12}$$

To obtain the potential employment series, we apply the HP filter to the economic population $P_t$ and the ratio of actual employment to the economic population $R_t$, obtaining Eqns. (7.10) and (7.11). Extracting the trend components hptrend_$P_t$ and hptrend_$R_t$, we derive the potential employment $LP_t$ from Eqn. (7.12).

$$Y_t = C + \alpha_0 Y_t^* + \sum_{i=1}^{6} \alpha_i X_{it} + \varepsilon \tag{7.13}$$

Substituting the capital stock, potential employment, parameter values, and constants into Eqn. (7.13) provides the logarithmic value of the potential output $\ln YP_t$ for each country.

$$\Delta Y_t = a \Delta Y_{Mt}^* \tag{7.14}$$

Finally, we empirically test the factors influencing economic growth using Eqn. (7.14). $Y_t$ represents a country's actual economic growth, $Y_t^*$ represents the country's potential economic growth, $X_{it}$ represents various factors affecting the actual economic growth, $C$ is the constant term, and $\varepsilon$ is the error term.

At a certain point in time, if a country implements significant macro control policies that cause substantial changes in influencing factors, it will alter the country's economic growth path. Under the original path, the output growth path $Y_1^A$ of Country A (a developing country) is lower than the output growth path $Y_2^B$ of Country B (a developed country). At time $Q_{t1}$, if Country B implements proactive macro control policies (or trade protectionist policies), in the short term, this will increase Country B's net exports $\left(\Delta T_{tBA}^G - \Delta X_{tAB}^G\right)$. In the long term, these policies can increase Country B's total factor productivity, leading to an increase in the potential output path to $Y_2^{B'}$. At this point, if Country A continues to develop along the original output growth path, the gap with Country B will widen, making economic catch-up increasingly difficult. In Fig. 7.3, if Country A chooses to implement supply-side reforms favorable to long-term economic growth at time $Q_{t2}$, such as optimizing resource allocation, industrial structure, and distribution structure, a proactive government can increase Country A's total factor productivity through regulation, enabling a leap in Country A's output growth path to $Y_1^{A'}$. Over time, Country A will achieve a comprehensive dynamic competitive advantage transition at point V at time $t^*$.

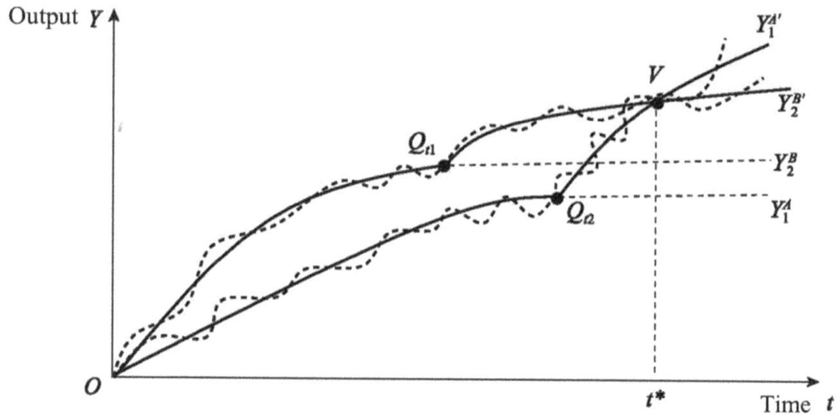


**Fig. 7.3** Transition of dynamic comprehensive competitive advantage

## 4 Country Case Studies

### *4.1 Analysis of the Latin American Economic Development Model*

1. The economic development process in Latin America

From the mid-nineteenth century to the eve of World War II, after achieving national independence, Latin American countries utilized the single economic base established by their former colonial powers and explored a development path centered on primary product exports. They further transitioned to an industrialization path focused on primary import substitution. After World War II, Latin American countries actively adjusted their economic development strategies, divided into the following three periods:

First Period: Broad Promotion of Import Substitution Industrialization

Starting in the 1950s, Latin American countries entered the golden period of import substitution industrialization. The national economy maintained a prolonged period of high-speed growth, with the per capita GDP growth rate achieving a "three-stage jump" from 1.7% in the 1950s to

2.2% in the 1960s and then to 3% in the 1970s. Main Latin American countries successively completed the framework and construction of their industrial systems, with the industrial production value accounting for 30% of GDP, and most Latin American countries successfully entering the middle-income stage.

Second Period: The "Lost Decade" After the Debt Crisis and Liberalization Reforms

During the development of import substitution industrialization in Latin American countries, many issues accumulated. Domestically, there were problems such as widening income gaps, high market protection, and lagging production efficiency. Internationally, they faced the failure to effectively take over labor-intensive industries relocated from developed countries, missing opportunities to absorb capital and technology, and ultimately being excluded from the international division of labor. Due to poor responses to the debt crisis that erupted in the 1980s, Latin American countries embarked on liberalization reforms, increasing their economic dependence on developed countries and international capital. Simultaneously, domestic issues erupted, and economic growth slowed, leading to the "lost decade" for Latin American countries.

Third Period: Post-import Substitution Strategy Implementation

In the 1990s, Latin American countries had to accept the unfair international division of labor and adopted a strategy combining export orientation with import substitution, somewhat returning to a resource-export-dependent development path. Some countries developed export-processing platforms targeting the US market. Meanwhile, the development of emerging countries such as China led to a sustained rise in resource prices, and Latin American countries' economic growth began to accelerate. Although the overall economy of Latin American countries warmed up, domestic issues remained prominent, and they were repeatedly adversely affected by financial crises, failing to explore new long-term competitive development paths. Particularly, extreme political instability and social conflicts in the Latin American region have been the most significant factors restricting the long-term stable development of national economies in these countries.

2. Manifestations of the MIT in Latin America

According to the World Bank report, the MIT in Latin America is characterized by the following three features. The first is that it includes numerous middle-income countries. Among the 33 economies in Latin America, 28 have reached middle-income levels. Of these, 68% are upper-middle-income countries, and 32% are lower-middle-income countries. The second is long-term low economic growth rates. Since the 1980s, the annual average economic growth rate in Latin America has been 1.2%, with a per capita economic growth rate of −0.9%. In the 1990s, these indicators recovered to 3.2% and 1.4%, respectively, and have risen again in the twenty-first century. However, their economic growth rates neither match those of emerging countries nor recover to their own levels from 30 years ago. The third is prolonged stagnation at middle-income levels. Some Latin American countries reached middle-income levels as early as the 1970s. By 2019, the time major Latin American countries had been stuck in the MIT had generally exceeded 40 years. Specifically, Brazil for 44 years, Mexico for 45 years, Colombia for 40 years, and Argentina for over 50 years.

The problems encountered in the urbanization process of Latin American countries are often referred to as "urban diseases." Due to the massive migration of rural populations to urban areas, the economic and social carrying capacity and the speed at which urban public services are improved cannot meet the demands of urbanization. The initial cities in Latin America emerged during the colonial period, incorporating a certain population and commercial system. Following their independence, the benefits generated by the export of primary products further promoted urban prosperity. By the 1950s, the urbanization rate in Latin American countries had exceeded 40%, passing through the global average of less than 30% at the time. During the period of import substitution industrialization, with economic prosperity providing ample material support, there was significant demand for urban development and population growth. Even during the "lost decade," the trend of urbanization in Latin America did not slow down, and by the twenty-first century, the urbanization rate had reached 80%, even higher than that of Europe.

3. Analysis of the main causes of Latin America falling into the MIT

(4) The failure to transition during the industrialization process in Latin American countries is considered the main reason for falling into the

MIT. The primary factors leading to the unsuccessful transitions during the four development phases in Latin America include: (1) Path Dependence Based on Initial Development Conditions; (2) Differences in Geopolitical Situations and External Demand Compared to East Asia; (3) Domestic Economic Systems and Preferences of Interest Groups; and (4) Intervention of Foreign Capital.

However, it is also important not to completely negate the industrialization process of Latin American countries.

Before the 1930s, the development path of exporting primary products chosen by Latin American countries stemmed from the unique economic structures established during the colonial period and expanded with national independence. This path matched the widespread international demand for Latin American primary products at the time. With the revenue from selling primary products globally and the introduction of foreign capital, Latin American countries built and improved infrastructure such as railways and ports, leveraging their abundant resources and labor advantages. During the Great Depression of 1929–1933, weak international demand severely impacted primary product exports from Latin America, forcing these countries to adopt an import substitution industrialization path to utilize the domestic market. The contraction in external demand led to a decline in primary product exports and reduced trade revenue, limiting their import capacity and forcing them to abandon the gold standard. Consequently, Latin American countries implemented the following methods:

(1) Active Monetary and Fiscal Policies: They provided credit, tax incentives, and adopted other supportive measures to strengthen domestic infrastructure construction and encourage the development of import substitution industries and their supporting sectors, fully promoting import substitution industrialization.
(2) Exchange Rate Controls and Trade Protection Policies: They imposed measures to control exchange rates for imported consumer goods and adopted trade protection policies to reduce imports, creating conditions for the development of domestic vulnerable industries.

In the early stages of import substitution industrialization in the 1950s, Latin American countries achieved an average annual economic growth rate of approximately 5.1%, with an industrial growth rate of 6.9%, demonstrating significant success with this strategy. However, after the initial "honeymoon period," inherent flaws in the import substitution industrialization model began to surface:

(1) Limited Overall Domestic Market Size: This constraint limited further industrial development.
(2) Dependence on Imported Production Equipment and Raw Materials: Increasingly severe foreign exchange shortages hindered the import of necessary industrial inputs.
(3) Fiscal Pressure from Government-Led Industrialization and Infrastructure Development: The government's role in driving industrialization and infrastructure projects imposed significant fiscal burdens.
(4) Lack of Market Competitiveness and Over-reliance on Monopolistic Profits by State-Owned Enterprises: Excessive protection led to a lack of market competitiveness and the inability of state-owned enterprises to participate in international competition and expansion.

Although Latin American countries attempted to shift toward export-oriented strategies and change the status quo, the inertia of the import substitution industrialization path was substantial. Past economic successes, combined with strong opposition from domestic vested interest groups, made the transition to an export-oriented model extremely slow and challenging.

By the early 1970s, the contradictions in Latin American countries had accumulated and developed to a very acute point, making transformation urgent. However, an unexpected event forcibly alleviated the outbreak of contradictions, once again delaying the pace of transformation. This unexpected event was the global oil crisis. The crisis brought new opportunities for Latin America's primary products, especially oil. Due to the massive influx of dollars, abundant fiscal revenue, inflow of international capital, and reduced capital costs, the willingness and motivation of Latin American countries to optimize fiscal and expenditure structures, open domestic markets, and participate in international market competition were further weakened. Latin American countries continued irreversibly down the path of import substitution industrialization, further developing deep import substitution of durable goods and capital goods. After the debt crisis erupted in the 1980s, relevant countries and international organizations forced Latin American countries to comprehensively reform their previous models and implement a series of policies under the neo-liberal framework. The rapid and comprehensive transformation of development models and policy systems caused severe economic and social shocks, ultimately leading Latin American countries into the MIT.

Many studies have pointed out that besides the choice of industrial development models, imbalanced income distribution is another important reason for Latin American countries falling into the MIT. Exploring the causes of income disparity in Latin American countries and how the income gap solidified and further expanded is crucial for understanding the adverse impacts of severe income inequality on their economic and social development. From the perspective of changes in national political and economic systems, the persistence of income inequality is influenced by three factors:

First, Severe land concentration laid the foundation for income inequality. In the early twentieth century, large landowners, who made up about 1.5% of the farming population in Latin American countries, occupied over 50% of the arable land. For instance, in Mexico, only 5% of farmers could own land, while the top 200 largest landowners controlled about 25% of the nation's arable land. Due to inadequate subsequent land reforms and a lack of attention to land and agricultural issues, severe income inequality emerged at the early stages of nation-founding in Latin American countries, exacerbating conflicts between different social classes and becoming a historical legacy.

Second, the centralization and bureaucracy in Latin American Countries is severe. Influenced by their former colonial powers, Latin American countries exhibit severe centralization and bureaucratic tendencies in their political practices. This leads vested interest groups to maintain the current structure of interests, hindering the market's ability to effectively allocate resources. Consequently, the national economy cannot proactively adapt to new domestic and international conditions, making it difficult for the lower classes to share in growth dividends and improve their income levels.

Third, the lower classes take the adverse consequences of radical and short-sighted economic policies. To secure electoral success, Latin American governments often adopt very radical economic policies to temporarily alleviate income disparity and issues arising from economic transformation. These include significantly increasing budgets, adopting extremely expansionary fiscal policies in the short term, and government-led wealth redistribution. Overly aggressive fiscal policies and monetary easing lead to a significant increase in short-term individual incomes. However, the affluent classes benefit more from government projects and further acquire resources, causing economic and political power to continue to shift covertly toward the wealthy, ultimately resulting in high unemployment and hyperinflation. The actual income of the lower classes decreases, creating a vicious cycle.

The formation of a debt crisis is typically due to domestic fiscal deficits and balance of payments deficits. In the case of Latin America, the latter was the primary cause, closely related to the region's industrialization path. The United States, as a global and regional power, has always considered Latin America its backyard, continuously exerting political and economic influence to control the region's rich resources and vast market. During the Great Depression, under the guidance of dollar diplomacy, the United States actively supported Latin American countries through their first debt crisis. Simultaneously, the US capital gradually took control of the issuance of government bonds, loan sources, and foreign direct investment in Latin American countries, increasing their dependency on the US capital. However, the Great Depression led to a decline in Latin American exports and reduced revenues, eroding their ability to repay international debts. Coupled with decreased national income leading to reduced imports and significant losses in tariff revenues, Latin American countries were forced to shift to an import substitution model. Subsequently, many Latin American countries declared their inability to continue fulfilling debt contracts, leading to the eruption of the second debt crisis.

(1) During the Latin American debt crisis, countries in the region were compelled to implement economic policies and advance a series of institutional reforms under the neo-liberal framework. Throughout this reform process, domestic and foreign cross-border capital in Latin America found common ground, promoting the integration of domestic and foreign capital. Foreign capital, through this integration, gained stronger control over Latin American resources, severely restricting domestic industrial development. After the debt crisis, creditor countries and lending banks demanded urgent adjustments from Latin American countries: (1) Vigorously Promote the Export of Primary Products: Expanding the scale of international trade revenues to repay foreign debts. (2) Restrict Imports and Constrain Domestic Demand: This led to the already

weakened domestic investments due to economic fatigue to redirect toward agricultural products, crude oil, minerals, and other primary product sectors. As a result, the manufacturing sector faced severe capital shortages, causing many manufacturing enterprises to struggle or go bankrupt. This led to a rapid expansion of primary product exports and a sharp reduction in the export of industrial goods, further solidifying Latin American countries' roles in the global industrial chain as suppliers of primary products.

(2) Private capital in Latin America also actively exploited the debt crisis to seize and consolidate social wealth: (1) Engaging in Financial Speculation: During the initial financial market turmoil, they utilized low exchange rate policies to conduct financial speculations and massively transferred funds overseas. By the late 1980s, capital flight from Latin American countries was extremely severe, with the proportion of fleeing capital relative to national debt remaining high, often exceeding the amount of national debt. Brazil, Argentina, Mexico, and Venezuela alone saw capital flight totaling USD219 billion. (2) Low-Cost Acquisition of State-Owned Enterprises and Resource Extraction Rights: Taking advantage of privatization reforms, they collaborated with foreign capital to acquire state-owned assets, enhancing their control over the economic lifeblood. (3) Benefiting from Expanded Resource Exports: Controlling resource extraction and export, they profited from export support measures and arbitraged with scarce foreign exchange. (4) Elevating the Position of Capital Relative to Labor: Wage growth lagged behind national income growth, and the bargaining power of labor unions was significantly weakened.

4. Lessons and insights from Latin American countries falling into the MIT

We can derive insights on how governments should guide economic development from the practices of the Latin American model. From the imbalanced economic development of Latin American countries and their policies that led to the MIT, the following experiences and lessons can be summarized:

(1) Utilizing the Natural Endowments: While a country's natural resources can indeed aid in its development, relying solely on static comparative advantages, especially for countries rich in natural or

labor resources, is insufficient. These countries must actively cultivate new dynamic comparative advantages.

(2) Addressing the "Three Rural Issues": In a dual economic structure, promoting industrialization must not neglect the "three rural issues" (agriculture, rural areas, and farmers). Balanced development between urban and rural areas is essential.

(3) Land Reform: Continuous reform to create land systems that meet current economic and social needs is crucial for solving the "three rural issues."

(4) Pursuing an Export-Oriented Economic Development Path: While an inward-oriented path like import substitution may lead to limited market scale, insufficient participation in international competition, and severe monopolies, it ultimately creates significant obstacles to reform. Therefore, a steadfast pursuit of an export-oriented development path is necessary.

(5) Critical View of the Washington Consensus: The Washington Consensus has severely misled governments about their role in economic development. Governments can utilize their capacity to regulate resources to promote economic development and upgrading, but they should avoid short-sighted behaviors and deficit-oriented policies.

(6) Wealth and Resource Reallocation: Economic transformation and upgrading will involve the redistribution of wealth and resources. It is imperative to prevent certain groups from seizing public resources during this process, thereby controlling the widening income gap.

(7) Stability as a Prerequisite for Development: Stability is a prerequisite for development. To smoothly advance economic development and upgrading, maintaining a stable political and social environment is essential. This helps avoid amplifying and worsening issues that arise during the transformation process, ultimately affecting the overall economic transition.

## *4.2 Analysis of the Southeast Asian economic Development Model*

1. The economic development dilemma in Indonesia

In 1945, Indonesia gained independence, and its economy, initially dominated by agriculture, gradually transformed into one driven by industry and services. This shift led to a continuous increase in national income and a steady decline in poverty rates. Indonesia's economic development can be divided into four distinct stages: the recovery phase from 1945 to 1955, the import substitution phase from 1956 to 1966, the export-oriented phase from 1967 to 1997, and the structural adjustment phase following the Asian financial crisis in 1998.

As early as 1989, Indonesia's per capita GDP had reached USD1200, close to the middle-income country threshold. However, the 1998 Asian financial crisis dealt a severe blow to Indonesia's economy, causing a serious recession. The value of the Indonesian Rupiah plummeted, and both the stock market and real estate market collapsed. By 1998, Indonesia's per capita GDP had fallen to USD435, making it one of the poorest countries in the world at that time. The significant income disparity in Indonesia led to prominent social conflicts, as well as severe ethnic and religious tensions. In response to the Asian financial crisis, the Indonesian government implemented a series of policy measures to adjust the economic structure. These measures included banking system reforms, adjustments to investment policies, improvements to the investment environment, changes in the economic development model, efforts to balance regional economic development, and upgrades to the industrial structure. These reforms helped maintain economic stability, prevent prolonged economic decline, and promote a shift in the economic development model, thus revitalizing Indonesia's economy. In recent years, Indonesia's per capita GDP growth rate has remained around 5%. Despite this progress, Indonesia's per capita GDP in 2018 was USD3932, still at the middle-income country level.

Indonesia, blessed with abundant natural resources, ranks fourth in the world in population and has a substantial pool of cheap labor, creating favorable conditions for economic growth. However, Indonesia still faces several critical issues in its economic development, including severe unemployment and poverty rates, regional development imbalances, incomplete market-oriented financial system reforms, and an irrational economic structure.

(1) Severe regional development imbalances

From 1976 to 2006, Indonesia's unemployment rate rose from 2.5% to 10.5%, with the unemployed population reaching 10.93 million. The persistently high unemployment rate has prevented the living conditions of Indonesia's low-income population from improving effectively, with nearly half of the population living on less than USD2 a day. Regionally, although Java Island accounts for only 6% of Indonesia's land area, it generates 56% of the country's GDP. The per capita GDP of Java is 6.8 times that of other regions, and it attracts 63% of the total foreign capital investment in the country.

(2) Incomplete market-oriented financial system reforms

Government investment plays a leading role in economic development, with banks under government control. However, the government has not issued loans according to market demand, leading to an increase in non-performing loans. Measures to alleviate bank bad debts by excessive currency issuance further caused fiscal imbalances and hyperinflation, putting Indonesia's economy at risk of total collapse. Although interest rate marketization reforms were later implemented, excessive market freedom and inadequate regulatory systems led to over-lending. The proportion of non-performing loans remained high, and an incomplete financial system was a primary reason why Southeast Asian countries are prone to economic crises.

(3) Irrational domestic industrial structure

The national economy relies heavily on labor-intensive export processing industries, with the development of high-tech industries relatively lagging and insufficient innovation capabilities. Most high-tech equipment is dependent on imports, and the service sector's share is low. Industrial structure upgrades have stagnated since 2005, with the development of industrial sectors supporting the national economy lagging behind. Premature deindustrialization has exacerbated the negative impact on Indonesia's economic growth. The Indonesian authorities are actively promoting infrastructure construction, accelerating approval processes, and optimizing investment environments to respond to the competitive international investment climate. They hope that through a series of economic structural adjustments, they can increase economic growth rates and strive to overcome the MIT as soon as possible. However, the results have been minimal.

2. The economic development dilemma in the Philippines

The Philippines was one of the first developing economies in Asia to begin industrialization. In the 1960s, the economic strength of the Philippines was second only to Japan in Asia, and by 1978, the country's per capita income had already reached the middle-income level. However, in the 1980s, the Philippines entered a prolonged period of economic stagnation, with an average economic growth rate of only 1.7% over ten years. Throughout the 1990s, the per capita economic growth rate in the Philippines was less than 3%. In 2019, the economic growth rate was 5.9%, with a per capita GDP of only USD3300. The Philippines is one of the world's largest sources of labor exports, with overseas workers making up 10% of the total population. The cash remittances from these overseas workers account for about 9% of the country's GDP, driving domestic consumption and contributing significantly to social stability. However, the proportion of investment in GDP has remained low, hindering the country's development and contributing to high unemployment rates.

The Philippines has long-standing structural contradictions in its economy, politics, and institutions, which severely constrain economic development. After the Spanish colonial era, large estates remained concentrated in the hands of a few, and multiple land reforms had minimal success. With advancements in production technology and the promotion of agricultural machinery, the need for agricultural workers decreased, leading many to either become domestic workers or join the ranks of the poor, with some forming anti-government militias. The unstable political environment has deterred investment and tourism, making sustainable economic development difficult. After the fall of Marcos in 1986, the Philippines returned to a democratic election model, with alternating governance by various political parties, but election-related bribery often occurred during this period.

3. The economic development dilemma in Thailand

In the 1950s, the Thai government aimed to establish a comprehensive national economic system and began promoting industrial development plans. The National Economic and Social Development Board was established in 1959 to carry out five-year plans. During the ten years following 1961, Thailand developed import substitution industries based on two five-year plans, achieving a peak annual economic growth rate of 8.4% and an industrial growth rate of 11%. This period is known as Thailand's industrial revolution period. After the 1985 Plaza Accord, the US dollar significantly depreciated, while the currencies of Japan and the "Four Asian Tigers" appreciated, which cause them to lose their advantage in exporting industrial goods. Meanwhile, Thailand received substantial investments in labor-intensive industries. The influx of massive foreign capital spurred rapid economic growth in Thailand, with an average annual economic growth rate of 11.6% from 1987 to 1990, 9% from 1991 to 1995, and 8.5% from 1995 to 2005, placing it among the fastest-growing economies in the world. By 1996, Thailand had entered the middle-income country group, but its economic growth began to slow down afterward. From 2006 to 2016, Thailand's average annual economic growth rate was 6.5%, and in 2018, the per capita GDP was USD7273, still far from that of developed countries.

The main factors constraining Thailand's economic development are political instability, a wide income gap, and a weak middle class. Additionally, Thailand suffered from severe regional economic imbalances, with the economic and political center in Bangkok significantly more developed than other regions, creating a scenario where a small portion of the population is very wealthy while the majority live in poverty. The poverty rate in Thailand is 9.6%, with the poor mainly concentrated in the northern and northeastern regions. The middle class in Thailand has not yet formed an independent political force. Since democratization in 1932, the ruling elite have been divided into three factions: the military, civilian officials, and the monarchy. In the absence of a strong middle class, the struggle between military personnel and civilian officials remains intense.

4. Lessons and insights from Southeast Asian countries falling into the MIT

(1) Insufficient technological innovation and talent hamper economic transformation

Compared to East Asian countries, Southeast Asian countries have experienced varying periods of rapid economic growth, but the growth rate of total factor productivity has remained relatively slow. TFP is a crucial indicator of technological innovation and economic growth. From 1970 to 1994, the TFP of the Philippines was negative, Indonesia's TFP did not exceed 1%, and Thailand's TFP was around 1.5%. This situation has not significantly changed. In 2018, the research and development (R&D) expenditure as a percentage of GDP in Indonesia, Thailand, and the Philippines was less than 0.5%. The number of researchers per million people was less than 400 in Thailand and less than 100 in both Indonesia and the Philippines.

(2) Severe income distribution imbalances and widening income gap

During the economic takeoff stages of Southeast Asian countries, income disparities began to emerge and worsened with economic stagnation. In Thailand, income distribution inequality is primarily reflected between regions and between urban and rural areas. The urban-rural gap is mainly related to Thailand's economic development strategy, which focuses on import substitution and export-oriented development while neglecting rural and agricultural development, resulting in lower income levels in rural areas. In 2019, Thailand's Gini coefficient was 0.44, and the Philippines' Gini coefficient was 0.48, both exceeding the international warning line of 0.4.

(3) Severe corruption and political instability drag on economic development

Brief economic takeoffs did not develop a middle class or establish mature constitutional systems in Southeast Asian countries, leading to unchecked government power and severe corruption. Corruption, interacting with social inequality, exacerbated social disorder. Indonesia lacked effective legal oversight mechanisms, had weak governance capabilities and strong local powers, all contributing to corruption. Since the twenty-first century, political instability in Thailand has directly impacted its key tourism industry.

(4) External competitive pressures make it hard to escape the MIT

In the 1970s, rapid economic growth in Europe and the United States increased global demand for primary products, benefiting ASEAN countries implementing export-oriented strategies. In the 1980s, investments and expansions by Japanese, South Korean, and Taiwan (China) small and medium-sized enterprises in Southeast Asia further boosted ASEAN's economic growth. However, in the late 1990s, the Asian financial crisis and the rise of China and India put immense pressure on ASEAN countries. The reliance on traditional industries to maintain economic growth declined, and the political and social environments in these countries were not conducive to economic transformation, making it difficult for ASEAN countries to escape the MIT. Thus, the transformation and upgrading of industrial structures are essential for economies to pass through the MIT. During this period, changes in political and social forces and their impact on economic transformation are crucial factors determining whether an economy can overcome the MIT.

### 4.3 *Analysis of the Economic Development Models of Major Developed Countries*

1. The process and experience of the United States passing through the MIT

At the end of the nineteenth century, after completing the first industrial revolution, the United States led the development of the electricity revolution, which resulted in remarkable economic growth. From 1869 to 1898, the US coal production increased by 800%, and total railway mileage increased by 567%. By 1890, the United States had significantly outpaced other countries in industrial production output, accounting for over 30% of the global industrial total. From 1920 to 1929, the industrial production output of the United States was equivalent to 79% of the combined industrial production output of the United Kingdom, France, and Germany, making it the leading world power.

The strong and sustained economic growth of the United States can be attributed to industrial structure adjustments, technological advancements, institutional innovations, and rational urbanization. In terms of industrial structure adjustments, the Civil War of the 1860s brought about an industrial revolution in the United States. Northern industrial capital emerged victorious, abolishing slavery and establishing a unified large market, which solidified the United States' position as the world's leading nation. After World War II, the US industrial economy matured further, gradually becoming a society where the service sector had the largest share. Regarding educational investment, the United States saw rapid increases in educational spending. From 1870 to 1916, public expenditure on basic education increased eightfold, and the number of higher education institutions grew from 563 to 1000. In terms of corporate institutional innovation, the development and maturation of modern corporate systems were key reasons for the enduring strength of the US economy. In 1819, Chief Justice John Marshall of the US Supreme Court established the legal status of corporations, which were legally viewed as having perpetual life. The promotion of limited liability contributed to the rapid spread of corporations in the United States. In 1882, 1890, and 1914, the US Congress enacted the Anti-Trust Act, the Sherman Act, and the Clayton Act, respectively, marking the federal government's stringent regulation of private companies. In terms of urbanization, the nineteenth century saw the United States transition from a rural to an urban society. The spatial structure of cities evolved from tightly clustered structures in the early development stages to dispersed structures with multiple centers. From 1860 to 1920, the urban population ratio rose from 19.8% to 51.2%, marking the completion of urbanization. With the improvement of the railway network, particularly the construction of transcontinental railroads, capital, labor, and material resources gradually flowed to the promising developed market, promoting the gradual coverage of industrialization and urbanization.

From an economic and institutional perspective, the historical process of the United States can be roughly divided into two major transformations: the first from 1870 to 1920, known as the "Gilded Age" and the "Progressive Era," transitioning from a model of capitalism under free competition to one under monopoly capitalism, and the second from the 1930s to World War II, during which the "New Deal" transitioned the US economy from monopoly capitalism to welfare capitalism. These two major transformations facilitated the transition of the United States from an era focused on essential goods to one centered on durable goods. The first transformation laid the economic foundation, and the second laid the social foundation. The technological innovations and industrial revolution of the "Gilded Age" spurred rapid economic growth, causing dramatic changes in industrial and social structures, widening income gaps, exacerbating social conflicts, and severe corruption, leading the United States into an overall credit crisis. The "Progressive Era" saw the establishment of monopoly capitalism, continued economic growth, financial oligarchs controlling economic lifelines, opposition to trusts, emphasis on free competition, expanded political participation, anti-corruption measures, and active promotion of the progressive movement in society. The "New Deal

Era," through more thorough institutional adjustments and comprehensive social construction, constrained costs, ensured livelihood security, seized opportunities to expand production, and formed a relatively stable middle class after World War II. These conditions gradually enabled the transition from a consumption model focused on essential goods to one centered on durable goods.

2. The process and experience of the United Kingdom passing through the MIT

The United Kingdom was the first country in the world to industrialize, and its industrial structure adjustment was relatively slow. In 1820, the industrial output of the United Kingdom passed through that of agriculture; around 1851, the number of industrial workers exceeded that of agricultural workers; by around 1914, the tertiary sector passed through the secondary sector in terms of both output and labor force; and by 1998, the United Kingdom's industrial structure adjustment was essentially complete, having taken nearly 150 years for the industrial revolution to develop.

The "British disease" began to manifest in the 1920s. Due to declining domestic market demand and export difficulties, the coal, textile, and shipbuilding industries stagnated, while domestic class struggles intensified, exacerbating internal conflicts. The economic crisis in the United States in the 1930s also affected the United Kingdom, further intensifying domestic conflicts. By mid-1932, the United Kingdom's unemployment rate had reached 23%, with 3 million unemployed. After World War II, the United Kingdom's control over its colonies weakened significantly, and the competitiveness of British exports did not improve, leading to a widening international trade deficit. In 1949, the British pound was devalued by 30.5%. Following World War II, the United Kingdom adopted Keynesian policies, using fiscal and monetary policies to intervene in the economy. While this created short-term prosperity, it also resulted in a heavy government spending burden, significant fiscal deficits, and unsustainable tax burdens on businesses. This led to low production incentives for businesses, declining employment rates, soaring prices, and severe trade deficits, plunging the UK economy into stagflation. By the late 1970s, the share of the state-owned economy in the United Kingdom had risen to 12%, and in industries such as communications, postal services, electricity, gas, and railways, the share was as high as 75%. Consequently, issues such as rigid government functions, excessive economic intervention, lack of competition mechanisms, and irrational resource allocation became prominent.

In the 1980s, the United Kingdom began extensive industrial structure optimization, focusing on the development of new industries such as finance, market services, real estate, patents, copyrights, trademarks, and design. The proportion of the service sector in GDP continually increased. In 1979, the Thatcher government promoted a free economy, implementing sweeping reforms to government regulations, weakening union power, and attracting investment. The United Kingdom's structural adjustment and reforms focused on reducing the state-owned sector and enhancing economic competitiveness through innovative systems. Effective policy measures included:

(1) Equity Reform: This included both internal and external equity participation, transforming enterprises from solely state-owned entities into private or mixed ownership forms. This helped introduce market mechanisms and prevent excessive government administrative intervention.
(2) Privatization of Government Functions: By converting administrative or service functions executed by central or local governments into private operations through agreements, costs were reduced while significantly improving efficiency and service quality.
(3) Combined State-Private Investment: For large-scale investments with long payback periods, private investment, management, and operations were introduced on the basis of state ownership to increase profitability.

By 1988–1989, the United Kingdom had emerged from the economic crisis. However, the Thatcher government failed the elections due to policies that harmed the interests of the middle and lower classes. Subsequent governments under Blair, Brown, and Cameron pursued the "Third Way," balancing the interests of the middle and lower classes while seeking reforms and innovation in the United Kingdom. This approach neither allowed the market to dominate all economic activities nor involved excessive, rigid government intervention. Exploring the neutral or center-left "Third Way" helped restore economic growth in the United Kingdom.

(1) In 1998, the United Kingdom's GDP composition was as follows: agriculture (2%), industry (31%), and services (67%). Economic

restructuring brought shocks to inefficient state-owned enterprises but created opportunities for emerging industries. For example, the telecommunications, computer industries, and related service sectors rapidly developed during this period. Through market competition, these industries increased their international competitiveness, which in turn promoted further domestic industrial innovation and upgrading. This positive cycle continuously optimized the industrial structure. The United Kingdom's development illustrates that during periods of social transformation, both economic restructuring and the accumulation of social conflicts are at their peak. The basic conditions for a country to successfully transfer from the late industrialization phase to a high-income stage include: (1) Promoting Technological Progress: Using technological advancements as an engine to drive industrial structure optimization and adjustment. (2) Reforming Market Mechanisms and Trade Systems: Reforming these systems to enhance economic efficiency and global integration. (3) Institutional Reforms to Promote Social Equity: Ensuring that social security systems are matched with current economic development levels and effectively avoiding the "welfare trap."

3. The process and experience of Germany passing through the MIT

Compared to the United Kingdom, Germany started its industrial revolution later but experienced rapid industrial development. In the late nineteenth century, Germany entered the Second Industrial Revolution, leveraging key industries such as steel, chemicals, and electricity to accelerate industrialization and enter an era of cluster innovation. Employment increased in emerging sectors, particularly in hydroelectric power, chemical, and gas industries. After enduring two world wars, Germany's economy was severely damaged, but the Marshall Plan and the Schuman Plan stimulated its recovery, leading to the development of a socialist market economy. By the late 1950s, Germany's economy began to take off, marking the main phase of transitioning from an industrialized country to a high-income welfare state, and the critical period for the maturation of the social market economy. The emphasis on technological innovation and education drove industrial structure optimization, enabling the pursuit of social harmony and balanced development.

Germany achieved industrial upgrading and technological innovation through the following five main approaches:

(1) Trade Liberalization Policies: Starting in the 1950s, Germany implemented trade liberalization policies that promoted industrial restructuring. This facilitated positive growth correlations between exports and industrial development, leading to a substantial increase in trade exports. By 1970, heavy industry accounted for 74% of Germany's total industrial output value.
(2) Focused on R&D to Establish Industry Positions: After the 1970s, faced with the oil crisis and weakened demand in the international heavy chemical industry market, Germany gradually shifted away from traditional heavy industries such as steel, shipbuilding, and refining. Instead, it focused on the R&D and innovation of low-energy, high-value-added heavy industries like vehicles and aircraft. Simultaneously, the proportion of the tertiary sector in GDP increased continuously.
(3) Green Industrial Transformation Strategies: In the 1990s, facing challenges from high-value-added products from the United States and Japan, as well as competition from cheap goods from emerging markets, the German government emphasized the development of high-tech fields such as biotechnology and micro-technology. This upgraded the industrial structure, forming international competitive advantages in the new round of industrial adjustments.
(4) Creating Favorable Conditions for SMEs: Germany fostered industrial transformation through the organic integration of government policies and market forces. Without intervening in the technological and economic activities of enterprises, the federal government formulated clear science and technology development strategies and implementation plans to guide enterprise development and social research.
(5) Dual-Track Vocational Education System: Germany established numerous world-class universities, equipped with top-tier technical and business education systems, enhancing the cultural and technical levels of workers at all levels. A diversified education system provided citizens with numerous development opportunities, promoted technological progress in industries, and laid the foundation for a decentralized job selection process, preventing blind pursuit of high academic qualifications.

One significant reason Germany successfully passed through the MIT is its establishment of an income distribution system that balances efficiency and equity. Germany's Gini coefficient exceeded 0.4 before World War II, but it gradually decreased after 1970, remaining below 0.3 in general. Germany's basic principles of income distribution was to prioritize efficiency with equity as a supplementary factor. Effective means of intervening in distribution include:

(1) Coordinating Labor Relations to Promote Employment: Labor and management formed stable social partnerships with relatively complete mechanisms at both the social and enterprise levels. Labor and management signed employment agreements and set wage levels through full negotiations. If labor disputes and conflicts could not be resolved, relevant administrative departments or social organizations would mediate and arbitrate based on fairness.
(2) High Tax Rate System: Aimed at reducing income disparities, Germany's tax system primarily levied personal income tax, which accounted for over 40% of total tax revenue. Personal income tax was progressive; higher incomes were taxed more, while lower incomes were taxed less or exempted. The majority of Germany's residents belonged to the middle class, and this "olive-shaped" social structure was crucial for social stability and development.
(3) Fiscal Measures for Regional Economic Balance: After World War II, Germany introduced policies and regulations to ensure balanced economic development across regions, ensuring residents in different areas could achieve roughly equal living conditions. Horizontal fiscal measures centered on inter-state fiscal transfers, while vertical measures supplemented federal fiscal transfers.
(4) Comprehensive Social Security System: Germany had one of the most developed welfare systems globally, benefiting over 90% of its residents. The social security system mainly included statutory pensions, healthcare, and unemployment insurance. Additionally, it covered family allowances and social assistance.
(5) Reputation as a "Lawful Economic Nation": Germany was one of the most economically developed, efficient, and orderly countries globally, thanks to the extensive economic laws and regulations issued by the government to reform, adjust, and manage the national economy. This had created an economic legal system compatible with the social market economy.

4. Insights from the historical processes of the main developed countries

The historical processes of the main developed countries provide us with several key insights:

(1) Transforming Economic Development Models: Enhancing the role of technological innovation and human capital in driving economic growth is crucial. This transformation involves shifting focus toward high-tech industries and innovation-driven growth.
(2) Emphasizing Education: Industrial specialization must be preceded by talent specialization. The improvement of labor force specialization and productivity plays a vital role in economic growth. Investment in education and training is essential to develop a skilled workforce that can adapt to and drive industrial advancements.
(3) Creating a Fair and Just Competitive Environment for Enterprises: It is important to ensure that small and medium-sized enterprises can compete on equal footing with large enterprises. Providing equal market conditions and opportunities for all enterprises fosters healthy competition and cooperation, which is beneficial for economic growth.
(4) Dynamic Adjustment of Industrial Structure: This provides sustained momentum for urbanization. Urbanization must be based on industrialization; however, once industrialization reaches a certain stage, its effect on urbanization diminishes. The vigorous development of the tertiary sector can then accelerate urbanization.
(5) Mitigating the Widening Income Gap: It is necessary to focus on the economic development of backward regions and establish a fair, standardized institutional framework compatible with the market system. Efforts should be made to protect the interests of the general public during economic development, ensuring that the benefits of growth are widely shared.

### 4.4 *Analysis of the East Asian Economic Development Model*

1. The development of Japan's industrial policy

Japan is the first country to successfully develop under the East Asian model, serving as a "leading goose" with demonstrative effects. Examining

Japan's modern history reveals significant differences from European countries like the United Kingdom, France, and Germany. Japan's bureaucratic system has been relatively stable, but high-ranking officials frequently change, with prime ministers and key officials often being replaced. The Japanese bureaucratic system is relatively independent of various social strata, maintaining a mutually utilitarian relationship rather than representing the interests of the wealthy or large conglomerates. Government policies primarily consider national interests and bureaucratic class interests. The driving force behind the Meiji Restoration was the samurai class, with most of them coming from various feudal domains. During this period, the lower classes and farmers did not form the main revolutionary force and remained subjects of rule. Thus, the social reforms at the beginning of the Meiji era were top-down, elite-driven transformations with a distinct characteristic of elite politics.

In the fourth year of Meiji, to learn from the advanced systems of the West and ensure the smooth progress of Japan's reforms, Japan dispatched a large government delegation to study the most enlightened and prosperous countries in Europe and Asia. They concluded that the fundamental path for national development lay in promoting industry and enriching the country. In 1874, the Japanese Cabinet formally proposed the *Proposal for the Promotion of Industry*, deciding to vigorously implement the policy of "Shokusan Kogyo" (promoting industry):

(1) Development of Mineral Resources: Expanding transportation and communication networks.
(2) Domestic Production of Imported Goods: Encouraging export industries such as raw silk and tea, establishing modern cotton spinning industries, and reducing the import of basic products as much as possible.

These policies achieved certain effects at the time, but Japan's "Shokusan Kogyo" policy ultimately failed, mainly due to the outflow of silver currency and financial difficulties. Japan's political elites focused on expanding industrial scale, which led to fiscal expenditures far exceeding fiscal revenues. From a revenue perspective, the government supported industrial development through tax exemptions, low-interest or interest-free loans, and the free transfer of state-owned fixed assets, covering various fields such as mining, steel, textiles, and transportation, resulting in significant fiscal revenue shortfalls. From an expenditure perspective, measures such as repairing the Yamagata Road with one official and two civilians, distributing compulsory education fees based on the number of households, and avoiding the destruction of traditional forces through conscription all increased fiscal and household expenditure burdens. However, during the "Shokusan Kogyo" period, the Japanese government established numerous model factories and nurtured a batch of industrial and technical talents, laying a foundation for the future development of Japanese enterprises.

Due to severe domestic resource shortages, Japan continuously sought external solutions and opportunities for expansion. Following the failure of internal industrial promotion, Japan formally began military expansion abroad. The policy of "rich country, strong army" led Japan onto the wrong path of outward aggression and development. Besides maintaining absolute monarchical power in the political structure, Japan also began preparing for external expansion in economic policies:

(1) Shift from Enriching the People to Enriching the Nation: The government's economic policies transitioned from focusing on the prosperity of the populace to the wealth of the nation.
(2) Compromise with the People's Party: The People's Party compromised with the government, sacrificing part of the interests of the represented enterprises. In return, the government provided opportunities to build railways, hydraulic projects, and telecommunications for enterprises, promising to share the profits of foreign wars.
(3) Full-Scale Development of Military-Related Industries: During this period, Japan's military factories developed rapidly, especially in the steel and machinery sectors. By 1879, artillery factories were established in Tokyo and Osaka, and in 1887, the Yokosuka shipyard was established. However, civilian mechanical industries did not significantly develop.

Japan embarked on a path of war profiteering, with investments, resources, and technology shifting to support military development. The compensation of 200 million taels of silver from the First Sino-Japanese War enabled Japan to establish the gold standard. Temporary wartime success lured Japan deeper into external aggression. However, sustainable national development requires not only top-down elite policies but also bottom-up support from the general populace.

The pre-World War II experiences of Japan provided several insights for post-war economic development:

(1) Outward-Oriented Economic Development Strategy: Clearly identifying an outward-oriented economic development strategy as the path to overcome resource constraints.
(2) Market-Led Development with Government Guidance: Government industrial policies should effectively mobilize economic resources and accelerate development, playing a guiding rather than dominating role. Private enterprises were more resilient than state-run enterprises.
(3) Prosperity of the People is the Basis for National Wealth: Ensuring that the pursuit of national wealth did not come at the expense of the lower classes.

Post-World War II, Japanese government policies aligned well with enterprise development. Japan entered a phase of rapid development after the war, benefiting from reflections on pre-war development paths and accurate assessments of the contemporary internal and external environments. The success of Japan's post-war industrial policies was largely due to adapting to circumstances, such as the Korean War special procurement that boosted industrial development. A key aspect was the effective integration of government industrial policies and enterprise development.

Taking the Japanese automobile industry as an example. The global automobile industry was already well-developed while Japan's was just beginning. Initially, due to the presence of imported cars from Ford and Chevrolet, Japanese domestic car sales were poor. The Japanese automobile industry went through a process of "importing, imitating, and innovating," with private enterprises driving the development and innovation. In 1955, Japan joined the General Agreement on Tariffs and Trade (GATT), fully opening its market to the outside world. Industries lacking international competitiveness were gradually eliminated in the global market context.

Japan's consumption revolution and technological innovation were the main drivers of economic development. Despite the growing demand for personal cars, the fledgling Japanese automobile industry faced significant competition from foreign cars. Japan adopted three main measures in response:

(1) Expanding Production: From 1958 to 1964, Toyota's investment increased from 4.9 billion yen to nearly 30 billion yen. In December 1959, the production at Toyota's Motomachi plant exceeded 10,000 cars for the first time.
(2) Reducing Car Prices: In 1959, Toyota controlled the prices of 11 popular car models at around 50,000 yen to promote these cars. In 1961, the Japanese government announced a policy to reduce production taxes, significantly lowering the prices of domestically produced cars. To enhance international competitiveness, Toyota decided in 1963 to reduce the prices of models other than the "Volkswagen" by 10,000 to 40,000 yen.
(3) Mergers and Restructuring: Toyota collaborated with Hino and Daihatsu in R&D, significantly enhancing product competitiveness.

Thanks to these measures, Japanese domestic car companies were not squeezed out after car import liberalization. At the same time, the performance and price advantages of Japanese domestic cars became evident, preparing them for future international market expansion. During the 1973 oil crisis, Japanese cars, known for their low fuel consumption, gained popularity in other developed markets. Japanese car companies seized this opportunity to continuously improve quality, gradually entering the mid-to-high-end car production ranks.

Therefore, the core of Japan's industrial policy was financial support, technical protection, and infrastructure development. Market monopoly is not a reasonable way to protect enterprises; instead, the government should create conditions for enterprise development through limited protection, enhancing the international competitiveness of domestic car companies.

2. South Korea's transformation and leap

In the 1950s, South Korea was still a backward and poor country. However, due to the smooth transformation of its economic and social structures, South Korea achieved more than 30 years of rapid economic growth and quickly overcame the MIT, joining the ranks of high-income countries. From 1961 to 1994, South Korea's average annual economic growth rate exceeded 8%, and its per capita income level steadily increased during this period. Paul Krugman pointed out that the "East Asian Miracle" achieved growth by increasing labor and capital inputs, but this growth did not result from improved efficiency. Due to the diminishing marginal returns of production factors, East Asian countries still lagged significantly behind Western countries in technology, and the world's economic center had not shifted to the Western Pacific. Looking at specific cases, latecomer countries must go through four essential development stages to achieve modernization:

(1) Low-Income Stage: Increased foreign direct investment, entering general manufacturing.
(2) Middle-Income Stage: Absorbing foreign technology, forming a manufacturing backbone.
(3) High-Income Stage: Possessing independent technological innovation capabilities and mastering high-end manufacturing technology and management methods.
(4) Global Leading Stage: Having globally leading capabilities in R&D, production, sales, and services.

Currently, countries like the United States, some Western European countries, and Japan are in the fourth stage. South Korea, overall, is in the third stage, but some of its industries have begun to enter the fourth stage, exhibiting the characteristics of this phase. From the development experiences of Japan and South Korea, it is evident that a key factor in overcoming the MIT is having strong independent innovation capabilities. Additionally, the development division of "government as an auxiliary, enterprises as the main force" is crucial. The South Korean government played an essential role in promoting social independent innovation. South Korea, founded in 1948, was one of the world's least developed countries. However, starting in the 1960s, it implemented an export-oriented economic development strategy, leading to rapid economic development known as the "Miracle on the Han River." This strategy helped South Korea join the ranks of upper-middle-income countries and gradually approach the level of high-income countries.

During this period, both the government and enterprises played indispensable roles, which can be summarized in the following four points:

(1) Setting Development Goals Aligning with Long-Term National Interests: The establishment of development goals that aligned with the long-term interests of the country was crucial.

(2) Leadership by Key Figures: Leaders such as Park Chung-hee, Chun Doo-hwan, and Roh Tae-woo played significant roles. They were committed to eradicating poverty, firmly promoting the transformation and upgrading of industrial structures, and vigorously pushing forward industrialization reforms.
(3) Support from Educated Bureaucratic Officials: Highly educated bureaucratic officials efficiently supported economic development.
(4) Fostering Large Business Conglomerates: Similar to Japan, the South Korean government nurtured numerous large business conglomerates during the process of promoting economic development. These conglomerates focused on developing capital-intensive industries and supporting super-large enterprise groups. After 2000, these large conglomerates began to demonstrate significant scale advantages in innovation.

However, prolonged industrialization in South Korea led to a shortage of labor. In 1988, South Korea enacted the Minimum Wage Act, setting legal standards for wage levels and increases. As a result, the wages of manufacturing workers increased by over 90% in the following six years. This massive "wage increase wave" caused many labor-intensive small and medium-sized enterprises to collapse and led to the relocation of South Korean international production lines overseas. Starting in the 1980s, South Korea began developing high-end manufacturing and established a strategy of "nation-building through science and technology." Subsequently, knowledge-intensive industries began to replace labor- and capital-intensive industries.

The South Korean government took a series of measures to encourage technological innovation, urbanization, social security, legal soundness, education, and healthcare:

(1) Organized Integration of Government, Industry, Academia, and Research: To promote social independent innovation, South Korea orderly integrated the roles of government, industry, academia, and research. The Basic Science and Technology Law was enacted to avoid wasteful and blind R&D investments. The National Science and Technology Committee, chaired by the President, coordinated dispersed R&D institutions across government departments to form the Science and Technology Innovation Headquarters. This headquarters was divided into the "Basic

Research Council," "Public Technology Research Council," and "Industrial Technology Research Council" by field. The headquarters was responsible for developing national strategic technology reserves, higher education institutions focused on basic research, and enterprises handled the practical application of various related technologies, forming a complete innovation system.

(2) Global IT Industry Competitiveness: According to global rankings by *The Economist*, South Korea's IT industry competitiveness ranks third globally, just behind the United States and Japan, indicating that South Korea has essentially achieved a technological development transformation.

(3) Universal Education: South Korea popularized high school education in the 1980s and university education in the 1990s, implementing educational equalization policies. Universities prioritize admission for poor students and offer scholarships and free accommodation. Additionally, South Korea focused on recruiting overseas tech talent to improve the overall quality of workers.

(4) Tax Policy Adjustments: Increased taxes on real estate and land property and raised personal income tax exemption limits. For enterprises, R&D investments could be tax-deductible to a certain extent.

(5) Comprehensive Social Security: Enacted various industrial promotion laws and the Equal Employment Act. Implemented three major social welfare and health insurance systems: universal health insurance, minimum wage system, and national pension system, along with four major social insurances: health insurance, pension insurance, employment insurance, and industrial accident insurance.

(6) Strategic Industry Support: Identified and attached importance to precision electronics, chemicals, and aerospace as strategic industries, and new materials, bioengineering, and information industries as future industries. Additionally, South Korea enacted the Public Official Ethics Law, requiring officials to disclose their assets to reduce corruption.

3. Land system reform in the urbanization transformation of Taiwan province in China

Land issues are crucial in rural areas, and addressing these issues is essential for sustained economic development and a country's progression into a higher-income stage. Successful countries or regions in the "East Asian model" have conducted detailed land system reforms to resolve land issues. Post-World War II Japan conducted two land reforms, promoting the Farmland Adjustment Act, the Farmland Adjustment Act Amendment Bill, and the Special Measures Act for the Creation of Owner-Farmers. Implementing the Farmland Law and the Land Use Promotion Law transformed land ownership into a system where ownership and usage rights were separated. It is well known that the Taiwan region in China has faced severe land conflicts. During the early stages of industrialization, issues included the transfer of land capital to industrial capital, labor identity, and competition for land between agriculture and industry. In the later stages of industrialization, problems such as rural labor outflow and lagging rural agricultural development became prominent. In response, the Taiwan region implemented measures such as the "375 Rent Reduction" and "Prosperous Rural Areas" initiatives, which essentially resolved the "three rural issues" and played a vital role in supporting economic transformation.

The economic take-off of East Asian economies such as Japan, South Korea, and China's Taiwan region began with land reforms. The main functions of successful land reforms include:

(1) Providing a Stable Environment for Social Development: Land reforms helped prevent large-scale migration from rural to urban areas, which could burden urban development.
(2) Orderly Transfer of Rural Population to Urban Areas: Gradual and organized urban migration provided a substantial labor force for industrial development.
(3) Ensuring Fair Distribution of Wealth: By ensuring that most farmers owned land, land reforms provided a basis for fair wealth distribution.

In June 1950, the Taiwan region implemented the "375 Rent Reduction," which limited landlords' rent to no more than 37.5% of farmers' total harvest. Additionally, arbitrary landlord practices such as tenant evictions, rent illegal possession, advance rent collection, and short rental periods were explicitly prohibited. Concurrently, a series of land governance policies, including the public ownership of land resources, were implemented. These policies strictly regulated landlords' reserved arable land, forcibly requisitioning excess land from landlords and redistributing it to farmers to ensure land ownership for tillers. The main achievements of these measures were as follows:

(1) Most Farmers Acquired Their Own Land: This increased farmers' labor enthusiasm, facilitating the adoption of new technologies and improving labor productivity.
(2) Clear Definition of Land Property Rights: This promoted fair income distribution and mitigated the exploitation of labor factors by capital factors to some extent.
(3) Land Compensation for Landlords: Landlords received compensation such as ten-year land bonds and stocks in industries like cement, forestry, and mining, guiding capital from land to industrial investments and contributing to national industrialization.

However, these land measures also had adverse effects:

(1) Difficulty in Mechanized Production: As industrialization progressed, mechanized and large-scale production became the mainstream. However, the extensive subdivision of land made mechanized production difficult, leading to increased production costs and reduced competitiveness of local agricultural products.
(2) Poverty Among Small Landlords: Overly low compensation measures impoverished a population of over two million small landlords, forcing them to sell government-compensated stocks at low prices, which were then acquired by the wealthy. This exacerbated wealth concentration among a few individuals, creating income distribution disparities.
(3) Grain-for-Fertilizer Policy: This policy indirectly lowered grain prices, seizing farmers' production surpluses to support public officials. The resulting meager farming income drove more farmers to migrate to cities.

The land reform in the Taiwan region of China supported local industrialization. By 1986, the contribution of industry to the region's economy had reached over 40%, a historical peak. Subsequently, the industrial contribution gradually decreased while the contribution of the service sector increased. By 1990, the leading economic sector had shifted from industry to services, with per capita GDP reaching USD8325. However, this period saw severe agricultural and rural decline, with significant labor outflows exacerbating rural development issues. In 1991, the Taiwan authorities introduced the Comprehensive Agricultural Adjustment Plan, adhering to the "three rural" principles and building prosperous rural areas. Following the region's accession to the WTO, the Mid-Term Agricultural Policy Plan aimed to shape new rural landscapes and lifestyles:

(1) Promoting Overall Rural Community Development: Emphasizing people-centered approaches to improve farmers' welfare and create comfortable living circles for farmers.
(2) Optimizing Rural Environments: Developing agricultural leisure and tourism industries to establish rural leisure and tourism circles.
(3) Adapting to Local Conditions: Developing resources based on regional characteristics, building modern rural industries, and forming unique rural industrial development circles.

In 2004, the Engel coefficient for urban and rural residents in the Taiwan region of China was roughly the same. However, the region had not yet found a reasonable and effective solution for intensive land use. The "land to the tiller" policy led to the rigidity of the farmland system, severely restricting the reform of the land transfer system. To address this, the Taiwan authorities no longer required the transferee of private farmland ownership to be a self-cultivating farmer, hoping to remove legal barriers to land transfer. However, the free buying and selling of high-quality farmland could lead to its conversion into non-agricultural land, potentially resulting in the significant loss of agricultural land resources. Some local representatives, in collusion with conglomerates, first purchased land under the policy conditions allowing free land transactions and then changed the land use to invest in real estate on agricultural land. Consequently, loopholes in the private land system facilitated the prevalence of land speculation activities.

4. Insights from the East Asian model

In October 1993, the World Bank published a special study titled "The East Asian Miracle: Economic Growth and Public Policy," which first introduced the concept of the "East Asian Model." This model primarily refers to the development patterns of the "Four Asian Tigers," namely, South Korea, Singapore, Taiwan (China), and Hong Kong (China) and Japan. It took Japan 15 years (1966–1981) to transition from the lower-middle-income stage to the high-income stage, South Korea 18 years (1977–1995), and Taiwan 16 years (1976–1992). Singapore and Hong Kong each took seven years to leap from the upper-middle-income stage to the high-income stage.

"The East Asian Miracle: Economic Growth and Public Policy" summarized the basic characteristics of the "East Asian Model" as follows: integration with the international economy, adapting to international development paths; correct economic development strategies with successful and effective government intervention; emphasis on human resource development and talent cultivation; active use of the region's high savings rate and foreign direct investment to achieve high investment returns; and a reverence for Confucian culture-centered Eastern values. The World Bank considers Japan the first case of overcoming the MIT, followed by South Korea, Singapore, Taiwan (China), and Hong Kong (China), which have become exemplary cases of successful development in the world economy.

The World Bank pointed out in its *World Development Report* that the East Asian Model was a development system combining a strong government with a free market. Historically, successful cases have almost always involved a cooperative relationship between the government and the market, where the market played the primary role, and the government corrected market failures in a timely manner. Institutional school scholars, represented by Robert Wade, believe that East Asian countries primarily aimed at economic development, advocated for economic nation-building, and centered their national strategies on catching up with Europe and the United States by implementing export-oriented development strategies. The unique cooperation between national and enterprise institutions in East Asia enabled rapid development. With the support of government industrial policies, East Asian countries promoted foreign trade and economic growth through the introduction of foreign capital and technology. In this model, the government mainly guides the market but does not replace it.

Although the East Asian Model has created economic development miracles, it has also brought significant problems, such as Japanese militarism and the welfare trap caused by excessive welfare policies. On the one hand, during the high-speed economic development stage, the high external dependency and insufficient domestic demand of these countries or regions led to increasing trade frictions and growing pressure for currency appreciation as their economic power developed, thereby reducing long-term competitiveness to some extent. On the other hand, currency appreciation accompanied by high savings rates would continuously drive up prices of living and asset prices, leading to inflation. Once the asset bubble bursts, the financial system inevitably suffers severe damage. Additionally, rising living costs due to inflation and high asset prices indirectly lower birth rates, and as the aging problem becomes increasingly serious, the demographic dividend gradually turns into demographic pressure, further suppressing consumption and investment. These issues became more prominent after South Korea, Japan, and Taiwan (China) successfully overcame the MIT. However, China is already facing these problems even before entering the high-income stage.

## 5 Empirical Analysis of the Middle-Income Trap Model: An International Perspective

Analyzing the cases of various countries reveals that the primary reasons for falling into the MIT in Latin America and Southeast Asia include distorted social structures, insufficient innovation, difficult transitions, inefficient administrative capabilities, imbalanced interest relationships, and lack of social security. In contrast, the experiences of developed Western countries and East Asian countries such as Japan and South Korea indicate that the conditions for successfully entering the high-income stage include balanced urban and rural development, scientific research advantages, high popularization of higher education, successful industrial transformation and upgrading, and the formation of a stable middle class. At the same time, experiences from various countries show that different social conditions are needed at the middle-income and high-income stages. The social conditions that support high speed economic growth during the middle-income stage often cannot sustain economic growth at the high-income stage. Sole reliance on factor-driven and efficiency-driven growth makes it difficult for a country to avoid the MIT. Innovation-driven growth is the main development measure for entering into the high-income stage. Therefore, overcoming the MIT requires addressing transformation pressures in various aspects of the country, necessitating more detailed research on balanced urban development, internet penetration, higher education development, improvements in research levels, the increase of proportion of services in total social output, and balanced income distribution.

We conducted regression analyses based on Eqn. (7.14) to examine the actual economic growth of 15 countries—the United States, the United Kingdom, Germany, France, Japan, South Korea, Brazil, Mexico, Indonesia, Malaysia, Thailand, the Philippines, Argentina, India, and China. We analyzed seven major influencing factors: potential economic growth, urbanization rate, higher education enrollment rate, the proportion of the service industry in GDP, internet user coverage rate, research investment as a percentage of GDP, and income inequality. Tables 7.3 and 7.4 present the summary of relevant development indicators for these countries.

The econometric results indicate that although the main factors promoting economic development vary across countries, these factors have a more significant impact on the economies of developed countries that have already overcome the MIT. In developed countries, urbanization, higher education enrollment rates, and the development of the internet significantly promote national economic development. In the United Kingdom, the growth of the service industry has greatly contributed to economic development; in Germany, the development of the internet is crucial to economic progress; in France, higher education enrollment rates, the expansion of the service industry, and increased research investment have significantly aided economic development; in Japan, higher education enrollment rates and internet development have clearly promoted economic growth. Among countries trapped in the MIT, only Thailand and the Philippines show relatively positive results. In Thailand, urbanization and internet development have had a significant driving effect on the economy; in the Philippines, higher education enrollment rates and the development of the service industry have propelled economic growth. In Brazil, the increase in urbanization has promoted economic development, while in Argentina, urbanization can foster economic growth. Mexico and Malaysia lack significant driving factors to promote their economic development. Additionally, the data show that issues of income inequality in Brazil, Thailand, and the Philippines have severely impacted their economic development.

Examining the two developing countries that are the focus of global attention today, India and China, as control groups reveals that currently, internet development and research investment in India have provided favorable support for economic development. However, low levels of urbanization, higher education enrollment rates, underdeveloped service industries, and significant income inequality are major obstacles to

**Table 7.3** Summary of relevant development indicators for selected countries

| *Indicator* | *USA* | *UK* | *Germany* | *France* | *Japan* | *South Korea* | *Brazil* | *Mexico* | *Indonesia* | *Malaysia* | *Thailand* | *Philippines* | *Argentina* | *India* | *China* |
|---|---|---|---|---|---|---|---|---|---|---|---|---|---|---|---|
| Urbanization rate above 60% | + | + | + | + | + | + | + | – | – | – | – | – | + | – | + |
| Internet user coverage rate above 80% | + | + | + | + | + | + | – | – | – | + | – | – | – | – | – |
| Higher education enrollment rate above 60% | + | + | + | + | + | + | – | – | – | + | * | – | + | – | – |
| Research investment as a percentage of GDP above 2.5% | + | – | + | + | + | + | – | – | + | * | * | – | + | + | – |
| Service industry accounting for over 60% of GDP | + | + | + | + | + | + | – | – | – | – | – | + | – | – | – |
| Gini coefficient below 0.4 | – | + | + | + | + | + | – | – | + | – | – | – | – | + | – |

Source: World Bank, Wind, Bank of China Research Institute

Note: Indicators that meet the condition are marked with "+," those that do not meet the condition are marked with "–," and missing data are marked with "*"

**Table 7.4** Results of empirical study

| *Country* | $Y_t^*$ | $X_{1t}$ | $X_{2t}$ | $X_{3t}$ | $X_{4t}$ |
|---|---|---|---|---|---|
| USA | 0.3334* | 0.0633** | 0.0015* | −0.0096 | 0.0012*** |
| Britain | 0.5278*** | 0.0077 | 0.0004 | 0.0153** | 0.0010 |
| Germany | 0.5180*** | −0.0109 | 0.0023 | 0.0008 | 0.0016** |
| France | 0.5655*** | −0.0073 | 0.0027*** | 0.0197*** | −0.0004 |
| Japan | 0.1812*** | 0.0052*** | None | −0.0030 | 0.0014*** |
| Brazil | 0.0506*** | 0.0628*** | −0.0008 | −0.0036 | 0.0510 |
| Mexico | 1.3286*** | −0.0157 | 0.0044 | −0.0007 | None |
| Argentina | 0.7017*** | 0.1331** | −0.0090** | 0.0017 | 0.0013 |
| Malaysia | 0.7985*** | 0.0169 | 0.0021 | −0.0087* | −0.0008 |
| Thailand | 0.1950*** | 0.0137** | 0.0037 | −0.0047 | 0.0063** |
| The Philippines | 0.4972 | −0.0629 | 0.0501* | 0.0836** | −0.0052 |
| India | 0.0001*** | −0.0926* | −0.0029** | −0.0184*** | 0.0061*** |
| China | 0.3239 | 0.0568** | −2.9529* | 2.9465* | 0.0010 |

| Country | $X_{5t}$ | $X_{6t}$ | $C$ | Adjusted $R^2$ |
|---|---|---|---|---|
| USA | 0.0737 | −0.0012 | 14.9058*** | 0.9966 |
| Britain | 0.0189 | 0.0020 | 12.914*** | 0.9881 |
| Germany | 0.0078 | −0.0011 | 14.4431*** | 0.9882 |
| France | 0.0788*** | 0.0069 | 9.4613*** | 0.9986 |
| Japan | −0.0308 | 0.0062 | 23.8166*** | 0.9795 |
| Brazil | None | −0.0084** | 8.92*** | 0.9988 |
| Mexico | −0.2990** | −0.0007 | −7.8477* | 0.9906 |
| Argentina | 0.0783 | None | −3.6370 | 0.9948 |
| Malaysia | −0.0414 | 0.0051 | 4.5476** | 0.9991 |
| Thailand | −0.0056 | −0.0087*** | 20.7230*** | 0.9950 |
| The Philippines | −5.1736* | −0.0034** | 10.5663 | 0.9798 |
| India | 0.1269** | −0.0140** | 26.5025*** | 0.9997 |
| China | −0.1350 | 0.0039 | 17.5298** | 0.9987 |

Note: $Y_t^*$ represents a country's potential economic growth; $X_{1t}$ represents urbanization rate; $X_{2t}$ represents higher education enrollment rate; $X_{3t}$ represents the proportion of service industry in GDP; $X_{4t}$ represents internet user coverage rate; $X_{5t}$ represents research investment as a percentage of GDP; $X_{6t}$ represents income inequality; C is the constant term. *, **, and *** indicate significance levels of 10%, 5%, and 1%, respectively. "None" indicates that results could not be obtained due to missing data in that category

economic growth. In China, urbanization and the development of the service industry have had a noticeable positive effect on economic growth. However, there is a significant deficiency in higher education enrollment rates, and there are no evident advantages in internet penetration, research investment, and income inequality mitigation to drive economic development.

## 6 China's Path to Pass Through the Middle-Income Trap

Through international comparative studies and theoretical model analysis, the following conclusions can be drawn: For China, to maintain steady growth and pass through the MIT, it is essential to comprehensively analyze relevant constraints and focus on strategic adjustments, narrowing income disparities, and enhancing innovation capacity.

### 6.1 *Key Factors Restricting China from Passing Through the MIT*

(1) Changes in the labor force and urban-rural structure

Since 1978, China's GDP has achieved sustained high-speed growth. Seen from the recent trends in the population size and age structure, the number and proportion of the working-age population have been continuously increasing, which correlates positively with the trend of China's GDP. Since the 1970s, China's population has been on a growth trajectory, especially the working-age population.[1] In 2019, the number of working-age people was approximately 1.77 times that of 1978, as shown in Fig. 7.4.[2]

However, China is gradually losing its demographic dividend. On the one hand, the number of migrant workers has been growing slowly in recent years. Although the number of migrant workers increased from 242 million in 2010 to 291 million in 2019, the incremental supply of migrant workers has been declining (see Table 7.5). From the income perspective, the average monthly income of farmers in 2019 was around 3962 yuan, an increase of 230% compared to 2010, with an average annual growth rate of 8.9 percentage points. There is no longer sufficient working-age labor output from rural areas, and the dual urban-rural structure's promotion of the demographic dividend is approaching a bottleneck. In addition, China is a country with a large population and relatively scarce per capita resources. Due to urbanization, rural arable land resources are continuously decreasing, and land quality is continuously declining. This has led to stagnation in farmers' income and slow rural economic development,

[1] Working-age population refers to the working-age population aged 15–64 years.

[2] Using the GDP of 1978 as the base, the GDP of each year is adjusted by the CPI.

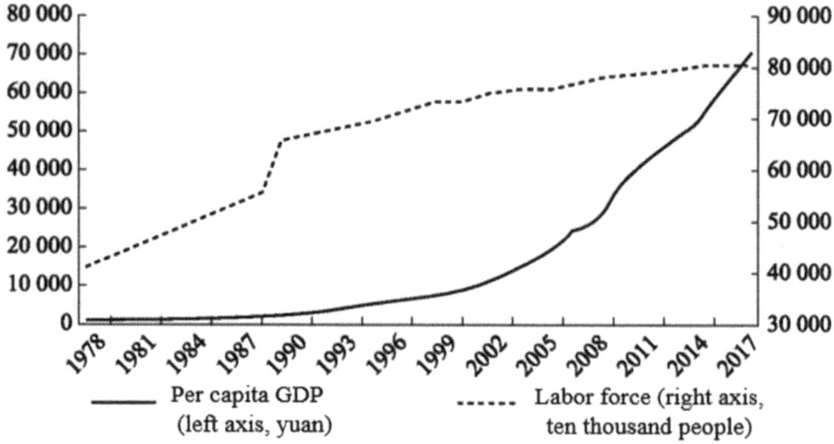


**Fig. 7.4** Working-age population and per capita GDP in China (1978–2019). (Source: Wind; Bank of China Research Institute)

posing a serious threat to China's food security. The pressure on land supply has brought more and more problems to the processes of urbanization and industrialization in China, gradually becoming one of the major factors restricting social development and the improvement of people's living standards.

In 2019, the employment structure of China's three industries was composed of 27%, 28%, and 45%, respectively, and the added value of the three industries was composed of 7%, 40%, and 53%, respectively. The huge disparity in returns among different industries reflects the huge income distribution gap in China. Agricultural development has clearly become a shortcoming in China's economic development, and the difficulty in overcoming the MIT lies in the insufficient development of rural areas and farmers. In 2019, China's urbanization rate of the permanent population exceeded 60% for the first time, but there were still about 500 million permanent residents in rural areas. Thus, rural development in the new era has become a major contradiction, and promoting urban-rural integrated development has become an inevitable choice to resolve contradictions and narrow the gap between the rich and the poor.

(2) Education investment

**Table 7.5** Changes in the number of migrant workers and urban employment (2001–2019)

| *Year* | *Number of migrant workers (ten thousand)* | *Annual growth rate (%)* | *Total urban employment (ten thousand)* | *Annual growth rate (%)* |
|---|---|---|---|---|
| 2001 | 8399 | 7.0 | 23,940 | 3.4 |
| 2002 | 10,470 | 24.7 | 24,780 | 3.5 |
| 2003 | 11,390 | 8.8 | 25,639 | 3.5 |
| 2004 | 11,823 | 3.8 | 26,476 | 3.3 |
| 2005 | 12,578 | 6.4 | 27,331 | 3.2 |
| 2006 | 13,212 | 5.0 | 28,310 | 3.6 |
| 2007 | 13,697 | 3.7 | 29,350 | 3.7 |
| 2008 | 14,041 | 2.5 | 30,210 | 2.9 |
| 2009 | 14,533 | 3.5 | 31,120 | 3.0 |
| 2010 | 24,223 | 5.4* | 34,693 | 3.5 |
| 2011 | 25,278 | 4.4 | 35,914 | 3.5 |
| 2012 | 26,261 | 3.9 | 37,102 | 3.3 |
| 2013 | 26,894 | 2.4 | 38,240 | 3.1 |
| 2014 | 27,395 | 1.9 | 39,310 | 2.8 |
| 2015 | 27,747 | 1.3 | 40,410 | 2.8 |
| 2016 | 28,171 | 1.5 | 41,428 | 2.5 |
| 2017 | 28,652 | 1.7 | 42,462 | 2.5 |
| 2018 | 28,836 | 0.6 | 43,419 | 2.3 |
| 2019 | 29,077 | 0.8 | 44,247 | 1.9 |

Source: National Bureau of Statistics, Bank of China Research Institute

"*" indicates data for 2010 calculated based on new statistical scope

It has been proven that human capital has a significant impact on labor productivity. However, while China's human capital is large in scale, its quality is uneven, making the level of education of the population one of the key factors restricting China's demographic dividend. According to statistical data, the proportion of education expenditure in China's fiscal expenditure as a percentage of GDP rose from 3.66% in 2010 to 4.04% in 2019 and has remained above 4% for several consecutive years. However, compared with some developed countries, there is still room for improvement in China's education investment (see Table 7.6). From the perspectives of China's urban-rural structure, population age structure, and education investment, China's aging population problem is becoming increasingly severe, and the demographic dividend is gradually disappearing, even potentially turning into a "demographic debt." Therefore, if

**Table 7.6** Proportion of government education expenditure to GDP in selected countries or regions (2010–2019); unit: %

| *Year* | *2010* | *2011* | *2012* | *2013* | *2014* | *2015* | *2016* | *2017* | *2018* | *2019* |
|---|---|---|---|---|---|---|---|---|---|---|
| China | 3.66 | 3.93 | 4.28 | 4.30 | 4.10 | 4.26 | 4.22 | 4.14 | 4.11 | 4.04 |
| USA | — | — | — | 4.93 | 4.96 | — | — | — | — | — |
| Iceland | 6.98 | 6.82 | 7.60 | 7.50 | 7.69 | 7.51 | 7.50 | 7.66 | — | — |
| South Korea | — | — | — | — | — | — | 4.33 | — | — | — |
| Britain | 5.70 | 5.60 | — | 5.53 | 5.60 | 5.56 | 5.43 | 5.44 | — | — |
| OECD | 5.39 | 5.11 | 4.99 | 5.14 | 5.14 | 5.11 | 5.01 | 4.99 | — | — |
| World average | — | 4.21 | 4.05 | 4.29 | 4.30 | 4.42 | 4.36 | 4.43 | 4.51 | 4.19 |

Source: Wind; Bank of China Research Institute

China cannot achieve the transformation of its demographic dividend and the upgrading of its economic structure, it is likely to fall into the MIT in the future, leading to a series of economic problems and conflicts.

(3) The driving force of economic growth continues to decline

Since the reform and opening up, China has maintained high-speed economic growth for many years. In 2010, China's economic aggregate surpassed Japan, becoming the world's second-largest economy, significantly narrowing the gap with developed countries in terms of total economic output (see Fig. 7.5). However, while the economy has developed rapidly, we also recognize that the driving force of China's economic growth is weakening, and the growth model urgently needs to be changed.

Investment is one of the important driving forces behind China's rapid economic growth. As shown in Fig. 7.6, in the economic structure proportion divided by the expenditure method, the share of final consumption in rural areas has been continuously decreasing, while the share of final consumption by urban residents has been steadily increasing, and government expenditure has remained relatively stable. Looking at capital expenditure, except for a rapid decline in the proportion of capital expenditure from 1975 to 1980, it has been rising continuously in other periods. In addition, in recent years, China has maintained a positive net export value. Another set of data shows that China's final consumption rate has fallen from 65% (in the 1980s) to less than 50% (after 2006), gradually rising since 2010 and maintaining around 55% in recent years. At the same time, the capital formation rate has grown from 30% to over

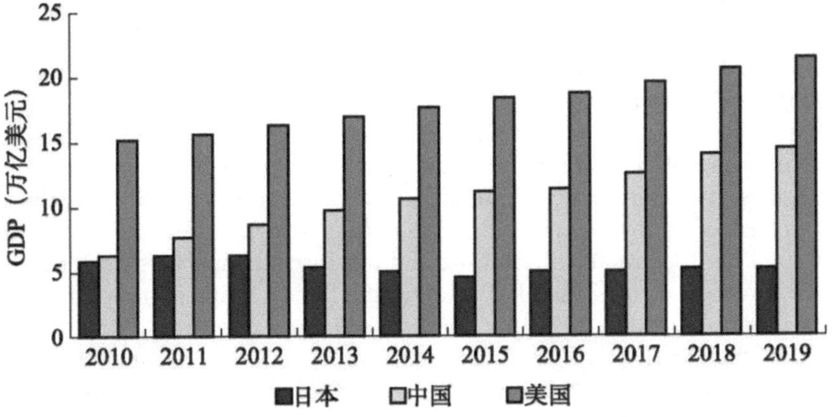


**Fig. 7.5** Comparison of economic aggregates between China and major developed countries (2010–2019). (Source: Wind; Bank of China Research Institute)

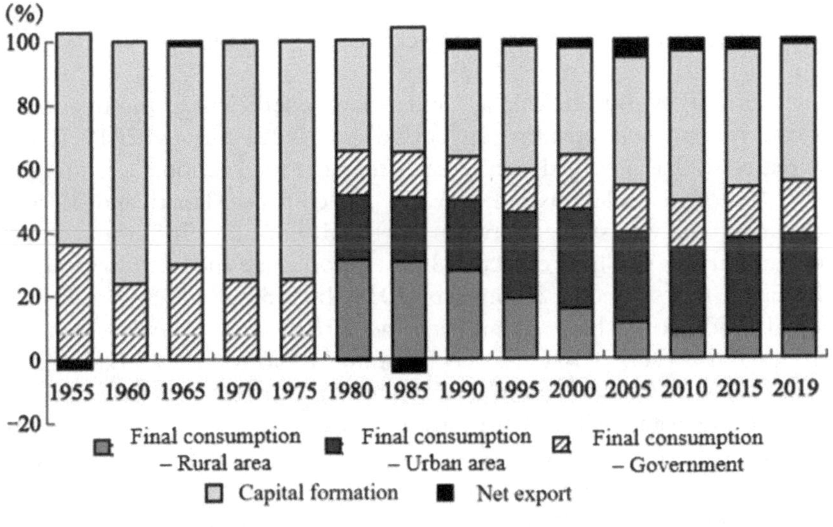


**Fig. 7.6** Proportion of China's economic aggregate by expenditure method (1955–2019). (Source: Wind; Bank of China Research Institute)

40%. This is because, since China joined the World Trade Organization, investment has become the main driving force of China's economic growth. However, the ultimate goal of economic growth is to improve people's living standards. Therefore, regardless of which factors play a major role in economic growth, they must ultimately serve the fundamental purpose of benefiting the people. In the context of unprecedented changes, the Chinese government has proposed a new development pattern that takes the domestic development as the mainstay and promotes mutual reinforcement of domestic and international markets. In terms of consumption scale, China has become the largest market for commodity retail in the world in 2019 and also has the largest consumption potential. From the perspective of investment, more and more industries are approaching investment bottlenecks. Therefore, it is necessary and feasible to gradually replace investment-driven economic growth with consumption-driven economic growth, and promoting growth through consumption will be essential to the sustainable development of China's economy.

(4) The income distribution gap continues to widen

According to World Bank data, China's Gini coefficient at the beginning of the reform and opening up period was 0.20, but by 2019 it had increased to 0.47 and had been greater than the international warning line of 0.40 for several consecutive years. In contrast, Japan and Europe remained relatively stable, between 0.24 and 0.36. In 1988, the top 10% income earners in China earned 7.3 times more than the bottom 10%, but this figure had surged to 30 times by 2019. Including hidden income, the actual ratio should be even higher. The *2019 China Household Finance Survey Report* shows that the savings rate of the top 10% high-income households in China is 60.6%, and their savings amount accounts for 74.9% of the total savings. Currently, China still has a social structure with a large proportion of the lower-income population and fewer people in other tiers, while the most stable and happiest social structure recognized worldwide is the "olive-shaped" social structure dominated by the middle class. Therefore, expanding the number of the middle class is a major task for optimizing China's future social structure.

### 6.2 *Pathways to Passing Through the MIT*

1. Pursuing new urbanization

Urbanization is an inevitable outcome of economic and social development, symbolizing the progress of industrialization and modernization. Actively and steadily advancing urbanization is a crucial strategy for solving issues related to agriculture, rural areas, and farmers (the "three rural issues"), promoting sustainable economic development in China, and building a moderately prosperous society in all respects. Urbanization development encompasses both the expansion of urban areas and the comprehensive improvement of urbanization quality, with the latter being the focal point. Specifically:

(1) Increase the scale and technological innovation capacity of urban industries.
(2) Integrate urban and rural industries to enhance the technological level of rural industries through collaborative technological innovation.
(3) With the integration of urban and rural industries, eliminate barriers in education, social security, and household registration, ultimately achieving resource sharing between urban and rural areas.
(4) Guide traditional farmers toward becoming modernized farmers, narrowing the differences in lifestyle between urban and rural areas.
(5) Improve the ecological environment of both urban and rural areas, fostering harmonious development between humans and nature.

New urbanization is a complex, systemic project involving urban management, land systems, regional development, agricultural modernization, and more. Promoting people-centered new urbanization is a multifaceted undertaking that requires consideration of the fundamental national conditions of the primary stage of socialism, touching on various aspects such as land systems, urban management, regional development, and agricultural modernization. We must adhere to the laws of development, act in accordance with the situation, and maintain a people-centered approach to urbanization construction. This involves promoting the coordinated development and rational division of labor among large, medium, and small cities and towns, optimizing the industrial layout comprehensively, adhering to the development philosophy that "lucid waters and lush mountains are invaluable assets," advancing green development, upholding low-carbon development, supporting ecological civilization construction, and developing beautiful towns with regional characteristics, ethnic culture, and historical memory, while promoting cultural heritage and protecting the unique features of towns.

2. Improving education quality comprehensively

According to the Chinese Ministry of Education, the enrollment rate for various forms of higher education in China reached 50% in 2019, entering the stage of mass education as defined internationally. In the future, the development goal of Chinese education should shift toward improving teaching quality and diversifying educational structures. Modern economic development poses new demands for higher education reform. With comprehensive economic development, the country's demand for talent has gradually shifted from a singular focus to a diversified one, requiring not only high-level technical and managerial talents across various industries but also mid-level technical talents, which are currently in more urgent demand. The integration of the education and research sector with the production sector is a result of the comprehensive development of the economy, science, and higher education. Higher education must cater to the needs of the real-world economy and serve the development of modern society. This involves strengthening the training of interdisciplinary talents and talents in short supply and encouraging higher education institutions to collaborate with research institutions, public institutions, and industry enterprises to cultivate talent, thus ensuring the integration of teaching and application.

China must optimize its education structure and address regional disparities: build world-class universities and disciplines, cultivate top-notch innovative talents, and strengthen the construction of universities with industry characteristics; focus on developing related specialties such as agriculture and forestry, water conservancy, geology and mining, petroleum, construction, transportation, resources, medicine, environment, teacher training, and service industries; balance the development of educational quality across regions; pay attention to the schooling level of colleges and universities in central and western China; enhance the educational infrastructure and teaching staff in these regions; and provide targeted support to western colleges to promote balanced development of higher education across regions.

China must enhance teaching capabilities and ensure educational quality: continuously conduct training courses to improve teachers' abilities; further refine the three-tier teacher training system at the national, provincial, and university levels; improve teaching standards and innovation capabilities, and advance changes in teaching methods and learning approaches; integrate IT technologies such as big data, cloud computing, and the internet with education and teaching; launch a batch of new high-quality online open courses; establish a teaching operation mechanism that combines online and offline teaching; and support the sharing of high-quality educational resources to benefit more learners.

3. Accelerating the development of the service industry

There is still untapped potential in China's service industry, and efforts should be made to continuously increase the proportion of service industry value-added in GDP, gradually forming an economy dominated by the service industry. Specific measures include:

(1) Guide urban and rural residents toward diversified consumption and broaden consumption fields. Promote the increase in service consumption proportion through expanding consumption scale and optimizing consumption structure.
(2) Use population urbanization as a carrier to promote the development of life service industries, thereby accelerating a new economic norm dominated by the service industry.
(3) Promote the transformation and upgrading of the manufacturing industry to provide intrinsic motivation for the production side.

The development of China's service industry should be primarily market-driven, supplemented by government regulation: on the one hand, continuously leverage the market's primary role in resource allocation; on the other hand, continuously strengthen the government's macro control capabilities. Meanwhile, the first thing should be to establish and improve the service system, set high-quality standards, and continuously expand service scope. For example, China should further raise and improve service standards in industries such as logistics, catering, postal services, and tourism. From a regulatory perspective, establishing a fair, just, and compliant regulatory system for the service industry is particularly important in expanding the social atmosphere of service consumption. For instance, protecting independent innovation and patent applications, strictly combating intellectual property infringements, safeguarding consumers' legitimate rights and interests, eliminating unreasonable charges, and strengthening the supervision and management of administrative and institutional fees—unreasonable charges should be abolished, and all revenues and expenditures should be made transparent and public for social oversight and inspection at any time.

Higher education institutions, vocational schools, research institutes, and related enterprises must work together to jointly cultivate talents, developing technical talents that meet market demands, open-minded talents familiar with international rules, and research talents with innovative capabilities. Meanwhile, through international exchanges and cooperation, China needs to establish talent service institutions that are internationally competitive. In terms of employment, China should encourage the construction and development of employment service institutions, continuously improve the employment service system, and provide relevant employment guidance for college graduates and job seekers. Additionally, it is crucial to actively address issues such as the transfer of surplus rural labor and the re-employment of laid-off urban workers by providing vocational training and cultivating a high-quality workforce to support the development of the service industry.

4. Encouraging and supporting the development of high-tech industries

In the current competitive international environment, high-tech industries play a foundational and transformative role. To overcome the MIT and narrow the gap with developed countries, China needs to actively support high-tech industries and encourage cooperation among research institutions to form scale advantages and promote close integration of production, education, and research. At present, most of China's research is focused on public technology and industrial technology, lacking fundamental research and practical application research. This leads to a lack of specialization due to insufficient foundational data, low conversion rates of research achievements, and limited contribution to social development. Therefore, strengthening collaborative innovation among the government, universities, and enterprises is the direction for reforming Chinese research institutions.

China should actively support high-tech industries and use them to drive the development of other industries. Decision-making should favor fields with broad industrial prospects and actively support emerging industries with future development potential, such as new energy, new materials, new medicine, information industry, biotechnology, and energy-saving and environmental protection industries. The government should establish a batch of competitive high-tech enterprises and provide protective policies for the initial development of high-tech industries to achieve breakthroughs in key technological fields. To encourage independent R&D by enterprises, the Chinese government can refer to the models of developed countries by signing agreements with enterprises, where the government entrusts R&D projects to enterprises, which in turn receive policy and financial support, thus strengthening their independent R&D capabilities. Internationally, efforts should be made to build the international image of China's high-tech industries, cultivate a batch of high-tech enterprises with international influence, and provide favorable policies and diplomatic assistance to help high-tech enterprises explore markets, thereby maintaining the image and interests of China's high-tech industries.

China should accelerate the cultivation of strategic emerging industries into leading and pillar industries, increasing their proportion in the industrial structure and using them as new drivers of economic growth. For example, the government should encourage the R&D of new information technology industries, new core internet devices, and new intelligent terminals; promote the development of the biotechnology industry and the industrialization of biopharmaceuticals; advance high-end equipment manufacturing, enhancing basic supporting capabilities; develop the new energy industry and utilize local conditions to develop and use bio-intelligence to achieve sustainable development; advance the new materials industry to achieve resource substitution; focus on the R&D of new energy vehicles; and promote the development, production, and marketing of high-efficiency, low-emission energy-saving and environmental protection vehicles. In the emerging industries related to the internet, apart from hot fields such as artificial intelligence, biotechnology, and virtual reality, the development of internet finance is also noteworthy. China should encourage the development of internet finance, including online banking, online futures, online payment, and online settlement. The development of internet finance in China focuses on innovation in financial models, emphasizing the development of new financial products and the release of funding supply and demand information on the internet, along with matching them accordingly. The financial system reforms behind this, such as the marketization of interest rates and exchange rates, also provide fundamental momentum for innovation in internet finance models.

5. Reducing the income gap and building a harmonious society

In recent years, the income gap among Chinese residents has been widening, deepening conflicts of interest between different groups. There remain significant disparities in basic public services between urban and rural areas, and between coastal regions and inland central and western regions. Public service facilities in rural communities are still lagging, and low-income groups and migrant workers enjoy lower levels of public services. Reducing China's income gap can mainly be addressed from the following aspects:

First, China must vigorously develop the economy to solve problems during the process of economic development. Since economic development has led to the widening of the income gap, the solution to the income gap must be sought within economic development. Only with economic development can the goal of partial affluence driving common prosperity be achieved, genuinely narrowing the income gap. However, we cannot stop developing the economy due to concerns about the income gap. We must adhere to economic development as the central focus. The economic foundation is the root cause of many issues. With economic development, the government can increase investment in scientific research and rely on technological progress to develop productive forces, thereby continuously improving production efficiency and accumulating wealth, laying the necessary prerequisites for narrowing the income gap.

Second, China must balance income disparities between different regions and pay attention to farmers' income levels. The development levels vary among provinces, with per capita income generally higher in the eastern regions than in the central regions, and higher in the central regions than in the western regions. The rural areas in the central and western regions suffer from significant labor loss and have relatively single economic models, making them more susceptible to weather and government support factors. The past urban-rural dualistic development model in China has also been a significant reason for the large income gap between urban and rural areas. In the early stages of economic development, we can rely on eastern urban development to drive economic growth. However, to overcome the MIT and reach high-income levels, we must focus on the economic development of the remote areas in the central and western regions.

Third, China must strengthen the construction of the legal system to achieve a development principle that prioritizes efficiency while considering fairness. Since the reform and opening up, China has been gradually improving and strengthening its legal system. However, phenomena such as non-compliance with laws and lax enforcement still occur. These issues not only affect social and economic efficiency but also create many social injustices, thereby provoking various social conflicts. Therefore, a sound legal system, strict law enforcement, and accountability for violations are essential guarantees for sustainable economic development and social harmony and stability.

Fourth, China must improve the socialist security system to raise the minimum living security level of the bottom population. The government can provide material assistance and social services to workers through the social security system, thus narrowing the income distribution gap. The social security system needs to be further improved in the future. Additionally, China must further enhance the basic pension security, medical security, unemployment insurance, and minimum living security systems to promote joint urban-rural development, enabling the broad masses of people to share the benefits brought by economic and social development and building a community of social interests. This approach can resolve social conflicts, achieve social stability, and provide strong guarantees for future economic development.

CHAPTER 8

# Theoretical Model of China's Reform: Model Construction, Interpretation, and China's Practices

The Third Plenary Session of the 11th CPC Central Committee in 1978 kicked off China's reform and opening up. After more than 40 years of exploration, China has basically established a socialist market economy. This is an unprecedented system change. Generally speaking, China is a country with vast territory, multi-nations, and weak economic foundation. However, in a complex environment where domestic and international challenges are intertwined, it has completed a rare system transformation in human history in a relatively short period of time and achieved the goal of economic take-off and industrialization. So there must be experience worth summarizing. From an international perspective, many countries have promoted similar transformation or market-oriented reforms, but most of them have only achieved a short-term prosperity, and many have encountered major setbacks or failures in their reforms. Therefore, China's successful experience in reform and opening up is particularly important and precious.

Generally speaking, reform is a substantial recalibration of the economic model, aimed at facilitating a transition from one economic paradigm to another by adjusting elements on both the supply and demand sides, among other pertinent domains. The pivotal condition for the success of such reforms hinges on whether the benefits of reform outweigh the costs. There are mainly two pathways to reform: the first is the shock therapy, an approach characterized by a rapid, immediate shift toward the targeted model; the second is a gradual approach that makes a phased


Z. Liang, *The Innovation of Economic Theory in China*,
https://doi.org/10.1007/978-981-95-2713-7_8

progression toward the new economic mode. Given that this transformation is a medium- to long-term endeavor, entailing structural adjustments at the supply side rather than mere short-term adjustments at the demand side. Therefore, empirical evidence tends to support the efficacy of gradual reforms. This contradicts the view point held by some Western economists that gradual reform may yield worse outcomes than rapid reform, yet it aligns with China's successful experience in its reform and opening up process. Considering the intricacies inherent in reform, discussions of reform abound from multiple angles, predominantly qualitative summarizations and analyses. There is, however, a relative dearth of studies employing models and engaging in quantitative analysis. With a focus on economic system reforms, our endeavor centers on developing a new perspective through the establishment of a quantitative theoretical model, thereby enabling a comprehensive analysis of the objectives, principles, pathways, and measures of reform.

## 1 Reform: The Propeller for China's Market Economy

The 40-year history of China's reform and opening up shows that reform is a systematic project, akin to a mathematical operation combining subtraction, addition, multiplication, and division. It is challenging to devise a perfect "top-down design"; therefore it is often the norm that the design of reforms to lag behind practical implementation. In its early stages, Deng Xiaoping's metaphor of "crossing the river by feeling the stones" outlined the route of reform. Over time, China has adhered to a decision-making philosophy that combines this exploratory "crossing the river by feeling the stones" approach with "top-down design." This dual strategy, embodying profound philosophical wisdom and proven effectiveness, has laid a solid foundation for the successful advancement of reforms.

After the Third Plenary Session of the 11th CPC Central Committee, reforms initially unfolded in rural areas and select localities, promptly enhancing agricultural productivity, leading to a gradual abundance of agricultural products, and yielding notably positive outcomes. By contrast, the urban economy did not exhibit marked improvements during the same period due to a delayed initiation of reforms. In October 1984, the Third Plenary Session of the 12th CPC Central Committee mentioned a planned commodity economy based on public ownership is the socialist economy. Subsequently, through continuous exploration, the 14th CPC National Congress in 1992 and the Third Plenary Session of the 14th CPC Central Committee in 1993 clarified the objective and basic framework for establishing a socialist market economic system. In 2013, the Third Plenary Session of the 18th CPC Central Committee proposed that the market plays a decisive role in resource allocation, essentially affirming the universal principles of a market economy. The Fifth Plenary Session of the 19th CPC Central Committee adopted the *Recommendations of the Central Committee of the Communist Party of China on Formulating the 14th Five-Year Plan for National Economic and Social Development and the Long-Range Objectives Through the Year 2035*, explicitly calling for deepening reforms comprehensively and constructing a high-standard socialist market economy. This decision was grounded in the profound changes in both domestic and international circumstances and signified a historic milestone in China's entry into a new phase of socialist market economic system construction.

Reform and opening up have propelled the establishment of China's market economic model, concurrently fueling the innovation of economic theories. China's reform in the past four decades was not a singular historical episode but a complex constellation of events. It is not only China's transformation, but also a grand experiment in human society. Practice has demonstrated that only through continuous development can economic issues be resolved, and socioeconomic progress is inherently intertwined with reform. While maintaining social stability, reform injects robust momentum into economic development. At the heart of reform lies the allocation of the relationship between the government and the market, steadily advancing market-oriented reforms, consistently streamlining administration and delegating powers. This process has given rise to the unique model of the Chinese socialist market economy, which, in turn, has fostered innovations in economic theory through practical application.

## 2 A Review of Reform-Related Economic Theories

Since the reform and opening up, China has embarked on a pivotal exploration of "Sinicizing" modern Western economic theories. This endeavor has not only provided a crucial historical reference for the development and refinement of socialism market economic theory, but also offered objective theoretical guidance for China's economic reform and development. In broad terms, China's reform efforts have not been confined by any single economic theory or ideology; instead, they represent a rational synthesis and elevation of multiple theories, with the outcome in practice serving as the ultimate arbiter of their validity. It is fair to say that, throughout China's four decades of reform experiences, a multitude of economic theories—including Marxist political economy, neoclassical economics, development economics, institutional economics, transition economics, etc.—have carried considerable relevance. Herein, we undertake a concise review of the principal economic theories implicated in China's reform practices.

### 2.1 *Reform from the Perspective of Marxist Political Economy*

Originating in nineteenth-century Europe, Marxist political economy focuses on the study of production relations. It represents a groundbreaking innovation in economic theory and serves as the ideological wellspring for the international communist movement, providing a scientific logical methodology for socialist construction. Marxist political economy is a theory that evolves with time. China's economists and people from all walks of life have systematically studied it and integrated its principles with China's specific national conditions. The adaptation has provided essential guidance for China's reform and opening up, as well as its economic and social development.

### 2.2 *Reform from the Perspective of Neoclassical Economics*

The neoclassical school, with its emphasis on resource allocation by markets, centers its analysis on the vital role of the "invisible hand" in guiding these allocations. This "invisible hand" refers to the market mechanism, which underscores that optimizing the allocation of economic factors is central to the functioning of a market economy. Conversely, government macroeconomic intervention can be seen as the "visible hand," stimulating growth by increasing inputs of productive factors. Taking the establishment of a socialist market economic system as its starting point, China has harnessed insights from the neoclassical theories on global economic integration and free trade. These concepts have served as important theoretical foundations for China's reform and opening up.

### 2.3 *Reform from the Perspective of Keynesian Theory*

From Adam Smith to John Maynard Keynes, Western economics has a long and rich history, evolving into a comprehensive system encompassing theories of growth, money, international trade, innovation, and development, among others. Keynesianism, particularly its theory of "effective demand" and the associated macroeconomic policies, has exerted significant influence on reform practices. Of notable impact is the content expounded in Paul Samuelson's book *Economics*. The theory played a pivotal role in popularizing Western economic thoughts and market economy practices in China, with its core tenets—theory of the market economy and macroeconomic regulation—profoundly shaping China's reforms. The formation of China's socialist market economy model, especially its macroeconomic regulatory framework, has drawn from Keynesian principles to a certain extent.

### 2.4 *Reform from the Perspective of Development Economics*

Development economics emerged in the 1940s with the aim of charting new paths to modernization, industrialization, and prosperity for impoverished or less developed countries and regions. The economists such as Zhang Peigang, Theodore W. Schultz, and W. Arthur Lewis are the representatives of the development economics school. In the early days of the founding of New China, despite undergoing socialist transformations, the economic foundation remained relatively underdeveloped. Up until the pre-reform and opening up period, China was still predominantly an agrarian nation with low levels of industrialization. Therefore, China's endeavor of reform and opening up could not have progressed without the pivotal guidance of theories rooted in development economics.

### 2.5 *Reform from the Perspective of Institutional Economics*

Since the initiation of reform and opening up, the fundamental driver of China's rapid economic growth has lain in the transformation of its economic mechanisms. The shift from a traditional planned economy to a socialist market economy ushered in profound changes in the economic system. Institutional economics originated with Ronald Coase's work *The Nature of the Firm*, which studies the distinct roles of firms and markets in economic interactions. China's reforms of state-owned enterprises (SOEs) have also borrowed ideas from related theories of institutional economics. The transformation of China's economic institutions has achieved an organic integration of "bottom-up institutional innovation" with "top-down institutional restructuring."

### 2.6 *Reform from the Perspective of Transition Economics*

China's economic system transformation has, to a certain extent, drawn inspiration from the theoretical guidance of transition economics. Transition economics studies the transition from planned to market economic systems, focusing on such economies as those in Central and Eastern Europe and China. Countries like Poland, Czechoslovakia (now the Czech Republic and Slovakia), Hungary, and Yugoslavia each developed their own economic reform theories, with a particular emphasis on issues including gradual reform, marginal substitution, liberation of power, and demonstration effects. Key thinkers in this realm included Oskar Lange, Ota Šik, Włodzimierz Brus, and János Kornai, among whom Kornai's theory of the economics of shortage exerted a significant influence on Chinese academic circles in the mid-to-late 1980s. These reform theories, largely originating from Eastern European nations, have in a way informed policy choices in China's reform and opening up process.

### 2.7 *Reform from the Perspective of Supply-side Economics*

During the 1970s and 1980s, the Reagan government in the United States and the Thatcher government in the United Kingdom championed supply-side economics as a response to the stagflation crisis plaguing the American and European economies. Supply-siders rejected Keynesianism on several grounds: First, adhering to Say's Law, they argued that supply generates demand. The school contended that attempting to stimulate demand without enhancing productive capacity would merely lead to inflation and failure to increase output. Second, they advocated for reducing tax burdens on both corporations and individuals to enhance corporate investment capability and incentive, alongside increasing personal incentives to work harder and save more. Third, they insisted that the money supply should be consistent with economic growth. Recognizing that excessive money issuance could fuel inflation, they called for prudent monetary management to maintain price stability. Fourth, they urged cuts in social welfare spending and government expenditures. They attributed rising unemployment, in part, to overly generous welfare programs that discouraged work, identifying this as a flaw in Keynesian thinking.

The supply-side school of economists advocate for reducing government intervention and strengthening the construction of a market economy and market competition. They oppose policies aimed at stimulating short-term demand, but instead focus on long-term value and innovative development to increase the effective supply and rational use of production factors. The supply-side school's propositions have successfully guided China's reform practices. It should be admitted that although the current supply-side structural reform that China is deeply promoting is quite different from the policy propositions of the supply-side school, it undoubtedly has certain reference significance.

## 3 Some Major Issues in the Process of China's Reform

China's reform and opening up has gone through four decades. During this period of time, China has accomplished a modernization process that took developed countries over a century, marking a monumental leap from a traditional to a modern society, from an agrarian to an industrial nation, and from a closed to an open society. Such a rapid transformation inevitably entails a myriad of unforeseen opportunities and challenges, presenting a double-edged sword for social stability. Historical precedents illustrate that periods of societal transition are fraught with diverse tensions and conflicts. If managed adeptly, these can spur the impetus for transformative change; conversely, without effective mechanisms to address these issues, crises may ensue. China's reform journey stands as a prime example, where debates and disagreements surrounding major issues have been integral to the reform process itself.

### *3.1 The Establishment of Reform Goals*

In the early stages of reform and opening up, China's leaders and economists universally recognized the necessity for reform, yet the specifics of how to proceed and the precise methods to employ were unclear. Naturally, there was no definitive roadmap, let alone a strategic objective outlining the transition from a traditional planned economy to a market economy. Throughout the reform process, China adhered to the approach of "crossing the river by feeling the stones," which was a continuous process of learning and exploration, as well as one that relied on practical implementation to propel reform forward. This involved harnessing the power of market mechanisms to forge new paths for reform, achieving breakthroughs in ideology and policy through practical application, and advancing reform dynamically in tune with the times or by "adapting to the current situation."

After more than a decade of exploration, establishing a socialist market economy emerged as the central objective of China's reforms in 1992. Deng Xiaoping once said, "Whether a market economy or a planned economy is not the defining characteristic distinguishing socialism from capitalism." Indeed, a completely free market economy does not exist in reality; increasingly, so-called market economies are enhancing the role of government. China embarked upon a historical phase characterized by the concurrent existence and mutual influence of markets and government action, with one sometimes prevailing over the other. In the practical operation of the economy, the notion of a completely free market economy or one entirely controlled by the government is inconceivable. When problems arise in the macroeconomy, it is quite difficult to figure out whether they are caused by the failure of the market economy or the failure of government intervention in the market. Indeed, China transcended the dichotomy that pits market economies against planned economies, achieving a harmonious integration of the two.

### *3.2 Early Debates About Plan and Market*

At the 1978 Theory-discussing Meeting of the State Council, many economists argued for giving greater play to the law of value, criticizing the leftist view that called for the eradication of commodity and monetary relations. On March 8, 1979, Chen Yun outlined in his *Plan and Market Issues* that both planned economy and market economy must exist throughout the entire socialist period. In November of the same year, when meeting with the vice president of Encyclopaedia Britannica Inc., USA, among others, Deng Xiaoping remarked, "A market economy cannot be said to belong solely to capitalism. Traces of a market economy emerged even in feudal societies. Socialism can also adopt a market economy." Clearly, Deng's views aligned fundamentally with Chen's, both of them emphasizing the introduction of market regulation and competition within the planned economy, thereby charting a course for China's economic reform and opening up.

Market-oriented reforms have created a miracle for China's economy, but some people still have doubts. If you plan ahead, you will succeed. If you don't, you will fail. Is it wrong to have plans when doing things and doing economics? It should be said that the essence of planned economy does not lie in whether there is a plan or not, but in the fact that it is a controlled economic model, which is the fundamental defect of traditional planned economy. At the same time, some people support the traditional planned economic model based on its characteristic of concentrating forces to accomplish major tasks, which can easily confuse people's understanding. China's goal of gradually establishing a socialist market economic system is of far-reaching significance. The essence of market economy is the autonomous activities of various market entities, which is an important source of market vitality, and the reform goal of market economy cannot be shaken.

The success of China's reform and opening up is a process of coordinated promotion of market construction and opening up. From planned pricing of products to market-determined product prices, from planned allocation of products and means of production to free transactions through the market, from unified allocation of production factors to free flow through factor markets, all these major changes are achieved through the dual-track system, that is, through the gradual transition of planned channels and market mechanisms and the rise and fall of the two. In general, the establishment of China's major markets has gone through a special process. In this process, the government gradually withdrew from direct participation in economic activities and turned to achieve healthy social development through redistribution. Of course, this requires a lot of meticulous work, including the formation of multiple market entities and price mechanisms, the construction of factor markets, and the transformation of macroeconomic control methods. All of these must be achieved through reform, which requires a process.

### *3.3 Debate on Whether to Insist on Reform*

Reform is not smooth; at times, it can be a tumultuous process. As the reforms of decentralization and incentivization progressed, their efficacy waned. And as the very act of reform inevitably disrupted original interest structures and challenged conventional socialist ideologies, it is necessary to find new breakthroughs and exploratory avenues. Domestically, the price liberalization reform of 1988 stumbled, culminating in a failed attempt to liberalize prices overnight. State-owned enterprises, operating under a contract responsibility system, generally saw dwindling performance, making their revitalization a daunting task amidst a narrowing margin for state concessions. Entering the early 1990s, extramural economic entities' competition exacerbated macroeconomic conditions, leading to substantial losses for SOEs. Internationally, the upheaval in Eastern Europe and the collapse of the Soviet Union prompted introspection on socialism's future and intensified debates around reform. Pro-reform factions faced mounting pressure amidst stalled progress and public discontent over official profiteering and soaring prices. Critics of reform, on the other hand, raised fundamental questions about the necessity and potential consequences of continued reform and opening up. Anti-marketization sentiments gained traction, dampening the impetus for further reform, and a sense of anxiety permeated society.

Nonetheless, the achievements of reform had gradually convinced many of its merits, and the ongoing process of reform and opening up had gathered irreversible momentum. Local governments and enterprises alike had benefited from decentralization and incentivization, and various non-state sectors of the economy—including urban collectives, individual businesses, and foreign-invested enterprises—had experienced rapid growth. Amidst this backdrop, there was an urgent need for a rallying call to consolidate consensus and propel the nation past the threshold of deeper reform and wider opening up.

Under this background, Deng Xiaoping made the "Southern Tour Speech" in 1992, carrying immense significance. Viewing the situation from a global economic perspective and geopolitical landscape, Deng resolutely endorsed the reform, asserting unequivocally, "Without adhering to socialism, without reform and opening up, without developing the economy, and without improving people's livelihood, there will be no alternative but a dead end." The speech emphasized that only through economic development and improvement of people's living standards could socialism be stabilized. It clarified that a market economy was not inherently capitalist, nor did a planned economy equate to socialism; socialism too could embrace a market economy.

In 1992, the 14th CPC National Congress established the goal of a socialist market economy, marking a significant step forward in China's market-oriented reforms and laying the groundwork for China's financial market system. In 2001, China's accession to the World Trade Organization (WTO) aligned its trade regime with global standards, further integrating the nation into the world economy. During the mid-1990s, ownership reform and asset restructuring centered on the principle of "grasping the large and releasing the small" initiated a process of "state retreat and private sector advance," fostering a diversified ownership base for the market economy. SOE reforms ushered in a new phase, demanding for innovative breakthroughs. The accomplishments of the 1990s reforms were prominently marked by the establishment of a basic framework for the socialist market economy, and China's accelerated integration into the global economy. The concerted efforts of steadfast market-oriented reforms and the continuous opening up of the economy propelled China's rapid growth. The country thus achieved an unprecedented economic boom, rapidly ascending to the world's second-largest economy.

### 3.4 The Choice of Reform Path: Gradual Reform Versus "Shock Therapy"

China, as the largest developing country, faced a crucial decision in its reform path to marketize its economy while preserving political cohesion and broad social stability. At the heart of economists' debates lay the question of whether China should opt for gradual reform or pursue radical reform. Gradual reform is characterized by gradualism in terms of timing, speed, and sequencing, embodying an evolutionary and phased approach to institutional change. Conversely, radical reform, also known as "shock therapy," entails swift and comprehensive systemic transformation within a shorter timeframe, featuring an evident discontinuous shift in institutional arrangements.

The economics community has produced numerous insightful findings in comparing the costs and benefits of gradual and radical reforms, yet consensus remains elusive. Jeffrey Sachs, a Harvard economist, is a prominent advocate for shock therapy, a strategy he formulated based on his consulting experiences in Latin American countries such as Bolivia. Sachs has argued that the Soviet Union and Eastern European countries should decisively and swiftly transition from a centrally planned to a market economy, implementing radical reforms all at once. His justifications included: (1) economic reform being an interconnected web affecting the whole, where piecemeal approaches fail due to each part's impact on others; (2) such a transformation strategy mitigating administrative resistance and pressures; (3) the scale of institutional adjustment necessitating fundamental systemic change; and (4) the dire economic situations in the Soviet Union and Eastern European countries requiring swift transformation, evidenced by the failures of gradualism in tackling inflation in Argentina, Brazil, and Peru. Sachs has viewed China's reforms as akin to "partial equilibrium" changes, primarily confined to the economic sphere and unsustainable in the long run, whereas Russian-style reforms, closer to a "general equilibrium" shift across economic and political domains, are deemed sustainable. However, economists like McKinnon (1994) have contested Sachs' overemphasis on structural factors, arguing that China's reform approaches and strategies are central to explaining its reform outcomes, with "initial conditions" being a pertinent but not decisive factor. Contrarily, Leseke Baserovich (2004) opines, based on the "Chinese model," that neither gradual nor radical reforms can be conclusively endorsed or dismissed. His reasoning hinged on: (1) different initial macroeconomic conditions at the outset of reforms; China encountered relatively mild imbalances when it initiated reforms in the late 1970s. (2) The success of China's economic reforms was primarily linked to the unique initial conditions. With approximately 80% of the farming population and the divisible nature of farming facilitating privatization, support of gradualism based on China's success logic was seen as a grave methodological error, overlooking the pivotal roles of special initial conditions and unique factors in economic development.

Lin Yifu et al. (1993) have contended that the "experimental promotion" approach to local reforms ensure control and stability throughout the reform process, minimizing risks. However, local reforms' progress relies on the state's coercion and administrative separation across sectors and regions, leading to uneven competition and market environments, fragmenting the integrity of market mechanisms, and exacerbating regional and sectoral disparities in development and income inequality. Fan Gang (1993), examining the origins and features of institutional change costs, has categorized them into implementation and friction costs. He argues that both radical and gradual reforms have advantages and disadvantages when comparing these costs. Radical reforms could swiftly complete institutional transformation and economic transition with potentially lower costs. Gradual reforms, however, prioritized control and stability throughout, balancing interests among different groups, fostering broad societal support for reform measures. In comparison, gradual reforms demonstrate a relative advantage over radical ones, with more evident success in China's practice. Scholars hold divergent views on radical versus gradual reforms, with no clear theoretical determination or ideological acceptance of superiority for either approach. Nonetheless, China's successful gradual reform provides a resounding answer. This model serves as a practical, viable alternative to the market fundamentalism and shock therapy often propagated by US academia and Washington think tanks, offering a proven path for other developing or transitioning economies. For China, it has facilitated the transition from a planned to a market economy while sustaining high growth rates and broad political and social stability. This chapter will discuss this rationality from a theoretical model perspective.

## 4 Theoretical Model of Reform: A Combination of an "Effective Market" and a "Proactive Government"

Essentially, reform is a process of economic system transformation, an ongoing process from the existent economic paradigm toward an envisioned ideal. The objective of reform is an aspirational economic model, with defining this target model of utmost importance. Reform is a systemic endeavor, necessitating answers to where to go, how to get there, and what principles to adhere to. In light of China's reform experiences, once the reform objectives and principles are delineated, the focus shifts to facilitating a smooth economic system transition via rational strategies and measures, culminating in the gradual emergence of a market economy model characterized by both an "effective market" and a "proactive government." Proceeding, a theoretical model for reform is constructed to address these queries.

### *4.1 Defining the Target of Reform: China's Market Economy Model*

Based on the Rational Comprehensive Economic Model (or Hybrid Economic Development Model) constructed by Zong Liang and Fan Ruoying (2018), which draws insights from the macroeconomic theory and ingeniously combines the concepts of an "effective market" with a "proactive government." It is a Rational Comprehensive Economic Framework, and a synthesis model for the modern market economy. The fundamental equation of this theoretical model is as follows:

$$\Delta Y_t = a\Delta Y_{Mt}^* + b\mu_{sl}\Delta A_t Y_{Mt}^* + b(\mu_d + \mu_{ss})(Y_t - Y_{Gt}^*) + b(\varepsilon_{dt} + \varepsilon_{st}) \quad (8.1)$$

Based on the dynamic macroeconomic growth model, in Eqn. (8.1) for calculating actual economic output growth $\Delta Y_t$, $a$ represents the market effect coefficient, and $b$ denotes the government effect coefficient. The coefficients $\mu_d$, $\mu_{ss}$, and $\mu_{sl}$ signify the government's regulatory impact on the demand side, short-term supply side, and long-term supply side respectively, while $\varepsilon_{dt}$ and $\varepsilon_{st}$ symbolize unobservable random shocks from the demand and supply sides. Given that a system dominated by market forces with manageable government intervention is considered optimal and efficacious, the targeted reform model aims to establish a market mechanism (Zong and Fan, 2018). In the mathematical model, varying weights of parameters $a$ and $b$ reflect differing degrees of market influence versus government intervention in real economies. Among different market economy models, the proportion of market elements can vary, theoretically ranging from 60%, 70%, to 90%, with a minimum threshold of 50%. Based on our calculations, broadly speaking, a market share of around 70% constitutes a highly favorable market economy model.

In the transformation of an economy, it is elusive initially to pinpoint an exact target. So we can only determine a general direction first, and then find the focus gradually throughout the reform process. As illustrated in Fig. 8.1, the ideal model for economic development is not static; it is intimately tied to the fundamental relationship between aggregate supply and aggregate demand, as well as the specific stage of social development. It is crucial to recognize that the evolution of economic models is a dynamic process, constantly in flux, yet within a given development stage, it exhibits a certain degree of stability. In other words, economic development models in human societies evolve progressively over time. By historical comparison and practical observations, slave societies represent a rudimentary form of market economy, and government intervention tended to increase in feudal societies. Conversely, in capitalist societies, government intervention lessened somewhat. From the historical evolution and practical experiences of economic models, a market economy model is the ideal pattern for economic development, serving as the objective of economic reforms.

The establishment of target for China's socialist market economy reform has been a continuous exploration, which can be represented through a diagram. As shown in Fig. 8.2, China's initial economic model

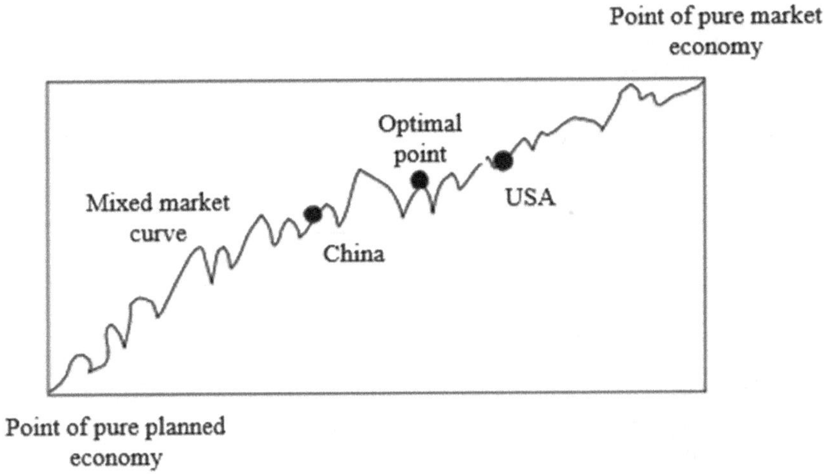


**Fig. 8.1** Dynamic transformation curve of economic development models

started around point A, with the ideal target located near point B, yet the actual reform trajectory led toward point O. This target embodies two layers of meaning: Firstly, it signifies the fundamental direction and the ideal endpoint, that is, the transition from point A to B. However, in the early stages, the precise ideal might not be clearly defined, and only a general direction can be set, leading to a practical path initially closer to point O. Secondly, it encompasses the process of gradually approaching the ideal target B from point A. This is because, initially, point B cannot be accurately identified and hard to attained in practice. The metaphor of "crossing the river by feeling the stones" implies exploring the path toward B while adhering to the fundamental direction. Conversely, "top-level design" broadly determines the position of B, also reflecting China's profound understanding that "reform is always a journey in progress."

### 4.2 *Clarifying the Principles and Pathways of Reform*

The principles guiding reform serve as constraints and benchmarks, mainly including the following: The first is to uphold the principle of promoting productive forces' development. This means adhering to a pragmatic approach, judging reforms not by their adherence to a particular theory or any precedent, but by their tangible contributions. The focus is on

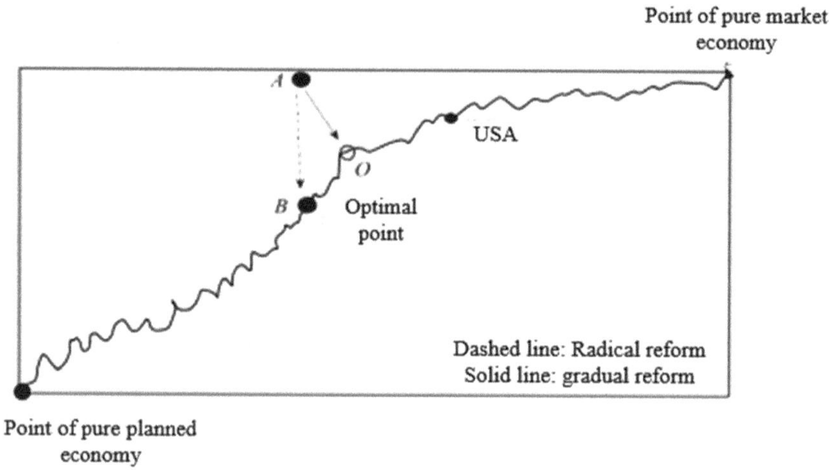


**Fig. 8.2** Target of reform

expanding the proverbial economic "pie," achieving tangible results. Any measure that yields clear benefits is deemed a good one, while those lacking efficacy are not. It echoes Deng Xiaoping's famous saying, "It doesn't matter if the cat is black or white, as long as it catches mice," akin to a doctor whose worth is proven by the ability to cure patients. The second is to embrace the principle that the benefits of reform can compensate the costs. Pursuing reforms that could just as easily be bypassed holds little merit and seldom yields optimal outcomes. Ideally, reforms commence where benefits are substantial and resistance is minimal, progress to those of moderate difficulty, and finally tackle the most challenging tasks—akin to the final push or the last mile. The third is to follow the principle of balancing risks and rewards in selecting reform pathways. Reforms inherently involve significant adjustments to existing interests; thus, pre-assessment of risks and rewards is paramount. Reform measures must first ensure a net increase in overall benefits, with losses contained and mitigated through targeted policies where necessary. By minimizing resistance and demonstrating positive outcomes, reforms garner broader support, fostering an environment conducive to sustained reform efforts.

The discussion now turns to the choice between gradual and radical reform paths. The establishment of economic models, market entities, and factor markets is typically not instantaneous. As depicted in Fig. 8.2, in the journey from point A to the ideal target B, two reform approaches exist: one is the radical reform, indicated by the dashed line, suggesting a direct leap without a discernible process; the other is the gradual reform, represented by the solid line, signifying a gradual progression requiring a series of steps. Reforms are typically an ongoing process of adaptation and approximation toward the target. In theory, both gradual and radical reforms have their merits, and the choice depends on the nature of the problem to be solved. Relatively, for short-term issues, localized markets, or cyclical problems, radical reforms might prove more efficacious. However, for more intricate problems involving structural and model transformations, which are long-term trends, gradual reforms are more efficacious. China's reform trajectory combines the two, primarily based on the gradual reform, in an organic manner. Analogous to a child's growth, regardless of the methods employed, maturity does not occur instantaneously but requires a gradual adaptation process, during which unique characteristics also form. Yet, at critical moments, targeted measures are necessary. Moreover, radical reforms, by moving too quickly, hinder assessment of risks and benefits, as well as where these benefits will accrue, thus relinquishing control over the process and outcomes. It's like releasing all fish in a lake at once, but who captures how much and with what outcome become uncertain. Gradual reform is a more effective strategy, which allows for controlled adjustment, enabling different interest groups to obtain their fair "share" of benefits. Radical reform implies a sudden change, while gradual reform manifests in a clear and phased process (see Fig. 8.3).

## 5 Analyzing the Objectives and Measures of Reform Based on the Theoretical Model

Different goals necessitate different reform measures. In the pursuit of establishing a market economy model, the primary measures are as follows:

### *5.1 Straightening Out the Relationship Between the Government and the Market*

Economic model transformation is both a dynamically evolving process and one that necessitates a degree of stability. As illustrated in the preceding models, this balance forms the core of the relationship. Consequently,

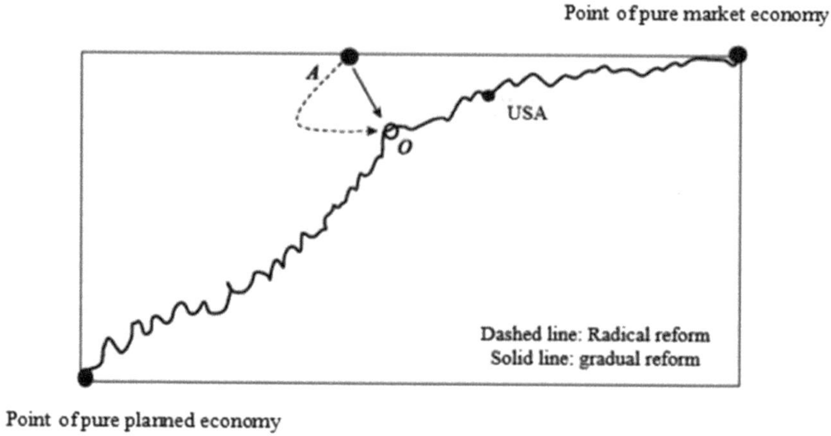


**Fig. 8.3** Pathways of reform

reforms must scrutinize the paramount relationship—that between the market and the government—and broadly delineate the reasonable threshold where the roles of the market and the government intersect. Generally, we encounter scenarios where government intervention tends to be relatively high, necessitating a gradual decentralization of power. In essence, streamlining administration and delegating powers constitute a fundamental direction, aimed at fostering an optimal market environment. Decisions should be made against market standards to discern what measures are rational and what are not, thereby facilitating structural optimization. It is imperative to analyze where the market proves efficient or fails and what the government must undertake or doesn't have to under certain circumstances, to clarify the approximate boundaries of government and market functions.

### 5.2 *Establishing and Improving Market Mechanism*

Establishing a market mechanism is a complex undertaking, as inferred from the earlier models, primarily governed by the first component of Eqn. (8.1), encompassing several key aspects: Firstly, to establish and reinforce a robust market, enabling the price mechanism to play a pivotal role. This market comprises both goods and factors of production, with the latter further divided into segments like financial markets. Secondly, to liberate market entities. Firms and individuals, acting as rational economic agents, are central players who engage in market competition driven by their self-interest. Thirdly, to improve the business environment and refine the competitive mechanism. For the market, to function effectively, a favorable business environment is imperative, forming the bedrock for healthy competition. Lastly, to formulate operational rules and standards for the market, adhering strictly to contractual obligations and integrity. All market participants must comply with these established rules and standards, while any irregularities in market competition must be rigorously addressed and rectified.

### 5.3 *Establishing and Refining the Regulatory Mechanism*

While previous sections have delved into this topic, a succinct summary is provided here. As indicated in the earlier model, for the third component of Eqn. (8.1), the crux lies in how to effectively leverage government intervention under market economy conditions to compensate for the inadequacies of market forces. This essentially involves constructing a regulatory system that seamlessly integrates supply-side and demand-side dynamics. This approach elevates Keynesian macroeconomic theory to a higher plane and aligns with Samuelson's logic of considering both aggregate supply and demand comprehensively. China's practices have exemplified the integration of supply-side and demand-side regulatory policies. Drawing from the policy mix table derived from the earlier models, macroeconomic regulation strategies contemplate not only shifts in economic structure but also cyclical factors. This approach accounts for the overlap of structural and cyclical issues. Consequently, the remedies for structural and cyclical problems diverge during economic upswings and downturns, differing from Keynesian theories that primarily focus on demand-side policies. In recent years, China's macro-policy implementations have showcased a nimble alternation between supply-side and demand-side measures in response to evolving economic phases, exemplifying a pragmatic application of this balanced approach.

### 5.4 *Technological Progress is Crucial to sustAined Economic Growth*

The second component in the preceding model directly pertains to total factor productivity or labor productivity, which constitute the crucial precondition for economies to achieve a leapfrog growth. It enables an upward shift in the long-term potential growth rate through the facilitative role of a "proactive government," thereby laying the groundwork for sustained real economic growth and significant transformations. The government's promotion of technological progress can be elucidated through two tiers: Firstly, the government needs to build a favorable environment for innovation. This includes incentivizing market entities to innovate through tax adjustments, allocating research and development funds to back fundamental research and technological innovations, and extending support to emerging yet less mature sectors in the market. Secondly, in line with the analysis of growth theories mentioned earlier, the government also functions as a brake, capable to transfer the entire trajectory of economic growth, and even facilitate a shift away from economic crises onto a path of healthy development. Absent from this intervention, the potential growth rate would follow a relatively fixed pattern, manifesting in evident convergence. Analogous to a train diverting to a safer route when encountering danger, this aligns with the concept we often encounter referred to as the "second curve."

## 6 Theoretical Model of Reform and Analysis of China's Practices

Practice has shown that traditional planned economic models have evident shortcomings, just as totally free market economies also present flaws. China's reform journey can be characterized as a continuous process of establishing a socialist market economic mechanism, one that progressively refines the functioning of both an "effective market" and a "proactive government." The success of China's reform and opening up represents China's exploration of the government-market relationship, a successful developmental model for the economy that validates the new trend of reconciling the once opposing roles of the government and the market into a unified force. Since the inception of reform and opening up, China has witnessed an unprecedented economic miracle, achieving rapid development while catering to the needs of over a billion people. The underlying reason for this feat resides in the invigorating power unleashed by the socialist market economic system. The 14th CPC National Congress established the socialist market economy as the target for economic system reforms. Thereafter, from the 15th to the 17th CPC National Congresses, we steadfastly adhered to this direction, advancing market-oriented reforms theoretically and practically, and essentially forming the micro foundations, competitive mechanisms, and pricing mechanisms of the socialist market economy. These reforms have optimized the fundamental role of resource allocation and the market's function in adjusting supply and demand, significantly enhancing economic vitality and promoting sustained and rapid development. China's reform practices resonate with the analyses conducted within our theoretical models.

### 6.1 Establishing Reform Goals and Criteria

Since the reform and opening up, China's economic development has undergone two pivotal transformations. First, a systemic transition from a traditional planned economy to a socialist market economy has taken place. Second, the mode of growth has shifted from extensive expansion to one focused on high-quality development. In 1992, the 14th CPC National Congress explicitly set the goal of our economic system reforms as the establishment of a socialist market economic system. This basic framework is fundamentally structured around five interconnected and mutually constraining components: enterprise systems, market systems, distribution systems, social security systems, and macroeconomic regulation systems.

Since the reform and opening up, the most visible transformation in China's economic and social landscape has been the shift from a traditional planned economy system to a socialist market economy. This transition has not only unleashed and greatly invigorated social productive forces, but also coincided with systematic changes in socioeconomic relations. These changes comprehensively depict the evolution of China's socioeconomic landscape and the restructuring of its economic fabric since the start of reform and opening up and represent the concentrated embodiment of China's economic reform endeavors.

### 6.2 Adhering to the Principle that "development is the top priority" and Seeking a Relatively Balanced Distribution of Benefits

China places great emphasis on the interplay between reform, development, and stability. From the 1980s to the global financial crisis in 2008, China maintained an average annual GDP growth rate of around 10% in most years. After 2008, China's economic growth rate gradually decelerated to its current level of roughly 5%. Annually, governments at different levels typically set economic growth targets, primarily focusing on GDP growth rates. While this approach has yielded noticeable results, it has also faced some criticism. As long as a high growth rate is sustained, China can expand employment, increase the stock of social wealth, raise the base for distributing national income, improve its citizens' well-being, and thereby garner broader support for ongoing reforms. Moreover, a higher growth rate facilitates a continuous rise in government revenue, which was particularly crucial for China's early economic development. In recent years, however, this situation has been changing; China's growth model is transitioning from one heavily reliant on labor and capital inputs to one more dependent on technological progress and innovation, from focusing on external drivers to focusing on internal ones, and from pursuing sheer GDP numbers to pursuing high-quality GDP growth. In line with the logic and experience of China's reform and opening up, the benchmark for judging the success of reforms is rapid economic development coupled with improved living standards for the people. Relevant institutional arrangements should be designed to equitably distribute the actual costs of reform and ensure that the benefits of such reforms are widely shared. This approach has won broad-based support for China's reform and opening up. Furthermore, given that there remains room for institutional transformation and structural upgrading in China, the potential for economic growth persists. As such, concerns raised by some economists about the "middle-income trap" are less likely to materialize, and it is probable that China will successfully navigate beyond this developmental hurdle.

### *6.3 Taking the Lead in Advancing Rural Reforms*

During the late 1970s and throughout the 1980s, farmers and rural areas in China took center stage in the nation's reform efforts. The innovation of the "household contract responsibility system," initiated by peasants in Xiaogang Village, Fengyang County, Anhui Province, shook the foundation of the existing People's Commune System, making a triumphant rural reform that laid the groundwork for China's sustained reform progress. Implementation of this system addressed long-standing issues regarding incentives for agricultural labor and management while gradually empowering households with increased autonomy and enabling them to retain the surplus from their labor. This rural reform significantly boosted the supply of agricultural products to cities, enriching and stabilizing a vast population of farmers, and thereby setting favorable conditions for subsequent reforms. Among these changes, the most dynamic groups migrated out of rural areas, transforming into a workforce employed in infrastructure construction and manufacturing sectors, becoming a vital part of the labor market. This migration supplied crucial manpower for the industrial sector's growth.

Reforms in rural areas triggered monumental shifts in China's social structure. By the late 1980s, multiple waves of migrant workers sparked massive population migrations unseen before in the country's history. Years of restrictive population management had amassed a substantial reserve of rural surplus labor. The concentrated release of this labor force and their urge to migrate to cities ignited the "migrant worker tide." The mobility of these migrant workers became a driving force of China's economic miracle. China's ascension to becoming the "world's factory" owes much to the contributions of these migrant workers. Moreover, the "migrant worker tide" continually fueled efforts to mitigate the urban-rural dual structure, significantly accelerating China's urbanization process. Urbanization rates climbed from 17.9% in 1978 to 51.3% in 2011, and by 2019, the urbanization rate of permanent residents exceeded 60% for the first time. Nonetheless, China's urbanization journey still has a long way to go, with its core lying in achieving equality of rights, truly transforming rural migrants into urban citizens.

The breakthroughs achieved in the rural reforms held comprehensive significance. The process was a combination of grassroots farmers' exploration and local governments' promotion, culminating in a nationwide policy after mutual consensus was reached. Initially, agricultural policies did not prioritize systemic reforms. However, the more relaxed political environment after the Third Plenary Session of the 11th Central Committee of the Communist Party provided fertile ground for substantial changes in rural management systems and operational methods. For example, bans on farmers were lifted, and rural economic policies were eased, granting farmers more options and autonomy. Simultaneously, the government consistently revised agricultural policies to benefit the people, incentivizing farmers with greater rewards. Consequently, most farmers chose the household contract responsibility systems, either contracting production quotas or fixed-amount contracts. If collectivization was likened to damming a river, then the household contract system represented an unstoppable breach of that dam, unleashing the productive forces of rural China.

This trend sparked intense debates across rural regions. Traditionally, adhering to collective economy was seen as a cornerstone of socialist values, and objections to whether "the household contract system still constituted socialism" were notable. However, proponents, including many central and local officials, outnumbered the dissenters. The rural reforms dramatically enhanced public satisfaction; a substantial number of farmers grew prosperous and settled, allowing policymakers to advance reforms steadily in a stable environment. The significance of the breakthroughs in rural reforms lay in its promotion of a major trend toward marketization: First, specialized households emerged, being occupied in commodity production and operation, including large-scale commercial ventures, fueling the rapid development of private enterprises. Second, it opened up long-distance trading, cross-regional commerce, and various markets. Third, the rise of township and village enterprises (TVEs) was a pivotal outcome of rural reforms. TVEs not only served as engines driving China's economic growth in the 1980s but also played a crucial role in transitioning toward a market economy.

### 6.4 *Steadily Advancing the Reform of State-owned Enterprises*

The reform of SOEs has virtually paralleled the entire course of China's reform era, evolving from decentralization and profit retention to "profit-to-tax conversion," then to contract responsibility systems, and eventually to shareholding reforms and the establishment of modern corporate systems. This journey has entailed prolonged exploration. Discussions surrounding SOE reforms must be intertwined with the broader context of the overall reform process. In 1978, China initiated enterprise reforms centered primarily on decentralization and profit retention. At that time, the main threads of enterprise reform comprised: (1) gradually endowing and expanding the operational autonomy of SOEs, until the modern corporate systems established; (2) promoting the transfer of benefits from the state to enterprises, thereby enhancing the motivation of enterprises as market entities; and (3) permitting and encouraging the development of non-public sector economies, actively attracting foreign investment, and fostering a healthy and competitive market environment.

In the 1980s, urban enterprise reforms shattered the "iron rice bowl" and "egalitarianism," earning widespread endorsement from workers who became active participants and beneficiaries of the reforms. However, entering the 1990s, amidst a wave of SOE closures, consolidations, transformations, bankruptcies, and privatization, a considerable portion of workers were laid off and forced to find their own livelihoods. Additionally, as these former workers aged, they lost the ability to secure reemployment, becoming reliant on the social security system. Consequently, this group confronted significant challenges and formed a certain resistance to further reforms.

China persists in the direction of establishing modern corporate systems. The integration of public ownership with the socialist market economy remains a significant area of ongoing exploration for China. Adherence to the corporate reform principles of "clear property rights, well-defined responsibilities, separation of government from enterprises, and scientific management" is crucial. Strengthening Party building within SOEs is a vital aspect of these reforms. Comprehensive understanding and implementing the Party's leadership in SOEs is no easy task. However, enhancing the Party's leadership does not imply micromanagement of every detail, but rather ensuring that the Party committees can direct and manage strategic, fundamental matters effectively. Strengthening the Party's leadership in SOEs means to, under the guidance of the Party, fully harness the initiative, proactivity, and creativity of the board of directors, shareholders' meetings, workers' congresses, and management teams. This, in turn, enhances the enterprises' economic performance, product quality, innovation capacity, and competitiveness. Only by achieving these enhancements can the genuine leadership of the Party be realized in practice.

### 6.5 *Endeavoring to Create a Fair Competitive Environment for all Types of Market Entities*

In Marxist political economy, the concept of ownership is of paramount importance and has shaped a particular mindset. From China's perspective, public ownership is an integral and distinctive feature of its economy. Prior to reform and opening up, China's public ownership mainly comprised state ownership and collective ownership, with the latter epitomized by the People's Commune System in rural areas. Western economies place significant emphasis on ownership as well, albeit often treating SOEs as outliers. In China's reform practice, the challenge has been to uphold the status of state ownership while striving to establish a relatively equitable competitive environment for all forms of ownership. This entails advancing SOE reforms while fully leveraging the critical roles of enterprises under diverse forms of ownership. The 18th CPC National Congress restated the principle of "two unwaveringly," that is, "unwaveringly consolidating and developing public ownership" and "unwaveringly encouraging, supporting, and guiding the development of non-public sector economies." Encouraging the common development of public ownership and various forms of ownership is a hallmark of the socialist market economy and a crucial experience garnered through practical exploration and innovation in China's socialist endeavor.

It should be acknowledged that throughout the reform process, while recognizing the advantages and even dominant position of the state-owned economy, China has actively sought substantial development for non-public sector economies, striving for a balance between them. Before reforms, the understanding of public ownership was simplistic, equating it to the sum of state and collective ownership. State ownership implied the entire population as the ultimate proprietors, with no other types of shareholders, and the representatives of the people being the administrative bodies of the state. State-owned enterprises were merely a specific form of this ownership. The Law of the People's Republic of China on State-owned Industrial Enterprises, promulgated in 1988 and later revised in 2009, reflected this shift, with the profound implication of substituting "state economy" for "public economy" being noteworthy. According to Marxist political economic theory, the fundamental distinction between socialism and capitalism in terms of ownership lies in the existence of ownership by the whole people, not merely state ownership. Entering the twenty-first century, with shareholding system reforms leading the way, state-owned enterprises embarked on a period of comprehensive development. A pivotal milestone was marked by the restructuring and listing of state-owned banks following China's accession to the WTO. While SOE reform remained a central theme, it was fundamentally different from the early 1980s, with contemporary SOEs primarily differentiated by shareholding proportions. Before reforms, collective ownership was characterized by collective laborers jointly owning the means of production and equally distributing the products of their labor. Post-reform, however, this model experienced differentiation and transformation.

Non-public sector economies have effectively played their roles as key market entities: (1) All kinds of non-public sectors have been growing rapidly, such as private, individual, and foreign-funded economies. The

1999 Constitutional Amendment affirmed their significance in China's socialist market economy. (2) The individual sectors experienced development and diversification. In the intensive market competition, some individual sectors flourished while others didn't. (3) The private entrepreneurs became the influential participants of the reform in regions like Guangdong and Zhejiang. (4) The foreign entrepreneurs, financiers, and bankers have encountered both privileged treatment and challenges in different stages of China's reforms. Generally, the foreign entrepreneurs are the participants, supporters, and beneficiaries of China's reforms, as they have experience from the developed economies. Looking ahead, we aim to stimulate vitality across all market players by not only invigorating SOEs and scaling up state capital through deeper reforms, but also continuously encouraging, guiding, and supporting non-public sector growth, improving the business environment for steady development across diverse economic models.

### *6.6 Actively Promoting the Decentralization Reform to Enhance Marketization Level*

Throughout its reform journey, China has placed great emphasis on introducing market mechanisms and fostering competition, with the aim of stimulating enthusiasm and enlivening its economy. Decentralization and profit retention have been key strategies implemented to enhance the dynamism of the economy. In the early stages of reform, Deng Xiaoping proposed allowing a portion of the population to "earn and live better first." Set against the backdrop where common prosperity is a core socialist value, this was a bold move. It courageously acknowledged disparities and, for the first time, positioned economic interests, rather than "revolutionary spirit," as the primary driver of economic development, with the ultimate goal of achieving common prosperity for all. This measure effectively tapped into people's long-suppressed profit motives and desires for prosperity, infusing new vitality into economic development and becoming a pivotal driver of economic reforms.

The reform of streamlining administration and decentralizing power is conducive to enhancing marketization levels and is an inevitable requirement for perfecting the socialist market economic system. Over the years, China has persistently advanced such reforms, leading to a substantial reduction in administrative approval items across various ministries and commissions of the State Council. Presently, the number of enterprise investment projects requiring central government approval is exceedingly limited, and those with centrally determined prices can be counted on one's fingers. These reforms have played a significant role in unleashing and developing social productive forces, promoting steady economic growth, and advancing social fairness and justice.

The report of the 19th CPC National Congress emphasized the urgency to accelerate the improvement of the socialist market economic system. To this end, it demanded resolute elimination of systemic and institutional hindrances that restrained the decisive role of the market in resource allocation, firmly grasping the "bull by the horns" of streamlining administration and delegating powers. Through the government's reduction and limitation of its powers, the reforms have continuously stimulated the vitality of market entities and social innovation, reinforcing the driving force for economic development and promoting growth that is of higher quality and more sustainable. Furthermore, deepening these reforms is also a major step toward optimizing the business environment and enhancing international competitiveness.

### 6.7 *Attaching Great Importance to Technological Progress*

In the course of reform, China has accorded high importance to the role of technological advancement, recognizing its vital contribution to economic growth. At the onset of reform and opening up, the country lagged significantly behind the United States, Europe, Japan, and South Korea in education, knowledge, and technology levels. Consequently, the contribution of technological progress to economic growth was exceptionally high. However, entering the 1990s, the marginal contribution of technological progress to China's economic growth began to decline. With China's accession to the WTO and the launch of a new round of opening up, the contribution of technological progress to economic growth resumed an upward trajectory. From the initiation of industrialization in the 1980s to 2007, China experienced an initial phase dominated by the introduction of advanced equipment and industrial technological upgrades. Subsequently, with a rapid increase in capital investment and the concurrent development of urbanization, real estate, and continued industrialization, the contribution of technological progress to economic growth progressively escalated. Meanwhile, China consistently augmented investments in education, science and technology, R&D, and emerging industries, yielding notable outcomes. Population growth, urbanization, the expansion of the real estate sector, and the heavy chemical industry fueled massive capital inputs, complemented by the impetus from technological advancements and export growth following WTO entry. Collectively, these factors propelled China's sustained and rapid economic growth from 1997 to 2007.

Currently, China is actively transitioning its economy toward innovation-driven development. The country's 13th Five-Year Plan underscored that "innovation is the primary driving force for development." In recent years, policies to promote mass entrepreneurship and innovation have been introduced successively, with initiatives such as the push for high-quality manufacturing development and the "Internet Plus" action plan steadily advancing. Emerging industry guidance funds and independent innovation demonstration zones are being established at an accelerated pace. Following years of concerted efforts, China has notably raised its level of science and technology and innovation. It now leads globally in the number of R&D personnel, with R&D expenditure climbing to 2.12% of GDP in 2017. Breakthroughs have been made in a series of significant technologies, including high-speed rail, nuclear power, 4G communications, and ultra-high voltage power transmission and transformation. China's colossal market size, comprehensive industrial system, and robust infrastructure provide ample room for innovation in technology, products, and industries.

### *6.8 Establishing and Improving Macroeconomic Management and Control Policies*

Since the reform and opening up, China has gradually refined its macroeconomic regulation system centered on countercyclical adjustments. Whether responding to the Asian Financial Crisis, the 2008 Global Financial Crisis, or mitigating the impacts of the COVID-19 pandemic, China's macroeconomic regulation policies have achieved notable effects. The theoretical foundation of traditional countercyclical adjustments lies in Keynes' theory of inadequate effective demand from the 1930s, leading to demand management policies being widely adopted as a paradigm of macroeconomic control worldwide. However, China's macroeconomic control policies are not simple adjustments to effective demand but encompass rational utilization of both aggregate supply and demand. Relative to traditional countercyclical adjustments, China's policies are more systematic, comprehensive, and rational, representing a significant innovation in macroeconomic control. China's relatively effective macroeconomic control has empowered the stable operation of its economy, enabling it to become one of the first countries to achieve economic recovery and growth post the 2008 financial crisis, with clear and evident outcomes. In 2020, China's new proposition of "improving the design and adjustment of macroeconomic controls across cycles" was a strategic choice made by the CPC Central Committee based on the domestic and international economic and financial environments in the new era, aiming to foster high-quality economic development. Proposing a new macroeconomic control approach from the perspective of high-quality economic development marks a significant policy innovation with substantial theoretical implications. The key to refining macroeconomic governance is to well manage the relationship between the government and the market, fully leverage the market's role in resource allocation, and better play the government's part.

## 6.9 *Emphasizing Coordinated Advancement of Reform and Opening Up*

In the new stage of refining the socialist market economic system, China confronts reforms that are risk-prone, require intricate coordination, and touch upon deep-seated interest relationships. Reforms in the political, cultural, and social systems are intricately linked with economic system reforms, heightening the demand for comprehensive and coordinated advancement of reforms. The success of China's reform is partly attributed to its execution within an open environment. In the early stages, while the reform lacked a clear roadmap, the direction for opening up was clear, primarily targeting developed countries or regions (especially the United States, Europe, and Japan), to fully utilize capital, technology, markets, and management expertise to propel China's rapid economic growth. Indeed, the establishment of diplomatic relations with the United States and the signing of a treaty with Japan facilitated favorable conditions for opening up, granting China access to major global markets. The reform and opening up in China has adopted a gradual, phased approach. Opening up not only attracted foreign investment but also introduced new rules, systems, management practices, and ushered in international competition, providing impetus for further reforms.

### *6.10 Advancing Comprehensive Reforms and Refining the Socialist Market Economic System*

China's sustained market-oriented reforms have fueled rapid economic growth, giving birth to the "Chinese miracle." Interpretations of China's "market-oriented reform model" vary considerably among scholars both domestically and internationally. Analyzing the characteristics of China's reforms reveals several points: First, following the order that economy first and politic later. It can ensure the government effectively steer the reform process and mediate stakeholders' interests. Second, reforms progressed incrementally through continuous experimentation, embodying the approach of "crossing the river by feeling the stones." This method allowed for comparing and competing between alternative options, took into account societal receptiveness to reform measures, and strived to benefit the majority through reforms. The "reforms outside the system" is a good example. When it is hard to promote the reform of the entities within the state-owned system, the emphasis can be placed on nurturing private enterprises, individual economies, and foreign-funded enterprises. These entities operated market-based and outside the traditional planned economy. It shows that different ownership forms under the market economic system are neutral. By the 1990s, the "inside" and "outside" economies were nearly on par, fostering intense competition that, in turn, pressured SOEs to reform. This path marks China's actual reform trajectory, with comprehensive deepening of reforms being a pivotal task in the future. In early 2021, the *Action Plan for Building a High-Standard Market System* issued by the state outlined a goal to essentially establish a unified, open, competitive, well-regulated, and effectively governed market system with high standard within five years. This endeavor promotes a harmonious integration of an "effective market" with a "proactive government," constituting a critical component of accelerating the refinement of the socialist market economic system and a key orientation for China's economic development during the 14th Five-Year Plan period.

CHAPTER 9

# Innovation in Globalization Theory and Reconstruction of International Trade Rules

Globalization has rendered the world a closely knit global village where interactions across borders are frequent and pervasive. Throughout history, the march of globalization has witnessed both triumphs and tribulations, yet it has persistently deepened, significantly contributing to the stability and growth of the global economy. Today, globalization confronts a pivotal crossroads: to proceed forward or revert to a path of "de-globalization." The COVID-19 pandemic at the end of 2019, while exacerbating certain anti-globalization tendencies, also underscored new dynamics propelling globalization. A rational, forward-looking perspective reveals that Globalization 4.0 is on the horizon, necessitating a more robust response to the realities and demands of our changing world. We have but one Earth, and it behooves us to strive for a world that is increasingly prosperous and equitable. China's Belt and Road Initiative (BRI) is not only a significant proposal but also embodies rich philosophical notions, thereby setting a shining example for Globalization 4.0. Amidst Western developed nations' resurgence of protectionist sentiments, exemplified by the Trump administration's "America First" policy and its instigation of a "global trade war," the reconstruction of international economic landscape is imperative. The evolving global economic landscape urgently requires a recalibration of theories, demanding frameworks that better align with contemporary realities to accurately interpret and forecast novel trends in global trade. Therefore, we should respond to the demands of our times by innovating globalization theories and



Z. Liang, *The Innovation of Economic Theory in China*,
https://doi.org/10.1007/978-981-95-2713-7_9

reconstructing international trade rules, thereby providing crucial support for a new form of globalization that sustains and fosters the stability and development of the global economy and finance.

While discussing globalization-related theories from a broad perspective, our core focus remains on economic globalization theory or international trade theory. It encompasses the globalization of production, trade, investment, and finance, enabling optimal allocation of factors such as goods, capital, and labor worldwide. A key feature of the contemporary world economy, globalization signifies a key development trend. New phenomena and challenges arising from economic globalization urgently call for explanation through the perspective of international economic theory, stimulating thoughtful reflections among economists. Our relevant theories and innovations are all built upon this foundation.

## 1 Evolution and Landscape of Globalization

Economic globalization has a long-standing history, tracing back to the Age of Discovery in the fifteenth century, accumulating over 500 years of evolution. A review of the economic globalization process since the nineteenth century reveals that it was typically propelled and shaped under the leadership of one or several economic and military powers. Despite various challenges throughout its course, economic globalization appears irreversible in essence today, albeit undergoing changes in its forms and contents.

### *1.1 Historical Trajectory of Globalization*

In the fifteenth century, European navigation ventures opened up new sea routes, providing the necessary conditions for expansion into the Americas, the East, and other global markets. The advent of the Renaissance in the sixteenth century significantly liberated thinking, broadening human horizons and transcending previous intellectual boundaries. Prior to the Industrial Revolution, the costs of logistics and information flow were high, with global trade primarily focusing on inter-regional transactions of finished consumer goods. Early Dutch and British East India Companies transported tea, silk, and spices from Asia to central European markets, fostering cultural exchanges between the East and West and yielding substantial trading profits. From the 1760s to mid-nineteenth century, the First Industrial Revolution unleashed a surge in productive capacity of capitalist countries, while technological breakthroughs significantly enhanced labor productivity, accelerating the pace of economic globalization. The Industrial Revolution established the United Kingdom as the preeminent economic and military power of the nineteenth century, and a leader in global free trade, though its overseas expansion often relied on colonialism and military force to propel international trade. Up until the eve of World War I, the globalization process fueled by the Industrial Revolution maintained rapid development, and the breakthroughs in transportation routes mark a major topic during this period.

Subsequently, the outbreaks of two World Wars and the impact of the 1929–1933 Great Depression caused various countries to adopt protective measures such as tariffs to safeguard domestic markets, thereby restricting the development of economic and trade globalization. It was not until the end of World War II that the international economic environment gradually stabilized, with peace and development becoming the dominant themes. Governments refocused on economic growth, and under supportive policies, production and trade efficiency rapidly increased. The division of labor in global industrial chains became more intricate, with capital investments led by multinational corporations spanning the globe, hastening the integration of emerging markets into the economic globalization framework. Competition and collaboration among industries became more diverse and sophisticated. The two World Wars indirectly facilitated the United States' rising over Europe as the economic pivot, with the country, as the strongest in terms of both economy and military might, steering the restructuring of the global economic and political orders. It established systems for resource allocation, trade regulations, and an international monetary and financial system centered on the US dollar. This era of globalization was characterized by a focus on international organizations and rule-based systems.

In the second half of the twentieth century, the rapid development of information technology significantly enhanced global trade connectivity. This gave rise to economies distinguished by different technological characteristics within the global value chain, including those with resource advantages, manufacturing prowess, service trade superiority, technological and consumption strengths. These developments subtly reshaped the world economic landscape. The surge in economic globalization, underpinned by the information revolution, disseminated the value chain theory widely. Technological advancements facilitated broader social benefits across production, trade, and finance. McKinsey & Company's research revealed that between 2009 and 2014, the internet contributed 21% to the GDP growth of developed countries, with 75% of this growth occurring in sectors outside but interconnected with tech industries. Studies by the International Telecommunication Union confirmed a clear correlation between ICT development and income growth, also verified by the application of advanced technologies. The theme of this era was characterized by a reduction in information costs.

The Fourth Industrial Revolution, aimed at enhancing resource productivity, reducing pollution, and promoting intelligence, found its technological breakthroughs in graphene, quantum information technology, biogenetics, AI, and virtual reality. This green industrial revolution promised a more efficient, environmentally sustainable globalization, transitioning the process from mere expansion to qualitative enhancement. The Davos Forum in January 2019, themed "Globalization 4.0: Shaping a New Global Architecture in the Age of the Fourth Industrial Revolution," marked the advent of Globalization 4.0, echoing the Fourth Industrial Revolution's principles. Technological progress and innovation necessitated comprehensive cooperation, rendering efficiency and eco-friendliness the new globalization tenets. Lower production and transport costs were essential for globalization, achievable through technological advancement, the ultimate driver of cost reduction. These advancements, in turn, enhanced the market fluidity of goods and factors. Across human history, four industrial revolutions dramatically cut international production and trade costs, fundamentally boosting the rapid development of economic globalization.

A graphical representation of the Global Economic Freedom Index from 1995 to 2019 is depicted in Fig. 9.1.

### *1.2 Development Landscape of Economic Globalization*

According to the Economist Intelligence Unit's *ICT Globalization Index Report 2014*, Europe and North America lead the current wave of globalization, with significant disparities in development levels among nations. Most Northern European countries, specifically the United Kingdom, the Netherlands, and Germany, rank high in the ICT globalization index. Conversely, Southern European countries like Italy and Spain lag behind in ICT trade openness and technology openness. The United States holds a relatively high position, ranking fourth globally. Meanwhile, emerging markets trail in the ICT globalization index, partly due to poor ICT infrastructure and immature conditions for reaping additional benefits. Among

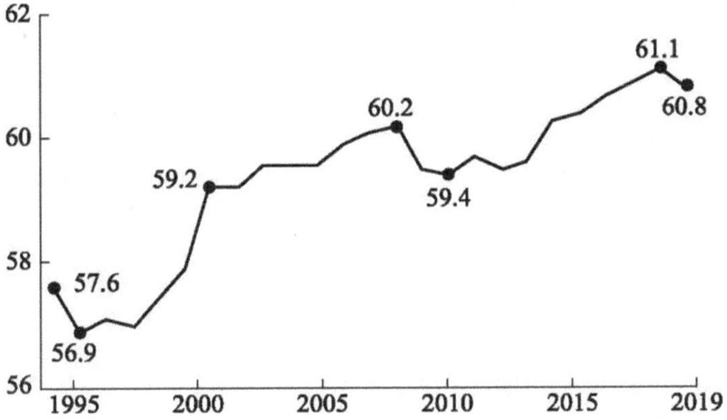


**Fig. 9.1** Global economic freedom index (1995–2019). (Source: Terry Miller, Anthony B. Kim, and James M. Roberts, *2019 Index of Economic Freedom*, Washington: The Heritage Foundation, 2019)

BRICS, China has the highest ICT globalization index yet ranks 12th globally. ICT trade openness, measured by the number of trade barriers and the volume of ICT imports and exports as a share of total trade, reflects a country's willingness and ability to engage in free trade. Here, China ranked second in 2014, behind the Netherlands, suggesting its ICT trade volume compensated for trade barriers, and it surpassed the United States as the largest ICT goods and services exporter in 2004. However, regarding foreign investment openness in the ICT sector, China ranks lower (18th), indicating China's certain investment barriers. For R&D globalization, Canada and the United States score highly, followed by Australia and China ranks ninth.

The Heritage Foundation defines the Index of Economic Freedom as the degree of close collaboration among human resources and organizations, comprehensively measuring a country's economic freedom. It includes factors like legal systems (property rights, judicial efficiency, government integrity), government size (taxation, spending, fiscal health), regulatory efficiency (business, labor, monetary freedom), and market openness (trade, investment, finance). Their *2019 Index of Economic Freedom* reports Hong Kong topping the list for 14 consecutive years with a score of 90.2 among 180 countries and regions, with Singapore, New Zealand, Switzerland, and Ireland above 80 points. Thirty-five countries scored over 70, accounting for 19.4%, while 21 countries scored below 50, representing 11.67%. Thus, 68.9% of countries and regions fell between 50 and 70. China scored 58.4 points in 2019, ranking 10th. Overall, global economic freedom slightly declined in 2019 compared to previous years, as shown in Fig. 9.2.

Different institutions have varying definitions and assessment frameworks for globalization. According to the 2019 Global Openness Index published by the Legatum Institute, Hong Kong still ranked first, followed by Singapore and the Netherlands. Hong Kong is regarded as having the most favorable conditions for business development, ranking third globally even in terms of market access and investment environment. As the second-largest economy and the most populous country in the world, China ranks 51st globally in terms of economic openness, up 13 places

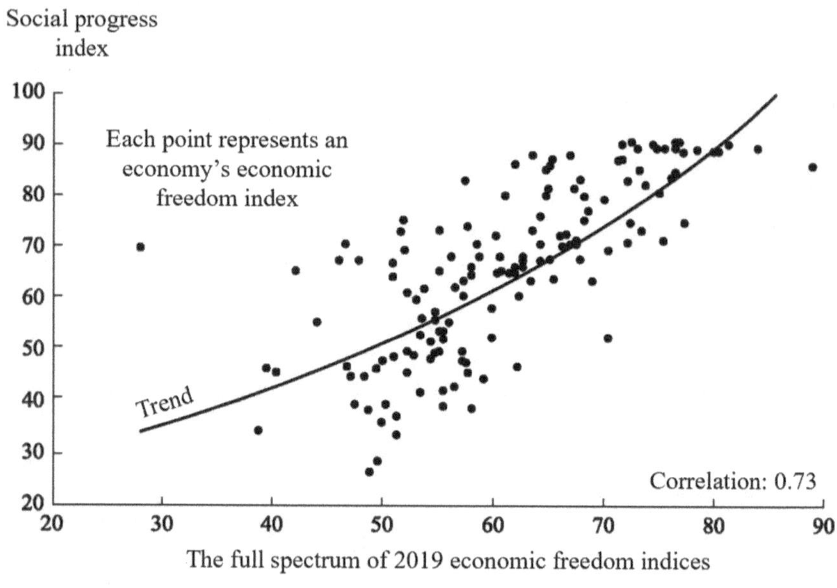


**Fig. 9.2** Overall performance of the economic freedom index in 2019. (Source: Terry Miller, Anthony B. Kim, and James M. Roberts, *2019 Index of Economic Freedom*, Washington: The Heritage Foundation, 2019, and Legatum Institute Foundation, *The Legatum Prosperity Index 2017*, 2017. Note: Among the economies listed, 146 appeared in both the Economic Freedom Index of 2019 and the Legatum Prosperity Index of 2017)

since 2019. With a large pool of skilled technical labor, it boasts an excellent environment for corporate innovation. Moreover, the Chinese government prioritizes the development of city clusters, with the largest city clusters concentrated in the Pearl River Delta, Yangtze River Delta, and Beijing-Tianjin regions.

Today, international production and trade globalization have penetrated into almost every corner of the world, becoming an integral part of daily life. Globally, industrial specialization, including division within industries, has continued to be refined. Countries leverage their comparative advantages to cross borders and optimize their supply chains, progressively demonstrating international characteristics in factors of production, products, production processes, and science and technology. Global free trade consistently reduces barriers and restrictions on goods and services, enabling countries participating in globalization to identify their competitive niches in international markets and fully utilize their comparative advantages and resource endowments. World Bank data shows that in 2018, global merchandise trade accounted for 46.12% of global GDP. The combination of international production and trade liberalization creates a compelling mechanism for economic restructuring and industrial transformation by upgrading sectors with lower efficiency and productivity and rejuvenating the economic system. Concurrently, global capital flows effectively address funding shortages in developing countries, with the inflow of capital also bringing advanced technologies and management expertise. This significantly contributes to talent cultivation domestically in these countries, boosts productivity, and rewards capital with substantial returns through the growth of local industries and economies.

### *1.3 Issues and Dilemmas of Economic Globalization*

1. The phenomenon of "de-globalization"

The rapid development of the information revolution in the latter half of the twentieth century, alongside the widespread dissemination of global value chain theory, significantly advanced globalization in areas such as trade, production, finance, and labor. This increased frequency and convenience of global material exchanges connected nations more closely than ever before, fostering mutual integration and influence. Nonetheless, historical progress has often been interrupted by various unpredictable events and crises, hindering or even reversing globalization's trajectory, a phenomenon we term "de-globalization." Events such as the 1997 Asian Financial Crisis, the 2008 Global Financial Crisis, and the 2009 European Debt Crisis, triggered by Greece's sovereign debt crisis, manifest the extensive destructive power of such crises, with economic stagnation rippling effects across multiple countries worldwide.

The 2008 Global Financial Crisis notably slowed the pace of economic globalization and even triggered instances of "de-globalization." Following the election of the US President Trump, who espoused an "America First" strategy, overt trade protectionism emerged. The United States also initiated a series of withdrawals from international agreements, including the Trans-Pacific Partnership (TPP) and the Paris Climate Agreement, replaced the North American Free Trade Agreement (NAFTA) with the United States-Mexico-Canada Agreement (USMCA), and instigated "trade wars" with multiple economies globally. In Europe, the United Kingdom officially completed its "Brexit" in early 2021, leaving a myriad of complex issues unresolved. These actions, typified by the withdrawals led by major capitalist nations such as the United States, embody classic "de-globalization" maneuvers.

The highly contagious COVID-19 pandemic, which broke out at the end of 2019, posed a grave threat to human life and health worldwide. Efficient transportation systems facilitated the virus' swift and widespread transmission. According to data released by the World Health Organization on April 13, 2021, by April 13, 2021 (Beijing time), there had been over 136.29 million confirmed COVID-19 cases and over 2.94 million deaths globally. Alarmingly, liberal democratic nations in the West became epicenters of the viral spread. Furthermore, the economic fallout from the pandemic gradually surfaced: in March 2020, the US stock market experienced historic fourfold "circuit breaks"; in 2020, major economies excluding China recorded negative GDP growth, with economic panic spreading swiftly in an environment of high data transparency, morphing into a monumental challenge to human development within the annals of globalization. Nevertheless, the advanced global logistics and machinery of the twenty-first century did address global resource allocation issues, with China, after effectively controlling its domestic outbreak, promptly assisting heavily affected nations. Faced with this crisis, the globally interconnected human society must employ rational thought, courage, wisdom, and unity to safeguard the significant interests of all nations and the global population.

2. Issues of innovation in international economic and trade theory and reconstruction of rules

For centuries, international trade theory, as a pivotal branch of economic theory, has garnered significant attention. It has evolved to encompass numerous formulated trade theories and framework systems to guide nations toward trade expansion, output growth, and welfare improvements. Some theories posit that, as economic globalization progresses, countries rich in scarce factors of production tend to oppose free trade, instead adopting protectionist policies to maintain domestic prices of these scarce resources and safeguard their home market conditions. In line with the Heckscher-Ohlin (H-O) theory, when a country's export commodity prices rise, the real return on its relatively scarce factor diminishes, whereas the return on its abundant factor increases. Thus, international trade enhances returns for abundant factors but deteriorates those for scarce ones. For instance, developed economies like the United States and Europe, with relatively fewer unskilled workers but abundant human and physical capital, have seen income increases from international free trade, yet this has concurrently depressed wages for unskilled labor, exacerbating income inequality. Consequently, to preserve domestic job opportunities and mitigate trade deficits, voices against globalization and free trade persist. Developing countries, in particular, are wary of the uneven structural impacts of globalization on their industries, and often implement protective measures to foster domestic industrial growth. These policy decisions, driven by societal interests, constitute major challenges to the globalization process.

Against the backdrop of economic globalization, bilateral and multilateral trade issues remain central to nations' developmental pursuits. Lately, protectionism in certain developed countries, epitomized by the Trump administration in the United States, guided by the "America First" principle, has sought to reshape the global economic and trade landscape through its trade negotiations and policy adjustments, exerting profound influences on international economic and trade theories and regulations. To secure its interests amidst globalization, the United States has even ignited a "global trade war," impacting the economic interests of numerous countries and regions. The US-China trade war that ignited in 2019 exemplifies a struggle for superpower interests, with repercussions felt across nations. In such conflicts, a gain for one nation in the trade war necessitates losses for others, compelling all stakeholder nations to weigh their interests and minimize damages. This evolving global economic landscape poses significant challenges to existing trade theories, urgently calling for advancements in international trade theory and the formulation of new frameworks that better align with contemporary realities, thereby enhancing our understanding and policy responses to global trade dynamics.

3. Impact of the COVID-19 pandemic on globalization

At a crucial juncture in the process of globalization, the COVID-19 pandemic has undeniably inflicted severe disruptions on global economic interactions, collaborative supply chains, and the movement of people and goods, casting a shadow over the prospects of globalization and prompting reflections on its future direction. Unprecedented, the pandemic has indeed dealt a massive blow to globalization, with its impacts resonating not only in the short term but also likely to shape the future trajectory of globalization. The sluggish global economy, compounded by the pandemic, has led some nations to adopt a pessimistic outlook on future economic prospects and intensified skepticism toward globalization. The pandemic's global spread has revealed the fragility of the global supply chains and distribution networks under production globalization, prompting countries, from a national security standpoint, to reconsider emergency supply systems, potentially giving rise to a trend of "limited globalization." Cautiously observed, the pandemic could amplify the risk of global populism, increasing resistance to globalization. As a cyclical social phenomenon, populism typically emerges during societal transitions and often intertwines with new social issues in novel historical contexts.

Nonetheless, it is crucial to acknowledge the emergence of new forces propelling globalization forward. COVID-19, perhaps the most challenging disaster in human history, has significantly impacted globalization, necessitating a collective global response. The pandemic has underscored the necessity of globalization through global mobilization and assistance to combat the virus. It has fostered greater global collaboration and joint efforts to curb the spread, further knitting the world together. Decisions made in one nation, be they medical or epidemiological, economic, or political, reverberate globally, implicating every country, emphasizing our shared fate. Collaborative problem-solving emerges as the pragmatic approach, and attempts to push others "overboard" for self-protection may lead to isolation and abandonment. We posit that nations should acknowledge the pandemic's impact on globalization but recognize that it does not signal globalization's demise. Globalization remains a defining characteristic of our era, with its overarching trend unaltered, though its forms and contents will undergo transformation.

## 2 A Review of Globalization Theory

### 2.1 *Theoretical Exploration of the Concept of "globalization"*

Globalization refers to the dynamic process of the intermingling of human resources, material resources, cultural resources, information resources, and technological advancements among different sectors, corporations, and governments across countries. It encompasses not only economic globalization but also political and cultural globalization. Currently, economic globalization stands as the focal point and crux of globalization studies, treating the world's resources as an integrated whole and increasingly becoming a vital aspect of economic research. The modern concept of "globalization," as understood today, originated in the 1970s, primarily entailing the integration of commodity markets, labor markets, and capital markets. In 2000, the International Monetary Fund (IMF) defined globalization in terms of four fundamental aspects: trade and international transactions, flows of capital and investment, population movements, and the dissemination of knowledge.

Economic globalization theories began to evolve and diversify in the West as early as the seventeenth century. Since the 1990s, the tide of globalization has penetrated all facets of human civilization's development, deepening and expanding continuously, bringing immense convenience to human life. Canadian philosopher Marshall McLuhan, in his 1964 book *Understanding Media*, introduced the term "global village," which is regarded as an early systematic articulation of the concept of globalization. He argued that contemporary globalization reached into everyone's lives through media, with old, isolated value systems and institutions being progressively supplanted by a participatory "new global village." In 1983, the term "globalization" was first publicly published and defined in detail by the American economist Theodore Levitt in his article "The Globalization of Markets." He elucidated that globalization involved the ongoing expansion and circulation of production, trade, and capital on a worldwide scale, facilitated by tremendous technological advancements that had become shared global resources, leading to profound transformations in the world economy under globalization's influence.

Early scholars grounded their understanding of globalization within capitalist relations of production, associating the origins of globalization with the historical progression of capitalism. They contended that the international free flow of capital in the 1970s initiated the dawn of economic globalization. The US scholar Arif Dirlik constructed a theoretical framework from an institutional perspective, viewing economic globalization as global capitalism, characterized by the unfettered development and flexible production of capitalist relations in the world market. Further, British scholar Leslie Sklair specified the concept of economic globalization, asserting that it denoted the worldwide proliferation and extension of an economic system centered on capitalist modes of production. However, the globalization process is not merely an economic expansion; it also facilitates the unification of politics, culture, and economics. Some scholars even perceive globalization as a privileged power within capitalist relations, emphasizing that globalization serves primarily as the internationalization of the bourgeoisie.

### 2.2 *Theoretical Discussions on the Nature of "Globalization"*

Many Western scholars contend that the essence of economic globalization lies in a "borderless economy," emphasizing its trans-class and supranational characteristics. Some scholars, however, express concerns regarding the economic globalization process. For example, neoliberal economist Robert Reich argues that economic globalization bolsters interactions among nations and regions in economic, political, and cultural dimensions, spurring reforms and expansions in international economic organizations, institutions, and the world economic order. Existing economic and political structures in various countries are undergoing changes influenced by globalization, challenging state authority through diminished economic autonomy and heightened roles of international organizations. Hans-Peter Martin and Harald Schumann, on the other hand, point out that since 1960, the gap between the richest countries and the poorest one-fifth of the world has doubled, suggesting that economic globalization has contributed to greater polarization and social instability to some extent.

However, a multitude of scholars acknowledge the dual-edged nature of economic globalization. Robert Solow, for instance, suggests that while globalization accelerates economic growth, expedites the diffusion of new technologies, and helps equalize living standards between wealthy and poor nations, it also erodes traditional economic cultures and poses threats to social stability. American scholar Langewiesche asserts that under economic globalization, consumers can access low-cost new goods and services from other regions, highly skilled workers who control economic information command high salaries, and workers in poor countries have opportunities to improve their living standards and incomes. Economist John H. Dunning offers the view that "global economic activity is irreversible unless halted by natural disasters or human calamities, as the dispersion of technology and technological progress itself is an irreversible process." Neoliberal economists argue that each country and region possesses its own comparative advantages, enabling them to produce specific goods and services for trade, thereby steering the world economy toward a win-win scenario rather than a zero-sum game, even if established interest groups are somewhat challenged and constrained by global competition.

### 2.3 *Major Western Schools of Thought on Globalization*

The dominant school of thought in current Western discussions on globalization is the Neoliberalism School, which primarily emphasizes the role of markets in globalization. Driven by the demands of productive force development, production factors start to freely circulate and be integrated in the world market, optimally allocating resources. The need for capital's outward expansion leads to the crossing of national boundaries by elements such as technology and information. Under a globalized pattern of international division of labor, production factors are reasonably allocated and combined on a global scale, generating more profits and value, thereby fueling rapid economic growth. Neoliberalists advocate deregulation of economies, encourage the free flow of international capital, and legitimize and defend the global expansion of capital, thus facilitating the spread of Western capital worldwide. Daniel Bell, in his 1950s work *The End of Ideology*, argued, "Neither the development of capitalism nor the expansion of free trade and world markets are the issues of our times. The confrontation and conflict among nations and peoples run counter to the theme of capitalist globalization." A key figure of neoliberalism, Francis Fukuyama, posited that liberalism was the dominant ideology and that the history of liberal democracy might be the endpoint of human history.

The Western Left approaches the study of economic globalization with skepticism. For example, British scholar Linda Weiss contends that neoliberalism's exaggerated portrayal of the positive effects of economic globalization is neither objective nor scientific. The regulatory functions of government and markets should not be overlooked due to an overemphasis on the role of globalization, nor should developing countries and lagging regions blindly deregulate, stripping society of necessary safeguards. The Dependency Theory prevalent in the 1970s adopted a relatively pessimistic view on the development prospects of marginalized and backward nations in the globalization process. It maintained that as long as the existing world economic structure centered on Western developed capitalism persisted, the pattern of less developed countries' dependency on developed ones in trade would not change. This dependency results in fundamentally different patterns of development between developed and less developed countries.

Transformationalist theories of globalization argue that economic globalization is the primary driver of social, political, and economic transformation and is instrumental in reshaping the modern world order (Giddens and Castells, 1996). The phenomenon of globalization does not reveal a single path; every individual and political entity is part of globalization, adhering to its rules. The "transformative" power generated by economic globalization leads to a drastic upheaval in the world order filled with contingencies and uncertainties, making it impossible to predict the direction of its evolution or the true character of the new global economic and political order it constructs (Ruggie, 1996).

Currently, in academic circles, a theory that significantly influences discourse and research on the fundamental issues of economic globalization is World Systems Theory, represented by American historian and sociologist Immanuel Wallerstein. Grounded in a holistic view of the world, Wallerstein posits that, given the world's interconnectedness, no nation or ethnic group throughout history has existed or developed in isolation; instead, they are interlinked, mutually dependent, and constraining one another. This theory focuses on analyzing the reciprocal impacts of different countries' economic, political, and social relations, emphasizing the transfer of surplus value and capital accumulation. It asserts that the essence of "capital accumulation" determines the expansion of capital globally, while "unequal exchange" gives rise to differential positions within the global economic system. World Systems Theory's perspective aligns relatively well with the objective reality of world development.

However, it tends to overly emphasize external factors affecting less developed countries, overlooking internal factors and unique processes inherent to specific human development histories within the process of economic globalization. This oversight renders World Systems Theory somewhat impractical.

### 2.4 *The Marxist World-Historical Perspective on Globalization*

Karl Marx, examining the development of capitalism and communism from the perspective of historical materialism, initiated his inquiry with an analysis of productive forces and relations of production. Building upon this foundation, he explored the cross-border flow of capital, international trade, and the world market, thereby formulating a theory of world history. World history, in this context, encompasses the entire course of human development, advancing in tandem with the development of social productive forces and the formation of the world market. As nations and ethnic groups interact, constraining and depending on one another, they progressively facilitate the integration of the world.

Marxist theory posits that the unfolding of world history is initiated by capitalism's development, which establishes the material foundations and prerequisites for world history, but its ultimate formation and goal lie in communism. Marxist world history theory fundamentally differs from Western globalization theories in that the former regards capitalism as merely the starting point and communism as the endpoint of development, while the latter lacks the fundamental aim of liberating all humanity, equating economic globalization with the completion of world history. Stephen Gill and Samir Amin, representatives of the Neo-Marxist approach to the globalization theory, argue that contemporary economic globalization represents the capitalist mode of production promoted by advanced capitalist countries of the West, marking a triumph of Western imperialism's global expansion in the present era. This outcome inevitably leads to an unjust and unfair international economic and political order, exacerbating wealth polarization, and turning governments into agents of international monopoly capital.

## 3 Evolution, Developments, and Challenges of International Trade Theory

International trade theory constitutes the core of the economic globalization theory and serves as a cornerstone for international economic and trade cooperation and integration. As a vital component of economic theory, the evolution and advancement of international trade theory have been under continuous scrutiny. To date, numerous trade theories and frameworks have emerged domestically and abroad to guide individual countries toward productive and trade practices that stimulate economic growth and enhance welfare. The progression of international trade theory has encompassed scholarly analyses of various aspects, including factor endowment advantages, cost advantages, conditions of trade competition, trade patterns, and trade policy measures. This evolution has fostered divergent schools of thought, advocating either free trade, protectionism, or a dialectical view combining both. Each proposed theory holds its strengths and limitations, necessitating further exploration and refinement.

### *3.1 Historical Evolution of International Trade Theory*

The roots of international trade theory lie in mercantilism, inherently embodying a blend of free trade and protectionism. The definitive inception of classical free trade theory is marked by Adam Smith's (1776) seminal work, *The Wealth of Nations*, introducing the concept of absolute advantage. Building upon this, David Ricardo (1817) has developed the comparative advantage theory, positing that countries should specialize in producing and exporting goods with relatively low costs while importing those with relative high costs, thereby mutually benefiting each other through trade. Free trade theory is predicated on a market economy, with comparative advantage at its core. Early globalization theories, exemplified by the classical trade theories of Adam Smith and David Ricardo, advocated for free trade between nations, trade liberalization, and international redistribution of natural endowments, forming the foundation for the growth of Western international trade and globalization theories. Notably, the logic derived from Smith's division of labor, absolute advantage, and Ricardo's comparative advantage theories points to globalization and is inconsistent with the contemporary trend of "de-globalization" and protectionism, which contradicts the principles espoused by the pioneers of market economics.

A more systematic factor endowment theory is outlined by Heckscher and Ohlin (1991), highlighting the diversity of products across nations as either capital-intensive (high K/L ratio) or labor-intensive (low K/L ratio). Bilateral trade, based on exporting products of comparative factor endowment advantage and importing those of disadvantage, laid the groundwork for factor analysis in globalization theory modeling. Based on the H-O theory, Samuelson (1949) has further demonstrated that under full factor mobility, factor and product prices will converge across nations. Leontief's (1953) input-output analysis reveals that the United States, a high capital-labor ratio (capital-intensive) country has exported more labor-intensive goods, giving rise to the "Leontief Paradox."

Since the 1960s, an increasing number of scholars have gradually relaxed the assumptions of neoclassical theory, emphasizing the importance of concepts like imperfect competition (Kravis, 1971; Melvin and Warne, 1973) and economies of scale (Balassa, 1966; Grubel and Lloyd, 1975) in the evolution of international trade. Ethier (1979) contends that economies of scale at the international level are more significant than those domestically. The pinnacle of the New Trade Theory, Paul Krugman (1979, 1980), systematically integrates imperfect competition and economies of scale into conventional trade theory models, and gradually develops the intra-industry trade theory that replaces inter-industry trade theory, allowing for resource optimization within industries among different firms (Krugman, 1979; Falvey, 1981). The Brander-Krugman model (Brander and Krugman, 1983) presupposes a Cournot game in international trade and analyzes the local equilibrium reached in such games. As a prominent proponent of the new trade protectionism, Krugman (1979) argues that trade liberalization does not directly enhance corporate productivity but instead facilitates the survival of efficient firms and elimination of inefficient ones. He stresses the need for nations to recognize the reality of "fair trade."

Further along, the "new" new trade theory emerged, with its principal representatives being the heterogeneous firm trade theory (Melitz, 2003) and the theory of the firm boundary. Melitz's (2003) theory of heterogeneous firm trade relaxes Krugman's (1979) assumptions of homogeneous firms and exogenously determines productivity, suggesting that trade liberalization promotes the elimination of less productive firms and fosters the growth of more productive ones, thereby elevating overall productivity levels. Antras' firm boundary theory introduces property rights and incomplete contracts, explaining the emergence of product cycles through a dynamic general equilibrium framework due to the incompleteness of international contracts.

Free trade ideology paved the way for globalization theory, with Say's Law of the nineteenth century dictating that free trade competition policy is essential for market equilibrium between aggregate supply and demand. The lifecycle trade model demonstrates that trade liberalization fosters physical capital accumulation and sustained economic growth, gradually narrowing the growth rate gap between developed and developing countries. The heterogeneous firm trade theory (Melitz, 2003) also argues that free trade encourages innovation intensity and enhances domestic firms to improve efficiency. Thus, trade liberalization not only benefits resource allocation within industries and across firms but also optimizes resource allocation within firms and among products (Mayer et al., 2011). The development of free trade theory provides a theoretical guide for open and free transactions in the global market, affirming the positive impact of globalization on global economic development.

In contrast to free trade, protective trade often arises when a relatively weaker party seeks appropriate safeguarding of its interests or a dominant party aims to secure extra profits, thereby forming a set of trade policy frameworks. Friedrich List (1841), a pioneer of classical protectionist theory, has argued that tariff reduction fosters the import of sophisticated industries while imposing tariffs can shield nascent domestic industries to a certain degree. Following the Great Depression of 1929–1933, John Maynard Keynes (1936) introduced super-protectionist theory to bolster the competitiveness of domestic industries. This theory underscores that trade surpluses should expand effective domestic demand. Strategic trade policy theory (Brander and Spencer, 1984) emphasizes the role governments should play, suggesting that when firms compete in trade markets, governments should provide assistance, subsidies, or incentivize market capture strategies.

Objectively, protectionist views offer theoretical guidance for countries to compete rationally under the umbrella of globalization, highlighting the roles of both governments and enterprises in global competition. In the global market, countries and their governments must not only recognize the fertile benefits of the global marketplace but also acknowledge the challenges and pitfalls of global competition, enhancing their protective awareness and capabilities in this arena.

Moreover, the contribution of New Structural Economics to international trade theory is significant and cannot be overlooked. This theory posits that the factor endowment structure, as in international trade theory, is equally crucial to macroeconomic analyses of a nation (Lin Yifu, 2012). Although the factor endowment structures of countries at varying stages of development are fixed at any given moment, over time, changes in the composition of capital, population, and other factors occur subtly. Consequently, when a country's technological and industrial development aligns with its original factor endowment structure, businesses incur lower production costs, thereby creating "comparative advantages" that enhance national competitiveness (Lin Yifu, 2017). New Structural Economics endeavors to explain how developing countries can leverage their "latecomer advantages" to achieve faster industrial and technological upgrading compared to developed countries.

### *3.2 Free Trade and Trade Protectionism*

Generally speaking, countries have exhibited varying inclinations toward free trade and protectionism at different periods. Starting with free trade, proponents argue that it enhances efficiency and optimizes resource allocation. Therefore, nations should refrain from restricting or granting preferential treatment to imports and exports of goods and services; they assert that "free trade" is the sole pathway to maximizing welfare. Theories supportive of free trade include classical trade theory, neoclassical trade theory, factor trade theory, economies of scale theory, life cycle theory, and intra-industry trade theory. Say's Law also advocates for free trade competition policies. Furthermore, from the perspectives of "learning by doing" (Arrow, 1962) and economies of scale, labor-abundant developing countries can accumulate substantial human capital through free trade (Young, 1991). Jones' life cycle trade model illustrates that trade liberalization favors capital accumulation and economic growth, fostering convergence in growth rates between developed and developing countries (Fischer, 1995). Heterogeneous firm trade theory (Melitz, 2003) posits that free trade spurs innovation and improves domestic firm productivity.

Protectionist viewpoints, on the other hand, advocate for policy measures that offer preferential treatment or impose restrictions on imports and exports to protect domestic market demand and minimize losses in international competition. List's trade protection theory underscores the role of tariffs in shielding infant industries. Keynes' super-protectionist theory highlights how trade surpluses can expand domestic effective demand. In the mid-to-late 1970s, amidst the oil crisis, a wave of "fair trade" oriented new protectionism resurfaced globally, again led by the United States (Krugman, 1979). This theory treats a country's productivity as exogenously given and unaltered by trade costs, concluding that trade liberalization does not enhance average firm productivity. Brander and Spencer (1984) have introduced strategic trade policy, proposing government assistance to firms in trade competition, subsidies, or support for market capture.

Extensive theoretical and empirical studies have attested to the superiority of free flow of factors and free trade. However, in the game of trade policy, both developed and developing countries resort to protectionist policies as per prevailing circumstances to safeguard their domestic industries' international competitive edge. Particularly since the global financial crisis, trade protectionist actions have surged (Georgiadis and Mehl, 2016). In the long term, free trade policies prove more beneficial than detrimental, but during economic downturns, temporary protectionist stances are common phenomena (Suhail, 2010). With the evolution of economic globalization and integration of international trade, free trade and protectionist theories have evolved to exhibit new tendencies toward unification.

From early mercantilism to Adam Smith's free trade theory, Friedrich List's protectionism, John Maynard Keynes' super-protectionist theory, and the neoliberals' trade theories, we observe the evolution, opposition, and fusion of free trade and protectionist theories across different epochs. Marx and Engels provided a dialectical perspective on the importance of integrating both approaches. Marx acknowledged the role of protective tariff systems in fostering modern industrial systems and advancing productive forces, yet from the standpoint of societal progress and revolution, he favored free trade. Engels saw the necessity of implementing protective tariffs during a nation's nascent stage, but argued that only through free trade could a nation achieve fuller development once it reached a certain level. Paul Samuelson opposed protectionism in his book *Economics with a Human Face*, yet in his article "Globalization in the Eyes of Mainstream Economists: The Ricardian-Mill Model," through numerical experiments with selective productivity states, he doubted free trade. His skepticism temporarily became key justification for some American protectionists. This skepticism essentially reflects that neither free trade nor protectionism alone adequately explains real-world international trade dynamics, with the powerful United States itself adopting a policy combining elements of both.

### 3.3 *Principal Strengths, Shortcomings, and Directions for Reform of International Trade Theory*

Broadly speaking, international trade theory has made significant strides in trade fundamentals, logical frameworks, and theoretical models, playing a pivotal role in shaping international trade architecture and promoting economic globalization. Its main strengths include:

(1) Comparative advantage and factor endowment theories underpin international trade, setting the theoretical foundation for establishing trade rules today. They have evolved from static to dynamic analyses, transforming singular comparative advantage into comprehensive competitive advantage, better reflecting real-world complexities.
(2) Free trade and protectionist theoretical systems have been developed, alongside corresponding policy tools, including explorations into hybrid models that integrate both approaches.
(3) Varied theoretical models have been scrutinized from multiple angles with relatively rigorous logic. Assumptions like heterogeneous firm trade, economies of scale, and imperfect competition have been progressively relaxed, aiming to construct models more reflective of reality.
(4) New Structural Economics, from a developmental perspective, examines the possibilities and conditions for a latecomer nation to surpass another, emphasizing the crucial roles of technology, industrial policies, and related factors.

Shortcomings of international trade theory:

(1) Difficulty in explaining real-world scenarios: In practice, no country has achieved absolute free trade, and few are willing to fully adopt trade protectionism. Neither free trade nor protectionist theories alone can comprehensively account for the variations in actual trade policies observed.
(2) Inadequate explanation for the contradiction and conflict between free trade and protectionism, with theoretical inconsistencies: The

conclusion that free trade maximizes welfare stands in stark contrast with the prevalence of protectionism in the global trade landscape. Most nations employ a mixed strategy combining elements of both free trade and protectionism.

(3) Lack of a comprehensive and cohesive theoretical framework: There exists no unified system that adequately reconciles discrepancies between theory and reality, making this a focal point for further theoretical exploration.

(4) Absence of dynamic theoretical models: Trade theories based on general equilibrium typically focus on specific states, limiting their explanatory power regarding dynamic real-world trade issues and the process of latecomer nations catching up. Existing theories posit that traded goods are determined by factor endowments, suggesting a static scenario where one country might perpetually produce aircraft while another shirts. Reality, however, witnesses ongoing shifts and rotations in national positions, epitomized by the Chinese proverb, "Thirty years on the east bank, thirty years on the west bank," highlighting the changing fortunes of regions over time.

Confronted with these challenges, existing globalization and trade theories fail to adequately address current international trade issues, necessitating the evolution of theoretical frameworks in light of new global trade dynamics and the practices of emerging economies. Given the obvious contradiction between the welfare-maximizing premise of free trade theories and the persistent rise of protectionism, there is an objective need for a new set of theoretical models of international trade that better elucidate the realities of globalized trade, thereby furnishing a foundation for stable international economic development and trade operations.

The directions for the transformation of international trade theory are outlined as follows:

(1) Proposing a New International Trade Theory Model: A fresh theoretical framework is needed to provide a more accurate explanation of the realities of international trade, thereby furnishing a foundation for its smooth operation and resolution of disagreements.

(2) Resolving the Dilemma Between Free Trade and Protectionism: The question of whether international trade should adhere to principles of free trade, protectionism, or a blend of both remains

pivotal. Without a clear resolution, inconsistent standards will persist. It is crucial to recognize that free trade and protectionist theories are not inherently contradictory but complementary. Their synthesis, to a certain extent, represents the future trajectory of trade theory development.

(3) Addressing Dynamic Determinants of Trade: Theories must adequately explain the ever-changing factors influencing trade. For economies, factor endowments are fixed at any given point but evolve over time, altering comparative advantages. The products traded between two nations should not be simplistically determined by static factor endowments but by their dynamic and combined competitive advantages, which are mutable and subject to shifts. Hence, the overtaking of one nation's product by another becomes a natural occurrence.

(4) Tackling Catch-Up and Realization Conditions: An efficient market, where prices reflect the relative scarcities of all factors, is a prerequisite for economic development guided by comparative advantage. A proactive government can capitalize on changing factor endowments, converting latent comparative advantages into competitive edges, breaking the "low-end lock-in," and achieving catch-up with another nation. Governments can, through reforms or targeted policies, continuously enhance the total factor productivity of key products, thus altering the dynamic composite competitive advantage in their favor.

## 4 Theoretical Model of International Trade from the Perspective of Rational Synthesis and Dynamically Synthesized Competitive Advantage

Building upon the review and analysis of the strengths and weaknesses of existing international trade theories, we aim to construct a novel theoretical model grounded in a perspective that integrates both free trade and protectionism. Our innovative proposition centers on dynamic composite competitive advantage as the cornerstone of international trade, asserting that the dynamic composite competitive advantages underlying trade products between two nations are not static, but rather mutable, capable of shifting over time and leading to reversals in trade relationships once a critical threshold is surpassed—a condition under which a nation leverages its latecomer advantage to catch up with another.

### 4.1 *Pathways and Foundations for Innovating Trade Theories*

It is evident under current international trade regulations that a nation does not adhere purely to either free trade or protectionism; the primary contention revolves around the degree of protectionist policies rather than their mere presence or absence. Consequently, future research should transcend the recurrent analytical paradigm that oscillates between these two extremes, moving beyond repetitive debates on free trade versus protectionism. Instead, it must propose a more comprehensive and practical trade theory model that espouses free trade as its guiding principle, complemented by limited protective measures in accordance with international norms, thereby establishing a cohesive theoretical framework. Our endeavor to formulate this innovative trade theory and its associated model proceeds along the path depicted in Fig. 9.3, which involves synthesizing the perspectives of free trade and protectionism in our discourse.

The rational synthesis economic model posits that an "effective market" and a "proactive government" are complementary. Drawing from the rational synthesis economic model, or the mixed development model,

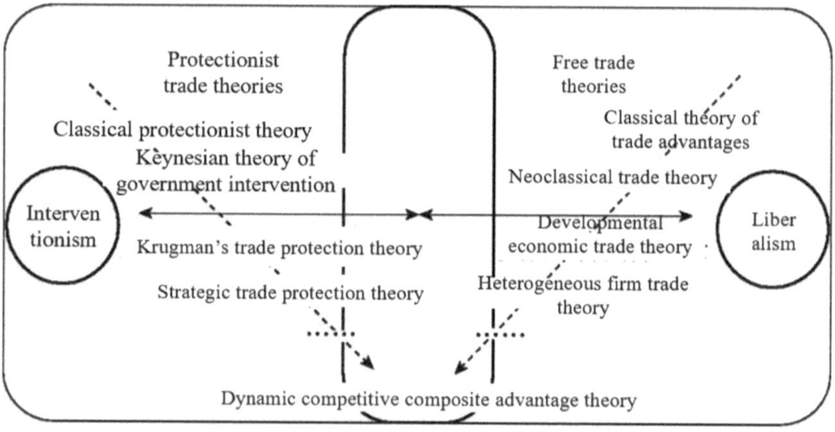


**Fig. 9.3** Evolution of and schools of thought on international trade theory. (Source: Compiled by the author)

constructed by Zong Liang and Fan Ruoying (2018), the refined basic formula of the model is presented as follows:

$$\Delta Y_t = a\Delta Y_{Mt}^* + b\mu_{sl}\Delta A_t Y_{Mt}^* + b\left(\mu_d + \mu_{ss}\right)\left(Y_t - Y_{Gt}^*\right) + b\left(\varepsilon_{dt} + \varepsilon_{st}\right) \quad (9.1)$$

This formula is referred to as the dynamic macroeconomic growth model (Zong Liang and Fan Ruoying, 2018). In Eqn (9.1), the dependent variable $\Delta \Upsilon_t$ represents the change in actual economic output growth $\Upsilon$ at time $t$; $a$ denotes the market effect coefficient; $b$ signifies the government impact coefficient; $\mu_d$,$\mu_{ss}$, and$\mu_{sl}$ represent the government's regulatory coefficients for the demand side, short-term supply side, and long-term supply side, respectively; $\Delta Y_{Mt}^*$ indicates the natural growth of output under market forces; $\Delta A_t$ represents the impact of technological advancement; $Y_t - Y_{Gt}^*$ denotes the deviation of natural output growth influenced by government actions; and $\varepsilon_{dt}$ and $\varepsilon_{st}$ are unobservable random shocks from the demand and supply sides, respectively. Interpreted from the perspective of real economies, a country at any given stage experiences an optimal balance between an "effective market" and a "proactive government," though pinpointing this ideal state is exceedingly challenging. Nations generally find themselves leaning toward either a freer market orientation or a more government-centric stance. The conceptual framework we propose for innovating international trade theory is grounded in the recognition that supply-side regulatory measures have implications not only for short-term economic fluctuations but also for the long-term trajectory of potential economic growth.

### 1.2 Constructing a New Theoretical Model for International Trade with Innovative Thinking

International trade arises from differences in products, factor endowments, and productivity levels between nations. In today's era of global integration, nurturing innovative thinking about international trade theory is important. We understand that free trade not only complements resource advantages between nations but also enhances consumption utility and welfare levels for both countries, forming the bedrock of international trade. Nevertheless, in trade practice, countries commonly implement policies aimed at protecting their domestic products' competitive conditions, thereby justifying the strategic use of government intervention. Therefore, the synergistic combination of free trade and protectionism constitutes a vital pathway for future theoretical innovation.

Starting from a simple 2 × 2 × 2 trade model: We assume that the global economic system comprises only two nations—a developing Country A and a developed Country B—and only two factors of production, labor ($L$) and capital ($K$). Each nation produces and trades a single good, denoted as $\Upsilon_i$ (where $i$ = 1, 2 ...), with the product $i_j$ determined by each country's endowment structure $\frac{L}{K}$. For instance, if the factor endowment ratios are $\frac{L_A}{K_A} > \frac{L_B}{K_B}$, then Country A has a relatively labor-intensive endowment structure, whereas Country B possesses a capital-intensive one. Specifically, it is supposed that Country A produces textiles ($i$ = $1$, $\Upsilon_1 = X$), then the production function for textile $X$ is:

$$X = f\left(L_A, K_A\right) = \lambda_A \times \left(\frac{L_A}{K_A}\right)^{\alpha} \tag{9.2}$$

Country B, on the other hand, produces technology products ($i$ = 2, $\Upsilon_2 = T$), then the production function for technology product $T$ is:

$$T = f\left(L_B, K_B\right) = \lambda_B \times \left(\frac{L_B}{K_B}\right)^{\beta} \tag{9.3}$$

Wherein, $\lambda$ symbolizes the level of production technology. Both countries produce quantities of their respective goods, part for self-sufficiency and part for export, under the assumptions of constant returns to scale and perfect competition in the market. Consequently, Country A specializes solely in producing (and trading) the labor-intensive textile product $X$, while Country B focuses on producing (and trading) the capital-intensive technology product $T$. At time $t$, the outputs of both nations can be represented by the following equations:

$$\Delta Y_{1,t}^{A} = \Delta X_t = \Delta X_{t,A} + \Delta X_{t,AB} \tag{9.4}$$

and

$$\Delta Y_{2,t}^{B} = \Delta T_t = \Delta T_{t,B} + \Delta T_{t,BA} \tag{9.5}$$

In these equations, $\Delta X_t = X_t - X_{t-1}$ denotes the change in the quantity of product $X$ produced in period $t$ compared to the previous period; thus, $\Delta X_t$ and $\Delta T_t$ represent the amounts of textile product $X$ and technology product $T$ produced by countries A and B, respectively, during a specific period (from $t-1$ to $t$). Further, on the right-hand side of the equations, $\Delta X_{t,A}$ represents the amount of textiles produced by Country A for domestic consumption, and $\Delta X_{t,\,AB}$ is the quantity exported to Country B; similarly, $\Delta T_{t,B}$ denotes the volume of technology goods produced by Country B for domestic use, and $\Delta T_{t,BA}$ is the amount exported to Country A. Additionally, it is assumed that all goods $\Upsilon_i$ produced by both countries fully satisfy domestic consumption and export demands.

Assuming both countries adhere to an identical consumption utility function denoted as $Uh$ (with $h = A, B$), the consumption utility functions for countries A and B can be expressed as follows.

For Country A:

$$U_A = X_A^{\theta} T_{BA}^{1-\theta} \tag{9.6}$$

For Country B:

$$U_B = \left(X_{AB}\right)^{\theta} \left(T_B\right)^{1-\theta} \tag{9.7}$$

The above consumption utility functions illustrate that the consumers' utility in both countries A and B is derived solely from the consumption of textile and technology goods. If the import and export volumes are equal, the international balance of payments equation for trade between the two countries can be formulated as:

$$P_{t,X} \Delta X_{t,AB} = P_{t,T} \Delta T_{t,BA} \tag{9.8}$$

This equation signifies that, within a given period and under this two-country model, the ratio of Country A's textile exports to Country B ($\Delta X_{t,AB}$) to Country B's technology exports to Country A ($\Delta T_{t,BA}$) equals the price ratio of technology product to textile product ($\Delta X_{t,\,AB}/\Delta T_{t,\,BA} = P_{t,\,T}/P_{t,\,X}$), implying that the value of Country A's textile exports to Country B ($P_{t,X}\Delta X_{t,AB}$) equals the value of Country B's technology exports to Country A ($P_{t,T}\Delta T_{t,BA}$). Alternatively, if imports and exports are unequal, a trade surplus or deficit exists, captured by the following equation:

$$P_{t,X}\left(\Delta X_{t,AB} - \Delta T_{t,AB}\right) = P_{t,T}\left(\Delta T_{t,BA} - \Delta X_{t,BA}\right) \tag{9.9}$$

Here, $\Delta T_{t,AB}$ denotes the quantity of technology goods imported by Country A from Country B.[1] The difference term $\Delta X_{t,AB} - \Delta T_{t,AB}$, representing the net exports of Country A to Country B after subtracting its imports from Country B, can be denoted as $\Delta \text{PureImp}_{t,A-B}$ or $\Delta \text{PIm}_{t,A-B}$. Similarly, $\Delta T_{t,BA} - \Delta X_{t,BA}$ represents Country B's net exports to Country A and can be represented as $\Delta \text{PIm}_{t,B-A}$. Thus, trade between the two countries is predicated on the principle of equitable exchange of net export values. However, adjustments in national policies and market interventions aimed at trade protection can disrupt the equilibrium of trade between the two nations. A country's total net exports consist of a natural, or potential, net export component under unaltered conditions and a component influenced by government policy. A detailed examination and analysis of this aspect will follow later.

### 4.3 *Transition Points of Dynamic Composite Competitive Advantage Under the New International Trade Theory Model*

Building upon the previously outlined framework for the new international trade model and incorporating insights from the dynamic macroeconomic growth model by Zong Liang and Fan Ruoying (2018), we can develop a trend model for output fluctuations under open economy conditions, taking into account the specifics of international trade. To summarize the law of complex real-world elements into a theoretical model, we first simplify a multi-factor environment of a nation and then present the fundamental logic formula under hypothetical conditions. The assumptions of this rational synthesis model include: (1) each country produces a single product, with Country A producing and trading

[1] Here, $\Delta T_{t,AB} \leq \Delta T_{t,BA}$ implies that the quantity of technology goods imported by Country A from B does not exceed the quantity of technology goods exported by Country B, indicating potential waste or welfare loss under the two-county model. Equation (9.8) particularly emphasizes the principle of equivalent exchange based on the net export values in the trade between the two nations.

product X and Country B producing and trading product T; (2) macro factors affecting output fluctuations are divided into two categories, the natural state's potential output growth fluctuation represented by $\Delta Y_t^*$ and all other influences on output growth fluctuations outside the natural growth path, primarily embodied by the government's influence $\Delta Y_t^G$ (where $\Delta Y_t^G = \Delta Y_t - \Delta Y_t^*$); (3) the influence on international trade (net exports $\Delta$PIm) is analyzed as an independent factor. The output fluctuation trend model for Country A is:

$$\Delta Y_{t,A} = a\left(\Delta Y_{t,A}^* + \Delta \mathrm{PIm}_{t,A-B}^*\right) + b\mu_{sl}\Delta A_{t,A}\left(\Delta Y_{t,A}^* + \Delta \mathrm{PIm}_{t,A-B}^*\right) \quad (9.10)$$
$$+ b\left(\mu_d + \mu_{ss}\right)\left(\Delta Y_{t,A}^G + \Delta \mathrm{PIm}_{t,A-B}^G\right) + \varepsilon_A$$

Similarly, under the framework of international trade analysis, the output fluctuation trend model for Country B can be defined as:

$$\Delta Y_{t,B} = a\left(\Delta Y_{t,B}^* + \Delta \mathrm{PIm}_{t,B-A}^*\right) + b\mu_{sl}\Delta A_{t,B}\left(\Delta Y_{t,B}^* + \Delta \mathrm{PIm}_{t,B-A}^*\right)$$
$$+ b\left(\mu_d + \mu_{ss}\right)\left(\Delta Y_{t,B}^G + \Delta \mathrm{PIm}_{t,B-A}^G\right) + \varepsilon_B \quad (9.11)$$

Eqns. (9.10) and (9.11) depict the composition of output fluctuation trends for both countries under consideration of international trade. The specific components of the output fluctuation calculation formula, using Country A as an example, according to (9.10), include $a\left(\Delta Y_{t,A}^* + \Delta \mathrm{PIm}_{t,A-B}^*\right)$ which reflects the potential self-supply output and potential net exports of product X under a purely market-driven scenario, embodying a nation's factor endowments. The term $b\mu_{sl}\Delta A_{t,A}\left(\Delta Y_{t,A}^* + \Delta \mathrm{PIm}_{t,A-B}^*\right)$ indicates the long-term effect of government's supply-side reforms on total factor productivity $\Delta A_{tA}$, signifying that a country's dynamic composite competitive advantage in a product can be transformed through appropriate government supply-side reforms. Specifically, the government's impact on dynamic composite advantage manifests in two parts: (1) altering the potential self-supply output and potential export growth path for Country

A's textiles; (2) the government's influence can even elevate Country A's output growth path, enabling Country A to surpass a previously higher-output-path Country B, marking this surpassing point as the turning point of dynamic composite competitive advantage (V-point),[2] illustrated in Fig. 9.4. The term $b\left(\mu_d + \mu_{ss}\right)\left(\Delta Y^G_{t,A} + \Delta \text{PIm}^G_{t,A-B}\right)$ represents the short-term effects of government regulation, i.e., policy adjustments to the supply-demand balance between the two countries. Specifically, government policies can influence the fluctuations in textile exports and technology imports. For instance, if Country A implements trade protectionist measures like raising tariffs, technology imports $\left(\Delta \text{PIm}^G_{t,A-B}\right)$ would increase, resulting in a short-term upward output fluctuation.

To visually illustrate the output fluctuation trends of two countries under open economy conditions, growth fluctuation paths for each country can be depicted based on Eqns (9.10) and (9.11). Initially, the output growth path $Y_t^A$ of Country A (a developing country) lags behind that of Country B (a developed country), represented by $Y_t^B$. At time $Q_{t1}$, Country B implements proactive macroeconomic policies (or trade protectionist measures), resulting in a short-term fluctuation that increases Country B's net exports ($\Delta P\text{Im}_{t,\,B-A}$). In the long run, this policy enhances Country B's total factor productivity, leading to an altered potential output growth path indicated as $Y_t^{B'\,'}$. If Country A maintains its original growth path, the gap between the two countries widens over time (represented by the dashed line showing Country A's unregulated output growth trajectory), making it increasingly difficult for Country A to catch up with Country B in terms of economic growth. In Fig. 9.4, if Country A opts for supply-side reforms conducive to long-term growth at time $Q_{t2}$, reallocating resources and restructuring its factor endowment configuration, and leverages a "proactive government" to exert long-term regulatory effects, enhancing its total factor productivity, Country A's output

[2] From the perspective of first-mover and late-mover advantages, the first term in Eqn (9.10) can be understood as a country's first-mover advantage, determined by its factor endowments, while the second term can be interpreted as its late-mover advantage, driven by changes in total factor productivity. The role of the government lies in creating conditions that facilitate a country's exploitation of its late-mover advantage, leveraging the second term to reach the turning point V of dynamic composite competitiveness. First-mover and late-mover advantages are possibilities rather than certainties, requiring appropriate policies to be realized. This viewpoint sheds light on Lin Yifu's New Structural Economics analysis of late-mover advantages, emphasizing the role of tailored strategies and policy environments in harnessing such advantages effectively.

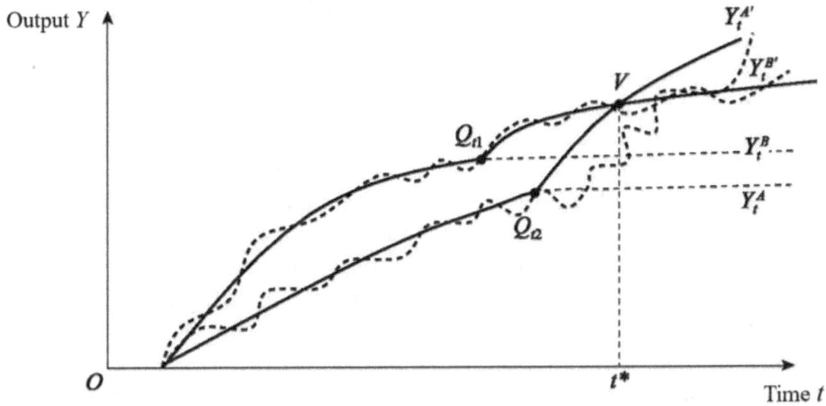


**Fig. 9.4** The transition point V for dynamic composite competitive advantage. (Source: Compiled by the author)

growth path experiences a leapfrog upgrade to $Y_t^{A'}$. As time progresses, Country A achieves the turning point V of dynamic composite competitiveness at time $t^*$, marking a turning point in its growth trajectory.

The core premise of the dynamic composite competitive advantage turning point in international trade theory and its innovative thinking posits that the products traded between two nations are not solely determined by factor endowments, but rather by their respective dynamic composite competitive advantages in these products. This dynamic composite competitive advantage is primarily shaped by two factors. The first is the initial factor endowment advantages a country possesses; the second is the government's regulatory policies that stimulate total factor productivity or technological innovation, leading to enhanced labor productivity and, consequently, an increase in the competitiveness of related products, reflecting the macro-policy's impact on export competitiveness. This dynamic composite advantage is mutable and features a turning point. The significance of the dynamic composite competitive advantage turning point lies in its implication that, in a given industry, a country may initially lack the factor endowments advantage, but if there's significant room for improvement in total factor productivity in that sector within the country, a favorable environment can be fostered for the industry's development, boosting its total factor productivity, and thereby enhancing the dynamic composite competitiveness of its products, turning them into key tradable commodities. This suggests that a nation's comparative competitive advantage in certain products or industries is not immutable or insurmountable; under sound government policy interventions, catching up and surpassing in industries is a normal phenomenon, debunking the notion that one nation can perpetually maintain superiority.

From the perspective of dynamic composite competitive advantage, governments of both nations typically manipulate, reform, or protect relevant products (such as textile or technology goods) competitively within the boundaries of international regulations, fostering a conducive demand-supply environment for product development, enhancing total factor productivity, and thereby altering the dynamic composite competitive landscape. This mirrors how nations can, within international rules, enhance their teams' competitive edge through various training measures. Before and after the turning point in the model, a structural shift occurs in the traded products between the two nations, highlighting the mutability and convertibility of advantageous products, where one nation's products can surpass those of the other. To revisit our earlier example, while, initially, Country A primarily produces and trades textiles and Country B specializes in technology goods, post-transition, capital-endowed Country B gains a more dynamic composite competitive edge in exporting labor-intensive products, inversely, labor-endowed Country A in exporting capital-intensive ones. The output trajectory manifests in Country A surpassing Country B, a natural progression.[3] Similarly, for related industries, it is normal for a nation to catch up and surpass in certain sectors; sustained superiority by one nation is not the norm.

### 4.4 *Reflections on International Investment Under the New Model Perspective*

The preceding analysis, focusing solely on trade, elucidates policies and rules pertinent to commerce. To expand our scope, we now take the investment dimension between the two nations into consideration. In the context of globalization, international investment stands alongside trade

[3] In 1953, Leontief observed that the United States, post-World War II, should have been exporting capital-intensive goods and importing labor-intensive ones, yet empirical analysis revealed the opposite, giving rise to the so-called Leontief Paradox. Our theory aligns with this observation, confirming that countries abundant in capital factors can indeed export labor-intensive products and import capital-intensive ones, thereby also validating this counterintuitive pattern.

as a pivotal strategy for developmental advancement. Capital's free flow enables nations to invest in global production chains, facilitating upgrades to their own industrial ecosystems and reaping direct capital profits. Moreover, countries gain access to substantial capital inflows and advanced technological support through foreign direct investments. Therefore, movements such as outward foreign direct investment, mergers and acquisitions, and financial portfolio investments freely traverse borders in response to national needs, with the volume of investment reflecting a country's comprehensive competitiveness. Government restrictions and scrutiny over foreign investments can impede this free flow. Advancing our analysis, we relax the assumption of limited product portfolios, supposing that Country A can produce a variety of products indexed by $\Upsilon_i$ (where $i = 1,3,5,\ldots$), and Country B produces $\Upsilon_j$ (where $j = 2,4,6,\ldots$), and extend the international trade market conditions to better align with realistic scenarios of economies of scale and imperfect competition, allowing for monopolistic competition among differentiated homogeneous goods. Integrating the international balance of payments Eqn (9.9) with the factor endowment production function (9.2), we derive:

$$\Delta Y_i = P_i \left( \Delta\lambda_A \left( \frac{L_A}{K_A} \right)_{BA}^{\alpha i} - \Delta\lambda_B \left( \frac{L_B}{K_B} \right)_{BA}^{\alpha j} \right) i \neq j \tag{9.12}$$

In summary, short-term capital movements affect product prices through mechanisms like exchange rates, indirectly impacting the volume of traded goods between the two nations. Conversely, long-term FDI can ameliorate a country's initial endowment conditions, stimulate improvements in total factor productivity, and enhance production efficiency and competitiveness. Ultimately, international direct investment reshapes the dynamics of traded goods by influencing their prices, facilitating complementarity of capital factors, enhancing production technologies, and thereby transforming the value of a country's foreign trade, represented by $\Delta \Upsilon_i$.

By expanding the previous two-country model, we find that the information product (O = $\Upsilon_3$) produced and exported by developing country A and the technology product (T = $\Upsilon_2$) produced and exported by country B will pose competition, after the two countries have undergone the transformation of dynamic comprehensive competitive advantages in their output growth paths. In an effort to safeguard its domestic product's competitive edge, Country B enacts policies influencing exchange rates, causing Country A's currency to appreciate, which in turn elevates Country A's export costs, thereby reducing the competitiveness of Country A's information product O in B's market. This leads to a decline in Country A's net exports of information products (i.e., $\Delta Y_i^A \leq 0$), resulting in a trade deficit. Simultaneously, Country B's currency depreciation renders its technology products T relatively cheaper in Country A's market, enhancing the trade volume of Country B's technology goods $\left(\Delta Y_j^B \geq 0\right)$, achieving a trade surplus. Incorporating investment considerations entails a suite of measures aimed at influencing the flow of production factors, product competitiveness, and market dynamics, encompassing market access, restrictions on technology transfer, conditions for mergers and acquisitions, factor mobility, and anti-monopoly measures. To preserve a fair competitive stance, less advantaged developing nations should adopt effective policies to shield their export industries from foreign policy interventions' detrimental effects, or engage in bilateral or multilateral trade agreements to ensure a steady progression toward the composite competitive advantage turning point, progressively narrowing the economic growth gap with developed nations.

### 4.5 *Key Innovations in International Trade Theory*

(1) Integration of Free Trade and Protectionism: Free trade not only complements resource advantages between nations but also elevates consumption utility and welfare levels, forming the bedrock of international trade. However, practical realities see widespread adoption of measures protecting domestic product competitiveness, making their complete abandonment impractical. Thus, combining free trade with carefully circumscribed protectionism constitutes a vital path for theoretical innovation.

(2) Evolution of Determinants of International Trade: Products traded between nations are not solely dictated by their factor endowments but determined by their dynamic composite competitive advantages. Factors influencing this dynamic composite competitive advantage encompass initial factor endowments, potential variations in total factor productivity, and supportive policies. It is crucial to recognize that dynamic composite advantages can change and feature a turning point. Comparative advantages in products

or industries are not insurmountable; under sound policy orchestration, catching up and surpassing in industries is a natural phenomenon.

(3) The Fair and Just Application of International Trade Rules: International trade rules exist to facilitate the smooth operation of trade and ensure a basic equilibrium of benefits. Free trade is an inevitable requirement for global interconnection, and limited protection may be applied to safeguard core national interests, but these protective measures must adhere to strict criteria and procedures. Fair trade does not equate to the maximization of one nation's interests; it necessitates functioning under the constraints and coordination of international rules, with no single country's laws extending beyond these rules to impose upon others. This preserves a broad balance in the international trade system, averting situations where the strong bully the weak. In practice, advanced economies should actively transfer some technologies to less developed ones to foster their growth, rather than resorting to protectionism under the guise of domestic law. This is a pivotal approach to realizing international fairness.[4]

Centering on the new theoretical model, we have focused our analysis on trade and investment, yet the economic and trade interactions between nations encompass a broader spectrum, including trade, investment, technology, finance, and more. Balance between two countries, therefore, is not simply a matter of trade and capital imbalances but a composite of multiple facets, with trade and investment forming the core and mainstay of economic ties. Fundamentally, economic and trade connections and adjustment measures between countries are closely intertwined with inter national rules and financial linkages, yet rule-based free trade remains the cornerstone of international trade, with rule-based and limited protection subject to stringent conditions and procedures. Fair trade cannot be about maximizing one country's interests; it indicates that any country's law should not transcend international rules and should not be used as a shield

[4] Economist Lewis (1967) once proposed that developed countries, by taking advantage of favorable trading conditions, would absorb surplus labor from developing countries through international trade and export capital in order to increase their own capital profit rates. This would further exacerbate the disadvantages faced by developing countries in international competition and also calls for developed countries to transfer appropriate technologies to achieve international fairness.

for protection. Hence, theoretical innovations reinforce the case for free trade and stand against protectionism. For instance, while there may be notable trade surpluses or deficits in Sino-American trade, a comprehensive view reveals a state of underlying balance. Advocating for a "one country first" ideology inherently poses the greatest unfairness to other nations and undermines international rules. Ultimately, cooperation for mutual benefit and promoting welfare for humanity form the ultimate goals of international trade. In the face of protectionist policies, China should fully harness its advantages in capital, labor, and other resources, actively enhance total factor productivity, foster industries with dynamic composite competitive advantages, and amplify the synergistic effects among comprehensive reforms, openness, and international trade. Continuously adhering to the "going global" strategy and the Belt and Road Initiative, China can propel its sustained and steady economic development.

## 5 China-US Trade Friction Through the Lens of the New Theoretical Model

### *5.1 The Landscape of the "US-China Trade War"*

Since the establishment of diplomatic relations between China and the United States, trade and investment cooperation have been continuously developing, with both nations evolving into significant international partners, benefiting from each other's strengths and achieving win-win outcomes. However, in recent years, the two countries have gradually initiated a trade war. In March 2018, the Trump administration in the United States, under the pretext of "China stealing American intellectual property," demanded additional tariffs on USD60 billion worth of goods imported from China, sparking the first round of bilateral trade friction. The second round of tariff hikes began in July 2018 when the United States imposed an additional 25% tariff on USD34 billion worth of Chinese goods exported to the United States. In retaliation, the Chinese Ministry of Commerce announced on the same day an additional 25% tariff on USD34 billion worth of American goods exported to China, notably including soybeans, one of America's top exports to China. Amidst the trade frictions, the two nations temporarily agreed to a truce. At the G20 Summit in Buenos Aires in December 2018, leaders from both countries reached a short-term consensus, agreeing to a 90-day negotiation period and a halt on introducing new trade measures during this time. Unfortunately, this respite was short-lived. In May 2019, the United States initiated the third round of the tariff war. President Trump announced on Twitter the imposition of a 25% tariff on an additional approximately USD200 billion worth of Chinese exports to the United States, making the total value of goods subject to tariffs to USD250 billion. In August of the same year, due to dissatisfaction with the Chinese government's purchase process of agricultural products, Trump announced on Twitter that starting from September, an additional 10% tariff would be imposed on all remaining Chinese exports worth USD300 billion. On August 6 the same year, the US Department of the Treasury designated China as a currency manipulator, as the Chinese Yuan fell below the 7 threshold against the US dollar. Subsequently, the Chinese government announced a suspension of purchases of American agricultural products and, on August 24, declared an additional 10% or 5% tariff on roughly USD75 billion worth of US exports to China. Moreover, it was decided that, effective from December 15, 12:01 a.m., tariffs on US automobiles and parts would be reinstated. The trade tensions culminated in a Phase One trade agreement signed between China and the United States on January 16, 2020. Subsequent to this agreement, the United States revoked the label of "currency manipulator" for China, marking a temporary cessation to the trade hostilities. For further details, refer to Table 9.1.

The outbreak of the US-China trade war has introduced substantial uncertainty to the economic and trade interactions between the two nations. This trade conflict is not a zero-sum game; instead, it results in a scenario where both parties, and potentially many others, lose out, inflicting harm on both countries and the global community at large. In response to the escalation of the US-China trade war, numerous international organizations have spoken up, attempting to highlight how a trade war between major powers could lead to a retreat in globalization. In April 2018, Christine Lagarde, the Managing Director of the International Monetary Fund, stated that the mutual threats of imposing tariffs between the world's two largest economies—the United States and China—would have a moderate direct impact on the global economy. However, she warned that greater threat lay in the uncertainty generated by such actions, which could stymie investments. If implemented, these tariff hikes would strike a blow to business confidence globally, given the interconnected nature of supply chains across the planet. In May 2019, a research team led by Gita Gopinath, the IMF's Chief Economist, published a report

**Table 9.1** Chronology of key events in the US-China trade war

| *Development stage* | *Timeline* | *United States* | *China* |
|---|---|---|---|
| Origin of dispute | March 22, 2018 | Trump accuses China of "stealing American intellectual property and trade secrets," proposing tariffs on USD60 billion worth of goods | China's Ministry of Commerce issues a list suspending duty concessions on US steel and aluminum products and ends tariff reductions on 128 categories of US imports, covering 7 types of goods |
| First round of rariffs | April 4, 2018 | The US government releases a list imposing 25% tariffs on 1333 items, totaling USD50 billion, of Chinese exports to the United States | China's State Council Tariff Commission decides to impose 25% tariffs on 106 categories of 14 types of US goods, including soybeans, automobiles, and chemicals |
| Initial negotiations | May 2018 | Both sides reach a temporary agreement to pause the trade war and issue a joint statement seeking reconciliation | |
| Second round of tariffs | July 6, 2018 | The United States imposes 25% tariffs on USD34 billion worth of Chinese goods, marking the official launch of Trump's tariff policy against China | China's Ministry of Commerce responds with retaliatory measures, imposing 25% tariffs on USD34 billion worth of US goods, including soybeans |
| Temporary truce | December 1, 2018 | At the G20 Summit, leaders from both countries agree to a 90-day negotiation period and a freeze on new trade measures during talks | |
| Third round of tariffs | May 5, 2019 | The Trump administration announces the imposition of a 25% tariff on an additional approximately USD200 billion worth of Chinese exports to the United States, bringing the total value of goods subject to tariffs to USD250 billion | On May 13, 2019, China's State Council Tariff Commission declares that starting from June 1, 2019, it will impose tariffs ranging from 5% to 25% on USD60 billion worth of US exports to China |
| Resumption of talks | June 29, 2019 | At the G20 Osaka Summit, leaders meet and agree to restart trade negotiations, with the United States halting new tariffs on Chinese goods | |

(*continued*)

**Table 9.1** (continued)

| *Development stage* | *Timeline* | *United States* | *China* |
|---|---|---|---|
| Fourth round of tariffs | August 1, 2019 | Unsatisfied with China's agricultural purchases, Trump tweets plans to impose a 10% tariff on the remaining USD300 billion of Chinese exports starting from September 1 | China halts purchases of US agricultural products and, on August 24, announces tariffs of 5% or 10% on about USD75 billion worth of US goods, plus the reinstatement of auto and auto parts tariffs from December 15 |
| Easing tensions | October 10, 2019 | Vice Premier Liu He leads a delegation to Washington for the 13th round of high-level economic and trade consultations. Later, the US Treasury Secretary announces suspension of the planned tariff hike from 25% to 30% on USD250 billion worth of Chinese goods, set for October 15 | |
| Phase one agreement | January 16, 2020 | China and the United States sign the Phase One Economic and Trade Agreement | |
| Post-agreement actions | February 10, 2020 | The US Trade Representative announces it will no longer treat 25 countries, including China, India, South Africa, and Brazil, as developing nations. Starting from February 28, China exempts additional tariffs on 65 US imports | |

Source: Compiled based on Wikipedia data

emphasizing that the trade tensions between the United States and China had negatively affected consumers and many producers in both countries. While tariffs reduced trade between the two nations, they had little net effect on the bilateral trade deficit. The report further cautioned that the escalating tensions could severely dampen business and financial market sentiment, disrupt global supply chains, and thereby jeopardize the anticipated recovery of global growth in 2019. That same month, United Nations Secretary-General Antonio Guterres underscored that in trade conflicts, there were no winners, only losers. He emphasized the critical importance of continuing to address trade disputes through multilateral dialogue and cooperation. A rules-based, non-discriminatory, and equitable trading system, he argued, not only was vital for safeguarding the interests of the poorest and the most vulnerable economies but also served the interests of all trading partners.

### 5.2 *The US-China Trade War Through the Lens of Traditional Trade Theory*

In 1776, Adam Smith's proposition of the absolute advantage theory in his seminal work *The Wealth of Nations* marked the rise of free trade theory. Building upon Smith's ideas, David Ricardo further advanced this theory in his *Principles of Political Economy and Taxation*, introducing the concept of comparative advantage, which represented a significant leap forward in free trade theory. Both texts contain analyses of protectionism, with Smith arguing that imposing high tariffs or outright bans on imports to protect domestic industries may encourage monopoly within the home market and redirect labor and capital toward those industries. However, he contended that such practices diverted national labor from more productive to less productive uses. Ricardo, on the other hand, pointed out that while protectionism shielded certain industries, it burdened consumers and other manufacturers with higher prices, an inefficient practice that misallocated capital into unproductive sectors and reduced overall output.

In the context of the US-China trade war, the United States' advocacy for increased tariffs and import restrictions initially raises government revenue but also elevates domestic prices of the targeted goods. Producers in the protected industries may see increased revenues and producer surplus, yet consumers face higher costs and then reduce their demand for these goods, leading to a loss in consumer surplus. Moreover, the vitality and diversity of the domestic market are compromised, with inefficient firms being shielded from competition at the expense of more productive uses of resources elsewhere, resulting in a misallocation of capital and labor.

Paul Samuelson, the 1970 Nobel laureate in economics and a known proponent of free trade, expressed a nuanced view in his 2004 article "Where Ricardo and Mill Rebut and Confirm Arguments of Mainstream Economists Supporting Globalization." He identified counterarguments to mainstream globalization proponents within Ricardo and Mill's models, suggesting that the development of trade with China could inflict lasting damage to US interests. This perspective is seen as the theoretical basis underpinning the US administration's initiation of the trade war with China.

Samuelson, focusing his analysis on Sino-American trade, outlined three main scenarios under conditions of free trade: First, in a relatively self-sufficient setting, both China and the United States, leveraging their comparative advantages, engage in free trade, leading to an increase in real incomes per capita for both nations through collaborative division of labor. Second, in export-oriented trade, technological advancements in sectors where China holds a comparative advantage boost global output. The United States, too, benefits from China's technological progress, seeing an increase in its real per capita income. However, this progress might inversely affect China's average income. Third, technological progress occurs in sectors where China used to be at a comparative disadvantage—an "import-biased" technological improvement. Upon engaging in free trade, if this product competes with the United States' similar products and reduces US output in that industry, China benefits, whereas the United States incurs losses, or even sustains long-term damage, as its previously advantageous market share is eroded. Post-publication of Samuelson's theory, concerns arose in the United States that future Sino-US trade might disadvantage the United States, prompting the adoption of protectionist measures and ultimately providing a theoretical foundation for launching the trade war with China.

However, relying solely on productivity evolution calculations in just a couple of sectors for theoretical analysis fails to capture the full picture and may overestimate the practical implications of such theories. Over the long term, free trade is undeniably beneficial for the income growth of both China and the United States, outweighing any drawbacks. It would be erroneous to generalize based on isolated events or to overly emphasize perceived disadvantages for the United States in free trade based on outcomes in just a few sectors. Instead, a continuous and dynamic understanding of events is needed, rationally acknowledging the broader advantages free trade brings to the US China's technological advancements and productivity enhancements are, in the long run, advantageous to both nations and contribute to global income growth. While China's notable progress in specific areas is a natural outcome of its active pursuit of development in today's globalized era and the evolutionary result of market competition, free competition also spurs the United States to advance its technology research to even higher levels rather than merely protecting current achievements.

### 5.3 *Analysis of the US-China Trade War from the Perspective of Rational Synthesis Model*

Drawing insights from the analysis of new theoretical models, we can summarize the key determinants of a nation's ability to achieve trade objectives into three main factors:

(1) Natural Factor Endowment Characteristics: This refers to factors such as capital and labor that form a crucial part of a country's competitiveness and often represent its first-mover advantage.
(2) Enhancement of Total Factor Productivity: This is pivotal in achieving dynamic composite competitive advantage between two trading nations. A "proactive government" can promote a country's potential output growth through policies fostering technological innovation, leading to a turning point in dynamic composite competitive advantage. Generally, the United States maintains a significant competitive edge in high-tech sectors, while China has approached a turning point in some areas.
(3) Market Compatibility and Policy Coordination: International trade is predicated on the synergy between the markets of both countries. The degree of compatibility directly influences gains or losses in trade competition and even impacts global trade welfare.

$$\Delta Y_t = a\left(\Delta Y_t^* + \Delta \mathrm{PIm}_t^*\right) + b\mu_{sl}\Delta A_t\left(\Delta Y_t^* + \Delta \mathrm{PIm}_t^*\right) + b\left(\mu_d + \mu_{ss}\right)\left(\Delta Y_t^G + \Delta \mathrm{PIm}_t^G\right) + \varepsilon_t \quad (9.13)$$

According to the Rational Synthesis Model (Zong Liang et al., 2019), the dynamic macroeconomic output growth of both China and the United States follows the fluctuation trajectory outlined in Eqn (9.13), which encompasses variations in natural output and net exports influenced by the countries' respective factor endowments, as well as the short-term impacts of government policies (such as macro-supply-side reforms) on output, their effects on societal demand, and the long-term implications for technological progress (total factor productivity). Consequently, the macroeconomic fiscal policies of both governments have an impact on the volatility path of output, thereby influencing the dynamic composite competitive advantage. As a developing nation, China leverages its inexpensive labor force as a factor endowment strength, enabling high productivity at low costs in manufacturing and thus securing an export advantage. However, with the ongoing refinement of its industrial structure, China's high-tech products are rapidly advancing and increasingly contributing to its export share. Referring to the *Report on China's Foreign Trade Situation (2019)* published by China's Ministry of Commerce, in 2018, China's exports of mechanical and electrical products reached 9.6 trillion yuan, accounting for 58.8% of total exports, while exports of high-tech products amounted to 4.9 trillion yuan, representing 30.1% of total exports. In recent years, China's high-tech products have demonstrated rapid growth and a bolstered export capability, indicative of the continuous upgrading and optimization of China's export trade structure.

In conjunction with Fig. 9.4, the initiation of the US-China trade war and the implementation of protectionist measures by the United States signal US intention during the $Q_{t1}$ phase to safeguard its domestic high-tech industries, undermine China's export advantages in high-tech products, and thereby enhance its own net export growth and TFP. Should China persist along its original output growth path, the disparity between it and the United States would widen, creating obstacles for the development of China's high-tech industries. Therefore, China must promptly adopt supply-side reforms conducive to sustained economic growth, reallocate resources, and restructure its endowment composition. A "proactive government," through its long-term regulatory function, can elevate China's TFP, facilitating a leapfrog evolution of China's output growth trajectory and realizing a dynamic composite competitive advantage shift at point V in the near future. China can attain the turning point of dynamic composite competitive advantage only through adjustments in its supply-side reforms, averting prolonged suppression and losses in specific industries imposed by the United States and achieving economic catch-up.

The primary competitive tools employed by the United States in this trade conflict fall under the umbrella of protectionist policies. The US government, waving the banners of "fair trade" and "reciprocal openness," denies the existence of developmental stage disparities, differences in resource endowments, and comparative advantage industries between the two nations. Under the slogan of "America First," the United States emphasizes unilateral trade protectionism and hegemonic policies, disregarding WTO's emphasis on mutually beneficial and balanced rules, obstructing fair transactions between China and the United States in areas such as trade, investment, and exchange rates. This strategy aims to widen the gap in our output development paths and delay or inhibit the arrival of the dynamic composite competitive advantage turning point in relevant fields for both countries.

Regarding the specific implementation strategies, US trade protection measures can be categorized into several aspects:

(1) Since 2017, the United States has implemented comprehensive taxation policies on trade products favorable to China through the application of tariff barriers and import quotas, aiming to reduce China's trade surplus.
(2) Concurrently, the United States provides substantial subsidies to industries where it holds a comparative advantage,[5] distorting the market and hindering fair international competition. In investment, the United States restricts Chinese investments and mergers and acquisitions in the United States under the guise of "national security reviews," interfering with the normal investment activities of Chinese enterprises and impeding the regular overseas development of China's leading companies.
(3) The US government, citing industry harm and intellectual property protection, bypasses the WTO's dispute settlement mechanism, initiates trade frictions based solely on domestic law, and employs laws like the Trade Expansion Act and Export Control Reform Act to launch "Section 301" and "Section 232" investigations against China, superimposing national laws over international trade rules and disrupting the global economic order.
(4) The United States also violates the spirit of contract, falsely accusing China and demanding forced technology transfers in an attempt to obscure the fact that the United States is the primary beneficiary in technological cooperation.
(5) The Trump administration further attempted to label China as a currency manipulator, aiming to raise China's trade costs, weaken the competitiveness of Chinese products, and dilute the US debt.

Scrutinizing the essence beneath the surface, analysis of the fundamental objectives behind the US-initiated trade war reveals that it is not merely an issue of balancing trade between China and the United States, but rather a question of how to maintain or indefinitely preserve its competitive edge. Frankly speaking, the United States intervenes in key areas to delay

[5] The range of industries benefiting from US government subsidies is extensive, encompassing 49 sectors where the United States holds an advantage, including aerospace, defense, automotive, computers and semiconductors, agriculture, among others.

or eliminate the dynamic composite competitive advantage turning point between China and the United States. At the heart of the trade friction between the two nations lies the shared aspiration to secure favorable conditions for international trade competition, thereby striving for composite competitive advantages in their respective key domains. Consequently, to preserve and uphold these advantageous positions, both countries actively employ various policy measures to safeguard their trade and investment activities, striving to achieve a state of relative equilibrium.

China's required responses entail the following measures:

(1) Balancing Principle with Flexibility: Approach the US-China trade war prudently, striving to confine it within the realm of economic and trade matters rather than allowing it to escalate into a comprehensive competition across all fronts. This necessitates a unified approach that combines steadfast principles with tactical adaptability.
(2) Maintaining Strategic Composure: Steadfastly resist tendencies toward either unwarranted optimism or excessive pessimism, enhancing the precision and effectiveness of measures taken. Focus on asymmetric strategies that yield clear and impactful results.
(3) Safeguarding National Dignity and Core Interests: Firmly uphold technological innovation and leverage the government's positive steering role in enhancing total factor productivity. Gradually narrow the growth gap with developed countries and expedite the transition to the dynamic comprehensive competitive advantage turning point.
(4) Preparedness for Escalation: Develop contingency plans tailored to varying intensities of the trade war—high-, medium-, and low-level scenarios. Holistically evaluate potential instruments and their pros and cons across trade, investment, technology, finance, international regulations, and diplomacy, deploying appropriate measures at opportune moments to introduce steady policy responses.
(5) Deepening Reforms and Expanding Opening-Up: Maintain stable and healthy economic development in China through ongoing reforms and expanded openness. Strengthen oversight of financial capital to prevent systemic risks stemming from irrational capital flows, ensuring sustained, stable economic growth and maximizing public welfare.

(6) Strengthening International Cooperation: Cultivate a favorable international environment by resolutely upholding and improving the multilateral trading system. Actively pursue win-win cooperation with other nations, particularly developing countries. Safeguard the legal rights and interests of foreign businesses in China and Chinese businesses abroad. Leverage China's large market to its fullest strategic advantage.

## 6 Reconstruction of International Trade Rules: The Way Forward

The global landscape is undergoing unprecedented transformation unseen in a century, characterized by a backlash against globalization, the resurgence of unilateralism, and the ascendancy of trade protectionism. Multilateral trade institutions and cooperation frameworks, painstakingly constructed over decades, now confront substantial pressures. The rules governing trade under the WTO, the bedrock of trade globalization, are witnessing a diminution in their impact on global economic growth. These signs collectively indicate that the current international trade rules are undergoing a transformative phase, necessitating recalibration to align with present realities. The world calls for a more equitable and rational framework of international trade rules to uphold order amidst the prevailing globalized trade dynamics. At its core, the reconstruction of international trade rules in the contemporary context represents a dynamic game between advanced economies and emerging ones, a contest for the authority to shape trade rule-making. As the leader in the global economy, the United States seeks to steer the reconstruction of international trade rules and pivot toward regional trade agreements as a platform to preserve its economic dominance. In the face of this evolving trade rule environment, China should, with a cool-headed assessment of the situation, actively seek strategies to promote the formulation of future trade rules that are fairer and more rational. Determining the direction of this restructuring of international trade rules poses a monumental task for the international community, one fraught with challenges and complexity, with profound and far-reaching implications for the global economy and finance. It is anticipated that all stakeholders will approach this process with a sense of responsibility toward fostering global trade development, treating it with the rationality and foresight it deserves.

### 6.1 *The Global Trade Landscape Grows More Diverse and Balanced, Yet Rule Competition Remains Central*

Propelled by the forces of globalization and digital informatization, the world's trade landscape is undergoing a once-in-a-century transformation, with changes in international trade rules mirroring the shifting demands of the global trade landscape. The rules governing international trade require recalibration to accommodate the needs of high-quality, high-standard commerce in the era of technological information. In recent years, powers such as the United States, the European Union, Japan, and China have actively sought to enhance their significance and influence within the global trade system through bilateral and regional negotiations, proposals, and declarations. Since its establishment in 1995, the World Trade Organization, or WTO for short, has significantly facilitated trade liberalization processes worldwide, effectively mediating and resolving disputes among nations and serving as a watchdog for trade policies. Nevertheless, the multilateral trading system centered on the WTO is far from perfect. Confronted with the demands of the new digital era, WTO members have gradually recognized the inadequacies and limitations of the existing system and the urgency for reform. Since 2018, members including the United States, the European Union, and Canada have initiated written opinions on WTO reforms, while China's Ministry of Commerce has presented three guiding principles and five propositions grounded in China's stance, manifesting a proactive engagement in the reshaping of international trade rules. Following a series of international consultations and negotiations, new rules for the global economy, trade, and investment are taking shape, imbued with distinct characteristics of the times. Looking ahead at the direction of WTO reforms, developed economies, such as Europe, the United States, and Japan, have clear priorities, primarily focused on enhancing their competitiveness and shaping digital trade rules. These economies argue that current WTO rules undermine the competitiveness of firms in the United States, Europe, and Japan, necessitating swift formulation of new international trade rules for rapidly growing sectors like the digital economy and services trade.

### 6.2 *Free Trade and Protectionism Will Coexist, with Free Trade Remaining Dominant*

In recent years, as the application of information science and technology spreads and international trade patterns evolve, the degree of globalization and integration in global trade has consistently risen. The entry into force of the Trade Facilitation Agreement (TFA) in 2017 stands as a significant milestone in the furtherance of international trade liberalization, recognized as one of the most substantial facilitation measures of the twenty-first century. It has facilitated a substantial reduction in the cost of international trade, enhancing economic benefits for WTO members and broadening the revenue potential for developing and least developed countries. The WTO estimates that full implementation of the TFA could increase global goods exports by USD1 trillion, with USD730 billion of that increase accruing to developing countries, while also reducing trade costs by an average of over 14%. Concurrently, however, a wave of unilateralism and protectionism, led by the United States, has swept across the globe, manifesting in intensified restrictive and protective trade policies such as the G20 nations actively implementing new trade restrictions that hikes tariff costs, imposing import bans, and establishing new export customs procedures. Since 2018, the United States has intensified unconventional trade protectionist measures targeting China, including the invocation of Section 301, Section 201, and the Entity List. Furthermore, this protectionist trend shows signs of spilling over into the investment domain.

An objective reality that may prevail is that within the framework of global trade rules, after free trade reaches a certain stage, tendencies toward protectionism tend to resurface. When protectionist barriers become formidable, calls for free trade intensify. World trade negotiates and progresses amidst this clash and friction between the two extremes, compromising and developing in a zigzag pattern. Given the diverse comparative advantages and interests among nations, a country typically advocates for free trade to penetrate foreign markets while seeking protectionism to safeguard its domestic market. Yet, the logic of market economies suggests that free trade should prevail as the mainstream. Meanwhile, a degree of protectionism will persist in each country to some extent. In light of this, international trade rules should not grapple with choosing between free trade and protectionism, but instead find an optimal balance between the two.

### 6.3 The "Three Zero" Principle Emerges as a Key Tenet, Yet Struggles to Escape Dual Standards Application

The "Three Zero" principle, encompassing zero tariffs, zero barriers, and zero subsidies, constitutes a pivotal component in current free trade agreement negotiations among regions such as Europe and North America, foreshadowing the direction of broader international trade rule reforms and underscoring the dominance of free trade ideology. However, the "Three Zero" principle does not imply a complete eradication of tariff barriers between economic zones, but rather symbolizes a trend in the evolution of international trade rules aimed at minimizing disruptive tariff barriers and industry subsidies that skew market prices. Evidence of this trend includes the 2018 US-Mexico-Canada Agreement (USMCA), seen as disruptor of WTO rules. Key provisions of the USMCA include zero-tariff agricultural trade and automotive parts among the three countries, and prohibitions on using export subsidies or WTO special agricultural safeguards on products exported to each other's markets. The USMCA diverges significantly from the objectives, principles, and governance mechanisms of the WTO, fundamentally subverting existing WTO rules. In 2019, then-President Trump proposed the "Three Zero Goals" at the G7 summit in Canada and incorporated them into the US-EU joint statement, outlining targets for non-auto industrial goods tariffs, subsidies, and non-tariff barriers between the two regions. Additionally, the EU-Japan EPA (Economic Partnership Agreement), signed on February 1, 2019, came into force, marking the birth of a new free trade zone covering over 600 million people, representing nearly 30% of global GDP and approximately 40% of total world trade. The EPA encompasses tariff elimination, dismantling of non-tariff barriers, expansion of service trade, opening of service markets, and e-commerce, with the EU gradually abolishing tariffs on almost 99% of Japanese imports, and Japan reciprocating by removing tariffs on about 94% of EU imports, excluding rice, wheat, beef, pork, dairy products, and sugar crops. While the "Three Zero" principle seems ideal, akin to pure free trade, it faces practical challenges. For instance, when the United States discusses the "Three Zero" principle with Europe and Japan, it exempts sectors like automobiles, while the EU cannot include agriculture, illustrating the adoption of "dual standards" where competitive sectors are subjected to the "Three Zero" rule, but those vital yet less competitive seek exceptions. Given the disparities in global competitiveness among nations and each country's core interests, international trade rules will inevitably combine free trade and protectionism over an extended period, differing only in their manifestations across varying circumstances. Developed nations possess individual strengths and are relatively advanced and similar in development levels, yet they also harbor enduring core interests and differences. The "Three Zero" principle merely represents a higher degree of free trade and a lower scope and intensity of protectionism.

### 6.4 *Global Digital Trade Emerges as the Trend in Global Commerce*

The development model of digital trade, exemplified by the Electronic World Trade Platform (e-WTP), is poised to become a prevalent trend. At the Boao Forum for Asia in March 2016, Alibaba first proposed the concept of establishing a World Electronic Trade Platform—a private sector-led, tripartite initiative involving governments, civil society, and businesses. The advent of the e-WTP fosters inclusive global cross-border e-commerce development, assisting more developing countries and small and medium-sized enterprises to engage in and access the global market. This indeed embodies the future trajectory of international trade.

As the world's largest and most influential trade organization, the WTO has embarked on negotiations on e-commerce to address the regulatory void in digital trade. On January 25, 2019, during an informal e-commerce gathering in Davos, Switzerland, 76 WTO members, including the United States, China, and the EU, signed the *Joint Statement Initiative on E-commerce*, signaling the initiation of negotiations on e-commerce topics within the framework of existing WTO agreements.

Digital trade is emerging as the focal point of competition for new international trade rules, with the construction of these rules presenting a formidable task. Advances in information technology have elevated the significance of digital investment and trade in international commerce, prompting nations, based on their own interests and economic contexts, to propose digital trade stances and claims aligned with their values in this round of rule-setting. The formulation of digital trade international rules centers on addressing new demands and standards arising in the twenty-first-century digital trade landscape, with particular emphasis on intellectual property protection, cross-border data flow, and personal information protection in the digital trade era. Developed economies like Europe and the United States, with a competitive edge in digital trade, are actively striving to dominate the formulation of new international digital trade norms. This ambition is currently reflected in regional trade agreements spearheaded by advanced economies like the United States and Europe. Of the over 40 regional agreements involving digital trade disclosed by the WTO, 32 agreements have a dedicated chapter for digital trade (e-commerce), with the United States leading 13 and the EU 7, while the rest are primarily signed among countries or regions that have already inked agreements with the United States or the EU.

As a global leader in information technology, the United States is not only a powerhouse in digital trade but also forcefully steering the modification and formulation of new-era international trade rules to solidify its competitive edge. Within US-led regional trade agreements, the crafting of digital trade rules extends beyond e-commerce to encompass areas such as intellectual property, information technology, investment, and cross-border service trade. For instance, the USMCA, revised and led by the United States, explicitly requires free flow of data, non-discriminatory treatment of digital products, and prohibits mandatory localization requirements. In contrast, the EU-Japan EPA demonstrates a more cautious approach from the EU regarding cross-border data flow and data localization, lacking a provision against data localization and instituting a three-year review period for data cross-border freedom. Nonetheless, the EU's introduction of the *General Data Protection Regulation* and the *Free Flow of Non-Personal Data Regulation* in 2018 suggests that future FTAs signed by the EU may incorporate similar clauses to those in USMCA.

### 6.5 Economic Globalization Progresses Toward a New Form of Standardized, Structured Modular Integration

With the continuous evolution of economic globalization, the scope and content of international trade theory research have expanded, making that the theory has become more grounded in reality and better equipped to explain phenomena under the backdrop of economic globalization, highlighting its role in driving the evolution and development of modern international trade theory.

Economic integration has four standardized forms: Free Trade Areas (FTAs), Customs Unions (CUs), Common Markets (CMs), and Economic Unions (like the EU). In the future, the world can further adopt standardized modules, enabling countries to choose according to their own situations and adjust relevant parameters to achieve common international trade standards, construct a new global economic order, and foster shared global development.

Structurally, globalization can be broadly divided into three tiers, with countries choosing their level of participation based on their development status and intentions. Mimicking Europe's tiered economic cooperation model, each tier entails distinct rights and obligations. The top-tier (A-Level) cooperation framework leads global trade trends, emphasizing fairness and justice. The mid-tier (B-Level) corresponds roughly to RCEP, focusing on significant trade and investment arrangements. The basic-tier (C-Level) pertains to general regional partnerships. In the future, joining an organization will entail standardized rights and obligations, bypassing complex negotiations for a straightforward selection process.

### 6.6 *China's Enhanced Role in the Restructuring of International Trade Rules*

As the largest developing country and a representative of emerging economies, China should actively participate in the process of formulating international trade rules to secure its rightful voice. CPC General Secretary Xi Jinping has emphasized that "adhering to and developing socialism with Chinese characteristics under new historical conditions... We must follow the global trend." Such thinking embodies the fundamental principles and direction China should adhere to amidst the once-in-a-century changes, the idea of building a community of shared future for mankind, and the determination to pursue a peaceful path of development. Facing WTO reforms and the advancement of regional trade agreements, China should strive to play a constructive role in the restructuring of international trade rules, contributing to global economic and financial stability.

First, actively support the reform of organizations like the WTO and persist in promoting changes to international trade rules through multilateral, bilateral, and regional channels. In China's *Position Paper on WTO Reform (2018)*, China clearly stated its stance supporting necessary reforms to "strengthen the WTO's authority and effectiveness, promote an open world economy, and build a community of shared future for mankind," proposing basic principles for reform such as maintaining the core values of the multilateral trading system. China actively promotes liberalization and facilitation of trade and investment, enhances mechanisms for resolving international trade disputes, and pushes for reforms in digital trade, service trade, and e-commerce rules.

Currently, some transformations in international trade rules, such as the shift from NAFTA to the USMCA, signal an increase in barriers for countries outside the agreement and the inclusion of clauses akin to “poison pills” that potentially infringe upon national sovereignty. While these changes may have short-term negative impacts on China, in the long run, they do not necessarily equate to anticipated losses. After more than 40 years of market-oriented reforms and opening up, China’s economy has made substantial progress, particularly in emerging technologies and digital information sectors, where it now possesses robust international competitiveness. While intensified international competition and trade wars may subject the Chinese market to external shocks, the effects are expected to be limited. In response to changes in international trade rules, China should look to the future, acknowledging potential short-term costs while confidently anticipating long-term gains. It should dynamically evaluate the effects of developing country provisions, actively participating in and driving the process of trade rule reforms. This approach ensures that China’s role is not just responsive but also proactive in shaping a fairer, more balanced, and sustainable global trade environment.

Second, we should strengthen regional economic and financial cooperation, striving to create a model for regional collaboration. Currently, numerous large-scale regional free trade agreements worldwide are dominated by developed countries. Geographically, these agreements largely encompass major advanced economies as well as dynamic emerging economies. As a significant developing nation, China should actively advance and engage in regional economic cooperation processes. The signing of the Regional Comprehensive Economic Partnership (RCEP) and the China-EU Bilateral Investment Treaty signifies a positive step, playing a crucial role in consolidating and expanding cooperation within these regions. China should collaborate with relevant countries and regions to establish RCEP and the China-EU investment treaty as global models; it should proactively push for a higher level of openness, facilitating the free flow and efficient utilization of global factors of production; continue to tap into the growth potential of our high-tech industries, gradually narrowing the gap with international counterparts.

Third, looking to the future, we need to maintain a keen focus on the development of digital industries. In the upcoming global economic landscape, digital industries will emerge as key economic drivers. China should adopt market-oriented policies appropriately, leveraging its strengths to seize the significant opportunities in developing digital industries.

Leveraging its status as a digital economy powerhouse, China should grasp the initiative in setting digital trade rules, reinforcing its path toward becoming a digital and trade powerhouse. By fully utilizing the features of its vast scale, evident technological superiority, and outstanding enterprise competitiveness in both the digital economy and digital trade, China should pioneer the establishment of a sound e-commerce regulatory and standard system; guide the formulation of international rules in areas such as the global payment and credit system, online consumer rights protection, taxation of digital products, unified logistics, and standard operations of cross-border e-commerce.

Fourth, globally, China should deepen cooperation with the majority of nations, striving for a leading position and a voice in constructing digital trade rules, committed to establishing a fair, transparent, and uniform regulatory framework. In the development of WTO digital trade rules, China should actively participate and drive the process, adhering to fair and reasonable WTO rules as the overarching principle for digital trade regulations. Meanwhile, in response to the needs of digital trade development, China should conclude supplementary bilateral and multilateral digital trade agreements, ensuring the rational and orderly conduct of digital trade worldwide. Currently, China has initiated comprehensive and multi-level trade strategies, integrating digital trade with the Belt and Road Initiative and tapping into the digital trade potential along BRI countries, while promoting the Cross-border Interbank Payment System (CIPS) as a vital financial infrastructure. Negotiations with BRI countries should incorporate China's digital trade propositions, strategically aiming to enhance its influence in discourse.

CHAPTER 10

# China's Market Economy Theory: Evolution and Theoretical Modeling

The theory of the socialist market economy was born and developed amidst the grand practice of China's reform and opening up and has been validated by the country's rapid economic development. It represents both an innovation in contemporary economic theory and its practical application. The theory has gone through several transformative phases—a tortuous progression, initial formation, steady growth, and in-depth exploration—refining itself in practice. It achieved the organic integration of the basic socialist system with the market economy and dual breakthroughs in the innovation of economic theory and successful practice. This has significantly enriched Marxist political economy and modern economic theory, offering a new benchmark for assessing market economy models. Looking ahead, the theory of the socialist market economy will continue to evolve, exerting a profound impact on the once-in-a-century global transformation and contributing to the building of a shared future for mankind.

In the year 2021, marking the centenary of the founding of the Communist Party of China, a powerful economic theory underpinned the extraordinary transformations of the past century and over 40 years of reform and opening up: the theory of the socialist market economy. Economic theories posited by figures such as Adam Smith, David Ricardo, and John Maynard Keynes were imprinted with the characteristics of their respective eras, addressing economic challenges specific to their nations. The unique conditions and distinct economic development model of



Z. Liang, *The Innovation of Economic Theory in China*,
https://doi.org/10.1007/978-981-95-2713-7_10

China dictate that Chinese economic theories diverge from Western ones, yet they also embrace inclusiveness. From a global perspective on economic thought, the question of whether socialism and a market economy can coexist has long been a contentious, worldwide dilemma. At the core of Western economic theory lies the dichotomy between the market and the state, an opposition established since Smith's time. The subsequent debates, whether the century-long dispute between Hayek and Keynes or the freshwater versus saltwater schools of thought, all boil down to choosing one or the other, with varying degrees of emphasis across different periods. The critical theoretical challenge lies in how to reconcile these two entities. The essence of the socialist market economy theory lies in harmonizing the relationship between the government and the market, representing a dialectical unity of these relations at a higher level. The theory of the socialist market economy stands as both a significant innovation in Marxist economic theory and a pivotal exploration that addresses economic conundrums through China's practical experiences.

## 1 Evolution of the Socialist Market Economy Theory: Blazing a Trail with Arduous Efforts

The formation and development of the socialist market economy theory can be broadly categorized into four distinct phases along its historical trajectory.

### 1.1 *The Stage of Twists and Turns (1949–1978): Rejection of Market Forces*

Before the founding of the People's Republic of China, a New Democratic economic system was in place, serving as a transitional bridge. Following the establishment of the PRC, a policy of "leaning to one side" was adopted in foreign affairs, emulating the Soviet model and instituting a highly centralized planned economy that completely dismissed the role of markets in resource allocation. Despite its evident drawbacks, the traditional planned economy was intensified after the Three Transformations to hasten socialist realization. However, this period also laid the foundation for our industrial infrastructure and later explorations into the socialist market economy theory.

### 1.2 Initial Formation Stage (1978–1992): Supplementary Role of the Market

The Third Plenary Session of the 11th CPC Central Committee in December 1978 signaled the start of both the reform and opening up era and the formal beginning of the development of socialist market economy theory. In 1979, Deng Xiaoping first discussed the relationship between planning and markets, asserting that it was erroneous to believe only capitalism could have markets; socialism too could foster a market economy. The Sixth Plenary Session of the 11th CPC Central Committee in 1981 introduced the guiding principle of "planned economy as the primary, market regulation as supplementary." This idea was incorporated into the 12th CPC National Congress report in 1982. The Third Plenary Session of the 12th CPC Central Committee introduced the concept of a "planned commodity economy" in 1984. In 1987, Deng Xiaoping suggested ceasing discussions on planned economy as the dominant force, marking the formal abandonment of the idea of the planned economy as the dominant force. In the same year, the 13th CPC National Congress initiated the transition from a planned to a socialist market economy under macro-regulated framework with the notion of "state regulation of the market, market guidance for enterprises."

### 1.3 Steady Development Stage (1992–2012): Fundamental Role of the Market

In 1992, Deng Xiaoping's Southern Tour remarks emphasized that "both planning and markets are economic tools" and that having more planning or market influence did not define the difference between socialism and capitalism. He debunked the conventional error of judging an economic system based on operational mechanisms, liberating Chinese economy in thinking. That year, the 14th CPC National Congress explicitly set the goal of establishing a socialist market economic system, marking the formal introduction of this theory. Subsequently, the Third Plenary Session of the 16th CPC Central Committee and the 17th and 18th CPC National Congresses advanced further measures to refine the socialist market economic system based on this guiding ideology.

### 1.4 *Advanced Exploration Phase (2012 to Present): The Decisive Role of the Market*

The Third Plenary Session of the 18th CPC Central Committee held in November 2013 marked a monumental theoretical breakthrough in the development of socialist market economy theory. Among the critical viewpoints presented in the *Decision of the Central Committee of the Communist Party of China on Some Major Issues Concerning Comprehensively Deepening Reform* was the assertion that "the market should play a decisive role in resource allocation and the government should play a better role." This statement transformed market's previous "fundamental role" in resource allocation to a "decisive role," elevating the market's function to an unprecedented level. While this change may seem straightforward, it conferred a special status and meaning to the concept of the "market." Simultaneously, it innovatively highlighted the interplay between the government and the market, emphasizing that managing this relationship is at the core of deepening systemic reforms comprehensively. Following the Third Plenary Session's commitment to deepen reforms, the 19th CPC National Congress and the Fourth Plenary Session of the19th CPC Central Committee further refined the theory. The19th CPC National Congress advocated for a new economic system characterized by "effective market mechanisms, vibrant micro-entities, and well-calibrated macro control." In 2019, the Fourth Plenary Session of the19th CPC Central Committee recognized the socialist market economic system as a prominent strength of China's national institutional system and governance framework, significantly enhancing the political standing of socialist market economy theory.

## 2 China's Market Economy: An Effective Model in the Interests of Future Generations

### 2.1 *Greatly Unleashing and Developing Social Productivity and Creating the Chinese Miracle*

Over the past 40 years of reform and opening up, China's economy has witnessed rapid growth, achieving globally recognized accomplishments, with the socialist market economy model demonstrating remarkable effectiveness. Economically, China has experienced a leapfrog growth, becoming the world's second-largest economy. The GDP soared from 67.9

billion yuan in 1952 to nearly 100 trillion yuan in 2018, with per capita GDP increasing from119 yuan to 66,000 yuan. China's near 10% high growth and social stability have created "two great wonders" in global economic development. In 2019, a 6.1% GDP growth rate was notable as a high growth pace; in 2020, amidst the COVID-19 pandemic, China was the sole major economy with positive growth, recording a 2.3% growth rate. This fully attests to the correctness and vitality of the socialist market economy theory. In the future, China's market economy model will further unleash and develop social productivity, continuously meeting people's ever-growing needs for a better life.

### 2.2 *Effective Market-oriented Reforms*

From the early exploration of the market economy model to the stage where the market plays a decisive role, China has gradually refined its socialist market economy system, forming a market economy model with Chinese characteristics. The key to China's success is the systematic and reasonable approach derived from practice, including: adherence to the basic principles of reform and opening up for continuity and stability; reliance on practice as the test of truth, problem-oriented approach, and development as the core principle for pragmatic and effective growth; the metaphor of "crossing the river by feeling the stones" and "black cat, white cat theory" ensuring the rationality of reform path. These innovative ideas and methods are not only effective in practice but also deeply rooted in economic logic, embodying the essence of successful practice and theoretical innovation. In this process, China has focused on handling special relationships in the market economy, achieving a qualitative leap, and enhancing the dimension of market economy thinking. Firstly, the "effective market" and "proactive government" work in concert, treating market and government roles as an integrated whole, a major innovation in practice. Scientifically leveraging market and government roles and emphasizing the market while doing a good job in macroeconomic regulation lays the groundwork for high-quality economic development. Secondly, rational comprehensive thinking is upheld. Analogies like the "black cat, white cat theory" and "target-driven planning," simple as they are, embody profound rationality and pragmatism. Moreover, by thoroughly studying theories and practices, formulating strategies tailored to China's reality, piloting them, then expanding based on success, or adjusting otherwise, China charts a feasible path for reform practice.

### 2.3 *Prudent and Steady Opening Up*

Since 1978, China has adhered to the fundamental policy of opening up, actively engaging in international cooperation, enhancing economic ties with the world, and integrating into globalization, significantly impacting the global economy. Currently, China is the leading goods trading nation, the largest holder of foreign exchange reserves, and the second largest in service trade, foreign direct investment attraction, and outbound investment. Reflecting on China's journey, its achievements can be divided into three phases:

First, Initial Opening (1978–2001): Focusing on processing trade and attracting foreign investment, China transitioned from a closed/semi-closed to a partially open state, with coastal special economic zones as pioneers, later extending to inland areas.

Second, Full Integration into Globalization (2001–2012): Joining the World Trade Organization in 2001 harmonized domestic regulations with international standards, deepened openness, and marked a new chapter. China shifted from unilateral to reciprocal openness with WTO members, balancing "bringing in" and "going out."

Third, Building a New Open Economy (2012 Onward): Since the 18th CPC National Congress, China's breakthroughs has included establishing free trade zones in Shanghai and Hainan Free Trade Port, initiating the Belt and Road Initiative, piloting comprehensive service sector liberalization in Beijing, advancing the Greater Bay Area, promoting Renminbi internationalization, and actively engaging in global economic governance reform. Since the 18th CPC National Congress, China has prioritized theoretical innovation, combining theory with practice. Concepts like the Belt and Road Initiative and the Community of Shared Future for Mankind guide China's future direction and global integration. Under the dual forces of theory and practice, China is building a higher-level open economy, adopting a more proactive strategy.

### 2.4 *Adhering to Rational Evaluation Criteria*

Throughout more than 40 years of reform and opening up, China has consistently relied on practice to verify truth. Under the socialist market economy theory, China has undergone profound transformations, demonstrating its influence and vitality. Whether in theoretical innovation or practical application, China has delivered satisfactory results to the world.

On assessing the suitability of the socialist market economy theory to China's national conditions, General Secretary Xi Jinping, in *Brief Reflections on the Significance of the Theses on Feuerbach*, posits that the maturity and completeness of socialist market economy theory must be judged by the criterion of China's reform and construction practice.

## 3 Defining Features of the Socialist Market Economy Theory: Back to Basics

### *3.1 Distinct Attributes of the Socialist System*

The decision of the Fourth Plenary Session of the 19th CPC Central Committee on *Several Major Issues on Adhering to and Improving the Socialist System with Chinese Characteristics and on Advancing the Modernization of the National Governance System and Governance Capacity* included the "socialist market economy system" in the basic socialist economic system for the first time, which is a very innovative discussion. How compatible is socialism with the market economy? This has been a persistent and significant question since the early days of reform and opening up, meriting thorough investigation. The practice and theory of reform and opening up over the past 40 years have proven that the socialist market economy theory does not conflict with the theories of Marx and other predecessors; instead, it has innovated Marxist economic theory and the basic socialist system. Regarding whether socialism can have a market economy, Deng Xiaoping noted at the start of reform and opening up that the planning and market mechanisms are merely tools and should not be used to determine whether an economy is "capitalist or socialist," and that the basic economic system of the country is what the market economy serves.

General Secretary Xi Jinping once said: "We are developing a market economy under the leadership of the Communist Party of China and the socialist system. We must never forget the qualifier of 'socialist'. The reason why it is called a socialist market economy is to adhere to the superiority of our system and effectively guard against the disadvantages of the capitalist market economy." This defines the fundamental relationship between the basic socialist system and the market economy. Therefore, the socialist market economy theory transforms the traditional planned economy into a market economy system regulated reasonably by the government, while also experiencing a "chemical reaction" of sublimation. As a theoretical innovation combining the basic socialist system and the socialist market economy, the socialist market economy theory possesses distinct attributes of the socialist system and the development potential of the market economy, leveraging the respective advantages of both and promoting tremendous progress in social productivity.

### 3.2 The Relationship Between Government and Market is No Longer Adversarial, but Organically Integrated

The history of human economic development shows that the market is the most efficient form of resource allocation, but it is realized under different market conditions. Therefore, under different market conditions, market economy models with their own characteristics can be established. China has established a socialist market economy system that suits its national conditions, which has strongly promoted the development of social productivity, the improvement of people's living standards, and the enhancement of comprehensive national strength. From a global perspective, the market economy is not omnipotent and has limitations. However, government intervention has also challenged traditional capitalist economy theories and even brought about significant political and ideological transformations. Unlike the West, which overemphasizes the role of the "invisible hand," on the one hand, it extensively uses the "visible hand" of government intervention, but on the other hand, it turns a blind eye to the government's role and even criticizes the government's role of other countries. The Chinese socialist market economy model emphasizes the combined and coordinated development of the "two hands" of the market and government. It can be said that China's socialist market economy developed by continuously adjusting the relationship between government and market. In 2013, the Third Plenary Session of the 18th Central Committee of the Communist Party of China proposed to let the market play a decisive role in resource allocation and better play the role of government. This was the first time it was proposed to let the market play a decisive role, establishing the "market" characteristic of the socialist market economy from the dimensions of quantity and proportion.

Properly handling the relationship between government and market is an intrinsic driving force and an urgent need for reform and development. Only by giving full play to the decisive role of the market in resource allocation, better playing the role of government, and allowing the "invisible hand" and the "visible hand" to work together and complement each other can we achieve market-determined factor prices and efficient and fair resource allocation, thereby achieving high-quality economic development. If China is to follow the path of the market economy, it naturally requires the decisive role of the market; otherwise, it will produce a large number of distortions and incur high institutional or social costs. However, how the government functions and the extent of its involvement are influenced by more factors, such as national conditions and stage of development; there should be a golden section point for the boundary of government and market functions. The roles of government and market are dynamic, and the proportion of their relationship varies across different countries, stages, and fields. However, as long as the market mechanism plays a leading role, it is considered a market economy model. On the one hand, it is necessary to establish an "effective market" to allow the market to play a decisive role and stimulate market vitality and innovation; on the other hand, it is necessary to have a "proactive government" that compensates for market failures and takes action in establishing a perfect market system framework, maintaining fair competition in the market, stabilizing the macroeconomic environment, and ensuring social welfare. In summary, the roles of government and market are complementary, mutually reinforcing, and indispensable.

### 3.3 *Coexistence of and Fair Competition Between Market Entities with Diverse Ownership*

The Fourth Plenary Session of the 19th Central Committee of the Communist Party of China emphasized: "We must adhere to the dominant role of public ownership, the joint development of various forms of ownership, the predominant role of distribution according to work, and the coexistence of various distribution methods, organically combining the socialist system with the market economy, and continuously unleashing and developing the productive forces, demonstrating the significant advantages of this approach." This indicates that public ownership is a distinctive feature of China's socialist market economy model, setting it apart from other market economy models. The 15th National Congress of the Communist Party of China achieved a breakthrough in the theory of ownership in China, clarifying the mixed ownership economic system of "public ownership playing the dominant role and various forms of ownership developing together." This system is not only an important foundation of the socialist market economy but also a key guarantee for achieving fair competition. The mixed ownership economy is an important form of realization for both public and non-public ownership economies. It is also a concrete manifestation of giving play to the decisive role of the market in resource allocation and better leveraging the role of the government.

In recent years, China has actively developed an economy of mixed ownership, gradually improved the property rights protection system, firmly supported the healthy development of the non-public sector, and significantly enhanced the vitality and creativity of various ownership economies. In summary, a competitive and neutral market environment has not yet been fully formed. In the future, as China advances market competition and enterprise reform, it will need to further strengthen the principle of competition neutrality, promote "ownership neutrality," oppose setting different rules for different forms of enterprise ownership, and continuously advance reforms in depth. General Secretary Xi Jinping pointed out at a recent entrepreneur symposium: "Market entities are the main participants in China's economic activities, the primary providers of employment opportunities, and the main drivers of technological progress, playing a very important role in national development." At the same time, the income distribution system, as a fundamental economic institution of China's economic development, represents the unity of fairness and efficiency, the structure of ownership of the means of production, and the important content and manifestation of common prosperity, and it is also the balance scale of the socialist market economy.

### 3.4 The Characteristic of High Openness is Conducive to Opposing Protectionism

Openness is a crucial characteristic of the socialist market economy system. China's market economy system has gradually taken shape through the practice of reform and opening up and should naturally integrate into the ongoing process of deepening reform and opening up. Over the past 40 years of reform and opening up, China has not only achieved significant institutional innovation and breakthroughs but also seen a significant increase in its economic strength, as well as continuous improvements in its international competitiveness and global voice. The Fourth Plenary Session of the 19th Central Committee of the Communist Party of China proposed "building a new system for higher-level open economy" and "implementing comprehensive opening up on a larger scale, in more areas, and at a deeper level." Currently, both the world and China are in a profound change that has not been seen in a century, with the unipolar pattern led by the United States diminishing, and economic globalization closely linking the development of countries around the world. However, in recent years, "anti-globalization" has gained momentum.

At present, economic globalization has penetrated almost every corner of the world, and the historical trend is irreversible. Seeking win-win cooperation and welfare for humanity is the ultimate goal of global economic and trade relations. International economic and trade relations should combine free trade, which plays a dominant role based on international rules, with limited protection.

## 4 Theoretical Model of China's Market Economy:Quantitative Rational Synthesis

Marx once emphasized that a discipline can only be considered a true science when it successfully applied mathematics. The qualitative description of China's market economy theory is relatively comprehensive, but it is relatively weak in the construction of mathematical models and quantification, which can affect its global recognition and acceptance. Therefore, a mathematical analysis of China's market economy theory would enhance its scientific validity and global recognition.

### *4.1 Mathematical Sublimation of the Logical Relationships in China's Market Economy Theory Model*

Based on this logic, we elevate the socialist market economy, which combines an "effective market" and a "proactive government," to the level of theoretical models and mathematical expressions. Given that the previous sections have established corresponding theories from the perspectives of the market economy and state intervention and both of them have played a good role within their respective scopes, we can view the market economy model as a combination of the market economy and government functions. By assigning different weights, we can demonstrate the differences in market economy models, thus establishing a corresponding rational comprehensive model after organically combining an "effective market" and a "proactive government." The core components of this model are represented by the following three equations:

$$\Delta Y_t = a\Delta Y_t^* + b\Delta Y_t \tag{10.1}$$

$$Y_t^* = f\left(K_t, L_t\right) = \lambda K_t^{\theta} L_t^{1-\theta} \tag{10.2}$$

$$Y_t^* = \Delta AS + \Delta AD \tag{10.3}$$

For simplicity, this section appropriately simplifies the market and government roles into mathematical forms and does not use the general form, but this simplification does not affect the basic conclusions. In Eqn. (10.1), $\Delta Y_t$ represents the changes in the total economic output level, where $\Delta Y_t = Y_t - Y_{t-1}$; $Y_t^*$ represents the potential output under conditions of a fully marketized economy and is the main part of the long-term trend; $\Delta Y_t^*$ represents the changes brought about by the government's role; the parameters $a$ and $b$ represent weights. In an ideal scenario of an "effective market" and a "proactive government," the sum of the two parameters equals 1. Any conditions that meet this can be regarded as a market economy model. In Eqn. (10.2), $\lambda$ is a constant; $K$ represents capital; $L$ represents labor; and the parameters $\theta$ and $1-\theta$ are the elasticity of capital output and the elasticity of labor output, respectively. In Eqn. (10.3), ΔAS represents shocks from the supply side, and ΔAD represents shocks from the demand side. Essentially, the rational comprehensive model changes the previous economic theory's premise based solely on a pure market economy, and it represents a significant innovation in thinking, demonstrating clear characteristics of rational comprehensiveness. We refer to the theoretical expression based on this model as Rational Comprehensive Economics.

### 4.2 *Economic Growth Model under China's Market Economy Theory*

The Rational Comprehensive Economic Model organically combines an "effective market" and a "proactive government." Its essence is the mathematical sublimation and model analysis of the socialist market economy mode. In a sense, it can also be regarded as the growth model of the socialist market economy. Therefore, the economic growth model under China's market economy theory is consistent with the Rational

Comprehensive Economic Model established by us, which is systematically elaborated in Chap. 4 of this book. The Rational Comprehensive Economic Model changes the premise of previous economic theories that were based solely on a pure market economy model, representing a significant innovation in research thinking. China's market economy theory shares common characteristics with other market economies but also has unique features determined by the attributes of its social system. These mainly include: first, the coexistence of a pluralistic market dominated by public ownership; second, the distribution mechanism aims for common prosperity to oppose excessive wealth disparity and achieve social equity; third, the government has a strong role in braking and macro control capabilities while emphasizing equality, public safety, social responsibility, and sustainable development; fourth, openness and inclusiveness are prominent. Mathematically, these specific characteristics equate to imposing corresponding constraints. It is important to note that they can make up for the deficiencies of the market and respond to market failures, which can be said to be high-quality economic growth equations that better combine an "effective market" and a "proactive government." Evidently, the socialist market economy growth model, though still evolving, embodies a dynamic and high-quality economic framework that synchronously integrates short-term dynamics with long-term perspectives, coordinating both aggregate supply and aggregate demand in a harmonized upgrade. However, this economic growth model is still being refined. We anticipate that over time, this economic growth model will guide the high-quality development of China's economy and present a new option for global economies.

By using the economic growth equations in Chap. 4, it is easy to understand that if discussions about total factor productivity, potential economic growth rate, and actual economic growth rate are elevated to a theoretical level, and the inherent logic of calculating actual and potential economic growth rates are flexibly used, one can form the most fundamental aspect of economic growth without government intervention. Increasing investment in education and technology is conducive to enhancing the potential economic growth rate, reflecting the government's capacity to alter the potential economic growth trend. Reform and opening up, precise judgments on significant medium and long-term development matters, five-year plans, and strong crisis handling capabilities essentially play the role of a government brake. Innovation in macro control policies has laid a solid foundation for achieving short-term economic growth while ensuring consistency with the basic logic and elements of the Real Business Cycle (RBC) derived from the long-term economic growth model.

### 4.3 A Golden Era of Development and Chinese Practices

Economics, as a science describing the dynamic functioning of economies, places central importance on theories of economic growth. Within a new logical framework, this theory better elucidates phenomena such as economic growth, business cycles, the middle-income trap, and the role of reforms. Specifically, the rational comprehensive model, grounded in China's market economy model, concludes that when a country or a group of major global economies enjoy a favorable foundation and environment during a certain period, along with the transformation and upgrading of both supply and demand sides, sustained growth can be achieved over a prolonged period if total factor productivity continually improves without severe imbalances or crises in supply and demand sides. Thus, theoretically, whether for the global economy or individual economies, a golden era of development can be anticipated if there is a synergistic upgrade and development of both the demand and supply sides, complemented by the progress of globalization and market expansion. China experienced such a prolonged golden era from the 1950s to the early 1970s and throughout the over four decades of reform and opening up.

For China to sustain another golden era of development in the future, several conditions must be met:

(1) The Chinese economy must maintain a favorable baseline condition.
(2) The government must implement effective measures to enhance labor productivity and steadfastly promote technological innovation.
(3) Dynamic equilibrium between aggregate supply and aggregate demand must be ensured.

The fundamental scenario entails stable short-term economic growth, long-term economic structural optimization, financial stability, significant risk prevention, and sustained high-quality economic growth. Meanwhile, external factors influencing China's economic development must be carefully considered, with efforts directed toward fostering a favorable external environment. Currently, there are instances of one country attempting to encircle and contain another. This action completely violates the principles of free trade and multilateral frameworks, potentially hindering China's smooth economic development. China should stand firm alongside all righteous nations in opposing trade protectionism, maintain strategic composure, focus on its internal affairs, and prepare for the advent of a new golden era of development.

## 5 Contribution of the Socialist Market Economy Theory: Drawing Upon the Strengths of Others

Throughout history, nations that have created economic miracles during their rise often formulate corresponding economic theories. After more than 40 years of reform and opening up, China naturally calls for theoretical innovations. The socialist market economy theory absorbs and learns from all economic theories conducive to its development, achieving theoretical innovations in economics while comprehensively deepening reforms, enriching Marxist political economy and contributing substantially to the treasury of modern economic thought.

### *5.1 Redefining the Relationship Between Market and Government: Moving from Opposition to Unity*

One of the central themes in the history of Western economic thought is the debate over the roles of market and government. Starting with Adam Smith, Western economics has traditionally placed government and market in opposition. Subsequent debates, whether it was the Hayek-Keynes debate or the division between Saltwater and Freshwater schools, revolved around choosing between the market and the government, idealizing the "invisible hand" of the market while confining and undermining the role of government—a single-dimensional logic. Since the advent of reform and opening up, China's successful model of integrating market and government in economic development has disproven the binary opposition between government and market, developing a new paradigm where the "invisible hand" and the "visible hand" work together. By allowing the market to play a decisive role in resource allocation and better leveraging government functions, a new relationship between market and government has been forged. China adheres to a dialectical unity between market and government, advocating for an "effective market" to invigorate market economy and a "proactive government" for macro control to address market failures. This theoretical breakthrough transcends the 200-year-old binary opposition between government and market in Western economic thought, charting a new course for macroeconomics and reconciling the relationship from opposition to unity.

### 5.2 *Innovating Macroeconomic Regulation Theory: Laying the Foundation for Addressing Market Failures*

Macroeconomic regulation is a concept introduced by China, with no direct equivalent in Western economic theory. The Third Plenary Session of the 18th CPC Central Committee innovatively stated: "Scientific macroeconomic regulation and effective government governance are inherent requirements for realizing the advantages of the socialist market economic system." The essence of macroeconomic regulation involves indirect intervention in economic operations, instead employing fiscal, financial, and monetary policies to adjust the overall economy, ensuring coordination and balance between supply and demand. Thus, the scope of macroeconomic regulation surpasses the concept of macroeconomic policy in Western economics, being more comprehensive and profound. Diverging from Keynesianism's exclusive focus on demand-side considerations, macroeconomic regulation attends to both demand and supply, constituting a regulatory system involving both supply-side and demand-side management. During the regulatory process, the government tailors its policies to address aggregate and structural issues, combining demand-side management and supply-side reforms accordingly.

CHAPTER 11

# Theoretical Model and Deductive Logic Analysis of the Integration of Market and Government

Economics, as a science that studies the laws governing the operation of the economy, has constructed a grand edifice of economic theories. However, due to the existence of numerous schools of thought within economics, a unified logic has not been formed, which has somewhat dimmed the luster of economics as a science. Since economics is a science that studies the relationships and operational laws among economic variables, its logic should be unified. There should not be two or more theories or explanations that are completely conflicted with each other for the same economic variable relationship. Economist Paul Krugman believes that we must accept the market's imperfections and the reality that a sophisticated, grand unified economic theory is still distant. This actually reflects his anticipation for the prospects of economic theory reform. In terms of the prospects for economic theory reform, whether it is possible to start from the simplest and most basic assumptions or axioms and construct an economic theory system with a unified logic, thereby realizing Krugman's dream, and also theoretically analyzing Say's Law, which serves as the foundation for the existence of a market economy, is an exploration that is attractive and worth pursuing.



Z. Liang, *The Innovation of Economic Theory in China*,
https://doi.org/10.1007/978-981-95-2713-7_11

# 1 The Theoretical Model of the Integration of an Effective Market and a Proactive Government, and the Chinese Story

As far as the logic of economic theory reform is concerned, induction and deduction are two different methods. Induction emphasizes moving from the particular to the general, while deduction focuses on starting from the general to conduct systematic analysis. The ultimate goal of both methods should be unified. If we can provide the most basic assumptions or axioms through induction, and then conduct systematic theoretical deduction through deduction, we can develop a unified economic theory system. By analyzing the scenarios and conditions under which various special theories are established, we can form a unified economic logic rather than each proposing their own logic based on specific assumptions. This is a task that economists cannot avoid.

## *1.1 Introduction*

The evolution of economic thought can be traced back to ancient times, with ancient Greece, Rome, and China all proposing corresponding doctrines. The birth of Adam Smith's *The Wealth of Nations* in 1776 marked an important milestone in the formation of modern economic theory. The Great Depression of the 1930s and the responses to it gave rise to the formation and development of Keynesian macroeconomic theory. After the 1970s, the stagflation caused by Keynesian effective demand theory highlighted its limitations, promoting the rise of supply-side school, the rational expectations school, and others. Although the Great Depression and the 2008 global financial crisis were quite different, both crises caused massive destruction, revealing the shortcomings of existing economic theories and instances of market failure. As early as the seventh century BC, Guanzi, a distinct economist who combined economic thought with practice, conducted preliminary explorations in the areas of market mechanisms, macro-regulation, and international trade theory, which are of great significance for understanding and innovating modern economic theories.

The evolution of economic theories and schools involves distinct stages, each characterized by representative schools emerging from the varying environments and perspectives of economists. The modern edifice of economic theory, while impressive, also leads to considerable confusion. We often ask which school's theories and methods should be employed when confronting a specific economic issue. Given that the relationship between the market and the government is a perennial topic of contention in economic theory, determining how to weigh their roles becomes paramount. It is particularly relevant to note that the Chinese narrative offers a unique key to enabling innovation in the theoretical understanding of the market-government relationship. In 2015, Chinese President Xi Jinping stressed the necessity of adhering to dialectics and the principle of "two points." He advocated for a continued focus on integrating the basic socialist system with a market economy, harnessing the advantages of both. President Xi emphasized the importance of an "effective market" alongside a "proactive government," striving to address this global economic conundrum through practical applications. This not only presents a significant challenge to economists but also outlines the path and methods for their endeavors.

The goal of economic theory is to study the causal relationships between key economic variables. In principle, this can be done through either inductive or deductive methods. Although these two approaches articulate the laws governing economic operations from different paths, they are fundamentally united in logic. For the grand system of economic theory, is it possible to first induce from experience and facts, propose basic propositions or axioms, and then use these axioms or assumptions as a foundation? By establishing corresponding mathematical models and deductive logic, could we systematically analyze economic principles under a unified logic? Professor Yu Yongding of the Chinese Academy of Social Sciences has emphasized,[1] "A successful theory cannot merely be an induction of certain experiences, although correct induction is very important. I believe that having a strong deductive nature is the most attractive aspect of economics or any theory." Therefore, a significant issue in the reform of economic theory is how to achieve a major breakthrough in the deductive logic of the theory. Forming a unified economic logic and theoretical system would make it more convincing.

We know that physicist Albert Einstein's Special Theory of Relativity is built on two basic assumptions: first, that all physical laws are the same in different inertial frames of reference; and second, the constancy of the speed of light, which remains the same in all inertial frames of reference in a vacuum. Based on these two fundamental assumptions, the entire theory

[1] Yu Yongding, "My Views on New Structural Economics" (2022)

was deduced through complete mathematical logic. So, can a similar method be applied to economic theory? By establishing corresponding basic assumptions or axioms, particularly those that can be universally accepted without the need for proof, and then using them as a foundation for theoretical deduction, this is an exploration that holds great promise.

### *1.2 On the Basic Assumptions (Axioms) of Economics*

All basic assumptions or axioms should describe objective factual characteristics, possess meanings that hold true under general conditions, and withstand scrutiny. This ensures the rationality of the inferences made from them. Therefore, the basic assumptions or axioms of economics are the cornerstone of economic theory and therefore are crucial.

1. Considerations on the standards of basic assumptions

If economic theory possesses theoretical cornerstones similar to those in the theory of relativity, then the basic assumptions (or axioms) serving as foundations must meet particular requirements; otherwise, achieving a level of self-evidence would be difficult. Basic scientific assumptions should conform to strict standards: universality, reality, necessity, and sufficiency. Universality means that no counterexamples exist in reality, ensuring the theory's consistency and rationality; reality means that the assumptions are a reasonable approximation to the reality, ensuring that relevant inferences or predictions stay within a reasonable range; necessity and sufficiency mean they are closely related to the most essential characteristics and must meet the criterion of "if and only if," ensuring consistency with rigorous mathematical logic. The classical economist Nassau William Senior emphasized the universality and reality of assumptions, providing strong support for this view.[2] Economic theories derived through deductive reasoning based on the assumptions that meet strict requirements inherently possess the basic characteristics of science.

[2] Nassau William Senior believed that theoretical political economics, or pure economics, should be based on a few general propositions that are the results of observation and consciousness, familiar to people, and whose conclusions are deduced logically, possessing universal truth. Therefore, the method of studying economics should be abstract and deductive reasoning, establishing the entire economic theory system from general propositions. *History of Economic Thought* (3rd Edition, Renmin University of China Press, edited by Yao Kaijian, p. 179).

There are numerous assumptions in various economic theories. An assumption provides certain premises or constraints, which accordingly determine the nature and boundaries. The conditions of an assumption are inversely related to the applicability of the theory; too many conditions reduce the theory's applicability. For the same issue, if there are many and very strict conditions, then the entire theory loses its generality and only applies to a very specific situation, thus losing its value. If limited assumptions are taken as the entire reality, then there is significant doubt about the logical basis of the theory. Just as if the foundation of a building is problematic, then even if the completed building may match some expectations, there will certainly be errors in terms of the overall structure or other related aspects.

The requirements for basic assumptions can be further analyzed from a mathematical perspective. Since economics studies the laws of economic operation, it can be expressed as a set of functions from a mathematical perspective. However, in reality, the involved factors are very complex. To facilitate theoretical analysis, it is necessary to refine the most essential characteristics, thus giving rise to assumptions or axioms. Generally speaking, the assumption function should belong to the set of real functions, and the ratio R of the assumption function to the real function should satisfy $0 < R \leq 1$ (this is an illustrative explanation, not a pursuit of mathematical rigor), to reflect the typical characteristics of the real function, being an abstraction of reality but not the entirety of reality. If the ratio of the assumption function to the real function is negative or greater than 1, then it is disconnected from reality and can represent partial factual characteristics at most, thus only partially explaining economic phenomena. Consequently, the inferences made are either difficult to fully reflect the real situation or provide conclusions that do not exist in reality. In a given scenario, the ratio of the assumption function to the real function should converge to a certain value and should not be a "discontinuity" of the function, presenting an absolute situation like the "rational economic man." No one can provide a situation that is or approximates the "rational economic man," meaning a typical "positive example" cannot be found.

2. The connotation of economic theory and analysis of basic assumptions

Views on the connotation of economics and its basic assumptions are not uniform, but there are several aspects that are crucial when considered collectively. Here, we focus on the concepts of economics and related important assumptions.

**Firstly, the definition or connotation of economics:** What exactly does economics study? Is it the study of scarcity, or the science of economic operation? This question seems simple but is very important and lies at the core of economic theory. It directly determines the scope and logic of research and is crucial for the entire process of theoretical derivation. Different schools may offer different definitions, but they mainly manifest as the two definitions mentioned above, and some definitions emphasize both meanings simultaneously. From a philosophical perspective, like other disciplines, the core of economics is the study of "states and changes," which actually provides the basic logic for the definition. Our principle is to agree with the most universal and basic meanings and not to endorse specific meanings, as specific meanings imply that economics studies a particular object. We should note that the title of Adam Smith's *An Inquiry into the Nature and Causes of the Wealth of Nations* intuitively tells us that economics studies the determinants and change laws in national wealth, without implying the study of scarcity. Scarcity belongs to a special meaning, because if economics is the study of scarcity, then the focus of research would be on resource allocation, and then in principle, many other aspects would be difficult to consider uniformly.

**Secondly, the assumption of the rational economic man:** This assumes that individuals are motivated by self-interest, striving to obtain the greatest economic benefits at the least economic cost. It can be said that the assumption of the rational economic man is the cornerstone upon which existing economic theories, especially market economy theories, are built. However, even those who believe in market economy theories agree that this assumption lacks a realistic foundation, or that it does not exist in reality. If a theory is based on an assumption that does not exist in reality, it is naturally difficult to satisfy people. Results deduced from an assumption that lacks a strong basis in reality are unlikely to align well with actual conditions. From the perspective of dialectical materialism, there should be logical unity among the reality of things, assumptions, and truth; otherwise, there will inevitably be a situation of various schools of thought arising from the same issue. However, in reality, we must acknowledge that theories based on the "rational economic man assumption" have indeed played an important role in market economies. This also indicates that assumptions are somewhat similar to important characteristics of reality or reflect certain key aspects of some phenomena. Therefore, theories based on this assumption offer partial explanations of reality and may be relatively accurate in certain situations that approximates to the reality, but this explanatory power should not be mistaken for a comprehensive one. Even Neoclassical economist Marshall's theories are not based on this strict assumption.[3]

Milton Friedman's 1953 work *The Methodology of Positive Economics* is a landmark book of its era. He emphasized that the realism of assumptions is independent of the validity of a theory, a view that is accepted but also highly controversial. One focus of the debate is whether economic assumptions should be realistic. Friedman argued that the less realistic, the better, while Samuelson believed that assumptions should reflect the real world. Coase offered a brilliant and compelling refutation, arguing that people accept a theory or doctrine not because it is proven by facts, but because the theory or doctrine provides us with inspirations, insights, new perspectives on the world, and new methods and paths for progress.

**The third is the assumption of perfect information**. In a market with perfect information, every individual engaged in economic activities (i.e., buyers and sellers) possesses complete information about the relevant economic conditions. Although there may be a trend toward this in reality, it is actually impossible to fully achieve.

3. What basic assumptions or axioms should economic theories be based on?

How should economic theories establish their most basic assumptions? This is a question worthy of in-depth study. Here, we examine the existing concepts and related assumptions of economics based on the strict standards previously mentioned. Current economic concepts and related assumptions often partially meet the standards. We believe they must reflect the most universal meanings in economics, rather than just specific aspects. From this perspective, defining economics as the study of the laws governing economic operations is more appropriate and satisfies the necessary and sufficient conditions. Defining economics as the study of scarcity is less appropriate. This is because, concerning the basic assumptions of the "rational economic man" and perfect information, even proponents

[3] He believes that "economists study an actual person, not an abstract or 'economic' person, but a person of flesh and blood." "A Review of the Ideas of 20 Influential Western Economists Who Changed the World," Bai Yongxiu and Ren Baoping, p. 158.

of market economies admit that these assumptions may not fully align with reality and are mainly established for theoretical convenience. Consequently, results derived from the models built on these assumptions will naturally deviate somewhat from reality.

Considering the various assumptions and the standards they should meet, we believe the following two basic assumptions or axioms are crucial, as they are both universal and realistic, satisfying the conditions of necessity and sufficiency.

The first basic assumption (axiom) is that economics is a science that studies the laws of economic operation, reflecting the dynamic relationships between economic variables.

The second basic assumption (axiom) is that market entities are a combination of rationality and irrationality, with rationality dominating. The pursuit of maximizing benefits is the basic tendency; the transformation of rights of market entities and elements comes with a cost; and the transaction costs are greater than zero, necessitating realization through equivalent exchange. Specialization is an inevitable choice in a market economy.

The first basic assumption (axiom) determines the economic laws and the relationships between economic variables, expressing the universal characteristics of economic operation in the real world. We know that Marx defined philosophy as the science of the universal laws of nature, society, and human thought. Correspondingly, economics is the science that studies the laws of economic operation, which is logically consistent. Defining economics as the study of scarcity gives it a very specific meaning, thus losing its universality. The second basic assumption (axiom) is the foundation of the market economy mechanism, determining the basic tendency of market entities to maximize benefits, the market-based approach to transfer rights, and the necessity of specialization. This assumption not only ensures the operation of the market economy mechanism but also aligns with reality. It avoids the strict conditions required by the "rational economic man" and encompasses the universal and realistic characteristics of Smith's theoretical logic, the "rational economic man" assumption, and Coase's theorem.

## 4. The logic of deriving economic principles from basic assumptions

Systematically analyzing economic principles from basic assumptions is a key task. We know that human understanding of science often begins with the local and gradually progresses to the whole. During this process, many people only recognize one or a few aspects, leading to confusion when facing the same issue due to different understandings. For example, during the COVID-19 pandemic, a large number of people faced the same problem, each with valid arguments, making the debate particularly pronounced. However, practice ultimately provided relatively reasonable conclusions for the relevant theories and logic. Professor Fang Fuqian has described this phenomenon in the field of economics.[4] As new theories are constantly established, the rational core of the original theories is retained, ultimately forming a relatively complete theoretical system. We will use the metaphor of blind men feeling an elephant to illustrate the basic logic of assumptions, modeling, and the analysis of principles.

**First, the establishment of basic assumptions.** By comprehensively inducing basic assumptions, we can define the research object and its essential characteristics. This is akin to many different blind men simultaneously feeling an elephant, or the same blind man feeling an elephant multiple times, ultimately providing a conclusion that closely represents the overall characteristics of the elephant, thus inducing corresponding assumptions or definitions, such as the elephant being an animal with a long trunk, tusks, and other features.

**Second, the formation and debate of partial theories.** It is very important to handle the relationship between the general and the specific. The general implies universality and broader applicability, although the generality of the whole is relative. The significance of the specific is that it provides the scope and boundaries of the research, making the research object concrete, which is also relative. For example, the research object of philosophy is the movement of the entire world, while the research object of economics is limited to the economic field. The specific essentially assumes that its external conditions remain unchanged or stable, based on which assumptions can be set and corresponding theories formed. In different processes of feeling the elephant, different theories or schools of thought are formed. For instance, those who felt the leg constructed the "leg theory" of the elephant, and those who felt the trunk constructed the "trunk theory" of the elephant. These theories are often based on

[4] *The Main Schools of Contemporary Western Economics* (Renmin University of China Press, Fang Fuqian, p. 12), any Western economic school's understanding of a specific economic issue is often only partially correct, and a complete and correct explanation cannot come from any single Western economic school or a single theory. This is like the blind men feeling the elephant; each person discovers only a part of the elephant, which is an organic part of the elephant's whole.

different assumptions, thus forming their respective theories. If the foundations and logic of understanding differ greatly, there may be significant debates, such as between the "leg theory" and the "trunk theory" of the elephant, which may have almost no common ground. If the same object is faced, different assumptions leading to different focuses and emphases will result in different schools of thought. For example, even if all feel the leg, different methods and parts felt might lead to varying theories or schools. However, this logic is sometimes very meaningful. In the subdivision of the research object, this logic can form different theories or disciplines, such as the subdivision of natural sciences including mathematics, physics, and chemistry. Therefore, defining the essential characteristics of the research object is crucial, and this is achieved through setting basic assumptions.

**Third, the formation and systematic explanation of a unified theoretical system.** The results of blind men touching the elephant should be able to reflect the true image of the elephant, including the overall and local features. This allows for the formulation of corresponding mathematical relationships or equations, and based on this, the deduction and analysis can fully reflect the main features of the elephant from the whole to the part. Mastering the overall image of the elephant can be achieved through two methods. On the one hand, the "nose theory" and the "leg theory" can be integrated to form a unified elephant theory to a certain extent; on the other hand, comprehensive analysis can be conducted based on the unified elephant theory, where the "nose theory" and the "leg theory" are merely special cases of the unified theory, and even new features that were previously unknown can be discovered through comprehensive analysis. From a mathematical perspective, this is equivalent to the general solution being a set or function of special solutions, which can explain the whole and special solutions can explain a specific aspect. The conclusion given by the theoretical elevation of many blind men touching the elephant and the deduction and analysis based on a complete understanding of the overall image of the elephant are unified. For example, the Neoclassical Synthesis should be a synthesis and elevation of classical and Keynesian theories. However, in the AD-AS model of the Neoclassical Synthesis, it is essentially an extension of the Keynesian theory AD model, a macroeconomic policy theory based on the logic of supply and demand in a market economy, which cannot reflect the elements of classical economics and seems to be inconsistent with the name of the Neoclassical Synthesis.

**Fourth, adherence to problem-oriented and practical testing.** Scientific exploration is a gradual process. When it is not possible to fully and clearly understand things, adhering to a problem-oriented approach is a better method for comprehensively understanding things and arriving at relatively unified conclusions. At this time, adhering to practical verification is very necessary and effective. The standard for determining whether economic theories are correct cannot simply rely on model results but should be based on practical outcomes. If the results do not match reality, then the assumptions or theories are likely problematic and require necessary adjustments. In the example of the elephant, if the given theory does not align with reality, it may explain the "legs and trunk" accurately but cause significant problems explaining the tusks, or even in extreme cases, describe the elephant as having a "horse's tail."

Economic theories should center on models that study causal relationships, as only causal connections can result in genuine equations. Economic causal relationships differ from the statistical relationships examined in econometrics. Causal relationships are fundamental and should serve as the basis for establishing theoretical models, while econometrics or statistics primarily play a role in validation. The statistical relationships illustrated by econometric models are merely correlations or predictive relationships and cannot be regarded as genuine economic causal relationships, though they remain meaningful.

### 1.3 Analysis of Theoretical Models Based on Two Basic Assumptions and Deductive Logic

Karl Marx once said, "A discipline is only truly scientific when it has reached the point where it can successfully apply mathematics." Therefore, if we can achieve a high degree of abstraction through assumptions by extracting the most universal, essential, and testable characteristics, and then use complete mathematical deduction to analyze and demonstrate economic principles, and finally apply these principles to guide practice, this would be a highly attractive task that could comprehensively enhance the scientific nature, recognition, and universality of economic theory.

1. The general logic and core equations of economic theory

From the first basic assumption, key equations that are universally significant in economic theory can be derived. In fact, Western scholars have proposed an equation as follows:

$$Y_t = F(K_t, L_t, A_t, N_t, S_t) \tag{11.1}$$

We know that the full title of *The Wealth of Nations* is "An Inquiry into the Nature and Causes of the Wealth of Nations," which essentially tells us that the object of economic study is to investigate the determinants and changes of wealth growth. Equation (11.1) can be seen as a specific expression of *The Wealth of Nations.* Here, $Y_t$ represents the total output of an economy, $K_t$, $L_t$, and $N_t$ represent capital, labor, and other stocks, respectively, and $A_t$ represents total factor productivity. $Y_t$ is the actual or potential total output.

If this formula is understood and interpreted in a broad sense, it will have more universal significance and value, that is, a function of $Y_t$ with related economic variables and with time. It is worth noting that if the variables in Eqn. (11.1) are understood as factors affecting economic growth, then this equation is quite extraordinary, as it can become an important foundation for economic theory or theories of economic growth. As a result, various schools of thought and theories of growth are merely variations and particularizations of this equation. Theoretically, this equation applies to various economic forms. However, due to the difficulty of mathematical treatment of general economic forms, the equation can only be said to have theoretical significance, and it is necessary to simplify it reasonably based on actual needs.

### 2. Theoretical model of the integration of market and government

We focus our research on the general market economy form, which satisfies the requirements of the second basic assumption. This allows us to decompose the various factors in the above formula into two categories: market and government roles, with the right-hand side of the equation mainly containing market and government effects. By determining the corresponding contributions through weights, we can form an economic growth equation that meets the criteria. It should be said that the above formula applies to various market economy models (such as the American model and the German model), but there will be certain differences in the parameters and variables under different market economy forms. In this way, we can uniformly consider the role of market and government in economic growth, determine the magnitude of their roles by assigning corresponding weights, and construct a relevant theoretical model.

In terms of market economy models, we can provide a set of simplified formulas, which are general market economic growth equations. For the sake of analysis, we will not use the general form here, but rather employ a specific form based on the logic of the market economy, which does not affect the results. The market effect part is based on the growth logic of Neoclassical Economics, and the government effect part is based on the growth logic of Keynesian theory, that is, the upgraded AD-AS model. It is composed of the following three equations:

$$\Delta Y_t = a\Delta Y_t^* + b\Delta Y_t \tag{11.2}$$

$$Y_t^* = f\left(K_t, L_t\right) = \lambda K_t^{\theta} L_t^{1-\theta} \tag{11.3}$$

$$\Delta \hat{Y}_t = \Delta AS + \Delta AD \tag{11.4}$$

Equation (11.2) can be seen as a simplification of Eqn. (11.1). The first part represents the effect of market factors, and the second part represents the effect of government factors. In Eqn. (11.2), $\Delta Y_t$ represents the change in the level of economic total output, $\Delta Y_t = Y_t - Y_{t-1}$. $\Delta Y_t^*$ represents the potential output under fully market economic conditions, which is the main part of the long-term trend. $\Delta \hat{Y}_t$ represents the change brought about by the government effect. The parameters $a$ and $b$ represent weights, and in an ideal "effective market and proactive government" situation, their sum is 1. In Eqn. (11.3), $\lambda$ is a constant, K represents capital, L represents labor, and the parameters $\theta$ and $1 - \theta$ respectively represent the capital output elasticity and labor output elasticity. In Eqn. (11.4), $\Delta AS$ represents shocks from the supply side, and $\Delta AD$ represents shocks from the demand side.

It is worth noting that, from a mathematical logic perspective, this equation set also reflects the integration of Neoclassical Economics and Keynesian Economics. However, there is a significant difference between this equation set and the logic of the Neoclassical Synthesis: firstly, the equation set embodies the combination of market and government roles, no longer merely reflecting the government's role in effective demand or the government part of the AD-AS model, but an equation that includes the complete role of both market and government, which can reflect the corresponding micro foundations. Secondly, the market and the government can both function relatively independently, with the government's role no longer being an auxiliary to the market's role. Thirdly, the equation is a complete equation based on mathematical logic, and to some extent, it can also be used to explain the basis and foundation for the Neoclassical Synthesis being considered by the mainstream economics.

This model differs from previous economic theories that were based solely on the premise of a pure market economy. The differences between the major schools of thought are reflected through the size of the market effect parameters. The above equation can be further processed to derive formula (11.5). Formula (11.5) can be seen as the growth equation of dynamic macroeconomic theory, based on the combined economic growth equation of market and government.

$$\Delta Y_t = (a + b\Delta A_t)\Delta Y_t^* + b(\mu_{ss} + \mu_d)(Y_t - Y_{t-1}) + b(\varepsilon_{st} + \varepsilon_{dt}) \quad (11.5)$$

In essence, formula (11.5) represents a significant innovation in thinking and can be called the market-government rational comprehensive model, with profound economic significance. It maintains consistency with the Neoclassical Synthesis based on the logic of a mixed economy, and we will refer to the theoretical exposition based on this model as "Rational Comprehensive Economics."

3. Analysis of government's role

**A re-evaluation and fine analysis of government's role is an important** foundation for comprehensively considering the roles of both the government and the market. Through an intuitive analysis of Fig. 11.1, economic growth at a certain point in time can be seen as the superposition of three parts, which is essentially a fine decomposition of the roles of government and market in economic growth. The first part represents the potential output under a free market or without government intervention; the second part represents the impact of government's role on long-term or potential economic growth; and the third part represents short-term economic fluctuations. From the perspective of transition, government also plays an important role, which is to release productivity significantly by promoting market-oriented reforms and promote a significant increase in the first part (potential growth rate without government intervention). During China's reform and opening up, especially in the initial stage, the economic growth effect brought about by market-oriented reforms was very obvious. Even today, relevant measures of China's market-oriented reforms can still effectively stimulate market vitality and promote

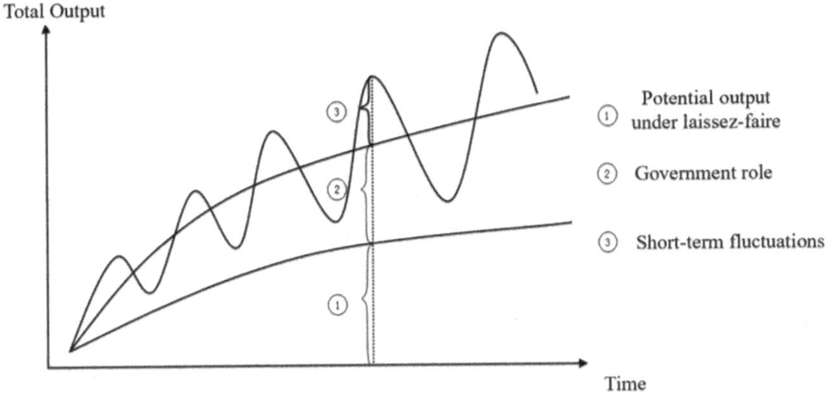


**Fig. 11.1** Decomposition of government and market roles

economic growth. However, it should be noted that this is the government's role in promoting transition and should be distinguished from the role of government as regulator under market economy conditions.

4. About the complete macro-regulation policy framework system and the corresponding empirical research

By constructing an economic theory analysis framework with the growth equation as the core, we can draw new conclusions. It is noteworthy that macro-regulation theory, as a control system integrating both supply-side and demand-side management, manages both sides throughout, with the policy emphasis varying at different stages according to the prominence of aggregate and structural economic issues. At the same time, there are also significant differences in terms of macroeconomic policy objectives. Keynesian theory outlines four major objectives of macroeconomic policy: economic growth, full employment, price stability, and balance of international payments. However, these objectives all stem from Keynesian effective demand theory and do not reflect indicators such as supply-side structural reform. Therefore, they should be appropriately adjusted: firstly, from the demand side, the two objectives of economic growth and full employment determined by Keynes can be unified as economic growth; secondly, from the supply side, the goal of structural optimization needs to be added; thirdly, from the perspective of imbalance and balance between aggregate supply and aggregate demand, an additional financial stability indicator should be included to coordinate price stability and maintain the risk bottom line; fourthly, the objective of balance of international payments can be retained, but its connotation needs to be further deepened. In summary, we can adjust the objectives of macro-regulation or macroeconomic policy to: economic growth, structural optimization, financial stability, and balance of international payments.

5. About the evaluation standards of market economy and the path choice for transition and reform

As can be seen from Fig. 8.1, various market economy models should all be located on the curve, with different positions reflecting different levels of marketization. Generally speaking, an economic entity with a market role weight exceeding 50% can be considered a market economy model. However, if it is an ideal market economy model, the weight of market role should be even higher. Clearly, the market economy model of China is not a "yes or no" difference from other typical market models, but a difference in "degree." It can be said that a system where the market plays a decisive role and that combines an "effective market" with a "proactive government" belongs to the market economy model. From this, we can draw an important conclusion that the market economy model is diverse. At the same time, attention should be paid to the optimal point or balance point between government and market, as this is also the reasonable boundary of government's role.

### 1.4 Unified Logical Analysis of the Evolution of Economic Theories and Schools

Economic theories are continuously evolving; the original theories should not be completely overturned. The reasonable and useful content should be retained and given new life in the new era, evolving into a part of the basic principles and the core of economic theory. The relationships and laws among the variables of an economic entity's economic operation should be fundamentally determined, and there should not be two or more economic theories and explanations, or even multiple contradictory situations. The complexity of history lies in the fact that from the early debates among economic schools to Hayek and Keynes' "century-long battle" in economics, to the later "salt and fresh water" debate, the disputes continue to this day. However, when we see that different schools always emphasize building their own theories on the basis of overturning others, it also seems very strange.

Each school of economics generally has its own basic logic, and due to differences in basic logic, there are obvious differences between different schools. Even within the same or similar schools, there may be certain differences. For example, there are obvious differences between classical economic theory and Keynesian theory; there are also differences even among different representatives of the classical economic school who emphasize the market. However, because our research object is the market economy mechanism, the relationship between government and market should be the focus and core of the research. Therefore, our goal is to grasp the main contradictions and solve the problem of the relationship between the market and the government. It is like a group of people holding bottles of saltwater, arguing fiercely about which one is saltier or less salty. A simple solution is to eliminate the saltiness differences caused by various special factors and focus on a clear core standard, such as the salt content per 100 grams of water. With this core standard, accurate comparisons can be made. Therefore, it is very important to find the comparable logic and core standards. From the perspective of rational integration of the market and the government, that is, using the aforementioned model and Eqn. (11.2) to analyze economic theories or schools according to a unified logic, we can clarify the evolution context, spectrum, and basic characteristics of economic schools.

1. About classical and neoclassical economics theories

The classical economic school represents a typical market economy theory, where the role of government is very limited and stable. This theory emphasizes that the optimal way of resource allocation is through complete market mechanisms (the invisible hand). Adam Smith's representative work, *The Wealth of Nations*, explores wealth growth and its determinants. The Neoclassical school, on the other hand, focuses on the market's role in resource allocation and systematically elaborates on the specific content of market mechanisms. The second basic assumption provides a foundation for establishing and improving the market economy mechanism. In this context, both classical and neoclassical economics belong to the school that emphasizes the absolute dominance of the market, with a very limited role for the government. This is equivalent to that the second term in Eqn. (11.2) has a relatively small weight, or approaches to zero, for example, at 5% level, or approaches to zero as represented by coefficient $a$ close to 1 and coefficient $b$ close to zero. For mathematical analysis, it is also convenient to assume a special case where $a = 1$ and $b = 0$, which yields results that are more in line with theoretical expectations. This is actually a common practice among the neoclassical economic school. Classical economists adhere to Say's Law, which posits that supply can automatically create demand, which is a special scenario where aggregate supply is significantly less than aggregate demand, and the market operates relatively normally (under certain conditions) in accordance with Eqn. (11.4).

2. About Keynesian theory

Keynes replaced the static equilibrium analysis method of classical economic theory with a comparative static analysis method in *The General Theory*, and replaced the price theory of the classical school with output and employment theory, thus proposing the theory of effective demand, which holds that demand determines output. The emergence of Keynesian theory led to a shift from free market to government intervention in Western countries and marked the birth of modern macroeconomics. Keynesian theory emphasizes the role of government while considering the market's role as a basic condition, which is equivalent to the first term in Eqn. (11.2) being relatively stable and considered a constant, while the second term is more important, focusing only on the second term; and treating the aggregate supply in Eqn. (11.4) as a fixed value, analyzing demand (AD), or more precisely, analyzing how effective demand affects economic growth. Therefore, from a model perspective, the main body of the Keynesian theory model is the AD model. At this point, the market plays a decisive role, which is relatively stable, but compared to the free market state, the role of the government in the Keynesian theory is significantly amplified. It means that $a$ can equal a certain value, for example, 0.7, but $b = 0.3$, which is clearly greater than zero. However, in the Keynesian theory model, there is no element or variable associated with $a$, making it difficult to analyze this, which leads to its being questioned for lacking a microeconomic foundation. The debate between Hayek and Keynes in the 1930s, known as the most important debate in the field of economic theory in the twentieth century, had a significant impact on economic and social development for a long period. The views of the two sides were clearly different, but the core was still the difference in the roles of the market and the government, specifically manifested as the difference in the proportion of *a* or *b* values.

3. Neoclassical synthesis—the logical basis of mainstream economics

Paul Samuelson (1973, 1979) attempted to integrate classical economics and Keynesian economics, and provided a more comprehensive explanation of the mixed economy. He proposed the aggregate supply-aggregate demand model[5] to explain the economic stagflation in the United States at that time, marking the formation of the Neoclassical Synthesis. Samuelson's AD-AS model was a comprehensive synthesis of the economic thoughts of various schools at that time, later incorporating Keynesianism, classical economics, monetarism, supply-side school, rational expectations school, and modern macroeconomics. It is worth noting that the AD-AS model should be seen as an extension of the Keynesian AD model, reflecting the comprehensive role of government in influencing aggregate demand and aggregate supply. However, it did not provide a mathematical explanation of how this integration was achieved within the classical school. Moreover, Samuelson still viewed the role of government as an auxiliary to the market, believing that the "visible hand" of government intervention in the economy should aim to fully play the role of the "invisible hand" of the market.

If a relationship can be expressed from a mathematical model or formula perspective, achieving a true synthesis would be more persuasive. However, if one only stays at the AD-AS model level, there is no problem in analyzing the role of government, but since it fails to consider the comprehensive role of the market, it becomes impossible to analyze the relevant market role and micro-foundations. In other words, Samuelson's model starts from Keynes' analysis of effective demand and expands to a more comprehensive AD-AS model. However, the model still only considers the government's role and does not achieve a complete integration with the classical school from a mathematical perspective. This still makes it, like other theories, a partial model, making it difficult to fully analyze the logic of economic theory. But Eqn. (11.2) provides a comprehensive

[5] Samuelson introduced the AD-AS model in his book *Economics* (12th edition) (1985, co-authored with Nordhaus), where he attempted to present this model as an alternative to the original IS-LM model, serving as the core method or tool for analyzing macroeconomic issues.

and clear expression, which can be seen as a unified model of the Neoclassical Synthesis, explaining the comprehensive role of the market and the government, as well as the micro-foundations, and also the logic of Neoclassical Synthesis being considered the mainstream economics.

Since the 1970s, there has been a special term in the American economics community—the "salt and fresh water" debate, which refers to the prolonged debate between the "salt water school" and the "fresh water school" in the mainstream economics community. The differences between the two are mainly reflected in their understanding of the relationship between the market and the government, their interpretation of economic fluctuations, and their advocacy for government intervention policies, etc. In essence, the "salt and fresh water" debate is a concentrated reflection of the development of modern macroeconomics in the debate between schools. Whether it is the "salt water" school or the "fresh water" school, from the above formula, it is essentially just a difference in relevant parameters or variables. Since the 2008 financial crisis, the macro environment faced by the global economy has undergone significant changes, which has further prompted the economics community to reflect on macroeconomic theory. Today, the macroeconomic theory is developing towards a unified and integrated direction.

4. Neoliberal economics

In the 1970s and 1980s, the American economy faced severe "stagflation," leading to doubts about Keynesian theory. Neoliberal economics emerged as a response, with monetarism, supply-side school, and rational expectations school as its typical representatives. Mathematically, this is akin to the market effect part in Eqn. (11.2) becoming larger, with the value of parameter $a$ increasing, for example, from $a = 0.80$ to $a = 0.70$, indicating a reduction in the government's role. Monetarism focuses on monetary factors in Eqns. (11.1) or (11.2), refining and specifying related monetary factors while treating other factors as constants. The supply-side economics school opposes Keynesianism, analyzing only the AS term in Eqn. (11.2), corresponding to the AD term in the Keynesian theory, which is also the logical basis for Say's Law and Keynes' Law.

Given the relevance between rational expectations theory and the real business cycle model (RBC model), we will only analyze the logic that holds for the RBC model. The RBC model posits that the production function is influenced by actual factors such as random technological shocks and policy shocks, leading to cyclical and fluctuating economic patterns. The RBC model's basic characteristic is that it integrates the growth theory and the fluctuation theory, breaking the binary division of short-term and long-term in macroeconomic analysis. To facilitate our analysis, we rewrite Eqn. (11.5) into the form of Eqn. (11.6).

$$Y_t = Y_t^* + \alpha A_t + \beta G_t + \varepsilon_t \quad (11.6)$$

Wherein, $Y_t^*$ is the potential growth rate under pure market conditions without government intervention; $\alpha A_t$ explains the impact of technological changes on potential output; $\beta G_t$ reflects the possible impact of policies; and the disturbance term $\varepsilon_t$ represents various random factors. From the above formula, it can be seen that the first term represents potential output under no shock conditions and can be represented by the production function, consistent with the Solow (R.M. Solow) growth model. The second term reflects the impact of technological shocks on potential output. The third term can be used to explain or study the impact of government policies; if policies have no impact, it implies policy neutrality.

From a global perspective, the market economy is not always powerful and has limitations. However, comprehensive government intervention also challenges traditional economic theories. In recent years, China's practice has proven that a complete transition to the traditional planned economy model is not feasible. It is necessary to move towards a market economy path, which is different from the so-called Western market economy model. In this model, the government should play a better role. The organic combination of the two is a more effective economic development model. The decisive role of the market is crucial, but the government's role should have an appropriate boundary.

5. Logical analysis of theories on economic growth and business cycles

Western economics has a long history and has formed a vast system, including theories on economic growth and business cycles, but these theories all have their own different premises or assumptions, equivalent to special solutions under certain conditions. If we can explain these theories with a unified formula or method, and use general solutions to explain special solutions, we can profoundly reflect the unity and scientific nature of economic theory. Here, we will take economic growth and business cycle theories as examples for simple explanation and illustration.[6]

**About the Solow Growth Model**: The economic growth theory is the core of economic theory, and Adam Smith's *An Inquiry into the Nature and Causes of the Wealth of Nations* can be seen as the logical starting point for economic growth theory, which can be used as a basis for deductive reasoning on the entire economic theory. Equation (11.1) or Eqn. (11.2) is essentially an economic growth equation, which can be transformed into various economic growth models based on different assumptions. For example, by transforming Eqn. (11.1) or Eqn. (11.2), considering that the potential growth rate is the focus, if we do not consider the government's short-term role or treat it as a constant, the equation can be converted into the familiar potential economic growth formula. Furthermore, when it comes to the government's role in structural changes on the supply side, we need to consider the impact of technological changes or changes in total factor productivity on potential economic growth, which can be transformed into the Solow economic growth model that considers technological progress.

**About Business Cycle Theory**: Business cycles should be the cyclical manifestation of actual economic growth and do not require a potential economic growth fluctuation that cannot be measured. Therefore, economic growth theory and business cycle theory are unified. Equation (11.2) as an overlay of economic growth trend and fluctuation reflects the cyclical fluctuations in actual economic growth. This is also the reason why theories on business cycles, such as those by Juglar, are generally concluded through statistical analysis of actual economic data, and it is also the logical basis and foundation for the unity of economic growth theory and business cycle theory under the RBC model. It is worth noting that Samuelson's multiplier-accelerator model deeply considers the interaction between multiplier and accelerator, establishing a macroeconomic dynamic system. This model shows cyclical fluctuations through the calculation of real data, thus reflecting the dynamics of the actual economy. Essentially, this is a simplified dynamic economic growth equation, and it provides solutions to economic growth, which are consistent with the basic logic of Eqn. (11.2). In a sense, Samuelson's multiplier-accelerator model not only explains business cycles but also, as a simplified dynamic economic

[6] Refer to *The Chinese Exploration of Economic Theory Innovation - From the Perspective of Theoretical Models* (published by Renmin University of China Press, May 2022).

equation, can be used to explain relevant theories on business cycles and to well argue the conditions for the establishment of Say's Law.

6. The relationship between the Chinese story and the theoretical model of market-government integration

Here, we briefly analyze the relationship between the Chinese story and the theoretical model of market-government integration. Since the beginning of reform and opening up, China has achieved rapid economic development, maintaining an average annual economic growth rate close to 10%, creating a "miracle" in human economic development history. The Third Plenary Session of the 18th CPC Central Committee proposed to make the market play a decisive role in resource allocation and better leverage the role of the government, which is a high-level summary of the socialist market economic model. China's successful practice has demonstrated a basic logic and concept of the coordination of government and market, and has promoted the relationship between government and market from opposition to unity. The Chinese story transcends the understanding of the relationship between government and market in Western economic theory, representing a new paradigm of economic theory innovation.

China's successful experience shows the world that since the roles of government and market can be combined, a theoretical model of an "effective market" combined with a "proactive government" can be constructed. This model also uses quantitative methods to tell the story of China's market economic theory innovation, thus achieving the sublimation of economic theory innovation. The innovative economic thinking from China's practice represents a unified economic logic, breaking the typical pattern of special logic commonly found in various economic schools. From the perspective of the theoretical model, the size of the market's role can be quantified, manifested as different proportions. When the market plays a decisive role, it means that the market's role should at least exceed 50%, but from the perspective of the market's efficient role, the rate is usually higher, for example, 70%. Theoretically, there will be a balance point or boundary for the roles of government and market in a specific economy, and in principle, the government's role should not exceed this boundary.

It is clear that the Chinese story and the theoretical model of market-government integration are consistent and unified. On the one hand, the

Chinese story is the source and driving force of the theoretical model, providing important basis and foundation for the construction of the theoretical model and promoting economic theory innovation based on China's experience. On the other hand, the theoretical model of market-government integration can well explain the logic of the Chinese story and guide China's practice. Moreover, since the economic theory sublimation and innovation based on China's practice are universal, it has broader applicability, providing new options for countries across the globe to choose their economic development models and theories.

### *1.5 The Future of Economic Theory Innovation and Transformation*

Economic theory should be a complete and unified theoretical system, as well as an evolving and innovating system. China's successful practice has provided an important source and impetus for the innovation and sublimation of contemporary economic theory, and the logic behind this innovation is universal. Economic theory innovation based on China's successful practice not only inherits and develops modern economic theory but also sublimates China's practical experience; it can guide the high-quality development of Chinese economy and also provide new choices for other countries or regions.

1. On the universality and authenticity of assumptions

Economic assumptions should be a highly generalized description of the essential characteristics of economic phenomena and should be the most basic assumptions. They should not only meet the unity of universality and authenticity but also fulfill the core requirements of necessity and sufficiency. Assumptions or axioms that embody these traits are the foundation for building economic theory and can become the "weapon" that enhances the scientific brand of economic theory. The rational economic man assumption is the cornerstone of existing economic theory, but it is inconsistent with people's experiences and perceptions and does not integrate with the practice of China's market economy. While the logic of pure market economy can be understood based on this assumption, it is difficult to accept that the logic of Keynesian theory, as an opposing force, also relies on this foundation. The Neoclassical Synthesis combines neoclassical theory with Keynesian theory, seemingly making the rational economic man assumption the basis for multiple economic schools. As Professor Lin Yifu emphasizes the rational economic man assumption as the starting point of modern economics, he also emphasizes the importance of studying different phenomena with an unconstrained attitude of always being prepared to adjust one's views.

Regarding the reality of assumptions, the industry generally agrees with Friedman's view. Friedman believes that as long as a theory's predictions are consistent with reality, the authenticity of its underlying assumptions is not the most important. We believe that how to measure the level of consistency between predictions and reality is crucial. Since assumptions can always describe some important features, they are necessarily effective in explaining some features or phenomena, but this does not prove their rationality for the whole. When different economists describe the characteristics of the same object using different assumptions, economic theory naturally presents a scene of various schools. Different schools often uphold the correctness of their theories by focusing on the aspects they can explain and criticize or oppose other theories accordingly.

2. The unity of economic theory and logic: Krugman's dream fulfilled

For economic theory, while we may not be able to provide a unified theory and logic similar to those in physics and mathematics, it should be said that the core logic and principles must still have a high degree of unity. The scientific truth and laws of the same object can be gradually improved in the process of understanding, but the highest level should be logical unity. Through both induction and deduction, two different methods of research on the same object should not yield two or more results. We believe that: the unity of ontology, dialectics, and epistemology should be maintained. The essence (the truth of things) is the logical foundation for the entire "unity" and determines the basic characteristics of epistemology and truth, which is the cornerstone for unifying the scattered doctrines within the same science. We hope that Chinese economists can make their due contributions to the innovation and development of economic theories and play a better role in the practice of China and even related countries based on the successful practice of the Chinese story, through the construction of a unified market-government integration model and theoretical system.

3. The relationship between market and government roles shifts from opposition to unity, finding the balance point of market and government relations

The relationship between market and government roles has always been a focal point of debate in Western economic theory. The root of this continuous debate lies in the lack of a common foundation for the premises of the debate, the existence of fundamental differences, and the fact that each side is essentially talking about their own perspectives. It is necessary to view the issue from a higher level of unity to reduce the differences. Since the market and the government have relatively independent and important roles, if a theory cannot explain the rationality of these roles, it indicates that the theory inherently has defects. Practice has already proven that both the market and the government can play important roles and should no longer be trapped in the "either-or" thinking. In the future, macroeconomics will further develop towards a unified and integrated direction based on a deeper understanding of the relationship between government and market, and it is crucial to grasp the balance point.

4. Building a unified rational synthesis model of market and government roles based on the reality of mixed economy

Given that the real economy is a mixed economy, it requires transforming the relationship between the market and the government from an opposing relationship to a higher level of unity, thereby establishing a theoretical model of the organic combination of market and government roles and proposing the corresponding macroeconomic policy system. This is just as the development of medicine which has led to the formation of a system of traditional Chinese medicine theory and techniques based on China's practice and a system of Western medicine theory and techniques based on Western practice. Both of the two branches of medicine have their advantages and limitations, and their organic combination is the direction of future development. For example, the understanding of light based on the assumption that light is a wave led to the establishment of the wave theory of light, while the assumption that light is a particle led to the establishment of corresponding theories. However, from a higher perspective, light has the dual properties of both wave and particle, and the establishment of the wave-particle duality theory allows for a comprehensive understanding of light phenomena.

The logic of China's market economy theory is an evolving theoretical system that will continue to improve in the practice of comprehensively deepening reform in China. In the future, it will play a more important role. China's market economy theory not only originated from the great practice of reform and opening up but also aligns with the trend of the unprecedented changes in the world over the past century. While playing the decisive role of the market, the better role of the government is both a rational choice and the most effective path for economic development. China's practical experience and theoretical innovation are an exploration of universal models and theories, providing new economic theory models and fair evaluation standards for not only China, but also countries around the world.

## 2 Theoretical Analysis of the Scenarios and Conditions for the Establishment of Say's Law

Say's Law is a crucial proposition in economic theory, considered to be the cornerstone of modern economic theory, especially market economy theory. The French economist Jean-Baptiste Say (1767–1832) expounded Say's Law in his 1803 book *Economic and Political Catechism*, which can be simply stated as "supply creates its own demand." However, its existence and the conditions under which it operates have been subject to debate. The debate on Say's Law mainly focuses on the qualitative aspects, with relatively little quantitative research. Proving or arguing it theoretically is a significant issue. In reality, we find that under certain conditions, there are situations very close to the establishment of Say's Law, which have corresponding explanatory power for reality. This section analyzes the scenarios and conditions for the establishment of Say's Law from the perspective of the multiplier-accelerator model.

### 2.1 Introduction

Say was one of the earliest scholars to examine capitalist business cycles from a macro perspective. It was insightful, especially when economic crises were not yet evident. The core idea of Say's Law is that supply creates demand, aimed at addressing a major issue frequently debated in the early nineteenth century, namely whether capitalism would lead to general overproduction.

1. Evolution and role of Say's Law

Say believed that the economy generally does not experience production overcapacity crises, let alone employment shortages. Most classical economists believed in Say's Law, but Malthus introduced the concept of effective demand to refute it. Marx's exposition of the economic crisis of overproduction was even more contrary to Say's Law. Marshall agreed with Say's Law that supply and demand were always equal, but there were also problems difficult to explain.

The 1929–1933 Great Depression challenged Say's Law, revealing its failure. The crisis showed that Say's Law did not hold true. Keynes criticized Say's Law from the perspective of effective demand theory in his 1936 book *The General Theory of Employment, Interest, and Money*. In Keynes' theory, savings and investment are mutually opposed, and savings do not necessarily lead to investment, and supply does not necessarily lead to demand, either. This negates the short-term applicability of Say's Law. Supply does not necessarily create demand, and ineffective supply only leads producers into a predicament. Severe oversupply will inevitably lead to an economic crisis. Keynes provided corresponding conclusions: demand automatically creates supply. Keynes believed that market does not operate as efficiently as assumed, and Say's Law only held true in the long term. We believe that the logic of Say's Law corresponding to Keynes' Law is itself evidence of its establishment under certain conditions.

Since the 1970s, the rise of Western neoliberalism, including supply-side school, rational expectations school, and other schools, has highly praised Say's Law. After the so-called rational expectations revolution in the 1970s, Say's Law has been revived as a core assumption in neolassical macroeconomics and is now prevalent in mainstream macroeconomics. In recent years, China's proposed supply-side structural reform, although logically different from Say's Law, also has some common characteristics.

2. Scholars' views and debates on Say's Law

Keynes believed that the classical school's faith in Say's Law and their neglect of effective demand resulted in a very fragile foundation for economic theory. The supply curve and the demand curve overlap, which is clearly impossible for either individual or total economies. Effective demand does not have a single equilibrium value but a series of infinitely many equally permissible equilibrium values. However, Keynes still believed that as long as the correct macroeconomic policies were implemented to make investment equal to savings under full employment, Say's Law could be established. This indicates that Keynes' criticism of Say's Law is not entirely justified, as he even believed that under certain conditions, Say's Law is valid, but he had not found the prerequisites for its establishment.

The supply-side school that emerged in the 1970s advocated restoring the role of "Say's Law," arguing that demand should be created by supply-side factors without increasing social productivity. They believed that stimulating demand alone without improving productivity would only lead to inflation and not increase output. This school believed that the 1929–1933 Great Depression was not due to insufficient effective demand but to a series of inappropriate policies implemented by Western governments at the time. They claimed that Say's Law was completely correct, while Keynes' Law was wrong. An important representative of the supply-side school, Arthur Laffer, emphasized the significant meaning of Say's Law, pointing out that it not only summarized classical economic theory but also confirmed that supply was the only source for maintaining actual demand. The rational expectations school also agreed with the logic of Say's Law, indicating the further "revival" of liberal thought, which sought to return to the era of "laissez-faire" in the capitalist world economy, allowing Adam Smith's "invisible hand" and "Say's Law" to guide economic operations.

In comparison, the supporters primarily explain their views from the supply side, emphasizing the rationality of Say's Law. The opponents criticize from the demand side, arguing that Say's Law neglects the characteristics, expectations, and influencing factors of demand, leading to the limitations of Say's Law. In the debate, it is a typical "either-or" situation, with one side emphasizing the overthrowing of the other's view. Overall, the debate on Say's Law mainly focuses on the qualitative aspects, with most scholars using their own theories to either endorse or criticize Say's Law. Few scholars conduct comprehensive analyses from the perspective of theoretical models to point out the scenarios and conditions under which Say's Law exists.

### 2.2 *Basic Proposition, Value, and Limitations of Say's Law*

Say, based on his fundamental logic of supply creating its own demand, arrived at an important conclusion: under economic freedom, the more developed the production, the greater the demand, the more popular the products, and the greater the profit.

1. Basic proposition of Say's Law

The main propositions of Say's Law include: first, "supply creates its own demand," with buying and selling always being in balance; second, production can create demand for products, and money serves as a medium of exchange; third, temporary oversupply of certain products is possible, but complete oversupply of the entire production is not, implying that capitalism does not have the possibility of economic crises. Deducting from Say's Law, if the market is not interfered with, producers will continue to use various production factors, eventually leading to full employment in the entire economy, where money only functions as a medium of exchange. In this so-called completely free market economy, since supply creates its own demand, the total social demand is always equal to supply, and the cash balance is zero, with actual economic growth equaling potential economic growth. Mathematically, Say's Law can be expressed as:

$$D_n \equiv S_n; \tag{11.7}$$

$$D_n - S_n \equiv \Delta M \equiv 0; \tag{11.8}$$

$$Y_t \equiv Y^* \tag{11.9}$$

Where $Y_t$ and $Y^*$ represent actual economic growth and potential economic growth, respectively. Clearly, if these equations can be proven mathematically, it would demonstrate the conditions under which Say's Law holds true, and which correspond to specific economic scenarios. Equation (11.7) represents the equilibrium level of supply and demand under certain conditions, while Eqn. (11.9) represents the long-term growth trend of the economy, equivalent to the absence or imperceptibility of short-term fluctuations.

2. The value and limitations of Say's Law

**As a pillar of economic theory, especially classical economics**, Say's Law originated in the early stages of capitalist development and has a specific historical background. In the late eighteenth to early nineteenth centuries, French capitalism was just in its infancy, the Industrial Revolution was booming, and the bourgeoisie accumulated enormous wealth, with very strong demand. However, due to continuous wars, France experienced a period of production slump, leading to severe shortages. Under these circumstances, demand was not the primary consideration, and supply increase was the most important basis for economic development. It is evident that while Say's Law considers both supply and demand, its focus is still on the supply side, which is a fundamental aspect of classical economics. Within the framework of classical and neoclassical economics, the theoretical research on economic growth naturally focuses on factors that affect potential economic growth rates, such as capital, labor, and technological inputs on the supply side, and actual economic growth rates naturally converge towards potential economic growth rates.

**As an important foundation for the existence of the market mechanism,** Say's Law emphasizes that free competitive capitalism has a self-regulating mechanism that will balance supply and demand in the production of goods. Interest rates can automatically regulate consumption, savings, and investment, making savings equal to investment. Ultimately, goods are always exchanged for other goods. This logic is an important foundation for the existence of the market mechanism and is generally accepted by classical economists, even Keynesianism does not completely negate it, and free-market economists regard it as a guiding principle. The faith in the market held by classical economic theory has been inherited by contemporary mainstream neoclassical macroeconomics, which uses the concept of general equilibrium to describe market mechanisms, implicitly assuming the validity of Say's Law. Ideas about production structure, scale, and the matching of supply and demand of Say's Law still have reference value for modern economic development.

**The limitations of Say's Law are as follows**: First, there are instances where Say's Law fails, especially during the 1929–1933 Great Depression, which clearly demonstrated the limitations of the market's self-regulating mechanism. Second, the emphasis on market mechanisms often leads to the neglect or dismissal of the government's role, disregarding the purpose of supply, which is to meet the changes in demand and its characteristics. This imbalance prevents a comprehensive consideration of economic growth that takes into account both aggregate supply and aggregate demand. Third, Say's Law does not specify the conditions under which it holds true, making it susceptible to selective interpretation and application.

3. Comments on the essence of Say's Law

Through the above analysis, we gain a clearer understanding of the essence of Say's Law: first, Say's Law is a special manifestation of the business cycle under certain conditions, which is a reality under those conditions. Its counterpart, in contrast, is the typical situation of an economic crisis. The analyses of both sides are based on their respective focuses, leading to the ongoing debate between the two sides. It is precisely because each side has grasped important characteristics that their respective theories have become the core foundations. Second, the logical basis of Say's Law is the logic of the business cycle, being the result of the cycle's invisible manifestation rather than its non-existence. It is not that there is no cycle, but rather that it appears as if there is no overproduction or economic crisis. Third, since the conditions under which Say's Law exists are simply cases where the business cycle does not significantly manifest itself, the essence of these conditions is that the business cycle does not manifest itself significantly, or that the amplitude of the cycle's fluctuations converges rapidly over time, leading to a long-term trend towards balance. Fourthly, the scenarios and theoretical models in which Say's Law holds true can be expanded from the perspective of the business cycle.

### 2.3 Building a Theoretical Model Based on the Extension of the Multiplier-Accelerator Principle

Here, we employ a theoretical model based on the extension of the multiplier-accelerator principle to analyze the manifestations of the business cycle under different conditions, especially when the business cycle exists but its amplitude converges rapidly over time, leading to the actual economic growth aligning with the potential economic growth. This approach aims to demonstrate the scenarios and conditions under which Say's Law holds true.

1. Basic logic for choosing the extension of the multiplier-accelerator principle to construct the theoretical model

The extension of the multiplier-accelerator principle provides a highly effective means to explain Say's Law. In terms of content, Say's Law asserts that capitalist cycles do not exist, indicating its close relationship with the existence and manifestation of business cycles. The verification can be conducted from the perspective of business cycles, followed by an elucidation of the basic relationship between supply and demand; the multiplier-accelerator principle is used to analyze business cycles and reveals the inherent connection between investment and consumption in economic operations. Therefore, the construction of the theoretical model aligns with the content of business cycle theory. In terms of the internal logical relationship, the core of Say's Law is the relationship between supply and demand, also involving the relationship between investment and savings. The multiplier-accelerator principle can dynamically analyze the relationship between supply and demand. In terms of implementation, the multiplier-accelerator principle are essentially simplified economic growth equations. The model's second-order difference equation effectively addresses the cyclical issue. Previous research by us using the multiplier-accelerator principle for business cycle studies has shown a good fit between the two.

2. Model construction based on the extension of the multiplier-accelerator model and the corresponding results

Samuelson (1939) proposed the multiplier-accelerator model, a simplified dynamic economic equation that holds significant importance for the analysis of business cycles. This model allows for the analysis of Say's Law, as expressed by the following set of equations:

$$\begin{cases} Y_t = C_t + I_t + G_t \\ C_t = cY_{t-1}\ (t = 0,1,2\ldots) \\ I_t = (a/c)(C_t - C_{t-1}) \end{cases} \tag{11.10}$$

Wherein, $Y_t$, $C_t$,$I_t$ and $G_t$ respectively represent total income, total consumption, total investment, and government spending. The marginal propensity to consume is represented by $c$, and the accelerator by $a$. The detailed derivation of this model is presented in the fifth part of Chap. 6 of this book, and the results are directly cited here.

The necessary condition for business cycles to exist is $\Delta < 0$, that is, the accelerator $a$ meets the following boundary conditions:

$$A_d = 2 - c - 2\sqrt{1-c} < a < 2 - c + 2\sqrt{1-c} = A_u \tag{11.11}$$

Wherein, $A_d$ represents the minimum value of $a$ that satisfies the condition for the existence of business cycles, while $A_u$ represents the maximum value of $a$ under the same condition. Based on the research findings of Ji Yao (2017) and China's actual economic data, we calibrated the marginal propensity to consume as 0.4, that is, c = 0.4. Subsequently, we calculated the boundary conditions for the accelerator $a$ based on the calibrated value:

$$A_d = 2 - 0.4 - 2\sqrt{1 - 0.4} = 0.05 \quad (11.12)$$

$$A_u = 2 - 0.4 + 2\sqrt{1 - 0.4} = 3.15 \quad (11.13)$$

$$Y_{\lambda+1} = (c + a)Y_{\lambda} - aY_{\lambda-1} + \bar{\text{C}} + \bar{\text{I}} + \bar{\text{G}} \quad (11.14)$$

The particular solution is:

$$Y_t^* = m^*\left(\bar{\text{C}} + \bar{\text{I}} + \bar{\text{G}}\right) \quad (11.15)$$

Where,

$$m = \frac{1}{1 - c} \quad (11.16)$$

Therefore, the solution to Eqn. (11.14) is:

$$Y_t = r^t\left(\text{c}_1 \cos \omega \text{t} + \text{c}_2 \sin \omega \text{t}\right) + \text{m}^*\left(\bar{\text{C}} + \bar{\text{I}} + \bar{\text{G}}\right) \quad (11.17)$$

When an economy is initially in equilibrium, i.e., $\Upsilon_0 = \Upsilon_{\text{initial}}$, and at time t = 1, it receives a shock that displaces $Y_1$ from $Y_0$ and $\Upsilon_1 = \Upsilon_{shock}$, then:

$$Y_0 = c_1 + \frac{1}{1 - c}\left(\bar{\text{C}} + \bar{\text{I}} + \bar{\text{G}}\right) = Y_{initial} \quad (11.18)$$

$$Y_1 = r^*\left(c_1 \cos \omega + c_2 \sin \omega\right) + \text{m}^*\left(\bar{\text{C}} + \bar{\text{I}} + \bar{\text{G}}\right) = Y_{shock} \quad (11.19)$$

The solutions are:

$$c_1 = Y_{initial} - m^*\left(\bar{\text{C}} + \bar{\text{I}} + \bar{\text{G}}\right) \quad (11.20)$$

$$c_2 = \left\{ \frac{1}{r}^{*} \left[ Y_{shock} - m^{*}\left(\bar{C}+\bar{I}+\bar{G}\right) \right] - \left( Y_{initial} - m^{*}\left(\bar{C}+\bar{I}+\bar{G}\right) \right) \cos\omega \right\} * \frac{1}{sinw} \quad (11.21)$$

Thus, given the values of *a*, *c*, $\bar{C}$, $\bar{I}$, $\bar{G}$, $\Upsilon_{initial}$ and $\Upsilon_{shock}$, the actual economic growth rate at a certain time point can be determined after the relevant calculations are performed.

### 2.4 *Theoretical Analysis of the Scenario and Conditions for the Validity of Say's Law*

Through Eqn. (11.17), we can analyze the scenarios and conditions under which Say's Law holds true. Business cycles manifest as cyclical fluctuations in economic growth, with different values of *a* determining various growth situations and characteristics, reflecting the consistency between actual and potential economic growth curves. Suppose an economy is initially in a steady state at t = 0, with $Y_0 = Y_{initial} = 2, a = c = 0.4, \bar{C} = \bar{I} = 1, \bar{G} = 1$. At t = 1, the economy is subject to a shock: the accelerator *a* changes to a new value *a′*, $Y_1 = \Upsilon_{shock} = 3$, while other variables remain unchanged, i.e., c = 0.4, $\bar{C} = \bar{I} = 1$, $\bar{G} = 1$, and $A_d = 0.05$, $A_u = 3.15$. For the possible values of *a*, we can discuss the following scenarios in detail.

1. Scenario 1: market failure or derailment

(1) **Scenario of Overheated Economy (*a′* > $A_u$)**: When the economy is hit by an overheating shock, and the new accelerator value *a′* exceeds $A_u$, the new accelerator value becomes too large, breaking the inherent cyclical nature. This leads to the failure of market mechanisms and government macro-regulation policies, necessitating special policy measures to restore normal economic operation. When investment intentions in the market become excessively exuberant, and the investment amount far exceeds what is required for normal economic functioning, an overheated economy occurs. In this case, *a′* surpasses the upper limit of $A_u$ = 3.15, causing the economy to deviate from the business cycle. Then, the aggregate supply will far exceed the aggregate demand due to increased investment, leading to a significant imbalance in supply and demand relations. In the short term, excessive increase in investment will result in rapid economic growth; however, in the

long term, insufficient demand will reduce the growth rate, leading to future economic depression. At this point, the government needs to promptly use macro-regulation to curb the growth of investment, reduce aggregate supply, and bring the accelerator $a$ down below the critical value $A_u$, helping to bring economic growth back into the cycle.

(2) **Scenario of Economic Recession or Crisis ($a' < A_d$)**: When the economy is hit by a shock, and the new accelerator value $a'$ falls below $A_d$, the new accelerator value becomes too small, also breaking the inherent cyclical nature. Consequently, normal market mechanisms and government macro-regulation policies fail, and special policy measures are required to restore normal economic operations. When investment intentions are too weak, and the investment amount is far below what is required for normal economic functioning, the economy loses momentum, which is commonly referred to as an economic recession or crisis. In this situation, $a'$ is below the lower limit of $A_d = 0.05$, causing the economy to deviate from the cycle, but the reasons are opposite to those for the above scenario: the aggregate supply falls far below the aggregate demand due to decreased investment, leading to an imbalance in supply and demand relations, weak investment and employment, and a significant slowdown in economic growth, resulting in a prolonged economic stagnation or recession. At this point, the government needs to stimulate investment growth through macro-regulation, increase aggregate supply, and expand demand by increasing income, bringing the accelerator $a$ up above the critical value $A_d$, helping to bring economic growth back into the cycle.

2. Scenario 2: normal state

The normal state refers to the expansionary phase of the business cycle ($1 < a' < A_u$): When the economy is hit by a shock, the new accelerator value $a'$ falls into the range of $A_d < a' < A_u$, and when $a' > 1$, the cyclical nature of economic operation exists. However, due to the large variation in amplitude over time, the economy may deviate from the normal state at certain times, though it still operates within the functioning mechanisms. Through general market mechanisms and government macro-regulation policies, the economy can return to normal operation. When $a$ is between the critical values $A_d$ and $A_u$ and $a > 1$, the cyclical operation of the economy is ensured. According to Eqn. (11.17), $r = \sqrt{\mathbf{a}''} > 1$ at this point, indicating that the amplitude $r^t$ of $\Upsilon_t$ in Eqn. (11.17) will continue to increase as $t$ increases. Mapping it to reality, under this scenario, the aggregate demand and the aggregate supply brought about by investment remain roughly in balance. Through market self-regulation and government macro-regulation, government policies and spontaneous investment can reach a balance, enabling the economy to grow smoothly, healthily, and sustainably. In this case, the economy operates within the boundary conditions of failure, and does not "derail." This is a common real-world situation for a country's economic operation. Analysis shows that the variation in amplitude is very important. When $a$ moves outside the range of $A_d < a < A_u$, overheating or an economic crisis will occur. Therefore, the range of $A_d < a < A_u$ is the boundary condition that ensures the market does not fail.

The following is an example of economic fluctuations caused by changes in the investment multiplier and accelerator under this scenario. Suppose the new accelerator value $a' = 1.3 > 1$, and substituting this value into Eqn. (11.17) yields the solution to Eqn. (11.14) as:

$$Y_t = (1.14)^t \left[-3\cos(0.20\pi t)_{+1.08}\ \sin(0.20\pi t)\right]_{+5} \tag{11.22}$$

Figure 11.2 visually demonstrates the fluctuation trend of Eqn. (11.22). As can be seen from the figure, due to $A_d < a' < A_u$ and r = 1.14 > 1, economic growth is cyclical, and economic fluctuations intensify over time. Mapping this scenario to reality, although economic growth may deviate significantly from the normal range at certain times, the presence of cyclical nature ensures that economic growth will "correct" and not "derail," thus remaining within the scope of government macro-regulation. In reality, due to the continuous changes in market conditions and government regulatory policies, the accelerator is also changing, and actual economic growth presents a situation that generally fluctuates around potential economic growth, with an irregular shape but generally a cyclical trend.

3. Scenario 3: scenario and conditions for the validity of Say's Law

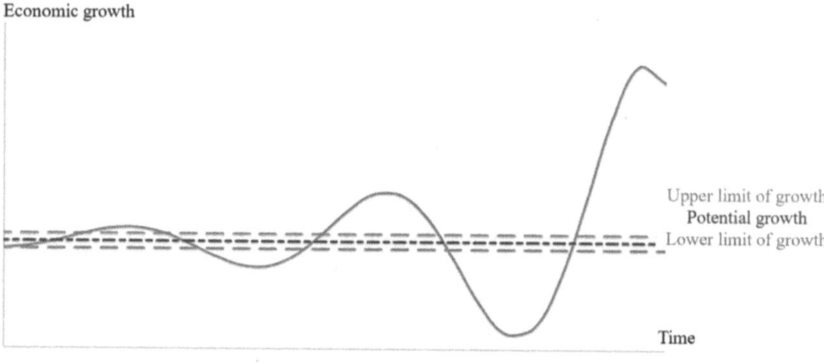


**Fig. 11.2** Business cycle in expansion

(1) Critical scenario and conditions for the validity of Say's Law ($a' = 1$): When the new accelerator $a'$ falls within the range of $A_d < a' < A_u$ and $a' = 1$, the investment intention and amount are in a reasonable range, and $r = \sqrt{a'} = 1$. This means that the amplitude $r^t$ of $Y_t$ in Eqn. (11.17) will not change with time, i.e., it will always be 1. Reflecting this in reality, in the short term, there will be a fluctuating imbalance between supply and demand, but the imbalance will be within a controllable range, and the market can spontaneously regulate the imbalance between supply and demand. In the long term, steady economic growth can be achieved, and economic growth shows cyclical fluctuations.

Below, we analyze an example of economic fluctuations caused by changes in the investment multiplier and accelerator under this scenario. Assuming the new accelerator value $a' = 1$, plugging this value into Eqn. (11.17) yields the solution to Eqn. (11.14) as:

$$Y_t = -3\cos\left(0.19\pi t\right)_{+0.80} \sin\left(0.19\pi t\right)\Big]_{+5} \quad (11.23)$$

Figure 11.3 shows the fluctuation trend of Eqn. (11.23). As can be seen from the figure, since $A_d < a' < A_u$ and $r = 1$, the amplitude remains constant at 1, and economic growth is cyclical with stable fluctuations. Reflecting this in reality, economic growth fluctuates around the potential growth value within a reasonable range, maintaining stable operation in a stable cyclical fluctuation. The corresponding conditions can be called the critical conditions for the validity of Say's Law, and there are high and low points of fluctuations, consistent with Hicks's analysis of the upper and lower limits of economic growth. Affected by various complex factors, it is difficult to achieve an ideal economic growth cycle in reality, i.e., $r = \sqrt{a} = 1$ , resulting in a typical cyclical economic growth pattern.

(2) Scenario and conditions for the validity of Say's Law ( $A_d < a < 1$): When the new accelerator a′ falls within the range of $A_d < a' < A_u$ and $a' < 1$, the investment intention and amount are in a reasonable range, and $r = \sqrt{a'} < 1$. This means that the amplitude $r^t$ of $Y_t$ in Eqn. (11.17) will decrease with time, and the economic fluctuation amplitude $r^t$ will narrow continuously until it approaches stable and non-fluctuating operation infinitely. This means that the supply-demand relationship tends towards a sustainable balanced state, and the overall economy presents a non-fluctuating state. In this scenario, Say's Law holds true. The following example illustrates this scenario: assuming the new accelerator value $a' = 0.9$, plugging this value into Eqn. (11.17) yields the solution to Eqn. (11.14) as:

$$Y_t = (0.95)^t \left[-3\cos(0.19\pi t)_{+0.65} \sin(0.19\pi t)\right]_{+5} \quad (11.24)$$

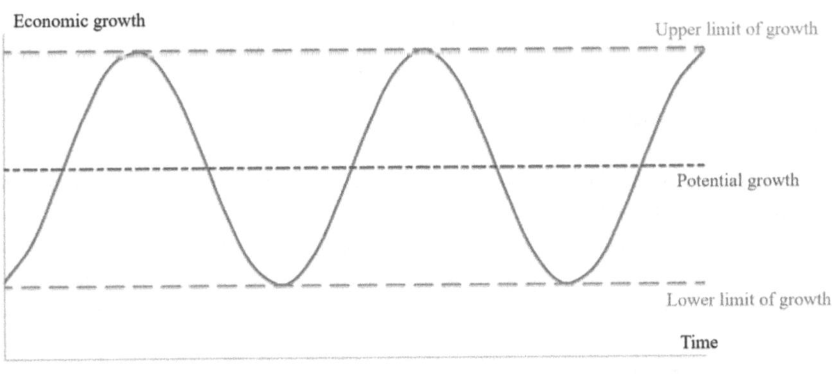


**Fig. 11.3** Business cycle under steady economic growth

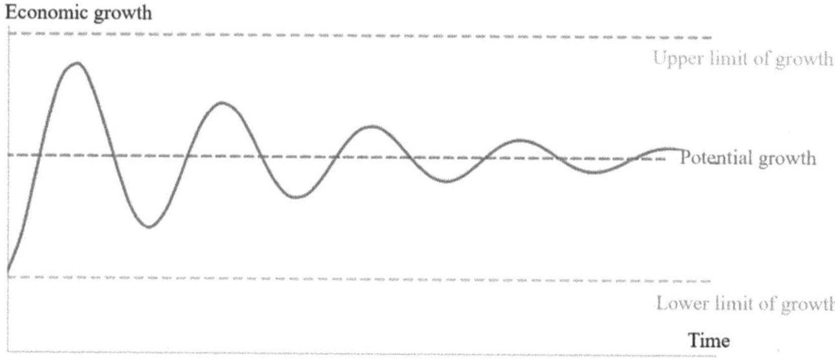


**Fig. 11.4** Business cycle under Say's Law

Figure 11.4 illustrates the business cycle under the condition where Say's Law holds true. It can be clearly observed that the amplitude $r^t$ plays a key role. Since r < 1, the amplitude $r^t$ exhibits a rapid decay over time. This implies that although there is a cyclical effect on economic growth, the fluctuation amplitude tends towards zero as time progresses, resulting in a macroscopic view where the cyclical effect is not prominently manifested. The macroeconomic growth is characterized by actual growth being consistent with potential growth, maintaining a growth momentum. Consequently, the cyclical fluctuations in the economy are very weak with almost no fluctuations, and economic crises do not occur. In the event of minor disturbances, the economy can naturally reach a new equilibrium state without intervention, much like the case where a small disturbance on the water surface can automatically revert to a balanced state.

4. Further explanation of the conditions for the validity of Say's Law

In summary, Scenario 1 represents a state of market failure or economic derailment, with the Great Depression of 1929–1933 being a typical example of this state. Scenario 2 is the usual state of an economy, while Scenario 3 reflects the critical state and general state for the validity of Say's Law. In the general state, the economy experiences cyclical fluctuations, but the amplitude decays rapidly over time, with the fluctuation term equal to zero, and economic growth gradually converges to a relatively fixed value, leading to the validity of the previously mentioned Eqns.

(11.7), (11.8), and (11.9), i.e., aggregate supply equals aggregate demand, money serves only as a medium of exchange, and actual economic growth is consistent with potential economic growth, reaching an equilibrium state. It appears as though there is no business cycle, and the economy can automatically reach a new equilibrium state after being disturbed. The conditions for the validity of Say's Law are: the accelerator $a$ is within a reasonable range of $A_d < a < A_u$, and $a$ is less than 1. If $a' = 0.5$ and the value of $r$ is smaller, the amplitude will quickly approach zero over time.

Specifically, when investment intention is not strong or when demand is sufficient, supply creates its own demand, resulting in cyclical fluctuations muted in the economy, maintaining a stable equilibrium. This is the basis for the validity of the equilibrium theory. This is similar to a swing with a certain resistance, where if no continuous force is applied, it quickly enters a stable state, as though it cannot swing at all. At this point, the business cycle is only presenting an invisible cyclical state, appearing as though it operates stably according to Say's Law, with no visible cycles or crises. However, this is only a surface phenomenon of cyclical fluctuations with the amplitude trending towards zero. If investment grows too quickly, the accelerator will increase, leading to significant changes in the supply-demand relationship. Once cyclical fluctuations become apparent, observable through actual data, it often indicates that the aforementioned balance has been disrupted and the economy has entered the usual state. At this point, by adjusting investment, it is possible to return to the general state where Say's Law holds true.

It is worth noting that Say's Law and Keynes's Law are not mutually exclusive or contradictory; rather, they are interdependent. Acknowledging one implies the validity of the other. If one does not hold true, the other should not either. The proof process is the same, with the difference lying in the focus of analysis: in demonstrating Say's Law, we consider the multiplier determined by the consumption propensity as given and focus on the role of the accelerator, which is the supply side's effect. However, when proving Keynes's Law, we treat the accelerator as relatively fixed and focus on the role of the multiplier or consumption.

We can further conclude that investment is an important variable affecting the business cycle and can be used as a significant tool for regulation and even transformation. When Scenario 1 occurs, the economic growth rate becomes disconnected from the cycle, indicating that for an economy to function normally, it is necessary to maintain investment within a reasonable range and for investment and consumption to maintain a reasonable balance. In this case, it is not advisable to overly emphasize expanding consumption, a situation that some countries, especially developed ones, commonly face. When encountering economic downturns, stagnation, or new regional development, initiating extraordinary investment is an effective means to help the economy reach a new level and cultivate new economic growth points. In Scenario 2, the inherent cyclical nature of the economy exists but manifests as a state of fluctuation, leading to the implementation of related policy measures. These policies, in turn, bring about changes in the accelerator, altering the characteristics of the fluctuations and forming the actual growth curve in reality which appears to fluctuate irregularly. An ideal policy would be to regulate economic growth within the business cycle and keep it close to the upper limit of growth. When the economy is in Scenario 3, the conditions for the validity of Say's Law are met, allowing for a rapid transition from a cyclical state to a stable state.

### 2.5 *Empirical Analysis of the Scenarios and Conditions for the Validity of Say's Law*

1. Empirical analysis based on US economic data

**Empirical Analysis 1: Examining the scenarios related to Say's Law conditions from US economic data (1946–1962).** Figure 11.5 shows the changes in US GDP from 1946 to 1962. The blue dots represent the actual US GDP, while the red line segments are the fittings based on the development of the actual GDP. If the fitting line segments are considered as the potential GDP growth trend, then the difference between the actual GDP and the fitted GDP can be used to represent the fluctuations in the economy. The blue dots in Fig. 11.8 show the difference between the actual GDP and the fitted GDP (Fig. 11.6).

Based on the model's expression Eqn. (11.10), by substituting the GDP, personal consumption expenditure, and total private domestic investment of the United States from 1946 to 1962 (see Table 11.1), we can calculate the personal consumption propensity to be 0.6324 and the accelerator to be 0.1706. Using the calculated personal consumption propensity and accelerator, and employing numerical methods to fit the actual economic fluctuations during this period, we obtain the red curve in Fig. 11.8.

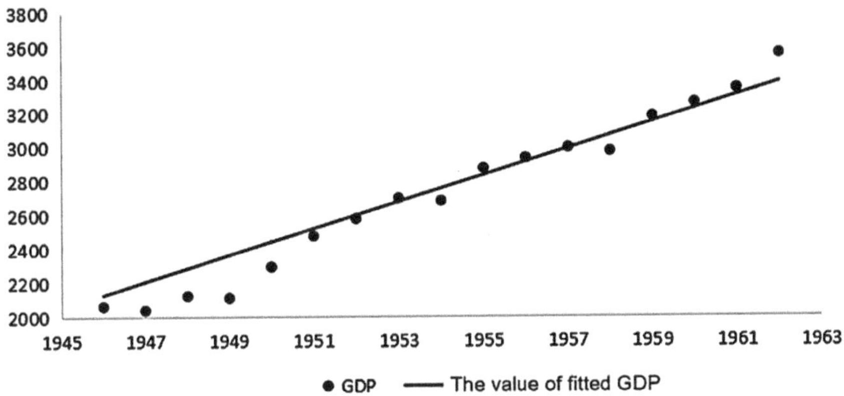


**Fig. 11.5** Actual vs. fitted GDP (1946–1962, United States, in billions of US dollars). (Data Source: Bureau of Economic Analysis, US Department of Commerce)

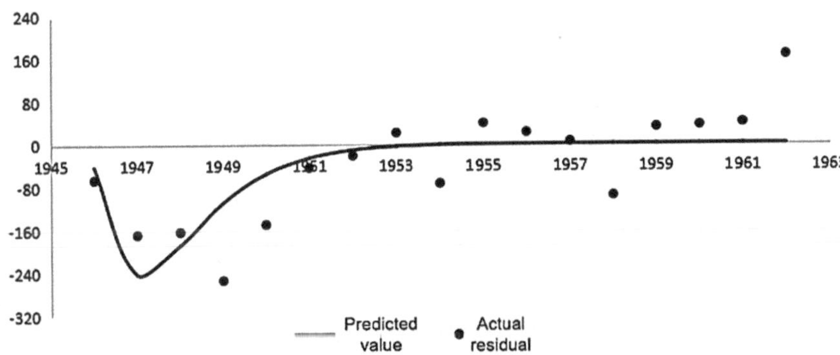


**Fig. 11.6** Residuals and multiplier-accelerator model fitting (1946–1962, United States, in billions of US dollars). (Data Source: Bureau of Economic Analysis, US Department of Commerce)

Relating the fitting results depicted in Fig. 11.8 to Scenario 3 in our model analysis, the US economy during this period met the fundamental conditions for Say's Law to hold: $<a' < 1$. Although the economy experienced cyclical fluctuations, the amplitude of these oscillations rapidly diminished over time, leading to a convergence of economic growth toward the potential GDP. This swift convergence towards

**Table 11.1** GDP calculated using expenditure approach and GDP components (1946–1962, United States, in billions of US dollars)

| *Year* | *GDP* | *Personal consumption expenditure* | *Total private domestic investment* |
|---|---|---|---|
| 1946 | 2059.8 | 1271.3 | 220.3 |
| 1947 | 2036.2 | 1295.6 | 212.1 |
| 1948 | 2120 | 1324.9 | 267.3 |
| 1949 | 2108 | 1361.7 | 206.7 |
| 1950 | 2291.1 | 1449.2 | 287.9 |
| 1951 | 2475.4 | 1471.9 | 288.6 |
| 1952 | 2576.7 | 1518.3 | 265 |
| 1953 | 2697.5 | 1590.3 | 279.9 |
| 1954 | 2681.9 | 1623.6 | 268.9 |
| 1955 | 2873.2 | 1743.4 | 331.1 |
| 1956 | 2934.4 | 1794.3 | 330.2 |
| 1957 | 2996.2 | 1838.8 | 317.8 |
| 1958 | 2974 | 1854.7 | 294.8 |
| 1959 | 3180.2 | 1960.5 | 351.4 |
| 1960 | 3262.1 | 2014.3 | 352.7 |
| 1961 | 3345.7 | 2055.6 | 353.8 |
| 1962 | 3550.7 | 2157.3 | 395.9 |

Data Source: Bureau of Economic Analysis, US Department of Commerce

"non-fluctuating" growth could have stemmed from the post-World War II boom in the US economy, where prolonged supply shortages relative to ample economic demand ensured the fulfillment of Say's Law that "supply creates its own demand."

**Empirical Analysis 2: Fluctuations during the era of neoliberalism and rapid technological advancement.** From the 1980s through the early 1990s, Reagan's administration espoused neoliberalism, reducing state intervention in businesses, which gradually rejuvenated the American economy. Following the collapse of the Soviet Union, the substantial investments previously allocated to the arms race with the USSR were redirected towards scientific and technological development. Waves of technological booms originating from the US swept across the globe, further solidifying America's position as the world's superpower. To eliminate the confounding effects of the Covid-19 pandemic, Figure 11.7 illustrates the changes in US GDP from 1980 to 2019. The blue dots represent the development of the US's actual GDP, while the red lines depict the fitting based on the development of actual GDP. If the fitted lines are taken as indicative of the underlying trend in potential GDP growth, the discrepancy between actual and fitted GDP values can be utilized to illustrate economic fluctuations. The blue dots in Fig. 11.8 specifically highlight the differences between actual and fitted GDP values, depicting the situation of economic volatility.

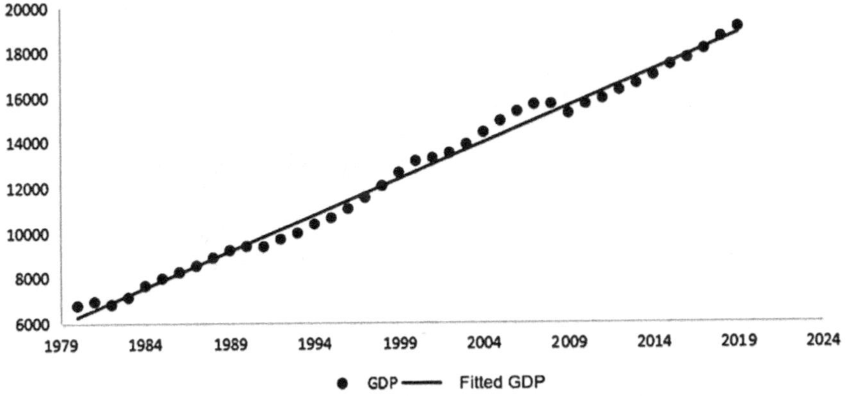


**Fig. 11.7** Actual vs. fitted GDP (1980–2019, United States, in billions of US dollars). (Data Source: Bureau of Economic Analysis, US Department of Commerce)

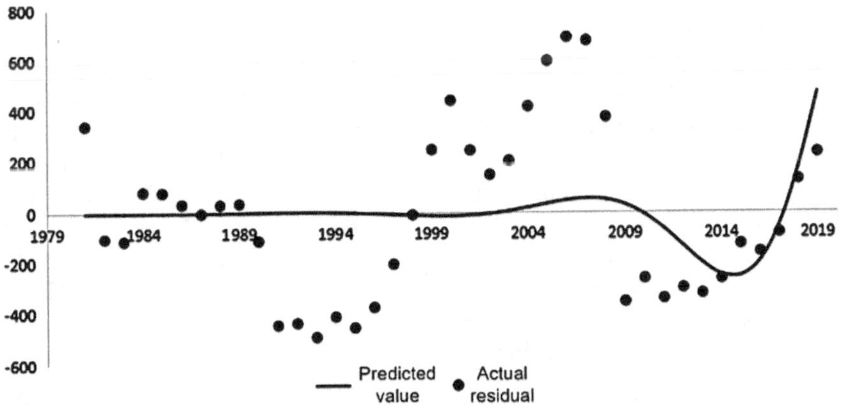


**Fig. 11.8** Residuals and multiplier-accelerator model fitting (1980–2019, United States, in billions of US dollars). (Data Source: Bureau of Economic Analysis, US Department of Commerce)

Based on the model's expression Eqn. (11.10), substituting the GDP, personal consumption expenditure, and total domestic private investment of the United States from 1980 to 2019 (as detailed in Table 11.2), we find marginal propensity to consume equals to 0.7323 and an accelerator equals to 1.5054. Utilizing the calculated marginal propensity to consume and accelerator, we apply numerical methods to fit the actual economic fluctuations of this period, as illustrated in Fig. 11.10, resulting in the red curve depicted in the chart.

The fitting results of Fig. 11.8 correspond to the second scenario in the model analysis. During this period, the US economy was generally in an expansionary business cycle ($1 < \alpha' < A_u$). At this stage, economic growth was cyclical, and economic fluctuations intensified over time. But economic growth kept "correcting" itself and did not "derail," remaining within the range of government's macro-regulation. The severe fluctuations in the economy at this stage might be attributed to the uncertainty of technological development and the fluctuating market expectations.

2. Empirical analysis based on Chinese economic data

**Empirical Analysis 1: China's economic development practice (1978–2008).** From the end of 1978 when China started reform and opening up and embarked on a path of economic development to 2008 when the Beijing 2008 Summer Olympics was successfully hosted, the country stunned the world with its extraordinary economic and social development.

Figure 11.9 depicts the changes in China's GDP from 1978 to 2008. The blue dots represent the evolution of China's actual GDP, while the red line segments are the fits based on the actual GDP growth. If the fitting line segments are taken as the potential trend of GDP growth, the difference between the actual GDP and the fitted GDP can be used to illustrate the economic fluctuations. The blue dots in Fig. 11.10 specifically show the difference between the actual GDP and the fitted GDP.

According to the model's expression Eqn. (11.10), by substituting China's GDP calculated using the expenditure approach, household consumption, and total capital formation (see Table 11.3) from 1978 to 2008, we can show that the personal consumption propensity equals to 0.4369 and the accelerator equals to 2.9315. Using the calculated personal consumption propensity and accelerator, and employing numerical

**Table 11.2** GDP calculated using expenditure approach and GDP components (1980–2019, United States, in billions of US dollars)

| *Year* | *GDP* | *Personal consumption expenditure* | *Total private domestic investment* |
|---|---|---|---|
| 1980 | 6763.5 | 4251.1 | 864 |
| 1981 | 6935.2 | 4310 | 940.1 |
| 1982 | 6810.1 | 4373.1 | 822 |
| 1983 | 7122.3 | 4620.7 | 898.7 |
| 1984 | 7637.7 | 4863.8 | 1144 |
| 1985 | 7956.2 | 5115.6 | 1143.2 |
| 1986 | 8231.7 | 5326.8 | 1145 |
| 1987 | 8516.4 | 5507.6 | 1177.6 |
| 1988 | 8872.2 | 5737.7 | 1206.6 |
| 1989 | 9198 | 5905 | 1255.4 |
| 1990 | 9371.5 | 6023.9 | 1223 |
| 1991 | 9361.3 | 6034.8 | 1142.1 |
| 1992 | 9691.1 | 6256.9 | 1225.3 |
| 1993 | 9957.7 | 6474.8 | 1323.3 |
| 1994 | 10,358.9 | 6725.7 | 1479.8 |
| 1995 | 10,637 | 6924.1 | 1527.3 |
| 1996 | 11,038.3 | 7164.4 | 1660.8 |
| 1997 | 11,529.2 | 7434.2 | 1850.2 |
| 1998 | 12,045.8 | 7829 | 2026.3 |
| 1999 | 12,623.4 | 8250.3 | 2198.7 |
| 2000 | 13,138 | 8665.8 | 2346.7 |
| 2001 | 13,263.4 | 8880.4 | 2214.6 |
| 2002 | 13,488.4 | 9106.2 | 2195.5 |
| 2003 | 13,865.5 | 9394.4 | 2290.4 |
| 2004 | 14,399.7 | 9748.6 | 2502.6 |
| 2005 | 14,901.3 | 10,093.8 | 2670.6 |
| 2006 | 15,315.9 | 10,386.2 | 2752.4 |
| 2007 | 15,623.9 | 10,638.7 | 2684.1 |
| 2008 | 15,643 | 10,654.7 | 2462.9 |
| 2009 | 15,236.3 | 10,515.6 | 1942 |
| 2010 | 15,649 | 10,716 | 2216.5 |
| 2011 | 15,891.5 | 10,898.3 | 2362.1 |
| 2012 | 16,254 | 11,047.4 | 2621.8 |
| 2013 | 16,553.3 | 11,211.7 | 2801.5 |
| 2014 | 16,932.1 | 11,515.3 | 2959.2 |
| 2015 | 17,390.3 | 11,892.9 | 3121.8 |
| 2016 | 17,680.3 | 12,187.7 | 3089.9 |
| 2017 | 18,076.7 | 12,478.2 | 3216 |
| 2018 | 18,609.1 | 12,837.3 | 3398.9 |
| 2019 | 19,036.1 | 13,092.3 | 3492.7 |

Data Source: Bureau of Economic Analysis, US Department of Commerce

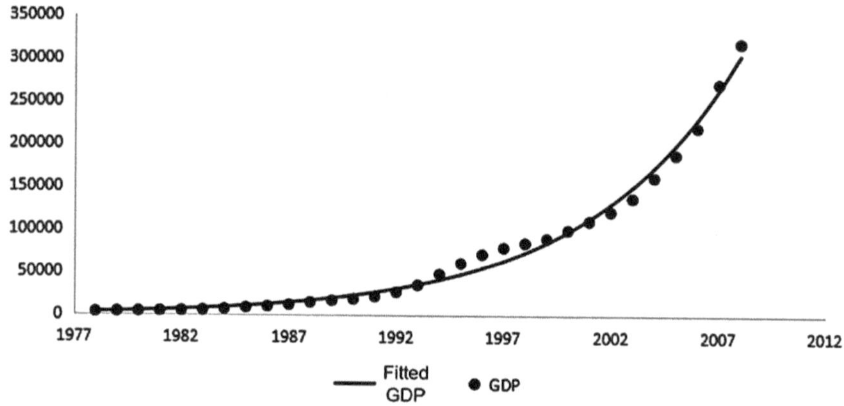


**Fig. 11.9** Actual vs. fitted GDP (1978–2008, China, in 100 million yuan). (Data Source: National Bureau of Statistics)

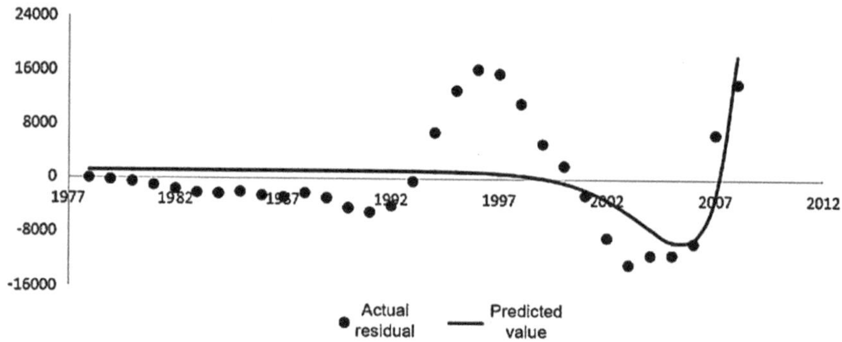


**Fig. 11.10** Residuals and multiplier-accelerator model fitting (1978–2008, China, in 100 million yuan). (Data Source: National Bureau of Statistics)

methods to fit the actual economic fluctuations during this period, we obtain the red curve in Fig. 11.10.

The fitting results of Fig. 11.10 correspond to the second scenario in the model analysis. During this phase, China's economy was generally in an expansionary business cycle ($1 < \alpha' < A_u$). At this stage, economic growth was cyclical, and economic fluctuations intensified over time, but did not "derail." The severe fluctuations in the economy at this stage

**Table 11.3** GDP calculated using expenditure approach and GDP components (1978–2008, China, in 100 million yuan)

| *Year* | *GDP calculated using expenditure approach* | *Household consumption* | *Total capital formation* |
|---|---|---|---|
| 1978 | 3605.6 | 1759.1 | 1383.3 |
| 1979 | 4047.3 | 2014 | 1488.3 |
| 1980 | 4540.5 | 2336.9 | 1587.5 |
| 1981 | 4921.6 | 2627.5 | 1626.3 |
| 1982 | 5386.3 | 2867.1 | 1718.4 |
| 1983 | 6034.2 | 3220.9 | 1922.2 |
| 1984 | 7290.1 | 3689.5 | 2502.2 |
| 1985 | 9108.1 | 4627.4 | 3554.4 |
| 1986 | 10,390.3 | 5293.5 | 3914.6 |
| 1987 | 12,198 | 6047.6 | 4543.7 |
| 1988 | 15,210.5 | 7532.1 | 5932.2 |
| 1989 | 17,250.5 | 8778 | 6392.4 |
| 1990 | 18,969.3 | 9435 | 6446.6 |
| 1991 | 21,997.2 | 10,544.5 | 7754 |
| 1992 | 27,140.3 | 12,312.2 | 10,625.4 |
| 1993 | 35,576 | 15,694.9 | 15,440.5 |
| 1994 | 48,410.3 | 21,443.2 | 19,479.4 |
| 1995 | 61,050.4 | 28,065.6 | 23,823 |
| 1996 | 71,541.5 | 33,644.1 | 26,960.1 |
| 1997 | 79,415.8 | 36,585.8 | 28,317.1 |
| 1998 | 84,790.8 | 38,768.5 | 29,659.7 |
| 1999 | 90,095.1 | 41,845.8 | 30,891.2 |
| 2000 | 99,799 | 46,863.3 | 33,667.1 |
| 2001 | 110,388.4 | 50,464.7 | 39,402.5 |
| 2002 | 121,326.7 | 54,667 | 44,005 |
| 2003 | 137,146.7 | 58,689.9 | 54,446.8 |
| 2004 | 161,355.6 | 65,724.8 | 67,725.6 |
| 2005 | 187,657.5 | 74,153.7 | 75,576 |
| 2006 | 219,597.5 | 82,842.4 | 87,578.6 |
| 2007 | 270,499.4 | 98,231.3 | 109,339.3 |
| 2008 | 318,067.6 | 112,654.7 | 134,941.6 |

Data Source: National Bureau of Statistics

might be attributed to people's sufficient confidence and high expectations for the future.

**Empirical Analysis 2: China's economic development practice (2008–2021).** After 2008, China's economic development entered a new stage. Figure 11.11 illustrates the changes in China's GDP from 2008 to

2021. The blue dots represent the development of China's actual GDP, while the red line segments are the fits based on the actual GDP growth. If the fitting line segments are considered the potential trend of GDP growth, the difference between the actual GDP and the fitted GDP can be used to represent the economic fluctuations. The blue dots in Fig. 11.12 specifically show the difference between the actual GDP and the fitted GDP.

According to the model's expression Eqn. (11.10), by substituting China's GDP calculated using the expenditure approach, household consumption, and total capital formation from 2008 to 2021 (see Table 11.4), we calculate the personal consumption propensity and the accelerator, which are equal to 0.4244 and 2.1952, respectively. Using the calculated personal consumption propensity and accelerator, and employing numerical methods to fit the actual economic fluctuations during this period, we obtain the red curve in Fig. 11.12.

The fitting results of Fig. 11.12 correspond to the second scenario in the model analysis. During this phase, China's overall economy was also in an expansionary business cycle ($1 < \alpha' < A_u$), but compared to the previous phase, the accelerator was smaller, and the amplitude was relatively smaller. The economic fluctuations during this phase were more moderate, which was possibly because that the market supply has exceeded demand, leading the economy to gradually return to rational growth.

From an empirical analysis perspective, among the selected data, only those for the United States from 1946 to 1962 basically meet the

**Fig. 11.11** Actual vs. fitted GDP (2008–2021, China, in 100 million yuan). (Data Source: National Bureau of Statistics)

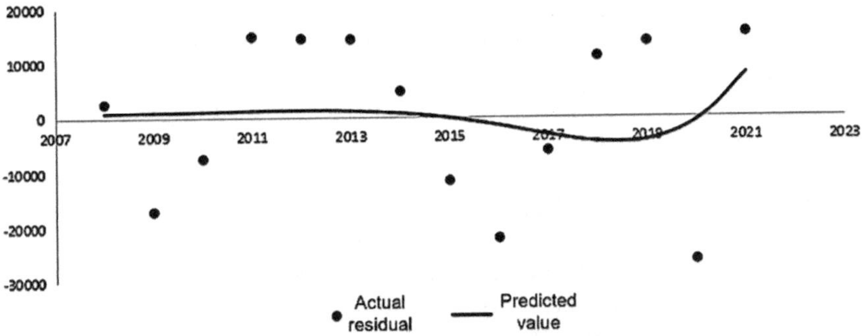


**Fig. 11.12** Residuals and multiplier-accelerator model fitting (2008–2021, China, in 100 million yuan). (Data Source: National Bureau of Statistics)

**Table 11.4** GDP calculated using expenditure approach and GDP components (2008–2021, China, in 100 million yuan)

| *Year* | *GDP calculated using expenditure approach* | *Household consumption* | *Total capital formation* |
|---|---|---|---|
| 2008 | 318,067.6 | 112,654.7 | 46,244.5 |
| 2009 | 347,650.3 | 123,121.9 | 51,416.7 |
| 2010 | 408,505.4 | 141,465.5 | 60,115.9 |
| 2011 | 484,109.3 | 170,390.8 | 74,356.5 |
| 2012 | 539,039.9 | 190,584.8 | 84,859.1 |
| 2013 | 596,344.5 | 212,477.3 | 94,186.4 |
| 2014 | 646,548 | 236,238.5 | 101,792.7 |
| 2015 | 692,093.7 | 260,202.4 | 111,718.2 |
| 2016 | 745,980.5 | 288,668.2 | 122,138.3 |
| 2017 | 828,982.8 | 320,689.5 | 135,828.7 |
| 2018 | 915,774.3 | 354,124.4 | 152,010.6 |
| 2019 | 990,708.4 | 387,188.1 | 165,443.6 |
| 2020 | 1,025,628.4 | 387,185.8 | 173,625.4 |
| 2021 | 1,145,282.9 | 438,015.2 | 181,673 |
| 2022 | 1,205,017 | 447,910.2 | 193,722.8 |

Data Source: National Bureau of Statistics

conditions of Say's Law. Chinese data represents the normal state of the economy and has a relatively high accelerator, which better reflects the actual situations of China's rapid economic growth over many years. After 2012, Chinese data was affected by changes in the supply-demand relationship, and the economic growth rate declined, a reasonable trend. The main stage data results show that the economy generally remained in Scenario 2, which also indicates that the validity of Say's Law is a relatively special case. The difference in accelerators reflects the different conditions and speeds of economic growth. The gap in savings propensities between China and the United States and the difference in accelerators suggest that consumption plays a greater role in the US economy's development, while investment plays a greater role in China's economy. However, the data did not show that the neoliberal era better met the conditions of Say's Law than the Keynesian theory era. If a more detailed analysis is required, it may be necessary to choose more reasonable data, for example, the data of the years closest to 1929–1933 and the years when neoliberal policies were most concentrated.

## 2.6 Conclusion and Significance

This section applies a theoretical model to analyze the scenarios and conditions for the validity of Say's Law, which represents a new approach and effectively interprets the foundation of market economy theory, possessing significant theoretical and practical value.

1. Say's Law is valid under certain conditions

Say's Law describes the important characteristics of economic operation under certain conditions, reflecting a special manifestation of the business cycle when aggregate supply is significantly less than aggregate demand (effective demand) and cannot rapidly increase. This state is essentially the equilibrium between aggregate supply and aggregate demand, with production determined by aggregate supply. Say's Law describes the long-term equilibrium state of economic operation, not the short-term fluctuations. The critical condition for the existence of the business cycle can be considered a condition of market failure. Once it deviates from this range or the amplitude increases over time, the economy enters an economic overheating or crisis state, which is difficult for the market to self-regulate to achieve balance and requires crisis or government intervention to achieve equilibrium. The theoretical limit state that the amplitude remains constant over time is rarely observed in reality. When economic operation is within the cyclical range and the amplitude quickly tends to zero over time, Say's Law holds true. At this point, the actual economic growth converges to the long-term potential growth, and the economic fluctuation amplitude tends to zero. The actual growth curve is essentially in line with the potential growth curve, satisfying all the corresponding conditions. In this case, the economy can automatically reach a new equilibrium state after being disturbed.

2. Say's Law is the result of the invisible expression of the business cycle

The business cycle is an objective reality with its boundary conditions. The length of the cycle varies, and the cycle may exhibit different characteristics at different stages due to various dominant factors. The business cycle is the result of the superposition of cycles caused by various dominant factors. When Say's Law is valid, since the amplitude of fluctuations tends to zero over time, the business cycle is manifested as invisible, meaning that the cyclical fluctuations are not visible, and the economic operation appears very stable. However, this is conditional; once investment is too fast or too slow, exceeding the defined conditions, the basic balance will be lost. If we consider a normal economy in isolation, maintaining a certain level of investment is a necessary condition for normal operation.

3. Say's Law and Keynes's Law have conjugate conditions for validity

The business cycle is jointly determined by the accelerator and the marginal propensity to consume. Say's Law and Keynes's Law are interdependent; they either both hold true or both do not. To prove the validity of Say's Law, the marginal propensity to consume can be taken as a given condition, and the accelerator determines the general characteristics of the business cycle: excessive investment will lead to a large accelerator, causing economic growth to lose its cyclical nature and present a state of economic overheating that is detached from the business cycle; conversely, lower investment will lead to a small accelerator, presenting a state of economic undercooling that is also detached from the business cycle. Investment growth may cause changes in the accelerator coefficient, thus initiating some changes in the business cycle and achieving the goal of smoothing the business cycle to some extent. To prove the validity of Keynes's Law, the accelerator can be considered relatively fixed, and the focus is on analyzing the roles of multiplier or consumption. In general, the relationship between investment and consumption should be dynamic balance and interaction.

4. Attention should be paid to the role of government in handling market failure

Say's Law emphasizes the complete effectiveness of the market and the natural balance of the market, advocating further research on the relationship and balance between supply and demand from the perspective of supply and demand. However, the relationship between supply and demand in modern economies has undergone significant changes, with oversupply and market failure being the norm, and the validity of Say's Law being an extremely special case. Therefore, while giving full play to the decisive role of the market, it is also necessary for the government to enhance its performance, achieving an organic combination of market and government functions, effectively dealing with market failure, and implementing macro-regulation policies from a higher perspective of considering both supply and demand, to achieve high-quality economic development.

5. The connotation of Say's Law is enriched under the new situation, and provides reference value for China's supply-side structural reform

China's statement on allowing the market to play a decisive role in resource allocation shares a commonality with the connotation of Say's Law. Allowing the market to function and enhance supply capacity will naturally create demand, thus providing a corresponding expression that should focus on the supply side. High-quality development is mainly reflected in the supply side, and supply-side structural reform must be driven by innovation. Say's thought has a reference value for promoting supply-side structural reform. The aim of supply-side structural reform is to achieve a reform of production factors through institutional adjustments, releasing the productivity of various factors. No matter what factor it is, its owner can be regarded as a market subject. No matter how he or she obtains income through the factor, it will eventually form demand. China's supply-side structural reform, which optimizes resource allocation from the supply side, is conducive to fostering new drivers of economic development. However, it should also be noted that currently, China's main problem is overcapacity, not insufficient production capacity, so the core task of China's supply-side structural reform is to improve and upgrade capacity, and it is necessary to consider the dynamic balance between aggregate supply and aggregate demand.

## 3 Theoretical Model Construction and Analysis of Economic Catching-up and Surpassing

The theoretical system of New Structural Economics (NSE) embodies the inheritance and development of modern economic theories, based on the sublimation of the practical experience of emerging economies like China. This theory lays the foundation for solving the problems of catching-up and surpassing. This section conducts a systematic analysis through the establishment of models: (1) Establishing the theoretical model of NSE from three different dimensions: constructing the theoretical growth model of NSE based on the logic of the Solow growth model; extending the economic growth equation of NSE based on the Real Business Cycle (RBC) model; and establishing corresponding equations from the perspective of the combination of "effective markets" and "proactive governments"; (2) Analyzing three important propositions of the NSE theory: the connotation and role of the factor endowment structure, the changes in comparative advantage and growth momentum, and the role of the government; (3) Analyzing three possible scenarios that a country's economy may encounter in the process of catching up or surpassing another country: being able to catch up or surpass, being in the critical zone of catching up or surpassing, and being unable to catch up or surpass.

### *3.1 Introduction*

NSE is an important theory proposed and advocated by Professor Lin Yifu and his collaborators. NSE advocates using historical materialism as a guide and adopting the methods of neoclassical economics. It starts with the factor endowment and its structure, which are given for each economy at a specific time and can change over time, to study the determinants and impacts of the economic structure and its changes, including industries and technologies that determine productivity, and infrastructure and institutional arrangements for transaction costs. Its main policy propositions are that developing economies should start from their own factor endowment structure, develop industries with comparative advantage, and under the joint action of "effective markets" and "proactive governments," promote the transformation and upgrading of the economic structure and the development of society and economy, in order to achieve the goal of gradually catching up with and even surpassing developed countries. This theory absorbs the ideas of comparative advantage and factor endowment theories and, based on the practical experience of emerging economies like China, has achieved theoretical sublimation, forming a self-contained NSE theoretical system, including a complete logical framework, main conclusions, and policy propositions.

Since its inception, NSE has received high praise from many Nobel economic laureates, including Joseph Stiglitz and Michael Spence. It is regarded as the third generation of development economics theory following "Structuralism" and "Neoliberalism," and has garnered widespread attention from various fields. It has also had a certain impact on policies and practices related to emerging economies, although it does have some shortcomings. For example, in terms of methodology and theoretical models, it is still difficult to satisfy, as there has been no systematic deductive logical analysis; the analysis of the connotation of the government's role is not refined enough, making it difficult to clearly define whether the role comes from the market or the government. This situation is normal, as NSE, as a new economic theory, still needs further development and improvement in the future. The successful practice of China is a reality that cannot be explained by Western economic theories, and new economic theories are needed to explain the "Chinese miracle" (Lin Yifu, 2012). Therefore, how to systematically analyze the theory of NSE from a model perspective, enhancing its credibility, logic, and universality, will be a major topic.

### 3.2 Theoretical Contributions and Unresolved Issues of New Structural Economics

New Structural Economics, based on the theories of comparative advantage and factor endowment from classical economics, and integrating the practical experience of emerging economies like China, fully considers the important role of the government in industrial policy and other aspects, and has constructed a self-contained theoretical system of NSE.

1. Important propositions of NSE

NSE actually contains the following important propositions: first, it accepts the assumption of rational economic man, which aligns with the basic logic of modern Western economic theories and models, and recognizes the important role of factor endowment in a country's economic development; second, at a certain point, different countries vary in their factor endowments and industrial structures, including capital, labor, and other factor endowments, as well as corresponding industrial structures, which are an important part of a country's comprehensive competitiveness; third, a country can achieve the optimization of its factor structure and the upgrading of its industrial structure, which is an important manifestation of its comparative advantage, and comparative advantage is dynamic. The government's industrial policies and investment in science and technology are key to achieving optimization and upgrading; fourth, under certain conditions, both the first-mover advantage and the late-mover advantage can exist and be realized; fifth, the role of the market and the role of the government are not opposed but complementary, or their relationship is one of unity of opposites. The conversion of comparative advantages between countries is normal. A country's government can change its comparative advantages through relevant industrial policies, and emerging economies can catch up with and even surpass developed countries, which is also an important manifestation of the advantages of being later.

2. Important contributions and innovative points of the NSE theory

The first contribution of NSE is a significant breakthrough in the "either or" paradigm regarding market and government roles. The NSE theory, based on the logic of neoclassical economics, emphasizes the importance of neoclassical economic principles, factor endowment, and comparative advantage theories while reflecting on the limitations of neoliberalism and structuralism. The theory breaks through the paradigm of either emphasizing market roles or highlighting government roles, starting from China's practice, and emphasizes the new paradigm of having both an "effective market" and a "proactive government," considering that the government can play an important role in industrial upgrading and economic structural transformation.

The second is the enrichment and development of the theories of comparative advantage and factor endowment. The theory of comparative advantage demonstrates the benefits of international division of labor but does not tell us what specific labor-intensive products to produce, how to produce them, or in what quantities. For a country, especially a large one, participating in international division of labor solely based on comparative advantage is not enough; the participation should be coordinated with efforts to achieve industrial upgrading. The NSE provides the relevant logic for policy choices. The theory determines the starting point of analysis as the factor endowment of an economy at a specific point in time, identifying industries with potential advantages, and considering that these potentially advantageous industries can be transformed into industries with competitive advantages. This makes the theories of comparative advantage and factor endowment more dynamic, representing an important innovative thinking.

The third is that the NSE theory considers both structural factors of economic growth, recognizing the roles of government and technological progress, and also considers cyclical factors, reflecting the total characteristics. The NSE theory emphasizes the dynamic logic of economic growth, interpreting the dynamic process of economic growth from a poor country to a rich one. Its analytical approach shares similarities with the logic of the Real Business Cycle theory, and the NSE theory's analysis of endogeneity also integrates the trend of the endogenous growth theory. Therefore, the theory represents an innovative development of modern growth theory and is an important innovation in the theory of development economics.

The fourth is the emphasis on the dynamic logic that developing countries can achieve catching up with or even surpassing developed countries. The NSE theory changes the logic that "developed countries have always been developed," considering it a dynamic process. From the dimensions of practice and theory, it analyzes the feasibility and paths for a developing country to catch up with or surpass developed countries. The theory discusses the first-mover and the late-mover advantages, emphasizing the importance of the latter, considering that government industrial policies play a crucial role, and that the government can formulate different industrial policies based on the different advantages of various industries.

3. Areas of improvement for NSE

The first is the need for improvement in methodology and logical foundation. Like other economic theories, NSE must be able to inductively analyze experience, propose basic propositions, and then establish corresponding deductive logic. Yu Yongding (2022) emphasizes, "A successful theory cannot merely be an induction of certain experiences, although correct induction is very important. I believe that having a strong deductive nature is the most attractive aspect of economics or any theory." If NSE could further improve its deductive logic, it would be more convincing.

The second is that the paradigm based on neoclassical economics is difficult to effectively match the Chinese practice characterized by the combination of market and government. The market plays a decisive role in resource allocation, but it is not always powerful, and the government can also play a role. The practical experience of China's reform and opening up has proven that the government can play an important role. Based on the paradigm of neoclassical economics, NSE highlights the role of the market but places a very limited role on the government within the theory. Zhu Fuqiang (2017) believes that Lin Yifu only maintains the positive role of the state within a limited scope, advocating that the state must promote limited industrial policies based on comparative advantages and nurture and support those private sectors with potential comparative advantages. If this logic is used to explain the rationality of the combination of the Chinese government and market, there are inherent deficiencies, leading to some issues that are difficult to explain.

The third is that the connotation of the factor endowment structure in NSE should be clearer, and the relationship between structural factors and growth momentum should be more explicit. NSE divides the endowment structure into three categories: factor endowment structure, institutional endowment structure, and natural endowment structure. For the convenience of analyzing industrial policies, the industries are divided into five categories: catch-up type, leading type, transitional type, overtaking type, and strategic type. We believe that the factor endowment structure should have clearer boundaries and not be overly expanded, for example, never considering institutions and infrastructure as endowment. The industrial structure can be the result of past factor endowments or a changing factor in the new stage, but it is difficult to consider it as the fundamental driving force of economic growth. Technological progress or changes in total factor productivity are the driving forces of economic growth.

The fourth is the lack of effective theoretical models. Zhang Jun (2013) believes that the ideas and policies of NSE are relatively clear, but NSE derives its theory based on the "rational economic man assumption" and "static comparative advantage" of neoclassical economics, explaining modern major economic phenomena with relatively traditional theories. This makes it difficult to explain the dynamic process of economic structure evolution, upgrading, and economic convergence. Overall, NSE still lacks a more convincing logic of deductive argumentation, and its theoretical models need further improvement.

### 3.3 *Exploration of the Construction and Analysis of NSE Theoretical Models*

The qualitative description of the NSE theory is relatively sufficient, but it is relatively weak in the construction of mathematical models and quantification, which can affect its recognition and acceptance. Therefore, it is very important to construct theoretical models to analyze the NSE theory. The full title of Adam Smith's *The Wealth of Nations* is *An Inquiry into the Nature and Causes of the Wealth of Nations*, which essentially explores the issue of wealth growth from a structural perspective. The logic of David Ricardo's theory of comparative advantage is reflected in the concept of comparative advantage, which is, in turn, reflected in factor endowment. Therefore, if comparative advantage is transformed into competitive advantage, and the economic growth rate becomes the major manifestation of competitive advantage, catching up and surpassing are just the results of differences in economic growth rates. The problem can be solved. Given that economic structure changes over a relatively long process, short-term changes do not affect the overall trend, the construction of NSE theoretical models can start from the perspective of potential growth, with the core being how structural factors determine and influence potential economic growth.

In this way, the issue of constructing theoretical models is transformed into: how to construct the economic growth equation of NSE theory? Here, we still use the previous relevant equations.

$$Y_t = \mathrm{F}\left(K_t, L_t, A_t, N_t, S_t\right) \tag{11.38}$$

This seemingly ordinary formula, if understood in a universal sense as the various factors affecting economic growth, can become an important foundation for economic theory or theories of economic growth. Various economic theories or growth theories and their logic are just its variations and specific manifestations. Here, we attempt to establish corresponding theoretical models from three different dimensions.

1. The first NSE theoretical model—based on the logic of the Solow growth model

If Eqn. (11.38) is simplified and reconstructed from a structural factor perspective, assuming other non-structural factors remain unchanged, a simple NSE economic growth equation can be obtained, which takes into account the role of factors and the impact of the government's industrial policies and technological investment on potential economic growth. A more straightforward expression is the familiar potential economic growth formula, which is expressed using the Solow model (R.M. Solow, 1956). The difference is that the "government's role" needs to be considered separately. This can then give the corresponding growth formula of the NSE theory:

$$Y_t = \mathrm{Y}_0^*\left(1+\frac{\mathrm{A}(\mathrm{t})-\mathrm{A0}}{\mathrm{A0}}\right) \tag{11.39}$$

At this point, it is assumed that technological progress without government intervention is stable, and the growth trend is also stable. Here, $\mathrm{Y}_0^*$ represents the potential growth rate under pure market conditions (without government intervention), while $\mathrm{Y}_0^*\frac{\mathrm{A}(\mathrm{t})-\mathrm{A0}}{\mathrm{A0}}$ represents the impact of government policies on technological progress during the period *t*, thereby changing the trend of potential growth rate (or the slope of growth).

Technology and industrial policies can promote a country to achieve a higher economic growth rate. For example, in Fig. 11.13, which considers a curved growth path, a less developed Country A, if it can achieve a point slope on the growth curve that is consistently higher than that of the more developed Country B, the difference in the slope of the growth curve will guide A's catching up and surpassing of B. The change in the slope of the growth curve is due to A's government policies in promoting

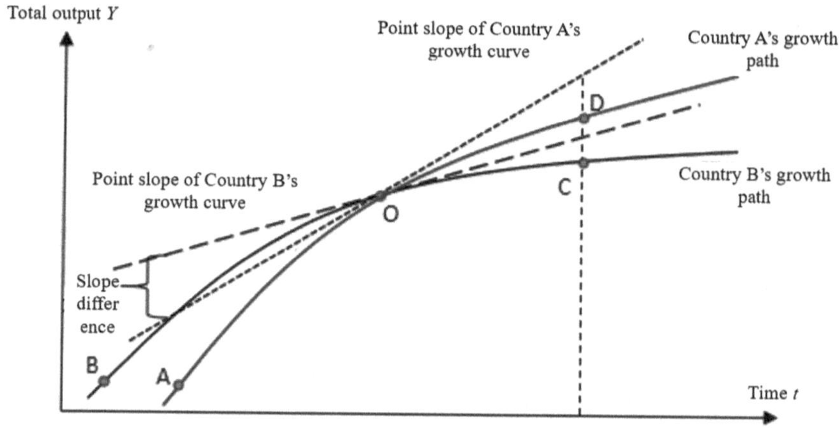


**Fig. 11.13** Changes in the slope of growth curve points lead to an upward shift in the growth path. (Source: Compiled by the author)

technological progress. If the point slope of A's growth curve becomes increasingly steeper, the difference in slope will increase, and the catching-up speed will become faster. This is the dynamic change of factor endowment advantages under policy regulation, which will eventually lead to changes in the economic growth rate of a country.

2. The second NSE theoretical model—based on the extension of the real business cycle model

The Real Business Cycle model can provide a reference for constructing the NSE theoretical model mainly because its basic logic is consistent with that of NSE. The basic feature of the RBC model is to integrate the growth theory with the business cycle theory, breaking the dichotomy of long-term and short-term in macroeconomic analysis, and reflecting the unity of growth and business cycle theories. The theory views actual shocks as the source of economic fluctuations and emphasizes the role of technological shocks rather than monetary shocks, and supply shocks rather than demand shocks in economic cycle fluctuations. Among the external shocks causing economic fluctuations, technological progress accounts for more than two-thirds.

The NSE theory is relatively consistent with this line of thought. If the government's industrial policies and technological investments are considered as shock factors, economic growth can be expressed as corresponding equations, mathematically represented as: the economic growth speed is related to the production function, macro-policies (industrial policies and technological shocks), etc. Therefore, we can give an extended NSE economic growth equation based on the idea of the RBC model:

$$Y_t = Y_t^* + a_t A_t + b_t g_t \tag{11.40}$$

Wherein, $Y_t^*$ represents the potential economic output without considering the government's role, reflecting the comprehensive effect of enterprises' self-sustaining capabilities; $a_t A_t$ represents the impact of technological progress, reflecting the increase in marginal products promoted by technological progress, which in turn affects the economic structure and growth trend. It can theoretically explain the role of factors such as industrial policies and technology policies that can bring about structural changes or changes in potential economic growth. The term $b_t g_t$ represents the relevant structural impact of macro-policies, such as the role of infrastructure and institutional changes, which is different from the direct role of factors.

3. The third NSE theoretical model—based on the perspective of rational comprehensive economic model

Previously, based on China's practice, we constructed the "Market and Government Rational Comprehensive Model," which is consistent with the basic logic of NSE. This theoretical model provides new options for the scenario description and theoretical analysis of NSE. From the perspective of the combination of China's "effective markets" and "proactive governments," we established a market and government rational comprehensive economic model (Zong Liang and Fan Ruoying 2018a, 2018b). By decomposing Eqn. (11.38) according to market and government factors (other factors considered constant), determining corresponding contributions through weighting, and conducting corresponding deductions, we can derive an economic growth equation that meets the criteria.

$$\Delta Y_t = a\Delta Y_{Mt}^* + b\left(\mu_d + \mu_{ss}\right)\left(Y_t - Y_{Gt}^*\right) + b\mu_{sl}\Delta A_t Y_{Mt}^* + b\left(\varepsilon_{dt} + \varepsilon_{st}\right) \tag{11.41}$$

In this way, in a certain period, a country's implementation of important macro-regulation policies can significantly change its own economic growth path. It is evident that the logic of economic growth is consistent with the logic of catching up and surpassing. If an economy can transform its growth path through reforms and technological innovation, raise its potential growth rate to a higher level, and achieve faster and more stable growth over a longer period through relevant macroeconomic policies and supporting measures, it is possible to achieve the goal of catching up with or surpassing another country.

According to the logic of NSE, from the perspective of factor endowment and industrial policy, and considering trends and fluctuations, Equation (11.41) can be simplified to obtain the NSE economic growth equation:

$$Y_t = Y_t^* + \alpha A_t + \beta G_t + \varepsilon_t \tag{11.42}$$

Wherein, $Y_t^*$ represents the potential output without government intervention (under pure market conditions), which can explain the role of factor endowment in economic growth under market conditions, essentially reflecting the self-sustaining capabilities of enterprises; $\alpha A_t$ explains the impact of government-promoted industrial and technological policies, reflecting changes in the economic structure and industrial upgrading; $\beta G_t$ represents the impact of macroeconomic policies and other related aspects, and can explain the role of infrastructure and institutional constraints; and the disturbance term $\varepsilon_t$ represents the impact of various random factors.

### 3.4 *Analysis of the Important Features, Scenarios, and Policy System of NSE*

1. Explanation of the important features of NSE

(1) About the connotation and role of factor endowment structure

From the perspective of theoretical models, the factor endowment of NSE should focus on factors such as labor, capital, and land resources, which are equivalent to the first and third categories. These factors directly influence potential economic growth and do not include institutional factors and infrastructure in the endowment structure. The industrial structure is different from the factor endowment structure to reflect the differences in growth momentum and factors affecting growth. The industrial structure is not only an inevitable result of a certain factor endowment but also an important lever for indirectly promoting technological progress and economic growth. Total factor productivity changes represent an important driving force for economic growth. In this way, technological progress is embodied within the economic operation system, and endogeneity is a natural result. An important concept in NSE, "self-sustaining capability," is equivalent to potential growth rate or potential output without government intervention. Understanding it in this way makes it easier to integrate the concept of "self-sustaining capability" into the entire system and explain it.

(2) About the changes in comparative advantage and growth momentum

The competitive conditions of a country's traded products in the base period are determined by its factor endowment, which is an embodiment of its comparative advantage. Comparative advantage based on factor endowment can be reflected in specific products, related industries, and industrial chains, ultimately manifesting as a country's comprehensive competitiveness. A country's product competitiveness is not simply determined by the factor endowment at a certain time point, but by the dynamic comprehensive competitive advantage of its related products, which is variable. The dynamic comprehensive competitive advantage mainly depends on the following facts: First, the factor endowment advantage of a country in the base period brings about corresponding comparative advantages; second, the government can promote technological innovation and industrial upgrading through industrial policies, increased investment in scientific research, and the development of education, continuously improving labor productivity or total factor productivity (Guo Qingwang et al., 2005), thereby enhancing the competitiveness of related products, and between countries, this manifests as an increase in competitiveness. That is, the government can change a country's products or industry's competitiveness through policies, thereby changing the corresponding dynamic comparative advantage.

The dynamic comprehensive competitive advantage of two countries can be changed, but there is a complex process and a turning point. The significance of the turning point is that regarding a certain product or industry, one country may initially not have another country's factor comparative advantage, but if there is a larger space for the total factor productivity of this industry to increase in the former country, it can create a favorable environment for the development of the industry from the supply side, improve the total factor productivity of the industry, and thus enhance the dynamic comprehensive competitive advantage of the product, becoming an important trade product. This means that catching up and surpassing in industries is a normal phenomenon, and there is no situation where a country's advantage continues indefinitely.

For the cases of countries A and B, assume that Country A developed later and had weaker factor endowment and structure, Country B developed earlier and had a stronger factor endowment structure and policy orientation, due to the differences in factor endowment structure, they grow along different trajectories. The party with weaker factor endowment in the base period (Country A) can only catch up or surpass the party with stronger factor endowment structure (Country B) through policy guidance or exogenous factors.

(3) About what can be done well and the role of government

We know that in Keynesian theory, while both aggregate supply and aggregate demand include the role of government policy, it is believed that the influence of government policy is only short-term, thus the government cannot change the environment in which factor endowments exist to stimulate the dynamic role of potential output growth. In reality, people may wonder: can government action influence the trend of potential economic growth? We briefly explain two typical views: one view is that the change in the trend of economic growth is the result of the market's own action. This view cannot explain why there is a change at this time when the market has always existed. The other view is that industrial policies have no effect on the change in the trend of economic growth. This theory is difficult to explain why, in so-called market-oriented countries, industrial policies or government intervention are becoming more prevalent. Regarding the "degree" of industrial policy, the necessity of industrial policy is obvious; it is not simply a question of whether to have it or not. However, it should also be noted that there needs to be a reasonable degree.

Regarding the concept of "first-mover advantage" and "late-mover advantage" and their realization, from the related diagrams, it can be seen that the factor endowment and the related industrial structure formed at the base period can be understood as a country's first-mover advantage, determined by the factor endowment. If used well, the first-mover advantage may be transformed into a competitive advantage; otherwise, it may be gradually surpassed. In contrast, as a relatively weaker country, due to the existence of reference experience, if with appropriate government's policies, it can promote the increase in total factor productivity and the upgrading of a certain industry through learning relevant experience, introducing advanced foreign technology, opening up and integrating into the international market, and increasing investment in science and technology, industrial policy, etc., which can be understood as the late-mover advantage. However, if without appropriate government's policies, it may also be inactive, always following behind. The government's active role lies in selecting a suitable breakthrough point for the industry, better utilizing its own existing foundation, and creating good conditions, which can stimulate the late-mover advantage of a country, achieving the transformation point of comprehensive dynamic competitive advantage more quickly. Of course, first-mover advantage and late-mover advantage are not inevitable, but only possible, and need reasonable policy support to be realized. To play the late-mover advantage and achieve catching up, it is often necessary to provide appropriate protection, rather than to advocate free trade, and when a country's competitiveness is strong, it usually advocates free trade. The protection theory of List and the theory of free trade of Adam Smith are reasonable under their respective conditions, which is a good example. In this way, we can better understand the industrial policy of NSE and the conclusions about first-mover advantage and late-mover advantage.

2. About achieving the goal of catching up and even surpassing

A country's government can achieve a relative shift in the competitive advantage of an industry by improving the market, stimulating market vitality, and creating a market environment conducive to industrial development, thereby achieving the goal of catching up with or even surpassing another country in a particular industry, or even in comprehensive economic strength. Considering that catching up or surpassing is more often manifested as a country's increase in comprehensive economic competitiveness, here we describe possible scenarios through the comprehensive economic competitiveness of countries A and B.

Scenario 1: Country A can catch up with or surpass Country B. In the base period, A and B have different factor endowments and comparative advantages, as well as growth rates. The former needs to maintain a continuous increase in new total output for many years to exceed the latter and achieve surpassing. It is crucial for the government of Country A to promote the upward trajectory of the potential growth rate curve through reforms, investment in education, technology, and industrial policies, which can enhance the potential growth rate and directly determine whether catching up is possible and the time required for catching up. Since both countries are developing, A catching up with and surpassing B usually requires a long time.

Scenario 2: Country A within the critical zone of catching up or surpassing. In the base period, A and B have different factor endowments and comparative advantages, as well as growth rates. It is crucial for the government of Country A to promote the upward shift of the potential growth rate curve, which is equivalent to enhancing the potential growth speed, but overall, the differences are relatively small and not stable. Then, there are two situations: one is that catching up or surpassing can be achieved, in which case the requirements for Country A's government policies are high to effectively promote long-term sustainable economic development. The other situation is that catching up or surpassing cannot be achieved; if the base-period conditions are significantly different, the potential for market and government action is relatively limited, and a "two steps forward, one step back" development process may occur.

Regarding the above situations, there is one point that needs to be noted: during the process of catching up with another country, a country may encounter the other country's suppression, which will increase the difficulty of catching up. Since catching up or surpassing involves a significant change in the economic status of A and B, it is a goal and opportunity for A, but it may be a risk and challenge for B. If B takes measures to prevent A from surpassing it, then the time required for A to surpass B will be longer.

Country A cannot catch up with or surpass Country B. If the base-period conditions of Country A are average, and its potential for market and government action is also limited, then it cannot promote the continuous increase in the potential growth rate of the economy. In this scenario, Country A will be unable to catch up with or surpass Country B.

3. International rules and related policy propositions

Due to the close correlation between comparative advantage and barriers between countries, which involves a country's comprehensive competitiveness and, in extreme cases, even its economic security, maintaining international balance requires international rules. Generally speaking, governments of different countries create a favorable supply and demand environment for their own products' development under the conditions permitted by international rules, through reforms, regulations, or reasonable protection policies, enhancing the competitiveness of related products and changing the dynamic comprehensive competitive advantage of the products. This is similar to how teams from different countries can improve their athletic performance through different training measures under the same international rules, but international rules should be universally recognized by the international community, rather than being an extension of the laws and regulations of a single country.

Comparatively, if a certain industry has long-term development potential, the party with the advantage tends to favor free trade, while the disadvantaged party may adopt certain protection measures. It is normal for a country to catch up with and surpass another country in its output, and it is not the case that one country's development can always be better. A country's government can gradually increase its total factor productivity through industrial policies and other measures, catching up with or surpassing another country, which is very realistic. The changes in the international status of countries throughout history have proven this point. If it were not so, there would not have been the early development of the UK, and there would not have been the subsequent prosperity of the United States. It would also be difficult to explain today's successful practice of China's reform and opening up and the current trade and economic conflicts between China and the United States.

### 3.5 *Brief Analysis of Empirical Issues of the NSE Theory*

The following is an explanation of the logical rationality of the NSE theory through three relevant actual situations.

1. Rationality of the NSE theory from the perspective of personal career development

Personal career development is similar to a country's economic growth, primarily depending on: first, one's own talents, which are the potential qualities, similar to factor endowment. The differences in potential qualities mean differences in potential capabilities, which are equivalent to the potential economic growth rate without government intervention. Second, education and training provided by teachers, parents, and social work, which are similar to the government's positive role, and industrial policies and technological investments are akin to support from families and society. These investments can greatly change a person's potential capabilities, causing the potential capability curve to shift (refer to Fig. 11.3). Of course, personal effort is also needed. If the education provided by teachers and parents is scientific and effective, with more opportunities for learning and practice, a person's potential capabilities can be greatly enhanced. Conversely, if the educational methods are inappropriate, a person's potential capabilities may decrease; third, of two people with differences or even significant differences in their base-period conditions, one can catch up with or even surpass the other in terms of career development after years of continuous changes, with appropriate opportunities. The saying "30 years on the east bank, 30 years on the west bank" vividly describes this situation.

2. China's continuous rapid economic development from 1978 to 2020 and comparison with the United States during the same period

In 1978, China's per capita GDP was only 381 yuan, making it a typical low-income country in the world at that time. By 2019–2021, this figure had continuously reached over 10,000 US dollars, placing China among the ranks of upper-middle-income countries. Over the past 40-plus years of reform and opening up, China's economy has experienced leapfrog development, maintaining its position as the world's second-largest economy. Its influence on the global economy has gradually increased, and the industrial structure has shifted from extensive and labor-intensive to high-quality, innovative, and developmental. Particularly after 2002, the government's contribution to actual economic growth has significantly increased (Zong Liang, Shi Yuan et al., 2022). At the same time, China has not experienced major economic or financial crises for decades, achieving an organic unity of quality, quantity, and speed in its economic development. From joining the WTO to proposing the "Belt and Road Initiative" and the concept of a community with a shared future for mankind, China's importance on the international stage has been on the rise, but it still lags behind the United States in some areas. This demonstrates that surpassing another country is a long and arduous process.

The NSE has formed a relatively complete theoretical system, and many of its important conclusions have originated from China's successful practice. This theory is integrated with China's economic development, providing appropriate guidance for promoting the high-quality development of China's economy. However, it should also be applicable to other countries or regions.

## 4 Externally Emphasizing Cooperation and Exchange, Internally Prioritizing Innovation and Development: China's Due Contributions

As a responsible global power, China will actively address the world's pressing issues and steadfastly promote the advancement of economic globalization.

First, innovation and upgrading will be the keywords for China's industrial development in the future. China is shifting from investment and factor-driven growth to innovation-driven development, integrating itself into the global innovation chain. Lacking core technologies in manufacturing and witnessing the erosion of its comparative advantage in labor-intensive industries due to soaring factor costs—a gap that Southeast Asian nations are progressively filling—China must focus on upgrading traditional industries and nurturing emerging strategic industries. Simultaneously, it will drive globalization centered on the liberalization and development of modern services. By implementing a strategy to expand domestic demand, China can leverage this to foster an innovation-driven economy, transitioning from a simple export-oriented model to a high-level open economy.

Second, China will persistently advocate for the propagation of the concept of a community of shared future for mankind. This vision offers a new blueprint for globalization, pursuing common interests and values for all humanity. While nations share interests and confront conflicts, globalization intertwines their destinies; in this era, common interests outweigh disputes. Peace, amity, and harmony have been ideals pursued and passed down by the Chinese nation for over 5000 years. Going forward, China will proactively take more international responsibilities, engage in global governance, and promote a universally recognized value system anchored in equality, inclusiveness, mutual benefit, and sustainability. It will uphold a global economic development model that is equitable and balanced. Amid the pandemic, disruptions to the flow of people, goods, and capital—pillars of global prosperity and development—call for active consultation and communication among nations. Major powers should set aside differences and collaborate to address the spread of the virus and its implications for global development.

Third, China will actively construct a multilateral global governance framework based on win-win cooperation. Post-World War II, developed nations dominated international economic rule-making, leading to a certain "institutional bias" in the global governance order that favored their interests. With the rise of emerging economies like China and the growing contribution of developing nations to global economic growth, they warrant greater say to protect their interests. Thus, China must push for reforms in global multilateral governance mechanisms, amplifying the voice of emerging economies, and strive to contribute its due share to the world economy.

# Postscript

The relationship between the market and the government has long been a focal point of the debate on economic theory. However, the Chinese narrative provides a unique key to unlocking innovative perspectives on economic theory. At the beginning of 2021, I undertook a key project from the Academy of Contemporary China and World Studies, focusing on telling the Chinese story about the integration of an effective market and an efficient government. This project offered a golden opportunity to delve deeper into this narrative. The Chinese story is not only captivating but also inspiring since it sows in people's minds the hope for the future. It presents new models and theoretical options for economic development in countries and regions around the world.

The practical work and theoretical exploration over the years drives me to dig into significant issues on economic theory, particularly the economic logic behind China's success and the origins of the diverse schools of economic thought. Centering on these complex questions, I have gradually developed a unique logical framework in my research. Adopting the theoretical models to condense China's successful practices into economic theory has been an especially fascinating endeavor. In recent years, I have engaged in in-depth discussions and research with several young experts from the Bank of China Research Institute and the financial sector and have my works published in related journals, which are well-received.



Z. Liang, *The Innovation of Economic Theory in China*,
https://doi.org/10.1007/978-981-95-2713-7

Hereby I would like to express my special gratitude for their contributions.

In my long-time exploration, I have received extensive support from the industry. I am deeply grateful to the following experts for their support: Ms. Chen Wenling, Chief Economist; Mr. Zhang Yansheng, Chief Researcher; Mr. Zhang Yongjun, Secretary-General of China Center for International Economic Exchanges; Mr. Li Daokui, Director of the Academic Center for Chinese Economic Practice and Thinking, Tsinghua University; Mr. Bai Chong'en, Dean of the School of Economics and Management of Tsinghua University; Professors Su Jian and Zhang Zheng from the School of Economics at Peking University; Professors Wang Jinbin and Lei Da from the School of Economics at Renmin University of China; Mr. Liang Qi, Member and Deputy Secretary of the Party Committee at Nankai University, and Professor Li Zhihui from the School of Economics of Nankai University; Mr. Nie Jun and Mr. Yu Zhen, respectively Dean and Vice Dean of the School of Economics, Wuhan University; Professors Du Li and Li Xiao from Jilin University; Mr. Liu Yuanchun and Ms. Liu Liya, respectively President and Vice President of Shanghai University of Finance and Economics; Mr. Ou Minggang from China Foreign Affairs University; Mr. Zhu Baoliang, former Chief Economist at the State Information Center; Mr. Ba Shusong, Executive Dean of the HSBC Financial Research Institute at Peking University and Chief Economist of China Banking Association; Mr. Feng Xingke, Secretary-General of the World Finance Forum; Director Chen Weidong, Deputy Directors E Zhihuan and Zhou Jingtong, and Senior Researcher Wang Jiaqiang of the Research Institute of Bank of China; Mr. Cao Yuanzheng, former Chairman of BOC International Research Company; Ms. Zhong Hong, Chief Economist at Bank of China (Hong Kong); Mr. Zhang Xingrong, Director of the China Yangtze River Delta Financial Research Institute; Mr. Wang Fanghong, Senior Researcher at the China Hainan Financial Research Institute; and Mr. Wang Zhifeng, Executive Director of Tencent Financial Research Institute.

I would like to extend my special thanks to my doctoral advisor, Professor Wu Nianlu, whose care and encouragement have provided me with the motivation to go on with my research and produce a work highly relevant to the era.

This book explores the theoretical development around the Chinese story characterized by reform and opening-up, offering new perspectives on China's market economy model and theory. I am particularly grateful to China Renmin University Press for its recommendation and to Palgrave Macmillan for its support so that the English edition has come out. My special thanks also go to three young experts from the Bank of China Research Institute: Dr. Fan Ruoying, Dr. Li Yingting, and Dr. Ping Jing, who were responsible for the translation and proofreading of the English manuscript. I would also like to express my gratitude to Professor Kevin H. Zhang from the University of Illinois Urbana-Champaign and Professor Wang Nianhua, Director of the Training Program Center.

Given that the topics discussed in this book are still evolving and our knowledge is limited, there might be inadequacies in the book. If you find any and point them out, I will very appreciate your advice and suggestions!

Zong Liang
March 2025

# References


Abboushi, Suhail. "Trade Protectionism: Reasons and Outcomes." Competitiveness Review, vol. 20, no. 5, 2010, pp. 384–394.

Acemoglu D., Restrepo P., "The Race between Man and Machine; Implications of Technology for Growth. Factor Shares, and Employment", American Economic Review, (2018): 1488–1542.

Aghion, P., & Howitt, P. (1992). A model of growth through creative destruction. Econometrica, 60 (2), 323–351.

Aghion, P., & Howitt, P. (1998). Capital accumulation and innovation as complementary factors in long-run growth. Journal of Economic Growth, 3 (2), 111–130.

Akerlof G A, Yellen J L. A Near-Rational Model of the Business Cycle, with Wage and Price Inertia [J]. Quarterly Journal of Economics, 1985, 100(Supplement): 823–838.

Arrow, K. J. The economic implications of learning by doing [J]. The Review of Economic Studies, 1962, 29:155–173.

Balassa, B. (1966). Tariff reductions and trade in manufactures among the industrial countries. American Economic Review, 56, 466–473.

Barro R. J., Gordon D. B. Rules, Discretion and Reputation in a Model of Monetary Policy [J]. Journal of Monetary Economics, 1983, 12(1): 101–121.

Barro R. J. A Capital Market in an Equilibrium Business Cycle Model [J]. Econometrica, 1989, 48(3): 645–662.

Barro, Robert J., and Xavier Sala-i-Martin. 2004. Economic Growth. 2nd ed. Cambridge, MA: The MIT Press.

Baserovich, A. (2004). Optical properties of nanomaterials. Advances in Materials Science, 18(3), 45–50.





Z. Liang, *The Innovation of Economic Theory in China*,
https://doi.org/10.1007/978-981-95-2713-7

Benigno G., Fornaro L. Stagnation Traps [J]. Review of Economic Studies, 2018, 85(3): 1565–1607.

Bernanke, B. S., & Mihov, I. (1998). Measuring monetary policy. The Quarterly Journal of Economics, 113(3), 869–902.

Black, Fischer. Exploring general equilibrium [M]. Cambridge, Mass: MIT Press, 1995.

Blanchard O. Do DSGE Models Have a Future? [J]. Policy Briefs, 2016-01-05: 1–12.

Blanchard O. Convergence? Thoughts About the Evolution of Mainstream Macroeconomics over the Last 40 Years [J]. NBER Macroeconomics Annual, 2025, 40: 3–48.

Brander, J. A., Krugman, P. R. (1983). A 'reciprocal dumping' model of international trade [J]. Journal of International Economics, 15(3–4), 313–321.

Brander, J., & Spencer, B. (1984). Tariff protection and imperfect competition [C]// KIERZKOWSKI H. Monopolistic competition and international trade. Oxford: Oxford University Press.

Burns, A. F., & Mitchell, W. C. (1946). Measuring Business Cycles. National Bureau of Economic Research (NBER), Studies in Business Cycles.

Calvo G. A. Staggered Prices in a Utility-maximizing Framework [J]. Journal of Monetary Economics, 1983, 12(3): 383–398.

Chari V. V., Kehoe P. J., McGrattan E. R. Business Cycle Accounting [J]. Econometrica, 2007, 75(3): 781–836.

Crafts N. The Rise and Fall of American Growth: Exploring the Numbers [J]. The American Economic Review, 2016, 106(5): 1228–1251.

Domar E. D. Capital Expansion, Rate of Growth and Employment [J]. Econometrica, 1946, 14(2): 137–147.

Domar E. D. Expansion and Employment [J]. American Economic Review, 1947, 37(1): 34–55.

Ethier, W. J. (1979). Internationally decreasing costs and world trade. Journal of International Economics, 9(1), 1–24.

Falvey RE. Commercial policy and intra-industry trade [J]. Journal of International Economics, 1981, 11(4): 495–511.

Frisch, R. (1931). Confluence analysis by means of complete regression systems [J]. Nordisk Matematisk Tidsskrift, 13 (1–2): 1–86.

Gambetti L., Musso A. Loan Supply Shocks and the Business Cycle [J]. Journal of Applied Econometrics, 2017, 32(4): 729–751.

Georgiadis, G., & Mehl, A. (2016). Financial globalisation and monetary policy effectiveness. Journal of International Economics, 103, 200–212.

Giddens, A., & Castells, M. (1996). The rise of the network society. Blackwell Publishers.

Giese G., Helmut W., "Graphical Analysis of the New Neoclassical Synthesis", SSRN Electronic Journal, 2006(9).

Grubel, H. G., & Lloyd, P. J. (1975). Intra-industry trade: The theory and measurement of international trade in differentiated products. Macmillan.

Hacker, Jacob S., and Paul Pierson. American Amnesia: How the War on Government Led Us to Forget What Made America Prosper. Simon & Schuster, 2016.

Han, L., & Wang, Z. (2005). Research on the efficiency of capital allocation in China's real economy. Economic Research Journal, (1), 77–84.

Hansen G., "Indivisible Labor and the Business Cycle", Journal of Monetary Economics, 1988(21).

Harrod R. F. An Essay in Dynamic Theory [J]. The Economic Journal, 1939, 49(193): 14–33.

Heckscher, E. F., & Ohlin, B. (1991). Heckscher-Ohlin trade theory (H. Flam & M. J. Flanders, Eds.). MIT Press. (Original works published 1919 & 1933)

Helpman E., Itskhoki O. Labour Market Rigidities, Trade and Unemployment [J]. The Review of Economic Studies, 2010, 77(3): 1100–1130.

Hodrick R. The Empirical Evidence on the Efficiency of Forward and Futures Foreign Exchange Markets [J]. Journal of International Economics, 1987, 25 (3–4): 283–308.

Hodrick R.J., Prescott E.C., et al., "Postwar U.S. Business Cycles: An Empirical Investigation", Journal of Money, Credit and Banking, 1997, 29(1).

Hsieh C., Hurst E., Jones C. I., et al. The Allocation of Talent and U. S. Economic Growth [J]. Econometrica, 2019, 87(5): 1439–1474.

Hodrick R. J., Prescott E. C., et al. Postwar U. S. Business Cycles: An Empirical Investigation [J]. Journal of Money, Credit and Banking, 1997, 29(1): 1–16.

Jiang, Yongji. "Japanese Scholars' Main Contributions to Mathematical Marxist Economics." Economic Perspectives, no. 2, 2010, pp. 12–20.

Joanne Chiu J., Russolillo S. China's Yuan Breaches Critical Level of 7 to the Dollar, Prompting Trump Critique [J]. WSJ, 2019-08-06: A1–A3.

Jorgenson D. W. Information Technology and The US Economy [J]. American Economic Review, 2001, 91(1): 1–32.

Juglar, C. (1862). Des crises commerciales et de leur retour périodique en France, en Angleterre et aux États-Unis. Paris: Guillaumin.

Justiniano A., Primiceri G. E., Tambalotti A. Investment Shocks and Business Cycles [J]. Journal of Monetary Economics, 2010, 57(2): 132–148.

Keynes J. M. The Means to Prosperity [M]. London: Macmillan, 1933.

Keynes J. M. The General Theory of Employment, Interest and Money [M]. London: Macmillan, 1936.

Kitchin J. Cycles and Trends in Economic Factors [J]. The Review of Economic Statistics, 1923, 5(1): 10–16.

King, M. A., & Robson, M. H. (1993). A dynamic model of investment and endogenous growth. Scandinavian Journal of Economics, 95 (3), 445–466.

Kiyotaki, N., & Moore, J. (1997). Credit cycles. Journal of Political Economy, 105(2), 211–248.

Kondratieff, N. D., & Stolper, W. F. (1935). The Long Waves in Economic Life. The Review of Economic Statistics, 17 (6), 105–115.

Kravis, I. B. A New Look at Economic Growth [J]. American Economic Review, 1971, 61(1): 15–25.

Krugman P R. Increasing returns, monopolistic competition, and international trade [J]. Journal of International Economics, 1979, 9(4): 469–479.

Krugman P R. Scale economies, product differentiation, and the pattern of trade [J]. American Economic Review, 1980, 70(5): 950–959.

Krugman P R. Import protection as export promotion: International competition in the presence of oligopoly and economies of scale [C]//Monopolistic Competition and International Trade. Oxford University Press, 1984: 184–196.

Krusell P., Boppart T. Labor Supply in the Past, Present, and Future: A Balanced-Growth Perspective [J]. Journal of Political Economy, 2019, 128(1): 1–49.

Kydland F. E., Prescott E. C. Time to Build and Aggregate Fluctuations [J]. Econometrica, 1982, 50(6): 1345–1370.

Laitner, J. (2000). Structural Change and Economic Growth. The Review of Economic Studies, 67(3), 545–561.

Leontief, W. (1953). Domestic production and foreign trade: The American capital position re-examined. The Quarterly Journal of Economics, 67(4), 331–349.

Li, L., Tang, Y., & Xiang, J. (2020). Measuring China's monetary policy uncertainty and its impact on the real economy. Emerging Markets Review, 44, 100714.

Lin, Y. F., Feder, G., Lau, L. J., & Luo, X. (1993). Rural reforms and agricultural growth in China. American Economic Review, 83(3), 34–51.

Lin, Justin Yifu. The Quest for Prosperity: How Developing Economies Can Take Off. Princeton University Press, 2012.

Liu, W., & Cai, Z. (2019). Economic cycles and long-term economic growth: China's experience and characteristics (1978–2018). Economic Perspectives, (7), 20–36.

Liua W. Macroeconomic Regulation in China and the New Agricultural Policy [J]. Problem of Agricultural Economy, 2004 (7): 23–28.

Loayza N., Oviedo A. M., Servén L. Regulation and Macroeconomic Performance [J]. Topics in Regulatory Economics & Policy, 2005, 15(4): 89–124.

Long J. B., Plosser C. I. Real Business Cycles [J]. Journal of Political Economy, 1983, 91(1): 39–69.

López-Salido D., Stein J. C., Zakrajšek E. Credit-Market Sentiment and the Business Cycle [J]. The Quarterly Journal of Economics, 2017, 132(3): 1371–1426.

Lucas R., "Expectations and the Neutrality of Money". Journal of Economic Theory, 1972, 4(2), 103–124.

Lucas R., "Models of Business Cycles", Economica, 1988, 55(218).
Lucas R. On the Mechanics of Economic Development [J]. Journal of Monetary Economics, 1988b, 22(1): 3–42.
Lucas R. Human Capital and Growth [J]. American Economic Review, 2015, 105(5): 47–52.
Matkiw N. G. Small Menu Costs and Large Business Cycles: A Macroeconomic Model of Monopoly [J]. Quarterly Journal of Economics, 1985, 100(2): 529–539.
Mayer T, Melitz M J, Ottaviano G I P. Market size, competition, and the product mix of exporters [R]. Cambridge: National Bureau of Economic Research, 2011.
McConnel M. M., Perez-Quiros G. Output Fluctuations in the United States: What Has Changed since the Early 1980's? [J]. American Economic Review, 2000, 90(5): 1464–1476.
McKinnon, R. I. (1994). The order of financial liberalization. Journal of International Finance, 22(5), 45–50.
Melitz, M. J. (2003). The impact of trade on intra-industry reallocations and aggregate industry productivity. Econometrica, 71(6), 1695–1725.
Melitz M., Ottaviano G. Market Size, Trade and Productivity [J]. The Review of Economic Studies, 2008, 75(1): 295–316.
Melvin, J. R., & Warne, R. W. (1973). Monopoly and the theory of international trade. Journal of International Economics, 3(2), 117–134.
Mike F., Kizilkaya O. Testing the Theory of PPP for Emerging Market Economies that Practice Flexible Exchange Rate Regimes [J]. Applied Economics Letters, 2019, 26(17): 1407–1411.
Pigou A. C., The Theory of Unemployment, London: Macmillan, 1933.
Ramsey, F. P. (1928). A mathematical theory of saving. The Economic Journal, 38(152), 543–559.
Ricardo, D. (1817). On the principles of political economy and taxation. John Murray.
Romer, P. M. (1990). Endogenous technological change. Journal of Political Economy, 98 (5), S71–S102.
Romer P., "The Trouble with Macroeconomics", The American Economist, 2016(1).
Rooney K. China Confirms It Is Suspending Agricultural Product Purchases in Response to Trump's New Tariffs [J]. CNBC, 2019-08-05: 1–5.
Ruggie, J. G. (1996). Winning the peace: America and world order in the new era. Columbia University Press.
Samuelson P. A. Where Ricardo and Mill Rebut and Confirm Arguments of Mainstream Economists Supporting Globalization [J]. Journal of Economic Perspectives, 2004, 18(3): 135–146.
Samuelson P. A. International Factor-Price Equalization Once Again [J]. Economic Journal, 1949, 59(234): 181–197.

Samuelson P. Interactions between the Multiplier Analysis and the Principle of Acceleration [J]. Review of Economics & Statistics, 1939, 21(2): 75–78.

Samuelson, P. A. (1973). Samuelson's "reply on Marxian matters". Journal of Economic Literature, 11(1), 64–68.

Samuelson, P. A. (1979). Why we should not make mean log of wealth big though years to act are long. Journal of Banking and Finance, 3, 305–307.

Schumpeter J. A., et al. The Theory of Economics Development [J]. Journal of Political Economy, 1934, 1(2): 120–130.

Schumpeter J. A. Business Cycles: A Theoretical Historical and Statistical Analysis of the Capitalist Process [J]. Journal of Political Economy, 1940(12): 647–655.

Smith, A. (1776). An inquiry into the nature and causes of the wealth of nations. W. Strahan and T. Cadell.

Solow R. M. A Contribution to the Theory of Economic Growth [J]. Quarterly Journal of Economics, 1956, 70(1): 65–94.

Solow R. M. Technical Change and Aggregate Production Function [J]. Review of Economics & Statistics, 1957, 39(3): 312–320.

Stiglitz J. E., "Where Modern Macroeconomics Went Wrong", Oxford Review of Economic Policy, 2018, 34(1–2).

Stock J. H., Watson M. W. Has the Business Cycle Changed and Why? [J]. NBER Macroeconomics Annual, 2002, 17: 159–218.

Swan T. W. Economic Growth and Capital Accumulation [J]. Economic Record, 1956, 32(2): 334–361.

Tang Z. Macroeconomic Regulation and State Intervention [J]. Contemporary Economic Research, 2000 (4): 15–20.

Wang, Qiaoru, et al. "Consistent Fluctuations, Regional Coordination, and Heterogeneous Differentiation of China's Provincial Economic Cycles." China Industrial Economics, no. 10, 2019, pp. 61–79.

Wang Z., Zhang S., Dallago B., Wang X. Enterprises and Ownership Reform in China [J]. The Singapore Economic Review, 2023, 69(3): 857–882.

Woodford M. Convergence in Macroeconomics: Elements of the New Synthesis [J]. American Economic Journal: Macroeconomics, 2009, 1(1): 267–293.

Young, A. (1991). Learning by doing and the dynamic effects of international trade. The Quarterly Journal of Economics, 106(2), 369–405.

Yu, Y. D. (2022). The reemergence of the issue of US 'external sustainability' and what should be China's responses. China Economic Journal, 15(3), 263–276.

Zhang, J. (2013). The Misunderstood Chinese Economy. Oriental Press.

Zhou L., Liu X. The new government–business relationship and corporate philanthropy: An analysis based on political motivation [J]. Eurasian Business Review, 2024, 14 (2): 189–212.

Zhu, F. Q. (2017). The Logic of Economic Growth: From the Perspective of New Structural Economics. Peking University Press.

安宇宏。朱格拉周期[J]. 宏观经济管理，2013 (4): 78–80.

卞志村，赵亮，丁慧。货币政策调控框架转型、财政乘数非线性变动与新时代财政工具选择 [J]. 经济研究，2019, 54 (9): 4–21.
蔡昉，刘浩。中国改革成功经验的逻辑[J]. 中国社会科学，2019, 40 (3): 4–23.
蔡继明，江永基。基于广义价值论的功能性分配理论[J]. 经济研究，2010 (6): 13–24.
蔡继明。从混合经济形成看两大经济思想体系融合[J]. 学术月刊，2015 (1): 63–71.
曹红辉。尽快建立”一带一路” 公共卫生国际合作机制[J]. 国际融资，2020 (5): 45–48.
曾辉，尹小兵。中国潜在GDP 估计的比较研究:基于1952—2008 年度和季度数据[J]. 南方金融，2009 (6): 32–36.
陈柏良，李闽榕。习近平总书记关于中国特色社会主义政治经济学的思想探源[J]. 政治经济学评论，2019, 10 (2): 3–20.
陈超凡.”东方凯恩斯” 管仲的经济哲思:浅谈管仲与凯恩斯经济思想之略同[J]. 价值工程，2010, 29 (33): 289–290.
陈德铭。全球化下的经贸秩序和治理规则[J]. 国际展望，2018 (6): 1-15+156.
陈杰，王立勇。改革开放以来我国宏观调控的有效性研究[J]. 宏观经济研究，2015 (3): 3–12.
陈钧浩。全球化经济的要素流动与国际贸易理论的发展方向[J]. 世界经济研究，2013 (17): 3–8.
陈乐一。对西方经济周期理论的一般考察[J]. 财经问题研究，1998 (4): 15–20.
陈诗一，陈登科。经济周期视角下的中国财政支出乘数研究[J]. 中国社会科学，2019 (8): 63–82.
陈晓光，张宇麟。信贷约束、政府消费与中国实际经济周期[J]. 经济研究，2010, 45 (12): 48–60.
程家玉. 《管子》的轻重理论与经济发展新常态[J]. 合作经济与科技，2018 (11): 4–6.
程霖，陈旭东。改革开放40 年中国特色社会主义市场经济理论的发展与创新[J]. 经济学动态，2018 (12): 36–48.
丛屹，蔡双立。从”摸着石头过河”到”道路自信”: 中国特色社会主义市场经济转型发展路径回溯、理论进路与热点问题高端研讨会综述[J]. 现代财经(天津财经大学学报), 2018, 38 (12): 3–15.
冯俊新，王鹤菲，何平，等。金融危机后西方学术界对宏观经济学的反思[J]. 经济学动态，2011 (11): 103–110.
傅殷才。当代西方”混合经济”理论[J]. 世界经济，1988 (1): 74–78.
郭杰，郭琦。信贷市场有限竞争环境中财政引发的国有部门投资的宏观影响:基于扩展RBC 模型的研究[J]. 管理世界，2015 (5): 11–23.
郭克莎，汪红驹。经济新常态下宏观调控的若干重大转变[J]. 中国工业经济，2015 (11): 5–18.
郭庆旺，贾俊雪。中国全要素生产率的估算:1979—2004 [J]. 经济研究，2005 (6): 51–60.

何青，钱宗鑫，郭俊杰。房地产驱动了中国经济周期吗?[J]. 经济研究，2015, 50 (12): 33–46.
何自力。推动供给侧结构性改革必须加强供给侧宏观调控[J]. 政治经济学评论，2016, 7 (2): 5–18.
洪银兴. 40 年经济改革逻辑和政治经济学领域的重大突破[J]. 经济研究参考，2018 (72): 3–10.
侯成琪，黄彤彤。影子银行、监管套利和宏观审慎政策[J]. 经济研究，2020, 55 (7): 56–72.
侯锦超。管仲的经济变革思想及其对后世的影响[J]. 经济师，2019 (11): 16–17.
胡家勇。试论社会主义市场经济理论的创新和发展[J]. 经济研究，2016, 51 (7): 4–16.
华冬芳，洪敏。中国经济周期波动的实证研究[J]. 统计与决策，2013 (1): 130–133.
黄树人。当前主流宏观经济学的基本特征:新古典主义与新凯恩斯主义比较的启示[J]. 经济评论，2002 (6): 43–47.
黄赜琳。中国经济周期特征与财政政策效应:一个基于三部门RBC 模型的实证分析[J]. 经济研究，2005 (6): 27–39.
纪敏，王月。对存货顺周期调整和宏观经济波动的分析[J]. 经济学动态，2009 (4): 29–33.
纪尧。基于马尔科夫机制转换理论的中国乘数— 加速数模型分析[J]. 统计与决策，2017 (3): 131–134.
简新华，余江。市场经济只能建立在私有制基础上吗?— 兼评公有制与市场经济不相容论[J]. 经济研究，2016, 51 (12): 22–35.
姜跃春，张玉环。新冠疫情不会中断经济全球化进程[J]. 世界知识，2020 (7): 28–29.
李浩，胡永刚，马知遥。国际贸易与中国的实际经济周期:基于封闭与开放经济的RBC 模型比较分析[J]. 经济研究，2007 (5): 17–26.
李腊生，关敏芳。我国政府经济刺激方案的结构性优化[J]. 财经科学，2010 (1): 50–57.
李琳，杨柳. 《管子》与《国富论》的经济思想比较[J]. 经济问题探索，2012 (10): 184–188.
李星伟。从乘数加速数模型角度看当前中国经济[J]. 现代商业，2011 (9): 168–169.
李扬。宏观调控再思考[J]. 新金融，2016 (1): 4–8.
梁琪，郝毅。地方政府债务置换与宏观经济风险缓释研究[J]. 经济研究，2019, 54 (4): 4–20.
梁琪，滕建州。中国宏观经济和金融总量结构变化及因果关系研究[J]. 经济研究，2006 (1): 11–22.
林宏宇。大疫呼唤大治，G20 特别峰会视角下的全球治理[J]. 人民论坛，2020 (10): 54–57.
林毅夫。中国经济学的理论发展与创新[J]. 经济导刊，2017 (7): 4–7.
林毅夫。新结构经济学的理论基础和发展方向[J]. 经济评论，2017 (3): 3–16.

刘安长。我国逆周期财政政策70 年:演进、镜鉴与展望[J]. 经济学家，2019 (12): 5–14.
刘斌。我国DSGE 模型的开发及在货币政策分析中的应用[J]. 金融研究，2008 (10): 1–19.
刘达禹，刘金全，赵婷婷。中国经济" 新常态" 下的宏观调控:基于世界经济景气变动的经验分析[J]. 经济学家，2016 (10): 19–27.
刘明远。西方主流宏观调控政策在中国的实践与反思[J]. 当代经济研究，2017 (6): 23–31.
刘瑞明，白永秀。晋升激励、宏观调控与经济周期:一个政治经济学框架[J]. 南开经济研究，2007 (5): 19–31.
刘伟，苏剑." 新常态" 下的中国宏观调控[J]. 经济科学，2014, 36 (4): 5–14.
刘伟，苏剑。供给管理与我国现阶段的宏观调控[J]. 经济研究，2007 (2): 4–15.
柳思维。改革开放与中国特色社会主义市场经济理论的创新[J]. 扬州大学学报(人文社会科学版), 2018, 22 (5): 28–35.
吕朝凤，黄梅波。国际贸易、国际利率与中国实际经济周期:基于封闭经济和开放经济三部门RBC 模型的比较分析[J]. 管理世界，2012 (3): 24–36.
马家喜。论我国市场经济波动中的典型朱格拉周期现象[J]. 理论导刊，2011 (11): 74–76.
马学锋。实际经济周期理论述评[J]. 经济问题探索，2002 (9): 11–14.
那艺，贺京同。从" 宏观经济学的麻烦" 看行为宏观经济学的兴起与发展[J]. 经济学动态，2017 (7): 85–97.
庞增安。社会主义市场经济理论的形成机制[J]. 南通大学学报(社会科学版), 2012, 28 (2): 117–122.
裴长洪。法治经济:习近平社会主义市场经济理论新亮点[J]. 经济学动态，2015 (1): 4–11.
秦宪文。论管仲经济思想的历史地位[J]. 经济理论与政策研究，2013 (1): 156–165.
秦宇。政府支出内生化的四部门乘数加速数模型:基于中国数据的实证分析[J]. 经济问题探索，2016 (4): 1–8.
邱斌，刘修岩。新常态背景下中国对外贸易转型升级的理论创新与政策研究会议综述[J]. 经济研究，2015 (7): 186–192.
裘翔，周强龙。影子银行与货币政策传导[J]. 经济研究，2014, 49 (5): 4–17.
邵彦敏。公有制观念的冲突:社会主义市场经济理论与英国工党市场社会主义理论比较[J]. 马克思主义研究，2011 (8): 74–81.
单豪杰。中国资本存量K 的再估算:1952—2006 年[J]. 数量经济技术经济研究，2008 (10): 17–31.
沈坤荣。经济增长理论的演进、比较与评述(上)[J]. 经济学动态，2006 (5): 71–77.
沈文玮，杨仁忠。从理论突破到体制创新:中国特色的社会主义与市场经济融合发展研究[J]. 现代财经(天津财经大学学报), 2018, 38 (11): 3–14.
沈越，邱晨曦。自由主义与干预主义的新综合:新兴新古典综合学派评析[J]. 经济学动态，2005 (12): 77–82.

宋华。管仲" 藏富于民" 及" 官山海" 的财政思想及启示[J]. 中外企业家，2014 (11): 236–237.
苏剑。基于总供求模型和中国特色的宏观调控体系[J]. 经济学家，2017 (7): 5–13.
苏云婷。新冠肺炎疫情背后:现实主义全球治理观回溯[J]. 北京科技大学学报(社会科学版), 2020 (2): 26–33.
孙小英，陈杰，杨荣。中国经济周期波动特征研究[J]. 当代经济，2009 (4): 14–15.
王国静，田国强。金融冲击和中国经济波动[J]. 经济研究，2014, 49 (3): 20–34.
王今朝。社会主义市场经济理论的创新发展[J]. 人民论坛，2019 (29): 84–85.
王强。反对" 私有化" 与发展私有经济:新时代中国特色社会主义市场经济的所有制理论研究[J]. 经济社会体制比较，2018 (3): 1–10.
王曦，王茜，陈中飞。货币政策预期与通货膨胀管理:基于消息冲击的DSGE 分析[J]. 经济研究，2016, 51 (2): 29–43.
王宣植。管仲财税思想的现代观点分析[J]. 管子学刊，2009 (2): 36–40.
王耀中，童文俊。凯恩斯主义经济学研究范式的演进[J]. 经济学动态，2003 (6): 61–65.
卫兴华。有关中国特色社会主义经济理论体系的十三个理论是非问题[J]. 经济纵横，2016 (1): 1–8.
吴超林。宏观调控的制度基础与政策边界分析:一个解释中国宏观调控政策效应的理论框架[J]. 中国社会科学，2001 (4): 54–64.
吴易风。社会主义市场经济重大理论与实践问题[J]. 学术研究，2017 (4): 5–14.
伍戈，刘琨。破解中国经济困局:基于总供给总需求的分析框架[J]. 国际经济评论，2013 (5): 120-134+7.
夏沐阳。管子经济思想对当下我国经济发展的价值剖析[J]. 中国市场，2016 (37): 156–157.
徐寅生。加快完善社会主义市场经济体制的理论认知与现实路径[J]. 行政与法，2020 (4): 1–8.
许志伟，薛鹤翔，车大为。中国存货投资的周期性研究:基于采购经理人指数的动态视角[J]. 经济研究，2012, 47 (8): 49–61.
杨农，郭辉铭。动态随机一般均衡模型理论与实证研究进展[J]. 经济学动态，2013 (8): 113–121.
杨小海，刘红忠，王弟海。中国应加速推进资本账户开放吗?— 基于DSGE 的政策模拟研究[J]. 经济研究，2017, 52 (8): 4–20.
尹响，易鑫，胡旭。人类命运共同体理念下应对新冠疫情全球经济冲击的中国方案[J]. 经济学家，2020 (5): 23–32.
余斌，吴振宇。中国经济新常态与宏观调控政策取向[J]. 改革，2014 (11): 15–23.
袁恩桢。社会主义市场经济理论研究[J]. 毛泽东邓小平理论研究，2006 (6): 25–30.
张斌。新冠肺炎疫情对宏观经济政策、财税改革与全球化的影响[J]. 国际税收，2020 (4): 33–38.
张晓晶。试论中国宏观调控新常态[J]. 经济学动态，2015 (4): 15–24.

张晓晶。通货膨胀形势、潜在增长率与宏观调控的挑战[J]. 经济学动态，2008 (1): 22–27.
张玉明，纪虹宇，刘芃。科学社会主义原则下中国特色社会主义市场经济对马克思理论的创新与发展[J]. 现代财经(天津财经大学学报), 2018, 38 (12): 15–26.
张再生。新冠肺炎疫情防控中的国家治理体系与治理能力建设[J]. 理论与现代化，2020 (2): 5–13.
赵可金.” 软战” 及其根源:全球新冠肺炎疫情危机下中美关系相处之道[J]. 美国研究，2020, 34 (3): 40-63+5.
庄丽婷。投资乘数加速数模型与我国经济周期波动探讨[J]. 价格月刊，2010 (4): 45–48.
庄子罐，崔小勇，龚六堂，邹恒甫。预期与经济波动:预期冲击是驱动中国经济波动的主要力量吗?[J]. 经济研究，2012, 47 (6): 46–59.
宗良，范若滢。宏观调控理论的创新思维、模型构建与中国实践[J]. 国际金融研究，2018 (11): 3–13.
宗良，范若滢。政府与市场” 两只手”: 宏观经济理论的历史演进、未来路径与理论模型[J]. 金融论坛，2018 (4): 3–14.
宗良，范若滢。经济学理论创新与黄金发展期[J]. 中国金融，2018 (14): 28–29.
宗良、范若滢。讲好” 有效市场” 与” 有为政府” 结合的中国故事[J]. 当代中国与世界，2022 (1): 45–52.
宗良，冯兴科，刘津含。美元加息对新兴市场国家的影响与对策[J]. 金融论坛，2019, 24 (5): 3–13.
宗良，郝毅，吴泽文。萨伊定律成立情景于条件的理论模型解析— 基于乘数-加速数模型和中国经济数据[J]. 国际金融研究，2025 (4): 18–29.
宗良、时圆、赵廷辰。现代经济增长理论的新思维— 基于传统模型的扩展与中国实践[J]. 国际金融研究，2022 (8): 3–13.
宗良，吴丹。国际贸易理论的创新思维与动态综合竞争优势转换:历史演进、理论创新和模型构建[J]. 武汉金融，2019 (7): 15–21.
邹至庄，王潇靓。中国宏观经济运行:从现象到规律[J]. 金融市场研究，2016 (5): 10–18.

Kolibri 360 GmbH
Ferdinand-Jühlke-Straße 7
99095 Erfurt, Deutschland
produktsicherheit@kolibri360.de